*Custom Textbook prepared for*

# DEPARTMENT OF INDUSTRIAL ENGINEERING AND OPERATIONS RESEARCH

**Columbia University**

## Volume I

*Includes Materials from:*

**Professor Soulaymane Kachani**

for

## IEOR E4003 & IEOR E4403

**Columbia University**

*FINANCIAL ACCOUNTING: A Valuation Emphasis*
Hughes–Ayres–Hoskin

*ADVANCED ENGINEERING ECONOMICS*
Park–Sharp–Bette

*VALUATION: Measuring and Managing the Value of Companies*
McKinsey & Company–Koller–Goedhart–Wessels

Cover images: © Columbia University.





To order books or for customer service, please call 1(800)-CALL-WILEY (225-5945).

ISBN 978-1-118-49057-0

10 9 8 7 6 5 4 3 2

# Preface

*New York, July 16th, 2012*

This book is intended for students in the Industrial Economics (IEOR E4003) and the Advanced Engineering & Corporate Economics (IEOR E4403) courses at Columbia University.

The fifth edition of this custom book better covers the broad range of topics discussed in these courses using four different sources as well as a subset of the lecture slides that I developed here at Columbia University, and that leverage my experience at McKinsey.

I would like to thank Alan Most at Wiley for his continued assistance in the publishing process. I would also like to thank Professor Ali Sadighian and my former students for their feedback.

I look forward to your suggestions as, together, we continue to improve these courses and this custom book.

Sincerely,

Soulaymane Kachani
Department of Industrial Engineering & Operations Research

# Table of Contents

## Part I: Interpreting Financial Statements



## Part II: Evaluating Economic Performance of Companies & Projects



## Part III: Corporate Finance



## Part IV: Additional Topics

## Outline

# Part I: Interpreting Financial Statements

- Lecture slides on financial analysis

- Chapters 1, 2, 3, 4, 5 and 6 of "Financial Accounting, A Valuation Emphasis" by Hughes, Ayres and Hoskin

# The Big Picture

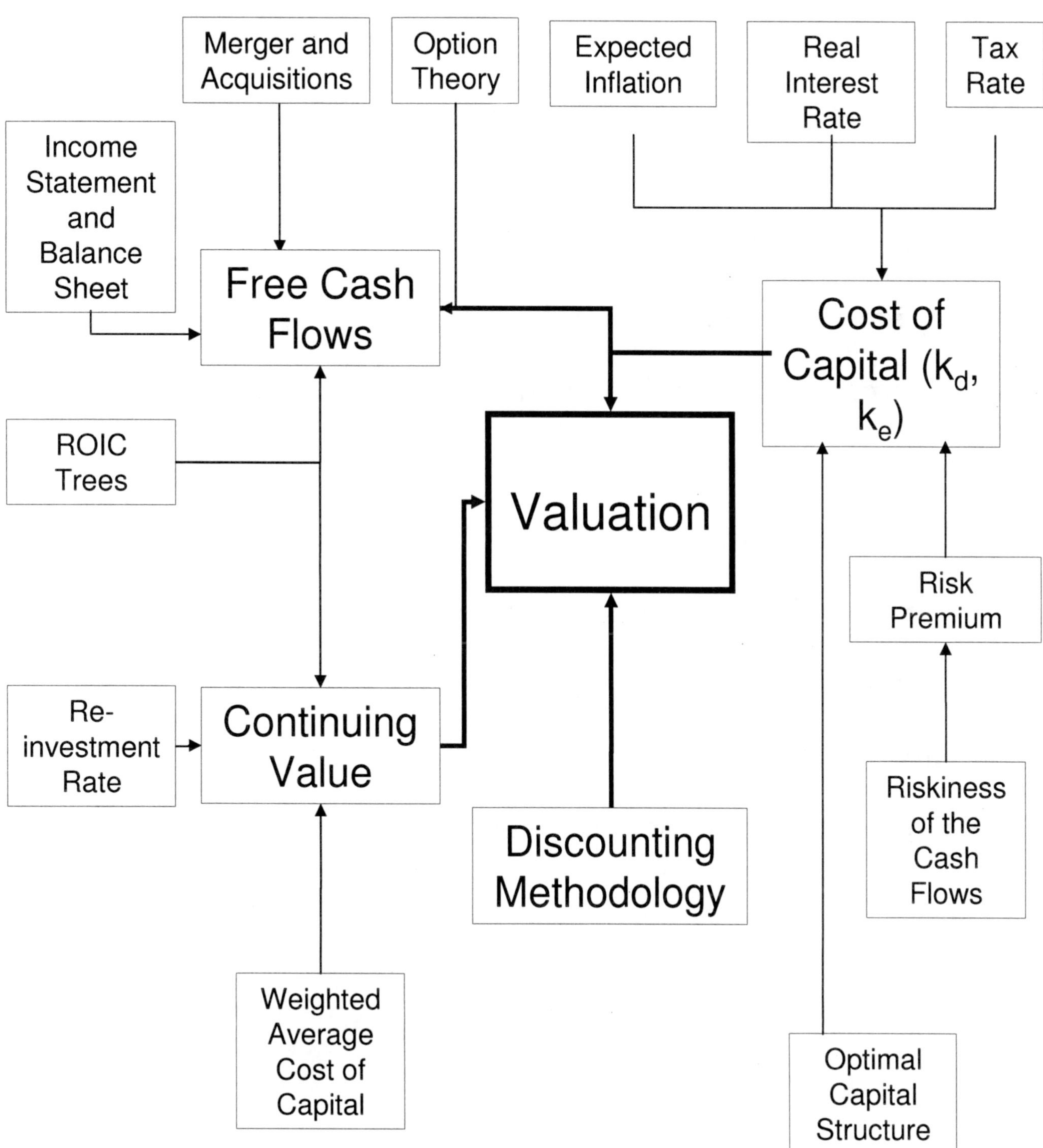

# Interpreting Financial Statements

- Cash Flow Cycle
- Balance Sheet
- Income Statement
- Sources and Uses Statement
- Cash Flow Statement
- Free Cash Flow
- Financial Statements and the Value Problem
- Balance Sheet Decomposition
- Sustainable Growth
- Financial Statement Footnotes

# Interpreting Financial Statements

## Key Concepts

1. **Understand the difference between financial accounting (governed by generally accepted accounting principles) and management accounting (governed by the needs of a particular company)**

- **GAAP: U.S.**
- **German accounting system**
- **IAS (International Accounting System)**

# Interpreting Financial Statements

## Key Concepts

➢ Financial accounting:

✓ **Not for managerial decision making**

✓ **Invented by bankers in Spain some 400 years ago**

✓ **External accounting**

➢ Management/Cost accounting:

✓ **For managerial decision making (sunk cost, opportunity cost)**

✓ **Internal accounting**

✓ **Company decides cost accounting systems**

✓ **Management information systems**

# Interpreting Financial Statements

## Key Concepts

2. **The financial accounting rules differ from a country to another. We will concentrate on major principles that are similar across all countries**

3. **We have to understand the difference between financial reporting (straight line) and tax reporting (accelerated)**

4. **Purpose of doing all of this: understand how to determine expected cash flows for business units and company valuation**

# Interpreting Financial Statements

## Three Main Accounting Principles

### 1. Realization principle / Accrual accounting

- **When is a sales revenue recognized in accounting?**
  1. Order received
  2. Service delivered
  3. Invoice sent
  4. Payment received

- **Can we estimate the market value of a company from financial statements?**

# Interpreting Financial Statements

## Three Main Accounting Principles

2. **Matching principle**

   - **Cost must be recognized when we have recognized the corresponding revenue**

   - **Problems with depreciation and future costs of guarantees**

3. **Principle of prudence**

   - **Do not overestimate your profits (you are allowed to underestimate your profits)**
     - ✓ R&D cost goes to the income statement: because you are not sure you are getting these benefits in the following years

# Interpreting Financial Statements

## Cash Flow Cycle

- **Close interplay between company operations and finances**

- **Property 1: *Financial statements are an important reflection of reality***

- **Property 2: *Profits do not equal cash***

# Interpreting Financial Statements

## Balance Sheet

- **Financial snapshot, at a point in time, of all the assets a company owns and all the claims against these assets**

**Assets = Liabilities + Shareholders' equity**

***Question: If a company is short in cash, can it spend some of its shareholders' equity? Why?***

# Interpreting Financial Statements

Standard Balance Sheet

| **Assets** | **Liabilities+S.E.** |
|---|---|
| ➢ Liquid assets | ➢ Short term borrowing |
| ➢ Accounts receivable | ➢ Accounts payable |
| ➢ Inventories | ➢ Net accruals |
| ➢ Net Fixed assets | ➢ Long-term debt |
| ➢ Other assets | ➢ Owners equity<br>➢ Paid-in capital<br>➢ Retained earnings |

# Interpreting Financial Statements

## Standard Balance Sheet

### Assets

- **Liquid assets**
  - Cash, Market securities
  - Belongs to shareholders
  - Companies need to justify why they are holding to high levels of liquids assets
- **Accounts receivable**
  - FIFO, LIFO
  - Financed by LTD
- **Inventories**
  - Financed by AP and STB
- **Net Fixed assets**
  - Financed from OE
- **Other assets**

  Intangible assets:
  - Patents
  - Trademarks
  - Human capital
  - Goodwill

### Financing

- **Short term borrowing**
- **Accounts payable**
  - Unpaid raw materials
- **Net accruals**
  - Unpaid energy bills and admin bills
- **Long-term debt**
- **Owners equity**
  - How much owners have invested in the company
  - Book value: may not include a lot of important value: e.g. trademark value (e.g. Coca Cola), human capital
  - **Paid-in capital**
  - Paid for by owner: investment
  - **Retained earnings**
  - Invested by owners instead of taking them in their pocket

# Interpreting Financial Statements

## Income Statement

- **A record of flow of resources *over time* commonly divided into two parts:**
  - **Operating segments**
  - **Non-operating segments**

- **At least 5 issues associated with Earnings (Net Income) reported in an income statement:**
  - **Accrual accounting**
  - **Inventory methods: FIFO, LIFO, Average method**
  - **Depreciation methods: Straight-line vs. Accelerated depreciation**
  - **Taxes**
  - **Research and Marketing, creation of trademarks and patents in the balance sheet**

# Interpreting Financial Statements

## Standard Income Statement

**Net Sales**

**Gross Profit**

**Operating Profit**

**Earnings Before Interest & Taxes (EBIT)**

**Earnings Before Taxes (EBT)**

**Earnings After Taxes (EAT) or Net Income**

# Interpreting Financial Statements

## Standard Income Statement

**Net Sales**

- Cost of Good Sold (COGS)

**Gross Profit**

- Administrative & Selling Expenses (SG&A)

- Depreciation

**Operating Profit**

+/- Extraordinary Gain/Loss

+ Other Income

**Earnings Before Interest & Taxes (EBIT)**

- Interest Expenses

**Earnings Before Taxes (EBT)**

- Provision for Income Taxes

**Earnings After Taxes (EAT) or Net Income**

## Interpreting Financial Statements

### Sources and Uses Statement

- **Answers two questions:**
  - **Where does a company get its cash?**
  - **How does a company spend its cash?**
- **Two-step approach:**
  - **Place two balance sheets for different dates and note all the changes in accounts**
  - **Segregate the changes in those that generate cash *(reduce an asset or increase a liability)* and those that consume cash *(increase an asset account or reduce a liability account)***

Sources = Uses

- **Question: *Is "Increase in cash" a source or a use of cash? Why?***

# Interpreting Financial Statements

## Statement of Cash Flows

- **Expands the Sources and Uses Statement, placing each source and use into 1 of 3 *(4)* categories**

- **Cash flows from operating activities**
- **Cash flows from investing activities**
- **Cash flows from financing activities**
- **Effect of exchange rate changes on cash**

# Interpreting Financial Statements

## Statement of Cash Flows

**Net Income**

Adjustment to net income:

1. \+ Depreciation
2. Changes in Working Capital
   1. **- Increase in Accounts receivable**
   2. **- Increase in Inventory**
   3. **+ Increase in Accounts Payable**
   4. **+ Increase in Accrued Liabilities**
3. Cash flow from investing
   1. **- Capital Expenditures**
   2. **- Increase in Other Assets**

**Total Cash Flow from Operations and Investing**

1. \- Dividends and Stock Repurchases
2. \+ Increase in Short Term Debt
3. \- Increase in Marketable Securities
4. \+ Increase in Long Term Debt

**Total Cash Flow from Financing**

**Increase in Cash**

# Interpreting Financial Statements

## Consolidation

- **Practically speaking, all large companies own other companies. To fully understand the impact of these ownership structures on companies' financial health, companies are required to publish consolidated financial statements. Typically, we divide the companies into three groups with respect to ownership levels:**
  - **Ownership > 50% (control the other company): these companies are fully consolidated and are called subsidiaries**
  - **50% ≥ Ownership ≥ 20% (include joint ventures): these companies are often called equity affiliates and they are accounted for by the equity method**
  - **Ownership < 20%: these companies are treated as financial investments**

## Interpreting Financial Statements

### Free Cash Flow

- **Fundamental determinant of the value of a business**

Free Cash Flow = **Total cash available for distribution to owners and creditors after funding all worthwhile investment activities**

= **EBIT (1 –Tax rate) + Depreciation – Capital Expenditures - Increases in Working Capital**

# Interpreting Financial Statements

## Statement of Free Cash Flow

**EBIT.(1-Tax Rate)**

Adjustment to EBIT.(1- Tax Rate):

1. + Depreciation
2. Changes in Working Capital
   1. **- Increase in Accounts receivable**
   2. **- Increase in Inventory**
   3. **+ Increase in Accounts Payable**
   4. **+ Increase in Accrued Liabilities**
3. Cash flow from investing
   1. **- Capital Expenditures**
   2. **- Increase in Other Assets**

**Free Cash Flow**

# Interpreting Financial Statements

## The Value Problem

➢ **Issues in using accounting data for financial decision making:**

- **Market Value vs. Book Value**
  - ✓Original costs vs. current values
    - Relevant & subjective vs. irrelevant & objective
  - ✓Forward-looking vs. backward-looking
    - Exception: Goodwill
- **Economic Income vs. Accounting Income**
  - ✓Realized vs. unrealized income
  - ✓Cost of equity

# Interpreting Financial Statements

## Balance Sheet Decomposition

- **This tool starts by dividing both investments and financing methods of a company into two parts**

  - **Investments**
    - ✓ Investments in fixed assets
    - ✓ Investments in the operating cycle = Working Capital Requirement

  - **Financing**
    - ✓ Short-term financing
    - ✓ Long-term financing

# Interpreting Financial Statements

## Balance Sheet Decomposition

➢ **Using the four elements we identified, we can divide the balance sheet into 3 separate blocks which affect each other**

- **Net Long-term Financing (NLF)**
  - ✓ Long-term Financing – Fixed Assets
  - ✓ Should be positive (cushion)
  - ✓ Bigger NLF: more conservative financing strategy (low risk) but more expensive
- **Working Capital Requirement (WCR)**
  - ✓ Accounts Receivable + Inventories – Accounts Payable – Net Accruals
  - ✓ Money needed to run the company day to day
- **Net Short-term Borrowing (NSB)**
  - ✓ Short-term Financing – Liquid Assets

**WCR = NLF + NSB**

# Interpreting Financial Statements

## Balance Sheet Structure

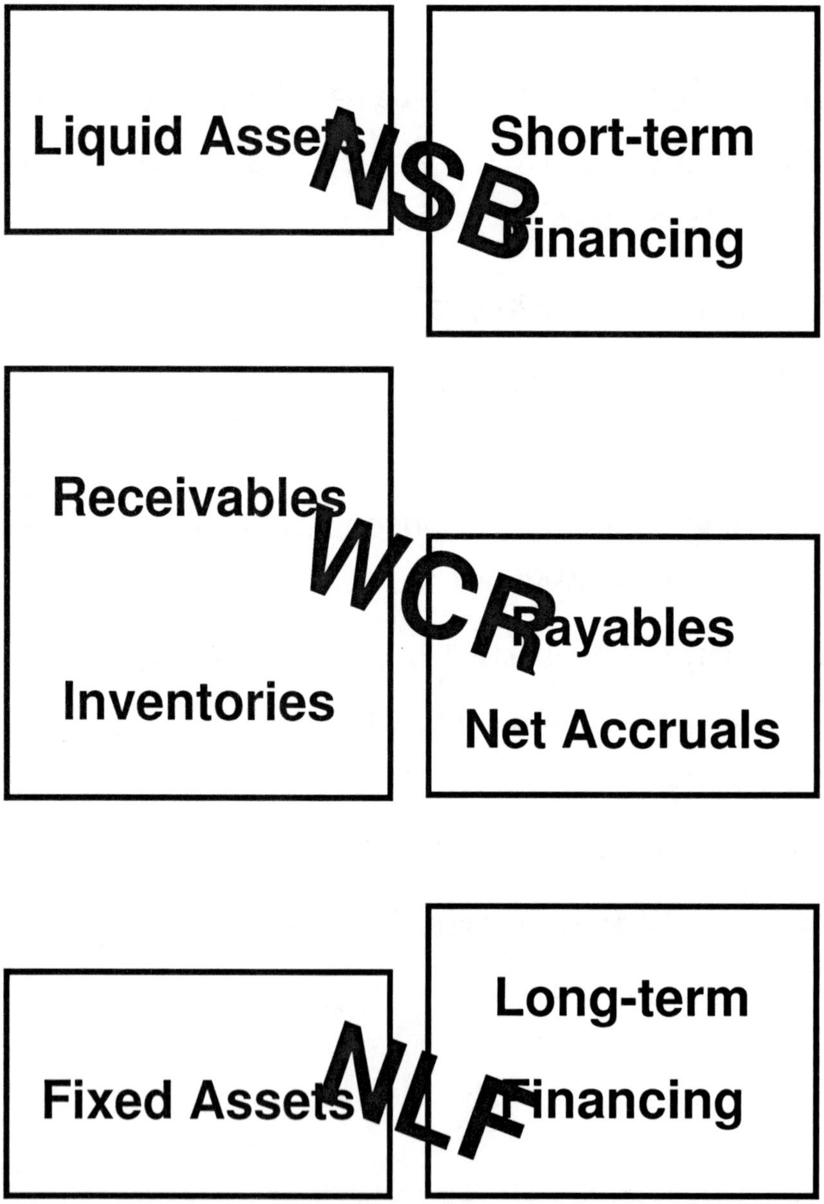

| Assets | | Financing |
|---|---|---|
| Liquid Assets | NSB | Short-term Financing |
| Receivables<br>Inventories | WCR | Payables<br>Net Accruals |
| Fixed Assets | NLF | Long-term Financing |

# Interpreting Financial Statements

## Concept of Sustainable Growth

➢ **What is the maximum growth rate, if no external financing sources exist?**

➢ **More precisely, sustainable growth computes the maximum growth rate a company can sustain without financial difficulties assuming that:**

- **The company cannot raise new equity financing**
  - ✓ Most applicable to small and medium size companies as well as government-owned companies
- **The company (or the banker) does not want to increase the financial risk of the company**
  - ✓ D/E ratio is constant
- **The operational efficiency of the company is constant**
  - ✓ Sales/Assets ratio is constant

# Interpreting Financial Statements

## Financial Statement Footnotes

- **Financial statements are not complete without footnotes which typically explain at least 3 different types of information**

  - **Explanations how the company has interpreted different financial accounting principles**

  - **More detailed information of income statement and balance sheet numbers**

  - **Off-balance sheet items which do not show up in the balance sheet such as:**
    - ✓ Operating leases
    - ✓ Pending lawsuits
    - ✓ Executive stock options
    - ✓ Financial instruments

# Outline

## Part I: Interpreting Financial Statements

- Lecture slides on financial analysis

- Chapters 1, 2, 3, 4, 5 and 6 of "Financial Accounting, A Valuation Emphasis" by Hughes, Ayres and Hoskin

CHAPTER 1

# Financial Reporting: The Institutional Setting

## LEARNING OBJECTIVES

After reading this chapter you should be able to:

1. Identify the types of business activities of publicly traded corporations reflected in financial accounting reports.
2. Explain the process governing the regulation of financial reporting and setting of Generally Accepted Accounting Principles (GAAP).
3. Describe the role of independent audits in monitoring compliance of financial reports with GAAP.
4. Recognize the economic consequences of accounting choices, and the link between owners' and managers' wealth and financial statement information.
5. Understand that a potential relationship exists between the value of a firm's stock and the information contained in financial reports, particularly the firm's statement of earnings.

**During the day of August 25, 2000, the stock price of Emulex, a computer** technology company, drastically dropped (see Exhibit 1.1) following an Internet story that it was under investigation by the Securities and Exchange Commission (SEC). The story also indicated that Emulex would restate its earnings downward as a result of the investigation. The stock quickly rebounded later that same day when investors learned that the story had been a hoax.

This event suggests that both earnings *per se*, and the credibility of that number are relevant to the stock market's assessment of a firm's value. Several questions come to mind: What are earnings? How are earnings linked to the market value of a company's stock? What role do the SEC and other institutions play in determining the reliability of reported earnings? These and many other questions pertaining to the construction of financial accounting information, and how that information relates to the value of the firm and the expectations of investors, lay at the heart of this text.

Exhibit 1.1

THE REAL WORLD

Emulex

Emulex Stock Price Movement. The Vertical Bars Reflect the Range of Price Movement on the Day Shown. The Horizontal Bars Show the Closing Price for the Day.

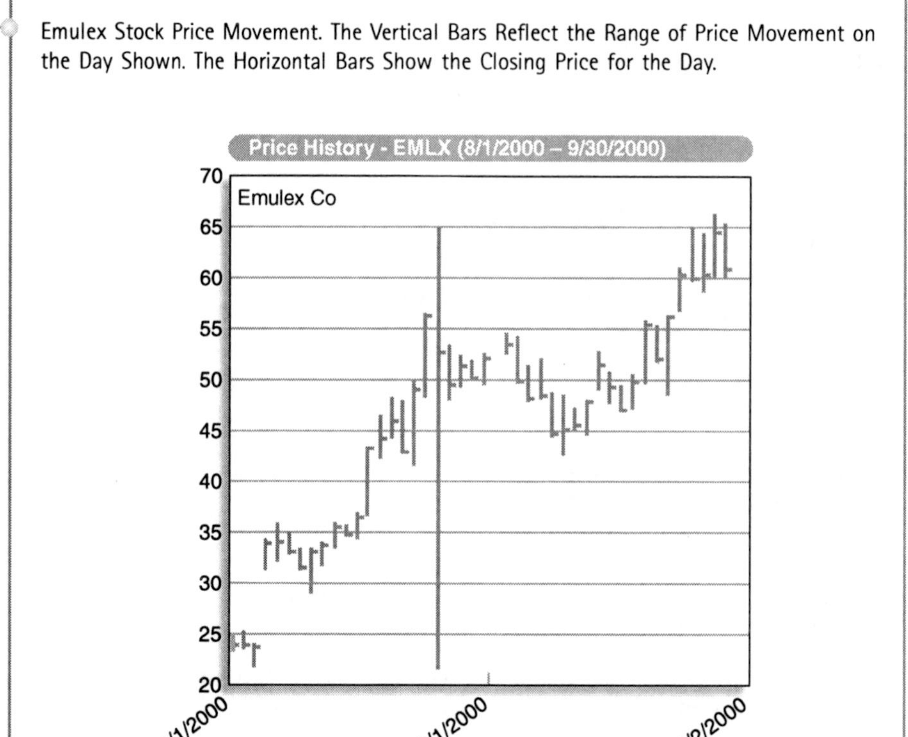


In this book, we focus on the presentation of accounting information for business entities (firms) and its interpretation by external decision makers, such as investors, financial analysts, and government regulators. Firms prepare periodic reports that are made available to such external parties. A key component of these reports consists of financial information generated from the firm's accounting system. This information is summarized in a set of financial statements and related notes. The false report on Emulex referred to one of these statements, the Earnings Statement.

The **earnings statement** for a firm reports its revenues and expenses for a given period of time. **Revenues** are the amounts collected, or relatively certain to be collected, from customers in return for providing goods or services. **Expenses** are the amounts paid, or expected to be paid, to vendors in return for resources that go into the production and marketing of goods or services (such as materials, salaries, and utilities). You may also see earnings referred to as *profits* or *net income.*

EARNINGS = REVENUE − EXPENSES

Although all types of business entities prepare financial statements, we will focus on corporations in this text. **Corporations** are distinguished from other business types (we provide a more complete description of various business types in Chapter 2) by the issuance of shares of **stock,** which represent ownership in the company. When companies initially form, investors (owners) exchange cash for shares of stock in the company. As an example, when Jeff Bezos formed Amazon.com, Inc. in the state of Washington on July 5, 1994, he invested $10,000 in exchange for 1,700,000 shares. Owners then profit from their investment by increases in the value of their shares or by receiving dividends from the company. **Dividends** can typically only be paid if the company has positive earnings on a cumulative basis and may be viewed as returning part of the earnings of the company to the owners. In Amazon.com's case, the company has not produced a profit yet and therefore has paid no dividends. The value of the shares has, however, fluctuated considerably over the life of the company consistent with changes in investors' expectations of the future earnings of Amazon. At the time of this writing Amazon's share price was $40.21 a share. As of April 4, 2003, Jeff Bezos owned almost 108 million shares of Amazon.

Because the return on investment to a firm's owners (stockholders) comes from future dividends and changes in share value and estimates of both are often based on earnings, earnings are of considerable importance to investors as they make decisions about whether to buy or sell shares of stock.

Because of their significance in our economy, we specifically focus on **publicly traded corporations,** which are those corporations whose shares trade in a public stock exchange, such as the New York Stock Exchange. Emulex is one example of a publicly traded corporation. Some other more recognizable publicly traded corporations include Starbucks, Nike, and Coca Cola. For publicly traded corporations, financial analysts make buy-and-sell recommendations to investors wishing to purchase or sell shares of stock. These buy-and-sell recommendations may influence investors' purchases and sales, and indirectly, the price of stock. For example, the incorrect Emulex story prompted some analysts to recommend that investors sell their stock. The increase in investors wishing to sell their stock, along with the decrease in those willing to buy the shares, led to price declines. Upon learning of the false report, the situation reversed, causing the price to adjust upward.

As evidenced by investors and analysts' reaction to the news that Emulex would have to restate its earnings, information about a company's earnings plays a key role in assessing a firm's value. For this reason, companies periodically make announcements (typically on a quarterly basis) about their most recent performance. See the announcement of Pepsico in Exhibit 1.2. Further, analysts routinely report their forecasts of earnings and ratios related to earnings, such as the *price-to-earnings ratio (P/E ratio),* which factor significantly into their assessment of the firm's value. For example, in July 2003, the P/E ratio for Pepsico was approximately 21:1, based on the current estimate for the following

**Exhibit 1.2**
First Quarter 2003 Performance Announcement by Pepsico

THE REAL WORLD

**Pepsico**

PEPSICO Q1 EARNINGS PER SHARE INCREASES 17 PERCENT TO 45 CENTS

Worldwide volume grew 3 percent
Division net revenues grew 5 percent, and 6 percent on a currency neutral basis
Division operating profits grew 7 percent, and 8 percent on a currency neutral basis, following 14 percent growth in Q1 2002
Total net income grew 13 percent

Note the prominence of earnings in this disclosure. Also note that because Pepsico has worldwide operations, many of its accounting numbers are influenced by currency differences around the world. Therefore, the company includes data both as reported and after some adjustment for currency differences.

year's earnings and the current stock price at the time. The P/E ratio can be viewed as the amount investors are willing to pay for each dollar of forecasted earnings. When the earnings in the ratio are the forecasted earnings, the ratio is more specifically known as the *forward* P/E ratio. If, instead, the calculation is based on the last reported earnings (i.e., the actual earnings) then the ratio is called the *trailing* P/E. We will discuss the interpretation of the P/E ratio later in the book.

As will become clearer as you progress through the book, earnings provides a measure of the value added to the owners' wealth as a result of the firm's activities. We describe next those firm activities captured by the accounting process.

## REPORTING ON THE ACTIVITIES OF THE FIRM

When assessing a firm's value, most analysts begin by reviewing the economic activities of the firm. All business firms engage in three basic kinds of activities: financing, investing, and operating. **Financing activities** are those activities directed at raising funds for the firm. Firms raise funds (sometimes called **capital**) from two basic sources: owners (*equity capital*) and lenders (*debt capital*). To raise funds from owners, corporations issue shares of stock. To raise funds from lenders, firms typically issue to the lenders a written promise indicating how the money will be repaid as well as the interest rate associated with the loan. There are many types of lenders, but one common lender would be a bank. For example, Skechers USA, Inc. was incorporated in 1992 and by the end of 2001 had $18,498,000 in loans payable to two banks.

A firm generally uses the funds obtained from its financing activities to engage in investing and operating activities. **Investing activities** typically consist of the firm's purchase of property and equipment to enable the company to make products or provide services. Firms may also purchase shares of stock of other companies. These purchases are also considered investing activities. **Operating activities** include those relatively short-term activities that the firm engages in to make and sell products and services. Representative of these activities are the collection of sales dollars from customers, the payment of salaries to employees, and the payment of utility costs.

The accounting process captures the financial effects of these activities. Individual economic events that affect the accounting system are called *transactions*. Financial statements are then constructed from the combined results of the transactions that occur during a particular period of time (e.g., a month, a quarter, a year). These statements reflect the transactions that have been recorded to date and, as such, form a historical record of the firm's activities. The challenge for analysts and investors is to utilize this historical record to assist in forecasting the future economic events that will, in turn, affect the firm's future earnings and hence its value.

Financial statement users make many significant decisions based on the information included in these reports. As a result, the information needs to be as accurate and comprehensive as possible. To ensure this, firms need to follow specific regulations when reporting their main activities. In the next section, we discuss the institutional environment in which accounting regulations are formulated and the key characteristics that are considered in setting accounting standards.

## REGULATION OF FINANCIAL REPORTING

Many financial statement users lack the influence to force a company to release information that they might need to make effective decisions. For instance, in the United States, large publicly traded corporations are owned by numerous individuals. The shareholders in these large companies typically do not work for the company and thus have little firsthand information about its day-to-day activities. They therefore rely upon the periodic financial statements issued by the company's management to obtain knowledge about the firm's activities. To ensure that owners or potential owners of public companies get relevant, reliable, and timely information regarding those companies, laws and regulations dictate much of the content of these reports.

The ultimate authority for regulating financial reports of publicly traded companies in the United States rests with the **Securities and Exchange Commission (SEC).** Prompted by the 1929 stock market crash, the U.S. Congress established the SEC to administer the 1933 Securities Act and 1934 Securities and Exchange Act. That is, Congress empowered the SEC with the legal authority to set disclosure and accounting standards that all publicly traded firms are obliged to follow.

To provide adequate disclosure, the SEC created a reporting structure (SEC's Regulation S-X and S-K) that all public companies must follow. For example, the regulations require an annual report (10K), quarterly reports (10Q), and a report of significant events (8K). The 8K report is often used to disclose earning announcements or public meeting with analysts. For instance, on August 6, 2003, American Express issued an 8K report that contained the Chief Executive Officer's presentation to the financial community regarding the company's second quarter results. All of the reports filed with the SEC are available electronically via the electronic filing site of the SEC known as EDGAR.

Although the SEC retains its authority over the disclosures of publicly traded firms, it delegates the primary responsibility for creating accounting standards to the **Financial Accounting Standards Board (FASB).** The FASB consists of individuals from the private sector, principally professional accountants. Since its inception in 1973, the FASB has generated several *Statements of Financial Accounting Concepts (SFACs),* putting forth broad objectives for financial reports (known as the FASB's *conceptual framework*), and many **Statements of Financial Accounting Standards (SFASs)** that address specific valuation and income measurement issues.

On occasion, the SEC intervenes in setting standards, through two series of publications: *Financial Reporting Releases (FRRs)* and *Accounting and Auditing Enforcement Releases (AAERs)*. In addition, SEC staff issue a series of bulletins, known as *Staff Accounting Bulletins (SABs)*, that reflect their opinion and interpretation of other releases. Congress may also become involved when it deems necessary. Collectively, the body of accounting concepts, standards, guidelines, and conventions governing the construction of financial statements and related disclosures are referred to as **Generally Accepted Accounting Principles (GAAP).**

## International Accounting Standards

The development of accounting standards has, in general, been a country-specific process. Each country has developed its own standards, which reflect its political, social, and economic environment. With the development of world markets for both products and capital, however, countries need a greater consensus with regard to financial reporting. To meet this need, the International Accounting Standards Committee (IASC) has been actively formulating international accounting standards.

The IASC is an independent, private-sector body that is funded by donations from accounting organizations around the world. Effective March 2001, a new organization emerged from the IASC, the International Accounting Standards Board (IASB). The IASB now establishes international accounting standards; as of 2002, the IASC/IASB issued 41 International Accounting Standards (IAS). The IASB will issue new standards known as International Financial Reporting Standards (IFRS). To promote the development of international accounting standards, the IASB developed relationships with the primary standard-setting bodies in numerous countries, including the FASB within the United States. In late 2002 the FASB and the IASB agreed to make their standards compatible with one another by January 1, 2005.

# DETERMINING GENERALLY ACCEPTED ACCOUNTING PRINCIPLES

Recognizing that it cannot set accounting standards for every economic event that might occur, the FASB developed the conceptual framework (FASB, SFAC No. 2, 1980) that serves as a guide for both standard setting and practice. The conceptual framework seeks to define the desirable characteristics of accounting information. Qualitatively, a number of characteristics shape the financial statement disclosures required under GAAP. Some of the key characteristics are:

- **Relevance** The information is capable of making a difference in a decision. Relevant information may derive value from its role in predicting future performance (*predictive value*) or in assessing past performance (*feedback value*).
- **Reliability** The information faithfully represents the economic events it is intended to portray. Reliable information is accurate, neutral (unbiased), and verifiable (see *Verifiability*).
- **Verifiability** Independent measurers using the same methods reach the same results. Verifiable information allows independent observers to agree on what a reported amount represents.
- **Neutrality** The information conforms to standards that are independent of the interests of any particular constituency. Neutral information is not withheld or modified to serve the company's or users' objectives.
- **Comparability** The information can be compared across firms in a meaningful manner. Comparable information does not distort similarities or differences as a consequence of how the company uses accounting methods.
- **Consistency** The information is determined under the same accounting methods from one period to the next. Consistent information is free of the effects of changing methods in its determination.

**Exhibit 1.3**
Qualitative Characteristics of Accounting Information

| PRIMARY QUALITIES | |
|---|---|
| **Relevance** | **Reliability** |
| Understandability | Decision Usefulness |
| Predictive Value | Verifiability |
| Feedback Value | Neutrality |
| Timeliness | Representational Faithfulness |
| **SECONDARY QUALITIES** | |
| Comparability | Consistency |

Trade-offs exist when applying these qualities to a particular economic event. Two of the primary qualities highlighted in Exhibit 1.3, relevance and reliability, are often the focus of these trade-offs. For example, the most relevant information about a company that sells a product in high demand but limited supply may be the number of backorders of the product. This information may be very *relevant* to assessing current firm value as a forecast of future sales, but may not be a very *reliable* measure of future sales. For example, a competitor may be able to supply the same or similar product in a more timely manner which would result in the backorder being cancelled. As a case in point, in mid-2002, Palm, Inc. was having difficulties providing sufficient quantities of a very popular color model of its handheld product. The major distributors (those who had the backorders) found that their customers would not wait and sought alternative distribution channels to get the model. One distributor was quoted in a press release saying "if we can't support our customers in a timely manner, the customer goes and finds the product online." As a result of these trade-offs, in determining specific accounting standards, such as when to recognize backorder sales of a product, the FASB must consider all of the qualities of the information and seek to determine an acceptable solution. In general, backorders are not recognized as sales under GAAP because they generally fail to meet the reliability criteria. However, backorders are still a very relevant piece of information and are often disclosed by firms in their press releases.

An ill-defined concept that also influences the content of financial statements is **materiality.** Materiality means that firms can use a flexible accounting approach for insignificant amounts. For example, firms should account for the purchase of an electric stapler, office equipment, as a long-term asset. However, most firms simply treat the stapler as an expense rather than as an asset. GAAP allows this simpler accounting treatment because treating the stapler cost as an expense would not (materially) affect our view of the firm's assets or expenses.

Financial statement users need to monitor how firms handle the materiality concept when assessing a firm's value and compliance with GAAP. In recent years, the SEC has been concerned that some firms misuse the concept of materiality by deciding that as long as an item is less than a certain percentage of income or assets that it is immaterial (5 percent is often quoted as a rule of thumb). In response, the SEC issued SAB 99 (in 1999), which states that misstatements are not considered immaterial simply because they fall beneath a certain threshold. Firms must consider many other aspects of the misstatement in determining whether to correct it or not. For instance, in SAB 99 two other factors that must be considered are (1) whether the misstatement has the effect of increasing management's compensation say, by satisfying requirements for the award of bonuses or other forms of incentive compensation (see our discussion concerning economic consequences later in this chapter for more information about this factor) and (2) whether the misstatement involves concealment of an unlawful transaction.

Finally, although not a quality explicitly sought under GAAP, financial statements tend to reflect conservatism. **Conservatism** indicates a firm's tendency to anticipate losses, but not gains; carry assets at values that are often low by comparison with current market prices or appraisal values; recognize liabilities in anticipation of obligations that may or may not arise; and delay recognition of revenues until uncertainties have been resolved. For example, under current GAAP, many construction companies recognize the profits from a long-term construction project over the period of construction. However, if they anticipate that there will be a loss on the overall contract at the end of the construction period, they recognize the loss immediately. To illustrate, Foster Wheeler LTD (a construction company specializing in petroleum processing facilities) reported this type of policy in their annual report:

> The Company has numerous contracts that are in various stages of completion. Such contracts require estimates to determine the appropriate cost and revenue recognition. However, current estimates may be revised as additional information becomes available. If estimates of costs to complete long-term contracts indicate a loss, provision is made currently for the total loss anticipated.

Note, however, that the conceptual framework explicitly states that firms must avoid misusing conservatism to understate assets or overstate liabilities.

At times, however, the conceptual framework fails to provide enough guidance. The FASB then moves to adopt a more specific standard for a particular economic event. To do this, the FASB follows a very public process of determining a new standard, encompassing three main stages:

1. The FASB analyzes the issue using the conceptual framework and other relevant existing standards. It then prepares a Discussion Memorandum laying out the alternatives with their pros and cons. The FASB elicits feedback of the Discussion Memorandum from interested parties such as investors, financial analysts, government regulators, corporate executives, and professional accountants.
2. After assessing the responses to this document, the FASB deliberates on the alternatives and issues an Exposure Draft of its proposed pronouncement. The FASB makes the Exposure Draft available for further public comment.
3. In the last step, the FASB incorporates any additional comments and then issues its pronouncement in the form of a Statement of Financial Accounting Standards (SFAS).

The process the FASB uses to set accounting standards is essentially political and subject to override by the SEC or the U.S. Congress. For example, during the oil crisis in the 1970s, the FASB issued SFAS 19 that eliminated certain accounting practices used by oil and gas producers. The new standard would have resulted in more volatile reported earnings for smaller companies engaged in significant exploration activities. Some opponents of the new standard argued that with more volatile earnings, smaller producers might be unable to raise capital to continue exploration, inconsistent with the national interest in encouraging exploration. The political pressures subsequently brought to bear resulted in the FASB rescinding the pronouncement it had originally issued (SFAS 52).

GAAP provides the framework and the specific rules for how the various activities of the firm should be recorded in their accounting system. However, if the firm does not follow these rules or they apply them inappropriately, investors and other readers of the financial statements could be misled about the performance of the firm. For this reason all publicly traded firms are required to present audited statements in their reports. The auditors provide the reassurance that the firm has appropriately applied GAAP. In the next section, we discuss the nature of the audit.

## INDEPENDENT AUDITS OF FINANCIAL STATEMENTS

All publicly traded companies must provide a report by independent auditors (see the report for Hasbro, Inc. in Exhibit 1.4). This report attests to the fairness of presentation (that the statements fairly represent the results of the

**Exhibit 1.4**
Hasbro, Inc. Auditors' Report

THE REAL WORLD

**Hasbro, Inc.**

The Board of Directors and Shareholders
Hasbro, Inc.:

We have audited the accompanying consolidated balance sheets of Hasbro, Inc. and subsidiaries as of December 29, 2002 and December 30, 2001 and the related consolidated statements of operations, shareholders' equity and cash flows for each of the fiscal years in the three-year period ended December 29, 2002. These consolidated financial statements are the responsibility of the Company's management. Our responsibility is to express an opinion on these consolidated financial statements based on our audits.

We conducted our audits in accordance with auditing standards generally accepted in the United States of America. Those standards require that we plan and perform the audit to obtain reasonable assurance about whether the financial statements are free of material misstatement. An audit includes examining, on a test basis, evidence supporting the amounts and disclosures in the financial statements. An audit also includes assessing the accounting principles used and significant estimates made by management, as well as evaluating the overall financial statement presentation. We believe that our audits provide a reasonable basis for our opinion.

In our opinion, the consolidated financial statements referred to above present fairly, in all material respects, the financial position of Hasbro, Inc. and subsidiaries as of December 29, 2002 and December 30, 2001 and the results of their operations and their cash flows for each of the fiscal years in the three-year period ended December 29, 2002 in conformity with accounting principles generally accepted in the United States of America.

As discussed in note 1 to the consolidated financial statements, effective December 31, 2001, the first day of the Company's 2002 fiscal year, the Company adopted the provisions of Statement of Financial Accounting Standards No. 142, "Goodwill and Other Intangibles."

/s/ KPMG LLP

Providence, Rhode Island
February 12, 2003

economic events that have affected the firm) and compliance of those statements with GAAP. **Auditors** are professional accountants who meet certification requirements set by states (i.e., Certified Public Accountants, or **CPAs** for short). Auditors must also follow procedures under the oversight of the American Institute of Certified Public Accountants (AICPA). The AICPA sets Generally Accepted Auditing Standards (GAAS) that define the auditor's responsibilities.

The auditor's opinion is important when using valuation techniques as it provides at least some level of assurance that the data being used to forecast future results are comparably prepared by companies.

In addition to assessing compliance with GAAP, auditors also examine the firm's internal controls, verify its principal assets, review for unusual changes in its financial statements, inquire with outside parties concerning the firm's exposure to losses, and determine the firm's ability to continue as a going concern. The term **going concern** means that the auditor expects that the firm will continue to operate into the foreseeable future; in other words, they do not expect the company to go out of business or file for bankruptcy. Investors and others might view the value of a company quite differently if they assumed it would soon quit operating. Auditors also consider the existence or prospect of fraud, though the firm's management has primary responsibility for its detection.

Auditors also apply the concept of materiality in their work. They typically limit their responsibility to material items when they state in their audit opinions that financial statements "present fairly, *in all material respects,* the financial position, results of operations, and cash flows" of a client firm.

Finally, auditors issue one of several types of reports. In an *unqualified opinion* the auditor expresses no reservations concerning the fairness of the financial statements and conformance with GAAP. A *qualified opinion* includes an exception to the conclusion of fairness or conformance with GAAP. Exceptions commonly relate to a deviation from GAAP or a limitation in the scope of the auditor's procedures under GAAS. An *adverse opinion* states that the financial statements do not fairly present the company's financial position and results of operations in conformity with GAAP. Under a *disclaimer,* the auditor does not express an opinion on the financial statements.

Firms appoint auditors and pay their fees. As a result, controversy exists on the independence of auditors whose fees are paid by the client. To help resolve these concerns, the accounting profession devised the *AICPA Code of Conduct* and a *peer review* process to monitor compliance with performance standards. In 2002, the U.S. Congress passed the Sarbanes-Oxley Act (SOX) to address these and other concerns about the auditing profession, partly in response to the Enron failure and the subsequent demise of Arthur Andersen (see Exhibit 1.5). The SOX created a Public Company Accounting Oversight Board that monitors auditing, quality control, and independence standards, and rules. For example, oversight of the public accountant must be done through the firm's audit committee, which must be composed of members who are independent of the company.

Independent audits help to ensure that the financial statements reflect those qualities of accounting information we discussed earlier. Owners, lenders, and managers face economic incentives in their interaction with a firm that may influence accounting decisions. In the next section, we discuss the economic consequences to owners, lenders, and managers from the accounting choices made by the firm. As illustrated by the Enron example, these consequences can be very significant.

Exhibit 1.5

THE REAL WORLD

Enron

In October, 2001 the SEC requested information from Enron Corporation regarding a set of transactions with several related parties. The transactions had the approval of Enron's auditors, Arthur Andersen. By the end of the month, the inquiry had turned into a formal SEC investigation. In an 8K filing (recall that 8K filings detail the occurrence of any material events or corporate changes that should be reported to investors or security holders) with the SEC on November 8, 2001, Enron agreed to restate its financial statements for 1997 through 2001 to record the effects of the related party transactions. The net effect: Enron reduced its owners' equity section by $1.2 billion. On December 2, 2001, Enron filed for protection from its creditors under Chapter 11 of the U.S. bankruptcy laws. In its continuing investigation the SEC requested audit working papers from Arthur Andersen (AA). The SEC then discovered that several individuals at AA had shredded documents related to the Enron audit. The government eventually filed an indictment for obstruction of justice against AA, and the company suffered the loss of numerous clients. AA was ultimately found guilty of obstructing justice and agreed not to audit publicly traded companies.

The loss in credibility of Enron's reported earnings, both past and present, along with the revelation of losses and exposure of business risks led investors to conclude that the stock was overvalued. As a result, Enron suffered such severe declines in its stock price and future prospects that the company was forced to declare bankruptcy.

## ECONOMIC CONSEQUENCES OF ACCOUNTING PRACTICES

Although GAAP places restrictions on accounting choices, firms still enjoy considerable flexibility in their selection and application of accounting methods. As a result, managers can and do affect the amounts reported in the financial statements. Allowing flexibility is a two-edged sword. On one hand, it makes it possible for financial statements to better reflect economic reality in the sense that one size does not fit all. On the other hand, it may provide the opportunity for firm owners or managers to manipulate information.

For example, lenders closely monitor a firm's activities to ensure that they will be repaid. One common way for owners to provide assurances to lenders and for lenders to protect themselves is to put restrictions into their lending contracts. These restrictions, called *covenants,* typically set minimums for certain accounting numbers or ratios that the firm must meet. The agreements typically state that the lender can make the loan immediately due if the firm violates these covenants. If a company found itself in danger of violating a covenant, there might be enough incentive to either change accounting methods or misreport transactions to avoid the violation. A mitigating factor on this behavior is that lenders often find it in their best interests to work with firms to restructure debt when violations occur (see Exhibit 1.6 regarding Cogent Communications Group).

As another example, compensation arrangements for a firm's management often include bonuses based on achieving a targeted amount of earnings. Under GAAP, managers commonly have sufficient discretion over accounting policies to significantly influence the recognition of revenues and expenses. In order to meet bonus targets, therefore, managers may advance the recognition of revenues or delay expenses as a means of reporting higher earnings. Other forms of discretion might include relaxing credit requirements customers must satisfy

**Exhibit 1.6**
Cogent Communications Group, Inc.—10K Report, April, 2003

THE REAL WORLD

**Cogent Communications Group**

*Breach of Cisco Credit Facility Covenant.* We have breached the minimum revenue covenant contained in our credit facility from Cisco Systems Capital. This breach permits Cisco Capital, if it wishes, to accelerate and require us to pay approximately $262.7 million we owed to Cisco Capital as of March 28, 2003. Should Cisco Capital accelerate the due date of our indebtedness, we would be unable to repay it. If it accelerates the indebtedness, Cisco Capital could make use of its rights as a secured lender to take possession of all of our assets. In such event, we may be forced to file for bankruptcy protection. We are currently in active discussions with Cisco Capital to restructure the Company's debt.

Note that violation of the covenant in this lending agreement had the potential to impose significant economic consequences to Cogent. You can imagine the pressure that this situation might exert on management to misstate revenues to be in compliance with the covenant. By June, however, Cogent had restructured its debt.

(to produce more revenues), postponing repairs and maintenance on equipment (to reduce expenses), and selling assets or retiring debt on which gains will be recorded (to increase income). These types of actions may actually reduce the firm's value. Although managers benefit by receiving a higher bonus, they do so at the expense of stockholders (lower firm value).

In compensation arrangements, firms try to design contracts that align the economic interests of managers with those of stockholders. One example is to provide some amount of a manager's compensation in the form of stock in the company. The idea is that managers will behave more like owners when managers' compensation includes stock. Stock could be awarded to managers directly. More frequently managers are given the option to buy shares of stock at a fixed price under what are called *stock option plans,* discussed later in the book. Often management compensation arrangements provide a combination of incentives, some based on earnings and some on stock price. For example, Intel compensates its executive managers with a combination of a base salary, a cash bonus tied to meeting an individual earnings performance target, a cash bonus tied to overall company earnings, and a stock option plan.

Other incentives to manipulate earnings may relate to lawsuits, labor negotiations, compliance with bank or insurance company regulations, and trade disputes with foreign rivals. For example, a firm facing litigation might prefer to ignore the likelihood of losing a lawsuit (by not recording a liability in advance of a settlement), thereby giving a false impression of the firm's value.

Many opportunities and incentives therefore exist for manipulating financial reports. One reason for allowing these opportunities to exist is that it may be too costly both to incorporate the level of detail required to set more stringent standards and to monitor compliance with those details. Another reason may be that allowing managers to select from a menu of accounting policies may provide an efficient means of communicating (*signaling*) information about the firm's future prospects when the economic consequences of a given policy depend on those prospects. For example, suppose that there are two companies in the same industry with similar debt agreements (including a restriction in their debt agreement that earnings must remain above $100,000). One firm has very good future sales prospects, and the other firm has very poor future sales prospects. If they both were faced with a decision about voluntarily (i.e., it was not a mandated change) adopting a new accounting policy that would reduce reported earnings in the future, the firm with good prospects would have little

Other countries differ on the matter of a separation between tax accounting and financial accounting. For example, Korean accounting policies for financial reporting correspond to those employed for tax purposes.

problem in adopting this policy as it expects to have good future earnings which would not force the company to violate its debt restrictions (even though it would reduce their future reported earnings due to the policy change). However, the firm with bad prospects would likely not adopt the new policy as it already is in a position to potentially violate the debt restriction (due to its poor future sales prospects) and the change in policy will make it even more likely. Therefore, by observing their decisions about the choice of accounting policy lenders might be able to infer the future prospects of companies and set the interest rates that they require accordingly.

Another economic consideration that managers face in the determination of accounting methods is the effect of the decision on the taxes paid by the company. All corporations pay taxes to the federal government (*Internal Revenue Service* or *IRS*) based on their earnings. The accounting rules for reporting earnings to the IRS are determined by the tax code and in some cases differ from GAAP. The company's objective in choosing its accounting policies for tax purposes is usually to minimize or delay its tax payments. In contrast, the company's objective in choosing its accounting policies for financial reporting purposes is to comply with GAAP. Although the norm is for firms to use different accounting methods for tax and financial reporting purposes, there is at least one case (LIFO inventory accounting) in which the method chosen for tax purposes is only permitted if that same method is used for reporting purposes. Accordingly, there may be a tax incentive that influences an accounting choice.

## FINANCIAL REPORTING AND VALUATION

As the discussion in this chapter suggests, financial accounting disclosures, especially earnings, provide information upon which financial analysts and investors at large may project a firm's future cash flows that, in turn, determine firm value. The central role of earnings as an important factor in determining firm value is evidenced by the prominence of earnings forecasts by financial analysts in the financial press and a vast empirical literature by academics that documents stock price reactions to information conveyed by changes in those forecasts, earnings announcements *per se,* and other related disclosures.

In the chapters that follow, we will seek to further an appreciation of the role that financial statements play in arriving at estimates of firm value. Our efforts in this regard culminate in Chapter 14 with the presentation of two principal approaches for mapping information contained in what are called *pro-forma financial statements* (statements based on forecasts of future operating, investing, and financing activities) into value estimates; specifically, *discounted cash flow (DCF)* analysis and *residual income (RI)* analysis. At this point, it is sufficient for you to begin to think of a firm's financial accounting disclosures as a starting point in assessing its future cash flow prospects.

## SUMMARY AND TRANSITION

As should be clear by now, accounting information, particularly earnings, plays a key role with investors in guiding their decisions to buy or sell stock. Analysts who advise investors also make significant use of accounting information in estimating the value of a share of stock as a basis for their buy or sell recommendations to investors. The reliability and relevance of accounting information are enhanced by a standard setting process involving both public (SEC) and private (FASB) sector bodies. Auditors provide additional assurance to investors that the accounting information is prepared in compliance with those standards.

Within the framework of generally accepted accounting principles, managers have considerable discretion over accounting policies adopted by the firm. Often managers' choices have economic consequences for themselves, their stockholders, and lenders. The nature of the consequences is driven by the contracts written between managers, stockholders, and lenders.

In the remainder of the book we will continue to visit valuation issues and to examine economic consequences issues as they arise. The next few chapters explain the construction of the financial statements contained in financial accounting reports and describe the major concepts underlying this construction. Considerable attention is given to the principal concepts used in the determination of earnings. These chapters are followed by an initial exposure to the techniques of financial analysis with a focus on the use of financial statements in assessing past performance and forecasting future performance. Later chapters consider a comprehensive set of valuation and income measurement issues in depth. The final chapter of the text provides basic introduction to the forecasting of financial statements and the two major approaches for valuing the firm based on components from those statements.

# END OF CHAPTER MATERIAL

## KEY TERMS

- Auditors
- Capital
- Conservatism
- Corporation
- Dividends
- Earnings Statement
- Expenses
- Financial Accounting Standards Board (FASB)
- Financing Activities
- Generally Accepted Accounting Principles (GAAP)
- Going Concern
- Investing Activities
- Materiality
- Operating Activities

Publicly Traded Corporations
Revenue
Securities and Exchange Commission (SEC)
Statement of Financial Accounting Standards (SFAS)
Stock

## ASSIGNMENT MATERIAL

### REVIEW QUESTIONS

1. Describe and illustrate the three major types of activities that firms engage in.
2. Discuss the meaning of Generally Accepted Accounting Principles, and describe the organizations that establish these principles.
3. What is the purpose of an auditor's opinion, and what types of opinions can auditors render?
4. Identify at least three major users of corporate financial statements, and briefly state how they might use the information from those statements.
5. List and briefly describe the major qualitative characteristics that accounting information should possess, according to the FASB concepts statements.
6. Discuss how materiality is used in the choice of accounting methods.
7. Describe what is meant by economic consequences of accounting practices and provide an example of how accounting choices can affect the welfare of parties with an interest in the firm.
8. How might differences in accounting standards across countries affect the analysis done by an analyst in predicting stock prices?
9. Describe what conservatism means in the construction of the financial statements of the firm.

### APPLYING YOUR KNOWLEDGE

10. For a manufacturing company, list two examples of transactions that you would classify as financing, investing, and operating.
11. The AMAX Company purchased land several years ago for $60,000 as a potential site for a new building. No building has yet been constructed. A comparable lot near the site was recently sold for $95,000.
    a. At what value should AMAX carry the land on its balance sheet? Support your answer with consideration for the relevance and reliability of the information that would result.
    b. If AMAX wanted to borrow money from a bank, what information about the land would the bank want to know?
12. You are the accounting manager for a U.S. company that has just been acquired by a German company. Helmut, the CEO of the German company, has just paid you a visit and is puzzled why American companies report on two different bases, one for reporting to their stockholders and another to the taxing authority, because in Germany these are one and the same. Draft a memo explaining to Helmut why there are two different bases

and a brief explanation for why they might involve different accounting rules.

13. Harmonization of accounting standards has been proposed on a global basis. As a CEO of an American company, what would you see as advantages and disadvantages of having the same set of standards across countries?

14. Suppose that the FASB proposed that inventory be accounted for at its current market price (i.e., what you could sell it for) rather than its historical cost. Provide an argument that supports or opposes this change on the basis of relevance and reliability.

15. Suppose that you started your own company that assembles and sells laptop computers. You do not manufacture any of the parts yourself. The computers are sold through mail order. Make a list of the information that you consider relevant to assessing your firm's performance. When you are through, discuss how you would reliably measure that performance.

16. Suppose that you own and operate your own private company. You need to raise money to expand your operations, so you approach a bank for a loan. The bank loan officer has asked for financial statements prepared according to GAAP. Why would the loan officer make such a request and, assuming that your statements were prepared according to GAAP, how could you convince the banker that this was so?

17. In order for a company's stock to be listed (i.e., traded) on most stock exchanges, the company's financial statements are required to be audited by a CPA firm. Why?

18. As a manager, suppose that you are responsible for establishing prices for the products your division sells. Under GAAP your firm uses a method of inventory costing called LIFO that means that the costs of the last units purchased are the first ones that are reported in the statement of earnings. Consequently, the costs that remain in inventory are those associated with the first purchases. Because inventory can build up over the years, some of these costs may be very old. How relevant would these old costs attached to ending inventory be to you as you decide how to price inventory in the coming year? If they are not relevant, what piece of information would be more relevant to you?

19. From time to time there have been calls from the user community for management to disclose their own forecasts of future results such as net income. As an external user of the financial statements, discuss the relevance and the reliability of this type of information.

20. Suppose a company decides to change accounting methods such that it reports its revenues sooner than it previously did. Discuss how this might effect investors' evaluation of the company's stock.

## USING REAL DATA

21. Amazon.com, Inc. has operated at a net loss since its formation, yet its stock has a positive value. Explain why investors would value the shares of Amazon at a positive value.

22. In early February 2001 Emulex Corporation revised its quarterly sales estimates downward. Prior to the revision Emulex had been expecting a 28 percent sales increase over the previous year and had shown 40 percent increases in sales annually for the last five years. Upon hearing this news, investors drove the price of Emulex down from $77.50 per share on a Friday to $40.25 on the following Monday. Explain why the valuation of Emulex dropped given this announcement.

23. In early February 2001 CISCO announced that it was missing its first quarter sales estimates. This was the first time since July 1994 that it had come in under its sales estimates, and it was the first time in more than three years that it had failed to beat its sales estimates. As an investor, how might you react to this news and how might this announcement affect the valuation of the company's shares?

## BEYOND THE BOOK

The Beyond the Book problems are designed to force you to find and utilize resources found outside the book.

24. Familiarize yourself with the resources that are available at your university to acquire information about corporations. Most universities have an electronic database that contains financial statement information. The following is a short list of resources that may be available:

    **LEXIS/NEXIS Database** This is an incredibly large database that contains all sorts of news and financial information about companies. It contains all of the SEC filings including the 10-K, 20-F (foreign registrants), and Proxy Statements. The financial information is in full text form.

    **CD-Disclosure** This database contains full text financial footnote information for thousands of companies but does not contain full text of the major financial statements.

    **EDGAR Filings** The EDGAR filings are electronic forms of the SEC filings that are included in the Lexis/Nexis database but are also accessible through the internet (www.sec.gov).

    **ABI Inform (UMI, Inc.)** This database contains full text information from numerous business periodicals.

25. Go to the FASB's website (www.fasb.org), locate the project activities section, and list the titles of the projects on its projects update list.

26. For a publicly traded company of your choosing, answer the following questions:

    a. What are the products (or product lines) and/or services that your company sells? Please be as specific as possible.

    b. Who are the customers of your company? Please be as specific as possible.

    c. In what markets, domestic and global, does your company sell its products and/or services?

    d. Who are the major competitors of your company?

    e. What are the major inputs your company needs to manufacture its products? Who are the suppliers of these inputs?

f. Are any of the items listed in the questions above changing substantially? Use a two-year time span as a window to address this question.

g. What has happened to the stock price of your company over the last two years?

To answer these questions it will be useful to collect a series of articles concerning your company over the most recent two-year period. Try to find at least five reasonably sized articles. Use these as references to write a two- to three-page background paper about your company.

CHAPTER 2

# Financial Statements: An Overview

## Learning Objectives

After reading this chapter you should be able to:

1. Understand the differences in the major forms of business organization, as well as some of the relative pros and cons for choosing a particular form of business.
2. Identify the nature of information contained in the main general-purpose financial statements: Statement of Financial Position, Statement of Earnings, Statement of Cash Flows, and Statement of Changes in Stockholders' Equity.
3. Explain the connection between statements of financial position at points in time and changes in financial position over time.
4. Describe the types of supplemental disclosures accompanying financial statements in a firm's annual report.

**On October 12, 2001, Polaroid Corporation filed for protection from creditors** under Chapter 11 of the U.S. bankruptcy laws. This action resulted from the financial difficulties that Polaroid faced when its sales declined significantly, starting in the fourth quarter of 2000. As Exhibit 2.1 shows, the value of the company's stock began its downward slide late in the first quarter of 2000. Note that the S&P 500 (Standard and Poor's) is an index of how the stock market performed overall during this same period. This correspondence between declining quarterly sales and relative stock price suggests that investors rely on information contained in financial statements. In this chapter, we begin to explore this relationship by describing the contents of those statements.

Polaroid's stock price movement relative to the S&P Index and trading volume from March 1999 through April 2002.

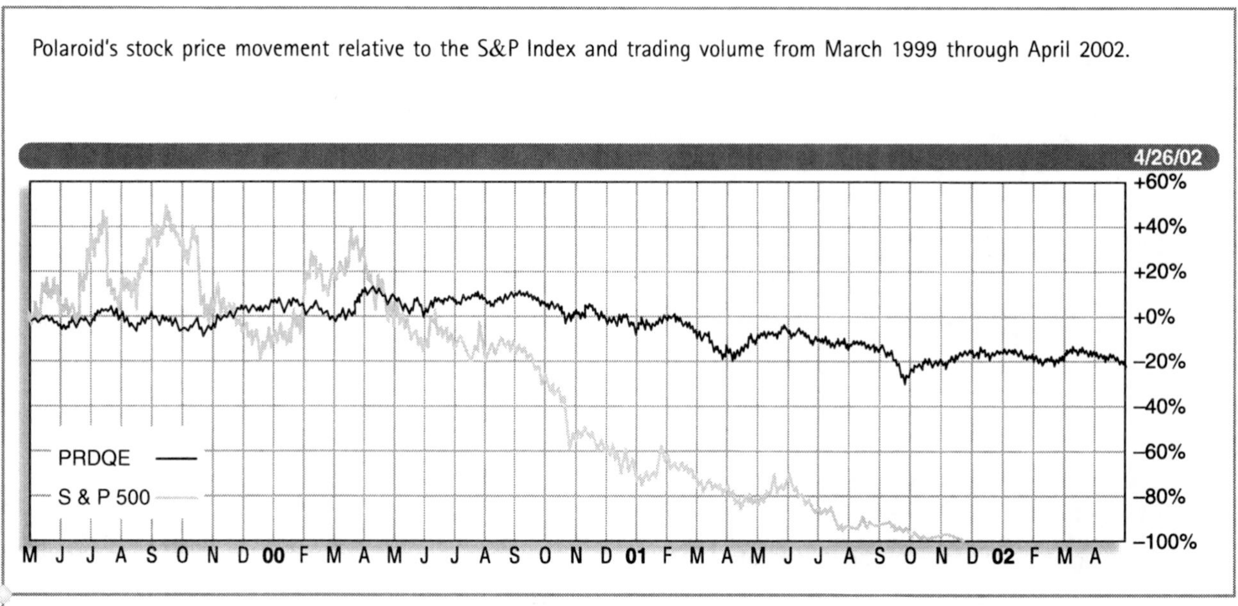


Exhibit 2.1

THE REAL WORLD

Polaroid

The changes in company value are very evident for a publicly traded corporation such as Polaroid since its stock price is published daily. This is not true for all forms of business. While we intend to focus on publicly traded corporations we would like to spend a little bit of time describing other forms of business so that you understand why the corporate form of business is the dominant one in the U.S. economy.

## FORMS OF BUSINESS ORGANIZATION

The corporate form of business is by far the most popular for large publicly traded firms. This popularity stems from three principal features:

- Limited liability for its capital suppliers
- Ease of transferring ownership
- Ease of access to additional ownership funds

**Limited liability** means that investors in the firm's equity securities generally cannot lose more than the amounts that they invest, should the firm perform poorly. This feature can be compared to the unlimited liability of owners of **sole proprietorships** (single owners) and **partnerships** (multiple owners). If a sole proprietorship or partnership cannot meet its obligations to creditors, then creditors may seek satisfaction of their claims from the owner's or partners' personal assets, respectively. As a result, hybrid forms of organization have emerged, such as *limited liability companies (LLCs)* and *limited liability partnerships (LLPs),* which, as their name suggests, include the limited liability feature of corporations. Many public accounting firms are organized as LLPs, such as PricewaterhouseCoopers, LLP and KPMG, LLP. Some relatively well known businesses are also organized as LLCs, such as Orbitz, LLC (the web-based travel service) and BMW of North America, LLC (an importer of BMW products in North America).

Corporations, particularly large ones, are typically owned by a vast number of individuals. This ownership structure spreads the limited risk of ownership over many investors. In the case of a sole proprietorship, the single owner bears all the unlimited risk, whereas in partnerships, the partners share that risk. This difference in the distribution of risks appears to have played an important role in the rise of corporations as the preferred type of business organization.

Transfers of ownership in publicly traded corporations can be easily accomplished through the purchase and sale of investors' equity securities, in other words, the trading of stock. To trade stock, a corporation lists its stock on major stock exchanges, such as the *New York Stock Exchange* or *NASDAQ*. These exchanges attract large numbers of investors, as they can easily and quickly acquire or sell securities as needed to maximize their economic welfare. From the firm's perspective, stock exchanges provide relatively easy access to one type of capital needed to fund its investment and operating needs. In contrast, ownership of sole proprietorships is more difficult to transfer, as it requires finding buyers without benefit of stock exchange services. Transferring ownership of partnerships is also more difficult. If an existing partner leaves or a new partner enters the business, the existing partnership must first be dissolved and a new one then created.

The corporate form of business also allows the firm to increase its equity capital by offering additional shares for sale. In a publicly traded corporation, this means that many individual investors, other then the present owners, might become owners in the firm. The larger set of investors in the public stock markets allows the company access to a considerable amount of resources as it grows. Sole proprietorships, in comparison, have limited access to additional funds as they are constrained by the owner's wealth and ability to borrow. Partnerships also are at a disadvantage, as they usually only raise ownership funds through additional contributions of the partners or by admitting new partners to the business.

The corporate form does possess a potentially significant negative consideration: taxes. Corporations are subject to corporate income taxation, whereas sole-proprietorship and partnership income is taxed only at the individual level. Because individual investors are taxed on the income they receive from corporations (in the form of dividends and capital gains), the net result is that corporate income is taxed twice, once at the corporate level and a second time at the individual level. This tax structure may influence who chooses to invest in corporations and how corporations' securities are priced relative to holdings in other forms of business entities.

The tax status of an entity has significant valuation implications, as taxes reduce cash flows.

Exhibit 2.2 summarizes some of the pros and cons of the main forms of business organization. Because of their dominance in the market, we focus on the reporting of publicly traded corporations in the remainder of the book. In the next section, we expand an understanding of corporations by discussing the nature of their financial statements.

**Exhibit 2.2**
Pros and Cons of Forms of Business Organization

| Form of Organization | Pros | Cons |
|---|---|---|
| Proprietorship | Income taxed once | Unlimited liability<br>Ownership transfer difficult<br>No sharing of risk<br>Limited access to additional ownership funds |
| Partnership | Income taxed once<br>Some sharing of risk<br>Some access to additional ownership funds | Unlimited liability<br>Ownership transfer difficult |
| Corporation | Limited liability<br>Ease of transfer of ownership<br>Relatively easy access to additional ownership funds | Double taxation |

# FINANCIAL ACCOUNTING REPORTS

As we discussed in Chapter 1, to conduct business, publicly traded corporations raise long-term funds from individuals and institutions through both lending agreements and the issuance of stock. Both lending agreements and stock represent claims on the resources (assets) that the corporation controls. Corporations also obtain short-term funds from other creditors; for example, suppliers often sell inventory to companies on credit. Such credit purchases are, in effect, short-term loans from the suppliers. Exhibit 2.3 shows the *balanced* relationship between the firm's resources on the one side, and claims to those resources on the other.

Financial statements provide information about the firm's resources and claims to resources at periodic points in time, and also about the changes to those resources and claims to resources from the firm's activities between those points in time. The major financial statements include the:

- Statement of Financial Position
- Statement of Earnings

**Exhibit 2.3**
Resources and Claims against Resources

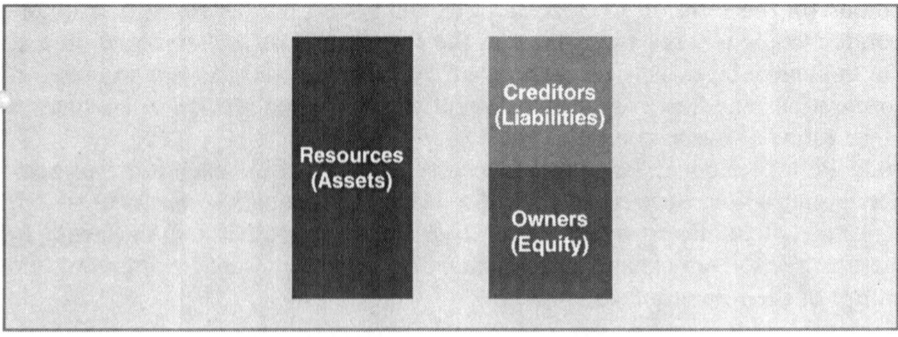

- Statement of Cash Flows
- Statement of Changes in Stockholders' Equity

Below we discuss each statement, as well as provide descriptions of many terms that each statement includes. In this chapter, we simply want to offer you a general sense of what each statement contains. We will provide more detailed explanations of the content in later chapters, so you need not try to fully understand them here.

## STATEMENT OF FINANCIAL POSITION

The Statement of Financial Position describes the firm's resources and claims to those resources as seen in Exhibit 2.3. Accounting expressions for resources, creditors, and owners are, respectively, **assets, liabilities,** and **stockholders' equity** (or **common stockholders' equity** or simply **owners' equity**).

### ASSETS

In simple terms assets are those resources owned by the company or those that the company has the right to use. From the accountant's point of view, assets are resources that have *probable future value* to the firm and are recognized under GAAP. Assets typically include *cash; accounts receivable* (amounts due from the firm's customers); *inventories* (for use in production or for sale); *plant, property, and equipment* (used to make products or provide services); and various *property rights* (the rights to use an economic resource such as a patent).

Accountants, however, do not consider some economic resources as assets because they fail to meet measurement criteria, such as the general criterion of reliability discussed in Chapter 1. For example, a brand image (e.g., the Coca Cola logo) created through advertising and customer satisfaction cannot be reliably valued and are not, therefore, recognized in the financial statements. Furthermore, the amounts at which resources are reflected as assets often differ from their current economic value. For example, the market or appraisal value of land some years after its acquisition might be greater than its recorded value (sometimes called the *carrying value*), as accounting standards stipulate that land be carried at its historical cost.

### LIABILITIES

In simple terms, liabilities represent the amounts owed to others. From the accountant's point of view they represent *probable future sacrifices* of resources. Liabilities may include bank borrowings (*notes payable* or *mortgages payable*), borrowings that are done through publicly traded securities known as bonds (*bonds payable*), amounts due to suppliers (*accounts payable*), and amounts due to others providing goods or services to the company during production, such as utility companies and employees (*utilities payable* and *salaries payable,* respectively). Sometimes the word **accrued** appears with the liability titles (e.g., *accrued warranty liability, accrued expenses*), implying that the amounts have been estimated. Customers may also have some claim on resources if they have prepaid for goods and services that the company must deliver in the future. These types of claims, typically called *deferred revenue, unearned revenues,* or simply *deposits,* reflect items such as prepaid magazine subscriptions.

Similar to assets, accountants also do not consider all economic obligations as liabilities. For example, if a company contracts with another company to purchase goods that will be delivered at a future date at a fixed price, current accounting standards do not require the company to recognize the obligation to pay the supplier when the contract is signed. As neither company has satisfied its part of the contract, neither company recognizes the contract in its accounting records. In accounting jargon, this kind of contract is known as a *mutually unexecuted contract.* Also, some liabilities are so uncertain that they may not meet the criteria for recognition. For instance, potential legal liabilities associated with lawsuits are often excluded from liabilities because it is very uncertain as to whether the company will actually have to pay a settlement.

As analysts try to predict the future cash flows of the firm, unrecorded liabilities may pose one of the more significant estimation challenges.

## STOCKHOLDERS' EQUITY

Unlike creditor and customer claims that a firm settles within some specified time frame, equity claims have no specified time period for payment. Stockholders of a corporation are not assured a specific set of payments. Instead, they usually only receive cash payments when the company declares a *cash dividend* (when the firm generates positive earnings) or when stockholders elect to sell their shares. As a result, stockholders' equity is sometimes referred to as a **residual claim,** because owners can only claim what is left over after all creditor claims have been met. It can also be thought of as the residual claim on assets after deducting liabilities. In other words, owners can claim the difference between what the company owns and what it owes. **Net assets** (also referred to as **net book value**) can be calculated through the accounting equation that we discuss next.

## THE ACCOUNTING EQUATION

As mentioned previously, the statement of financial position (often called a **balance sheet**) reports a firm's assets, liabilities, and stockholders' equity at a particular point in time. Further, a characteristic of a balance sheet is that the sum of assets equals the sum of liabilities and stockholders' equity (hence the word "balance"). This characteristic of the balance sheet is commonly referred to as the **accounting equation** (recall that Exhibit 2.3 illustrates this).

$$\text{Assets} = \text{Liabilities} + \text{Stockholders' Equity}$$

It follows from this equation that stockholders' equity equals assets less liabilities. That is:

$$\text{Stockholders' Equity} = \text{Assets} - \text{Liabilities}$$

Stockholders' equity is also called *net assets* or *net book value.* To illustrate a statement of financial position, based on the accounting equation, let's next look at a real company, Ross Stores.

## STATEMENT OF FINANCIAL POSITION: ROSS STORES

Exhibit 2.4, Ross' 10K report, describes the company's business and operating goals. Reviewing this information first helps to provide insight into the information included in the financial statements.

Exhibit 2.5 shows Ross' Statement of Financial Position for the year ended February 1, 2003. Note that Ross presents two columns of data, one at the beginning of the year (2/2/2002) and the other at the end of the year (2/1/2003). The SEC requires two years of balance sheet data for annual reports. Further, the SEC requires firms to report the balance sheet data as of the end of their **fiscal** (financial) **year.** The fiscal year often ends on the same date as the calendar year, December 31. However, as with Ross, this need not be the case. Due to the seasonal nature of their business, many retail firms use year-ends other than December 31, for example, Tommy Hilfiger Corp (March 31), Wal-Mart (January 31), American Greetings (February 28), and Starbucks (September 30). Finally, note that the accounting equation is satisfied at both points in time. In fact, the accounting equation needs to be satisfied at all points in time in an accounting system.

Ross presents what is known as a **classified balance sheet.** This type of balance sheet lists assets in order of how quickly they can be converted into cash, sometimes referred to as **liquidity order.** In addition, a classified balance sheet also segregates assets into **current** and **noncurrent** categories. **Current assets** are cash and assets that are expected to be converted into cash or expire within one year or one operating cycle of the business, whichever is longer. For a manufacturing firm, the *operating cycle* is the time between the initial acquisition of raw materials and the collection on the sale of the inventory that is sold. Inventory is a current asset because it will be sold and converted into cash during the firm's current operating cycle, which, for most firms, is less than one year. Note that for certain kinds of inventory (e.g., any long-term construction project such as submarines and aircraft) the operating cycle could be longer than a year. This type of inventory would still meet the definition of a current asset as the inventory is sold within an operating cycle.

**Exhibit 2.4**
Ross Stores Business (from 10K)

THE REAL WORLD

**Ross Stores**

Ross Stores, Inc. ("Ross" or "the Company") operates a chain of off-price retail apparel and home accessories stores, which target value-conscious men and women between the ages of 25 and 54 primarily in middle-income households. The decisions of the Company, from merchandising, purchasing, and pricing, to the location of its stores, are aimed at this customer base. The Company offers brand-name and designer merchandise at low everyday prices, generally 20 percent to 60 percent below regular prices of most department and specialty stores. The Company believes it derives a competitive advantage by offering a wide assortment of quality brand-name merchandise within each of its merchandise categories in an attractive easy-to-shop environment.

**Exhibit 2.5**
Ross Stores—Statement of Financial Position (in thousands)

THE REAL WORLD
**Ross Stores**

| | 2/1/2003 | 2/2/2002 |
|---|---|---|
| ASSETS | | |
| CURRENT ASSETS | | |
| Cash and cash equivalents (includes $10,000 of restricted cash) | $ 150,649 | $ 40,351 |
| Accounts receivable | 18,349 | 20,540 |
| Merchandise inventory | 716,518 | 623,390 |
| Prepaid expenses and other | 36,904 | 30,710 |
| Total Current Assets | 922,420 | 714,991 |
| PROPERTY AND EQUIPMENT | | |
| Land and buildings | 54,772 | 54,432 |
| Fixtures and equipment | 412,496 | 351,288 |
| Leasehold improvements | 232,388 | 209,086 |
| Construction-in-progress | 61,720 | 24,109 |
| | 761,376 | 638,915 |
| Less accumulated depreciation and amortization | 358,693 | 307,365 |
| | 402,683 | 331,550 |
| Other long-term assets | 36,242 | 36,184 |
| Total Assets | $1,361,345 | $1,082,725 |
| LIABILITIES AND STOCKHOLDERS' EQUITY | | |
| CURRENT LIABILITIES | | |
| Accounts payable | $ 397,193 | $ 314,530 |
| Accrued expenses and other | 114,586 | 92,760 |
| Accrued payroll and benefits | 99,115 | 70,413 |
| Income taxes payable | 15,790 | 11,885 |
| Total Current Liabilities | 626,684 | 489,588 |
| Long-term debt | 25,000 | — |
| Deferred income taxes and other long-term liabilities | 66,473 | 48,682 |
| STOCKHOLDERS' EQUITY | | |
| Common stock, par value $.01 per share Authorized 300,000,000 shares Issued and outstanding 77,491,000 and 78,960,000 shares | 775 | 790 |
| Additional paid-in capital | 341,041 | 289,734 |
| Retained earnings | 301,372 | 253,931 |
| | 643,188 | 544,455 |
| Total Liabilities and Stockholders' Equity | $1,361,345 | $1,082,725 |

Consistent with the nature of its business, Ross' assets include cash; accounts receivable, representing amounts due from its customers; merchandise inventories, representing costs of goods waiting to be sold; and property and equipment, representing the long-term investments in property and equipment that are necessary to its merchandising activities. In each case, these assets reflect an expected future benefit. For accounts receivable, it is the cash Ross expects to collect from customers. For merchandise inventories, it is the cash or receivables that Ross expects to arise from sales. For property and equipment, it is the sales that Ross expects to generate from their stores.

As with the asset section, the balance sheet classifies liabilities into a current and noncurrent section. Similar to current assets, **current liabilities** are liabilities that become due, or expected to be settled, within one year. Ross' liabilities are consistent with the nature of its business. They include accounts payable, principally representing amounts due to vendors of merchandise that it sells; accrued payroll, representing amounts owed to employees; accrued expenses, representing amounts owed to others for providing certain services, for example, utilities; and income taxes payable, representing amounts owed to the taxing authorities. Ross' liabilities also include long-term debt, representing amounts borrowed to finance its investment and operating activities.

As noted above, stockholders' equity represents the residual claim after liabilities have been met. **Common stock** and **additional paid-in capital** combined represent the amount contributed by stockholders when they purchased shares from the company. The remaining portion of stockholders' equity, **retained earnings,** represents the accumulated amount of net income less dividends distributed to stockholders since the company formed.

As explained earlier, not all resources that Ross controls may be reported as assets on its balance sheet. GAAP restricts what items can appear on the balance sheet, as well as the values assigned to those items that do appear. For example, Ross' slogan "Dress for Less" may have value for its company recognition. However, difficulties in how to measure the economic benefits of slogans or brand names generally prevent their recognition as assets in an accounting sense. Going back to the example of Polaroid that started this chapter, Polaroid states that patents and trademarks are valued at $1 on its financial statements. This treatment recognizes that these assets have value, but by only recognizing them at $1 there is no material effect on the interpretation of the financial statements. Polaroid therefore indicates to its financial statement readers that these items have value even though the company cannot report them under GAAP.

Recall that the accounting values for assets and liabilities may not reflect their current market values. Because stockholders' equity must equal assets less liabilities, it therefore follows that the book value of stockholders' equity does not necessarily equal its market value. For example, if we divide stockholders' equity from Ross' balance sheet ($643,188) by the number of shares of Ross' common stock outstanding (77,491), we obtain a **book value per share** of $8.35 at February 1, 2003. However, Ross' stock price during the year ended February 1, 2003 ranged from $32.76 to $46.88 a share.

The amount in the common stock accounts represents a par value assigned to the shares at issuance and has little economic significance. Par value should not be confused with market value of the firm's stock. Market value takes into account the entire equity of stockholders and is not limited to the portion of initial contribution labeled as par value.

Market values are not used to value owners' equity in the financial statements as it would be circular logic to value stockholders' equity at market prices that, in principle, depend on the information contained in financial reports.

## FLOW STATEMENTS—CHANGES IN FINANCIAL POSITION

Changes in the firm's financial position from one point in time to another can be broadly classified into those related to *operating, investing,* and *financing activities.* Three statements describe these changes in the financial position of the firm: the Statement of Earnings, the Statement of Cash Flows, and the Statement

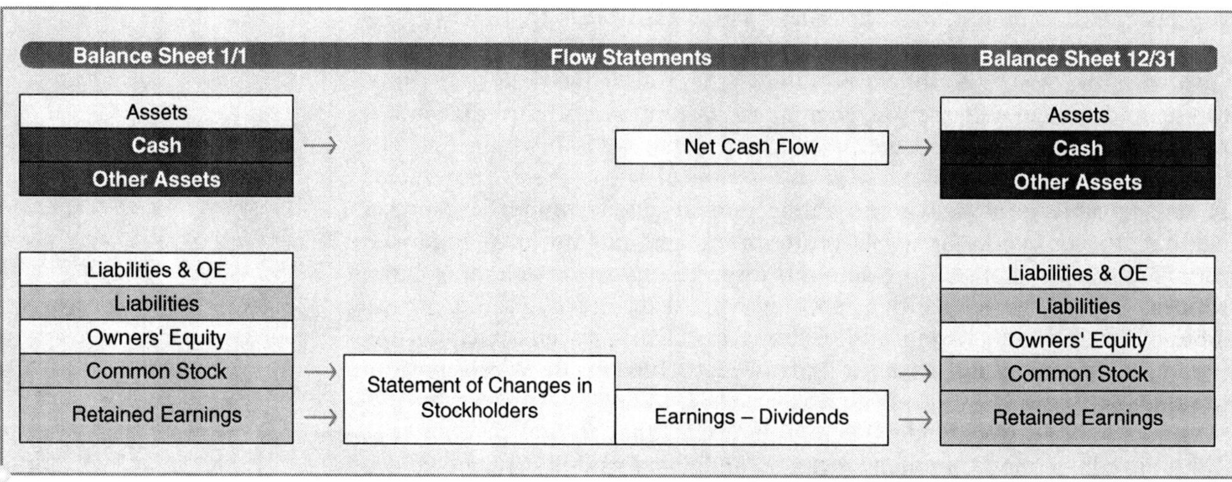


**Exhibit 2.6**
Financial Statement Connections

of Changes in Stockholders' Equity. Exhibit 2.6 shows the relationships of the three flow statements to the balance sheet at the beginning and end of the period.

## STATEMENT OF EARNINGS

The Statement of Earnings (sometimes called the *Statement of Income,* or *Income Statement*) explains changes in stockholders' equity arising from the firm's operating activities. It reports *revenues* from sales of goods and services to customers and the *expenses* of generating those revenues. Revenues are generally recognized at the point at which the company transfers the risks and benefits of ownership of the goods or services to the buyer. For most product firms, this happens at the date the product is delivered to the customer. Expenses are often classified into costs directly related to the goods sold **(cost of goods sold),** other operating expenses (including selling and administrative costs), financing costs (e.g., interest), and income taxes.

At the time revenues are recognized, the firm records the increase in assets that it has received in exchange for its goods or services. These assets are typically either cash or, if the customer is granted credit, accounts receivable. In some cases, a customer may pay for a product or service in advance of its receipt (e.g., school tuition). When this occurs, the firm cannot recognize the revenue from the sale until the product or service is delivered (as we will discuss in Chapter 4). Therefore, the receipt of cash results in the creation of a liability that represents this deferred revenue (the obligation of the firm to deliver the product or service in the future). Later, when revenue is recognized on the income statement, this liability account is reduced.

When expenses are recognized, they may be associated with decreases in assets (such as the decrease in inventory when cost of goods sold is recognized) or increases in liabilities (such as when salary expense is recognized before salaries are paid to employees).

**Net income** (loss) (also referred to as *net earnings*), then, is the excess of revenues (expenses) over expenses (revenues):

Net Income = Revenues − Expenses

Net income (loss) increases (decreases) owners' equity because it is added to the balance in retained earnings. Note that earnings can either be positive (income) or negative (loss).

Accounting recognition of the revenues and expenses that go into the determination of net income are governed by the **accrual concept** of accounting. As explained more fully in Chapter 4, under this concept, revenues are recorded as *earned,* not necessarily when cash is received, and expenses are recorded as *incurred,* not necessarily when cash is paid.

The accrual concept is very important to fully understand because analysts often use earnings as a starting point to forecast future cash flows of the firm.

Let's look at the Statement of Earnings for Ross for three fiscal years (Exhibit 2.7). Ross prepares what is known as a single-step income statement. This type of income statement combines all revenues in one section and all expenses except income taxes in a second section. *Sales* are amounts charged to customers for merchandise. *Costs and Expenses* include *costs of goods sold, general and administrative costs,* and *interest expense.* As is the case for most retailers, costs of goods sold include costs associated with buying and distributing merchandise and building occupancy costs. General and administrative costs include salaries, wages, employee benefits, and other expense of managing the firm's activities. Interest expense pertains to the debt that appears on Ross' balance sheet and is therefore considered a nonoperating item. *Earnings before taxes* is then computed (subtracting all expenses from sales). The tax on this income is shown just prior to *Net earnings,* often referred to as the *bottom line.*

Net earnings summarizes the effect of Ross' operating activities on stockholders' equity. It is added to the balance of retained earnings at the end of the previous year in arriving at the balance at February 1, 2003. Because stockholders' equity equals net assets (assets less liabilities), net assets must also

**Exhibit 2.7**
Ross Stores—Statement of Earnings

THE REAL WORLD

**Ross Stores**

| For the years ended (in thousands) | 2/1/2003 | 2/2/2002 | 2/3/2001 |
|---|---|---|---|
| SALES | $3,531,349 | $2,986,596 | $2,709,039 |
| COSTS AND EXPENSES | | | |
| Cost of goods sold, including related buying, distribution, and occupancy costs | 2,628,412 | 2,243,384 | 2,017,923 |
| General, selling, and administrative | 572,316 | 485,455 | 438,464 |
| Interest expense, net | 279 | 3,168 | 3,466 |
| | 3,201,007 | 2,732,007 | 2,459,853 |
| Earnings before taxes | 330,342 | 254,589 | 249,186 |
| Provision for taxes on earnings | 129,164 | 99,544 | 97,432 |
| Net earnings | $ 201,178 | $ 155,045 | $ 151,754 |

reflect the results of operations. Intuitively, we can see that sales prices charged to customers not only increase net income (and hence owners' equity) in the form of revenues, but also increase assets by increasing either cash or accounts receivable. Likewise, salaries and wages of employees not only decrease net income (owners' equity) in the form of operating expenses, but either decrease assets by decreasing cash or increase liabilities by increasing accrued payroll. This two-sided effect of revenues or expenses is essential to preserve the relationship in the accounting equation. (This concept is discussed in detail in Chapters 3 and 4 so do not be concerned if it seems difficult to grasp at this point.)

## STATEMENT OF CASH FLOWS

The Statement of Cash Flows also describes changes in financial position, specifically the changes in cash. This statement shows how investing, financing, and operating activities affect cash. Investment activities relate to the acquisition or disposal of long-term assets such as property and equipment. Financing activities relate to the issuance and repayment or repurchase of debt and equity. The operating activities section reports the cash inflows and outflows associated with the sales of goods and services to customers.

Under current accounting standards, the operating section of the statement can be presented in one of two forms: a **direct method,** under which the direct cash inflows and outflows are shown, or an **indirect method** (by far the most common), under which net income under the accrual concept is adjusted to its cash flow equivalent. Exhibit 2.8 illustrates the direct method of the Statement of Cash Flows for Rowe Companies (a group of companies that provides home furnishings). In contrast, Exhibit 2.9 shows the indirect method of the Statement of Cash Flows for Ross. Chapter 5 provides a more complete discussion of the differences in these two methods.

Looking at Exhibit 2.9, note how the operating section differs from the one presented in Exhibit 2.8. For the Ross Statement of Cash Flows, the operating section starts with net earnings, which is then adjusted to its cash flow equivalent (net cash provided by operating activities). Further note how the net earnings and the net cash provided by operating activities differ in each year. For instance, in 2003, net income was $201,178 (000s), whereas cash flow from operations was $332,445 (000s).

The investing section contains additions to property and equipment made during the year. Though not in Ross' case, this section may also include amounts invested in temporary investments or costs of acquiring the net assets of another firm. The financing section shows the proceeds and payments on long-term debt, the cash payments of dividends, the proceeds from the issuance of stock for employee stock plans (recall that we mentioned these in Chapter 1 as a common way to compensate certain managers), and repurchases of Ross' own shares.

Now that we have completed a look at three of the major financial statements for Ross, it is useful to revisit the diagram in Exhibit 2.6 that showed the connections among the balance sheet, income statement, and cash flow statement.

**Exhibits 2.8**
Statement of Cash Flows: Direct Method

THE REAL WORLD

**Rowe Companies**

The Rowe Companies Annual Report 2003
CONSOLIDATED STATEMENTS OF CASH FLOWS

| Year Ended (in thousands) | 11/30/2003 | 12/1/2002 | 12/2/2001 |
|---|---|---|---|
| Increase (Decrease) in Cash | | | |
| Cash flows from operating activities: | | | |
| Cash received from customers | $300,299 | $336,853 | $329,558 |
| Cash paid to suppliers and employees | (287,266) | (317,217) | (331,014) |
| Income taxes received (paid), net | 1,352 | 2,839 | 585 |
| Interest paid | (5,225) | (4,028) | (2,397) |
| Interest received | 225 | 347 | 480 |
| Other receipts—net | 942 | 1,340 | 1,109 |
| Net cash and cash equivalents provided by (used in) operating activities | 10,327 | 20,134 | (1,679) |
| Cash flows from investing activities: | | | |
| Payments received on notes receivable | 100 | 125 | 125 |
| Increase in cash surrender value | (121) | (150) | (179) |
| Proceeds from sale of Mitchell Gold | 39,573 | – | – |
| Proceeds from sale of property and equipment | – | – | 1,056 |
| Capital expenditures | (3,995) | (3,323) | (3,317) |
| Payments under earn-out and related obligations (Note 2) | (15,759) | – | – |
| Net cash provided by (used in) investing activities | 19,798 | (3,348) | (2,315) |
| Cash flows from financing activities: | | | |
| Restricted cash released from (deposited to) collateral for letters of credit | 264 | (1,938) | – |
| Net borrowings (repayments) under line of credit | – | (9,368) | 5,368 |
| Draws under revolving loans | 12,570 | 3,994 | 6,865 |
| Proceeds from issuance of long-term debt | – | 39,442 | – |
| Repayments under revolving loans | (20,751) | (10,244) | (3,821) |
| Payments to reduce long-term debt | (18,759) | (47,874) | – |
| Payments to reduce loans on cash surrender value | (16) | – | – |
| Proceeds from loans against life insurance policies | – | – | 3,014 |
| Proceeds from issuance of common stock | 3 | 38 | 27 |
| Dividends paid | – | – | (1,379) |
| Purchase of treasury stock | (2) | (19) | (16) |
| Net cash provided by (used in) financing activities | (26,691) | (25,969) | 10,058 |
| Net increase (decrease) in cash and cash equivalents | 3,434 | (9,183) | 6,064 |
| Cash at beginning of year | 274 | 9,457 | 3,393 |
| Cash at end of year | $ 3,708 | $ 274 | $ 9,457 |

**Exhibit 2.9**
Ross Stores—Statement of Cash Flows

THE REAL WORLD
**Ross Stores**

| For the years ended (in thousands) | 2/1/2003 | 2/2/2002 | 2/3/2001 |
|---|---|---|---|
| CASH FLOWS FROM OPERATING ACTIVITIES | | | |
| Net earnings | $201,178 | $155,045 | $151,754 |
| Adjustments to reconcile net earnings to net cash provided by operating activities: | | | |
| Depreciation and amortization of property and equipment | 53,329 | 49,896 | 44,377 |
| Other amortization | 12,847 | 12,725 | 10,686 |
| Deferred income taxes | 17,375 | 12,633 | 10,015 |
| Change in assets and liabilities: | | | |
| Merchandise inventory | (93,128) | (63,824) | (59,071) |
| Other current assets net | (4,003) | (16,901) | (980) |
| Accounts payable | 81,958 | 54,064 | 5,751 |
| Other current liabilities | 54,541 | 34,384 | (26,836) |
| Other | 8,348 | 4,867 | 7,653 |
| Net cash provided by operating activities | 332,445 | 242,889 | 143,349 |
| CASH FLOWS USED IN INVESTING ACTIVITIES | | | |
| Additions to property and equipment | (133,166) | (86,002) | (82,114) |
| Net cash used in investing activities | (133,166) | (86,002) | (82,114) |
| CASH FLOWS USED IN FINANCING ACTIVITIES | | | |
| Borrowings (repayments) under lines of credit | 0 | (64,000) | 64,000 |
| Proceeds from long-term debt | 25,000 | 0 | 0 |
| Issuance of common stock related to stock plans | 50,863 | 54,581 | 14,303 |
| Repurchase of common stock | (149,997) | (130,676) | (169,324) |
| Dividends paid | (14,847) | (13,595) | (12,389) |
| Net cash used in financing activities | (88,981) | (153,690) | (103,410) |
| Net increase (decrease) in cash and cash equivalents | 110,298 | 3,197 | (42,175) |
| Cash and cash equivalents: | | | |
| Beginning of year | 40,351 | 37,154 | 79,329 |
| End of year | $150,649 | $ 40,351 | $ 37,154 |
| SUPPLEMENTAL CASH FLOW DISCLOSURES | | | |
| Interest paid | $ 409 | $ 3,332 | $ 3,352 |
| Income taxes paid | $ 91,875 | $ 61,433 | $100,359 |

## ARTICULATION OF THE FINANCIAL STATEMENTS

Exhibit 2.10 presents an update of Exhibit 2.6; we have now included the dollar amounts for the key components of these connections. Note how earnings and dividends affect the balance in retained earnings. However, in Ross' case, retained earnings is also affected by the repurchase of shares of its own stock. (We will discuss this type of transaction in Chapter 12.) Ross' Statement of

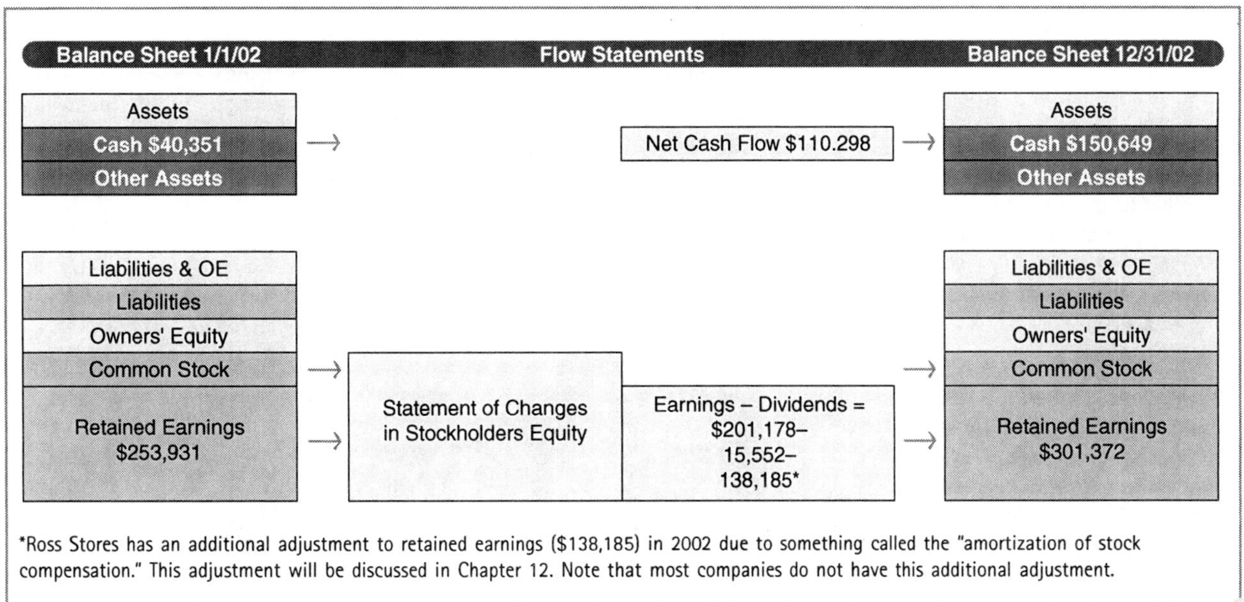


*Ross Stores has an additional adjustment to retained earnings ($138,185) in 2002 due to something called the "amortization of stock compensation." This adjustment will be discussed in Chapter 12. Note that most companies do not have this additional adjustment.

**Exhibit 2.10**
Financial Statement Connections–Ross

Changes in Stockholders' Equity, discussed next, provides these same direct connections between the beginning and ending balances in the accounts, as well as changes in those accounts.

**THE REAL WORLD**

**Ross Stores**

## STATEMENT OF CHANGES IN STOCKHOLDERS' EQUITY

The Statement of Changes in Stockholders' Equity provides details about all of the transactions that affect stockholders' equity, including such items as stock issuance, stock repurchases, net income, and dividends. Exhibit 2.11 shows Ross' Statement of Changes in Stockholders' Equity. Each column represents a particular account within stockholders' equity. The rows represent the balance and the transactions that have occurred over the most recent three years. Recall that retained earnings are increased by net income and decreased by dividends declared to stockholders (except for the adjustment for the repurchase of stock that we have already mentioned).

## OTHER STATEMENT DISCLOSURES

A company's annual report to shareholders contains more than the financial statements themselves (see Exhibit 2.12). For example, footnotes describe significant accounting policies employed by the firm (see Exhibit 2.13), as well as elaborate on items that appear in the statements. The report of the firm's auditors attests to the fairness of the financial statements and their conformance

| | Common Shares | Stock Amount | Additional Paid-In Capital | Retained Earnings | Total |
|---|---|---|---|---|---|
| BALANCE AT JANUARY 29, 2000 | 88,774 | $888 | $234,635 | $237,908 | $473,431 |
| Common stock issued under stock plans, including tax benefit | 1,854 | 18 | 14,285 | | 14,303 |
| Amortization of stock compensation | | | 9,894 | | 9,894 |
| Common stock repurchased | (10,101) | (101) | (22,690) | (146,533) | (169,324) |
| Net earnings | | | | 151,754 | 151,754 |
| Dividends declared | | | | (12,511) | (12,511) |
| BALANCE AT FEBRUARY 3, 2001 | 80,527 | 805 | 236,124 | 230,618 | 467,547 |
| Common stock issued under stock plans, including tax benefit | 3,378 | 34 | 54,547 | | 54,581 |
| Amortization of stock compensation | | | 11,881 | | 11,881 |
| Common stock repurchased | (4,945) | (49) | (12,818) | (117,809) | (130,676) |
| Net earnings | | | | 155,045 | 155,045 |
| Dividends declared | | | | (13,923) | (13,923) |
| BALANCE AT FEBRUARY 2, 2002 | 78,960 | 790 | 289,734 | 253,931 | 544,455 |
| Common stock issued under stock plans, including tax benefit | 2,341 | 23 | 50,840 | | 50,863 |
| Amortization of stock compensation | | | 12,241 | | 12,241 |
| Common stock repurchased | (3,810) | (38) | (11,774) | (138,185) | (149,997) |
| Net earnings | | | | 201,178 | 201,178 |
| Dividends declared | | | | (15,552) | (15,552) |
| BALANCE AT FEBRUARY 1, 2003 | 77,491 | $775 | $341,041 | $301,372 | $643,188 |

**Exhibit 2.11**
Ross Stores—Statement of Changes in Stockholders' Equity (in thousands)

THE REAL WORLD

**Ross Stores**

with regulatory guidelines. Further, although not formally part of the company's financial statements, management provides its own assessment of the past year's operating results, liquidity, and capital expenditures, as well as financing strategies. Management provides this information through the management's discussion and analysis section of the annual report, commonly known as the *MD&A section*.

**Exhibit 2.12**
Typical Contents of an Annual Report

Message from Chief Executive Officer
Description of Principal Products or Services
Financial Highlights
Management's Discussion and Analysis
Statement of Financial Position
Statement of Earnings
Statement of Cash Flows
Statement of Changes in Stockholders' Equity
Notes to Financial Statements
Statement of Management's Responsibilities
Auditor's Report
Other Corporate Information

**Exhibits 2.13**
Ross Stores Footnotes: Summary of Significant Accounting Policies

THE REAL WORLD
**Ross Stores**

**Merchandise Inventory.** Merchandise inventory is stated at the lower of cost (determined using a weighted average basis) or net realizable value. The Company purchases manufacturer overruns and canceled orders both during and at the end of a season which are referred to as packaway inventory. Packaway inventory is purchased with the intent that it will be stored in the Company's warehouses until a later date, which may even be the beginning of the same selling season in the following year. Packaway inventory accounted for approximately 44 percent and 43 percent of total inventories as of February 1, 2003 and February 2, 2002, respectively.

**Cost of Goods Sold.** In addition to the product cost of merchandise sold, the Company includes its buying and distribution expenses as well as occupancy costs related to the Company's retail stores, buying, and distribution facilities in its cost of goods sold. Buying expenses include costs to procure merchandise inventories. Distribution expenses include the cost of operating the Company's distribution centers and freight expenses related to transporting merchandise.

**Property and Equipment.** Property and equipment are stated at cost. Depreciation is calculated using the straight-line method over the estimated useful life of the asset, typically ranging from five to 12 years for equipment and 20 to 40 years for real property. The cost of leasehold improvements is amortized over the useful life of the asset or the applicable lease term, whichever is less. Computer hardware and software costs are included in fixtures and equipment and are amortized over their estimated useful life generally ranging from five to seven years. Reviews for impairment are performed whenever events or circumstances indicate the carrying value of an asset may not be recoverable.

Analysts must understand the accounting choices that firms make in order to interpret their financial statements and to make fair comparisons across firms. The summary of significant accounting policies footnote is very important in conveying this information about the choices the firm has made.

Beyond the annual report, additional financial information is made publicly available through filings with the SEC. These filings include prospectuses accompanying new stock issues, annual 10K reports (such as Exhibit 2.4), and 10Q reports (a 10Q reports contains quarterly financial statement information). These reports typically offer greater detail than the annual report. For example, these filings might include information on competition and risks associated with the firm's principal business, holdings of major stockholders, compensation of top executives, and announcements of various events.

## THE INFLUENCE OF FINANCIAL STATEMENTS

Financial statements embody the standards by which other information is often constructed. For example, professional security analysts project revenues and estimate research and development spending. Given that such forecasts and projections pertain to information that will ultimately surface in financial statements (see the report for Archer Daniels in Exhibit 2.14), these reports are likely to reflect the same accounting principles. In other words, the influence of financial reports extends well beyond their contents

**Exhibit 2.14**
Archer Daniels Midland Operating Earnings Up

THE REAL WORLD

**Archer Daniels**

January 19, 2001

DECATUR, Ill. Jan 14 (Reuters)—Archer Daniels Midland Co., the largest U.S. grain producer, said on Friday its fiscal second-quarter operating earnings rose 22 percent, beating forecasts, as sales in ethanol, feed, and cocoa products boosted results.

This type of additional disclosure may potentially affect the company's stock valuation as it indicates changes in the expectations of future results ("beating forecasts"). How much the valuation changes depends, in part, on whether the increase in earnings is sustainable in the future. Although no obvious price reaction resulted on the day after this announcement, the price of ADMs stock rose from around $8 a share to $15 a share between October 2000 and February 2001. This clearly indicates the increased prospects of the company.

as such. There is a confirmation aspect to reports provided by the firm that becomes apparent as you look closely at financial information from other sources.

We opened the chapter relating how Polaroid suffered a drop off in sales, starting in the fourth quarter of 2000. Exhibit 2.15 shows the quarterly sales figures for Polaroid (taken from Polaroid's 10Q reports) over the period from the first quarter of 1998 through the second quarter of 2001. Notice the seasonal pattern of Polaroid's sales. That is, in a given year, Polaroid always realizes its highest sales in the fourth quarter, typically significantly up from the third quarter. However, in 2000, fourth-quarter sales are only slightly higher than those in the third quarter. This departure from the previous trend would be important to investors and analysts as they assessed the value of Polaroid's shares in the fourth quarter of 2001 and beyond. Note that sales then dramatically fell in the first and second quarters of 2001, leading up to Polaroid's declaration of bankruptcy in the third quarter of 2001. Sales are just one of the items that analysts would look at to understand earnings and the market value of Polaroid, but in this case perhaps, the most significant one.

**Exhibit 2.15**
Polaroid's Sales by Quarter

THE REAL WORLD

**Polaroid**

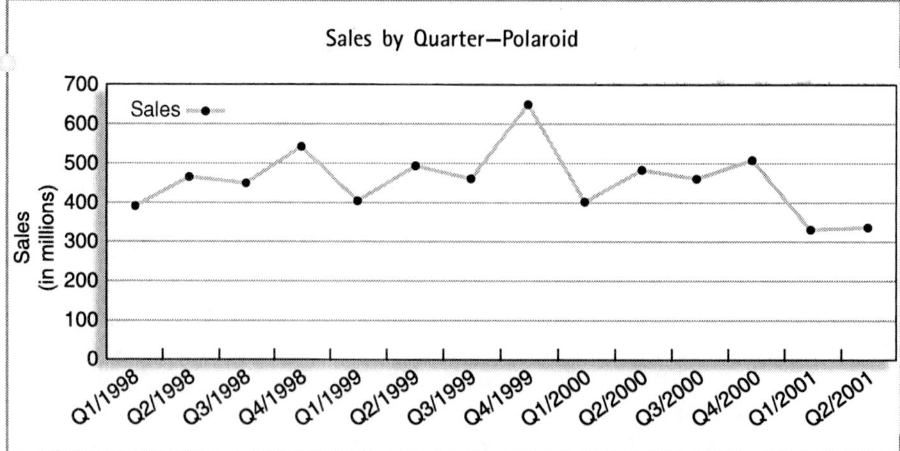

## SUMMARY AND TRANSITION

In this chapter, we provided an overview of the corporate form of business and the major financial statements prepared under GAAP as a way to set the stage for examining the construction and use of financial accounting reports in the chapters that follow. As we described, corporations have become the dominant form of business entity due to such features as limited liability and the ease with which ownership can be transferred and capital can be raised.

The main general-purpose financial statements considered include a Statement of Financial Position, which describes the financial position in terms of its assets, liabilities, and stockholders' equity of the firm at a point in time; a Statement of Earnings, which describes the results of the firm's operations in terms of its revenues and expenses from one point in time to another; a Statement of Cash Flows, which describes the firm's investment, financing, and operating activities in terms of their effects on cash; and a Statement of Changes in Stockholders' Equity, which describes transactions affecting contributed capital and retained earnings in further detail.

Our description of these financial statements provides a first glimpse of the typical items comprising the resources that a firm may control (assets) and the claims to those resources held by creditors and owners (liabilities and stockholders' equity, respectively). We identified changes in assets and liabilities arising from the operating activities of the firm as composed of revenues and expenses, leading to the bottom-line number, net income or earnings. Other changes pertained to investment and financing activities. We also reviewed further details of changes in stockholders' equity. In Chapter 3, we describe the mechanics of the accounting system and how to analyze the effects of a particular transaction on these financial statements of the firm. Chapter 4 provides further detail on the measurement and reporting of revenues and expenses. Our coverage of the construction of financial statements then concludes with methods for distinguishing operating, investing, and financing cash flows.

# END OF CHAPTER MATERIAL

## KEY TERMS

Accounting Equation
Accrual Concept
Accrued
Additional Paid-in Capital
Assets
Balance Sheet
Book Value per Share
Classified Balance Sheet
Common Stock
Common Stockholders' Equity
Cost of Goods Sold
Current Assets
Current Liabilities
Direct Method
Fiscal Year
Indirect Method
Liabilities
Limited Liability
Liquidity Order
Net Asset
Net Book Value
Net income

Noncurrent Assets
Owners' Equity
Partnership
Residual Claim
Retained Earnings
Sole Proprietorship
Statement of Cash Flows
Statement of Changes in Stockholders' Equity
Statement of Earnings
Statement of Financial Position
Stockholders' Equity

## ASSIGNMENT MATERIAL

### REVIEW QUESTIONS

1. Describe the pros and cons for organizing a business as a corporation rather than a partnership.
2. Describe and illustrate the three major categories of items that appear in a typical statement of financial position.
3. Describe the purpose of the four main financial statements that are contained in all annual reports.
4. What is the meaning of the term net assets?
5. Why might certain economic resources not be considered assets by accountants? Provide an example.
6. What is the accounting equation?
7. What is meant by a classified balance sheet?
8. How do accountants distinguish between current and noncurrent assets and liabilities?
9. Explain the meaning of retained earnings.
10. Why might the book value of a company be different from the market value of the company?
11. What is net income?
12. What are the two methods for reporting cash flow from operations that are allowed under GAAP?
13. What is comprehensive income?
14. How is other comprehensive income reported in the financial statements?

### APPLYING YOUR KNOWLEDGE

15. Compare and contrast the statement of earnings and the cash flow statement.

Use the following abbreviations to respond to question 16:
CA—Current Assets
NCA—Noncurrent Assets
CL—Current Liabilities
NCL—Noncurrent Liabilities
CS—Capital Stock
RE—Retained Earnings

NI—Income statement item

CF—Cash flow statement item

16. Classify the following items according to where the item would appear in the financial statements:
    a. Inventory
    b. Taxes Payable
    c. Interest Expense
    d. Dividends
    e. Sales to customers
    f. Manufacturing Equipment
    g. New issuance of common stock
    h. Cash
    i. Bonds Payable (debt due in ten years)
    j. Employee's Wages

Use the following abbreviations to respond to question number 17:

O—Operating Item

F—Financing Item

I—Investing Item

17. Classify each of the following transactions as to whether they are operating, financing, or investing activities:
    a. Cash collected from customers
    b. Repayment of debt
    c. Payment of dividends
    d. Purchase of a truck (by a manufacturing company)
    e. Purchase of a truck (by a truck dealer)
    f. Purchase of shares of stock of another company
    g. Sale of a plant
    h. Utility expenses are incurred
18. Compute the missing balance sheet amounts in each of the following independent situations:

| | A | B | C | D |
|---|---|---|---|---|
| Current Assets | ? | $650,000 | $230,000 | $40,000 |
| Noncurrent Assets | 250,000 | ? | 400,000 | ? |
| Total Assets | ? | 1,050,000 | ? | 190,000 |
| Current Liabilities | 50,000 | 500,000 | 300,000 | 25,000 |
| Noncurrent Liabilities | ? | 90,000 | ? | 10,000 |
| Owners' Equity | 225,000 | ? | 80,000 | ? |
| Total Liabilities and Owners' Equity | 350,000 | ? | ? | ? |

**19.** Compute the missing amounts in the reconciliation of retained earnings in each of the following independent situations:

| | A | B | C | D |
|---|---|---|---|---|
| Retained Earnings Dec. 31, Year 1 | $20,000 | $100,000 | ? | $40,000 |
| Net Income | 15,000 | ? | 400,000 | 22,000 |
| Dividends Declared and Paid | 6,000 | 35,000 | 250,000 | ? |
| Retained Earnings Dec. 31, Year 2 | ? | 115,000 | 300,000 | 52,000 |

**20.** For each of the following companies, list at least two types of assets and one type of liability that you would expect to find on their balance sheet (try to include at least one item in your list that is unique to that business):

**a.** The Washington Post Company—This is a company that is primarily in the newspaper business but also has operations in television stations, cable systems, *Newsweek* magazine, as well as some other smaller operations.

**b.** International Paper—This is a company that is primarily in the forest products business, selling both paper and wood products.

**c.** SBC—This is a telecommunications company.

**d.** Hartford Financial Services Group—This is a multiline insurance company.

**e.** Philip Morris Companies, Inc.—This is a company that is primarily in the tobacco business but has also diversified into foods, beer, financial services, and real estate.

**f.** Citibank—This is a major commercial bank.

**g.** Delta—This is a major airline.

**21.** For each of the companies listed in question number 20 list at least two line items that you would expect to find on their income statement (try to include at least one item in your list that is unique to that business).

**22.** For each of the companies listed in question number 20 list at least two line items that you would expect to find on their cash flow statement (try to include at least one item in your list that is unique to that business).

**23.** Suppose that your best friend wanted to start a new business providing desktop publishing services to customers. Your friend has some savings to start the business but not enough to buy all of the equipment that she thinks she needs. She has asked you for some advice about how to raise additional funds. Give her at least two alternatives and provide the pros and cons for each alternative.

**24.** Suppose that you and a friend form a partnership in which you both contribute the same amount of cash and you agree to share in profits on a 50–50 basis. Further suppose that you are responsible for running the day-to-day operations of the firm but your friend is a silent partner in the sense that he doesn't work in the business (he has another job). Because you have no other job, the partnership agrees to pay you $1,500 per month. How should the partnership treat this payment, as a distribution of profits or as an expense of doing business? What difference would it make to the distribution to you and your partner?

## USING REAL DATA

Base your answer to problems 25–28 on the data from Polaroid provided here.

| POLAROID CORP. Balance Sheet | 12/31/1999 | 12/31/2000 |
|---|---|---|
| Assets | | |
| Current Assets | | |
| Cash and cash equivalents | $ 92,000,000 | $ 97,200,000 |
| Receivables, less allowances of $23.9 in 1999 and $23.8 in 2000 (Note 6) | 489,700,000 | 435,400,000 |
| Inventories (Notes 5 and 6) | 395,600,000 | 482,500,000 |
| Prepaid expenses and other assets (Note 4) | 130,800,000 | 103,500,000 |
| Total Current Assets | 1,108,100,000 | 1,118,600,000 |
| Property, Plant, and Equipment: | | |
| Land | 14,700,000 | 6,900,000 |
| Buildings | 322,700,000 | 313,500,000 |
| Machinery and equipment | 1,620,100,000 | 1,597,500,000 |
| Construction in progress | 65,500,000 | 49,600,000 |
| Total property, plant and equipment | 2,023,000,000 | 1,967,500,000 |
| Less accumulated depreciation | 1,423,800,000 | 1,398,300,000 |
| Net Property, Plant, and Equipment | 599,200,000 | 569,200,000 |
| Deferred Tax Assets (Note 4) | 243,700,000 | 279,500,000 |
| Other Assets | 89,000,000 | 75,700,000 |
| Total Assets | $2,040,000,000 | $2,043,000,000 |
| Liabilities and Stockholders' Equity | | |
| Current Liabilities | | |
| Short-term debt (Note 6) | $ 259,400,000 | $ 363,700,000 |
| Payables and accruals (Note 7) | 338,000,000 | 334,100,000 |
| Compensation and benefits (Notes 10 and 11) | 138,100,000 | 76,700,000 |
| Federal, state and foreign income taxes (Note 4) | 14,700,000 | 18,800,000 |
| Total Current Liabilities | 750,200,000 | 793,300,000 |
| Long-term debt (Note 8) | 573,000,000 | 573,500,000 |
| Accrued postretirement benefits (Note 11) | 234,800,000 | 222,700,000 |
| Other long-term liabilities | 111,500,000 | 78,300,000 |
| Total Liabilities | 1,669,500,000 | 1,667,800,000 |
| Preferred stock, Series A and D, $1 par value, authorized 20,000,000 shares; all shares unissued | – | – |
| Common stockholders' equity (Note 9) | | |
| Common stock, $1 par value, authorized 150,000,000 shares (75,427,550 shares issued in 1999 and 2000) | 75,400,000 | 75,400,000 |
| Additional paid-in capital | 395,200,000 | 363,100,000 |
| Retained earnings | 1,208,800,000 | 1,219,500,000 |
| Accumulated other comprehensive income | (48,900,000) | (68,900,000) |
| Less: Treasury stock, at cost (30,811,263 and 29,895,578 shares in 1999 and 2000, respectively) | 1,259,700,000 | 1,213,800,000 |
| Deferred compensation | 300,000 | 100,000 |
| Total common stockholders' equity | 370,500,000 | 375,200,000 |
| Total Liabilities and Common Stockholders' Equity | $2,040,000,000 | $2,043,000,000 |

| POLAROID CORP. Income Statement | 12/31/1998 | 12/31/1999 | 12/31/2000 |
|---|---|---|---|
| Net Sales | $1,845,900,000 | $1,978,600,000 | $1,855,600,000 |
| Cost of goods sold | 1,108,400,000 | 1,170,500,000 | 1,055,900,000 |
| Marketing, research, engineering, and administrative expenses (Note 2) | 736,500,000 | 700,500,000 | 696,400,000 |
| Restructuring charges/(credits) (Note 2) | 50,000,000 | – | (5,800,000) |
| Total Costs | 1,894,900,000 | 1,871,000,000 | 1,746,500,000 |
| Profit/(Loss) from Operations | (49,000,000) | 107,600,000 | 109,100,000 |
| Other income/(expense): | | | |
| Interest income | 2,900,000 | 2,700,000 | 5,500,000 |
| Other | 64,800,000 | (19,500,000) | 28,600,000 |
| Total other income/(expense) | 67,700,000 | (16,800,000) | 34,100,000 |
| Interest expense | 57,600,000 | 77,400,000 | 85,300,000 |
| Earnings/(Loss) before Income Tax Expense | (38,900,000) | 13,400,000 | 57,900,000 |
| Federal, state and foreign income tax expense (Note 4) | 12,100,000 | 4,700,000 | 20,200,000 |
| Net Earnings/(Loss) | ($51,000,000) | $8,700,000 | $37,700,000 |

| POLAROID CORP. Cash Flow | 12/31/1998 | 12/31/1999 | 12/31/2000 |
|---|---|---|---|
| Cash Flows from Operating Activities | | | |
| Net earnings/(loss) | $ (51,000,000) | $ 8,700,000 | $ 37,700,000 |
| Depreciation of property, plant, and equipment | 90,700,000 | 105,900,000 | 113,900,000 |
| Gain on the sale of real estate | (68,200,000) | (11,700,000) | (21,800,000) |
| Other noncash items | 62,200,000 | 73,800,000 | 22,900,000 |
| Decrease/(increase) in receivables | 79,000,000 | (52,700,000) | 41,800,000 |
| Decrease/(increase) in inventories | (28,400,000) | 88,000,000 | (100,600,000) |
| Decrease in prepaids and other assets | 39,000,000 | 62,400,000 | 32,900,000 |
| Increase/(decrease) in payables and accruals | 25,300,000 | (16,500,000) | 9,200,000 |
| Decrease in compensation and benefits | (21,000,000) | (72,500,000) | (105,000,000) |
| Decrease in federal, state, and foreign income taxes payable | (29,900,000) | (54,000,000) | (31,500,000) |
| Net cash provided/(used) by operating activities | 97,700,000 | 131,400,000 | (500,000) |
| Cash Flows from Investing Activities | | | |
| Decrease/(increase) in other assets | (25,400,000) | 16,500,000 | 4,500,000 |
| Additions to property, plant, and equipment | (191,100,000) | (170,500,000) | (129,200,000) |

| | 12/31/1998 | 12/31/1999 | 12/31/2000 |
|---|---|---|---|
| Proceeds from the sale of property, plant, and equipment | 150,500,000 | 36,600,000 | 56,600,000 |
| Acquisitions, net of cash acquired | (18,800,000) | – | – |
| Net cash used by investing activities | (84,800,000) | (117,400,000) | (68,100,000) |
| Cash Flows from Financing Activities | | | |
| Net increase/(decrease) in short-term debt (maturities of 90 days or less) | 131,200,000 | (86,200,000) | 108,200,000 |
| Short-term debt (maturities of more than 90 days) | | | |
| Proceeds | 73,000,000 | 41,800,000 | – |
| Payments | (117,200,000) | (24,900,000) | – |
| Proceeds from issuance of long-term debt | – | 268,200,000 | – |
| Repayment of long-term debt | – | (200,000,000) | – |
| Cash dividends paid | (26,500,000) | (26,600,000) | (27,000,000) |
| Purchase of treasury stock | (45,500,000) | – | – |
| Proceeds from issuance of shares in connection with stock incentive plan | 6,000,000 | 300,000 | 100,000 |
| Net cash provided/(used) by financing activities | 21,000,000 | (27,400,000) | 81,300,000 |
| Effect of exchange rate changes on cash | 3,100,000 | 400,000 | (7,500,000) |
| Net increase/(decrease) in cash and cash equivalents | 37,000,000 | (13,000,000) | 5,200,000 |
| Cash and cash equivalents at beginning of year | 68,000,000 | 105,000,000 | 92,000,000 |
| Cash and cash equivalents at end of year | $105,000,000 | $92,000,000 | $ 97,200,000 |

**25.** Find the following amounts in the statements of Polaroid:

**a.** Net sales in 2000

**b.** Marketing, research, engineering, and administrative expenses incurred in 2000

**c.** Interest expense in 2000

**d.** Income tax expense in 1999

**e.** Net income in 1999

**f.** Inventories at the end of 2000

**g.** Payables and accruals at the beginning of 2000

**h.** Retained earnings at the end of 2000

**i.** Accumulated other comprehensive income at the end of 2000

**j.** Long-term borrowings at the beginning of 2000

**k.** Cash produced from operating activities in 2000

l. Cash payments to acquire property, plant, and equipment in 2000
m. Dividends paid in 2000
n. Cash proceeds from new borrowings in 2000
o. Cash produced or used for investing activities in 2000
p. Amount of other comprehensive income in 2000

26. What is the trend in net income for the three years presented?
27. What is the trend in cash flow from operations for the three years presented?
28. What is the trend in net sales for the three years presented?

Base your answers to problems 29–35 on the data for Werner Enterprises provided here.

WERNER ENTERPRISES, INC.
CONSOLIDATED BALANCE SHEET
(In thousands, except share amounts)

| | 2000/12/31 | 1999/12/31 |
|---|---|---|
| ASSETS | | |
| Current assets: | | |
| Cash and cash equivalents | $ 25,485 | $ 15,368 |
| Accounts receivable, trade, less allowance of $3,994 and $3,236, respectively | 123,518 | 127,211 |
| Receivable from unconsolidated affiliate | 5,332 | – |
| Other receivables | 10,257 | 11,217 |
| Inventories and supplies | 7,329 | 5,296 |
| Prepaid taxes, licenses, and permits | 12,396 | 12,423 |
| Current deferred income taxes | 11,552 | 8,500 |
| Other | 10,908 | 8,812 |
| Total current assets | 206,777 | 188,827 |
| Property and equipment, at cost | | |
| Land | 19,157 | 14,522 |
| Buildings and improvements | 72,631 | 65,152 |
| Revenue equipment | 829,549 | 800,613 |
| Service equipment and other | 100,342 | 90,322 |
| Total property and equipment | 1,021,679 | 970,609 |
| Less accumulated depreciation | 313,881 | 262,557 |
| Property and equipment, net | 707,798 | 708,052 |
| Notes receivable | 4,420 | – |
| Investment in unconsolidated affiliate | 5,324 | – |
| Other noncurrent assets | 2,888 | – |
| | $ 927,207 | $896,879 |
| LIABILITIES AND STOCKHOLDERS' EQUITY | | |
| Current liabilities: | | |
| Accounts payable | $ 30,710 | $ 35,686 |
| Short-term debt | – | 25,000 |
| Insurance and claims accruals | 36,057 | 32,993 |
| Accrued payroll | 12,746 | 11,846 |
| Income taxes payable | 7,157 | 926 |
| Other current liabilities | 14,749 | 14,755 |
| Total current liabilities | 101,419 | 121,206 |

| | 2000/12/31 | 1999/12/31 |
|---|---|---|
| Long-term debt | 105,000 | 120,000 |
| Deferred income taxes | 152,403 | 130,600 |
| Insurance, claims, and other long-term accruals | 32,301 | 30,301 |
| Commitments and contingencies | | |
| Stockholders' equity Common stock, $.01 par value, 200,000,000 shares authorized; 48,320,835 shares issued; 47,039,290 and 47,205,236 shares outstanding, respectively | 483 | 483 |
| Paid-in capital | 105,844 | 105,884 |
| Retained earnings | 447,943 | 404,625 |
| Accumulated other comprehensive loss | (34) | – |
| Treasury stock, at cost; 1,281,545 and 1,115,599 shares, respectively | (18,152) | (16,220) |
| Total stockholders' equity | 536,084 | 494,772 |
| | $ 927,207 | $896,879 |

**WERNER ENTERPRISES, INC.**
**CONSOLIDATED STATEMENTS OF INCOME**
**(In thousands, except per share amounts)**

| | 2000/12/31 | 1999/12/31 | 1998/12/31 |
|---|---|---|---|
| Operating revenues | $1,214,628 | $1,052,333 | $863,417 |
| Operating expenses: | | | |
| Salaries, wages, and benefits | 429,825 | 382,824 | 325,659 |
| Fuel | 137,620 | 79,029 | 56,786 |
| Supplies and maintenance | 102,784 | 87,600 | 72,273 |
| Taxes and licenses | 89,126 | 82,089 | 67,907 |
| Insurance and claims | 34,147 | 31,728 | 23,875 |
| Depreciation | 109,107 | 99,955 | 82,549 |
| Rent and purchased transportation | 216,917 | 185,129 | 139,026 |
| Communications and utilities | 14,454 | 13,444 | 10,796 |
| Other | (2,173) | (11,666) | (11,065) |
| Total operating expenses | 1,131,807 | 950,132 | 767,806 |
| Operating income | 82,821 | 102,201 | 95,611 |
| Other expense (income): | | | |
| Interest expense | 8,169 | 6,565 | 4,889 |
| Interest income | (2,650) | (1,407) | (1,724) |
| Other | (154) | 245 | 114 |
| Total other expense | 5,365 | 5,403 | 3,279 |
| Income before income taxes | 77,456 | 96,798 | 92,332 |
| Income taxes | 29,433 | 36,787 | 35,086 |
| Net income | $ 48,023 | $ 60,011 | $ 57,246 |
| Average common shares outstanding | 47,061 | 47,406 | 47,667 |
| Basic earnings per share | $ 1.02 | $ 1.27 | $ 1.20 |
| Diluted shares outstanding | 47,257 | 47,631 | 47,910 |
| Diluted earnings per share | $ 1.02 | $ 1.26 | $ 1.19 |

WERNER ENTERPRISES, INC.
CONSOLIDATED STATEMENTS OF CASH FLOWS
(In thousands)

| | 2000/12/31 | 1999/12/31 | 1998/12/31 |
|---|---|---|---|
| Cash flows from operating activities: | | | |
| Net income | $ 48,023 | $ 60,011 | $ 57,246 |
| Adjustments to reconcile net income to net cash provided by operating activities: | | | |
| Depreciation | 109,107 | 99,955 | 82,549 |
| Deferred income taxes | 18,751 | 22,200 | 14,700 |
| Gain on disposal of operating equipment | (5,055) | (13,047) | (12,251) |
| Equity in income of unconsolidated affiliate | (324) | – | – |
| Tax benefit from exercise of stock options | 130 | 663 | 389 |
| Other long-term assets | (2,888) | – | – |
| Insurance, claims, and other long-term accruals | 2,000 | (500) | 1,472 |
| Changes in certain working capital items: | | | |
| Accounts receivable, net | 3,693 | (32,882) | (868) |
| Prepaid expenses and other current assets | (8,474) | (8,725) | (5,186) |
| Accounts payable | (4,976) | (12,460) | 3,979 |
| Accrued and other current liabilities | 10,160 | 16,762 | (4,090) |
| Net cash provided by operating activities | 170,147 | 131,977 | 137,940 |
| Cash flows from investing activities: | | | |
| Additions to property and equipment | (169,113) | (255,326) | (258,643) |
| Retirements of property and equipment | 60,608 | 84,297 | 86,260 |
| Investment in unconsolidated affiliate | (5,000) | – | – |
| Proceeds from collection of notes receivable | 287 | – | – |
| Net cash used in investing activities | (113,218) | (171,029) | (172,383) |
| Cash flows from financing activities: | | | |
| Proceeds from issuance of long-term debt | 10,000 | 30,000 | 40,000 |
| Repayments of long-term debt | (25,000) | – | – |
| Proceeds from issuance of short-term debt | – | 30,000 | 20,000 |
| Repayments of short-term debt | (25,000) | (15,000) | (20,000) |
| Dividends on common stock | (4,710) | (4,740) | (4,201) |
| Repurchases of common stock | (2,759) | (3,941) | (9,072) |
| Stock options exercised | 657 | 2,188 | 1,335 |
| Net cash provided by (used in) financing activities | (46,812) | 38,507 | 28,062 |
| Net increase (decrease) in cash and cash equivalents | 10,117 | (545) | (6,381) |
| Cash and cash equivalents, beginning of year | 15,368 | 15,913 | 22,294 |
| Cash and cash equivalents, end of year | $ 25,485 | $ 15,368 | $ 15,913 |
| Supplemental disclosures of cash flow information: | | | |
| Cash paid during year for: | | | |
| Interest | $ 7,876 | $ 7,329 | $ 4,800 |
| Income taxes | 3,916 | 13,275 | 26,100 |
| Supplemental disclosures of noncash investing activities: | | | |
| Notes receivable from sale of revenue equipment | $ 4,707 | $ – | $ – |

WERNER ENTERPRISES, INC.
CONSOLIDATED STATEMENTS OF STOCKHOLDERS' EQUITY
(In thousands, except share amounts)

| | Common Stock | Paid-in Capital | Retained Earnings | Accumulated Other Comprehensive Loss | Treasury Stock | Total Stockholders' Equity |
|---|---|---|---|---|---|---|
| BALANCE, December 31, 1997 | $387 | $104,764 | $296,533 | $ – | ($6,566) | $395,118 |
| Purchases of 592,600 shares of common stock | – | – | – | – | (9,072) | (9,072) |
| Dividends on common stock ($.09 per share) | – | – | (4,428) | – | – | (4,428) |
| Five-for-four stock split | 96 | (96) | – | – | – | – |
| Exercise of stock options, 119,391 shares | – | 670 | – | – | 1,054 | 1,724 |
| Comprehensive income: | | | | | | |
| Net income | – | – | 57,426 | – | – | 57,246 |
| BALANCE, December 31, 1998 | 483 | 105,338 | 349,351 | – | (14,584) | 440,588 |
| Purchases of 302,600 shares of common stock | – | – | – | – | (3,941) | (3,941) |
| Dividends on common stock ($.10 per share) | – | – | (4,737) | – | – | (4,737) |
| Exercise of stock options, 198,526 shares | – | 546 | – | – | 2,305 | 2,851 |
| Comprehensive income: | | | | | | |
| Net income | – | – | 60,011 | – | – | 60,011 |
| BALANCE, December 31, 1999 | 483 | 105,884 | 404,625 | – | (16,220) | 494,772 |
| Purchases of 225,201 shares of common stock | – | – | – | – | (2,759) | (2,759) |
| Dividends on common stock ($.10 per share) | – | – | (4,705) | – | – | (4,705) |
| Exercise of stock options, 59,255 shares | – | (40) | – | – | 827 | 787 |
| Comprehensive income (loss): | | | | | | |
| Net income | – | – | 48,023 | – | – | 48,023 |
| Foreign currency translation adjustments | – | – | – | (34) | – | (34) |
| Total comprehensive income | – | – | 48,023 | (34) | – | 47,989 |
| BALANCE, December 31, 2000 | $483 | $105,844 | $447,943 | ($34) | ($18,152) | $536,084 |

**29.** Verify that total assets equal total liabilities and owners' equity for Werner in 2000.

**30.** Find the following amounts in the statements of Werner:

**a.** Revenues in 2000

**b.** Salaries, wages, and benefits incurred in 2000

**c.** Interest expense in 2000

**d.** Income tax expense in 1999

e. Net income in 1999
f. Inventories at the end of 2000
g. Accounts payable at the beginning of 2000
h. Retained earnings at the end of 2000
i. Long-term borrowings at the beginning of 2000
j. Cash produced from operating activities in 2000
k. Cash payments to acquire property, plant, and equipment in 2000
l. Dividends paid in 2000
m. Cash proceeds from new borrowings in 2000
n. Cash produced or used for investing activities in 2000

31. Does Werner finance the firm mainly from creditors (total liabilities) or from owners (owners' equity) in 2000? Support your answer with appropriate data.
32. List the two largest sources of cash and the two largest uses of cash in 2000. (Consider operations to be a single source or use of cash.)
33. Suggest some reasons why income was $48,023 (000) in 2000, yet cash flow from operations was $170,147 (000).
34. What is the comprehensive net income for Werner in 2000?
35. On December 31, 2000, find the price of Werner's stock (use the library or the web) and compute the total market value of the company's stock that is outstanding based on the number of shares that were outstanding as of that date. Compare this value with the book value of owner's equity on Werner's balance sheet as of that date. If these numbers are different, offer an explanation for this discrepancy.

Base your answers to problems 36–42 on the data for Emulex Corporation provided here.

| EMULEX CORP.: Balance Sheet | 2001/07/01 | 2000/07/01 |
|---|---|---|
| Assets | | |
| Current assets: | | |
| Cash and cash equivalents | $ 36,471,000 | $ 23,471,000 |
| Investments | 148,204,000 | 128,234,000 |
| Accounts and other receivables, less allowance for doubtful accounts of 1,298 in 2001 and 844 in 2000 | 40,239,000 | 24,332,000 |
| Inventories, net | 38,616,000 | 12,635,000 |
| Prepaid expenses | 2,527,000 | 1,021,000 |
| Deferred income taxes | 1,579,000 | 453,000 |
| Total current assets | 267,636,000 | 190,146,000 |
| Property and equipment, net | 18,379,000 | 6,927,000 |
| Long-term investments | 38,805,000 | 29,293,000 |
| Goodwill and other intangibles, net | 590,316,000 | 0 |
| Deferred income taxes and other assets | 2,878,000 | 3,629,000 |
| Total Assets | $918,014,000 | $229,995,000 |

| | 2001/07/01 | 2000/07/01 |
|---|---|---|
| Liabilities and Stockholders' Equity | | |
| Current liabilities: | | |
| Accounts payable | $ 29,253,000 | $ 17,869,000 |
| Accrued liabilities | 11,749,000 | 6,355,000 |
| Income taxes payable and other current liabilities | 300,000 | 320,000 |
| Total current liabilities | 41,302,000 | 24,544,000 |
| Deferred income taxes and other liabilities | 26,000 | 0 |
| | 41,328,000 | 24,544,000 |
| Commitments and contingencies (note 9) | | |
| Stockholders' equity: | | |
| Preferred stock, $0.01 par value; 1,000,000 shares authorized (150,000 shares designated as Series A Junior Participating Preferred Stock); none issued and outstanding | 0 | 0 |
| Common stock, $0.10 par value; 120,000,000 shares authorized; 81,799,322 and 72,466,848 issued and outstanding in 2001 and 2000, respectively | 8,180,000 | 7,247,000 |
| Additional paid-in capital | 861,461,000 | 155,190,000 |
| Deferred compensation | (12,366,000) | 0 |
| Retained earnings | 19,411,000 | 43,014,000 |
| Total stockholders' equity | 876,686,000 | 205,451,000 |
| Total liabilities and stockholders' equity | $918,014,000 | $229,995,000 |

| EMULEX CORP.: Income Statement | 2001/07/01 | 2000/07/01 | 1999/07/01 |
|---|---|---|---|
| Net revenues | $245,307,000 | $139,772,000 | $68,485,000 |
| Cost of sales | 120,812,000 | 73,346,000 | 40,138,000 |
| Cost of sales—inventory charges related to consolidation | 0 | 0 | 1,304,000 |
| Total cost of sales | 120,812,000 | 73,346,000 | 41,442,000 |
| Gross profit | 124,495,000 | 66,426,000 | 27,043,000 |
| Operating expenses: | | | |
| Engineering and development | 27,002,000 | 14,727,000 | 11,766,000 |
| Selling and marketing | 16,734,000 | 10,077,000 | 6,953,000 |
| General and administrative | 12,111,000 | 6,923,000 | 4,279,000 |
| Amortization of goodwill and other intangibles | 52,085,000 | 0 | 0 |
| In-process research and development | 22,280,000 | 0 | 0 |
| Consolidation charges, net | 0 | 0 | (987,000) |
| Total operating expenses | 130,212,000 | 31,727,000 | 22,011,000 |
| Operating income (loss) | (5,717,000) | 34,699,000 | 5,032,000 |
| Nonoperating income | 14,301,000 | 9,131,000 | 480,000 |
| Income before income taxes | 8,584,000 | 43,830,000 | 5,512,000 |
| Income tax provision | 32,187,000 | 11,016,000 | 247,000 |
| Net income (loss) | ($23,603,000) | $32,814,000 | $5,265,000 |

| EMULEX CORP.: Cash Flow | 2001/07/01 | 2000/07/01 | 1999/07/01 |
|---|---|---|---|
| Cash flows from operating activities: | | | |
| Net income (loss) | ($23,603,000) | $32,814,000 | $5,265,000 |
| Adjustments to reconcile net income (loss) to net cash provided by operating activities: | | | |
| Depreciation and amortization | 4,801,000 | 1,814,000 | 1,648,000 |
| Gain on sale of strategic investment | (1,884,000) | 0 | 0 |
| Stock-based compensation | 1,756,000 | 0 | 0 |
| Amortization of goodwill and other intangibles | 52,085,000 | 0 | 0 |
| In-process research and development | 22,280,000 | 0 | 0 |
| Loss (gain) on disposal of property, plant, and equipment | 400,000 | 112,000 | (750,000) |
| Deferred income taxes | (536,000) | (5,643,000) | 0 |
| Tax benefit from exercise of stock options | 32,188,000 | 16,661,000 | 0 |
| Impairment of intangibles | 0 | 175,000 | 125,000 |
| Provision for doubtful accounts | 435,000 | 435,000 | 86,000 |
| Changes in assets and liabilities: | | | |
| Accounts receivable | (15,714,000) | (7,679,000) | (5,033,000) |
| Inventories | (25,007,000) | (1,552,000) | (1,177,000) |
| Prepaid expenses and other assets | (111,000) | (701,000) | 18,000 |
| Accounts payable | 5,882,000 | 6,474,000 | 4,486,000 |
| Accrued liabilities | 4,006,000 | 2,064,000 | (2,987,000) |
| Income taxes payable | (37,000) | (32,000) | 215,000 |
| Net cash provided by operating activities | 56,941,000 | 44,942,000 | 1,896,000 |
| Cash flows from investing activities: | | | |
| Net proceeds from sale of property, plant, and equipment | 0 | 30,000 | 2,999,000 |
| Additions to property and equipment | (11,657,000) | (5,703,000) | (1,953,000) |
| Payment for purchase of Giganet, Inc., net of cash acquired | (15,530,000) | 0 | 0 |
| Purchases of investments | (524,091,000) | (637,892,000) | (115,380,000) |
| Maturity of investments | 491,009,000 | 595,745,000 | 0 |
| Proceeds from sale of strategic investment | 5,484,000 | 0 | 0 |
| Net cash used in investing activities | (54,785,000) | (47,820,000) | (114,334,000) |
| Cash flows from financing activities: | | | |
| Principal payments under capital leases | (12,000) | (18,000) | (76,000) |
| Net proceeds from issuance of common stock under stock option plans | 9,742,000 | 4,083,000 | 184,000 |
| Proceeds from note receivable issued in exchange for restricted stock | 1,114,000 | 0 | 0 |
| Net proceeds from stock offering | 0 | 0 | 132,838,000 |
| Net cash provided by financing activities | 10,844,000 | 4,065,000 | 132,946,000 |
| Net increase in cash and cash equivalents | 13,000,000 | 1,187,000 | 20,508,000 |
| Cash and cash equivalents at beginning of year | 23,471,000 | 22,284,000 | 1,776,000 |
| Cash and cash equivalents at end of year | $36,471,000 | $23,471,000 | $22,284,000 |

| | 2001/07/01 | 2000/07/01 | 1999/07/01 |
|---|---|---|---|
| Supplemental disclosures: | | | |
| Noncash investing and financing activities | | | |
| Fair value of assets acquired | $ 7,832,000 | | |
| Fair value of liabilities assumed | 8,136,000 | $ 0 | $ 0 |
| Common stock issued and options assumed for acquired business | 661,678,000 | 0 | 0 |
| Cash paid during the year for: | | | |
| Interest | $ 352,000 | $ 21,000 | $ 60,000 |
| Income taxes | 221,000 | 32,000 | 53,000 |

**36.** What is Emulex's fiscal year-end date?

**37.** Find the following amounts in the statements of Emulex:

a. Net sales in 2001

b. Cost of sales in 2001

c. Interest expense in 2001

d. Income tax expense in 2001

e. Amortization of goodwill in 2001 and in 2000

f. Net income in 2001

g. Inventories at the end of 2001

h. Goodwill at the end of 2001

i. Additional paid-in capital at the end of 2001

j. Cash from operating activities for 2001

k. Cash from investing activities for 2001

l. Cash from financing activities for 2001

**38.** Does Emulex finance its business primarily from creditors or from owners? Support your answer with appropriate data.

**39.** In 2001 Emulex purchased a new business. How did Emulex pay for this acquisition?

**40.** What is the trend in sales and net income over the last three years, and can you provide an explanation for why there is a loss in 2001?

**41.** Does Emulex pay dividends on its stock?

**42.** On July 1, 2001 find the stock price of Emulex's stock (use the library or the web) and compute the total market value of the company's stock that is outstanding, based on the number of shares that were outstanding as of that date. Compare this value with the book value of owner's equity on Emulex's balance sheet as of that date. If these numbers are different, offer an explanation for this discrepancy.

## BEYOND THE BOOK

**43.** For a company of your choosing, answer the following questions:

a. What are the major sections included in your annual report?

b. What are the three most important points made in the letter to the shareholders?

c. What are the titles to the major financial statements included in the report?

d. What are the total assets, total liabilities, and total stockholders' equity of the firm? What percent of the company's total assets are financed through liabilities?

e. What were the net sales in the most recent year? Is this up or down from the prior year (answer in both dollar and percentage amounts)?

f. What is the net income and earnings per share in the most recent year? Is this up or down from the prior year (answer in both dollar and percentage amounts)?

g. Are any of the following items reported in the income statement: discontinued operations, extraordinary items, accounting method changes? If so, which ones?

h. What is the net cash provided (used) by operating, financing, and investing activities for the most recent year?

i. What is the last day of your company's fiscal year end?

j. Who are the independent auditors, and what type of opinion did they give the company?

44. Refer to the footnotes that accompany the company you chose in 43.

a. In the section "Summary of Significant Accounting Policies," what key policies are discussed?

b. Does your company have long-term debt? If so, what is the interest rate?

c. If your company has inventory, what do the footnotes tell you about the inventory?

d. From the footnotes, does it appear that there are any obligations that the company may have that do not appear to be reflected as liabilities on the balance sheet? If so, what are they?

CHAPTER 3

# The Accounting Process

## Learning Objectives

After reading this chapter you should be able to:

1. Recognize common business transactions and understand their impact on general-purpose financial statements.
2. Understand the dual nature of accounting transactions as reflected in the accounting equation.
3. Explain the basic construction of the Statement of Financial Position, the Statement of Earnings, and the Statement of Cash Flows.
4. Distinguish between economic events that are commonly recognized in accounting as transactions and those that are not.
5. Apply the concept of nominal or temporary accounts to record revenues and expenses, and identify their relationship to the Statement of Earnings and Statement of Financial Position.
6. Describe the accounting cycle and recognize the timing issues inherent in reporting financial results.

**On March 2, 2001, investors reacted very favorably to an initial public offering** (an Initial Public Offering or IPO is the first time a private company decides to issue shares to the public) from AFC Enterprises, Inc. The company operates and franchises quick-service restaurants, bakeries, and cafés (3618 in the United States and 27 in foreign countries) under the names Popeye's Chicken & Biscuits, Church's Chicken, Cinnabon, Seattle's Best Coffee, and Torrefazione Italia. The company also sells specialty coffees at wholesale and retail under the Seattle Coffee brand name. Sales totaled about $2.4 billion in 2000.

Although originally issued at $17, AFC shares opened at $19.50, climbed as high as $20.75, and ended the day at $20.38 on the Nasdaq Stock Market. The company had originally expected the shares to be offered at between $15 and $17. After the IPO, AFC had 29.5 million shares outstanding. You can see that with almost 30 million shares issued, AFC raised a substantial amount of money to fund its operations.

Investors and analysts use financial statements to guide their predictions and investment decisions. For example, when a company such as AFC Enterprises decides to issue stock to the public, it files information (in a document called a *prospectus*) containing past and projected financial performance. Investors, potential investors, managers, and other stakeholders rely on this financial statement information to help determine the company's value. As a result, these users must understand the process and assumptions underlying the construction of financial statements in order to make sound decisions based (in part) on these statements.

In the following pages, we present the fundamental aspects of the *double-entry accounting system* for constructing financial statements. The mechanical aspects of recording transactions are sometimes referred to as *bookkeeping*. You may well question why you should be concerned with this bookkeeping aspect of accounting, especially in light of today's computerized technology. The answer: You need to understand what the preparers are doing so that you can better interpret the output of their work, the financial statements. Let's start first with the balance sheet accounts, which underlie the financial statements.

# BALANCE SHEET ACCOUNTS

Most of the balance sheet accounts are categorized as assets, liabilities, or stockholders' equity. Before examining specific transactions, let's review these in more detail.

## ASSETS

The Financial Accounting Standards Board (FASB) Concepts Statement Number 6 (CON 6) defines an asset as follows (FASB, SFAC No. 6, 1985):

> Assets are probable future economic benefits obtained or controlled by a particular entity as a result of past transactions or events.

Probable future economic benefits means that a firm expects either future cash inflows or smaller cash outflows to result from the asset. For example, a prepaid expense, such as the premium on an insurance policy, is considered to be an asset because the coverage that the policy provides benefits future periods. However, as we noted in Chapter 2, some items have economic value but are not recognized as assets. For instance, if a firm faces uncertainty about future realization of cash flows, an item might not be recognized as an asset (e.g., research and development expenditures). Pepsico spends a significant amount of money each year for marketing its products. While this may create value for the business (brand recognition), they expense their advertising costs as they are incurred. Or, an item may be valuable to an entity but not owned or controlled by that entity, such as skilled employees.

Most assets originate as the result of a transaction with a party outside of the firm. A firm generally recognizes assets at the price it paid to acquire the assets. Exhibit 3.1 lists assets commonly found on a balance sheet:

**Exhibit 3.1**
Common Assets

*Cash* The amount of money that the firm has, including the amounts in checking and savings accounts.

*Marketable Securities* Short-term investments, such as stocks and bonds, in the securities of other companies.

*Accounts Receivable* Amounts owed to the firm that result from credit sales to customers.

*Inventory* Goods held for resale to customers.

*Prepaid Expenses* Expenses that have been paid for, but have not been used, such as rent paid in advance and insurance premiums.

*Property, Plant, and Equipment (PP&E)* Buildings, land, and equipment to be used for business operations over several years.

*Intangible Assets* Assets that have value, but do not have a physical presence, such as patents, trademarks, and goodwill.

*Deferred Tax Assets* Amounts of expected future tax savings.

## LIABILITIES

In contrast to assets, liabilities are amounts recognized in accounting that result in expected future outflows of cash or delivery of goods or services. Exhibit 3.2 lists some of the more common balance sheet liabilities. Similar to assets, liability recognition also usually involves a transaction with an external party. FASB Con 6 defines liabilities as follows (FASB, SFAC No. 6, 1985):

> Liabilities are probable future sacrifices of economic benefits arising from present obligations of a particular entity to transfer assets or provide services to other entities in the future as a result of past transactions or events.

**Exhibit 3.2**
Common Liabilities

*Accounts Payable* Amounts owed to suppliers from the purchase of goods on credit.

*Notes Payable* Amounts owed to a creditor (bank or supplier) that are represented by a formal agreement called a note. Notes payable can be either short-term (due in less than one year) or long-term (due more than one year in the future).

*Accrued Liabilities* Amounts that are owed to others relating to expenses that the company has incurred, but are not paid in cash as of the balance sheet date, such as interest payable or a warranty liability.

*Taxes Payable* Amounts currently owed to taxing authorities.

*Deferred Taxes* Amounts that the company expects to pay to taxing authorities in the future.

*Bonds Payable* Amounts owed to a creditor that are paid out over longer periods; they generally involve fixed interest payments as well as a large payment at the end of some specified period. Some bonds payable can be traded on exchanges in the same way as stock is traded. Bonds payable are generally long-term in nature, meaning that they are payable in a period more than one year from the date of issuance.

## STOCKHOLDERS' EQUITY

We would not expect a company to accumulate large amounts of cash, even if the company is very profitable. This is because cash as an asset does not generate high rates of return. Thus, management, seeking to maximize shareholders' wealth, generally keeps only as much cash as it requires to meet its operating needs and to make the repayment of its debt. Additional amounts may be held in anticipation of further investments.

Owners' or stockholders' equity is the last main category on the balance sheet. Stockholders' equity consists of two major components: contributed capital and retained earnings. **Contributed capital** reflects the amount of capital that a firm's owners have invested in the business. This amount is typically the sum of the **par** or **stated value** of stock issued, plus the amounts in excess of par, **additional paid-in-capital.** The sum of common stock plus additional paid-in-capital represents the total investment by shareholders at the time the company issued the stock.

**Retained earnings** is the total amount of earnings (revenues minus expenses) recorded in the accounting system to date, but not yet distributed to shareholders as dividends. Dividends are distributions of earnings to shareholders and are not considered an expense to the company. Remember that retained earnings are not cash. A company may have substantial earnings yet have no cash for at least two reasons. First, accounting rules require that earnings be recognized on an accrual basis. For example, firms sometimes recognize revenues before receiving cash (as in sales on account), and sometimes recognize expenses before paying cash out (as in wages owed to employees). Second, a company may use its cash to invest in noncash assets (e.g., a new computer system or repay debt).

## NOMINAL ACCOUNTS

Balance sheet accounts (sometimes called **real** or **permanent accounts**) include a number of assets, liabilities, and stockholders' equity accounts such as those discussed in the previous sections. **Nominal accounts** (or **temporary accounts**) are accounts that a firm uses to determine its earnings. These accounts consist of revenue and expense accounts such as sales, cost of goods sold, wage and salary expenses, and selling and administrative expenses. Ultimately, these accounts affect a permanent account, namely retained earnings. (We'll discuss how this is accomplished later.) However, at this point, it is worth noting that the reason that revenue and expenses are considered to be temporary accounts is that the balances in these accounts are transferred (or *closed*) to retained earnings at the end of each accounting period. By closing revenue and expense accounts each period, the balances in these accounts reflect only the firm's operating performance for one period at a time. The retained earnings account contains cumulative earnings less dividends distributed to stockholders since the firm's inception.

Now that you have a good understanding of the types of accounts, let's see next how firms use them to record transactions.

# ACCOUNTING FOR TRANSACTIONS

The starting point in constructing financial statements is the accounting recognition of **transactions,** or economic events. Most, but not all, transactions are triggered by an exchange between the firm and another party. Accounting recognition of these transactions take the form of an **entry,** which indicates the financial effects of that event on accounts that appear on the firm's financial statements.

Recall from Chapter 2 that the accounting equation states that

Assets = Liabilities + Stockholders' Equity

When firms record transactions in the accounting system, this equality must always be maintained.

To analyze transactions, you can use two approaches. The first approach is based on the accounting equation. Each transaction is analyzed in terms of how it affects assets, liabilities, and stockholders' equity (we'll illustrate this approach later in this chapter). The equation approach is only useful when first learning accounting, so you can more easily see how transactions affect the accounting equation and financial statements. However, this approach quickly becomes unwieldy and inefficient when dealing with a large number of transactions and accounts. As a result, most firms use the second approach, the double-entry accounting system.

## DOUBLE-ENTRY ACCOUNTING SYSTEM

The **double-entry accounting system** expresses account balances and changes in account balances using terms called **debits** and **credits.** Although it requires some investment of your time and effort to be able to use debits and credits, having this skill is extremely useful. Once you understand the double-entry accounting system, you can efficiently assess the effects of a variety of types of transactions on a company's financial statements, as well as address valuation and income measurement issues.

The system of using debit and credits serves as the basis of virtually every accounting system worldwide. Further, the Sarbane's Oxley Act requires that top management certify to the fundamental accuracy of their company's financial statements. Such certification requires that management possess a basic understanding of the accounting process, in order to be able to communicate with the preparers of financial statements. Understanding the process of generating financial statements is an essential component of financial literacy.

### T-ACCOUNTS

A debit means simply an entry or balance on the left-hand side of an account, and a credit is an entry or balance on the right-hand side of an account. Increases and decreases in specific accounts can be expressed by debit and credit entries following set conventions. The conventions that dictate the rules for debits and credits are structured so that all accounting transactions will maintain the equality of the accounting equation at all times. The basic form of an account can be represented using a so-called **T-account** of the following form (note that we have represented the balance on the debit side of the account but also recognize that the balance could appear on either side of the account):

| Account Title | |
|---|---|
| Balance<br>Debit | Credit |
| Balance | |

A T-account shows the beginning and ending balance in an account, as well as the debit and credit entries for transactions affecting the account during a particular period of time. Whether an account is increased or decreased by a debit or credit depends on whether the account represents an asset, liability, or stockholders' equity, in other words, has a debit or a credit balance. As Exhibit 3.3 shows, assets are increased by debit entries and decreased by credit entries. Liabilities and stockholders' equity accounts (capital stock, additional paid in capital, and retained earnings) are increased by credits and decreased by debits.

As shown in Exhibit 3.3, we normally expect asset accounts to carry a debit balance, while liability and stockholders' equity accounts normally carry a credit balance. One way to think about these results is that the accounting equation shows assets on the left side (debit) and liabilities and stockholders' equity on the right (credit). An exception is retained earnings. A profitable company will have a credit balance in this account, but it can have a debit balance if it incurs a cumulative net loss. Finally, remember that to maintain the accounting equation, the sum of all debit account balances must equal the sum of all credit account balances.

## JOURNAL ENTRIES

In a double-entry accounting system, firms typically track transactions as they occur in a chronological listing known as a **journal.** Each entry in the journal, known as a **journal entry,** summarizes both sides of a transaction (debit and

**Exhibit 3.3**
T-Accounts

T-Accounts for Assets, Liabilities, and Stockholders' Equity

| Assets | | Liabilities | |
|---|---|---|---|
| Beginning balance<br>Debits increase | Credits decrease | Debits decrease | Beginning balance<br>Credits increase |
| Ending balance | | | Ending balance |

| Capital Stock (common stock + paid-in-capital) | | Retained Earnings | |
|---|---|---|---|
| Debits decrease | Beginning balance<br>Credits increase | Debits decrease | Beginning balance<br>Credits increase |
| | Ending balance | | Ending balance |

credit). By convention, in a journal entry, the debit portion of the entry is shown first, followed by the credit portion. (See the sample journal entries that follow.) The credit entry is slightly indented from the debit to make the entry clear. The total debits for a transaction must equal the total credits for that transaction.

| | | |
|---|---|---|
| Title of Account Debited | Amount Debited | |
|    Title of Account Credited | | Amount Credited |

For example, the journal entry to record the purchase of \$100 of inventory for cash would appear as follows:

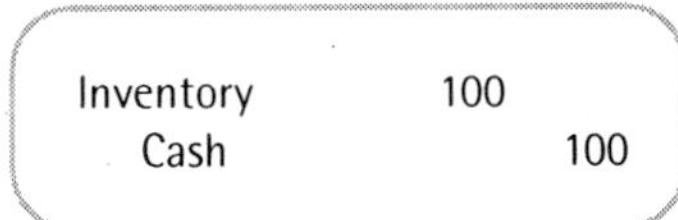


We will explain this transaction later, but for now just recognize the form of the journal entry.

After recording journal entries, they are then posted to the T-accounts. Posting simply means transferring the information in the journal entry to the appropriate T-accounts. (In this text, we will often simplify this two-step approach by recording the transaction directly to the T-account, bypassing the journal entry step.) The set of T-accounts that a company uses is collectively referred to as the **ledger.**

To illustrate the application of the accounting equation, journal entries, and T-accounts, assume that a company borrows \$50,000,000 cash from a bank and signs a promissory note. This note specifies an interest rate and when the amount borrowed must be repaid. Using the accounting equation approach, we view this transaction as shown here (shown in millions of dollars):

| Assets | = | Liabilities | + | Stockholders' Equity |
|---|---|---|---|---|
| | | Notes | | |
| Cash | | Payable | | |
| +50 | = | +50 | | |

Notice that the asset (Cash) is increased, and the liability (Notes Payable) is also increased. Observe also that we maintain the equality of the accounting equation. The journal entry for this transaction would appear as follows:

| | | |
|---|---|---|
| Cash | 50 | |
|    Notes Payable | | 50 |

The debit to the Cash account means that cash (an asset) has increased by $50 and the credit to Notes Payable (a liability) means that account is increased as well. Posting this journal entry to the appropriate T-accounts, the transaction would be recorded as:

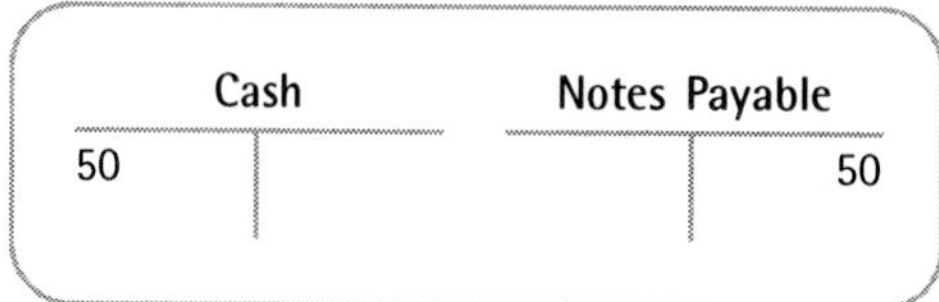


Observe that both the T-account and the journal entry maintain the equality of total debits and total credits. Note also that dollar signs ($) are generally omitted from journal entries and T-accounts. Journal entries are a useful way to represent individual transactions, while T-accounts illustrate the effect of a series of transactions on the accounts that comprise a company's financial statements.

## COMPUTERIZED ACCOUNTING

The basic accounting process, still used today, has existed for centuries. Before computers, firms literally recorded accounting entries in paper journals, and then posted the individual components of those entries to paper ledger accounts. You can easily imagine the large amount of paperwork involved in a manual accounting system, even for a modestly sized business. Although today's accounting systems are computerized, they continue follow the same basic process. Transactions still give rise to entries in some form (a journal), from which summaries (ledger) by account can be created, which then serve as a foundation for the construction of financial statements.

Modern accounting systems are structured much differently than in the past and may be simply one part of a company's software system. These sophisticated systems provide a wide variety of management tools. For example, some systems may instantly determine the impact of a revenue or expense transaction on a company's income statement and balance sheet. There are several companies that provide very sophisticated systems, and Oracle is one of those companies. Exhibit 3.4 provides a description of Oracle's business.

Even though computers have eased the paperwork requirements of accounting systems, you still need to know how they work. Let's look at an example that illustrates the accounting process and the preparation of financial statements.

**Exhibit 3.4**
Oracle Corporation: Description of Business (Oracle 10-K, 2003)

**THE REAL WORLD**
**Oracle Corporation**

> We are the world's largest enterprise software company. We develop, manufacture, market, and distribute computer software that helps our customers manage and grow their businesses and operations. Our offerings include new software licenses, software license updates, and product support and services, which include consulting, advanced product services, and education. We also offer an integrated suite of business applications software and other business software infrastructure, including application server, collaborative software, and development tools.

## AN ILLUSTRATION OF TRANSACTION ANALYSIS

Biohealth, Inc., is a hypothetical, wholesale health-products distributor (similar to an actual company in the health supply industry). As is often true for publicly traded companies, Biohealth is denoted by its *ticker symbol,* in this case BHT, used on the stock exchanges where the company's stock trades. BHT distributes (not manufactures) a wide variety of healthcare products and prescription medicines to hospitals, retail chains, and other health-related outlets. It also provides software solutions to a variety of businesses in the healthcare sector for managing their ordering and inventory. BHT was incorporated on December 20, 20X0 and began operations the following January.

The following economic events/transactions occurred in December prior to the start of BHT's operations:

1. BHT issued 250 million shares of common stock with a par value of $1 per share for $6.50 per share.
2. BHT acquired fixtures for $540 million. BHT estimates that the fixtures will be used for nine years.
3. The purchase of fixtures was partially financed with a $400 million note due in five years. The loan carries an interest rate of 7 percent.[1]

These transactions reflect BHT's start-up financing and investing activities. Let's look at them more closely.

### ANALYSIS OF FINANCING AND INVESTING ACTIVITIES

Exhibit 3.5 summarizes the impact of these initial three transactions on the accounting equation. Notice how the accounts to the left of the equal (=) sign are added together, as well as the accounts to the right of the equal sign, to

| | Assets | | = | Liabilities | | | |
|---|---|---|---|---|---|---|---|
| #-Type | Cash | Fixtures | = | Notes payable | Common Stock | Paid-in Capital | Retained Earnings |
| Bal. 12/20/20X0 | 0 | 0 | = | 0 | 0 | 0 | 0 |
| 1-Financing | 1,625 | | = | | 250 | 1,375 | |
| 2-Investing | (540) | 540 | = | | | | |
| 3-Financing | 400 | | = | 400 | | | |
| Bal. 12/31/20X0 | 1,485 | 540 | = | 400 | 250 | 1,375 | 0 |

**Exhibit 3.5**
Impact of BHT's Financing and Investing Activities on the Accounting Equation (in millions of dollars)

[1]A note is a loan accompanied by a written promise to repay the amount owed. Interest on notes is always expressed in terms of an annual rate even if the note is for a period longer or shorter than one year. For example, the total interest on a six-month $1,000 note with an interest rate of 5 percent would be $1,000 × .05 × 6/12 = $25.

determine the ending balance. On each line of the exhibit, from individual transactions to ending balances, the accounting equation holds. Negative amounts, as shown in Exhibit 3.5, are enclosed in parentheses.

### Issuing Stock (Transaction 1)

The first transaction increases Cash by $1,625 million (250 million shares × $6.50/share), increases Common Stock by $250 million (250 million shares × $1/share), and increases Additional Paid-In Capital by $1,375 million (the difference between cash and par value). We classify this transaction as a financing activity because it relates to how the company funds its operating and investing activities. Note that dollar figures are reported in millions, a common practice in financial statements.

### Purchasing Fixtures (Transaction 2)

The second transaction increases assets (Fixtures) by $540 million, and decreases Cash by $540 million. This transaction is an investing activity. Investing activities involve purchase and sale of assets that are used over multiple periods such as property, plant, and equipment. Note that later in the chapter we classify fixtures under property, plant, and equipment (PPE).

### Borrowing Funds (Transaction 3)

Although the third transaction relates to the investing activity in Transaction 2, it, by itself, is a financing activity. Here, the company borrows funds to finance its purchase of fixtures. Note that interest is not recognized yet on the loan as it is a charge that the firm incurs with the passage of time. Investing and financing activities often occur simultaneously. For example, America Online (AOL) acquired all of Time-Warner's common stock in January 2000. We classify AOL's stock acquisition of Time Warner as an investing activity because America Online now controls the assets of Time Warner. However, we also classify this as a financing activity, as AOL funded this transaction by issuing additional shares of AOL stock.

### Using Journal Entries and T-Accounts to Record Transactions

We show the journal entries and T-accounts for the first three BHT transactions in Exhibits 3.6 and 3.7, respectively. The journal entry for Transaction 1 summarizes

**Exhibit 3.6**
Journal Entries for BHT's Financing and Investing Transactions (in millions of dollars)

| | Account | Debit | Credit |
|---|---|---|---|
| **Transaction #1** | | | |
| | Cash | 1,625 | |
| | Common Stock | | 250 |
| | Additional Paid-in Capital | | 1,375 |
| **Transaction #2** | | | |
| | Fixtures | 540 | |
| | Cash | | 540 |
| **Transaction #3** | | | |
| | Cash | 400 | |
| | Notes Payable | | 400 |

**Exhibit 3.7**
T-Accounts for BHT's Financing and Investing Transactions (in millions of dollars)

| Cash | | | |
|---|---|---|---|
| Bal. | 0 | | |
| (1) | 1,625 | 540 | (2) |
| (3) | 400 | | |
| Bal. | 1,485 | | |

| Fixtures | | |
|---|---|---|
| Bal. | 0 | |
| (2) | 540 | |
| Bal. | 540 | |

| Notes Payable | |
|---|---|
| | Bal. 0 |
| | 400 (3) |
| | Bal. 400 |

| Common Stock | |
|---|---|
| | Bal. 0 |
| | 250 (1) |
| | Bal. 250 |

| Additional Paid-In Capital | |
|---|---|
| | Bal. 0 |
| | 1,375 (1) |
| | Bal. 1,375 |

BHT's issuance of stock by showing an increase in BHT's Cash (debit to Cash) and increases in both Common Stock and Additional Paid-in Capital (credits to those accounts). The journal entry for Transaction 2 reflects an increase in assets (Fixtures) by a debit to Fixtures and a decrease in Cash by a credit to Cash. Finally, the journal entry for Transaction 3 shows an increase in Cash and an increase in Notes Payable by a debit to Cash and a credit to Notes Payable, respectively.

As Exhibit 3.7 shows, each T-account includes the sum of all transactions affecting the account to date. The beginning balances in the accounts are zero as the company just started business at the beginning of this period. Finally, note that the sum of the debit balances equals the sum of the credit balances.

Observe that the three investing and financing transactions had no effect on the retained earnings account because none of them involved the generation of revenues or concurrent expenses. Earlier in the chapter, we mentioned the notion of permanent and nominal accounts. However, no nominal accounts have been affected by transactions thus far.

Now that we've recorded the journal entries and posted them to the ledger (T-accounts), we can use this information to construct the financial statements.

## CONSTRUCTING THE FINANCIAL STATEMENTS

Exhibit 3.8 shows BHT's Balance Sheet as of 12/31/20X0, summarizing the financial statement position of the firm. The balance sheet omits the beginning of the period, because the balances are all zero. Further, we don't need to prepare an income statement, as none of the initial three transactions produced revenue or expenses.

Exhibit 3.9 shows BHT's Statement of Cash Flows for the month ended 12/31/20X0. The statement indicates that the firm has not yet produced any cash flows from operating activities. Also, note that the total change in cash equals

**Exhibit 3.8**
Biohealth, Inc. (BHT) Balance Sheet (in millions) as of 12/31/20X0

| | |
|---|---|
| Assets | |
| Current Assets: | |
| Cash | $1,485 |
| Property, Plant, and Equipment: | |
| Fixtures | 540 |
| Total Assets | $2,025 |
| Liabilities and Stockholder's Equity | |
| Liabilities: | |
| Notes Payable | $ 400 |
| Total Liabilities | 400 |
| Stockholders' Equity | |
| Common Stock | 250 |
| Additional Paid in Capital | 1,375 |
| Retained Earnings | 0 |
| Total Stockholders' Equity | $1,625 |
| Total Liabilities and Stockholders' Equity | $2,025 |

**Exhibit 3.9**
Biohealth, Inc. (BHT) Statement of Cash Flows (in millions) for the Month Ending 12/31/20X0

| | |
|---|---|
| Cash Flow from Investing Activities | |
| Purchase Fixtures | ($540) |
| Cash Flow from Financing Activities | |
| Proceeds from Issuance of Common Stock | 1,625 |
| Proceeds from Loan | 400 |
| Total Cash from Financing Activities | 2,025 |
| Net Change in Cash | $1,485 |
| Cash Balance 12/20/20X0 | 0 |
| Cash Balance 12/31/20X0 | $1,485 |

the cash balance at the end of 12/31/20X0, because the company started with no cash on hand. Finally, the beginning cash balance is as of 12/20/20X0, the date the company formed. Normally, in a month-ending statement, the date would have been 12/1/20X0.

## ANALYSIS OF OPERATING ACTIVITIES

Now that we've examined BHT's initial financing and investing activities, let's next look at a series of transactions occurring in BHT's first year of operation, starting on 1/1/20X1. The following events occurred during 20X1 (all figures are in millions of dollars).

4. BHT purchased inventory costing $34,340 on account.
5. BHT sold goods for $35,724 on account.
6. The cost of the inventory sold was $30,420.
7. BHT received $33,260 in customer payments on accounts receivable.
8. BHT paid $29,200 on its accounts payable.
9. BHT paid $4,800 to lease warehouse space for inventory storage for the year and for other miscellaneous selling and administrative costs.
10. Depreciation expense on the fixtures was $60 ($540/9 years).
11. BHT paid interest on the note payable of $28.
12. BHT declared and paid dividends of $150.

Most of these transactions are operating transactions because they relate to BHT's profit-generating activities. Operating transactions can involve revenue and expense accounts (nominal accounts), but they may also involve only asset or liability accounts. For example, Inventory and Accounts Payable accounts are affected when a company buys inventory on credit. While this acquisition of inventory might be viewed as an investing activity, accounting standards classify it as operating because the company holds the inventory for resale in the short term. We classify assets such as Accounts Receivable, Inventory, and Prepaid Expenses as operating assets in part because they are short-term or current in nature, and in part because they relate to the operating cycle of the business. In contrast, we do not regard marketable securities as operating assets.

Recall from Chapter 2 that classification as a current asset generally means that we expect the asset to be converted into cash or consumed within one year or within one operating cycle of the business, whichever is longer. Similarly, obligations such as accounts payable and other short-term payables are considered operating liabilities in part because they will be paid in less than one year (current liabilities) and in part because they relate to operating activities. However, debt may also be classified as current if it is to be repaid within a year. Thus, some but not all changes in various current assets and current liabilities are considered to be operating transactions.

Before examining how we recognize these operating transactions in the accounting system, we need to first discuss revenues and expenses in more detail.

## Revenues and Expenses

*Revenues* reflect the sales value of goods or services sold by an enterprise. *Expenses* are the costs related to generating revenue, such as the cost of inventory sold and employee wages. Recall that net income is the difference between revenues and expenses. The cumulative amount of net income, minus dividends paid to shareholders over all accounting periods to date, appears on the balance sheet in the form of retained earnings. Exhibit 3.10 shows the changes of Retained Earnings in the balance sheet.

While we could immediately proceed to talk about the nominal accounts (revenue and expense accounts) and how to incorporate them into our entries,

**Exhibit 3.10**
Retained Earnings Flow through the Balance Sheet

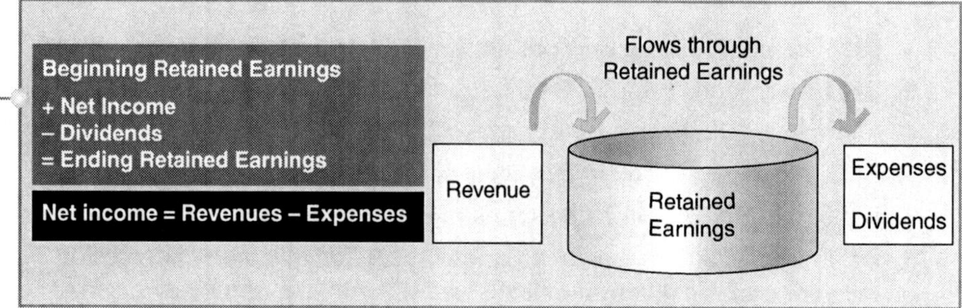


Summary Impact of Operating Activities on the Accounting Equation

| Transaction #- explanation | Assets | | | | | = | Liabilities | | CS | PIC | Retained Earnings |
|---|---|---|---|---|---|---|---|---|---|---|---|
| | Cash | AR | Inventory | PPE | (AD) | = | AP | NP | CS | PIC | Revenue – Expenses |
| Balance 12/31/20X0 | 1,485 | | | 540 | | = | | 400 | 250 | 1,375 | |
| 4. Purchase inventory | | | 34,340 | | | = | 34,340 | | | | |
| 5. Sales revenue | | 35,724 | | | | = | | | | | 35,724 |
| 6. Cost of sales | | | (30,420) | | | = | | | | | (30,420) |
| 7. Cash collection | 33,260 | (33,260) | | | | = | | | | | |
| 8. Payment for inventory | (29,200) | | | | | = | (29,200) | | | | |
| 9. S&A expenses | (4,800) | | | | | = | | | | | (4,800) |
| 10. Depreciation expense | | | | | (60) | = | | | | | (60) |
| 11. Interest expense | (28) | | | | | = | | | | | (28) |
| 12. Dividend paid | (150) | | | | | | | | | | (150) |
| Balance 12/31/20X1 | 567 | 2,464 | 3,920 | 540 | (60) | = | 5,140 | 400 | 250 | 1,375 | 266 |

**Exhibit 3.11**
Impact of BHT's Operating Transactions on the Balance Sheet

we take a two-step approach to analyzing operating transactions. In the section that follows, we will focus our attention on the permanent accounts as portrayed in the accounting equation to examine BHT's operating transactions. We will, therefore, portray revenue and expense events in terms of their (ultimate) impact on the Retained Earnings account (a permanent account) on the balance sheet. Accordingly, we treat revenues as direct increases (credits) to retained earnings and expenses as direct decreases (debits) to retained earnings as shown in Exhibit 3.11. It is important that you understand the ultimate effects on the permanent accounts, and it is often easier to focus on this effect first before we look more closely at nominal accounts. Following the accounting equation analysis of the transactions, we will present a more in-depth discussion of the nominal accounts and then illustrate the same transactions using journal entries and T-accounts, including the nominal accounts. If you prefer to consider the balance sheet equation effects and the journal entries simultaneously, then prior to reading about the transactions that follow, skip ahead to the section called "Nominal Accounts Revisited" and read about nominal accounts. You can then simultaneously follow the accounting equation effects in Exhibit 3.11 as well as the journal entry effects in Exhibit 3.15.

## Using the Accounting Equation to Analyze Operating Activities

Exhibit 3.11 summarizes the effects of Transactions 4 through 12 using the accounting equation. We use the following abbreviations for the balance sheet accounts: AR, Accounts Receivable; PPE, Property, Plant, and Equipment; AD, Accumulated Depreciation; AP, Accounts Payable; NP, Notes Payable; CS, Common Stock; PIC, Paid-In Capital; and RE, Retained Earnings.

### Purchasing Inventory on Account (Transaction 4)

Transaction 4 involves the credit (on account) purchase of inventory for resale. We consider this an operating activity because BHT expects to sell the inventory during the upcoming year for a price that exceeds its cost, generating profit for the company. The purchase is "on account," meaning that BHT pays for the inventory after its purchase. The result is that BHT has a liability, Accounts Payable, for the cost of the inventory purchased. The impact on the accounting equation is as follows:

4. Purchase of inventory on account

| | | Assets | | | = | Liabilities | | | Stockholders' Equity | |
|---|---|---|---|---|---|---|---|---|---|---|
| Cash | AR | Inventory | PPE | (AD) | = | AP | NP | CS | PIC | RE |
| | | 34,340 | | | = | 34,340 | | | | |

Purchasing inventory does not constitute an expense. The inventory holds future value and is owned by the firm. Therefore, it should be recorded as an asset. The cost of purchasing inventory eventually becomes an expense (cost of goods sold) at the time that BHT sells the inventory to a customer, that is, at the point when the firm no longer owns it (see Transactions 5 and 6).

### Selling Inventory on Account (Transaction 5)

Transaction 5 involves the sale of inventory on account. "On account," in this context means that BHT did not collect cash at the time of the sale but expects to do so at some future date. The amount owed to BHT, accounts receivable, represents an asset. This new asset for BHT stockholders results in an increase in stockholders' equity. Further, BHT sells its inventory for more than its cost. We refer to the gross sales value of inventory sold as **sales revenue.** At the same time, the stockholders lost an existing asset (inventory). The cost of inventory sold is accounted for separately as an expense called **cost of goods sold** (see Transaction 6, which follows). The difference between the gross sales value of the inventory (sales revenue) and its cost (cost of goods sold) is **gross profit** to BHT. The gross profit amount affects BHT's stockholders' equity in the form of an increase in retained earnings. The impact of the sales revenue itself on the accounting equation is as follows:

5. Recognize sales revenue for sales on account

| Assets | | | | | = | Liabilities | | Stockholders' Equity | | |
|---|---|---|---|---|---|---|---|---|---|---|
| Cash | AR | Inventory | PPE | (AD) | = | AP | NP | CS | PIC | RE |
| | 35,724 | | | | = | | | | | 35,724 |

The recognition of revenues can often be a source of confusion and, potentially, manipulation. In some cases companies improperly recognize revenues and the SEC can force them to restate their earnings. Such an example is that of Lucent Technologies, as illustrated in Exhibit 3.12.

### Recognizing Cost of Goods Sold (Transaction 6)

As previously mentioned, cost of goods sold is an expense related to generating the revenues recorded in Transaction 5. By accounting convention, a firm reports this expense in the same period as the related revenue. In this way, cost of goods sold is matched with the related revenue. An asset (inventory) was given up, so stockholders' equity also decreases. Specifically, this transaction decreases retained earnings. The impact on the accounting equation is shown as follows:

6. Recognize cost of goods sold

| Assets | | | | | = | Liabilities | | Stockholders' Equity | | |
|---|---|---|---|---|---|---|---|---|---|---|
| Cash | AR | Inventory | PPE | (AD) | = | AP | NP | CS | PIC | RE |
| | | (30,420) | | | = | | | | | (30,420) |

**Exhibit 3.12**

**THE REAL WORLD**

**Lucent Technologies**

In February 2001, Lucent Technologies, Inc. announced its cooperation with the SEC in a probe of the company's accounting practices. On November 21, 2000, Lucent had indicated that $125 million in improperly booked sales could reduce its results for the fourth quarter ended September 30, 2000. The announcement resulted in a 16 percent drop in the company's stock value. After an internal review, Lucent announced on December 21, 2000, that it was reducing previously reported fourth-quarter revenues by $679 million to $8.7 billion.

The fact that firms generally recognize revenues at the time of sale, rather than at the time of collection, could have important implications for the valuation of companies. Some companies may erroneously or fraudulently recognize sales by an accounting entry even when no legitimate sale has taken place. To minimize this type of opportunistic behavior, a firm's financial records are subject to examination by external auditors, internal control systems, and oversight by external members of a firm's board of directors. Further, legal sanctions apply to those firms that are found to have engaged in such behavior. However, as the Lucent example illustrates, none of these mechanisms are perfect.

Observe that neither the revenue or expense recognition for these transactions affected cash, due to accrual accounting. As we explain fully in Chapter 4, under this concept, a firm recognizes revenues when they have been earned. In this case, revenue recognition occurs when the inventory is delivered to the buyer and the firm can reasonably expect to collect cash in the future, not necessarily when BHT receives the cash. Similarly, a firm recognizes expenses not when it pays out cash, but when the cost (expenditure) can be matched to revenues (implying there is no future benefit to be received). Thus, a firm records inventory as assets upon purchase, and then records the cost of inventory sold as an expense when revenue is earned.

While some firms can calculate the cost of goods sold at the time of sale, many firms determine the cost of goods sold at the end of the period through the following calculation:

Cost of Goods Sold Calculation:

Cost of Goods Sold = Cost of Beginning Inventory + Purchases − Cost of Ending Inventory

## Collecting Receivables (Transaction 7)

Transaction 7 indicates the collection of cash for sales on account. This transaction involves an exchange of one type of an asset (accounts receivable) for another (cash), and therefore has no effect on retained earnings. BHT already recognized the revenue from the sale when the sale took place.

7. Recognize collection of cash from past sales

| Assets | | | | | = | Liabilities | | Stockholders' Equity | | |
|---|---|---|---|---|---|---|---|---|---|---|
| Cash | AR | Inventory | PPE | (AD) | = | AP | NP | CS | PIC | RE |
| 33,260 | (33,260) | | | | = | | | | | |

## Paying Accounts Payable (Transaction 8)

Transaction 8 records the payment for the inventory and other items that BHT purchased on account during the year.

8. Record payments on account

| Assets | | | | | = | Liabilities | | Stockholders' Equity | | |
|---|---|---|---|---|---|---|---|---|---|---|
| Cash | AR | Inventory | PPE | (AD) | = | AP | NP | CS | PIC | RE |
| (29,200) | | | | | = | (29,200) | | | | |

### Paying Selling and Administrative Costs (Transaction 9)

Transaction 9 involves the payment of cash for rent and other selling and administrative expenses that BHT incurred during the year. Because these cash expenditures do not result in assets with future value, these costs immediately become expenses. These expenses affect the accounting equation as follows:

9. Payment of cash for rent and selling and administrative expenses

| Assets | | | | | = | Liabilities | | Stockholders' Equity | | |
|---|---|---|---|---|---|---|---|---|---|---|
| Cash | AR | Inventory | PPE | (AD) | = | AP | NP | CS | PIC | RE |
| (4,800) | | | | | = | | | | | (4,800) |

### Depreciating Fixtures (Transaction 10)

When a firm purchases plant and equipment, it records these items as assets because they provide future benefits to the firm. Plant and equipment contribute to the production of products or services that can be sold in later periods. This productive capacity of plant and equipment, however, diminishes over time. As a result, for accounting purposes, the costs incurred in acquiring the plant and equipment should be expensed over the life of the plant and equipment. Specifically, accounting standards require that the costs incurred should be allocated to expense over the *useful life* of the asset using a rational and systematic method. We call these methods **depreciation methods,** and the expense that results **depreciation expense.** GAAP allows several depreciation methods, which we'll discuss in more detail in Chapter 9. These methods require several estimates. Exhibit 3.13 illustrates the disclosure made by Hasbro, Inc. regarding the use of estimates.

For example, the *straight-line depreciation* method assumes an equal amount of the cost of the asset is to be used up each year of its useful life. The method also factors in the possibility that the asset has some remaining estimated value

**Exhibit 3.13**
Hasbro, Inc. and Subsidiaries

THE REAL WORLD

Hasbro, Inc.

Notes to Consolidated Financial Statements

**(1) Summary of Significant Accounting Policies**

Preparation of Financial Statements

The preparation of financial statements in conformity with generally accepted accounting principles requires management to make estimates and assumptions that affect the amounts reported in the financial statements and notes thereto. Actual results could differ from those estimates.

Within GAAP, managers must make some significant estimates, such as the useful life and salvage value of a firm's property, plant, and equipment. Hasbro's disclosure reminds its financial statement readers of the estimates that management makes and the impact of these estimates on those statements.

at the end of its useful life, referred to as *salvage value.* A firm using this method therefore calculates depreciation expense dividing the original cost, less the salvage value, by the number of years of useful life. If BHT uses the straight-line method, with fixtures having a useful life of 9 years and a zero salvage value, its depreciation expense for the fixtures is [(Original Cost − Salvage)/Useful Life = ($540 − 0)/9 years = $60 million/year].

A firm records depreciation by an entry to Depreciation Expense (for the moment, retained earnings) and an entry to an account called Accumulated Depreciation. Accumulated Depreciation is a contra-asset account. **Contra-asset accounts** have credit balances and are an offset to a related asset account. In this case, the original cost of the fixtures is shown in the PP&E account. The entry shows Accumulated Depreciation as a direct reduction of this account. BHT reports the contra-asset on the balance sheet as a subtraction from the related asset account. The impact of recording depreciation on the accounting equation is shown as follows:

The use of the accumulated depreciation account is helpful for analysis because it allows the financial statement user to observe the original cost of an asset from the asset account and then, using the information in the accumulated depreciation account, infer such information as the age of plant and equipment and how long before they may need to be replaced.

10. Recognition of depreciation expense

| | | Assets | | | = | Liabilities | | | Stockholders' Equity | |
|---|---|---|---|---|---|---|---|---|---|---|
| Cash | AR | Inventory | PPE | (AD) | = | AP | NP | CS | PIC | RE |
| | | | | (60) | = | | | | | (60) |

We show the Accumulated Depreciation account as a negative amount. On the balance sheet, after the first year's depreciation is recorded, the asset and related accumulated depreciation accounts for fixtures would appear on the balance sheet as follows:

| | |
|---|---|
| Fixtures | $540 |
| Less | |
| Accumulated depreciation | (60) |
| Net fixtures | $480 |

At the end of the second year, the accumulated depreciation account would show that two years of depreciation had been recognized, and fixtures and related accumulated depreciation on the balance sheet would appear as:

| | |
|---|---|
| Fixtures | $540 |
| Less | |
| Accumulated depreciation | (120) |
| Net Fixtures | $420 |

By keeping the accumulated depreciation separate from the original cost of the fixtures, the financial statement reader can estimate both how close assets are to being fully depreciated and the years remaining in the asset's estimated useful life. This information may be helpful predict when a firm will need to replace or upgrade equipment. For example, suppose a company discloses that its depreciation expense is \$60 million, the asset is being depreciated using the straight-line method over nine years, and its accumulated depreciation is \$300. We can then estimate that the asset's remaining useful life is 4 years (9 − (300/60) = 4). If a company does not list accumulated depreciation on the balance sheet, but instead shows property, plant, and equipment net of accumulated depreciation, a breakdown between the asset and related accumulated depreciation accounts is often provided in the firm's footnotes to the financial statements.

### Paying Interest (Transaction 11)

When a firm borrows funds, it must pay for the use of the funds in the form of interest payments. In this case, we assume that the loan has simple interest at a rate of 7 percent per annum and is paid in cash. Thus, the interest on the loan is \$28 million (\$400 × .07) and affects the accounting equation as follows:

11. Payment of interest expense

| Assets | | | | | = | Liabilities | | Stockholders' Equity | | |
|---|---|---|---|---|---|---|---|---|---|---|
| Cash | AR | Inventory | PPE | (AD) | = | AP | NP | CS | PIC | RE |
| (28) | | | | | = | | | | | (28) |

While we treat interest as an operating activity, others argue that interest expense should be considered a financing activity because it relates to borrowing funds. In fact, we employ this view in Chapter 14 when we consider valuing a firm. However, the FASB states that interest should be classified as an operating activity for cash flow purposes.

### Dividends (Transaction 12)

Dividends return a certain amount of the profits to owners in the form of cash. A company's Board of Directors frequently declares dividends on a quarterly basis. However, a firm usually does not pay dividends at the date they are declared. Instead, a firm often pays them within the month following declaration. To deal with this delay, a firm creates a new liability, Dividends Payable. Dividends are not an expense of doing business and are not reported on the income statement. However, they do directly reduce retained earnings, as the owners are withdrawing a part of their profits from the firm. We will discuss dividends in more detail later in the text. Here, however, for simplicity, we assume that BHT pays dividends immediately in cash.

12. Declaration of dividends

| | | Assets | | | = | Liabilities | | | Stockholders' Equity | |
|---|---|---|---|---|---|---|---|---|---|---|
| Cash | AR | Inventory | PPE | (AD) | = | AP | NP | CS | PIC | RE |
| (150) | | | | | = | | | | | (150) |

Now that we've examined how BHT's operating transactions affected the accounting equation, we're ready to look at the respective journal entries and T-accounting. However, before we can do that we need to provide more detail of the accounts used to record the firm's profit-measurement activities. In other words, we need to discuss nominal accounts.

## Nominal Accounts Revisited

Recall that stockholders' equity consists of contributed capital and retained earnings. To record changes in retained earnings that result from a firm's operating activities, a firm uses *nominal accounts,* separate revenue and expense accounts, whose balances are transferred to retained earnings at the end of the accounting period. As mentioned earlier, the idea is to measure operating performance one period at a time, as retained earnings reflects *cumulative* revenues and expenses over all accounting periods. By using these nominal accounts, a firm can better analyze the inflows and outflows pertaining to the operating activities of the company for the accounting period just completed.

A firm uses separate accounts for each category of revenue and expense. A firm can then more easily determine the amounts to be included in the various line items on its income statement. Consistent with the usual effects of revenues increasing retained earnings and expenses decreasing retained earnings, revenues are increased by credits, while expenses are increased by debits. Accordingly, revenue accounts will normally have a credit balance, and expense accounts will normally have a debit balance. T-accounts for revenues and expenses are shown below:

T-Accounts for Revenues and Expenses

| Revenues | | Expenses | |
|---|---|---|---|
| Debits Decrease | Credits Increase | Debits Increase | Credits Decrease |

Exhibit 3.14 summarizes the normal balance in each type of account and indicates how the account is affected by debit (left) and credit (right) entries.

With this improved understanding of nominal accounts, we're ready to resume analyzing BHT's operating transactions, now by using journal entries and T-accounts.

**Exhibit 3.14**
Normal Account Balances and Debit and Credit Effects on Accounts

| Account Type | Normal Balance | Debit Entries | Credit Entries |
|---|---|---|---|
| Asset | Debit | Increase | Decrease |
| Liability | Credit | Decrease | Increase |
| Common Stock | Credit | Decrease | Increase |
| Paid-in-Capital | Credit | Decrease | Increase |
| Retained Earnings | Credit | Decrease | Increase |
| Revenue | Credit | Decrease | Increase |
| Expense | Debit | Increase | Decrease |

### Using Journal Entries and T-Accounts to Record Transactions

We show the journal entries and T-accounts for Transactions 4 through 12 in Exhibits 3.15 and 3.16, respectively. Note in Exhibit 3.16 that the beginning balances at the start of 20X1 carry forward from the end of the previous year (20X0). Further, note that the retained earnings account does not include entries other than the dividends declared at this point. This is because the nominal accounts, revenue and expense, have not yet been closed. These accounts will be closed and their balances moved to retained earnings after preparing the income statement. (We'll provide more details on the closing process in the next section.)

**Exhibit 3.15**
Journal Entries for Operating Transactions

| | Debit | Credit |
|---|---|---|
| Transaction #4 | | |
| Inventory | 34,340 | |
| Accounts Payable | | 34,340 |
| Transaction #5 | | |
| Accounts Receivable | 35,724 | |
| Sales | | 35,724 |
| Transaction #6 | | |
| Cost of Sales | 30,420 | |
| Inventory | | 30,420 |
| Transaction #7 | | |
| Cash | 33,260 | |
| Accounts Receivable | | 33,260 |
| Transaction #8 | | |
| Accounts Payable | 29,200 | |
| Cash | | 29,200 |
| Transaction #9 | | |
| S&A Expenses | 4,800 | |
| Cash | | 4,800 |
| Transaction #10 | | |
| Depreciation Expense | 60 | |
| Accumulated Depreciation | | 60 |
| Transaction #11 | | |
| Interest Expense | 28 | |
| Cash | | 28 |
| Transaction #12 | | |
| Retained Earnings | 150 | |
| Cash | | 150 |

**Exhibit 3.16**
Added Operating Transactions to BHT's T-Accounts

| Cash | |
|---|---|
| Bal. 1,485 | |
| | 29,200 (8) |
| (7) 33,260 | 4,800 (9) |
| | 28 (11) |
| | 150 (12) |
| Bal. 567 | |

| Account Receivable | |
|---|---|
| Bal. 0 | |
| (5) 35,724 | |
| | 33,260 (7) |
| Bal. 2,464 | |

| Inventory | |
|---|---|
| Bal. 0 | |
| (4) 34,340 | 30,420 (6) |
| Bal. 3,920 | |

| Fixtures | |
|---|---|
| Bal. 540 | |

| Accumulated Depreciation Fixtures | |
|---|---|
| | Bal. 0 |
| | 60 (10) |
| | Bal. 60 |

| Note Payable | |
|---|---|
| | Bal. 400 |

| Account Payable | |
|---|---|
| | Bal. 0 |
| (8) 29,200 | 34,340 (4) |
| | Bal. 5,140 |

| Capital Stock | |
|---|---|
| | Bal. 250 |

| Paid-in Capital | |
|---|---|
| | Bal. 1,375 |

| Retained Earnings | |
|---|---|
| | Bal. 0 |
| (12) 150 | |

| Sales Revenue | |
|---|---|
| | Bal. 0 |
| | 35,724 (5) |
| | Bal.35,724 |

| Cost of Sales | |
|---|---|
| Bal. 0 | |
| (6) 30,420 | |
| Bal. 30,420 | |

| S&A Expense | |
|---|---|
| Bal. 0 | |
| (9) 4,800 | |
| Bal. 4,800 | |

| Depreciation Expense | |
|---|---|
| Bal. 0 | |
| (10) 60 | |
| Bal. 60 | |

| Interest Expense | |
|---|---|
| Bal. 0 | |
| (11) 28 | |
| Bal. 28 | |

Note: Beginning account balances include the financing and investing activities prior to the start of 20X1.

## CONSTRUCTING THE FINANCIAL STATEMENTS

Exhibit 3.17 shows a balance sheet for 12/31/20X1 compared to 12/31/20X0. Although total assets have dramatically increased, cash has decreased. Note also that the ending balance in retained earnings is determined using the closing entries discussed in the next section. An income statement and statement of cash flows follow in Exhibits 3.18 and 3.19, respectively. BHT provides an income statement only for the year ending 12/31/20X1, as the firm did not begin operations during 20X0. BHT provides cash flow statements for 20X0 and 20X1 for comparative purposes. As briefly discussed in Chapter 2, BHT, like most firms, prepares the cash flow statement using the *indirect approach* (we'll cover this in more depth in Chapter 5). That is, BHT determines its cash from operations

**Exhibit 3.17**
Balance Sheet for Biohealth, Inc. (BHT)

| | As of 12/31/20X1 | As of 12/31/20X0 |
|---|---|---|
| Assets | | |
| Current Assets: | | |
| Cash | $ 567 | $1,485 |
| Accounts Receivable | 2,464 | 0 |
| Inventory | 3,920 | 0 |
| Total Current Assets | 6,951 | 1,485 |
| Property, Plant, and Equipment (Fixtures) | 540 | 540 |
| Less: Accumulated Depreciation | (60) | 0 |
| Net Property Plant and Equipment | 480 | 540 |
| Total Assets | $7,431 | $2,025 |
| Liabilities and Stockholders' Equity | | |
| Liabilities: | | |
| Current Liabilities: | | |
| Accounts Payable | $5,140 | $ 0 |
| Long-Term Debt: | | |
| Notes Payable | 400 | 400 |
| Total Liabilities | 5,540 | 400 |
| Stockholders' Equity | | |
| Common Stock | 250 | 250 |
| Additional Paid-In Capital | 1,375 | 1,375 |
| Retained Earnings | 266 | 0 |
| Total Stockholders' Equity | 1,891 | 1,625 |
| Total Liabilities and Stockholders' Equity | $7,431 | $2,025 |

**Exhibit 3.18**
Income Statement for Biohealth, Inc. (BHT)

| | Year Ending 12/31/20X1 |
|---|---|
| Sales Revenue | $35,724 |
| Less: Cost of Goods Sold | (30,420) |
| Gross Profit | 5,304 |
| Selling and Administrative Expenses | (4,800) |
| Depreciation Expense | (60) |
| Interest Expense | (28) |
| Net Income | $ 416 |
| Earnings per Share[2] | $ 1.66 |

[2]Earnings per share is the amount of earnings per share of common stock outstanding. There are some specific requirements regarding how this is computed that will be discussed later. However, in this case it is simply net income/shares of common stock outstanding, or $416,000,000/250,000,000.

**Exhibit 3.19**
Statement of Cash Flows for the Years Ending 20X1 and 20X0 Biohealth, Inc. (BHT)

| | Year Ending 12/31/20X1 | Year Ending 12/31/20X0 |
|---|---|---|
| Cash from Operations: | | |
| Net Income | $416 | $ 0 |
| Add: Noncash Expenses | | |
| Depreciation | 60 | 0 |
| Less: Changes in Current Assets and Current Liabilities: | | |
| Increase in Accounts Receivable | (2,464) | 0 |
| Increase in Inventory | (3,920) | 0 |
| Increase in Accounts Payable | 5,140 | 0 |
| Total Cash from Operations | (768) | 0 |
| Cash from Investing | | |
| Purchase Fixtures | 0 | (540) |
| Total Cash from Investing | 0 | (540) |
| Cash from Financing | | |
| Borrow on Long-Term Note | 0 | 400 |
| Dividend Payments | (150) | |
| Issue Stock | 0 | 1,625 |
| Total Cash from Financing | (150) | 2,025 |
| Total Change in Cash | ($918) | $1,485 |

starting with net income and then adjusting for noncash operating transactions. Note that the activities in 20X0 were limited to financing and investing activities, as no BHT operations occurred during this start-up period.

The cash flow statement for 20X1 illustrates why cash decreased even though the company earned a profit. Although dividends somewhat reduced cash during the period, operations proved to be the primary driver of the decline in cash, as it had a negative cash flow of $768. This decrease was caused primarily by the increase in accounts receivable and inventory. Increasing inventory requires cash to buy or make the inventory, and the increase in accounts receivable reflects uncollected revenues, resulting in less cash. Offsetting this was the positive effect of the increase in accounts payable during the period. When a company buys things on credit (thereby increasing accounts payable), it conserves cash. Finally, depreciation also produced a minor effect. Depreciation expense is added back to net income. Although it is an expense and it decreases net income, it does not use cash.

## CLOSING ENTRIES

After preparing the income statement, the balances in the temporary revenue and expense accounts must be transferred to the retained earnings account (a permanent account). This will reset the balance in each temporary account to zero, to start the next accounting period. For example, the accounting period for BHT was from 1/1/20X1 through 12/31/20X1. The entries that accomplish the transfer of balances from the revenue and expense accounts to retained earnings are called **closing entries.** We'll distinguish closing entries in this text by lettering the entries rather than numbering them.

Sometimes companies use a single temporary account, the **income summary account,** to accumulate balances from all the income statement accounts. Firms often find it useful to summarize the net of the revenues and expenses during the closing process to calculate taxes. Firms use the income summary account only during the closing process; it carries a zero balance at all other times. The balances from all the individual revenue and expense accounts are closed to this summary account. The balance in the income summary account is then closed to retained earnings. Exhibit 3.20 shows the journal entries and T-accounts to close the revenue and expense accounts for BHT. After making these closing entries, the balances in the revenues, expenses, and income summary accounts return to zero.

**Exhibit 3.20**
Closing Entries for BHT Revenue and Expense Accounts Period Ended 12/31/20X1

**Journal Entries**

| Account Titles | | Debit | Credit |
|---|---|---|---|
| a. Sales Revenue | | 35,724 | |
| | Income Summary | | 35,724 |
| b. Income Summary | | 35,308 | |
| | Cost of Sales | | 30,420 |
| | S&A Expenses | | 4,800 |
| | Depreciation Expense | | 60 |
| | Interest Expense | | 28 |
| c. Income Summary | | 416 | |
| | Retained Earnings | | 416 |

**Closing Entries T-Accounts**

Sales Revenue

| Debit | Credit |
|---|---|
| | Bal. 35,724 |
| (a) 35, 724 | |
| | Bal. 0 |

Cost of Sales

| Debit | Credit |
|---|---|
| Bal. 30,420 | |
| | 30,420 (b) |
| Bal. 0 | |

S&A Expenses

| Debit | Credit |
|---|---|
| Bal. 4,800 | |
| | 4,800 (b) |
| Bal. 0 | |

Depreciation Expense

| Debit | Credit |
|---|---|
| Bal. 60 | |
| | 60 (b) |
| Bal. 0 | |

Interest Expense

| Debit | Credit |
|---|---|
| Bal. 28 | |
| | (28) (b) |
| Bal. 0 | |

Retained Earnings

| Debit | Credit |
|---|---|
| | Bal. 0 |
| (12) 150 | 416 (c) |
| | Bal. 266 |

Income Summary

| Debit | Credit |
|---|---|
| | Bal. 0 |
| (b) 35,308 | 35,724 (a) |
| (c) 416 | |
| | Bal. 0 |

Finally, just prior to making closing entries, a firm typically makes **adjusting entries.** Adjusting entries improve the accuracy of firm's financial statements, by enabling it to meet the accrual concept. For example, BHT's recording of depreciation is one type of adjusting entry. Other adjusting entries include the recognition of interest expense that has not been paid and wages that have been incurred but not paid. We'll discuss adjusting entries again in Chapter 4 and Appendix A covers adjusting entries in more detail.

## THE ACCOUNTING CYCLE

The accounting cycle refers to the series of steps in the accounting process, which a firm repeats each time it prepares financial statements. While accounting systems may differ from very simple systems in a sole proprietorship, to multibillion-dollar systems in large companies, the process remains essentially the same:

1. *Identify transactions.* As we indicated earlier, some economic events are not recognized in accounting as transactions. For example, if Dell signed a contract with another company to furnish a large number of computers to the company over a period of time, this would be an event of economic consequence to Dell, but it would not be recorded as an accounting transaction.
2. *Journalize transactions.* A journal entry provides a summary of a particular event's impact on assets, liabilities, and stockholders' equity.
3. *Post journal entries to ledger accounts.* In this book, we use T-accounts to represent ledgers. In real accounting systems, ledger accounts can take many forms, but the key to thinking about the ledger is to realize that it carries forward all of the transactions that affect a particular account. In the case of permanent accounts as seen on the balance sheet (assets, liabilities, and various stockholders' equity accounts), the balances carry-forward over accounting periods. For example, the balance in accounts receivable at the end of 20X0 is the same as the balance at the beginning of 20X1. In contrast, the nominal or temporary accounts (revenues and expenses) will start each accounting period with a zero balance.
4. *Prepare period-end adjusting entries and then post them to ledger accounts.* An example would be recording depreciation.
5. *Prepare the income statement.*
6. *Close nominal accounts to retained earnings.*
7. *Prepare the balance sheet and cash flow statement.*

One final issue with regard to the accounting cycle is the frequency with which financial statements should be prepared. On one hand, a firm should prepare financial statements as often as necessary to provide timely information to management, stockholders, creditors, and others with an interest in the firm. On the other hand, a firm must balance the benefits of having up-to-date information with the cost of preparing the statements. In some businesses, management may need up-to-date information, in which case daily reports may be necessary. This is becoming more common as the cost of compiling timely information continues to decrease. In other businesses, a monthly statement may be sufficient.

Regardless of what time period a firm selects, firms will follow the same procedures as outlined in this chapter.

Companies whose stock is traded on a public exchange and who fall under the authority of the SEC are required to file financial statements quarterly, as well as on an annual basis. The frequency with which a firm prepares its financial statements is sometimes expressed in terms of how often the firm closes its books. If it closes its books monthly, the accounting cycle for the firm is one month, and the nominal (temporary) accounts are reset on a monthly basis. However, although a company may close its books more frequently than at year-end, annual financial statements require that revenues and expenses be accumulated over the entire year. Thus, firms do interim closings only for purposes of preparing interim statements.

## ANALYZING FINANCIAL STATEMENTS

Understanding the accounting cycle will help you to use the information in the financial statements more effectively. To illustrate, as an investor or potential investor, you can obtain financial statements, but not information about the individual transactions that gave rise to those statements. However, by understanding the accounting process, you may be able to deduce some of the major transactions by analyzing the financial statements.

Say you looked at Exhibits 3.17, 3.18, and 3.19 without knowing BHT's transactions. By understanding the accounting process, you would be able to observe the following:

- Cash has declined for the year despite the fact that BHT reported a profit.
- The balance sheet shows an increase in Accounts Receivable, suggesting that cash collection from sales was less than the revenue recognized.
- The balance sheet shows an increase in Inventory, indicating that the company is purchasing more inventory than it is selling.
- Accounts Payable increased during the year, suggesting that the company is purchasing more inventory than it is paying to suppliers.

As BHT formed in 20X0, we would not be surprised by these findings, as they are typical of a new business. However, in an established company, significant changes in balance sheet accounts may signal information about the company's future cash flows. For example, if a company records large amounts of sales on account, and accounts receivable increases more rapidly than the sales, the company may not be collecting its accounts receivable on a timely basis or it may have relaxed its credit policies. This may signal future cash flow problems (defaults by customers). Similarly, increasing inventory coupled with decreasing (or less rapidly) increasing sales may signal that a company is having difficulty selling its inventory. In Chapter 6, we continue to consider how to assess past performance based on the information contained in financial statements, as well as to predict future performance.

As you progress through this text, you will appreciate more fully the power of the information conveyed about a company in its financial statements and the value to you of understanding the concepts underlying financial statement construction. Of particular importance is predicting transactions' impact on each of the major financial statements. For example, as a manager, you might consider generating additional sales by providing a more liberal credit policy (e.g., allowing customers with weaker credit to purchase goods on account). With a good knowledge of accounting, you could anticipate the effects of such a change in credit policies on the financial statements. In this particular case, you would likely see increased sales on the income statement, coupled with increased accounts receivable because weaker credit customers might pay more slowly or not at all. You might also see cash flows decline even if sales increased. This could occur due to a combination of two factors, slower sales collections and a need to purchase and pay for more inventory to sell to customers who have not yet paid. Thus, this business decision would impact all of the major financial statements.

## SUMMARY AND TRANSITION

This chapter provided an overview of the accounting process used to generate financial statements. Understanding the framework of accounting allows you to readily determine the impact of economic events on the financial statements. This knowledge will allow you as a manager or investor to make sound decisions using information generated from the accounting process.

The accounting process contains two basic concepts: duality and the nominal (temporary) account. The concept of duality portrays accounting events in terms of the dual effects on the resources of the firm (its assets), the claims of creditors (its liabilities), and the owners' wealth (stockholders' equity). The duality concept is apparent in the accounting equation and the requirements that debits equal credits in the accounting representation of each transaction. Nominal accounts are used to describe changes in stockholders' equity that result from operating activities, principally revenues and expenses.

Understanding the accounting process is necessary to understanding the information conveyed in the financial statements that are the final product of that process. However, apart from the accounting process itself, there are many accounting choices and judgments that affect the implementation of that process and, thereby, shape the content of those statements. Chief among these are the recognition criteria which determine when an economic event should get recognized in the accounting system (such as the timing of recognizing revenues and expenses) and the valuation principles that determine the values of the assets and liabilities of the firm that meet the recognition criteria. These choices and judgments are addressed in the chapters that follow.

# END OF CHAPTER MATERIAL

## KEY TERMS

Additional Paid-In Capital
Adjusting Entries
Closing Entries
Contra-Asset Account
Contributed Capital
Cost of Goods Sold

Credits
Debits
Depreciation Expense
Depreciation Methods
Double-Entry Accounting System
Entry
Journal
Journal Entry
Ledger
Nominal Accounts
Par Value
Permanent Accounts
Retained Earnings
Sales Revenue
Stated Value
Summary Account
T-Account
Temporary Accounts
Transactions

## ASSIGNMENT MATERIAL

### REVIEW QUESTIONS

1. Explain what double-entry accounting means and provide an example.
2. Define an asset, according to GAAP.
3. Define a liability, according to GAAP.
4. Describe what owners' equity represents.
5. Discuss how retained earnings changes over time.
6. What is a permanent account?
7. What is a nominal or temporary account?
8. What is the proper form for a journal entry?
9. What is a ledger?
10. What is depreciation?
11. How is straight-line depreciation calculated?
12. What is a contra-asset account and how is it used in the context of depreciation?
13. "Expense accounts have debit balances, and debit entries increase these accounts." Reconcile this statement with the normal effects of entries on owners' equity accounts and the resulting balances.
14. Describe the closing process.
15. Discuss why one firm might close their books monthly and another might close them weekly.

### APPLYING YOUR KNOWLEDGE

15. Explain why you agree or disagree with the following statement: "Retained earnings are like money in the bank; you can always use them to pay your bills if you get into trouble."
16. Respond to each of the following statements with a true or false answer:
    a. Debits increase liability accounts.
    b. Revenues are credit entries to owners' equity.

c. Cash receipts from customers are debited to accounts receivable.
d. Dividends declared decrease cash at the date of declaration.
e. Dividends are an expense of doing business and should appear on the income statement.
f. Selling goods on account results in a credit to accounts receivable.
g. Making a payment on an account payable results in a debit to accounts payable.

17. For each of the transactions below, indicate which accounts are affected and whether they increase or decrease.
    a. Issue common stock for cash.
    b. Buy equipment from a supplier on credit (short term).
    c. Buy inventory from a supplier partly with cash and partly on account.
    d. Sell a unit of inventory to a customer on account.
    e. Receive a payment from a customer on his or her account.
    f. Borrow money from the bank.
    g. Declare a dividend (to be paid later).
    h. Pay a dividend (that was previously declared).
18. For each of the following transactions, indicate how income and cash flow are affected (increase, decrease, no effect) and by how much:
    a. Issue common stock for $1,000.
    b. Sell, on account, a unit of inventory for $150 that cost $115. The unit is already in inventory.
    c. Purchase equipment for $500 in cash.
    d. Depreciate plant and equipment by $300.
    e. Purchase a unit of inventory, on account, for $100.
    f. Make a payment on accounts payable for $200.
    g. Receive a payment from a customer for $75 on his or her account.
    h. Declare a dividend for $400.
    i. Pay a dividend for $400.
19. Show how each of the following transactions affects the balance sheet equation:
    a. Borrow $1,500 from the bank.
    b. Buy land for $20,000 in cash.
    c. Issue common stock for $5,000. The par value of the stock is $1,500.
    d. Buy inventory costing $3,000 on account.
    e. Sell inventory costing $2,500 to customers, on account, for $3,500.
    f. Make a payment of $250 to the electric company for power used during the current period.
    g. Declare a dividend of $350.
    h. Depreciate equipment by $500.
20. Show how each of the following transactions affects the balance sheet equation:
    a. Issue common stock for $10,000. The stock has no par value attached to it.

b. Receive a payment from a customer on his or her account in the amount of $325.

c. Make a payment to the bank of $850. Of this amount, $750 represents interest and the rest is a repayment of principal.

d. Return a unit of inventory costing $200 that was damaged in shipment. You have already paid for the unit and have requested a refund from the supplier.

e. Dividends of $175 that were previously declared are paid.

f. Purchase equipment costing $1,800. You pay $600 in cash and give the supplier a note for the balance of the purchase price.

g. Sales on account of $15,000 are reported for the period.

h. A count of physical inventory at the end of the period indicates an ending balance of $575. The beginning balance was $485, and the purchases for the period were $11,500. Record the cost of goods sold.

21. For each of the following transactions, indicate how each immediately affects the balance sheet equation and what other effects there will be in the future as a result of the transaction:

a. Purchase equipment.

b. Borrow money from the bank.

c. Purchase inventory on account.

d. Sell inventory on account to customers.

e. Buy a patent for a new production process.

22. Indicate the effects of the following transactions on the balance sheet equation developed in the chapter. Assume that the fiscal year end of the firm is December 31.

a. Borrow $2,500 from the bank on 1/1/X1.

b. Pay interest on the bank loan on 12/31/X1. The interest rate is 10 percent.

c. Buy equipment on 1/1/X1 for $2,000. The equipment has an estimated useful life of five years and an estimated salvage value at the end of five years of $500.

d. Record the depreciation for the equipment as of 12/31/X1, assuming the firm uses the straight-line method.

e. Sales for the period totaled $5,500, of which $3,500 were on account. The cost of the products sold was $3,600.

f. Collections from customers on account totaled $2,800.

g. Purchases of inventory on account during 20X1 totaled $2,700.

h. Payments to suppliers totaled $2,900 during 20X1.

i. Dividends were declared and paid in the amount of $100.

23. Indicate the effects of the following transactions on the balance sheet equation developed in the chapter. Assume that the fiscal year end of the firm is December 31.

a. Issue common stock for $25,000, with a par value of $8,000.

b. Sales recorded for the period totaled $60,000, of which $25,000 were cash sales.

c. Cash collections on customer accounts totaled $37,000.

d. Sign a contract to purchase a piece of equipment that costs $1,200, and put a downpayment of $100 on the purchase.

e. Dividends of $1,300 are declared.

f. Dividends of $1,150 that had previously been declared are paid.

g. Depreciation of $3,300 was taken on the property, plant, and equipment.

h. Purchase $31,350 of inventory on account.

i. Inventory costing $35,795 was sold.

24. Indicate whether each of the following accounts normally has a debit or a credit balance:

a. Accounts Receivable

b. Accounts Payable

c. Sales Revenue

d. Dividends Declared

e. Dividends Payable

f. Depreciation Expense

g. Common Stock (par value)

h. Cost of Goods Sold

i. Loan Payable

25. For each of the following accounts indicate whether the account would normally have a debit or a credit balance:

a. Cash

b. Accounts Payable

c. Common Stock

d. Sales Revenues

e. Inventory

f. Cost of Goods Sold

g. Paid-In Capital

h. Retained Earnings

i. Accumulated Depreciation

26. For each of the following transactions construct a journal entry:

a. Inventory costing $1,500 is purchased on account.

b. Inventory costing $1,200 is sold on account for $1,800.

c. Accounts receivable of $800 are collected.

d. The firm borrows $10,000 from the bank.

e. The firm issues common stock for $2,500 and $1,500 is considered par value.

f. New equipment costing $3,500 is purchased with cash.

27. The T. George Company started business on 1/1/X2. Listed below are the transactions that occurred during 20X2.

Required:

a. Construct the journal entries to record the transactions of the T. George Company for 20X2.

b. Post the journal entries to the appropriate T-accounts.

c. Prepare a balance sheet and income statement for 20X2.

d. Prepare the closing entries for 20X2.

Transactions:

1. On 1/1/X2, the company issued 10,000 shares of common stock for $175,000. The par value of the stock is $10 per share.
2. On 1/1/X2, the company borrowed $125,000 from the bank.
3. On 1/2/X2, the company purchased (for cash) land and a building costing $200,000. The building was recently appraised at $140,000.
4. Inventory costing $100,000 was purchased on account.
5. An investment was made in Calhoun Company stock in the amount of $75,000.
6. Sales to customers totaled $190,000 in 20X2. Of these, $30,000 were cash sales.
7. Collections on accounts receivable totaled $135,000.
8. Payments to suppliers totaled $92,000 in 20X2.
9. Salaries paid to employees totaled $44,000. There were no unpaid salaries at year end.
10. A count of inventories at year end revealed $10,000 worth of inventory.
11. The building was estimated to have a useful life of 20 years and a salvage value of $20,000. The company uses straight-line depreciation.
12. The interest on the bank loan is recognized each month and is paid on the first day of the succeeding month; that is, January's interest is recognized in January and paid on February 1. The interest rate is 12 percent.
13. The investment in Calhoun Company paid dividends of $5,000 in 20X2. All of it had been received by year end.
14. Dividends of $15,000 were declared on 12/15/X2 and were scheduled to be paid on 1/10/X3.

28. The Hughes Tool Company started business on 10/1/X3. Its fiscal year runs through September 30 of the following year. Following are the transactions that occurred during fiscal year 19X4 (the year starting 10/1/X3 and ending 9/30/X4).

Required:

a. Construct the journal entries to record the transactions of the The Hughes Tool Company for fiscal year 20X4.

b. Post the journal entries to the appropriate T-accounts.

c. Prepare a balance sheet and income statement for fiscal year 20X4.

d. Prepare the closing entries for fiscal year 20X4.

Transactions:

1. On 10/1/X3, J. Hughes contributed $100,000 to start the business. Hughes is the sole proprietor of the business.
2. On 10/2/X3, Hughes borrowed $300,000 from a venture capitalist (a lender who specializes in start-up companies). The interest rate on

the loan is 11 percent. Interest is paid twice a year on March 31 and September 30.

3. On 10/3/X3, Hughes rented a building. The rental agreement was a two-year contract that called for quarterly rental payments of $20,000, payable in advance on January 1, April 1, July 1, and October 1. The first payment was made on 10/3/X3 and covers the period from October 1 to December 31.
4. On 10/3/X3, Hughes purchased equipment costing $250,000. The equipment had an estimated useful life of seven years and a salvage value of $40,000.
5. On 10/3/X3, Hughes purchased initial inventory with a cash payment of $100,000.
6. Sales during the year totaled $800,000, of which $720,000 were credit sales.
7. Collections from customers on account totaled $640,000.
8. Additional purchases of inventory during the year totaled $550,000, all on account.
9. Payments to suppliers totaled $495,000.
10. Inventory on hand at year end amounted to $115,000.
11. J. Hughes withdrew a total of $40,000 for personal expenses during the year.
12. Interest on the loan from the venture capitalist was paid at year-end, as well as $20,000 of the principal.
13. Other selling and administrative expenses totaled $90,000 for the year. Of these, $20,000 were unpaid as of year end.

29. The A.J. Smith Company started business on 1/1/X4. The company's fiscal year ends on December 31. Following are the transactions that occurred during 20X4.

Required:

a. Construct the journal entries to record the transactions of the The A.J. Smith Company for fiscal year 20X4.
b. Post the journal entries to the appropriate T-accounts.
c. Prepare a balance sheet and income statement for fiscal year 20X4.
d. Prepare the closing entries for fiscal year 20X4.

Transactions:

1. On 1/1/X4, the company issued 25,000 shares of common stock at $15 per share. The par value of each share of common stock is $10.
2. On 1/1/X4, the company purchased land and buildings from another company in exchange for $50,000 in cash and 25,000 shares of common stock. The land's value is approximately one-fifth of the total value of the transaction.
3. Equipment worth $100,000 was purchased on 7/1/X4, in exchange for $50,000 in cash and a one-year, 10 percent note, principal amount $50,000. The note pays semiannual interest, and interest was unpaid on 12/31/X4.

4. The equipment is depreciated using the straight-line method, with an estimated useful life of 10 years and an estimated salvage value of $0.
5. The buildings purchased in transaction 2 are depreciated using the straight-line method, with an estimated useful life of 30 years and an estimated salvage value of $40,000.
6. During the year, inventory costing $200,000 was purchased, all on account.
7. Sales during the year were $215,000, of which credit sales were $175,000.
8. Inventory costing $160,000 was sold during the year.
9. Payments to suppliers totaled $175,000.
10. At the end of the year, accounts receivable had a positive balance of $10,000.
11. On March 31, 20X4, the company rented out a portion of its building to Fantek Corporation. Fantek is required to make quarterly payments of $5,000 each. The payments are due on April 1, July 1, October 1, and January 1 of each year, with the first payment on 4/1/X4. All scheduled payments were made during 20X4.
12. Selling and distribution expenses amounted to $30,000, all paid in cash.
13. During the year, inventory worth $10,000 was destroyed by fire. The inventory was not insured.
14. The company calculates taxes at a rate of 30 percent. During the year, $3,000 was paid to the taxing authority.
15. Dividends of $4,000 were declared during the year, and $1,000 remained unpaid at year end.

30. The accounting system closing process takes some amount of time at the end of the accounting period in order to check for errors, make adjusting entries, and prepare the financial statements. In recent years there has been a real push to speed up this process for most firms. Discuss the incentives that companies might have to implement in order to make this a faster process.

31. During the year-end audit process, the auditing firm may find errors and omissions in the recording of transactions and will then ask management to make an adjusting entry to correct for these errors. In light of the purpose of the audit opinion, discuss plausible arguments that management might give to convince the auditor to waive making these suggested adjustments.

32. Suppose that a company has a bonus plan in which managers can earn a bonus if they meet certain net income targets. If the management team has discretion as to which depreciation method they might use, with the straight-line reporting the least amount of depreciation in the early years of the life of the asset, discuss the incentives that management would have in choosing a depreciation method. Also discuss how owners might protect themselves from any self-serving behavior on the part of management.

**33.** Discuss how creditors might protect their interests (relative to owners) when they negotiate their lending agreement with the firm.

## USING REAL DATA

**34.** Base your answers to the following questions on the financial statements of Russ Berrie.

**RUSS BERRIE & Co., Inc.: Income Statement**

| | 12/31/2001 | 12/31/2000 | 12/31/1999 |
|---|---|---|---|
| Net sales | $294,291,000 | $300,801,000 | $287,011,000 |
| Cost of sales | 132,611,000 | 132,908,000 | 123,216,000 |
| Gross profit | 161,680,000 | 167,893,000 | 163,795,000 |
| Selling, general and administrative expense | 112,570,000 | 106,991,000 | 108,023,000 |
| Information system write-off | 0 | 0 | 10,392,000 |
| Investment and other income net | (8,560,000) | (10,202,000) | (8,587,000) |
| Income before taxes | 57,670,000 | 71,104,000 | 53,967,000 |
| Provision for income taxes | 17,496,000 | 23,163,000 | 17,531,000 |
| Net income | $ 40,174,000 | $ 47,941,000 | $ 36,436,000 |

**RUSS BERRIE & Co., Inc.: Balance Sheet**

| | 12/31/2001 | 12/31/2000 |
|---|---|---|
| Assets | | |
| Current assets | | |
| Cash and cash equivalents | $148,872,000 | $ 77,794,000 |
| Marketable securities | 94,181,000 | 141,032,000 |
| Accounts receivable, trade, less allowance of $3,454 in 2001 and $3,460 in 2000 | 63,481,000 | 58,673,000 |
| Inventories, net | 37,374,000 | 47,430,000 |
| Prepaid expenses and other current assets | 4,550,000 | 5,508,000 |
| Deferred income taxes | 6,705,000 | 6,003,000 |
| Total current assets | 355,163,000 | 336,440,000 |
| Property, plant, and equipment, net | 24,623,000 | 26,745,000 |
| Inventories—long-term, net | 2,284,000 | 0 |
| Other assets | 4,574,000 | 3,824,000 |
| Total assets | $386,644,000 | $367,009,000 |
| Liabilities and Shareholders' Equity | | |
| Current liabilities | | |
| Accounts payable | 5,376,000 | 4,913,000 |
| Accrued expenses | 20,003,000 | 20,313,000 |
| Accrued income taxes | 6,848,000 | 7,192,000 |
| Total current liabilities | 32,227,000 | 32,418,000 |

| | 12/31/2001 | 12/31/2000 |
|---|---|---|
| Commitments and contingencies | | |
| Shareholders' equity | | |
| Common stock: $0.10 stated value; authorized 50,000,000 shares; issued 2001, 25,682,364 shares; 2000, 25,413,626 shares | 2,587,000 | 2,541,000 |
| Additional paid-in-capital | 73,794,000 | 63,103,000 |
| Retained earnings | 392,272,000 | 381,479,000 |
| Accumulated other comprehensive loss | (4,165,000) | (4,310,000) |
| Unearned compensation | (75,000) | (149,000) |
| Treasury stock, at cost (5,632,014 shares at December 31, 2001 and 5,557,514 shares at December 31, 2000) | (109,996,000) | (108,073,000) |
| Total shareholders equity | 354,417,000 | 334,591,000 |
| Total liabilities and shareholders' equity | $386,644,000 | $367,009,000 |

**RUSS BERRIE & Co., Inc.:**
**Cash Flow**

| | 12/31/2001 | 12/31/2000 | 12/31/1999 |
|---|---|---|---|
| Cash flows from operating activities: | | | |
| Net income | $ 40,174,000 | $47,941,000 | $36,436,000 |
| Adjustments to reconcile net income to net cash provided by operating activities: | | | |
| Depreciation and amortization | 4,021,000 | 3,998,000 | 5,008,000 |
| Information system write-off | 0 | 0 | 10,392,000 |
| Provision for accounts receivable reserves | 1,828,000 | 2,298,000 | 2,534,000 |
| Income from contingency reserve reversal | 0 | (2,544,000) | 0 |
| Other | 415,000 | 390,000 | (456,000) |
| Changes in assets and liabilities: | | | |
| Accounts receivable | (6,636,000) | 414,000 | (9,058,000) |
| Inventories, net | 7,772,000 | (3,123,000) | 894,000 |
| Prepaid expenses and other current assets | 958,000 | 3,995,000 | (197,000) |
| Other assets | (166,000) | 78,000 | (1,460,000) |
| Accounts payable | 463,000 | (1,315,000) | 1,979,000 |
| Accrued expenses | (310,000) | (631,000) | 421,000 |
| Accrued income taxes | (344,000) | 1,086,000 | (1,099,000) |
| Total adjustments | 8,001,000 | 4,646,000 | 8,958,000 |
| Net cash provided by operating activities | 48,175,000 | 52,587,000 | 45,394,000 |
| Cash flows from investing activities: | | | |
| Purchase of marketable securities | (97,335,000) | (48,959,000) | (46,365,000) |
| Proceeds from sale of marketable securities | 144,331,000 | 45,567,000 | 60,017,000 |

| | 12/31/2001 | 12/31/2000 | 12/31/1999 |
|---|---|---|---|
| Proceeds from sale of property, plant, and equipment | 89,000 | 79,000 | 116,000 |
| Capital expenditures | (2,405,000) | (4,087,000) | (8,435,000) |
| Net cash provided by (used in) investing activities | 44,680,000 | (7,400,000) | 5,333,000 |
| Cash flows from financing activities: | | | |
| Proceeds from issuance of common stock | 10,737,000 | 2,155,000 | 2,416,000 |
| Dividends paid to shareholders | (29,381,000) | (17,764,000) | (16,861,000) |
| Purchase of treasury stock | (1,923,000) | (15,619,000) | (44,292,000) |
| Net cash (used in) financing activities | (20,567,000) | (31,228,000) | (58,737,000) |
| Effect of exchange rate changes on cash and cash equivalents | (1,210,000) | (1,073,000) | (146,000) |
| Net increase (decrease) in cash and cash equivalents | 71,078,000 | 12,886,000 | (8,156,000) |
| Cash and cash equivalents at beginning of year | 77,794,000 | 64,908,000 | 73,064,000 |
| Cash and cash equivalents at end of year | $148,872,000 | $77,794,000 | $64,908,000 |
| Cash paid during the year for: | | | |
| Interest | $ 196,000 | $ 127,000 | $ 118,000 |
| Income taxes | 17,841,000 | 22,077,000 | 18,630,000 |

a. Determine the amount of dividends declared during fiscal 2001.

b. Determine the amount of dividends paid during fiscal 2001.

c. Assuming that all sales were on account, determine the amount of cash collected from customers.

d. Assuming that the only transactions that flow through the accounts payable to suppliers and others are purchases of inventory and assuming that all additions to inventory were purchases of inventory, determine the cash payments to suppliers.

e. The other comprehensive income account reflects the translation of Russ Berrie's foreign subsidiaries. What has been the experience with these subsidiaries over time—have they resulted in net gains or net losses from translation?

f. In 1999, the company wrote off the cost of some of its information systems. How significant was this write-off (express your answer as a percent of income before the write-off)? How might an analyst factor this loss into his or her evaluation of the company's stock?

g. How does the company finance its business (use data to support your answer)?

h. How healthy is the company from a cash flow perspective?

35. Use the data from the financial statements of the GAP to answer the following questions:

a. Determine the amount of dividends declared during the year ended 2/2/2002.

b. Determine the amount of dividends paid during the year ended 2/2/2002.

c. The GAP reports the ratio of each expense line item relative to net sales on its income statement. Use these data to discuss how profitable GAP has been over the last three years in selling its products.

d. What has been the trend in revenues and earnings over the last three years (use data to support your answer)?

e. How does the company finance its business (use data to support your answer)?

f. How healthy is the company from a cash flow perspective?

g. If you were an analyst, how might you react to the trends you see in income, debt, and cash flows over the years presented?

GAP, Inc. Income Statement
($ in thousands except share and per share amounts)

| | 52 Weeks Ended | | 53 Weeks Ended | | 52 Weeks Ended | |
|---|---|---|---|---|---|---|
| | Feb. 2, 2002 | % to Sales | Feb. 3, 2001 | % to Sales | Jan. 29, 2000 | % to Sales |
| Net sales | $13,847,873 | 100.00% | $13,673,460 | 100.00% | $11,635,398 | 100.00% |
| Costs and expenses | | | | | | |
| Cost of goods sold and occupancy expenses | 9,704,389 | 70.1 | 8,599,442 | 62.9 | 6,775,262 | 58.2 |
| Operating expenses | 3,805,968 | 27.5 | 3,629,257 | 26.5 | 3,043,432 | 26.2 |
| Interest expense | 109,190 | 0.8 | 74,891 | 0.5 | 44,966 | 0.4 |
| Interest income | (13,315) | (0.1) | (12,015) | (0.0) | (13,211) | (0.1) |
| Earnings before income taxes | 241,641 | 1.7 | 1,381,885 | 10.1 | 1,784,949 | 15.3 |
| Income taxes | 249,405 | 1.8 | 504,388 | 3.7 | 657,884 | 5.6 |
| Net earnings (loss) | ($7,764) | (0.1%) | $877,497 | 6.4% | $1,127,065 | 9.7% |

GAP, Inc. Balance Sheet

| | Feb. 2, 2002 | Feb. 3, 2001 |
|---|---|---|
| Assets | | |
| Current assets: | | |
| Cash and equivalents | $1,035,749,000 | $408,794,000 |
| Merchandise inventory | 1,677,116,000 | 1,904,153,000 |
| Other current assets | 331,685,000 | 335,103,000 |
| Total current assets: | 3,044,550,000 | 2,648,050,000 |
| Property and equipment | | |
| Leasehold improvements | 2,127,966,000 | 1,899,820,000 |

| | Feb. 2, 2002 | Feb. 3, 2001 |
|---|---|---|
| Furniture and equipment | 3,327,819,000 | 2,826,863,000 |
| Land and buildings | 917,055,000 | 558,832,000 |
| Construction-in-progress | 246,691,000 | 615,722,000 |
| | 6,619,531,000 | 5,901,237,000 |
| Accumulated depreciation and amortization | (2,458,241,000) | (1,893,552,000) |
| Property and equipment, net | 4,161,290,000 | 4,007,685,000 |
| Lease rights and other assets | 385,486,000 | 357,173,000 |
| Total assets | $7,591,326,000 | $7,012,908,000 |
| Liabilities and shareholders' equity: | | |
| Current liabilities | | |
| Notes payable | $ 41,889,000 | $ 779,904,000 |
| Current maturities of long-term debt | 0 | 250,000,000 |
| Accounts payable | 1,105,117,000 | 1,067,207,000 |
| Accrued expenses and other current liabilities | 909,227,000 | 702,033,000 |
| Total current liabilities | 2,056,233,000 | 2,799,144,000 |
| Long-term liabilities: | | |
| Long-term debt | 1,961,397,000 | 780,246,000 |
| Deferred lease credits and other liabilities | 564,115,000 | 505,279,000 |
| Total long-term liabilities | 2,525,512,000 | 1,285,525,000 |
| Shareholders' equity: | | |
| Common stock $.05 par value | | |
| Authorized 2,300,000,000 shares; issued 948,597,949 and 939,222,871 shares; outstanding 865,726,890 and 853,996,984 shares | 47,430,000 | 46,961,000 |
| Additional paid-in capital | 461,408,000 | 294,967,000 |
| Retained earnings | 4,890,375,000 | 4,974,773,000 |
| Accumulated other comprehensive losses | (61,824,000) | (20,173,000) |
| Deferred compensation | (7,245,000) | (12,162,000) |
| Treasury stock, at cost | (2,320,563,000) | (2,356,127,000) |
| Total shareholders' equity | 3,009,581,000 | 2,928,239,000 |
| Total liabilities and shareholders' equity | $7,591,326,000 | $7,012,908,000 |

GAP, Inc. Cash Flow

| Cash Flows from Operating Activities | 52 Weeks Ended Feb. 2, 2002 | 53 Weeks Ended Feb. 3, 2001 | 52 Weeks Ended Jan. 29, 2000 |
|---|---|---|---|
| Net earnings (loss) | ($7,764,000) | $877,497,000 | $1,127,065,000 |
| Adjustments to reconcile net earnings (loss) to net cash provided by operating activities: | | | |
| Depreciation and amortization | 810,486,000 | 590,365,000 | 436,184,000 |
| Tax benefit from exercise of stock options and vesting of restricted stock | 58,444,000 | 130,882,000 | 211,891,000 |
| Deferred income taxes | (28,512,000) | (38,872,000) | 2,444,000 |

| | 52 Weeks Ended Feb. 2, 2002 | 53 Weeks Ended Feb. 3, 2001 | 52 Weeks Ended Jan. 29, 2000 |
|---|---|---|---|
| Change in operating assets and liabilities: | | | |
| Merchandise inventory | 213,067,000 | (454,595,000) | (404,211,000) |
| Prepaid expenses and other | (13,303,000) | (61,096,000) | (55,519,000) |
| Accounts payable | 42,205,000 | 249,545,000 | 118,121,000 |
| Accrued expenses | 220,826,000 | (56,541,000) | (5,822,000) |
| Deferred lease credits and other long-term liabilities | 22,390,000 | 54,020,000 | 47,775,000 |
| Net cash provided by operating activities | 1,317,839,000 | 1,291,205,000 | 1,477,928,000 |
| Cash flows from investing activities: | | | |
| Net purchase of property and equipment | (940,078,000) | (1,858,662,000) | (1,238,722,000) |
| Acquisition of lease rights and other assets | (10,549,000) | (16,252,000) | (39,839,000) |
| Net cash used for investing activities | (950,627,000) | (1,874,914,000) | (1,278,561,000) |
| Cash flows from financing activities: | | | |
| Net increase (decrease) in notes payable | (734,927,000) | 621,420,000 | 84,778,000 |
| Proceeds from issuance of long-term debt | 1,194,265,000 | 250,000,000 | 311,839,000 |
| Payments of long-term debt | (250,000,000) | 0 | 0 |
| Issuance of common stock | 139,105,000 | 152,105,000 | 114,142,000 |
| Net purchase of treasury stock | (785,000) | (392,558,000) | (745,056,000) |
| Cash dividends paid | (76,373,000) | (75,488,000) | (75,795,000) |
| Net cash provided by (used for) financing activities | 271,285,000 | 555,479,000 | (310,092,000) |
| Effect of exchange rate fluctuations on cash | (11,542,000) | (13,328,000) | (4,176,000) |
| Net increase (decrease) in cash and equivalents | $ 626,955,000 | ($41,558,000) | ($114,901,000) |
| Cash and equivalents at beginning of year | 408,794,000 | 450,352,000 | 565,253,000 |
| Cash and equivalents at end of year | $1,035,749,000 | $408,794,000 | $ 450,352,000 |

**36.** Use the financial statements of Hasbro to answer the following questions:

**a.** Determine the amount of dividends declared during fiscal year 2001.

**b.** Determine the amount of dividends paid during fiscal year 2001.

**c.** Assuming that all sales were on account, determine the amount of cash collected from customers.

**d.** Assuming that the only transactions that flow through the accounts payable to suppliers and others are purchases of inventory, and assuming that all additions to inventory were purchases of inventory, determine the cash payments to suppliers.

**e.** What has been the trend in revenues and earnings over the last three years (use data to support your answer)?

**f.** How does the company finance its business (use data to support your answer)?

**g.** How healthy is the company from a cash flow perspective?

**h.** If you were an analyst, how might you react to the trends you see in income, debt, and cash flows over the years presented?

| HASBRO, Inc. Income Statement | 12/30/2001 | 12/30/2000 | 12/30/1999 |
|---|---|---|---|
| Net revenues | $2,856,339,000 | $3,787,215,000 | $4,232,263,000 |
| Cost of sales | 1,223,483,000 | 1,673,973,000 | 1,698,242,000 |
| Gross profit | 1,632,856,000 | 2,113,242,000 | 2,534,021,000 |
| Expenses | | | |
| Amortization | 121,652,000 | 157,763,000 | 173,533,000 |
| Royalties, research and development | 335,358,000 | 635,366,000 | 711,790,000 |
| Advertising | 290,829,000 | 452,978,000 | 456,978,000 |
| Selling, distribution, and administration | 675,482,000 | 863,496,000 | 799,919,000 |
| Restructuring | (1,795,000) | 63,951,000 | 64,232,000 |
| Loss on sale of business units | 0 | 43,965,000 | 0 |
| Total expenses | 1,421,526,000 | 2,217,519,000 | 2,206,452,000 |
| Operating profit (loss) | 211,330,000 | (104,277,000) | 327,569,000 |
| Nonoperating (income) expense | | | |
| Interest expense | 103,688,000 | 114,421,000 | 69,340,000 |
| Other (income) expense, net | 11,443,000 | 7,288,000 | (15,616,000) |
| Total nonoperating expense | 115,131,000 | 121,709,000 | 53,724,000 |
| Earnings (loss) before income taxes and cumulative effect of accounting change | 96,199,000 | (225,986,000) | 273,845,000 |
| Income taxes | 35,401,000 | (81,355,000) | 84,892,000 |
| Net earnings (loss) before cumulative effect of accounting change | 60,798,000 | (144,631,000) | 188,953,000 |
| Cumulative effect of accounting change, net of tax | (1,066,000) | 0 | 0 |
| Net earnings (loss) | $ 59,732,000 | ($144,631,000) | $ 188,953,000 |

| HASBRO, Inc. Balance Sheet | 12/30/2001 | 12/30/2000 |
|---|---|---|
| Assets: | | |
| Current assets | | |
| Cash and cash equivalents | $ 233,095,000 | $ 127,115,000 |
| Accounts receivable, less allowance for doubtful accounts of $49,300 in 2001 and $55,000 in 2000 | 572,499,000 | 685,975,000 |
| Inventories | 217,479,000 | 335,493,000 |
| Prepaid expenses and other current assets | 345,545,000 | 431,630,000 |
| Total current assets | 1,368,618,000 | 1,580,213,000 |
| Property, plant, and equipment, net | 235,360,000 | 296,729,000 |
| Other assets | | |
| Goodwill, less accumulated amortization of $269,496 in 2001 and $225,770 in 2000 | 761,575,000 | 803,189,000 |
| Other intangibles, less accumulated amortization of $398,183 in 2001 and $347,149 in 2000 | 805,027,000 | 902,893,000 |

| | 12/30/2001 | 12/30/2000 |
|---|---|---|
| Other | 198,399,000 | 245,435,000 |
| Total other assets | 1,765,001,000 | 1,951,517,000 |
| Total assets | $3,368,979,000 | $3,828,459,000 |
| Liabilities and shareholders' equity: | | |
| Current liabilities | | |
| Short-term borrowings | $ 34,024,000 | $ 226,292,000 |
| Current installments of long-term debt | 2,304,000 | 1,793,000 |
| Accounts payable | 123,109,000 | 191,749,000 |
| Accrued liabilities | 599,154,000 | 819,978,000 |
| Total current liabilities | 758,591,000 | 1,239,812,000 |
| Long-term debt | 1,165,649,000 | 1,167,838,000 |
| Deferred liabilities | 91,875,000 | 93,403,000 |
| Total liabilities | 2,016,115,000 | 2,501,053,000 |
| Shareholders' equity | | |
| Preference stock of $2.50 par value. Authorized 5,000,000 shares; none issued | 0 | 0 |
| Common stock of $.50 par value. Authorized 600,000,000 shares; issued 209,694,630 shares in 2001 and 2000 | 104,847,000 | 104,847,000 |
| Additional paid-in capital | 457,544,000 | 464,084,000 |
| Deferred compensation | (2,996,000) | (6,889,000) |
| Retained earnings | 1,622,402,000 | 1,583,394,000 |
| Accumulated other comprehensive earnings | (68,398,000) | (44,718,000) |
| Treasury stock, at cost, 36,736,156 shares in 2001 and 37,253,164 shares in 2000 | (760,535,000) | (773,312,000) |
| Total shareholders' equity | 1,352,864,000 | 1,327,406,000 |
| Total liabilities and shareholders' equity | $3,368,979,000 | $3,828,459,000 |

HASBRO, Inc. Cash Flow

| | 12/30/2001 | 12/30/2000 | 12/30/1999 |
|---|---|---|---|
| Cash flows from operating activities: | | | |
| Net earnings (loss) | $59,732,000 | ($144,631,000) | $188,953,000 |
| Adjustments to reconcile net earnings (loss) to net cash provided by operating activities: | | | |
| Depreciation and amortization of plant and equipment | 104,247,000 | 106,458,000 | 103,791,000 |
| Other amortization | 121,652,000 | 157,763,000 | 173,533,000 |
| Deferred income taxes | 38,697,000 | (67,690,000) | (38,675,000) |
| Compensation earned under restricted stock program | 2,532,000 | 2,754,000 | 0 |
| Loss on sale of business units | 0 | 43,965,000 | 0 |
| Change in operating assets and liabilities (other than cash and cash equivalents): | | | |
| Decrease (increase) in accounts receivable | 99,474,000 | 395,682,000 | (11,248,000) |
| Decrease (increase) in inventories | 109,002,000 | 69,657,000 | (44,212,000) |

| | 12/30/2001 | 12/30/2000 | 12/30/1999 |
|---|---|---|---|
| Decrease (increase) in prepaid expenses and other current assets | 45,936,000 | (84,006,000) | (26,527,000) |
| (Decrease) increase in accounts payable and accrued liabilities | (194,525,000) | (292,313,000) | 193,626,000 |
| Other, including long-term advances | (14,272,000) | (25,083,000) | (147,729,000) |
| Net cash provided by operating activities | 372,475,000 | 162,556,000 | 391,512,000 |
| Cash flows from investing activities: | | | |
| Additions to property, plant, and equipment | (50,045,000) | (125,055,000) | (107,468,000) |
| Investments and acquisitions, net of cash acquired | 0 | (138,518,000) | (352,417,000) |
| Other | (7,734,000) | 82,863,000 | 30,793,000 |
| Net cash utilized by investing activities | (57,779,000) | (180,710,000) | (429,092,000) |
| Cash flows from financing activities: | | | |
| Proceeds from borrowings with original maturities of more than three months | 250,000,000 | 912,979,000 | 460,333,000 |
| Repayments of borrowings with original maturities of more than three months | (250,127,000) | (291,779,000) | (308,128,000) |
| Net (repayments) proceeds of other short-term borrowings | (190,216,000) | (341,522,000) | 226,103,000 |
| Purchase of common stock | 0 | (367,548,000) | (237,532,000) |
| Stock option and warrant transactions | 8,391,000 | 2,523,000 | 50,358,000 |
| Dividends paid | (20,709,000) | (42,494,000) | (45,526,000) |
| Net cash (utilized) provided by financing activities | (202,661,000) | (127,841,000) | 145,608,000 |
| Effect of exchange rate changes on cash | (6,055,000) | (7,049,000) | (5,617,000) |
| Increase (decrease) in cash and cash equivalents | 105,980,000 | (153,044,000) | 102,411,000 |
| Cash and cash equivalents at beginning of year | 127,115,000 | 280,159,000 | 177,748,000 |
| Cash and cash equivalents at end of year | $233,095,000 | $127,115,000 | $280,159,000 |
| Supplemental information | | | |
| Interest paid | $103,437,000 | $ 91,180,000 | $ 64,861,000 |
| Income taxes paid (received) | ($34,813,000) | $ 95,975,000 | $108,342,000 |

## BEYOND THE BOOK

**37.** Find the 10-K, proxy statement, and annual report of a typical company in the manufacturing business. Answer the following questions:

**a.** From either the 10-K or annual report, discuss how important inventory is in relationship to other assets on the firm's balance sheet. Also address how important property, plant, and equipment is to the firm.

**b.** How does the company finance its business?

**c.** Compare the information provided in the 10-K and annual report and discuss at least five things that are in the 10-K that are not in the annual report. If you were a stockholder, would you want to know these things and why?

d. From the proxy statement, what were the major issues (at least four) that were discussed at the annual meeting?

e. What is the total compensation paid to the five highest-paid employees? Who was the highest paid? What percent of sales was the total paid? Does this seem reasonable and why?

f. How many directors does the company have? How old are they and what percent of the board is female? How much do the directors get paid to attend meetings?

38. For the company you selected in problem 31, find at least three articles that discuss the nature of the markets for this company and the forecast of what the future may be for this sector of the economy. Write a one-page summary of your findings.

CHAPTER 4

# Income Measurement and Reporting

## Learning Objectives

After reading this chapter you should be able to:

1. Understand and apply the accrual basis of accounting and the related recognition and matching concepts.
2. Explain the operating cycle and its relation to accrual accounting.
3. Discuss revenue recognition methods and the reasons why revenue is recognized at different times for different economic events.
4. Identify links between accrual accounting and firm valuation.
5. Construct accrual entries for both revenue and expense transactions.
6. Explain how the income statement format reflects the concept of separating transitory items from operating earnings.

**In late May 2001, ConAgra Foods announced that accounting and conduct** matters at its United Agri Products Company (UAP) subsidiary would result in the restatement of its financial results. Certain accounting adjustments would also result in a restatement for fiscal 1998. The restatement reduced revenues and earnings for fiscal years 1998, 1999, and 2000, and increased revenues and earnings in fiscal year 2001. ConAgra restated its earnings due to accounting irregularities in its UAP subsidiary that related, in part, to its revenue recognition practices. In the days leading up to the announcement, ConAgra's stock price fell by approximately 6 percent. Clearly, as ConAgra's press release illustrates, investors and analysts pay close attention to the earnings reported by publicly traded companies.

To further your understanding of the earnings reported by companies, we examine the concepts of accrual-basis accounting in this chapter. Specifically, we examine the recognition criteria for revenues and expenses, and related implications for the recognition of assets and liabilities. We compare and contrast this accrual-basis recognition of revenues and expenses with the timing of the actual cash flows that result from these transactions.

You need to understand accrual accounting and how it differs from a cash basis for at least two reasons. First, investors and analysts often use forecasts of earnings to estimate future cash flows, which, in turn, affects their assessments of a firm's value. Second, owners often use earnings and stock prices (which may depend on earnings) to measure management performance. Accrual accounting, however, allows managers sufficient latitude to influence the performance measures upon which they are evaluated and paid. As a result, owners must understand this latitude in setting management compensation arrangements, and investors and analysts must do so in assessing firm value.

Let's begin with a discussion of the general concepts of accrual-based accounting.

## ACCRUAL ACCOUNTING

In **accrual-basis accounting,** a firm recognizes revenues and expenses in the period in which they occur, rather than in the period in which the cash flows related to the revenues and expenses are realized. In contrast, **cash-basis accounting** recognizes revenues and expenses in the period in which the firm realizes the cash flow. For example, under the accrual basis, a firm that sells goods to customers on credit recognizes the sales revenue at the point of physical transfer of the goods. Under the cash basis, however, the firm waits to recognize the sale until it collects the cash. As the diagram in Exhibit 4.1 illustrates, this difference in timing of revenue recognition can have a significant impact on the period in which the revenues are reported if the date of delivery of the goods falls in a different accounting period than the collection of cash. Because the cash might be collected in an accounting period later than the period in which the goods were delivered, it is clear that the choice of when to recognize revenue may have a significant impact on the statement of earnings.

Firms use accrual-basis accounting because it provides information about future cash flows that is not available under the cash method. In our sales example, investors want to know the firm's sales, even if the cash has not been collected, in order to better predict the future cash flows upon which the value of the firm depends. Similarly, a company's expected future payments are also relevant information. However, accrual accounting, while more informative than the cash basis, also involves considerable judgment. As a result, accounting standard setters developed criteria to assure that firms use similar assumptions in

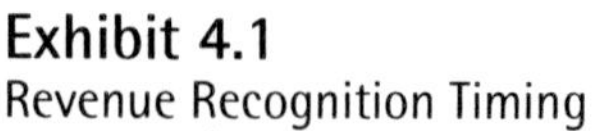

**Exhibit 4.1**
Revenue Recognition Timing

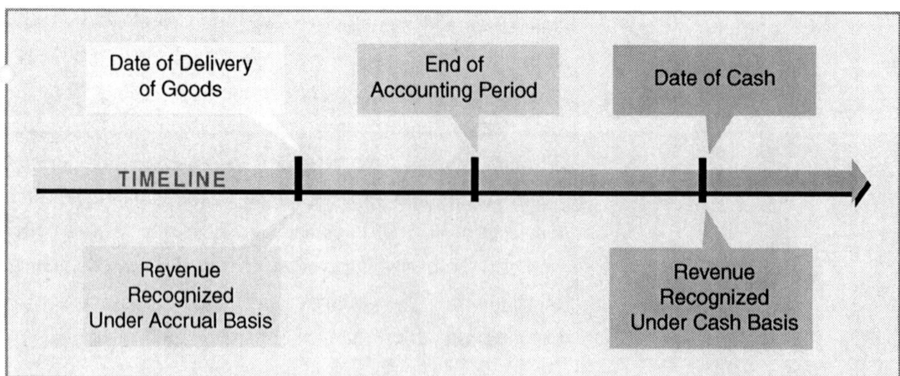

their judgments. In that way, the resulting revenue and expense numbers will be as consistent as possible with the qualitative characteristics of accounting information discussed in Chapter 1, such as neutrality, reliability, and verifiability.

The FASB's criteria are intended to guide all recognition decisions. These criteria detail what items should be recognized in the financial statements and when the items should be recognized. The following criteria apply to all financial statement components, including revenues, expenses, assets, liabilities, and stockholders' equity accounts:

*Definition:* The item meets the definition of an element of financial statements.

*Measurability:* The item has a relevant attribute measurable with sufficient reliability.

*Relevance:* The information about the item is capable of making a difference in user decisions.

*Reliability:* The information about the item is representationally faithful, verifiable, and neutral.

The above criteria include the concept of an attribute. *Attributes* are characteristics of financial statement items that we might choose to measure. For instance, inventory possesses several attributes. One of them is the cost the company incurs to either make or buy the inventory. A second attribute is the current selling price of the inventory. Whatever attribute we choose to measure, however, the recognition criteria require it to be "relevant." Often, accounting regulators must determine which attribute is the most relevant and reliable to report in the financial statements. We continue to address this issue as we progress through the text.

Recall in Chapter 3 that we defined assets, liabilities, and owners' equity. Later in this chapter we define revenues and expenses. All these definitions are based on the concepts of accrual accounting. Double-entry accounting links the recognition of revenues, expenses, assets, and liabilities. Let's look more closely at how revenue and expense recognition reflects these accrual-accounting concepts.

## REVENUE RECOGNITION

**Revenue recognition** refers to the point in time at which revenue should be reported on the statement of earnings, a crucial element of accrual accounting. Typically, firms implement accrual accounting by first determining the revenues to be recognized and then matching the costs incurred in generating that revenue to determine expenses. It follows that the timing of revenue and expense recognition determines the earnings that are reported. Given that the information conveyed by earnings is a factor in estimating the value of the firm, revenue recognition is particularly important to analysts, investors, managers, and others with an interest in those estimates.

It is reasonable to imagine that these individuals desire earnings to be reported as early as possible in order to gain access to information upon which they can improve their estimates. However, this desire is likely to be tempered by an understanding that revenue recognized in advance of collecting the cash from customers implies some uncertainty that could be avoided if revenue recognition can be delayed until those collections are made. In other words, there is a trade-off between early access to information and the level of uncertainty contained in the revenue and related expenses reported on the statement of earnings. For example, an extreme view would argue that when a firm purchases inventory, it immediately adds value to the company because the goods can be sold later for a profit. Therefore, the firm should recognize the revenue (profit) upon inventory purchases, assuming that future sales will occur. The difficulty with this argument, of course, is the considerable uncertainty about both the timing and the amount of revenue that may be realized from future sales. For example, a company might purchase or manufacture inventory and be unable to sell it because of changing demand or excess supply.

Consider the electronic game industry in 2001. Three competitors, Microsoft, Sony, and Nintendo, sought industry dominance with the XBox, Playstation 2, and the Game-Cube, respectively. Manufacturers of these products needed to determine how many units to manufacture, set prices for the product, make arrangements with distributors (such as Toys Я Us, Wal-Mart, and Target), and ship the product in sufficient numbers to satisfy customers. Furthermore, the companies needed to consider the costs of product warranties and returns of unsold products. Finally, the three firms assumed that third-party software manufacturers would be able to offer a sufficient quality and variety of games on the different platforms to satisfy consumer demand. All of these factors worked to create substantial uncertainty about the profits from a particular product line. Thus, it would be difficult for any of these companies to argue that sales should have been recognized at the time they manufactured the products.

Because of the tension between the desire to recognize the value added by investment and production activities as early as possible, and the uncertainties involved in accurately portraying these results, accounting standard setters developed **revenue recognition criteria.** These criteria establish the requirements that must be met in order to recognize revenue on a company's books.

## REVENUE RECOGNITION CRITERIA

GAAP requires that revenues be recognized at the earliest point in the firm's operating cycle, at which it meets the following criteria:

- Revenue is realized or realizable
- Revenue is earned by the enterprise

**Realized** or **realizable** means that an exchange of goods or services has taken place, the seller has either received cash or the right to receive cash, and collection is reasonably assured. **Earned** means that the goods or services have been delivered, and related obligations are substantially complete. In applying the earned criteria, a firm must apply judgment in determining whether the risks and rewards of ownership of the product have effectively been transferred to the buyer. That is, has there been substantial performance by both the seller and the buyer such that the earnings process is essentially complete? For instance, Werner Enterprises, a major trucking company, recognizes "operating revenues and related direct costs when the shipment is delivered." Because Werner is

> At the time of this writing, the FASB is considering an approach for revenue recognition that is more closely linked to changes in assets and liabilities than the notions of realization and completion of the earnings process. Concerns with the present criteria for revenue realization are that they are sometimes in conflict with concepts of assets and liabilities, imprecisely defined, and difficult to consistently apply when the revenue generating process involves multiple steps.

Exhibit 4.2

THE REAL WORLD

Target Corporation

Target Corporation—Revenues

Revenue from retail sales is recognized at the time of sale. Leased department sales, net of related cost of sales, are included within sales and were $33 million in 2000, $31 million in 1999, and $29 million in 1998. Net credit revenues represent revenue from receivable-backed securities, which is comprised of finance charges and late fees on internal credit sales, net of the effect of publicly held receivable-backed securities. Internal credit sales were $5.5 billion, $5 billion, and $4.5 billion in 2000, 1999, and 1998, respectively.

responsible for transporting the goods of the customer, management judges that the earning process is only complete when the goods are ultimately delivered.

The revenue recognition criteria can be met at different points in a firm's operating cycle depending on the nature of the business. In the following sections, we illustrate some common points of revenue recognition used by various industries.

### At Point of Delivery

A fairly common point of revenue recognition for manufacturing and retail firms is at the point when they deliver a product or service to a customer. As we noted previously, Werner, Inc. reports its revenue when the shipment is delivered. This is the point at which the customer accepts the risks and rewards of ownership of the asset, and at which point Werner ceases its obligation to the customer (the revenue has been earned). Further, the customer is now obligated to pay Werner for the delivery (the revenue is realizable).

Target's revenue recognition policy as shown in Exhibit 4.2 is more complex than that of Werner. Target derives its revenues not only from product sales but also from interest on credit sales to customers. However, for its product sales, the method of revenue recognition is at the time of delivery (which is also the time of sale). Target's 2000 income statement (shown later in Exhibit 4.11) reports sales of $36,362 million and net credit revenues of $541 million.

### As Service Is Provided or Cost Incurred

For a firm that sells subscriptions, cash may be received in advance. The firm recognizes the revenue as it incurs costs in the fulfillment of those subscriptions. For example, Reader's Digest sells magazine subscriptions to individuals and newstands. In a footnote to its 2003 annual report, the company describes its revenue recognition methods as reported in Exhibit 4.3. As the footnote describes, Reader's Digest has three primary sources of revenue. It uses a

Exhibit 4.3

THE REAL WORLD

Readers Digest

Footnote on Revenue Recognition

Sales of our magazine subscriptions, less estimated cancellations, are deferred and recognized as revenues proportionately over the subscription period. Revenues from sales of magazines through the newsstand are recognized at the issue date, net of an allowance for returns. Advertising revenues are recorded as revenues at the time the advertisements are published, net of discounts and advertising agency commissions.

Because circulation numbers drive the rates that magazines charge to advertisers, magazine publishers sometimes overstate their sales. This practice of overestimating monthly sales has led advertisers to be unwilling to pay the full cost for ads that are published or to demand refunds when new figures reveal that the estimated sales figures were missed. A publisher would need to recognize this reduction in revenues through an estimate of refunds. For instance, the following is the revenue recognition policy for Primedia, Inc. and it indicates that revenues are stated less an amount (provisions) for rebates, adjustments, and so forth.

"Advertising revenues for all consumer magazines are recognized as income at the on-sale date, net of provisions for estimated rebates, adjustments and discounts."

different recognition method for each type of revenue. The company recognizes subscriptions over the subscription period, newsstand sales at the issue date, and advertising revenues upon advertisement publication. The collection of cash does not determine the timing of revenue recognition. In the case of subscriptions, the revenue is earned as the goods are furnished to the purchaser. In the case of newsstand sales, the shipments are determined on a standing order (based on past sales), and newsstands pay only for the magazines that they sell. Thus, recognizing revenues at the issue date means that accurate estimation of the number of magazines to issue and of returns is critical to accurate revenue recognition. Finally, advertising revenues are recognized when the magazine is published (which constitutes providing the service to those purchasing advertisements).

### Based on Contractual Agreements

Firms sometimes retain a substantial financial interest in the product or service, even after the initial sale. For example, Krispy Kreme, a typical franchiser, provides a significant amount of service related to establishing the business between the time of signing the agreement and the opening of the business. The company typically provides financing to the purchaser, allowing franchise fees to be paid in installments. Krispy Kreme defers revenues from the initial franchise fee until the opening of the new store is complete (i.e., the revenue has been earned).

Retail land sales also pose unique accounting problems. Retail land sales involve the sale of undeveloped land. Sales contracts may offer buyers below-market interest rates and attractive financing terms, with the land serving as collateral for the sale (sometimes called a *collateralized sale*). Because of uncertainties regarding the future costs of developing the land as well as the collectibility of the receivable (particularly when there are low down payments), accounting regulators established criteria to determine the conditions under which revenue from a retail land sale could be recognized at the signing of a sales contract. For example, footnotes to Amrep Corporation's annual report (reported in Exhibit 4.4) illustrate a typical disclosure in the case of retail land sales.

### At Time of Production

When both the value and the assurance of sale can be estimated at the time of production, such as in certain agricultural and mining operations, a firm recognizes revenue at that point. Often, the company has a supply contract with

**Exhibit 4.4**

**THE REAL WORLD**

**Amrep Corporation**

**Revenue Recognition Footnote**

Land sales are recognized when the parties are bound by the terms of the contract, all consideration (including adequate cash) has been exchanged, and title and other attributes of ownership have been conveyed to the buyer by means of a closing. Profit is recorded either in its entirety or on the installment method depending on, among other things, the ability to estimate the collectibility of the unpaid sales price. In the event the buyer defaults on the obligation, the property is taken back and recorded in inventory at the unpaid receivable balance, net of any deferred profit, but not in excess of fair market value less estimated cost to sell.

a buyer that establishes the price of the commodity to be delivered and a time schedule for its delivery. For example, Kinross Gold Corporation (Kinross Annual Report 2000) notes that "Gold and Silver in inventory, in transit and at refineries, are recorded at net realizable value and included in accounts receivable with the exception of Kubaka bullion. The estimated net realizable value of Kubaka bullion is included in inventory until it is sold."

### As Cash Is Collected

In most cases, revenue recognition criteria are met prior to collection. Firms can reasonably estimate collections at the time of sale, and the revenue is thus realizable. However, for some circumstances, collection of the receivable is sufficiently in doubt that revenue cannot be recognized at the time of sale. Recognition prior to collection would therefore not reflect the underlying economic reality. In these cases firms can use two methods to recognize revenue and related expenses as cash is collected: the installment method and the cost recovery method.

With the **installment method,** a firm recognizes gross profits in proportion to cash payments received. With the **cost recovery method,** a firm defers gross profit recognition until enough cash is collected to recover the costs. For example, assume that Wilson Land Company sells a home site for $100,000 that cost Wilson $60,000. The purchaser agrees to pay Wilson for the land in three payments of $40,000, $30,000, and $30,000. Exhibit 4.5 shows the amount of gross profit recognized each year under the installment method and the cost recovery method.

Either method results in the same total gross profit over three years. How, then, to determine the appropriate method of revenue recognition in a particular case? Firms generally use the cost recovery method only when considerable uncertainty exists about ultimate collection of the total sales price (so no profit is recognized until the costs have been covered). The decision, then, becomes whether to recognize a real estate sale under the installment method or at the time of sale. As a rule, retail land sales should only be recognized at the time of sale if both collection is assured and the seller has no remaining obligations to the buyer.

### During Construction

In the long-term construction industry, major projects can take years to complete. Thus the operating cycle in this industry is very long, requiring special income recognition methods: the completed contract method and the percentage completion method. Under the **completed contract method,** a firm waits to recognize revenues and expenses until the project is complete. Under the **percentage**

**Exhibit 4.5**
Installment Method versus Cost Recovery Method

Profit % = ($100,000 − 60,000)/$100,000 = 40%

| Year | Installment method gross profit | Cost recovery method gross profit |
|---|---|---|
| 1 | 40% × $40,000 = $16,000 | $0 ($40,000 cost recovered) |
| 2 | 40% × $30,000 = $12,000 | $10,000 ($20,000 cost recovered) |
| 3 | 40% × $30,000 = $12,000 | $30,000 |
| Total | $40,000 | $40,000 |

**Exhibit 4.6**
Revenue Recognition Using Percentage of Completion Method (dollars in billions)

| Year | Degree of Completion | Revenue Recognized | Expenses Recognized | Gross Profit Recognized |
|---|---|---|---|---|
| 1 | $8/$15 = 53.33% | .533 × $20 = $10.67 | $8 | $2.67 |
| 2 | $4/$15 = 26.67% | .267 × $20 = $5.33 | $4 | $1.33 |
| 3 | $3/$15 = 20.00% | .20 × $20 = $4.00 | $3 | $1.00 |
| Total | 100.00% | $20.00 | $15 | $5.00 |

**of completion method,** a firm recognizes revenues and expenses in proportion to the degree of completion of the project. Degree of completion is typically measured by the cost incurred to date relative to the total estimated cost. For example, assume that Horning Construction agrees to build a casino. The purchaser agrees to pay $20 billion to Horning for the project. Horning expects to spend three years building the casino and estimates the following costs: Year 1, $8 billion; Year 2, $4 billion; Year 3, $3 billion. Exhibit 4.6 shows the amount of revenue and expenses recognized each year under percentage of completion.

Under the completed contract method, Horning Construction would recognize all of the revenue and expense at the end of year 3, at contract completion. Typically, though, firms use the completed contract method for short construction periods. However, to use the percentage completion method, firms must be able to accurately estimate costs to obtain reliable profit forecasts. As a result, if there is a high degree of cost uncertainty, the completed contract method may be used even for long-term contracts.

Although the percentage of completion and completed contract methods are the more common, firms sometimes use other methods of accounting for long-term construction contracts, such as the installment and cost recovery methods described earlier. Firms will likely use the installment method when the uncertainty pertains largely to assurance of collection (buyer's performance) rather than the reliability of future cost estimates (seller's performance). The cost recovery method is especially conservative and appropriate in cases where considerable uncertainty exists about collection and future costs.

Now that we have reviewed several aspects of revenue recognition, let's turn to the related issue of expense recognition.

## EXPENSE RECOGNITION

The **matching concept** requires that firms recognize both the revenue and the costs required to produce the revenue (expenses) at the same time. The implications of this are two-fold. First, it means that firms must defer some costs on the balance sheet until they can be matched with sales. In some cases, though, direct matching with sales is not practical. In these cases, firms often expense the deferred costs based on the passage of time. Second, firms will not incur some costs at the time of the sale (e.g., warranty costs). Firms will thus need to estimate these costs, and accrue an expense to give proper matching with the revenue reported.

Perhaps the best example of direct matching is when a retail or wholesale company recognizes revenue at the time of delivery. Here, a related expense, **cost of goods sold,** which represents the cost of inventory that the company had on its balance sheet as an asset prior to the sale, must also be recognized. Target provides an example of such a company. Its cost of goods sold can be seen in Exhibit 4.11 (later in the chapter).

Matching is applied differently depending on the type of cost. Some costs, such as costs of goods sold, can be matched directly with sales. However, other costs, such as executive salaries, insurance, and depreciation of various assets used in the business, can be more difficult to directly link to revenue. In this case, firms usually either charge the costs to income as incurred (e.g., salaries and various administrative costs) or allocate the costs systematically over time periods (e.g., depreciation, interest, insurance). Werner, Inc. (the trucking company mentioned earlier) provides a service to its customers, so it has no cost of goods sold. However, if you review the income statement for Werner, you would see sales-related expenses such as salaries, fuel costs, and depreciation on its trucks, which are related to the delivery service it provides to its customers.

With expense recognition, GAAP guidelines focus on whether or not a cost should be treated as an asset (a **deferred expense**) or as an expense. For example, Prepaid Legal Services pays its sales force an advance of up to three years' worth of commissions on new customer sales. In the years prior to 2001, Prepaid treated these prepayments as deferred expenses (assets) and then expensed these deferred expenses over time to match them with revenues from the provided legal services. However, in 2001 the SEC concluded that Prepaid's accounting methods were not in accordance with GAAP arguing that the future revenue from these sales was highly uncertain. Effective in its third quarter 10-Q filing with the SEC as shown in Exhibit 4.7, Prepaid changed its accounting

**Exhibit 4.7**

**THE REAL WORLD**

**Prepaid Legal Services**

In the November 14, 2001, 10-Q filing of Prepaid Legal Services, the following disclosure was made:

As previously reported, in January 2001 and May 2001, the staff of the Division of Corporation Finance of the Securities and Exchange Commission (SEC) reviewed the Company's 1999 and 2000 Forms 10-K, respectively. On May 11, 2001, the Company received a letter from the staff of the Division of Corporation Finance advising that, after reviewing the Company's Forms 10-K, it was the position of the Division that the Company's accounting for commission advance receivables was not in accordance with GAAP. The Company subsequently appealed this decision to the Chief Accountant of the SEC. On July 25, 2001, the Company announced that the Chief Accountant concurred with the prior staff opinion of the Division of Corporation Finance. The Company subsequently announced that it would not pursue any further appeals and that it would amend its previously filed SEC reports to restate the Company's financial statements to reflect the SEC's position that the Company's advance commission payments should be expensed when paid. As previously discussed, the change in accounting treatment reduced total assets from $247 million at December 31, 2000 to $93 million, reduced total liabilities from $100 million to $48 million (due to the elimination of deferred taxes related to the receivables) and therefore reduced stockholders' equity from $147 million to $45 million. The elimination of the receivables reduced 2000 net income from $43.6 million, or $1.92 per diluted share, to $20.5 million, or $.90 per diluted share. The Company expects to amend its 2000 Annual Report on Form 10-K in the near future to reflect the change in accounting for commission of advance receivables and restate all periods included in the 2000 Form 10-K. The financial statements and the explanation thereof contained in this Form 10-Q reflect the change in the accounting treatment for advance payments made to associates.

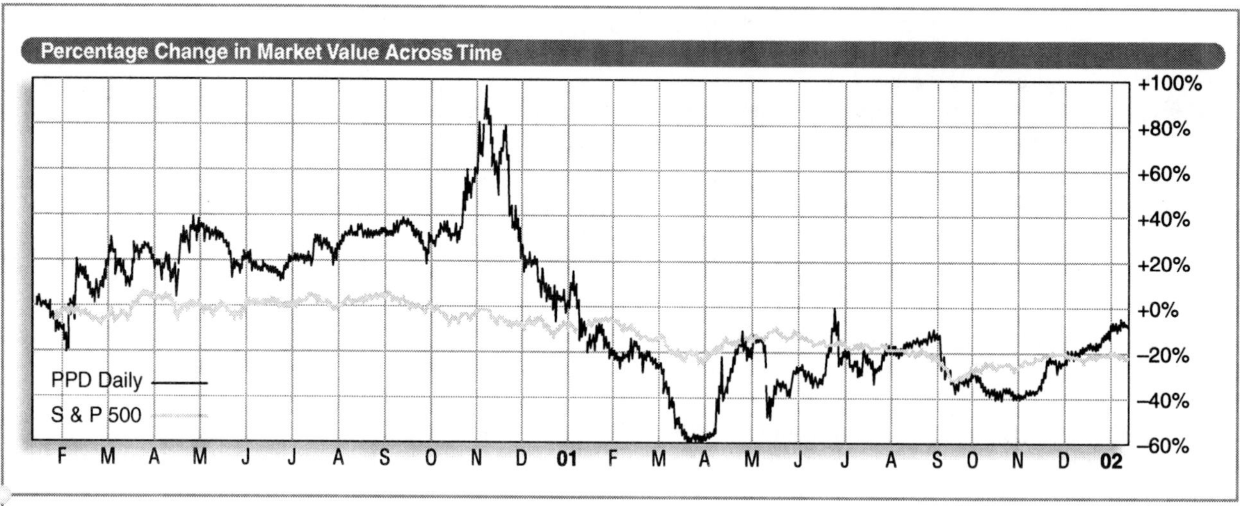


**Exhibit 4.8**
Prepaid Legal Services Inc.

THE REAL WORLD

methods to conform with the SEC ruling. The company now expenses the commissions in the period in which they were paid.

The concern over Prepaid's accounting methods stemmed back to December 2000, when a research report questioned the firm's economic viability. The graph in Exhibit 4.8 demonstrates the changes in value that took place between the issuance of this report and the change of policy in late 2001.

Now that we've discussed accrual-accounting concepts, let's next look at how firms put into practice these revenue and expense recognition criteria.

## RECORDING ACCRUAL ENTRIES

In this section, we use four common types of economic events to illustrate how accrual accounting is applied and how the cash flow timing differs for each event. Exhibit 4.9 summarizes these revenue and expense events, and provides a simple example of each. Let's look more closely at each of these transactions.

### REVENUES THAT ARE RECEIVED IN CASH BEFORE THEY ARE EARNED

In this situation the firm must record the cash received as an asset. However, as the firm cannot yet treat the transaction as earned revenue, it must postpone the recognition of revenue. The firm will, therefore, record a liability, **deferred revenue** (or *unearned revenue* or *customer deposits*), that represents an obligation to provide goods or services to the customer in the future. This obligation clearly meets the definition of a liability in that it most definitely represents a future sacrifice of resources to the firm. Recall our earlier illustration of Reader's Digest and its revenue recognition of subscriptions.

To illustrate the entries to be made for this type of transaction, let's return to our BHT example from Chapter 3. Suppose that BHT receives $20 million

**Exhibit 4.9**
Common Accrual Accounting Events

| Revenue Events | Example |
|---|---|
| Cash that is received in advance before the revenues are recognized as having been earned | Magazine subscriptions are usually paid in advance and earned when the publisher delivers the magazines. |
| Revenues that are recognized as having been earned before the revenues are received in cash | Sales on account, interest revenue on notes is earned with the passage of time and paid at regular intervals. |
| **Expense Events** | **Example** |
| Expenses that are paid in advance before they are recognized as having been incurred | Insurance is generally paid in advance to cover a future period. The expense is incurred with the passage of time as dictated by the policy. |
| Expenses that are recognized as having been incurred before they are paid in cash | Salary expense is incurred when the employees work, even though they may be paid later, such as once every two weeks. |

in cash from customers for goods to be delivered in the future. BHT would make the following journal entry at the time cash is received:

| | | |
|---|---|---|
| Cash | 20 | |
| Deferred Revenue | | 20 |

Later, when BHT earns the revenues (likely at delivery), the firm would make the following entry:

| | | |
|---|---|---|
| Deferred Revenue | 20 | |
| Revenue | | 20 |

## REVENUES THAT ARE EARNED BEFORE THEY ARE RECEIVED IN CASH

For most firms, revenue recognition criteria are most often met before the firms collect the cash. Here, the firm records revenues on its income statement and also an asset (accounts receivable). Accounts receivable meets the definition of an asset as the firm has probable future value in the right to receive cash from the customer at some point in the future. Recall in Chapter 3 that we showed you this type of transaction for BHT, as follows:

| | | |
|---|---|---|
| Accounts Receivable | 35,724 | |
| Sales | | 35,724 |

As another example, consider interest accrued on a note receivable. A firm earns revenue (interest) on the note with the passage of time, periodically receiving cash. If the cash hasn't yet been received, the firm would record interest revenue and an asset (typically called interest receivable). To illustrate, suppose that BHT allows a customer to pay its bill over a longer period than normal by issuing a note receivable for the amount of the sale (say $100). Further, suppose that this note specifies that the customer pays 5 percent interest. At the end of the first year, the customer would owe an additional $5 for the interest ($100 × 5%). BHT records this earned revenue (assuming it hadn't been paid yet) as follows:

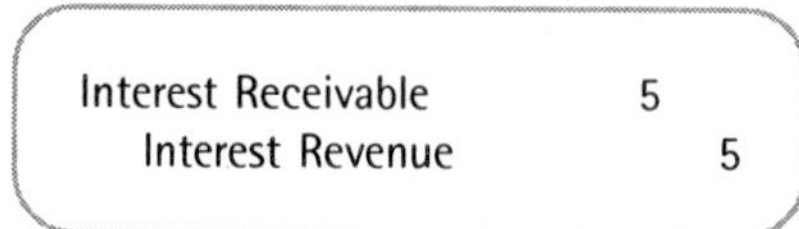

| | | |
|---|---|---|
| Interest Receivable | 5 | |
| Interest Revenue | | 5 |

When BHT collects the interest, it makes the following entry:

| | | |
|---|---|---|
| Cash | 5 | |
| Interest Receivable | | 5 |

## EXPENSES THAT ARE PAID IN CASH BEFORE THEY ARE INCURRED

Cash payment often precedes the incurrence of an expense, such as with prepaid insurance. Insurance companies usually require payment of insurance policy premiums in advance of the coverage. If the firm has just paid its premium, then it should record the reduction in cash and the creation of an asset, typically called prepaid insurance. Prepaid insurance meets the definition of an asset: the insurance provides probable future value in terms of coverage (protection from risk) over the remaining period of the policy. The firm will then convert the prepaid insurance into an expense with the passage of time. For example, if BHT pays $150 for an insurance policy covering its plant, property, and equipment for the following year, it records the following entry at the date of payment:

| | | |
|---|---|---|
| Prepaid Insurance | 150 | |
| Cash | | 150 |

As time passes, the insurance is consumed as coverage expires. If six months have passed and half of the coverage, or $75 worth of the amount prepaid, has been consumed, BHT would make the following entry:

| | | |
|---|---|---|
| Insurance Expense | 75 | |
| Prepaid Insurance | | 75 |

### EXPENSES THAT ARE INCURRED BEFORE THEY ARE PAID IN CASH

Salary expense is often incurred prior to it being paid, as most firms issue checks to employees after services have been received. If employees have worked for the firm, but haven't been paid, the firm should record an expense and a liability (salaries payable) indicating its obligation to pay the employees at a later date. To illustrate, if BHT employees earned $25 during the last week of December but will not be paid until the end of the first week in January, BHT would make the following entry on December 31:

| | | |
|---|---|---|
| Salaries Expense | 25 | |
| Salaries Payable | | 25 |

When BHT pays the employees, it would make the following entry:

| | | |
|---|---|---|
| Salaries payable | 25 | |
| Cash | | 25 |

The flexibility within GAAP as it relates to accrual entries might allow management to understate discretionary or estimated expenses or overstate estimated revenues in order to meet analysts' forecasts or internal performance targets. Considerable attention has been given to the implications of management's discretion within GAAP on earnings forecasts, estimates of firm value, and management compensation.

Note that the initial entry in each of the previous four examples results in the creation of an asset or liability. These accrual-based assets and liabilities would not exist under the cash basis. In fact, most assets and liabilities that exist on a GAAP-prepared balance sheet, except cash, arise as a consequence of accrual-based accounting. These include receivables (revenue recognized before cash is received), inventories, prepaid expenses, property and equipment, intangible assets (cash paid before expense is recognized), payables and accrued liabilities (expense recognized before cash is paid), and deferred revenues (cash received before revenue is recognized).

Almost all of the transactions we have just discussed involve the use of an adjusting entry. Recall from our discussion in Chapter 3 that adjusting entries are made at the end of the period for transactions that do not involve an exchange with an external party. For example, when BHT recorded its deferred revenue, this entry was triggered by the receipt of cash. However, the later recognition of deferred revenue on the income statement was not accompanied by an exchange event and therefore was recorded via an adjusting entry. Similarly, the recording of prepaid insurance was triggered by the cash payment of the premium, while the recognition of insurance expense was recorded via an adjusting entry by the accountant after it was determined how much of the insurance coverage had expired. For a more detailed discussion of various adjusting entries refer to Appendix A.

## VALUATION IMPLICATIONS OF INCOME RECOGNITION

Reported net income plays an important role in determining a company's value. Simply put, net income from an accrual-accounting is informative about future cash flows to the business that, in turn, implies future potential cash flows to investors. The stream of future cash flows to investors determines the value of a company (as we describe more fully in Chapter 14). A company must generate positive cash flows for investors either in the form of dividends or an increased stock price in order to remain a viable business.

Both revenue and expense recognition involve assumptions and estimation. Accounting standards seek to provide relevant and timely information about a company to assist in forecasting its future while at the same time assuring the reliability of the information in the face of estimation and uncertainty. The criteria for revenue and expense recognition seek to balance these desired attributes in providing guidelines for the determination of earnings. Nevertheless, the link between current income and future cash flows remains uncertain. To improve our understanding of the imprecise relation between current earnings and future cash flows, let's look at the income statement more closely.

## INCOME STATEMENT FORMAT

Financial statements should provide information that helps current and potential investors, creditors, and other users to assess the amount, timing, and uncertainty of prospective net cash flows to the firm. The income statement reports on a company's financial performance and provides information about future expected cash flows.

GAAP does not specify the format of the income statement in detail. As a result, the degree to which specific line items are combined into the aggregate line items that appear on the statement (sometimes referred as the degree of aggregation), as well as the labels used for the aggregate items, vary widely across firms. Because this can make statement interpretation challenging for the novice financial statement user, let's take a closer look at the line items.

### LINE ITEM DEFINITIONS

When looking at the income statement, you should first determine which items relate to the core operations of the business, or are *persistent,* and which are *transitory,* or unrelated to the company's core operations. Investors value persistent profits more highly than transitory ones as they are more likely to continue in the future. For example, a business might report a loss from a lawsuit that involves a substantial cash outlay. However, this one-time cost has different implications for the value of the firm than a loss caused by operations (e.g., when product's costs exceed its sales). Thus, proper classification of items as continuing/recurring or noncontinuing/nonrecurring provides investors and financial statement users with more accurate forecasts of future cash flow.

To this end, the FASB provides direction in its definition (FASB Concepts No. 6, "Elements of Financial Statements") of revenues and expenses (FASB, SFAC No. 6, 1985):

- *Revenues:* "inflows or other enhancements of assets of an entity or settlements of its liabilities (or a combination of both) from delivering or producing goods, rendering services, or other activities that constitute the entity's ongoing major or central operations."
- *Expenses:* "outflows or other using up of assets or incurrences of liabilities (or a combination of both) from delivering or producing goods, rendering

services, or carrying out other activities that constitute the entity's ongoing major or central operations."

- *Gains:* "increases in equity (net assets) from peripheral or incidental transactions of an entity and other events and circumstances affecting the entity except those that result from revenues or investments by owners."
- *Losses:* "decreases in equity (net assets) from peripheral or incidental transactions of an entity and from all other transactions and other events and circumstances affecting the entity except those that result from expenses or distributions to owners."

## INCOME STATEMENT LABELS

The degree of aggregation and labeling of income statement items varies widely across companies. For example, some companies will explicitly list items such as gross profit, income from continuing operations, and other subcategories, while others simply list all revenues and subtract all costs. Income statements that provide greater detail and breakdown of costs by category are referred to as **multiple step.** Those that simply list revenue and expenses in two broad categories are called **single step.** Because valuing companies requires the ability to estimate future cash flows to owners, financial disclosures that help users to discern which revenues and costs are related to core continuing activities are most useful to financial statement users.

In general, multiple-step income statements include the following categories:

- Gross Profit
- Income from Continuing Operations
- Nonrecurring Items
- Extraordinary Items
- Accounting Changes and Errors

Let's look at each of the categories in more detail.

### Income from Continuing Operations

**Income from continuing operations** is the difference between a company's operating revenues and its operating expenses. It does not include revenues from nonoperating sources nor from operations that a company discontinues. For example, Exhibit 4.10 shows the income statement for Albertson's, Inc., a large national grocery store chain. Note the line "Operating Profit," which reflects income from continuing operations. However, while Albertson's expects most of the operating items to continue from period to period, the company also lists several items that might not be considered recurring: "Merger-Related and Exit Costs," "Litigation Settlement," and "Impairment Store Closures." Albertson's separately discloses these one-time or limited-term items to allow analysts to adjust these charges out of the operating profits before trying to use the historical data to forecast future operating profits.

Exhibit 4.11 shows an income statement for Target for 2000 including comparative results for 1999 and 1998. Note that a complete income statement also includes earnings per share information (described later in the chapter). Target

**Exhibit 4.10**
Albertson Corporation Consolidated Statement of Earnings (millions except per share data)

THE REAL WORLD

**Albertson Corporation**

| In millions except per share data | 52 weeks 02/01/2001 | 52 weeks 02/01/2000 | 52 weeks 01/28/1999 |
|---|---|---|---|
| Sales | $36,762 | $37,478 | $35,872 |
| Cost of sales | 26,336 | 27,164 | 26,156 |
| Gross profit | 10,426 | 10,314 | 9,716 |
| Selling, general, and administrative expenses | 8,740 | 8,641 | 7,846 |
| Merger-related and exit costs | 24 | 396 | 195 |
| Litigation settlement | | 37 | |
| Impairment-store closures | | | 24 |
| Operating profit | 1,662 | 1,240 | 1,651 |
| Other (expense) income: | | | |
| Interest, net | (385) | (353) | (337) |
| Other, net | (3) | 12 | 24 |
| Earnings before taxes and extraordinary items | 1,274 | 899 | 1,338 |
| Income taxes | 509 | 472 | 537 |
| Earnings before extraordinary items | 765 | 427 | 801 |
| Extraordinary loss on extinguishment of debt, net of tax benefit of $7 | | (23) | |
| Net earnings | $ 765 | $ 404 | $ 801 |

**Exhibit 4.11**
Target Corporation Consolidated Results of Operations (millions except per share data)

THE REAL WORLD

**Target Corporation**

| | 2000 | 1999 | 1998 |
|---|---|---|---|
| Sales | $36,362 | $33,212 | $30,203 |
| Net credit revenues | 541 | 490 | 459 |
| Total revenues | 36,903 | 33,702 | 30,662 |
| Cost of sales | 25,295 | 23,029 | 21,085 |
| Selling, general, and administrative expenses | 8,190 | 7,490 | 6,843 |
| Depreciation and amortization | 940 | 854 | 780 |
| Interest expense | 425 | 393 | 398 |
| Earnings before income taxes and extraordinary charges | 2,053 | 1,936 | 1,556 |
| Provision for income taxes | 789 | 751 | 594 |
| Net earnings before extraordinary charges | 1,264 | 1,185 | 962 |
| Extraordinary charges from purchase and redemption of debt, net of tax | – | 41 | 27 |
| Net earnings | $ 1,264 | $ 1,144 | $ 935 |
| Earnings before extraordinary charges | $ 1.40 | $ 1.32 | $ 1.07 |
| Extraordinary charges | – | (.04) | (.03) |
| Basic earnings per share | $ 1.40 | $ 1.28 | $ 1.04 |
| Earnings before extraordinary charges | $ 1.38 | $ 1.27 | $ 1.02 |
| Extraordinary charges | 0 | (.04) | (.03) |
| Diluted earnings per share | $ 1.38 | 1.23 | .99 |

reports cost of sales; selling, general, and administrative expenses; depreciation; and amortization and interest expense. These reflect typical categories for a retail or wholesale company that sells products. However, Target's income statement does not explicitly show operating earnings. Thus Target's income statement readers must determine from the account titles, placement on the financial statement, and the disclosures provided in Target's footnotes which items represent Target's operating income.

Note that Target shows "Net Credit Revenues" in its total revenue section. This is interest income that represents income from Target's financing operations. Financing is one of Target's core operations, so analysts would probably classify this as a part of operating revenues. If, however, firms report interest income primarily from investment activities, the revenue would be classified as nonoperating or other revenue.

### Nonrecurring Items

In addition to separating operating from nonoperating items, investors also want to identify recurring versus nonrecurring items. Unusual or infrequent revenues and/or expenses should be highlighted to signal financial statement users that the items do not have the same kind of information about future cash flows as do normal recurring ones. Some firms simply label unusual items as such. In other cases, accounting standard setters provide specific guidelines for how to report such items.

GAAP requires three items to be shown after the computation of tax expense: **discontinued operations, extraordinary items,** and the **cumulative effect of changes in accounting principles.** Because these items appear below both operating and nonoperating items and after the computation of tax expense, they are often referred to as "below the line" items. Because they are shown after the tax computation, firms show these items on a net of tax basis. For example, Target reported an extraordinary charge of $41 million in 1999. This $41 million represents the net amount after subtracting the tax effect.

### Discontinued Operations

Results from discontinued operations represent amounts related to a line of business, such as a product, that a company decides to discontinue. The income statement items related to discontinued operations include (1) any gain or loss from operations of the discontinued business after the decision is made to discontinue and prior to actual termination of operations, and (2) any gain or loss on disposal of the business. In December, 2002, H.J. Heinz decided to spin off its pet snacks, U.S. tuna, U.S. retail private label soup and private label gravy, College Inn broths, and its U.S. infant feeding businesses. The income statement for Heinz in Exhibit 4.12 reflects the discontinued operations.

> Note that analysts often consider certain items as nonrecurring beyond those specified for GAAP purposes when they are valuing the firm. For instance, if a firm recorded a restructuring charge during the period, it wouldn't earmark this item as extraordinary but it is nonrecurring. If an item is less than likely to recur, then an analyst would put less weight on this item when determining value.

### Extraordinary Items

Extraordinary items are both unusual in nature and infrequent in occurrence. These gains and losses are not expected to recur, and hence are segregated from operations. Because management may have an incentive to classify all bad news as extraordinary, the FASB developed guidelines that specify when a firm may classify an item as extraordinary. For example, the "unusual" nature criteria guidelines specify that the item must be unusual within the existing context of

**Exhibit 4.12**
H.J. HEINZ Co. Income Statement

THE REAL WORLD
**H.J. Heinz**

| 52 Weeks Ended (in 000s): | Apr-30-03 | May-1-02 | May-2-01 |
|---|---|---|---|
| Sales | $8,236,836 | $7,614,036 | $6,987,698 |
| Cost of products sold | 5,304,362 | 4,858,087 | 4,407,267 |
| Gross profit | 2,932,474 | 2,755,949 | 2,580,431 |
| Selling, general, and administrative expenses | 1,758,658 | 1,456,077 | 1,591,472 |
| Operating income | 1,173,816 | 1,299,872 | 988,959 |
| Interest income | 31,083 | 26,197 | 22,597 |
| Interest expense | 223,532 | 230,611 | 262,488 |
| Other expense/(income), net | 112,636 | 44,938 | (5,358) |
| Income from continuing operations before income taxes and cumulative effect of change in accounting principle | 868,731 | 1,050,520 | 754,426 |
| Provision for income taxes | 313,372 | 375,339 | 190,495 |
| Income from continuing operations before cumulative effect of change in accounting principle | 555,359 | 675,181 | 563,931 |
| Income/(loss) from discontinued operations, net of tax | 88,738 | 158,708 | (70,638) |
| Income before cumulative effect of change in accounting principle | 644,097 | 833,889 | 493,293 |
| Cumulative effect of change in accounting principle | (77,812) | – | (15,281) |
| Net income | $ 566,285 | $ 833,889 | $ 478,012 |

The issues surrounding extraordinary items highlight the difficulties involved in determining operating earnings or income from continuing operations. Management has an incentive to classify losses as extraordinary and to suggest that the losses will not persist into the future, and to move nonoperating and one-time gain items to revenues to make them appear as if they will recur. Accounting and auditing standards are intended to minimize these opportunities.

the business. Tornado damage in Oklahoma City, Oklahoma, would likely not be considered extraordinary because these storms frequently occur in Oklahoma. The possibility of tornado damage would therefore be considered a normal business risk of locating in Oklahoma. However, tornado damage in New Hampshire might meet these criteria.

GAAP also occasionally specifies extraordinary-item treatment for transactions that would not normally meet the criteria. For example, from 1975 through 2001, when companies retired debt early and incurred a book gain or loss, they reported these items as extraordinary. These gains and losses had no future cash flow implications. However, early retirements of debt have become so common that the FASB recently concluded that gains and losses on debt retirements should no longer be classified as extraordinary.

The FASB concluded that events related to the terrorist attack on the World Trade Center on September 11, 2001 were not extraordinary. The event would clearly be classified as unusual and infrequent, but the FASB was not convinced that the costs associated with this event were easily measurable. Further, the FASB was concerned that managers of poorly performing firms (particularly in the airline industry) would be tempted to classify all of their operating losses as extraordinary. Firms can still give significant footnote disclosure to explain any event that they believe significantly impacted their operations during the fiscal year. The obvious difficultly for analysts is to sort out which of the firm's results are expected to continue and which were related to this one-time event.

### Accounting Changes and Errors

Accounting changes and errors comprise a third category of item that can result in separate disclosure. Accounting changes can occur from a change in accounting principle or from a change in estimate. Changes in accounting estimates do not require any restatements and may not even be disclosed. However, voluntary changes in accounting principle require firms to provide an adjustment for the effects of the change in prior years. In the year of the change, there will be a catch-up adjustment, known as the *cumulative effect* of the accounting principle change. Firms report this catch-up adjustment in a matter similar to that used for disposal of a segment of a business and extraordinary items. Accounting errors in prior period do require the restatement of prior periods through an adjustment to the beginning balance of the retained earnings account. These are called **prior period adjustments.**

## PRO-FORMA EARNINGS

Recently, the SEC increased its focus on companies' misuse of accounting to mislead investors. One area of concern has been the presentation of pro forma earnings that represent a company in a more favorable light than actual earnings. **Pro forma earnings,** also called "as if" earnings, are earnings restated to reflect certain assumptions different from those in the actual earnings statement. For example, Waste Management, Inc. reported net income of $30 million for the third quarter of 2001. However, in its press release announcing its third quarter earnings, Waste Management reported pro forma earnings of $225 million. Items that the company eliminated from the pro forma earnings included consulting fees and truck painting.

In the November 2001 press release, Waste Management, Inc. announced financial results for its third quarter ended September 30, 2001. Revenues for the quarter were $2.90 billion as compared to $3.12 billion in the one-year-ago period. Included in the third quarter revenues was $203 million from operations which have since been sold. Net income reported for the quarter was $30 million, or $.05 per diluted share, for the third quarter 2000. On a pro forma basis, after adjusting for unusual costs and certain other items, including a charge related to the agreement to settle the class action lawsuit, third quarter 2001 net income was $225 million, or $.36 per diluted share as compared with $208 million or $33 per diluted share, in the one-year-ago period. Note that this disclosure offers significant information about which items are nonrecurring (e.g., sold operations and the lawsuit settlement). Also note that the company failed to include these items in its pro-forma disclosure.

## EARNINGS PER SHARE

GAAP requires firms to disclose **earnings per share** in the income statement. (See the disclosure of Target in Exhibit 4.11.) There are two components of earnings per share, basic earnings per share and fully-diluted earnings per share. **Basic**

**earnings per share** is simply net income divided by the weighted average number of shares of common stock outstanding for a company. Hence, it measures the per share earnings accruing to shareholders. A company reports **fully-diluted earnings per share** when it has stock options and other instruments that are convertible into shares of common stock that could potentially reduce the common shareholder's proportionate share of earnings if the instruments were converted. For example, when a company provides an executive stock option plan, more shares outstanding will occur if and when the executives exercise their options. This will reduce the proportionate equity in earnings of current shareholders. The fully-diluted earnings per share figure provides an estimate of this type of dilution. It calculates how low earnings per share might become if everything is converted. We'll provide a more detailed discussion of earnings per share and its computation in Chapter 12.

Analysts often focus on per share earnings when forecasting earnings and, as we discussed, the ability to meet earnings forecasts can significantly affect a company's share price.

## COMPREHENSIVE INCOME

FASB Concepts Statement 6 (FASB, SFAC No. 6, 1985) defines **comprehensive income** as the change in equity of a firm due to transactions and other events and circumstances from nonowner sources. It includes all changes in equity except those resulting from investments by owners and distributions to owners. At first glance, this appears to be a definition of earnings. The difference is that accounting standards allow for some items that affect owners' equity to bypass the income statement and be recorded directly in stockholders' equity.

Primarily, these transactions relate to holding gains and losses on certain investments in equity securities and the balance sheet effects of foreign currency translations. Foreign currency translation gains and losses occur when a company has a subsidiary in another country whose accounting records are maintained in a currency other than the U.S. dollar. When the results of this subsidiary are combined to produce the consolidated financial statements of the company, they must be translated from the currency in which they are kept to U.S. dollars by applying various exchange rates. This translation produces gains and losses in dollar terms that must be accounted for and reported. In many circumstances, these gains and losses bypass the income statement and end up in comprehensive income. Accounting standards require that comprehensive income be reported separately from earnings, usually disclosed in the Statement of Shareholders' Equity.

## SUMMARY AND TRANSITION

Understanding the basis for recognition of revenues and expenses, as well as how those are presented, is critical to analyzing and using financial statements for decision making. The income statement provides useful information about future cash flows, but that information must also be both timely and reliable. In some cases, the trade-offs for more timely information may reduce the certainty of the information presented. As we saw in this chapter, a firm might wait and recognize revenues on long-term construction contracts until it receives cash. However, months or even years may lapse between the time construction begins and the contract price is fully collected. This lag reduces the usefulness of the information. Financial accounting standards are not intended to eliminate uncertainty, but they are intended to balance the conflict between the goals of providing relevant and timely information with information that is reliable and accurate.

At a conceptual level, accrual accounting seeks to recognize revenues as earned, rather than as the cash is received, and expenses as incurred, rather than as the cash is paid. To implement this concept, those who set the standards have devised criteria for revenue and related expense recognition that identify where in the operating cycle recognition is appropriate.

The usefulness of earnings in valuing the firm is enhanced by separating continuing/recurring operating items from more transitory noncontinuing/nonrecurring ones, such as profits or losses from discontinued operations, restructuring charges, and extraordinary items. The effects of accounting changes should also be identified to improve estimates of future earnings numbers.

# END OF CHAPTER MATERIAL

## KEY TERMS

Accrual-Basis Accounting
Cash-Basis Accounting
Revenue Recognition
Revenue Recognition Criteria
Realized/Realizable
Earned
Installment Method
Cost Recovery Method
Completed Contract Method
Percentage Completion Method
Matching Concept
Cost of Goods Sold
Deferred Expense
Deferred Revenue
Multiple-Step Income Statement
Single-Step Income Statement
Income from Continuing Operations
Discontinued Operations
Extraordinary Items
Cumulative Effect of Changes in Accounting Principles
Prior Period Adjustment
Pro Forma Earnings
Earnings per Share
Basic Earnings per Share
Fully-Diluted Earnings per Share
Comprehensive Income

## ASSIGNMENT MATERIAL

### REVIEW QUESTIONS

1. What advantages and disadvantages do you see in using the cash basis of accounting rather than the accrual basis?
2. Respond to each of the following statements with a true or false answer:
   a. Dividends declared decrease cash immediately.
   b. The cash basis recognizes expenses when they are incurred.
   c. There is no such thing as a prepaid rent account on the cash basis.

d. Dividends are an expense of doing business and should appear on the income statement.

e. On the accrual basis, interest should only be recognized when it is paid.

3. Explain how a prepaid expense (such as rent) gets handled under accrual basis accounting.
4. Explain how an accrued expense (such as interest) gets handled under accrual basis accounting.
5. Suppose that a firm's accounting policy was to recognize warranty expense only when warranty service was provided. Discuss whether this meets the matching concept under accrual basis accounting and other ways that this transaction might be handled.
6. Diagram a typical operating cycle of a manufacturing firm and briefly explain what assets and liabilities are likely to be created as a result of this operating cycle.
7. List the two major revenue recognition criteria that exist under GAAP.
8. Describe the concept of revenue being "earned" and contrast it with the concept of revenue being "realized."
9. Explain the difference between the percentage completion method and the completed contracts method.
10. Explain the difference between the installment method and the cost recovery method.
11. Explain the meaning of the matching concept.

## APPLYING YOUR KNOWLEDGE

12. Brickstone Construction Company signs a contract to build a building in four years for $40,000,000. The expected costs for each year are:

| | |
|---|---|
| Year 1: | $ 9,750,000 |
| Year 2: | 12,025,000 |
| Year 3: | 6,500,000 |
| Year 4: | 4,225,000 |
| Total | $32,500,000 |

The building is completed in year 4. Compute for each year, the total revenue, expenses, and profit under:

a. The Percentage of Completion Method

b. The Completed Contract Method

13. Sandra Carlson sold her house, which cost her $210,000, to Bob Fletcher for $300,000. Bob agreed to pay $60,000 per year for a period of five years. Compute the revenue, expense, and profit for each of the five years (ignoring interest):

a. The Installment Method

b. The Cost-Recovery Method

14. Imperial Corporation purchases a factory from Superior Manufacturing Company for $1,500,000. The cost of the factory on Superior's book is $975,000. The terms of agreement are that yearly installment payments of $705,000, $505,000, $455,000, and $255,000 will be made over the next four years. Each of these payments includes an interest payment of $105,000 per year. Compute the revenue, expense, and profit for each of the four years accruing to Superior Manufacturing Company as per:

    a. The Installment Method

    b. The Cost Recovery Method

15. Cruise Shipping, Inc. agreed to rebuild the *Santa Marice;* an old cargo ship owned by the Oceanic Shipping Company. Both parties signed the contract on November 28, Year 1, for $120 million which is to be paid as follows:

    $12 million at the signing of the contract
    $24 million on December 30, Year 2
    $36 million on June 1, Year 3
    $48 million at completion, on August 15 Year 4.

    The following cost were incurred by Cruise Shipping, Inc. (in millions):

| | |
|---|---|
| Year 1: | $19.2 |
| Year 2: | 38.4 |
| Year 3: | 24.0 |
| Year 4: | 14.4 |
| Total | $96.0 |

    a. Compute the revenue, expense, and profit for each of the four years (ignoring interest) for Cruise Shipping, Inc. as per:

        1. The Installment Method
        2. The Cost-Recovery Method
        3. The Percentage of Completion Method
        4. The Completed Contract Method

    b. Which method do you think should be employed by Cruise Shipping, Inc. to show the company's performance under the contract? Why?

16. Computronics Corporation received a contract on March 3, Year 1 for setting up a central communication and pricing center for a small university. The contract price was $1,000,000 which is to be paid as follows:

    $150,000 at the signing of the contract
    $ 60,000 on July 1, Year 1
    $ 30,000 on December 31, Year 1
    $ 80,000 on March 25, Year 2
    $100,000 on August 25, Year 2
    $180,000 on December 31, Year 2
    $400,000 on June 30, Year 3

The system was completed on June 30, Year 3.
Estimated and actual costs were:

$150,000 for the six months ending June 30, Year 1
$225,000 for the six months ending December 31, Year 1
$262,500 for the six months ending June 30, Year 2
$75,000 for the six months ending December 31, Year 2
$37,500 for the six months ending June 30, Year 3

Total $750,000

a. Compute the revenue, expense, and profit for each of the six months as per:
   1. The Percentage of Completion Method
   2. The Completed Contract Method
   3. The Installment Method
   4. The Cost-Recovery Method

b. Which method should be used by Computronics Corporation? Why?

17. Forte Builders, a construction company, recognizes revenue from its long-term contracts using the percentage completion method. On March 29, 20X3, the company signed a contract to construct a building for $500,000. The company estimated that it would take four years to complete the contract and would cost the company an estimated $325,000. The expected costs in each of the four years are as follows:

| Year | Cost |
|---|---|
| 20X3 | $113,750 |
| 20X4 | 97,500 |
| 20X5 | 81,250 |
| 20X6 | 32,500 |
| Total | $325,000 |

On December 31, 20X4, the date Forte closes its books, the company revised its estimates for the cost in 20X5 and 20X6. It estimated that the contract would cost $200,000 in 20X5 and $100,000 in 20X6 to complete the contract. Compute the revenue, expense, and profit/loss for each of the four years.

18. Samson Industries purchased furniture and appliances from the Metal and Wood Company for $75,000 under the following payment plan which called for semiannual payments over two years:

| Payment | Amount |
|---|---|
| 1 | $33,600 |
| 2 | 16,800 |
| 3 | 22,400 |
| 4 | 11,200 |
| Total | $84,000 |

Each payment contains interest (assume that the proportionate share of interest in each payment is the same as the proportion of that payment to the total payments). Assuming that the cost of the furniture and appliances is $60,000, compute the revenue, expense, and profit that Metal and Wood Company would report for each of the installment payments under:

a. The Installment Method

b. The Cost-Recovery Method

19. On June 21, 20X1, Tristar Electric Company signed a contract with Denton Power, Incorporated to construct a small hydroelectric generating plant. The contract price was $10,000,000, and it was estimated that the project would cost Tristar $7,850,000 to complete over a three-year period. On June 21, 20X1, Denton paid Tristar $1,000,000 as a default-deposit. In the event that Denton backed out of the contract, Tristar could keep this deposit. Otherwise the default-deposit would apply as the final payment on the contract (assume for accounting purposes that this is treated as a deposit until completion of the contract). The other contractual payments are as follows:

| Date | Amount |
|---|---|
| 10/15/X1 | $3,150,000 |
| 4/15/X2 | 1,350,000 |
| 12/15/X2 | 1,800,000 |
| 3/15/X3 | 1,755,000 |
| 8/10/X3 | 945,000 |
| Total | $9,000,000 |

Estimated costs of construction were as follows:

| Year | Amount |
|---|---|
| 1 | $3,532,500 |
| 2 | 2,747,500 |
| 3 | 1,570,000 |

The contract was completed on January 10, 20X4. Tristar closes its books on December 31 each year. Compute the revenue, expense, and profit to be recognized in each year using:

a. The Installment Method

b. The Cost-Recovery Method

c. The Percentage Completion Method

d. The Completed Contracts Method

20. Financial analysts frequently refer to the quality of a firm's earnings. Discuss how the quality of two firms' earnings might differ depending on the revenue recognition method that the two firms use.

21. Suppose that a firm is currently private but is thinking of going public (i.e., issuing shares in a publicly traded market). Discuss the incentives that the

firm might have to misstate its income statement via its revenue recognition policies.

22. Suppose that you are the sales manager of a firm with an incentive plan that provides a bonus based on meeting a certain sales target. Explain how meeting your sales target is influenced by the revenue recognition principles of the firm.

23. Suppose that you are a sales manager of a U.S.-based firm that sells products in Israel, which has traditionally had a high inflation rate. This means that the exchange rate of shekels per dollar typically increases dramatically from year to year. If your compensation is a function of sales as measured in dollars, what risks do you face in meeting your targets and how might you mitigate the risks that you face in meeting those targets?

24. Explain the incentives that a firm has in choosing its revenue recognition method for both financial reporting and tax purposes.

25. In the toy industry it is common to allow customers to return unsold toys within a certain specified period of time. Suppose that a toy manufacturer's year end is December 31 and that the majority of its products are shipped to customers during the last quarter of the year in anticipation of the Christmas holiday. Is it appropriate for the company to recognize revenue upon shipment of the product? Support your answer citing references to revenue recognition criteria.

26. Suppose that an importer in Seattle buys goods from a supplier in Hong Kong. The goods are shipped by cargo vessel. For goods that are in transit at year end, what recognition should the Seattle importer make of these goods in its financial statements? Support your answer based on revenue recognition criteria.

27. Suppose that a company recognizes revenues at the time that title passes to its inventory and that it ships its inventory FOB (free on board) shipping point (i.e., title passes at the shipping point). Suppose at year end that it has loaded a shipment of goods on a truck that is parked on the grounds of the company based on a firm purchase order from a customer. How should the firm treat this inventory in its financial statements at year end?

28. Firms often sell their accounts receivable to raise cash to support their operations. Suppose that a firm sells its accounts receivable with recourse. Recourse means that the buyer can return the account receivable to the selling company if it cannot collect on the receivable. How should this transaction be treated in the financial statements of the selling company?

29. Suppose that ESPN (the sports channel) sells $10,000,000 in advertising slots to be aired during the games that it broadcasts during the NCAA basketball tournament. Suppose further that these slots are contracted for during the month of September with a downpayment of $2,000,000. The ads will be aired in March. If the fiscal year end of ESPN is December 31, how should ESPN recognize this revenue in its financial statements?

30. Suppose that The GAP (a clothing retailer) sells gift certificates for merchandise. During the Christmas holiday period, suppose that it issues $500,000 in gifts certificates. If the firm's fiscal year end is December 31, how should it recognize the issuance of these gift certificates in its financial statements at year end?

31. Suppose that the XYZ Software company produces an inventory tracking software that it sells to manufacturing companies. Further suppose that the software sells for $100,000 each and it requires the company to provide customization to the buyers' operations, which can take several months. If the fiscal year end is September 30 and the company sells ten units of the product in August, how should it recognize these "sales" in the financial statements at year end?
32. Suppose that you are the auditor of ABC Manufacturing Company and during your audit of the firm's inventory you observe a significant amount of inventory that appears to be extremely old. How would you recommend that the firm deal with this inventory and how will it affect the revenues and expenses recognized during the period? Explain the incentives that the management of the firm might have for keeping the inventory in its warehouse.
33. Assume that a company is discontinuing a line of products due to lack of profitability. It is not sure whether this discontinuance meets the criteria for separate recognition as a discontinued line of business. The alternatives are to incorporate the losses from this line within normal operations or report them as a separate line item called "discontinued operations." As a stock analyst, discuss how the alternatives might affect your analysis of the company's stock.

## USING REAL DATA

34. Zale Corporation sells fine jewelry and giftware in a chain of stores nationwide. The following footnotes appeared in the 2001 annual report along with the income statement below:

**Revenue Recognition**

The Company recognizes revenue in accordance with the Securities and Exchange Commissions Staff Accounting Bulletin No. 101, Revenue Recognition in Financial Statements (SAB 101). Revenue related to merchandise sales is recognized at the time of the sale, reduced by a provision for returns. The provision for sales returns is based on historical evidence of the Company s return rate. Repair revenues are recognized when the service is complete and the merchandise is delivered to the customers. Net Sales include amortized extended service agreements (ESA) which are amortized over the two-year service agreement period. ESA revenue and related expenses were previously netted in selling, general, and administrative expenses. Prior periods sales and cost of sales have been restated to reflect ESA revenue. The amortized ESA revenues were $25.0 million, $20.8 million, and $16.8 million for the years ended July 31, 2001, 2000, and 1999, respectively, and related ESA costs were $12.5 million, $10.8 million, and $9.5 million for the years ended July 31, 2001, 2000, and 1999, respectively.

Advertising Expenses are charged against operations when incurred and are a component of selling, general, and administrative expenses in the consolidated income statements. Amounts charged against operations were $78.5 million, $66.4 million, and $49.0 million for the years ended July 31, 2001, 2000, and 1999, respectively, net of amounts contributed by vendors to the Company. The amounts of prepaid advertising at July 31, 2001 and 2000, are $6.0 million and $6.4 million, respectively, and are classified as components of other assets in the Consolidated Balance Sheet.

**Unusual Charges—Executives**

Effective September 6, 2000, Robert J. DiNicola retired as Chairman of the Board but remained as a nonemployee member of the Board. In connection with his severance arrangement, the Company agreed to pay certain benefits of approximately $1.9 million consisting principally of an amount equivalent to one year of salary and bonus and other severance-related benefits including the accelerated vesting of certain options held by Mr. DiNicola.

Additionally, the Board approved the provision to Mr. DiNicola by the Company of a full recourse, $2.2 million interest-bearing loan at 8.74 percent for the sole purpose of purchasing 125,000 stock options prior to their expiration. The Company also extended the exercise period on an additional 500,000 stock options set to expire on September 6, 2002 to the earlier of the original ten-year term (to expire July 9, 2007), the maximum term pursuant to the Company's stock option plan, or two years after Mr. DiNicola leaves the Board of Directors. Based on the intrinsic value of these stock options on the modification date, no compensation charge was recorded by the Company.

Effective February 12, 2001, Beryl B. Raff resigned as Chairman of the Board and Chief Executive Officer. In connection with her resignation, the Company agreed to pay certain benefits of approximately $2.5 million consisting principally of an amount equivalent to three years of salary and other severance-related benefits including accelerated vesting of certain options and restricted stock.

Robert J. DiNicola was reappointed as Chairman of the Board and Chief Executive Officer, effective February 21, 2001, under a three-year contract with terms substantially consistent with his previous contract when he held the same position. In August 2001, the Company entered into a five-year employment agreement with Mr. DiNicola effective upon Mr. DiNicola's reelection as Chairman of the Board and Chief Executive Officer, replacing the earlier employment agreement. In April 2001, the Company extended a $2.1 million, three-year interest bearing loan at 7.25 percent to Mr. DiNicola for the purpose of purchasing a home. In August 2001, the loan was modified and extended with the entire principal amount to be repaid in August 2006.

**Nonrecurring Charge**

Upon the return of Robert J. DiNicola as Chairman and Chief Executive Officer on February 21, 2001, the Company performed an in-depth review to determine the inventory that was not of a quality consistent with the strategic direction of the Company's brands. As a result of that review, the Company recorded a nonrecurring charge in Cost of Sales of $25.2 million to adjust the valuation of such inventory and provide for markdowns to liquidate or sell-through the inventory.

| ZALE CORP.: Income Statement | 07/31/2001 | 07/31/2000 | 07/31/1999 |
|---|---|---|---|
| Net sales | $2,068,242,000 | $1,814,362,000 | $1,445,634,000 |
| Cost of sales | 1,034,970,000 | 930,826,000 | 746,663,000 |
| Nonrecurring charge | 25,236,000 | 0 | 0 |
| Gross margin | 1,008,036,000 | 883,536,000 | 698,971,000 |
| Selling, general, and administrative Expenses | 804,780,000 | 630,687,000 | 509,570,000 |
| Depreciation and amortization expense | 58,290,000 | 42,431,000 | 29,478,000 |
| Unusual item—executive transactions | 4,713,000 | 0 | 0 |
| Operating earnings | 140,253,000 | 210,418,000 | 159,923,000 |
| Interest expense, net | 6,857,000 | 32,178,000 | 30,488,000 |
| Earnings before income taxes | 133,396,000 | 178,240,000 | 129,435,000 |
| Income taxes | 51,348,000 | 66,726,000 | 48,503,000 |
| Net earnings | $ 82,048,000 | $ 111,514,000 | $ 80,932,000 |

**a.** Provide support for Zale's revenue recognition policy for its extended service agreements.

**b.** From an analyst's point of view, discuss why the change in reporting ESA's as part of revenue rather than as an offset to expenses would be important.

c. From an analyst's point of view, discuss why the disclosure of advertising costs by year might be important.

d. From an analyst's point of view, discuss how you might use the disclosures concerning the unusual and nonrecurring charges to assist you in predicting the stock price for Zale.

35. Lands' End, Incorporated is a direct merchant of clothing and other cloth products that are sold primarily through catalog mailings. The cost of catalog production and mailing is fairly substantial for a company such as Lands' End. Discuss how the costs associated with catalog production and mailing should be treated for accounting purposes. Frame your answer in terms of the revenue recognition criteria and the matching concept discussed in this chapter.

36. Many consumer electronics retailers have offered extended warranty contracts to their customers. These contracts typically provide warranty coverage beyond the manufacturer's warranty period, usually anywhere between 12 and 60 months from the date of purchase. The cost of these contracts is generally collected at the time of the purchase of the product. The following is the revenue recognition Disclosure for Best Buy, Inc.:

**Revenue Recognition**

We recognize revenues from the sale of merchandise at the time the merchandise is sold. We recognize service revenues at the time the service is provided, the sales price is fixed or determinable, and collectibility is reasonably assured.

We sell extended service contracts, called Performance Service Plans, on behalf of an unrelated third party. In jurisdictions where we are not deemed to be the obligor on the contract at the time of sale, commissions are recognized in revenues at the time of sale. In jurisdictions where we are deemed to be the obligor on the contract at the time of sale, commissions are recognized in revenues ratably over the term of the service contract.

Discuss why Best Buy's revenue recognition policy, with regard to commissions on Performance Service Plans, is different in different jurisdictions. Base your defense on the nature of the transaction and the revenue recognition criteria found in GAAP. In jurisdictions in which they are the obligor, what might happen to them should the third party not be able to live up to this agreement?

37. In the early 1990s a new business emerged to help individuals deal with the financial burdens of terminal illnesses, such as AIDS. If a terminally ill person has a life insurance policy, an investor group of companies could buy the insurance policy from the individual for a lump sum settlement amount. The seller could then use the proceeds to pay their bills. The buyer agrees to continue to make the premium payments until the individual dies and then collects the proceeds of the insurance policy upon death. These types of agreements are called viatical settlements. Depending on the estimated life span of the individual and the creditworthiness of the insurance company, the buyer might offer somewhere between 25 to 80 percent of the face value of the policy.

a. If you were an investor, how would you decide how much to pay for a given viatical agreement?

b. Having agreed on a price, how would you recognize revenue from this agreement (assume for the purposes of this question that there is more than one year from the inception of the agreement to the death of the seller) over the life of the contract?

c. Given your revenue recognition method outlined in part b, how would you treat the payment of premiums over the life of the contract?

d. Discuss any ethical dilemmas that the buyers of viatical agreements might face in the conduct of their business.

## BEYOND THE BOOK

38. Using an electronic database, search for a company that has changed its revenue recognition methods during the last three years. Answer the following questions:

a. Describe the method that was used before the change as well as the new method.

b. Does the company give a reason for the change? If so, describe the change; if not, speculate on why the change occurred.

c. How significant an effect did the change have on the firm's financial statements? As an investor, how would you view this change?

d. Did the auditor agree with the change? Do you agree and why?

Prepare a short two- to three-page paper to respond to these questions.

CHAPTER 5

# Financial Statements: Measuring Cash Flow

## Learning Objectives

After reading this chapter you should be able to:

1. Understand and interpret the information about operating, investing, and financing activities found in the cash flow statement.
2. Explain the relationship between the cash flow statement and changes in balance sheet accounts.
3. Construct a cash flow statement using the indirect method.
4. Define free cash flows and explain how they can be determined from the Statement of Cash Flows.

**Moody's Investor Service announced it was reviewing the debt rating for** Georgia-Pacific (GP), citing concerns with Georgia-Pacific's weakening cash flow. Mark Gray, an analyst with Moody's said, "We looked at the company's position and we were concerned about the scope of the asset sales to Willamette and the weakening cash flow over the near term that would limit their debt reduction ability."

The announcement of Moody's review of Georgia-Pacific's debt rating highlights the importance of strong cash flows to a company's value. A downgrade in debt raises the cost of borrowing for Georgia-Pacific as well as lowers equity values. In this chapter we discuss the content and meaning of the information contained in the statement of cash flows.

Broadly speaking, the statement of cash flows reflects the operating, investing, and financing activities of the firm described in Chapter 1. As such, the statement of cash flows provides different information than the income statement that focuses on changes in stockholders' equity arising from operations. The cash flow statement explains changes in cash in terms of changes in noncash accounts appearing on successive balance sheets. These changes are not limited to those involving operations, but include those involving investing and financing.

Further, with respect to operating activities, the cash flow statement offers a different perspective than reflected on the income statement. As we discussed in Chapter 4, firms determine net income on an accrual basis by the application of revenue and expense recognition criteria. Recall that under the accrual basis of accounting, revenue may be earned and expenses incurred before or after the cash flows to which they relate. Net income, therefore, reflects the revenues earned and the expenses incurred by the firm as a result of its operating activities during the period, *not* the operating cash inflows and outflows. Operating cash flows may precede or follow the recognition of revenues or expenses on the income statement. Timing issues thus separate the recognition of income from the actual cash flows of the firm.

For example, if a firm's sales grow rapidly but a significant lag exists between the cash outflows to make the company's product and the inflows from the sales collections, the firm may experience a severe liquidity crisis. In other words, a firm may possess insufficient available cash to make the required payments for items such as salaries and accounts payable. This liquidity crisis may then spark the need to obtain additional financing to pay bills and to support the company's growth. If analysts focused on only the income statement, they would miss the liquidity crisis. Further, as the income statement does not report on the investing and financing activities of the firm, analysts would not see any attempts made by the firm to address the liquidity crisis (e.g., through additional financing or a slowdown in investing). The cash flow statement not only makes any liquidity crisis transparent, it also indicates how a firm addresses the crises. Because it contains such crucial data, let's take a closer look at the information a typical cash flow statement provides.

## CASH FLOW STATEMENT COMPONENTS

SFAS 95 (FASB, SFAS No. 95, 1987) requires that all companies issue a cash flow statement and provides guidelines regarding its format. The Statement of Cash Flows provides information about changes in cash flows from all sources: operating, investing, and financing activities of an entity.

### CASH FLOW FROM OPERATING ACTIVITIES

Cash flow from operations includes cash inflows from sales of goods and services to customers, and cash outflows from expenses related to the sales of goods and services to customers, such as cost of goods sold and selling and administrative expenses. In fact, cash from operations can be viewed as a measure of cash-basis

| TECH DATA CORP.: Cash Flow | 01/31/2002 | 01/31/2001 | 01/31/2000 |
|---|---|---|---|
| Cash flows from operating activities: | | | |
| Cash received from customers | $17,511,511,000 | $20,114,486,000 | $16,788,960,000 |
| Cash paid to suppliers and employees | (16,406,265,000) | (20,047,551,000) | (16,684,316,000) |
| Interest paid | (55,871,000) | (94,823,000) | (69,554,000) |
| Income taxes paid | (72,745,000) | (62,048,000) | (34,176,000) |
| Net cash provided by (used in) operating activities | 976,630,000 | (89,936,000) | 914,000 |
| Cash flows from investing activities: | | | |
| Acquisition of businesses, net of cash acquired | (183,000) | (19,198,000) | (42,898,000) |
| Expenditures for property and equipment | (28,466,000) | (38,079,000) | (59,038,000) |
| Software development costs | (20,719,000) | (22,705,000) | (18,381,000) |
| Net cash used in investing activities | (49,368,000) | (79,982,000) | (120,317,000) |
| Cash flows from financing activities: | | | |
| Proceeds from the issuance of common stock, net of related tax benefit | 36,432,000 | 35,539,000 | 19,663,000 |
| Net (repayments) borrowings on revolving credit loans | (1,118,167,000) | 248,712,000 | 99,447,000 |
| Proceeds from issuance of long-term debt, net of expense | 284,200,000 | 0 | 0 |
| Principal payments on long-term debt | (634,000) | (557,000) | (162,000) |
| Net cash (used in) provided by financing activities | (798,169,000) | 283,694,000 | 118,948,000 |
| Effect of change in year end of certain subsidiaries (Note 3) | 0 | 0 | 23,626,000 |
| Effect of exchange rate changes on cash | (10,091,000) | (6,637,000) | 0 |
| Net increase in cash and cash equivalents | 119,002,000 | 107,139,000 | 23,171,000 |
| Cash and cash equivalents at beginning of year | 138,925,000 | 31,786,000 | 8,615,000 |
| Cash and cash equivalents at end of year | $ 257,927,000 | $ 138,925,000 | $ 31,786,000 |

**Exhibit 5.1**
Direct Method Cash Flow Statement

**THE REAL WORLD**
**Tech Data Corp.**

earnings because it measures the cash inflows from sales in the period of collection and the cash outflows for expenses in the period of payment.

There are two approaches to presenting cash flow from operations, the **direct method** and the **indirect method.** Under the direct method, a firm first reports cash received from revenue-producing activities, and then subtracts its cash payments for expenses. Exhibit 5.1 illustrates this type of statement (see the shaded operating section). Notice that the company shown (Tech Data, a distributor of hardware and software products) combined its operating cash outflows to employees and suppliers into a single line item.

In contrast, the indirect method starts with net income and shows the adjustments necessary to arrive at cash flows from operations. Exhibit 5.2 shows this method in the statements of Tofutti Brands, Inc. (a producer of soy-based products).

FASB 95 allows the use of either method, as both methods produce identical results of cash from operations. However, most firms use the indirect approach. As a result, FASB 95 requires firms that report under the direct

**Exhibit 5.2**
Indirect Method Cash Flow Statement

THE REAL WORLD
**Tofutti Brands**

| TOFUTTI BRANDS, Inc.: Cash Flow | 12/29/2001 | 12/29/2000 | 12/30/1999 |
|---|---|---|---|
| Cash flows from operating activities: | | | |
| Net income | $ 1,150,000 | $ 956,000 | $ 850,000 |
| Adjustments to reconcile net income to net cash flows from operating activities: | | | |
| Provision for bad debts | 40,000 | 60,000 | 60,000 |
| Accrued interest on investments | 0 | (34,000) | (3,000) |
| Deferred taxes | (119,000) | (176,000) | 332,000 |
| Change in assets and liabilities: | | | |
| Accounts receivable | (625,000) | (105,000) | 64,000 |
| Inventories | 92,000 | (342,000) | 17,000 |
| Prepaid expenses | (1,000) | (1,000) | 5,000 |
| Accounts payable and accrued expenses | 9,000 | 17,000 | (51,000) |
| Accrued compensation | 0 | 175,000 | 115,000 |
| Income taxes payable | (144,000) | 209,000 | 103,000 |
| Net cash flows from operating activities | 402,000 | 759,000 | 1,492,000 |
| Cash flows from investing activities: | | | |
| Proceeds from redemption of investments | 269,000 | 0 | (250,000) |
| Other assets | (144,000) | (22,000) | (22,000) |
| Net cash flows from investing activities | 125,000 | (22,000) | (272,000) |
| Cash flows from financing activities: | | | |
| Notes payable | (8,000) | (22,000) | (18,000) |
| Issuance of common stock | 35,000 | 50,000 | 84,000 |
| Purchase of treasury stock | (436,000) | (247,000) | 0 |
| Net cash flows from financing activities | (409,000) | (219,000) | 66,000 |
| Net change in cash and equivalents | 118,000 | 518,000 | 1,286,000 |
| Cash and equivalents, at beginning of period | 2,211,000 | 1,693,000 | 407,000 |
| Cash and equivalents, at end of period | $ 2,329,000 | $2,211,000 | $1,693,000 |
| Supplemental cash flow information: | | | |
| Interest paid | | $ 2,000 | $ 5,000 |
| Income taxes paid | $ 750,000 | $ 579,000 | $ 151,000 |

method to also disclose the operating section data prepared under the indirect method (see Exhibit 5.3). Compare the net cash from operations in both Exhibits 5.1 and 5.3, and note how the amounts are identical. However, you can see that the indirect method disclosure (Exhibit 5.3) provides more information about investments in current operating assets net of operating liabilities than the direct method (Exhibit 5.1).

| TECH DATA CORP.: Cash Flow | 01/31/2002 | 01/31/2001 | 01/31/2000 |
|---|---|---|---|
| Reconciliation of net income to net cash provided by (used in) operating activities: | | | |
| Net income | $ 110,777,000 | $177,983,000 | $127,501,000 |
| Adjustments to reconcile net income to net cash provided by (used in) operating activities: | | | |
| Depreciation and amortization | 63,488,000 | 63,922,000 | 57,842,000 |
| Provision for losses on accounts receivable | 40,764,000 | 41,447,000 | 40,877,000 |
| Special charges (Note 13) | 27,000,000 | 0 | 0 |
| Deferred income taxes | (11,848,000) | (1,789,000) | 1,306,000 |
| Changes in assets and liabilities: | | | |
| Decrease (increase) in accounts receivable | 314,000,000 | (313,197,000) | (202,790,000) |
| Decrease (increase) in inventories | 702,219,000 | (146,093,000) | (220,585,000) |
| (Increase) in prepaid and other assets | (6,248,000) | (11,603,000) | (25,430,000) |
| (Decrease) increase in accounts payable | (264,722,000) | 11,863,000 | 136,748,000 |
| Increase in accrued expenses | 1,200,000 | 87,531,000 | 85,445,000 |
| Total adjustments | 865,853,000 | (267,919,000) | (126,587,000) |
| Net cash provided by (used in) operating activities | $976,630,000 | ($89,936,000) | $ 914,000 |

**Exhibit 5.3**
Indirect Method Disclosure under Direct Method

THE REAL WORLD
**Tech Data**

## CASH FLOW FROM INVESTING ACTIVITIES

Investing activities involve the cash flow effect of transactions related to a company's long-term assets and investments. Examples include cash paid or received to purchase or sell property, plant, and equipment; investments in securities of other companies; and acquisitions of other companies. The investing activities section provides information about how a company uses its cash to generate future earnings. Investments represent opportunities for future earnings growth. For a growth company, we would normally expect cash from investing activities to be a net outflow, although this depends on the company's growth strategy.

For example, in Tech Data's cash flow statement (Exhibit 5.1), you see significant annual investments in property and equipment, and software development. Contrast this with Tofutti's cash flow statement (Exhibit 5.2), which includes little activity in the investing section. The company primarily leases its facilities (the cash flows from leasing would appear in the operating section) and therefore does not have significant investments in plant and equipment.

The investment section of the cash flow statement is where you would also see investments in other companies including acquisitions. You can see this kind of activity in Tech Data's statements. Note that in most acquisitions the investment cash flow occurs on the date of acquisition. Subsequent to the date of acquisition, the cash flows from operating the newly acquired company will start to appear in the operating section. At the date of acquisition, the firm reports new assets and liabilities from the acquisition (e.g., receivables, inventory, PP&E, accounts payable) that would appear in the firm's balance sheet as of the acquisition date. If a firm acquired a new company mid-year, then the net change in certain asset accounts (such as inventories) would include the changes due to operations and the changes due to the acquisition.

### CASH FLOW FROM FINANCING ACTIVITIES

This section of the cash flow statement provides information about transactions with owners and creditors. Financing activities include issuance and repayment of debt such as loans, bank advances, and bonds payable, as well as issuances and repurchases of stock and payments of dividends.

Tofutti (Exhibit 5.2) shows relatively minor outflows of cash to repay notes payable. The remaining transactions relate to issuance of stock and repurchase of shares that are held in its treasury account. Tech Data's statements (Exhibit 5.1) show significantly more activity related to long-term debt.

Now that you can identify the components of the cash flow statement, how do you use its information? One of the best ways is by understanding the mechanics of preparing a cash flow statement. Going through the preparation process can shed light on how a firm generates and uses cash. Additionally, reconciling a firm's cash flow statement to its balance sheet and income statement can be a useful tool for financial statement analysis.

## PREPARATION OF THE STATEMENT OF CASH FLOWS

In this section, we'll show how to prepare a cash flow statement (indirect method) using Biohealth, Inc. (BHT), the fictitious wholesale company we discussed in previous chapters. Exhibit 5.4 shows the balance sheets for BHT at 12/31/20X2 and 12/31/20X1. Exhibit 5.5 shows the income statement for BHT for the year ending 12/31/20X2.

We use a T-account worksheet to determine the net effects of the transactions for BHT for 20X2 on the cash account, as shown in Exhibit 5.6. Note that we use this worksheet only to assist in the construction of the cash flow statement. Do not confuse this worksheet with the firm's accounting system that contains the actual entries made to the system. In fact, you can also use a simple spreadsheet instead of a T-account worksheet.

The first step is to place the beginning and ending balances of all of the accounts from the balance sheet in the T-accounts, as shown in Exhibit 5.6. Then, we analyze the changes in the various accounts on the balance sheet and classify them into operating, investing, and financing activities. In order to do this, we rely on information from the income statement as well as any additional information provided about the company's operating, financing, and investing transactions. For example, the following additional information applies to the transactions of BHT for the year ending 12/31/20X2:

**Exhibit 5.4**
BHT Balance Sheet

| Biohealth, Inc. (BHT)<br>Balance Sheet ($ in millions) | As of 12/31/20X2 | As of 12/31/20X1 |
|---|---|---|
| Assets | | |
| Current assets: | | |
| Cash | $ 1,510 | $ 567 |
| Accounts receivable | 3,650 | 2,464 |
| Inventory | 4,400 | 3,920 |
| Prepaid expenses | 360 | 0 |
| Total current assets | 9,920 | 7,101 |
| Property, plant, and equipment (PPE) | 950 | 540 |
| Less: accumulated depreciation | (210) | (60) |
| Net property plant and equipment | 740 | 480 |
| | $10,660 | $7,581 |
| Liabilities and Stockholders' Equity | | |
| Liabilities: | | |
| Current liabilities: | | |
| Accounts payable | $ 6,671 | $5,140 |
| Long-term debt: | | |
| Notes payable | 950 | 400 |
| Total liabilities | 7,621 | 5,540 |
| Stockholders' equity | | |
| Common stock | 300 | 250 |
| Additional paid-in capital | 1,950 | 1,375 |
| Retained earnings | 789 | 266 |
| Total stockholders' equity | 3,039 | 2,041 |
| | $10,660 | $7,581 |

**Exhibit 5.5**
BHT Income Statement

| Biohealth, Inc. (BHT)<br>Income Statement | Year ending 12/31/20X2 |
|---|---|
| Revenues | $43,850 |
| Less: Cost of goods sold | (37,272) |
| Gross profit | 6,578 |
| Selling and administrative expenses | 5,320 |
| Depreciation expense | 150 |
| Interest expense | 85 |
| Net income | $1,023 |

**Exhibit 5.6**
BHT Cash Flow T-Account Worksheet

### BHT Cash Flow T-Account Worksheet Set Up

**Cash**

| | Debit | Credit |
|---|---|---|
| Bal. | 567 | |
| Operating: | | |
| Investing: | | |
| Financing: | | |
| Bal. | 1,510 | |

**Accumulated Depreciation–PPE**

| Debit | Credit | |
|---|---|---|
| | 60 | Bal. |
| | 210 | Bal. |

**Accounts payable**

| Debit | Credit | |
|---|---|---|
| | 5,140 | Bal. |
| | 6,671 | Bal. |

**Accounts receivable**

| | Debit | Credit |
|---|---|---|
| Bal. | 2,464 | |
| Bal. | 3,650 | |

**Notes payable**

| Debit | Credit | |
|---|---|---|
| | 400 | Bal. |
| | 950 | Bal. |

**Inventory**

| | Debit | Credit |
|---|---|---|
| Bal. | 3,920 | |
| Bal. | 4,400 | |

**Common Stock**

| Debit | Credit | |
|---|---|---|
| | 250 | Bal. |
| | 300 | Bal. |

**Prepaid Expenses**

| | Debit | Credit |
|---|---|---|
| Bal. | 0 | |
| Bal. | 360 | |

**Additional Paid-in capital**

| Debit | Credit | |
|---|---|---|
| | 1,375 | Bal. |
| | 1,950 | Bal. |

**PPE**

| | Debit | Credit |
|---|---|---|
| Bal. | 540 | |
| Bal. | 950 | |

**Retained Earnings**

| Debit | Credit | |
|---|---|---|
| | 266 | Bal. |
| | 789 | Bal. |

1. All inventory is purchased on credit from suppliers.
2. All sales to customers are for credit.
3. Borrowed $550 million during 20X2.
4. Issued 50 million shares of $1 par stock at $12.50 per share during 20X2.
5. Declared and paid $500 million in dividends to shareholders during 20X2.

Items 1 and 2 simply summarize common assumptions and need not correspond to the transactions that actually occurred. Items 3 through 5 provide information that you would find in the Statement of Stockholders' Equity and Notes to the Financial Statements.

We are now ready to create the worksheet entries for the cash flow statement. The basic approach is to examine each balance sheet account (other than cash) that changed and then assess its effect on cash. Next, we create a worksheet entry to show this effect on cash along with the corresponding change in the balance sheet account. Once we analyze all of the balance sheet accounts and complete the worksheet entries, we should have the basis of our cash flow statement. Let's start now with determining the worksheet entries for the operating section and then proceed through the investing and financing sections.

## WORKSHEET ENTRIES FOR CASH FROM OPERATIONS

The starting point typically begins with analyzing the change in retained earnings. In the indirect approach, we record net income in the Cash account of the worksheet (as well as in the Retained Earnings account, to ensure that debits equal credits) as if it increased cash. We know, however, that not all revenues increase cash and not all expenses use cash. Therefore, subsequent entries will make adjustments to correct for the noncash components of earnings.

We obtain net income from the income statement in Exhibit 5.5, giving us the first entry:

| | | | |
|---|---|---|---|
| (1) | Cash | 1,023 | |
| | Retained Earnings | | 1,023 |

We now need to correct our "mistake" of reporting net income as if it were all cash. We start with adjustments to correct the revenue portion of net income.

### Adjusting Net Income

Changes in current assets and liabilities in the operating section serve to correct line items in the net income number to their cash flow equivalent. For revenues, these adjustments serve to undo the effects of recognizing revenues when earned rather than as the cash is received, and for expenses the effects of recognizing them when incurred rather than when paid. We can thus view increases in current operating assets as requiring cash (and decreases providing cash) and increases in current operating liabilities as providing cash (and decreases requiring cash). Exhibit 5.7 summarizes the effects of these changes. With this understanding of adjustments, let's return now to our BHT example.

**Exhibit 5.7**
Adjustments to Net Income Using the Indirect Method

**Positive adjustments to income to determine cash from operations result from:**

Decreases in current operating assets (A/R, inventory, prepaid assets, etc.)
Increases in current operating liabilities (A/P, Salaries Payable, etc.)*

**Negative adjustments to income to determine cash from operations result from:**

Increases in current operating assets other than cash
Decreases in current operating liabilities

*Notes Payable and the Current Portion of Long-Term Debt are typically not considered to be a part of operating liabilities even though they are generally classified as current liabilities. Also, there are instances where operating liabilities are classified as noncurrent and changes in those liabilities are included in the operating section of the cash flow statement.

### Revenue Adjustments to Net Income

Because sales revenue is recorded on an accrual basis, not when cash is collected, we need to adjust income for the difference between sales revenue recognized and cash collected on accounts receivable (AR). This difference can be found in the change in the accounts receivable balance. In the case of BHT, accounts receivable increased, meaning that cash collections on account were less than the amount of sales recognized. Recall that we assume that all sales are on account. Therefore, we calculate cash collections on accounts receivable as follows:

Cash Collections = Beginning AR + Sales − Ending AR
= Sales − (Ending AR − Beginning AR)
= Sales − Change in AR

For BHT, cash collections for 20X1 are therefore:

Cash Collections = $2,464 + $43,850 − $3,650
Cash Collections = $43,850 − ($3,650 − $2,464)
= $43,850 − $1,186 = $42,664

Management could possibly report fraudulent earnings by reporting nonexistent sales and accounts receivable. Note however that the increase in sales that result from this behavior would be offset by the increase in receivables in the determination of operating cash flows; i.e., operating cash flows are unaffected by accruals per se. It would be far more difficult to implement fraud that affected cash flows.

Because cash collections are less than sales, when we reported net income in the cash account, we overstated the effect of sales on cash. As a result, we need to adjust by reducing cash for the increase in accounts receivable. A simpler alternative to the previous calculation would be to identify the change in the accounts receivable account. With a net debit to the accounts receivable account, by default, we would need to credit the Cash account for this difference, thereby reducing the amount reported in net income in the Cash account from Transaction 1. The entry to record this is:

| | | | |
|---|---|---|---|
| (2) | Accounts receivable | 1,186 | |
| | Cash | | 1,186 |

This negative adjustment to cash matches the increase in the current operating asset, accounts receivable.

### Cost of Goods Sold Adjustment to Net Income

After revenues, cost of goods sold is typically the first expense that appears on the income statement. Understanding the cash flow impact of the cost of inventory sales requires considering two separate timing relationships: (1) the relationship between the purchase of inventory (INV) and its recognition as a cost when sold, and (2) the relationship between the purchase of inventory and the payment for that inventory.

Recall from Chapter 3 the cost of goods sold equation:

$$\begin{aligned}\text{Cost of Goods Sold} &= \text{Beginning Inventory} + \text{Purchases} - \text{Ending INV}\\ &= \text{Purchases} - (\text{Ending INV} - \text{Beginning INV})\\ &= \text{Purchases} - \text{Change in INV}\end{aligned}$$

Because we assume that all inventory is purchased on accounts payable (AP), we therefore calculate cash paid for purchases as:

$$\begin{aligned}\text{Payments} &= \text{Beginning AP} + \text{Purchases} - \text{Ending AP}\\ &= \text{Purchases} - (\text{Ending AP} - \text{Beginning AP})\\ &= \text{Purchases} - \text{Change in AP}\end{aligned}$$

The difference between the expense (cost of goods sold) on the income statement and the cash paid to suppliers can be explained by the change in accounts payable less the change in inventory:

$$\begin{aligned}&\text{Cost of Goods Sold} - \text{Payments}\\ &\quad = (\text{Purchases} - \text{Change in INV}) - (\text{Purchases} - \text{Change in AP})\\ &\quad = \text{Purchases} - \text{Purchases} - \text{Change in INV} + \text{Change in AP}\\ &\quad = \text{Change in AP} - \text{Change in INV}\end{aligned}$$

The cost of goods sold for BHT was \$37,272 during the current year. We can apply the above equations to calculate the purchases for the period as \$37,752 (= CGS + Ending INV − Beginning INV = 37,272 + 4,400 − 3,920). Then we can use the purchases to calculate the payments for the period as \$36,222 (= Purchases + Beginning AP − Ending AP = 37,752 + 5,140 − 6,671). The difference between the cost of goods sold reported in income and the payments is therefore \$1,051 (\$37,272 − 36,222). Notice that this amount equals the difference between the change in AP (1,531) and the change in INV (480).

Again, we can avoid calculations by recording an entry that explains the change in the balance of both inventory and accounts payable with the corresponding entry to the operating section of the cash account, as follows:

| | | | |
|---|---|---|---|
| (3) | Inventory | 480 | |
| | Cash | | 480 |

The change in accounts payable is:

| | | | |
|---|---|---|---|
| (4) | Cash | 1,531 | |
| | Acct. Payable | | 1,531 |

### Depreciation Adjustment to Net Income

Depreciation is a noncash expense that a firm recognizes for financial reporting. It represents the allocation of the cost of plant and equipment over its useful life. Because depreciation expense is noncash, the amount of expense is added back to earnings to arrive at cash from operations. Sometimes depreciation is mistakenly thought of as a source of cash. This is incorrect in that depreciation does not generate cash for a business. Rather, it is an expense that does not require the use of cash (beyond the amount previously reported as an investment activity on earlier cash flow statements).

For many companies, depreciation is a large expense. Hence, cash from operations may be considerably larger than net income. However, because BHT is a wholesaling company and it leases its warehouses, it does not have proportionately as much depreciation as companies with large amounts of plant and equipment (e.g., in Exhibit 5.3 you can see a fairly substantial adjustment for depreciation for Tech Data Corp.). The entry to add back the depreciation expense to net income is:

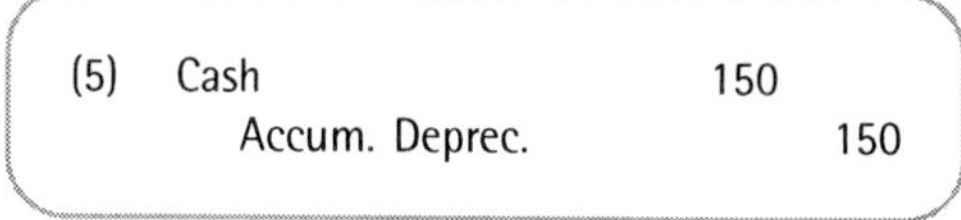

| | | | |
|---|---|---|---|
| (5) | Cash | 150 | |
| | Accum. Deprec. | | 150 |

### Prepaid Expense Adjustment to Net Income

BHT also had an increase in its prepaid expenses account. While we could calculate the differences between expenses related to this prepayment and the actual cash flows as we did with inventory, we can again avoid this. Instead, we simply determine how the balance in this operating asset account changes and record the appropriate entry, as follows:

| | | | |
|---|---|---|---|
| (6) | Prepaid Expenses | 360 | |
| | Cash | | 360 |

This completes the adjustments for the operating activities for BHT, as there are no other operating asset or liability accounts to consider. Other companies might also have accrued expenses, such as salaries payable, that would require adjustment. Further, GAAP requires firms to recognize all interest and tax cash flows in the operating section, so we might also have to adjust for changes in accounts such interest payable, taxes payable, and deferred taxes.

## WORKSHEET ENTRIES FOR CASH FROM INVESTING

Only one investing activity occurred for BHT for the year ending 20X2: the acquisition of property, plant, and equipment. The entry is:

| | | Debit | Credit |
|---|---|---|---|
| (7) | Property, Plant, and Equipment | 410 | |
| | Cash | | 410 |

Analyzing the cash from investing, however, may be more complex for a company that acquires or disposes of multiple groups of assets during a period. When a company disposes of a long-term asset such as property, plant, and equipment, it may report a gain or loss in the income statement from that transaction. Notice that the cash inflow from this sale should appear in the investing section. However, the gain or loss will appear in net income (and therefore will have been included in the cash account as part of net income in Transaction 1). Should this occur, we would need to remove the gain or loss from the operating section as the cash flows associated with these transactions should appear in the investing section. To remove a gain, we would credit the cash account; to remove a loss, we would debit the cash account.

## WORKSHEET ENTRIES FOR CASH FROM FINANCING

BHT had several financing transactions during 20X2, including payment of dividends of $500 million. Recall that dividends are a distribution to shareholders, and as such are not an expense to the company. Hence, dividends are considered a financing transaction. When the board of directors declares dividends, an entry is made debiting retained earnings and crediting dividends payable. Later, when the dividend is actually paid to stockholders, dividends payable is debited and cash is credited. Because there is no dividends payable account, we know that all declared dividends have also been paid. Thus, the aggregate entry to record this in the worksheet is:

| | | Debit | Credit |
|---|---|---|---|
| (8) | Retained earnings | 500 | |
| | Cash | | 500 |

BHT also issued a note payable. This is also a financing activity that increases the amount of cash available to BHT to fund its operations. The entry is:

| | | Debit | Credit |
|---|---|---|---|
| (9) | Cash | 550 | |
| | Note payable | | 550 |

**Cash**

| | | Debit | Credit | | |
|---|---|---|---|---|---|
| Bal. | | 567 | | | |
| **Operating:** | | | | | |
| Net Income | (1) | 1,023 | 1,186 | (2) | AR Increase |
| Increase in AP | (4) | 1,531 | 480 | (3) | Inventory Increase |
| Depreciation Expense | (5) | 150 | 360 | (6) | Increase in Prepaid Expenses |
| **Investing:** | | | | | |
| | | | 410 | (7) | Purchase PPE |
| **Financing:** | | | | | |
| Issue note payable | (9) | 550 | | | |
| Issue common stock | (10) | 625 | 500 | (8) | Pay Dividends |
| Bal. | | 1,510 | | | |

**Accumulated Depreciation–PPE**

| | Debit | Credit | |
|---|---|---|---|
| | | 60 | Bal. |
| | | 150 | (5) |
| | | 210 | Bal. |

**Accounts Payable**

| | Debit | Credit | |
|---|---|---|---|
| | | 5,140 | Bal. |
| | | 1,531 | (4) |
| | | 6,671 | Bal. |

**Accounts Receivable**

| | | Debit | Credit |
|---|---|---|---|
| Bal. | | 2,464 | |
| | (2) | 1,186 | |
| Bal. | | 3,650 | |

**Notes Payable**

| | Debit | Credit | |
|---|---|---|---|
| | | 400 | Bal. |
| | | 550 | (9) |
| | | 950 | Bal. |

**Inventory**

| | | Debit | Credit |
|---|---|---|---|
| Bal. | | 3,920 | |
| | (3) | 480 | |
| Bal. | | 4,400 | |

**Common Stock**

| | Debit | Credit | |
|---|---|---|---|
| | | 250 | Bal. |
| | | 50 | (10) |
| | | 300 | Bal. |

**Prepaid Expenses**

| | | Debit | Credit |
|---|---|---|---|
| Bal. | | 0 | |
| | (6) | 360 | |
| Bal. | | 360 | |

**Additional Paid-In Capital**

| | Debit | Credit | |
|---|---|---|---|
| | | 1,375 | Bal. |
| | | 575 | (10) |
| | | 1,950 | Bal. |

**PPE**

| | | Debit | Credit |
|---|---|---|---|
| Bal. | | 540 | |
| | (7) | 410 | |
| Bal. | | 950 | |

**Retained Earnings**

| | Debit | Credit | |
|---|---|---|---|
| | | 266 | Bal. |
| (8) | 500 | 1,023 | (1) |
| | | 789 | Bal. |

**Exhibit 5.8**
T-Account Worksheet Entries for BHT

**Exhibit 5.9**
Statement of Cash Flows for the Years Ending 20X2 and 20X1 Biohealth, Inc (BHT)

| | Year ending 12/31/20X2 | Year ending 12/31/20X1 |
|---|---|---|
| Cash from operations: | | |
| Net income | $1,023 | $416 |
| Add: noncash expenses | | |
| Depreciation | 150 | 60 |
| Changes in current assets and liabilities | | |
| Increase in accounts receivable | (1,186) | (2,464) |
| Increase in inventory | (480) | (3,920) |
| Increase in prepaid expenses | (360) | |
| Increase in accounts payable | 1,531 | 5,140 |
| Total cash from operations | 678 | (768) |
| Cash from investing | | |
| Purchase fixtures (PPE) | (410) | (0) |
| Total cash from investing | (410) | (0) |
| Cash from financing | | |
| Issuance of long-term note | 550 | 0 |
| Issuance of common stock | 625 | |
| Dividends | (500) | (150) |
| Total cash from financing | 675 | (150) |
| Total change in cash | 943 | (918) |
| Cash balance 1/1/20X2 | 567 | 1,485 |
| Cash balance 12/31/20X2 | $1,510 | $567 |

The final financing transaction affecting cash is the issuance of common stock. We record this as follows:

| | | Debit | Credit |
|---|---|---|---|
| (10) | Cash | 625 | |
| | Common Stock | | 50 |
| | Additional Paid-In Capital | | 575 |

At this point, we have analyzed all of the changes in the balance sheet accounts other than cash and, therefore, also explained all of the changes in cash. Exhibit 5.8 shows our completed worksheet entries. We can now construct the cash flow statement from the information contained within the Cash account in Exhibit 5.8. Exhibit 5.9 shows our completed cash flow statement for 2002, along with the cash flow statement from the prior year (which we presented in Chapter 3).

### SUMMARY OF CASH FLOW STATEMENT PREPARATION—INDIRECT METHOD

To summarize, the preparation of the cash flow statement involves the following steps:

Cash from operations:
- Net income
- Add:
  - Depreciation and amortization
  - Losses on sales of noncurrent assets and liabilities
  - Decreases in current operating assets other than cash
  - Increases in operating liabilities
- Deduct:
  - Gains on sales of noncurrent assets and liabilities
  - Increases in current operating assets other than cash
  - Decreases in current operating liabilities

Cash from investing:
- Add:
  - Proceeds from sales of noncurrent assets and nonoperating current assets
  - Proceeds from sales of other companies
- Deduct:
  - Purchases of noncurrent assets and nonoperating current assets
  - Acquisitions of other companies

Cash from financing:
- Add:
  - Issuance of debt (borrowings)
  - Issuance of stock
- Deduct:
  - Debt repayments
  - Dividends
  - Stock repurchases

## ARTICULATION OF THE CASH FLOW STATEMENT

As we said earlier, reconciling a firm's cash flow statement to its balance sheet and income statement can be a useful analytical tool. In simple cases, such as for Tofutti, the adjustments for changes in the various assets and liabilities that appear on the cash flow statement **articulate** with (are the same as) the corresponding changes in the balance sheet of the company. Exhibit 5.10 shows the balance sheet of Tofutti and includes a column that shows the net changes in the assets and liabilities of the firm. The operating items are highlighted. To demonstrate the articulation, look at the net change in inventories, accounts payable, and accrued expenses, and compare these changes with the net adjustments on the cash flow statement in Exhibit 5.2. Note that both the decrease in inventory and the increase in accounts payable result in a positive adjustment to net income consistent with the information in Exhibit 5.10.

The one account that does not appear to articulate is accounts receivable, where you will observe a change on the balance sheet of $585,000 and a change

**Exhibit 5.10**
Articulation with Balance Sheet

**The Real World**

**Tofutti Brands, Inc.**

TOFUTTI BRANDS, Inc.:
Balance Sheet

| | 12/29/2001 | 12/29/2000 | Net Change |
|---|---|---|---|
| Assets | | | |
| Current assets: | | | |
| Cash and equivalents | $2,329,000 | $2,211,000 | $ 118,000 |
| Short-term investments | 0 | 269,000 | (269,000) |
| Accounts receivable, net of allowance for doubtful accounts of $325,000 and $270,000, respectively | 1,461,000 | 876,000 | 585,000 |
| Inventories | 816,000 | 908,000 | (92,000) |
| Prepaid expenses | 10,000 | 9,000 | 1,000 |
| Deferred income taxes | 478,000 | 359,000 | 119,000 |
| Total current assets | 5,094,000 | 4,632,000 | 462,000 |
| Other assets: | | | |
| Other assets | 325,000 | 181,000 | 144,000 |
| | $5,419,000 | $4,813,000 | $606,000 |
| Liabilities and stockholders' equity | | | |
| Current liabilities: | | | |
| Notes payable | $ 0 | $ 8,000 | ($8,000) |
| Accounts payable and accrued expenses | 155,000 | 146,000 | 9,000 |
| Accrued compensation | 375,000 | 375,000 | 0 |
| Income taxes payable | 187,000 | 331,000 | (144,000) |
| Total current liabilities | 717,000 | 860,000 | (143,000) |
| Commitments and contingencies | | | |
| Stockholders' equity: | | | |
| Preferred stock—par value $.01 per share; authorized 100,000 shares, none issued | 0 | 0 | 0 |
| Common stock—par value $.01 per share; authorized 15,000,000 shares, issued and outstanding 6,091,267 shares at December 29, 2001 and 6,354,567 shares at December 30, 2000 | 61,000 | 64,000 | (3,000) |
| Less: Treasury stock, at cost (18,100 shares and 122,400 shares at December 29, 2001 and December 30, 2000, respectively) | (38,000) | (247,000) | 209,000 |
| Additional paid-in capital | 3,156,000 | 3,763,000 | (607,000) |
| Accumulated earnings | 1,523,000 | 373,000 | 1,150,000 |
| Total stockholders' equity | 4,702,000 | 3,953,000 | 749,000 |
| Total liabilities and stockholders' equity | $5,419,000 | $4,813,000 | $606,000 |

of ($625,000) on the cash flow statement. However, the adjustment for the provision for bad debts in the cash flow statement also affects the accounts receivable account, because accounts receivable is reported net of the effects of bad debts on the balance sheet. Therefore, if you net the $40,000 adjustment for bad debts on the cash flow statement with the change in accounts receivable of ($625,000), you get the same change in net accounts receivable of $585,000

Although not all countries require preparation of a cash flow statement, cash flows are increasingly important in international markets. Many companies voluntarily disclose cash flow statements. International accounting standards (IAS Number 7) state that the cash flow statement is a basic financial statement that explains the change in cash and cash equivalents during a period. In some countries, a funds flow statement is presented. The funds statement is similar to the cash flow statement, but it reconciles changes in total working capital rather than cash.

reported on the balance sheet. We will revisit the issue of accounting for bad-debts in Chapter 7. The cash statement will not always articulate with the balance sheet primarily due to acquisitions and foreign currency translation, both of which are beyond the scope of this book.

## SUPPLEMENTAL DISCLOSURES TO THE CASH FLOW STATEMENT

Companies often report supplemental disclosures on the cash flow statement. For example, GAAP requires firms to report all interest cash flows in the operating section. However, because users might want to view these amounts as financing cash flows, GAAP requires that firms disclose the dollar amount of interest cash flows that exist in the operating section. Many firms (like Tofutti) do this by providing supplemental cash flow information at the bottom of the statement, as shown in Exhibit 5.2. Other firms provide this information in a footnote to the financial statements. GAAP also requires all tax cash flows to be reported in the operating section, even though you could argue that they apply to all three sections. As a result, GAAP requires supplemental disclosure of the tax cash flows (again, see Exhibit 5.2).

In addition, a firm may engage in transactions that do not directly affect cash. However, if a transaction is considered a significant noncash activity, GAAP requires the firm to disclose this type of transaction as supplemental information. For example, Polaroid disclosed that, in 2000, it recorded noncash items of $22.9 million in cash flow from operating activities that consisted primarily of $12.0 million for the issuance of shares relating to their Retirement Savings Plan.

## INTERPRETING THE CASH FLOW STATEMENT

The cash flow statement provides both insights into the effectiveness with which a company manages its cash flows, as well as signals of the underlying quality of its earnings flows. Management of cash flows is an important activity in a business. If a company's operating cash inflows are insufficient to meet operating cash outflow demands, a company may be forced to engage in additional borrowing or issuance of stock, or sale of long-term assets to meet cash needs. If the firm cannot raise sufficient cash from these sources, it may be forced into bankruptcy. For example, Kmart Corporation filed Chapter 11 bankruptcy following a slow holiday season in 2001. One source of the company's problem was the inability to pay suppliers on a timely basis due to the declining sales.

In the case of Tofutti (Exhibit 5.2), you can see that net income increased each year over the most recent three-year period of time. However, you also can observe that cash from operating activities has declined over this same period. To understand why, look to the adjustments to net income. Observe that in 2000 the three largest negative adjustments were for inventories, deferred taxes, and accounts receivable.

Although we discuss deferred taxes in greater depth later in Chapter 10, the simple explanation for now is that federal tax laws often allow or require different accounting methods to be used in calculating taxable income than those methods used to report under GAAP. In the case of depreciation, for example, the tax code provides a benefit to businesses in the form of allowing for more rapid depreciation write-offs for tax purposes than firms use for financial reporting. As a result, tax payments are deferred because taxable income (i.e., income reported for tax purposes) is usually less than income before taxes reported for financial accounting purposes. Hence, tax payments are less than the tax expense reported on net income. The difference between the actual tax liability and the tax expense reported for financial reporting is reported as an account called "deferred taxes." Notice for Tofutti that the adjustment for deferred taxes goes in different directions in different years. Negative adjustments mean that there were net, noncash, income-improving effects during the year as a result of deferred taxes, and vice versa for positive adjustments.

While taxes are a difficult item to fully explain at this point, we can provide interpretation for the other two items. The negative adjustments for both the inventory and accounts receivable balance mean that they are increasing over the year. One explanation might be an increase in the firm's sales. Looking at the income statement for Tofutti (Exhibit 5.11), sales did significantly increase in 2000 over 1999. In fact, Tofutti's sales showed a growth of approximately

**Exhibit 5.11**
Income Statement

THE REAL WORLD

**Tofutti Brands, Inc.**

TOFUTTI BRANDS, Inc.:
Income Statement

| | 12/29/2001 | 12/29/2000 | 12/30/1999 |
|---|---|---|---|
| Net sales | $16,254,000 | $13,343,000 | $11,912,000 |
| Cost of sales | 10,550,000 | 8,192,000 | 7,349,000 |
| Gross profit | 5,704,000 | 5,151,000 | 4,563,000 |
| Operating expenses: | | | |
| Selling | 1,896,000 | 1,724,000 | 1,521,000 |
| Marketing | 391,000 | 277,000 | 199,000 |
| Research and development | 483,000 | 397,000 | 376,000 |
| General and administrative | 1,381,000 | 1,288,000 | 1,043,000 |
| | 4,151,000 | 3,686,000 | 3,139,000 |
| Operating income | 1,553,000 | 1,465,000 | 1,424,000 |
| Other income | 268,000 | 103,000 | 12,000 |
| Income before income tax | 1,821,000 | 1,568,000 | 1,436,000 |
| Income taxes | 671,000 | 612,000 | (586,000) |
| Net income | $1,150,000 | $956,000 | $850,000 |

12 percent. However, the net change in inventories of $342,000 (see the cash flow statement, Exhibit 5.2) to bring the balance in inventories to $908,000 (see the balance sheet, Exhibit 5.10) seems to be approximately a 60 percent increase in inventories. This seems out of line with the growth in sales. You would want to, therefore, seek a better explanation for what happened to inventories during 2000. Tofutti explains in its 10-K that part of this increase in inventory was the result of introducing new products (as well as an increase in sales).

In 2001 the largest single adjustment ($625,000) is in accounts receivable, while inventories actually show a decline. Again, looking at the income statement, you can see that sales grew substantially in 2001. This provides some explanation for the growth in accounts receivable, but the growth in accounts receivable is much higher (67 percent) than the annual sales growth (22 percent). If you read Tofutti's annual report, you will see that management indicates that sales increased significantly in the last quarter of the year that led to the high level of accounts receivable at year end. This is obviously good news in terms of future prospects as sales are going up significantly.

However, notice that in the current period this immense growth is starting to put a strain on cash from operations. This is not unusual for a rapid-growth company, but is something that the company must take into consideration in its planning to make sure that it does not end up in a cash crisis. Because Tofutti has a significant balance in its cash account (which has also been increasing over this period of time), it seems to be in no immediate danger of a cash crisis.

Interestingly, Tofutti reported a smaller amount of bad debt expense in 2001 than in 2000 despite a considerable increase in accounts receivable. Bad debt expense reported in 2001 was $40,000 compared to $60,000 in 2000 and 1999. In Tofutti's statement, the provision for bad debts (sometimes called bad debt expense) is a deduction in arriving at net income, for the company's estimate of the sales made during the period that it does not expect to collect (customers who never pay their bill). As such it is a noncash expense.

Further, as the balance sheet shows, although Tofutti's allowance for uncollectible accounts increased about 20 percent from 2000 to 2001, it did not increase proportionately to the increase in accounts receivable. This is a potential concern because a relationship usually exists between sales, accounts receivable, and the amount of estimated bad debt expense recognized (we discuss this in more depth in Chapter 7). If Tofutti underestimated its bad debt expense during 2001, the reported net accounts receivable may be too high, leading to overstated assets and earnings for Tofutti. The fact that a significant portion of Tofutti's increased earnings has not been collected may be a red flag, signaling to investors that future cash flows may not be as strong as the income statement alone suggests.

In summary, cash from operations can provide important information about a company's current and future prospects. GAAP guidelines for revenue and expense recognition are intended to result in earnings that, in part, reflect expected future cash flows, but both revenue and expense recognition rules, even if appropriately applied, involve significant estimation. Furthermore, managers may manage earnings to meet targeted earnings numbers or analyst's forecasts. As a result, careful study of cash from operations, together with the other financial statement information, may provide clues about a company's performance not evident from either statement alone. A company with increasing receivables, inventory, and payables may show positive earnings. However, if the company fails to generate cash and pay its creditors, the company may have financial distress regardless of the earnings reported.

## VALUATION IMPLICATIONS OF THE CASH FLOW STATEMENT

Cash flows can have significant implications for the valuation of firms, and firms like Procter & Gamble often refer to cash flow in their announcements of performance as shown in Exhibit 5.12.

The cash flow statement provides information not directly available from either the income statement or the balance sheet. In order for a company to retain and grow in value, it must not only earn a profit, it must also generate cash that can be used to invest in growing the business or paying dividends to shareholders. The cash flow statement provides insights not only into the sources of a company's cash, but how it uses that cash. Analysts look at both sources of information to help determine the company's ultimate profit potential.

Many companies even report performance in terms of cash flows as well as earnings. Cemex reported the following information about its 2001 fourth-quarter results (the term EBITDA stands for Earnings Before Interest, Taxes, Depreciation, and Amortization): "Cash earnings increased 11% to US$446 million, compared to US$400.5 million in the fourth quarter of 2000; lower interest expense enabled cash earnings to outpace EBITDA growth." Note that the "cash earnings" referred to in the Cemex disclosure is close to the cash from operations a firm would report on its cash flow statement except that it is before taxes and there are no adjustments for the changes in the working capital accounts (i.e., accounts receivable, inventories, accounts payable).

Analysts' estimates of the market value of firm typically rely on projections of free cash flows to equity holders as the principal input. **Free cash flows** to equity holders are the cash flows from operating activities, less cash flows used for investing activities, plus cash flows from debt financing activities, and less the increase in cash needed to sustain operations. Equivalently, if the entire increase in cash is required by operations, then free cash flows to equity holders

**Exhibit 5.12**

**THE REAL WORLD**

**Procter & Gamble**

CINCINNATI, January 31, 2002—The Procter & Gamble Company today reported that it exceeded consensus expectations for second quarter results. P&G delivered on the high end of its financial guidance for the October–December quarter, behind record quarter unit volume. For the quarter ended December 31, 2001, unit volume grew five percent versus the prior year led by double-digit growth in the health and beauty care businesses. Excluding acquisitions and divestitures, unit volume increased four percent. Net sales were $10.40 billion, up two percent versus one year ago. "We are seeing clear improvements in our results, and we're pleased to have met our commitments once again," said P&G President and Chief Executive A. G. Lafley. "We're continuing our unyielding focus on delivering better consumer value on our brands, building core categories, reducing the company's cost structure, and improving our cash flow."

are cash distributions to stockholders (dividends and stock repurchases), net of cash proceeds from stock issues. The concept is that these are cash flows that would be available to stockholders each period to provide a return to them.

To illustrate the calculation of free cash flows, consider the calculation of the free cash flows for our BHT example (refer back to Exhibit 5.11 for the line items on the cash flow statement):

| | |
|---|---|
| Cash from operations: | $678 |
| Cash from investing: | (410) |
| Cash from borrowing: | 550 |
| Change in cash: | (943) |
| Total free cash flows to equity: | ($125) |

Observe that the total free cash flows to equity (stockholders) can also be determined by subtracting proceeds from the issuance of stock from dividends ($500 − $625 = −$125). Note that we are assuming the entire change in cash ($943) is needed to support operations.

## SUMMARY AND TRANSITION

In order to help determine firm value, earnings must provide a signal of future cash flows. This means that earnings should be indicative of the firm's ability to generate future cash flows. This does not imply a one-to-one correlation between the pattern of operating cash flows and earnings, but it does suggest that revenues should reflect cash inflows in a systematic manner and that expenses should likewise reflect operating cash outflows. One way to think about earnings is as a smoothing of cash flows. The cash flow statement makes the association between earnings and operating cash flows more apparent than it might be otherwise.

Cash flows from investing activities are also important. In order to grow, companies must generally invest in long-term assets. The cash flow statement provides information about asset replacements as well as investments in new assets. The difference between operating cash flows and investing cash flows is a measure of the extent to which the company is able to finance its growth internally.

Cash flows from financing activities show amounts raised externally from creditors and stockholders, net of repayments and dividends. Careful analysis of this section provides indications of the company's debt commitments and dependency of stockholders in obtaining the cash necessary to sustain operating and investing activities.

We will return to an analysis of the information contained in the cash flow statement in the next chapter. As is probably evident from reading this chapter, full understanding of the cash flow statement can be daunting. While the cash flow statement can be complex, an investment in understanding its information is worth the time for anyone with a serious interest in interpreting and using financial statements. The cash flow statement can be a useful tool to help filter the information provided in the balance sheet and income statement in order to get a more complete view of a company's past and future expected performance.

# END OF CHAPTER MATERIAL

## KEY TERMS

Articulate
Direct Method
Free Cash Flows
Indirect Method

## ASSIGNMENT MATERIAL

### REVIEW QUESTIONS

1. Discuss why it is important for firms to prepare a cash flow statement in addition to an income statement.
2. Discuss how a firm's receivables, inventory, and payables policies affect cash flow relative to the income produced in a given period.
3. What is meant by a lead/lag relationship in terms of the cash flow statement?
4. For a firm with a cash flow problem, list at least three potential reasons for the problem, and suggest a possible solution for each of these reasons.
5. Describe the three major categories of cash flows that are required to be disclosed by SFAS 95.
6. Discuss the difference between the direct and indirect (reconciliation) methods for constructing the operation section of the cash flow statement.
7. Depreciation is a source of cash. Explain your reasons for agreeing or disagreeing with this statement.

### APPLYING YOUR KNOWLEDGE

8. In what section of the cash flow statement (operating, investing, or financing) would each of the following items appear?
   a. Purchase of net plant, property, and equipment
   b. Proceeds from a bank loan
   c. Collections from customers
   d. Dividends to stockholders
   e. Proceeds from the sale of marketable securities (stocks and bonds)
   f. Retirements of debt
   g. Change in accounts receivable
   h. Net income
   i. Gain/loss from the sale of plant, property, and equipment
   j. Cash proceeds from the sale of plant, property, and equipment
9. Explain why a high sales growth rate can create significant cash flow problems for a company.
10. Explain the timing of the cash flows related to the purchase, use, and ultimately the sale of property, plant, and equipment.

11. Discuss the classification of interest cash flows in the statement of cash flows under SFAS No. 95 and discuss why you believe this is either appropriate or not.

12. For each of the transactions listed below,

    a. Indicate the effect on balance sheet categories in the following format:

| Trans. # | Cash | Other Current Assets | Noncurrent Assets | Current Liabilities | Noncurrent Liabilities | Owners' Equity |
|---|---|---|---|---|---|---|

    b. State, for the transactions affecting cash, whether they relate to an operating, investing, or financing activity.

    Transactions:

    1. Credit purchases, $10,000
    2. Cash paid to suppliers, $8,000
    3. Credit sales, $25,000
    4. Cost of goods sold, $15,000
    5. Cash payments received on accounts receivable, $18,000
    6. Salaries accrued, $1,500
    7. Salaries paid (previously accrued), $1,000
    8. Machine purchased for $800 in cash
    9. Depreciation expense, $200
    10. Borrowed (long-term) $5,000 to purchase plant
    11. Interest of $50 is accrued and paid on the amount borrowed for the purchase of the plant
    12. Debentures worth $1,000 are issued
    13. Equipment having book value of $700 is sold for $700 cash
    14. Dividends declared, $350
    15. Dividends paid, $200
    16. Insurance premium for the next year paid, $175
    17. 1000 shares of stock issued at $1 per share
    18. Rent received for building, $250
    19. Income taxes accrued and paid, $325

13. For each of the transactions listed below,

    a. Indicate the effect on balance sheet categories in the following format:

| Trans. # | Cash | Other Current Assets | Noncurrent Assets | Current Liabilities | Noncurrent Liabilities | Owners' Equity |
|---|---|---|---|---|---|---|

    b. State, for the transactions affecting cash, whether they relate to an operating, investing, or financing activity.

    Transactions:

    1. 5,000 shares of common stock are issued at $10 per share.
    2. Plant, property, and equipment worth $120,000 is purchased for $50,000 in cash and the balance in common stock.

3. Rent payments of $5,000 are received in advance.
4. Sales contracts for $100,000 are signed and a $25,000 deposit is received in cash.
5. Merchandise inventory worth $85,000 is purchased on account.
6. Goods worth $15,000 were found defective and returned to suppliers. These goods had been purchased on account.
7. Sales were $175,000 of which $100,000 was on account.
8. Cash is paid to suppliers in the amount of $60,000.
9. Equipment recorded at $10,000 was destroyed by fire.
10. The company purchased 500 shares of X Company stock at $5 per share for short-term investment purposes.
11. The company purchased 2,000 shares of Z Company at $8 per share in an effort to buy a controlling interest in the company (a supplier).
12. Interest expense for the year amounted to $2,500 and was paid in cash.
13. The sales contract in question 4 was cancelled. $10,000 of the deposit was returned and the rest was forfeited.
14. A bank loan for $75,000 was taken out and is due in five years.
15. Equipment with a cost of $50,000 was sold for $60,000. The $60,000 was in the form of a note.
16. During the year, warranty services costing $3,500 were provided to customers. A provision for warranty services was provided in a separate transaction.
17. Depreciation for the year totaled $20,000.
18. Dividends of $10,000 were declared and $5,000 remained unpaid at year end.
19. Patents on a new manufacturing process were purchased for $5,000.
20. Research and development expenses amounted to $15,000 and were charged to expense as incurred.

14. Compute the cash flow from operations in each of the following cases:

| | I | II | III |
|---|---|---|---|
| Sales Revenues | $25,000 | $35,000 | $65,000 |
| Depreciation Expense | 3,000 | 5,000 | 20,000 |
| Cost of Goods Sold | 15,000 | 38,000 | 41,000 |
| Other Expenses | 1,500 | 700 | 1,200 |
| Dividends Paid | 3,000 | – | 1,000 |
| Increase (Decrease) in: | | | |
| Inventories | 5,000 | (10,000) | 15,000 |
| Accounts Receivable | 3,500 | 1,000 | (2,000) |
| Prepayments | (500) | (1,000) | 1,800 |
| Salaries Payable | (10,000) | 5,000 | (15,000) |
| Interest Payable | (5,000) | (500) | 5,000 |
| Other Current Liabilities | 8,000 | (10,000) | 800 |

**15.** Compute the cash flow from operations in each of the following cases:

| | I | II | III |
|---|---|---|---|
| Sales Revenues | $175,000 | $200,000 | $225,000 |
| Cost of Goods Sold | 100,000 | 185,000 | 195,000 |
| Depreciation | 20,000 | 15,000 | 10,000 |
| Interest Expense | 5,000 | 25,000 | 15,000 |
| Dividends Paid | 8,000 | – | 5,000 |
| Profit (Loss) on Sale of PP&E | – | (10,000) | 25,000 |
| Increase (Decrease) in: | | | |
| Common Stock | 10,000 | 5,000 | – |
| Bonds Payable | 20,000 | (30,000) | (15,000) |
| Interest Payable | (25,000) | (5,000) | 10,000 |
| Accounts Payable | (25,000) | 10,000 | 15,000 |
| Accounts Receivable | 50,000 | (40,000) | 35,000 |
| Inventories | (10,000) | (15,000) | 25,000 |
| PP&E | 100,000 | (50,000) | – |

**16.** Financial statement data for Dennison Corporation for 20X8 is as follows:

**Dennison Corporation**
**Comparative Balance Sheets**

| | 12/31/X7 | 12/31/X8 |
|---|---|---|
| Assets | | |
| Cash | $25,500 | $4,400 |
| Accounts Receivable | 59,000 | 35,000 |
| Inventories | 30,000 | 50,000 |
| Total Current Assets | 114,500 | 89,400 |
| Property, Plant, and Equipment | 165,000 | 180,000 |
| Accumulated Depreciation | (61,900) | (80,400) |
| Total Noncurrent Assets | 103,100 | 99,600 |
| Total Assets | $217,600 | $189,000 |
| Liabilities and Owners' Equity | | |
| Accounts Payable | $38,600 | $28,500 |
| Salaries Payable | 24,000 | 12,000 |
| Total Current Liabilities | 62,600 | 40,500 |
| Bank Loan | 50,000 | 40,000 |
| Total Liabilities | 112,600 | 80,500 |
| Common Stock | 100,000 | 100,000 |
| Retained Earnings | 5,000 | 8,500 |
| Total Liabilities and Owners' Equity | $217,600 | $189,000 |
| Income Statement | | |
| Sales | | $185,500 |
| Expenses: | | |
| Cost of Goods Sold | 87,500 | |
| Salaries Expense | 48,000 | |
| Depreciation Expense | 23,500 | |
| Interest Expense | 8,000 | |
| Loss on Sale of PP&E | 5,000 | |
| Total Expenses | | 172,000 |
| Net Income | | $13,500 |

Additional Information:

1. Equipment originally costing $35,000 was sold for $25,000.
2. Dividends declared and paid during the year were $10,000.

Required:

Prepare a statement of cash flows for Dennison Corporation for the year ended 12/31/X8, supported by a T-account worksheet. Use the indirect approach to prepare the operating section.

17. Financial statement data for Matrix, Incorporated is as follows:

**Matrix, Incorporated**
**Balance Sheets**

| | 12/31/X3 |
|---|---|
| Assets | |
| Cash | 15,500 |
| Accounts Receivable | 10,000 |
| Trade Notes Receivable | 5,000 |
| Inventories | 20,500 |
| Total Current Assets | 51,000 |
| Property, Plant, and Equipment | 160,000 |
| Accumulated Depreciation | (35,500) |
| Total Noncurrent Assets | 124,500 |
| Total Assets | $175,500 |
| Liabilities and Owners' Equity | |
| Accounts Payable | 5,000 |
| Salaries Payable | 18,000 |
| Total Current Liabilities | 23,000 |
| Bonds Payable | 50,000 |
| Total Liabilities | 73,000 |
| Common Stock | 100,000 |
| Retained Earnings | 2,500 |
| Total Liabilities and Owners' Equity | $175,500 |

**Matrix, Incorporated**
**Trial Balance for the Year Ended 12/31/X4**

| | Debits | Credits |
|---|---|---|
| Cash | $2,900 | |
| Accounts Receivable | 12,500 | |
| Prepaid Rent | 6,000 | |
| Inventories | 18,900 | |
| Cost of Goods Sold | 275,500 | |
| Depreciation Expense | 10,000 | |
| Rent Expense | 12,000 | |
| Interest Expense | 15,000 | |
| Salaries Expense | 24,000 | |
| Property, Plant, and Equipment | 160,000 | |
| Accumulated Depreciation | | $ 45,500 |
| Accounts Payable | | 13,800 |

| | Debits | Credits |
|---|---|---|
| Interest Payable | | 9,000 |
| Salaries Payable | | 6,000 |
| Bonds Payable | | 10,000 |
| Common Stock | | 100,000 |
| Retained Earnings | | 2,500 |
| Sales | | 350,000 |
| Totals | $536,800 | $536,800 |

Required:

a. Prepare an income statement and a reconciliation of retained earnings for the year ended 12/31/X4.

b. Prepare a balance sheet for the year ended 12/31/X4.

c. Prepare a statement of cash flows for the year ended 12/31/X4 supported by a T-account worksheet. Use the indirect approach to prepare the operating section.

18. The financial statement data for Crescent Manufacturing Company is as follows:

**Crescent Manufacturing Company**
**Comparative Balance Sheets**

| | 12/31/X0 | 12/31/X1 |
|---|---|---|
| Assets | | |
| Cash | 17,800 | 12,800 |
| Marketable Securities | 125,000 | 25,000 |
| Accounts Receivable | 38,600 | 69,600 |
| Prepaid Insurance | 6,000 | – |
| Inventories | 43,300 | 93,300 |
| Total Current Assets | 230,700 | 200,700 |
| Property, Plant, and Equipment | 225,000 | 300,000 |
| Accumulated Depreciation | (36,300) | (86,300) |
| Total Noncurrent Assets | 188,700 | 213,700 |
| Total Assets | $419,400 | $414,400 |
| Liabilities and Owners' Equity | | |
| Accounts Payable | 12,600 | 15,000 |
| Interest Payable | 8,000 | 5,600 |
| Dividends Payable | 20,000 | 30,000 |
| Total Current Liabilities | 40,600 | 50,600 |
| Mortgage Payable | 100,000 | 75,000 |
| Bonds Payable | 75,000 | 75,000 |
| Total Liabilities | 215,600 | 200,600 |
| Common Stock | 250,000 | 250,000 |
| Treasury Stock | (50,000) | (60,000) |
| Retained Earnings | 3,800 | 23,800 |
| Total Owners' Equity | 203,800 | 213,800 |
| Total Liabilities and Owners' Equity | $419,400 | $414,400 |

| | 12/31/X0 | 12/31/X1 |
|---|---|---|
| Income Statement | | |
| Sales | $508,000 | |
| Interest Revenue | 12,500 | |
| Gain on Sale of Marketable Securities | 25,000 | |
| Total Revenues | | $545,500 |
| Expenses: | | |
| Cost of Goods Sold | 330,000 | |
| Depreciation Expense | 50,000 | |
| Insurance Expense | 12,000 | |
| Interest Expense | 43,500 | |
| Salaries Expense | 60,000 | |
| Total Expenses | | 495,500 |
| Net Income | | $ 50,000 |

Additional Information:

1. 10,000 shares of Sigma Company, which were purchased at a cost of $10 per share, were sold at a price of $12.50 per share.
2. Dividends declared during the year amounted to $30,000 and remained unpaid at year end.

Required:

Prepare a statement of cash flows for Crescent Manufacturing Company for the year ended 12/31/X1 supported by a T-account worksheet. Use the indirect method to prepare the operation section.

19. The Balance Sheet for Simco Corporation as of the beginning and the end of the 20X1 appears below. During the year, no dividends were declared or paid, there was no sale of PP&E and no debt repaid. Net Income for the period was $35,000 and included $25,000 in depreciation expenses. Prepare a statement of cash flows for Simco Corporation for the current year and also prepare a T-account worksheet supporting the cash flow statement. Use the cash reconciliation approach.

**SIMCO CORPORATION**
**Balance Sheet**

| | 12/31/X0 | 12/31/X1 |
|---|---|---|
| Assets | | |
| Current Assets | | |
| Cash | $ 10,000 | $ 8,000 |
| Accounts Receivable | 86,000 | 100,000 |
| Inventories | 102,000 | 112,000 |
| Total Current Assets | 198,000 | 220,000 |
| Property, Plant, and Equipment | 485,000 | 600,000 |
| Less: Accumulated Depreciation | 125,000 | 150,000 |
| Total PP&E | 360,000 | 450,000 |
| Total Assets | $558,000 | $670,000 |

| | 12/31/X0 | 12/31/X1 |
|---|---|---|
| Liabilities and Owners' Equity | | |
| Current Liabilities | | |
| Accounts Payable | $ 78,000 | $ 95,000 |
| Wages Payable | 30,000 | 40,000 |
| Total Current Liabilities | 108,000 | 135,000 |
| Long-Term Debt | | |
| Bonds Payable | 100,000 | 125,000 |
| Total Liabilities | 208,000 | 260,000 |
| Owners' Equity | | |
| Common Stock | 150,000 | 175,000 |
| Retained Earnings | 200,000 | 235,000 |
| Total Liabilities and Owners' Equity | $558,000 | $670,000 |

**20.** Comparative Balance Sheets of Marvel Cosmetics Company for 20X2 are as follows:

MARVEL COSMETICS COMPANY
**Comparative Balance Sheet**

| | 12/31/X1 | 12/31/X2 |
|---|---|---|
| Assets | | |
| Current Assets | | |
| Cash | $ 188,000 | $ 200,000 |
| Accounts Receivable | 133,000 | 120,000 |
| Trade Notes Receivable | 61,000 | 70,000 |
| Inventory | 326,000 | 439,000 |
| Total Current Assets | 708,000 | 829,000 |
| Noncurrent Assets | | |
| Land | 500,000 | 525,000 |
| Machinery | 238,000 | 483,000 |
| Accumulated Depreciation | (97,500) | (143,000) |
| Total Noncurrent Assets | 640,500 | 865,000 |
| Total Assets | $1,348,500 | $1,694,000 |
| Liabilities and Owners' Equity | | |
| Current Liabilities | | |
| Accounts Payable | $ 158,000 | $ 145,000 |
| Interest Payable | 10,000 | 17,500 |
| Total Current Liabilities | 168,000 | 162,500 |
| Noncurrent Liabilities | | |
| Debentures | 200,000 | 350,000 |
| Total Liabilities | 368,000 | 512,500 |
| Owners' Equity | | |
| Common Stock | 550,000 | 650,000 |
| Retained Earnings | 430,500 | 531,500 |
| Total Owners' Equity | 980,500 | 1,180,500 |
| Total Liabilities and Owners' Equity | $1,348,500 | $1,694,000 |

Additional Information:

a. Net Income is $151,000 and includes depreciation expenses of $105,500.

b. Dividends declared and paid during the year were $50,000.

c. A machine costing $80,000 was sold at its book value of $20,000.

d. There was no Repayment of long-term debt.

Prepare a Statement of Cash Flows for Marvel Cosmetics Company for the year ended 12/31/X2, supported by a T-account worksheet.

21. The financial statement data for Pharmex Pharmaceutical Company for 20X5 is as follows:

| PHARMEX PHARMACEUTICAL COMPANY | 12/31/X4 | 12/31/X5 |
|---|---|---|
| Comparative Data | | |
| Debits | | |
| Cash | 80,000 | 50,000 |
| Accounts Receivable | 185,000 | 235,000 |
| Inventories | 296,000 | 325,000 |
| Machinery | 545,000 | 555,000 |
| Total | 1,106,000 | 1,165,000 |
| Credits | | |
| Accumulated Depreciation | 122,500 | 172,500 |
| Accounts Payable | 97,500 | 82,500 |
| Bonds Payable | 150,000 | 175,000 |
| Common Stock | 350,000 | 400,000 |
| Retained Earnings | 386,000 | 335,000 |
| Total | 1,106,000 | 1,165,000 |
| Income Statement Data | | |
| Sales | | 1,052,000 |
| Gain on Sale of PP&E | | 15,000 |
| Cost of Goods Sold | | 878,000 |
| Depreciation Expense | | 75,000 |
| Interest Expenses | | 60,000 |
| Rent Expense | | 85,000 |

Additional Information:

Acquisition cost of new machinery is $135,000. Old machinery having an original cost of $125,000 was sold at a gain of $15,000. Dividends of $20,000 were declared and paid.

a. Prepare an income statement including a reconciliation of retained earnings for the year ended 12/31/X5.

b. Prepare a statement of cash flows for Pharmex Pharmaceuticals Company for the year ended 12/31/X5 supported by a T-account work sheet.

22. From the perspective of a bank loan officer, discuss why the cash flow statement may or may not be more important in your analysis of a company that is applying for a loan.

23. From the perspective of a stock analyst, discuss why the cash flow statement may or may not be more important in your analysis of a company for which you must make a recommendation.

## USING REAL DATA

24. Use the data in the cash flow statement for Amazon.Com, Inc. to answer the questions that follow.

Amazon.com, Inc.
Consolidated Statements of Cash Flows
(in thousands)
Years Ended December 31,

| | 2001 | 2000 | 1999 |
|---|---|---|---|
| Cash and cash equivalents, beginning of period | $822,435 | $ 133,309 | $ 71,583 |
| Net loss | (567,277) | (1,411,273) | (719,968) |
| Adjustments to reconcile net loss to net cash used in operating activities: | | | |
| Depreciation of fixed assets and other amortization | 84,709 | 84,460 | 36,806 |
| Stock-based compensation | 4,637 | 24,797 | 30,618 |
| Equity in losses of equity-method investees, net | 30,327 | 304,596 | 76,769 |
| Amortization of goodwill and other intangibles | 181,033 | 321,772 | 214,694 |
| Noncash restructuring-related and other | 73,293 | 200,311 | 8,072 |
| Loss (gain) on sale of marketable securities, net | (1,335) | (280) | 8,688 |
| Other losses (gains), net | 2,141 | 142,639 | – |
| Noncash interest expense and other | 26,629 | 24,766 | 29,171 |
| Cumulative effect of change in accounting principle | 10,523 | – | – |
| Changes in operating assets and liabilities: | | | |
| Inventories | 30,628 | 46,083 | (172,069) |
| Prepaid expenses and other current assets | 20,732 | (8,585) | (54,927) |
| Accounts payable | (44,438) | 22,357 | 330,166 |
| Accrued expenses and other current liabilities | 50,031 | 93,967 | 95,839 |
| Unearned revenue | 114,738 | 97,818 | 6,225 |
| Amortization of previously unearned revenue | (135,808) | (108,211) | (5,837) |
| Interest payable | (345) | 34,341 | 24,878 |
| Net cash used in operating activities | (119,782) | (130,442) | (90,875) |
| Investing Activities: | | | |
| Sales and maturities of marketable securities | 370,377 | 545,724 | 2,064,101 |
| Purchases of marketable securities | (567,152) | (184,455) | (2,359,398) |
| Purchases of fixed assets, including internal use software and web-site development | (50,321) | (134,758) | (287,055) |

| | 2001 | 2000 | 1999 |
|---|---|---|---|
| Investments in equity-method investees and other investments | (6,198) | (62,533) | (369,607) |
| Net cash provided by (used in) investing activities | (253,294) | 163,978 | (951,959) |
| Financing Activities: | | | |
| Proceeds from exercise of stock options and other | 16,625 | 44,697 | 64,469 |
| Proceeds from issuance of common stock, net of issuance costs | 99,831 | – | – |
| Proceeds from long-term debt and other | 10,000 | 681,499 | 1,263,639 |
| Repayment of long-term debt and other | (19,575) | (16,927) | (188,886) |
| Financing costs | – | (16,122) | (35,151) |
| Net cash provided by financing activities | 106,881 | 693,147 | 1,104,071 |
| Effect of exchange-rate changes on cash and cash equivalents | (15,958) | (37,557) | 489 |
| Net increase (decrease) in cash and cash equivalents | (282,153) | 689,126 | 61,726 |
| Cash and cash Equivalents, end of period | $540,282 | $ 822,435 | $ 133,309 |
| Supplemental cash flow information: | | | |
| Fixed assets acquired under capital leases | $ 4,597 | $ 4,459 | $ 25,850 |
| Fixed assets acquired under financing agreements | 1,000 | 4,844 | 5,608 |
| Equity securities received for commerical agreements | 331 | 106,848 | 54,402 |
| Stock issued in connection with business acquisitions and minority investments | 5,000 | 32,130 | 774,409 |
| Cash paid for interest | 112,184 | 67,252 | 30,526 |

a. Why is net cash provided by operating activities less negative than net income for the three years presented?

b. What specific items contributed most to the greater net loss in 2000 than in the other two years?

c. How were investment activities in 1999 financed?

d. What trend do you observe for debt and related cash paid for interest over the three years presented?

e. What general concerns do you have about the future operating activities of the company based on your review of the cash flow statement for the three years presented?

**25.** Use the data in the cash flow statement for Barnes Group, Inc. to answer the questions that follow.

| BARNES GROUP, Inc.: Cash Flow | 12/31/2001 | 12/31/2000 | 12/31/1999 |
|---|---|---|---|
| Operating activities: | | | |
| Net income | $19,121,000 | $35,665,000 | $28,612,000 |
| Adjustments to reconcile net income to net cash provided by operating activities: | | | |
| Depreciation and amortization | 37,045,000 | 35,871,000 | 30,602,000 |
| Loss (gain) on disposition of property, plant, and equipment | 2,093,000 | (1,960,000) | (857,000) |
| Changes in assets and liabilities: | | | |
| Accounts receivable | 11,378,000 | 1,087,000 | (1,731,000) |
| Inventories | (3,629,000) | (7,631,000) | 1,980,000 |
| Accounts payable | 13,634,000 | (5,415,000) | 17,356,000 |
| Accrued liabilities | (5,552,000) | 1,026,000 | (9,524,000) |
| Deferred income taxes | 6,510,000 | 5,863,000 | 3,655,000 |
| Other | (13,700,000) | (12,649,000) | (7,296,000) |
| Net cash provided by operating activities | 66,900,000 | 51,857,000 | 62,797,000 |
| Investing activities: | | | |
| Proceeds from disposition of property, plant, and equipment | 1,093,000 | 2,744,000 | 1,929,000 |
| Capital expenditures | (22,365,000) | (26,575,000) | (27,222,000) |
| Business acquisitions, net of cash acquired | (1,036,000) | (104,935,000) | (92,239,000) |
| Redemption of short-term investments | – | – | 2,566,000 |
| Other | (4,286,000) | (5,776,000) | (2,019,000) |
| Net cash used by investing activities | (26,594,000) | (134,542,000) | (116,985,000) |
| Financing activities: | | | |
| Net (decrease) increase in notes payable | (1,583,000) | (5,201,000) | 5,249,000 |
| Payments on long-term debt | (28,000,000) | (60,000,000) | (70,000,000) |
| Proceeds from the issuance of long-term debt | 22,765,000 | 150,000,000 | 159,000,000 |
| Proceeds from the issuance of common stock | 2,845,000 | 3,920,000 | 1,486,000 |
| Common stock repurchases | (8,798,000) | (9,197,000) | (22,351,000) |
| Dividends paid | (14,806,000) | (14,677,000) | (14,564,000) |
| Proceeds from the sale of debt swap | 13,766,000 | – | – |
| Net cash (used) provided by financing activities | (13,811,000) | 64,845,000 | 58,820,000 |
| Effect of exchange rate changes on cash flows | (930,000) | (2,489,000) | (1,206,000) |
| Increase (decrease) in cash and cash equivalents | 25,565,000 | (20,329,000) | 3,426,000 |
| Cash and cash equivalents at beginning of year | 23,303,000 | 43,632,000 | 40,206,000 |
| Cash and cash equivalents at end of year | $48,868,000 | $23,303,000 | $43,632,000 |

**a.** What changes in assets and liabilities contributed most to the increase in net cash provided by operating activities in 2001 over that in 2000?

**b.** How were business acquisitions financed in 1999 and 2000?

**c.** What changes in financing activities do you observe in 2001 by comparison to the two previous years?

**d.** What is your general assessment of the company's ability to finance its investing activities from operating cash flows beyond 2001?

**26.** Use the data in the cash flow statement for GAP, Inc. to answer the questions that follow.

| GAP, Inc.: Cash Flow | 52 Weeks Ended Feb. 2, 2002 | 53 Weeks Ended Feb. 3, 2001 | 52 Weeks Ended Jan. 29, 2000 |
|---|---|---|---|
| Cash flows from operating activities: | | | |
| Net earnings (loss) | $ (7,764,000) | $877,497,000 | $1,127,065,000 |
| Adjustments to reconcile net earnings (loss) to net cash provided by operating activities: | | | |
| Depreciation and amortization | 810,486,000 | 590,365,000 | 436,184,000 |
| Tax benefit from exercise of stock options and vesting of restricted stock | 58,444,000 | 130,882,000 | 211,891,000 |
| Deferred income taxes | (28,512,000) | (38,872,000) | 2,444,000 |
| Change in operating assets and liabilities: | | | |
| Merchandise inventory | 213,067,000 | (454,595,000) | (404,211,000) |
| Prepaid expenses and other | (13,303,000) | (61,096,000) | (55,519,000) |
| Accounts payable | 42,205,000 | 249,545,000 | 118,121,000 |
| Accrued expenses | 220,826,000 | (56,541,000) | (5,822,000) |
| Deferred lease credits and other long-term liabilities | 22,390,000 | 54,020,000 | 47,775,000 |
| Net cash provided by operating activities | 1,317,839,000 | 1,291,205,000 | 1,477,928,000 |
| Cash flows from investing activities: | | | |
| Net purchase of property and equipment | (940,078,000) | (1,858,662,000) | (1,238,722,000) |
| Acquisition of lease rights and other assets | (10,549,000) | (16,252,000) | (39,839,000) |
| Net cash used for investing activities | (950,627,000) | (1,874,914,000) | (1,278,561,000) |
| Cash Flows from financing activities: | | | |
| Net increase (decrease) in notes payable | (734,927,000) | 621,420,000 | 84,778,000 |
| Proceeds from issuance of long-term debt | 1,194,265,000 | 250,000,000 | 311,839,000 |
| Payments of long-term debt | (250,000,000) | — | — |
| Issuance of common stock | 139,105,000 | 152,105,000 | 114,142,000 |
| Net purchase of treasury stock | (785,000) | (392,558,000) | (745,056,000) |
| Cash dividends paid | (76,373,000) | (75,488,000) | (75,795,000) |
| Net cash provided by (used for) financing activities | 271,285,000 | 555,479,000 | (310,092,000) |
| Effect of exchange rate fluctuations on cash | (11,542,000) | (13,328,000) | (4,176,000) |
| Net increase (decrease) in cash and equivalents | 626,955,000 | (41,558,000) | (114,901,000) |
| Cash and equivalents at beginning of year | 408,794,000 | 450,352,000 | 565,253,000 |
| Cash and equivalents at end of year | $1,035,749,000 | $408,794,000 | $ 450,352,000 |

**a.** What trend do you observe in net income for the three years presented?

**b.** Why does net cash provided by operating activities not display the same trend as noted in your answer to a.?

**c.** What other information from the cash flow statements can be used to explain the substantial increase in depreciation and amortization from 2001 to 2002?

**d.** How would you describe the events pertaining to debt that occurred in 2002?

**27.** Use the data in the cash flow statement for Polaroid Corporation to answer the questions that follow.

| POLAROID CORP.: Cash Flow | 12/31/1998 | 12/31/1999 | 12/31/2000 |
|---|---|---|---|
| Cash flows from operating activities: | | | |
| Net earnings/(loss) | $ (51,000,000) | $ 8,700,000 | $37,700,000 |
| Depreciation of property, plant, and equipment | 90,700,000 | 105,900,000 | 113,900,000 |
| Gain on the sale of real estate | (68,200,000) | (11,700,000) | (21,800,000) |
| Other noncash items | 62,200,000 | 73,800,000 | 22,900,000 |
| Decrease/(increase) in receivables | 79,000,000 | (52,700,000) | 41,800,000 |
| Decrease/(increase) in inventories | (28,400,000) | 88,000,000 | (100,600,000) |
| Decrease in prepaids and other assets | 39,000,000 | 62,400,000 | 32,900,000 |
| Increase/(decrease) in payables and accruals | 25,300,000 | (16,500,000) | 9,200,000 |
| Decrease in compensation and benefits | (21,000,000) | (72,500,000) | (105,000,000) |
| Decrease in federal, state, and foreign income taxes payable | (29,900,000) | (54,000,000) | (31,500,000) |
| Net cash provided/(used) by operating activities | 97,700,000 | 131,400,000 | (500,000) |
| Cash flows from investing activities: | | | |
| Decrease/(increase) in other assets | (25,400,000) | 16,500,000 | 4,500,000 |
| Additions to property, plant, and equipment | (191,100,000) | (170,500,000) | (129,200,000) |
| Proceeds from the sale of property, plant, and equipment | 150,500,000 | 36,600,000 | 56,600,000 |
| Acquisitions, net of cash acquired | (18,800,000) | – | – |
| Net cash used by investing activities | (84,800,000) | (117,400,000) | (68,100,000) |
| Cash flows from financing activities: | | | |
| Net increase/(decrease) in short-term debt (maturities 90 days or less) | 131,200,000 | (86,200,000) | 108,200,000 |
| Short-term debt (maturities of more than 90 days) | | | |
| Proceeds | 73,000,000 | 41,800,000 | – |
| Payments | (117,200,000) | (24,900,000) | – |
| Proceeds from issuance of long-term debt | – | 268,200,000 | – |
| Repayment of long-term debt | – | (200,000,000) | – |
| Cash dividends paid | (26,500,000) | (26,600,000) | (27,000,000) |
| Purchase of treasury stock | (45,500,000) | – | – |
| Proceeds from issuance of shares in connection with stock incentive plan | 6,000,000 | 300,000 | 100,000 |
| Net cash provided/(used) by financing activities | 21,000,000 | (27,400,000) | 81,300,000 |
| Effect of exchange rate changes on cash | 3,100,000 | 400,000 | (7,500,000) |
| Net increase/(decrease) in cash and cash equivalents | 37,000,000 | (13,000,000) | 5,200,000 |
| Cash and cash equivalents at beginning of year | 68,000,000 | 105,000,000 | 92,000,000 |
| Cash and cash equivalents at end of year | $105,000,000 | $92,000,000 | $97,200,000 |

**a.** Why is the upward trend in net earnings/(loss) not reflected in net cash provided/(used) by operating activities for the three years presented?

**b.** How were net additions to property, plant, and equipment in 2000 principally financed?

c. What would be a reasonable estimate of the change in property, plant, and equipment during 2000?

d. What indications are there that the company will need to seek external financing in 2001?

**28.** Use the data in the cash flow statement for Tech Data Corporation to answer the questions that follow.

| TECH DATA CORP.: Cash Flow | 01/31/2002 | 01/31/2001 | 01/31/2000 |
|---|---|---|---|
| Cash flows from operating activities: | | | |
| Cash received from customers | $17,511,511,000 | $20,114,486,000 | $16,788,960,000 |
| Cash paid to suppliers and employees | (16,406,265,000) | (20,047,551,000) | (16,684,316,000) |
| Interest paid | (55,871,000) | (94,823,000) | (69,554,000) |
| Income taxes paid | (72,745,000) | (62,048,000) | (34,176,000) |
| Net cash provided by (used in) operating activities | 976,630,000 | (89,936,000) | 914,000 |
| Cash flows from investing activities: | | | |
| Acquisition of businesses, net of cash acquired | (183,000) | (19,198,000) | (42,898,000) |
| Expenditures for property and equipment | (28,466,000) | (38,079,000) | (59,038,000) |
| Software development costs | (20,719,000) | (22,705,000) | (18,381,000) |
| Net cash used in investing activities | (49,368,000) | (79,982,000) | (120,317,000) |
| Cash flows from financing activities: | | | |
| Proceeds from the issuance of common stock, net of related tax benefit | 36,432,000 | 35,539,000 | 19,663,000 |
| Net (repayments) borrowings on revolving credit loans | (1,118,167,000) | 248,712,000 | 99,447,000 |
| Proceeds from issuance of long-term debt, net of expense | 284,200,000 | – | – |
| Principal payments on long-term debt | (634,000) | (557,000) | (162,000) |
| Net cash (used in) provided by financing activities | (798,169,000) | 283,694,000 | 118,948,000 |
| Effect of change in year end of certain subsidiaries (Note 3) | – | – | 23,626,000 |
| Effect of exchange rate changes on cash | (10,091,000) | (6,637,000) | – |
| Net increase in cash and cash equivalents | 119,002,000 | 107,139,000 | 23,171,000 |
| Cash and cash equivalents at beginning of year | 138,925,000 | 31,786,000 | 8,615,000 |
| Cash and cash equivalents at end of year | $ 257,927,000 | $ 138,925,000 | $ 31,786,000 |

| TECH DATA CORP.: Cash Flow | 01/31/2002 | 01/31/2001 | 01/31/2000 |
|---|---|---|---|
| Reconciliation of net income to net cash provided by (used in) operating activities: | | | |
| Net income | $ 110,777,000 | $177,983,000 | $127,501,000 |
| Adjustments to reconcile net income to net cash provided by (used in) operating activities: | | | |
| Depreciation and amortization | 63,488,000 | 63,922,000 | 57,842,000 |
| Provision for losses on accounts receivable | 40,764,000 | 41,447,000 | 40,877,000 |

| | 01/31/2002 | 01/31/2001 | 01/31/2000 |
|---|---|---|---|
| Special charges (Note 13) | 27,000,000 | – | – |
| Deferred income taxes | (11,848,000) | (1,789,000) | 1,306,000 |
| Changes in assets and liabilities: | | | |
| Decrease (increase) in accounts receivable | 314,000,000 | (313,197,000) | (202,790,000) |
| Decrease (increase) in inventories | 702,219,000 | (146,093,000) | (220,585,000) |
| (Increase) in prepaid and other assets | (6,248,000) | (11,603,000) | (25,430,000) |
| (Decrease) increase in accounts payable | (264,722,000) | 11,863,000 | 136,748,000 |
| Increase in accrued expenses | 1,200,000 | 87,531,000 | 85,445,000 |
| Total adjustments | 865,853,000 | (267,919,000) | (126,587,000) |
| Net cash provided by (used in) operating activities | $976,630,000 | $ (89,936,000) | $ 914,000 |

**a.** How does the format of the cash flow statements for this company differ from the format used by most companies?

**b.** What changes do you note in the reconciliation of net income to net cash provided by (used in) operating activities that most explain the dramatic increase in net cash provided by those activities?

**c.** How did the company finance its investing activities in 2000 and 2001?

**d.** Where were the funds obtained to repay borrowings on revolving credit loans in 2002?

**e.** What evidence is there that the company has reversed its growth during 2002 from what it was during the previous two years?

## BEYOND THE BOOK

**29.** For a company of your own choosing, answer the following questions related to its cash flow statement:

**a.** What is the trend in net income for the three years presented?

**b.** What is the trend in cash from operations for the three years presented?

**c.** In the most recent year, explain why the cash from operations differs from net income.

**d.** What other cash needs did the firm have in the most recent time period outside of operations?

**e.** Where did the company get the cash to cover the needs identified in part (d)?

**f.** What concerns do you have about the financial health of the company from your analysis of the cash flow statement?

CHAPTER 6

# Financial Statement Analysis

## Learning Objectives

After studying this chapter students should be able to:

1. Understand how to adjust financial statements to give effect to differences in accounting methods.
2. Be able to calculate and interpret common financial ratios.
3. Evaluate a firm's short-term and long-term debt repayment abilities and its profitability.
4. Have a basic understanding of methods of forecasting future revenues or earnings.
5. Understand the concept of present value and its application to valuing free cash flows and residual earnings.

**In late 2001 Starbucks Corp. announced that it had beat analysts' expectations** and reported a first quarter profit (for the quarter ended September 30, 2001) of 25 cents a share. The analysts' previous estimate was 23 cents a share. In the same announcement Starbucks also reported record revenues of $667 million, up 26 percent from $529 million in the same period a year ago. Earnings were $49 million, up 41% over the same period a year ago of $34.7 million. Starbucks also indicated that it had raised its own projections of the year's fiscal earnings by a penny per share.

Despite the very sizeable increase in revenues and earnings over the previous year for Starbucks, note that analysts' forecasts nearly matched Starbucks' reported amounts and thus we would expect very little adjustment to Starbucks' market value as a result of this disclosure. The prominence of revenues in this earnings release is consistent with analysts viewing changes in revenues as a measure of growth and, hence, as a key factor in forecasting future performance.

In virtually all cases, financial statement users are concerned with predicting future outcomes of a firm. However, these forecasts usually begin with an assessment of the firm's *past performance.* In this chapter, we'll show you how financial statement analysis provides this link from evaluating past performance to forecasting future expectations.

## OVERVIEW OF FINANCIAL STATEMENT ANALYSIS

**Financial statement analysis** refers to a set of procedures for transforming past data from a firm's published financial statements into information useful for future decisions. Many different types of decisions are based on financial statement analysis, such as whether to extend credit, buy or sell securities, or reward managers for their performance.

Financial statement analysis typically involves making **inter-temporal** (across time) and **cross-sectional** (across firms) comparisons. Inter-temporal comparisons help to identify trends in past data as well as reveal areas of concern that may warrant special attention. Cross-sectional comparisons (of a firm with its main rivals) indicate relative performance that may have a bearing on future market share. One complication in making both types of comparisons using raw financial statement data is the effect of changes or differences in firm size. For instance, if we were analyzing the pizza business and wanted to compare Domino's, Sbarro, and Bertucci's, they are very different in size with revenues of $1,275 million, $360 million, and $162 million, respectively. Analysts commonly adjust for such differences by using financial ratios in making these comparisons.

Another complication is that accounting policies may vary across time or across firms. When this occurs, analysts may need to adjust for these variations by restating financial statements in order to place them on a common basis. Such restatements answer the question of what the firm's financial statements would look like "as if" they had been prepared under the same set of accounting policies.

Once analysts transform the data into ratios and understand the trends that may be present, they next assess future prospects by constructing **operating forecasts,** for example, the forecast of net income from operations. A formal approach to forecasting extrapolates past operating data through statistical models that take advantage of inter-temporal relationships present in that data (these models are often called *time-series models*). Less formal approaches rely more on analysts' subjective judgments of future trends. Regardless of the approach used, operating forecasts should factor in the outlook for the industry and the economy as a whole, the company's business plan, and the nature of competition.

Exhibit 6.1
Consolidated Statements of Income

THE REAL WORLD

AnnTaylor Stores Corporation

| | 02/01/2003 | 02/01/2002 | 02/01/2001 |
|---|---|---|---|
| Net sales | $1,380,966,000 | $1,299,573,000 | $1,232,776,000 |
| Cost of sales | 633,473,000 | 651,808,000 | 622,036,000 |
| Gross margin | 747,493,000 | 647,765,000 | 610,740,000 |
| Selling, general, and administrative expenses | 612,479,000 | 576,584,000 | 501,460,000 |
| Amortization of goodwill | – | 11,040,000 | 11,040,000 |
| Operating income | 135,014,000 | 60,141,000 | 98,240,000 |
| Interest income | 3,279,000 | 1,390,000 | 2,473,000 |
| Interest expense | 6,886,000 | 6,869,000 | 7,315,000 |
| Income before income taxes | 131,407,000 | 54,662,000 | 93,398,000 |
| Income tax provision | 51,249,000 | 25,557,000 | 41,035,000 |
| Net income | $ 80,158,000 | $ 29,105,000 | $ 52,363,000 |

We're now ready to take a closer look at financial statement analysis. We'll use the data from AnnTaylor Stores Corporation (see Exhibits 6.1 and 6.2) to illustrate the process of financial statement analysis. Our first step is to review the financial statements to determine if they need to be restated.

## CREATING COMPARABLE DATA FOR FINANCIAL STATEMENT ANALYSIS

Analysts must often consider how a firm's financial statements would appear if it used a different accounting method. For example, analysts may seek to undo the effects of overly aggressive income recognition ("as if" restatements), assess the effects of an impending change in accounting policy, or compare the performance of firms that employ different accounting methods. These adjustments can be quite complex in some situations. A full understanding of restatements requires a level of understanding of accounting that is beyond the scope of this book. However, a basic knowledge of accounting is sufficient to understand the idea of restatements and how to make basic restatements. Here we provide examples of some common restatements. Let's review how analysts create comparable data for each of these situations.

### "AS IF" RESTATEMENTS

A useful technique in restating revenues, expenses, or income is to determine first how balances of related accounts appearing on comparative balance sheets would be affected; then, adjust the item in question by the change in the difference between the beginning and ending balances. For example, suppose a company recognized revenue for sales of goods or services at the time of delivery, despite considerable uncertainty about future collections from customers. Analysts determine the effect on the company's revenues, if it

**Exhibit 6.2**
Consolidated Balance Sheets

THE REAL WORLD

**AnnTaylor Stores Corporation**

| | 02/01/2003 | 02/01/2002 |
|---|---|---|
| Current assets: | | |
| Cash and cash equivalents | $ 212,821,000 | $ 30,037,000 |
| Accounts receivable, net | 10,367,000 | 65,598,000 |
| Merchandise inventories | 185,484,000 | 180,117,000 |
| Prepaid expenses and other current assets | 46,599,000 | 50,314,000 |
| Total current assets | 455,271,000 | 326,066,000 |
| Property and equipment, net | 247,115,000 | 250,735,000 |
| Goodwill, net | 286,579,000 | 286,579,000 |
| Deferred financing costs, net | 4,170,000 | 5,044,000 |
| Other assets | 17,691,000 | 14,742,000 |
| Total assets | $1,010,826,000 | $883,166,000 |
| Liabilities and stockholders' equity: | | |
| Current liabilities | | |
| Accounts payable | $ 57,058,000 | $ 52,011,000 |
| Accrued salaries and bonus | 27,567,000 | 12,121,000 |
| Accrued tenancy | 10,808,000 | 10,151,000 |
| Gift certificates and merchandise credits redeemable | 25,637,000 | 21,828,000 |
| Accrued expenses | 30,125,000 | 37,907,000 |
| Current portion of long-term debt | | 1,250,000 |
| Total current liabilities | 151,195,000 | 135,268,000 |
| Long-term debt, net | 121,652,000 | 118,280,000 |
| Deferred lease costs and other liabilities | 23,561,000 | 17,489,000 |
| Stockholders' equity common stock, $.0068 par value; 120,000,000 shares authorized; 48,932,860 and 48,275,957 shares issued, respectively | 332,000 | 328,000 |
| Additional paid-in capital | 500,061,000 | 484,582,000 |
| Retained earnings | 296,113,000 | 218,600,000 |
| Deferred compensation on restricted stock | (3,968,000) | (9,296,000) |
| | 792,538,000 | 694,214,000 |
| Treasury stock, 4,050,972 and 4,210,232 shares, respectively, at cost | (78,120,000) | (82,085,000) |
| Total stockholders' equity | 714,418,000 | 612,129,000 |
| Total liabilities and stockholders' equity | $1,010,826,000 | $883,166,000 |

adopted the less-aggressive procedure of delaying recognition until cash was received, as follows:

> Revenue (as if recognized at time of collection) =
> Revenue (as Reported) + Decrease (−Increase) in Accounts Receivable

Consider the data from AnnTaylor. From Exhibit 6.1 we find reported revenues of $1,381.0 (all numbers in millions, rounded to the nearest hundred thousand). From Exhibit 6.2, we compute a decrease in accounts receivable of \$55.2 (\$10.4 − \$65.6). Thus, if AnnTaylor recognized revenue as it collected cash from customers, revenues would equal \$1,436.2 (\$1,381.0 + \$55.2).

Inventories provide another illustration. Different firms often value inventories under different methods, such as the "first-in, first-out" (FIFO) and "last-in, first-out" (LIFO) methods. For instance, Ford Motor Company uses LIFO, whereas Dell Computer uses FIFO. As discussed in more detail in Chapter 8, LIFO usually results in higher costs of goods sold and lower inventory levels on the balance sheet than FIFO. However, GAAP requires firms that apply the LIFO method to include a disclosure explaining the net difference in inventory values as a result of applying these two methods. Firms often report this difference, known as the LIFO reserve, in a footnote. Using these data, you can calculate what the cost of goods sold would have been under FIFO using the following calculation:

Cost of goods sold (as if FIFO had been used) =
Cost of goods sold (as reported, LIFO) + Decrease (−Increase) in LIFO Reserve

One last illustration of the adjustment process relates to a company's accounting treatment of warranty expenses. Most companies, for example Ford Motor Company, recognize warranty costs (on an estimated basis) as expenses at the time of sale rather than when paid. Suppose, however, that an analyst wants to determine a company's warranty settlement cost. In this case, we adjust the expense under the former treatment to determine the amount of claims settled as follows:

Warranty Expense (as if recorded when settled) =
Warranty Expense (as reported) + Decrease (−Increase) in Warranties Payable

**THINKING GLOBALLY**

## International Accounting Issues

Because countries employ different accounting standards, analysts frequently need to make adjustments before conducting a cross-sectional analysis across countries. For example, Canadian companies selectively capitalize (record as assets) research and development (R&D) costs at the time these costs are incurred, while U.S. companies are required by GAAP to write off (record as expenses) those costs immediately.

If research and development (R&D) costs were initially recorded as an asset (as they might be under Canadian standards) and subsequently amortized as an expense, then one could calculate what R&D expense would be reported under the U.S. policy (which requires immediate recognition as an expense when the expenditures are made) as shown below:

R&D Expense (U.S.) = R&D Amortization Expense (Canadian)
+ Increase (−Decrease) in Unamortized R&D Costs (Canadian)

Note that adjustments made to the income statement might also affect the calculation of income taxes, and therefore all as-if adjustments should also include adjustments for the tax effects.

Note that all of these adjustments focus on the income statement. In each case, however, to maintain the accounting equation, an impact also occurs on the balance sheet through an adjustment of an asset or a liability account. Further, because these adjustments affect net income, a change also occurs in retained earnings. For example, if a company begins accruing an expense that it previously recognized only when paid, then the balance in accrued liabilities increases, expenses on the income statement also increase, and the balance in retained earnings decreases by the reduction in net income.

Finally, note that some changes in the timing of revenue and expense recognition materially affect only the balance sheet. For example, as mentioned, Canadian companies are allowed to capitalize (record as an asset) some research and development (R&D) costs and then later amortize the costs to income. Suppose that a particular Canadian company capitalized costs in an amount equal to its amortization expense in the year you are analyzing. If you were to adjust the statements to conform to U.S. GAAP (where the firm must expense all R&D as incurred), the adjusted expense would be the same as the original expense and therefore there would be no effect of this adjustment on the income statement. However, the balance sheets would still differ as both assets and retained earnings would be lower if no R&D costs had ever been capitalized. In other words, balance sheet restatements reflect the cumulative effects (the effects of applying the new method in all prior years) of differences in accounting methods, whereas income statement restatements reflect only the current year effect.

## MANDATED ACCOUNTING CHANGES

Accounting rule changes by the FASB and the SEC frequently occur. Accordingly, analysts need to be aware of the consequences of these changes on the financial statements. However, analysts are assisted with this task as follows:

- The FASB and the SEC typically specify how firms must handle these mandated changes within the financial statements.
- Firms usually document these changes in the footnotes of the financial statements in the period in which the change is made.
- The FASB and the SEC often require that firms also restate past financial statements to give effect to the mandated change in question.
- In some cases, these changes require that the cumulative effects on income of applying the new rules be shown as a separate line item in the income statement for the year in which the change is made.
- Auditors call attention to accounting rule changes in their report to stockholders.

Hence, a question seldom arises as to whether a change has occurred.

The greater challenge for analysts in dealing with mandated accounting changes is to evaluate the economic consequences of the change. For example, suppose a firm previously issued debt containing a covenant (a contractual restriction) that requires net worth (stockholders' equity) determined under GAAP to stay above a specified level. Now suppose that the FASB changes a rule governing revenue recognition, with the result of reducing the firm's net income to the point where it violates the covenant. To avoid this, the firm might have to cut its dividend. This might cause the value of the company's stock to fall due to an increase in risk, because of the reduction of cash flows (dividends) to shareholders.

Another consequence of a change to a more conservative method of revenue recognition might be to alter the incentives (often earnings-based bonuses) to managers provided by compensation contracts. For example, consider an executive who receives a bonus if reported income exceeds a certain level. If the accounting change makes it highly unlikely that this level will be reached in the year of change, no matter how much effort the executive applies, he or she may decide to postpone initiatives until the following year when it is more likely that he or she would receive the bonus. This reduced effort may negatively affect firm value.

## DISCRETIONARY ACCOUNTING CHANGES

Within the GAAP framework, managers have considerable discretion in their choices of accounting treatments. Further, evidence suggests that managers make use of their discretion in responding to incentives and furthering the interests of shareholders (when their incentives are aligned). Beyond the consideration of the comparability of the data that result when the change occurs, the bigger issues for analysts are the motivation of the firm's management and the potential for significant economic consequences.

For example, consider firms in an industry that seeks trade relief. These firms must show they have been injured by the anticompetitive practices of foreign rivals. Managers in these companies would have an incentive to make accounting decisions that lower their reported income, in order to demonstrate such injury. Evidence (Lenway and Rayburn, *Contemporary Accounting Research,* 1992) does indicate that in the mid-1980s, U.S. semiconductor producers generally had higher negative accruals coincident with petitions alleging dumping by Japanese producers.

Accounting treatments may also influence real investment and financing decisions. For example, firms generally do not recognize changes in the market value of debt (sometimes referred to as unrealized holding gains and losses) that result when interest rates in the economy change. However, a company seeking to increase or decrease its reported income for reasons mentioned above might decide to retire its debt early, causing the recognition of the gain or loss.

Finally, note that accounting decisions might serve as signaling devices, whereby a firm may be able to persuade investors that it has more favorable future cash flow prospects. For example, as we will see in Chapter 8, if a firm uses the LIFO method of valuing inventories for tax purposes, it must also use this same method for reporting to its shareholders (in periods of rising prices, LIFO results in lower reported net income and therefore lower tax payments). Theorists suggest that firms choosing to forego the tax benefits of LIFO by using FIFO for reporting purposes (and hence for tax purposes) may be signaling that they have stronger cash flow prospects than comparable firms that use LIFO.

Once analysts complete reviewing a firm's financial statements, and restating as necessary, calculating ratios can lead to more meaningful information. In the next section, we'll see how to use ratios to analyze a firm's past performance, which is the next step in financial statement analysis.

> Firms using LIFO could mimic the firms with stronger cash flow prospects by also choosing FIFO. However, they may find the loss of tax benefits to outweigh the benefits of not having investors learn that they have weaker cash flow prospects.

## USING FINANCIAL RATIOS TO ASSESS PAST PERFORMANCE

To assess a firm's past performance from periodic financial statements, analysts must first adjust the contents for inter-temporal changes or cross-sectional variations in firm size. For example, it does not mean much when assessing operating efficiency to compare income either over time for a firm that is changing in size or between small and large firms. Analysts remove effects of scale (size) by employing financial ratios. Financial ratios are often broadly organized into those that assess profitability and those that assess debt-repayment ability.

### ASSESSING PROFITABILITY

From an investor's perspective, **rate of return on equity (ROE)** presents a comprehensive accounting measure of a firm's performance. For a company with only common stock outstanding (we consider other types of stock in Chapter 12), we determine ROE as follows:

$$\text{ROE} = \frac{\text{Net Income}}{\text{Average Stockholders' Equity}}$$

Because a firm earns net income over a period of time, the denominator of this ratio also reflects the level of stockholders' investment over this same period of time. Hence, it makes sense to calculate the average amount invested during the period in the denominator. Most analysts compute the average as simply the sum of the beginning and ending balances of stockholders' equity, divided by two. The implicit assumption in this computation is that the change in balances remained uniform over the period. If the change in balances varied over the period, analysts might then use more sophisticated averaging techniques.

ROE is an accounting measure of the profitability of the firm's past investments. We can compare this measure to the expected rate of return investors require in order to buy the firm's stock, called the cost of equity. Investors measure returns on the firm's stock from market data such as dividends and changes in market prices. The expected rate of return on the firm's stock depends on the risks that equity holders cannot eliminate through holding a well-diversified portfolio (in other words, a portfolio of a wide variety of stocks); something that we discuss further in Chapter 14. An ROE greater than the cost of equity suggests that the firm has been successful in finding projects to invest in whose returns exceed investors' expectations. However, a firm's ability to consistently find projects that result in an ROE in excess of its cost of equity is likely to be limited by competitors attracted to the same projects. Accordingly, in the long run we would anticipate that ROE would converge toward the cost of equity and that the ROE of firms in the same industry would converge to the industry average.

ROE can be decomposed into both a measure of the efficiency with which a firm uses its assets to generate income and of the capital structure of the firm.

$$\text{ROE} = \frac{\text{Net Income}}{\text{Average Assets}} \times \frac{\text{Average Assets}}{\text{Average Stockholders' Equity}}$$

The first component is commonly referred to as **rate of return on assets (ROA),** and the second component is commonly referred to as **financial leverage.** Thus, a shorthand expression for ROE is:

$$\text{ROE} = \text{ROA} \times \text{Leverage}$$

ROA can be further decomposed into profit margin and asset turnover:

$$\text{ROA} = \frac{\text{Net Income}}{\text{Sales}} \times \frac{\text{Sales}}{\text{Average Assets}}$$

or:

$$\text{ROA} = \text{Profit Margin} \times \text{Total Asset Turnover}$$

This decomposition allows us to distinguish between operating strategies that emphasize profit per dollar of sales (profit margin) versus sales per dollar of investment in assets (total asset turnover).

For AnnTaylor, we calculate ROE and ROA as follows:

$$ROE = \frac{80.2}{(714.4 + 612.1)/2} = 12.1\%$$

$$ROA = \frac{80.2}{1{,}381} \times \frac{1{,}381}{(1{,}010.8 + 883.2)/2} = 8.5\%$$

$$ROA = 5.8\% \times 1.46 = 8.5\%$$

ROA, as a measure of return on investment on assets, is complicated by employing a numerator (net income) that includes the return to debtholders in the form of interest expense. An alternative measure, more focused on the efficiency of assets employed in the firm's operating activities, is the **rate of return on capital (ROC).** Here, the numerator of ROC uses operating income. Operating income can be obtained by adding back interest expense, net of taxes, to net income. Because this ratio is an after-tax ratio, we must adjust for taxes related to interest expense. In the denominator, debt and stockholders' equity replace total assets, to represent the net assets contributed by the firm's capital suppliers (total assets less operating liabilities, i.e., liabilities other than debt).

$$\text{ROC} = \frac{\text{Net Income} + \text{Interest Expense} \times (1 - \text{tax rate})}{\text{Average Debt} + \text{Average Stockholders' Equity}}$$

We calculate ROC for AnnTaylor as follows:

$$ROC = \frac{80.2 + 6.9 \times (1 - 51.2/131.4)}{((121.7 + 23.6 + 1.3 + 118.3 + 17.5)/2 + (714.4 + 612.1)/2)} = 10.3\%$$

We obtain the tax rate by comparing the tax expense reported by AnnTaylor ($51.2) with the income before tax ($131.4), resulting in a tax rate of 39 percent (51.2/131.4). We determine the total debt by adding together the long-term debt and the deferred lease cost and other liabilities on the balance sheet (including the current portion of long-term debt from the current liability section). We can then compare the above measure to the composite market return required by the suppliers of both debt and equity capital, commonly referred to as the company's **weighted average cost of capital (WACC).** However, this calculation is beyond the scope of this book. We will provide more discussion on estimating the cost of equity capital in Chapter 14.

Shareholders of a firm leverage their investment by borrowing additional funds from debtholders to invest in additional assets. **Trading on equity** refers to the use of leverage to generate a higher ROE for shareholders. Because ROC provides a measure of the return to investments in assets (before distributions to any capital suppliers), shareholders can generate higher returns to themselves (ROE) as long as ROC on assets financed through debt exceeds the after-tax interest rate charged by debtholders, in other words, the cost of debt capital. Whether stockholders will benefit from trading on equity in the long run depends on the trade-off between the added risk of their position and the added expected return. Note that AnnTaylor generated a ROE of 12.1 percent, versus a ROA of 8.5 percent and a ROC of 10.3 percent. This indicates that they have used leverage to their shareholders' advantage, as ROE is greater than either ROA or ROC.

Recall from the decomposition of ROA that we calculate profit margin by dividing net income by sales. To further explore factors that influence profit margin, we can prepare a common size income statement. A **common size income statement** expresses each component of net income as a percent of sales. Exhibit 6.3 presents common size income statements for AnnTaylor.

The advantage of a common size statement is that it allows analysts to identify factors responsible for changes in profit margin. For example, rising product costs that are not passed on to customers might be reflected in higher cost of sales, as a percent of sales, and lower gross profit margins. Similarly, holding unit costs constant, a change in pricing policy might be evident from a comparison of gross profit margins. Administrative and marketing efficiencies may

**Exhibit 6.3**
Common Size Income Statement

**THE REAL WORLD**

**AnnTaylor Stores Corporation**

| | 02/01/2003 | 02/01/2002 | 02/01/2001 |
|---|---|---|---|
| Net sales | 100.0% | 100.0% | 100.0% |
| Cost of sales | 45.9% | 50.2% | 50.5% |
| Gross margin | 54.1% | 49.8% | 49.5% |
| Selling, general, and administrative expenses | 44.4% | 44.4% | 40.7% |
| Amortization of goodwill | 0.0% | 0.8% | 0.9% |
| Operating income | 9.8% | 4.6% | 8.0% |
| Interest income | 0.2% | 0.1% | 0.2% |
| Interest expense | 0.5% | 0.5% | 0.6% |
| Income before income taxes | 9.5% | 4.2% | 7.6% |
| Income tax provision | 3.7% | 2.0% | 3.3% |
| Net income | 5.8% | 2.2% | 4.2% |

also become more apparent when the direct effects of growth in sales are removed.

In Exhibit 6.3, Net Income (as a percent of sales in 2003) is 5.8 percent, the same amount we calculated in the Profit Margin Ratio component of ROA. Net Income in 2003 presents a significant improvement as indicated by the increase in profit margin to 5.8 percent from the 2.2 percent in 2002. Reviewing the common size income statement, we identify this change as a direct result of a significant improvement in the cost of sales relative to sales revenues (50.5 percent to 45.9 percent), as well as a decline in the amortization of goodwill (which disappeared in 2003).

As another example of how to interpret the common size income statement, in Exhibit 6.4 find the common size income statement for Amazon.com for the years 2000 through 2002. Note that Amazon was able to maintain its gross profit percentage at approximately 25 percent over the three years. However, it cut its total operating expenses from 55 percent of sales to 24 percent of sales over

**Exhibit 6.4**
Amazon.com, Inc. Common Size Income Statement

**THE REAL WORLD**

**Amazon.Com, Inc.**

Amazon.com, Inc.
Common Size Income Statement

| | 12/31/2002 | 12/31/2001 | 12/31/2000 |
|---|---|---|---|
| Net sales | 100% | 100% | 100% |
| Cost of sales | 75% | 74% | 76% |
| Gross profit | 25% | 26% | 24% |
| Operating expenses: | 0% | 0% | 0% |
| Fulfillment | 10% | 12% | 15% |
| Marketing | 3% | 4% | 7% |
| Technology and content | 5% | 8% | 10% |
| General and administrative | 2% | 3% | 4% |
| Stock-based compensation | 2% | 0% | 1% |
| Amortization of goodwill and other intangibles | 0% | 6% | 12% |
| Restructuring-related and other | 1% | 6% | 7% |
| Total operating expenses | 24% | 39% | 55% |
| Loss from operations | 2% | −13% | −31% |
| Interest income | 1% | 1% | 1% |
| Interest expense | −4% | −4% | −5% |
| Other income (expense), net | 0% | 0% | 0% |
| Other gains (losses), net | −2% | 0% | −5% |
| Net interest expense and other | −5% | −4% | −9% |
| Loss before equity in losses of equity method investees | −4% | −17% | −40% |
| Equity in losses of equity-method investees, net | 0% | −1% | −11% |
| Loss before change in accounting principle | −4% | −18% | −51% |
| Cumulative effect of change in accounting principle | 0% | 0% | 0% |
| Net loss | −4% | −18% | −51% |

this same period. Note further that this resulted in the conversion of an operating loss of 31 percent from operations in 2000 to a gain of 2 percent from operations in 2002. While Amazon has still shown a net loss, this analysis implies that it has demonstrated significant progress in trying to achieve profitability from its operations.

## ASSESSING TURNOVER RATIOS

Total asset turnover, as depicted in the decomposition of ROA, equals sales divided by total assets. The concept of a turnover is that we invest in assets to sell goods and services. We then expect that our investment in assets will be converted (or turned over) into sales. For AnnTaylor this ratio is 1.46, indicating that the investment in total assets is converted or turned over into sales 1.46 times a year. This ratio reflects significant averaging, as property and equipment turns over much less than 1.46 times a year and merchandise inventories turn over much more frequently. As a result, analysts seeking a better understanding of the company's performance in managing its operating assets may find it useful to consider more specific asset turnover ratios, including accounts receivable and inventory turnovers.

We calculate accounts receivable turnover and inventory turnover as follows:

$$\text{Receivables Turnover} = \frac{\text{Sales}}{\text{Average Receivables}}$$

$$\text{Inventory Turnover} = \frac{\text{Cost of Goods Sold}}{\text{Average Inventories}}$$

This type of ratio provides a measure of how many times a firm converts a particular asset into a sale (inventory turnover) or how much a firm needs a particular type of asset to support a given level of sales (accounts receivable turnover). In effect, asset turnover ratios reflect the ability of the company to efficiently use its assets to generate sales.

Often, we convert turnover ratios into an alternative form to represent the number of days that a firm, in a sense, holds an asset, as follows:

$$\text{Days Receivables} = \frac{\text{Average Receivables}}{\text{Average Sales per day}}$$

or:

$$\text{Days Receivables} = \frac{365}{\text{Receivables Turnover}}$$

$$\text{Days Inventory} = \frac{\text{Average Inventories}}{\text{Average Cost of Goods Sold per day}}$$

or:

$$\text{Days Inventory} = \frac{365}{\text{Inventory Turnover}}$$

Decreases in receivables and inventory turnover ratios, or increases in days receivables and inventory, may indicate collection and sales problems, respectively.

Similarly, accounts payable turnover reflects the efficiency with which a firm manages its credit from its suppliers, or alternatively, how much credit the firm needs in support of its sales efforts. We calculate this ratio as follows:

$$\text{Payables Turnover} = \frac{\text{Cost of Goods Sold}}{\text{Average (Accounts) Payable}}$$

$$\text{Days Payables} = \frac{\text{Average (Accounts) Payable}}{\text{Average Cost of Goods Sold per day}}$$

or:

$$\text{Days Payables} = \frac{365}{\text{Payables Turnover}}$$

Other turnover ratios consider various asset groupings such as:

$$\text{Working Capital Turnover} = \frac{\text{Sales}}{\text{Average Current Assets} - \text{Average Current Liabilities}}$$

$$\text{Capital Assets Turnover} = \frac{\text{Sales}}{\text{Average Plant, Property, and Equipment}}$$

Here again, lower turnover ratios may indicate deterioration in operating efficiency.

We calculate the applicable turnover ratios for AnnTaylor as follows:

$$\text{Receivables Turnover} = \frac{1{,}381}{(10.4 + 65.6)/2} = 36.3$$

$$\text{Days Receivables} = \frac{365}{36.3} = 10$$

$$\text{Inventory Turnover} = \frac{633.5}{(185.5 + 180.1)/2} = 3.4$$

$$\text{Days Inventory} = \frac{365}{3.4} = 107.3$$

$$\text{Payables Turnover} = \frac{633.5}{(57.1 + 52.0)/2} = 11.6$$

$$\text{Days Payables} = \frac{365}{11.6} = 31.4$$

$$\text{Working Capital Turnover} = \frac{1{,}381}{(455.3 + 326.1)/2 - (151.2 + 135.3)/2} = 5.6$$

$$\text{Capital Assets Turnover} = \frac{1{,}381}{(247.1 + 250.7)/2} = 5.5$$

Looking at these ratios, we can make several observations about AnnTaylor. The days in receivables seems to be relatively small. However, recognize that many of AnnTaylor's sales are for cash. Therefore, by including total sales in the numerator of the turnover ratio we have overstated the sales that result in receivables. This results in an understatement of the days to collect from credit sales. Further recognize that AnnTaylor's credit sales are typically via a nonproprietary credit card and those are immediately converted into cash. Inventory turns over more than three times a year. For a clothing retailer such as AnnTaylor, this makes sense as its product line changes from one season to the next. It also appears that AnnTaylor receives approximately 30 days of credit from their suppliers as the days of payables is slightly over 30 days.

In addition to turnover ratios, we can prepare a common size balance sheet to assess the investments being made in asset categories as well as the amounts and forms of financing. A **common size balance sheet** expresses each line item as a percent of total assets. Exhibit 6.5 presents common size balance sheets for AnnTaylor.

**Exhibit 6.5**
Common Size Balance Sheet

THE REAL WORLD

**AnnTaylor Stores Corporation**

| | 02/01/2003 | 02/01/2002 |
|---|---|---|
| Current assets | | |
| Cash and cash equivalents | 21.1% | 3.4% |
| Accounts receivable, net | 1.0% | 7.4% |
| Merchandise inventories | 18.3% | 20.4% |
| Prepaid expenses and other current assets | 4.6% | 5.7% |
| Total current assets | 45.0% | 36.9% |
| Property and equipment, net | 24.4% | 28.4% |
| Goodwill, net | 28.4% | 32.4% |
| Deferred financing costs, net | 0.4% | 0.6% |
| Other assets | 1.8% | 1.7% |
| Total assets | 100.0% | 100.0% |
| Liabilities and stockholders' equity: | | |
| Current liabilities | | |
| Accounts payable | 5.6% | 5.9% |
| Accrued salaries and bonus | 2.7% | 1.4% |
| Accrued tenancy | 1.1% | 1.1% |
| Gift certificates and merchandise credits redeemable | 2.5% | 2.5% |
| Accrued expenses | 3.0% | 4.3% |
| Current portion of long-term debt | 0.0% | 0.1% |
| Total current liabilities | 15.0% | 15.3% |
| Long-term debt, net | 12.0% | 13.4% |
| Deferred lease costs and other liabilities | 2.3% | 2.0% |
| Stockholders' equity common stock, $.0068 par value; 120,000,000 shares authorized; 48,932,860 and 48,275,957 shares issued, respectively | 0.0% | 0.0% |
| Additional paid-in capital | 49.5% | 54.9% |
| Retained earnings | 29.3% | 24.8% |
| Deferred compensation on restricted stock | −0.4% | −1.1% |
| | 78.4% | 78.6% |
| Treasury stock, 4,050,972 and 4,210,232 shares, respectively, at cost | −7.7% | −9.3% |
| Total stockholders' equity | 70.7% | 69.3% |
| Total liabilities and stockholders' equity | 100.0% | 100.0% |

In looking at this common size balance sheet, a couple of questions arise. For example, why have accounts receivable and inventory declined? If production costs have declined as shown on the income statement, perhaps the carrying value of inventory has also declined. This, however, does not explain the change in accounts receivable. As sales have actually increased during the year, we would have to investigate further to understand this change. By reading the details of the 10-K report for AnnTaylor, we discover that the firm sold the receivables associated with its proprietary credit card in fiscal year 2003 (we will refer to the fiscal year as the year in which the fiscal year ended, e.g., AnnTaylor ended fiscal year 2003 on February 1, 2003). This resulted in the much lower level of receivables at the end of 2003.

Analysts are often led to search other sources of information to answer the questions that are raised by financial statement analysis such as the changes in accounts receivable for AnnTaylor.

In terms of its financing, the common size balance sheet indicates that AnnTaylor finances its assets with approximately 12 percent long-term debt and 70 percent equity (relative to total assets). This leads us to the next section in which we focus on the ability of the company to pay its long-term debt.

## ASSESSING DEBT REPAYMENT ABILITY

Analysts assessing a company's debt-paying ability often separate short-term and long-term debt-paying ability. While this distinction may be somewhat arbitrary, a qualitative difference exists in how we measure the ability of a firm to repay debt that either matures before cash flows are generated by future operations or concurrently with those flows.

## SHORT-TERM DEBT

Measures of the firm's ability to meet current obligations from existing assets include:

$$\text{Current Ratio} = \frac{\text{Current Assets}}{\text{Current Liabilities}}$$

$$\text{Quick Ratio} = \frac{\text{Cash, Marketable Securities, and Receivables}}{\text{Current Liabilities}}$$

$$\text{Cash Ratio} = \frac{\text{Cash and Cash Equivalent Investments}}{\text{Current Liabilities}}$$

These ratios primarily differ by the ease and speed with which assets included in the numerator can be converted to cash. Inventories are the furthest removed, as sales of inventory often give rise to receivables before producing cash. Receivables are closer to being converted to cash but are less easily converted than marketable securities. Low ratios may suggest future problems in repaying short-term liabilities as they become due.

The following ratios reflect AnnTaylor's short-term debt-repayment ability:

$$\text{Current Ratio} = \frac{455.3}{151.2} = 3$$

$$\text{Quick Ratio} = \frac{212.8 + 10.4}{151.2} = 1.5$$

$$\text{Cash Ratio} = \frac{212.8}{151.2} = 1.4$$

Due to the significant changes in cash and receivables that we noted earlier, these ratios may differ somewhat in the current year. In fact, when we compute them for the prior year, the ratios are 2.4, 0.7, and 0.2, respectively.

## LONG-TERM DEBT

In the long term, a firm's ability to meet obligations is closely related to its ability to generate cash flows from operations. Interest coverage ratios consider the ability of the firm either to earn sufficient income or produce sufficient cash to make interest payments on the long-term debt.

$$\text{Interest Coverage} = \frac{\text{Income before Interest and Tax Expenses}}{\text{Interest Expense}}$$

The interest coverage ratio is based on net income, a long-run predictor of cash from operations but is not a cash flow measure itself. Some analysts also compute the cash equivalent ratio as follows:

$$\text{Interest Coverage} = \frac{\text{Cash from Operations before Interest and Tax Payments}}{\text{Interest Payments}}$$

Why do we compute income or cash before taxes? Recall that a firm meets its interest requirements before taxes are assessed. Low interest coverage ratios imply a greater risk of being unable to service debt as a consequence of fluctuations in operating results.

A different perspective on repayment ability focuses on debt capacity as measured by balance sheet leverage ratios:

$$\text{Debt Equity Ratio} = \frac{\text{Short-term Debt} + \text{Long-term Debt}}{\text{Stockholders' Equity}}$$

The debt-equity ratio predominantly measures the financial risk when assessing the risk/expected return trade-off relevant to investors. The more debt a company has, the more interest payments the company will be obligated to pay before common stock investors can earn a return on their investment.

The following ratios reflect AnnTaylor's long-term debt repayment ability and financial risk:

$$\text{Interest Coverage} = \frac{151.4 + 6.9}{6.9} = 20$$

$$\text{Debt Equity Ratio} = \frac{121.6}{714.4} = .2$$

We calculate the cash flow measure of interest coverage from information contained in the cash flow statement (not included here). In the statement, we see that cash from operations equaled \$155.5 in 2003. In the supplemental disclosure to the statement, we find interest payments of \$1.3 and tax payments of \$40.1 (all figures in millions). We therefore calculate the cash measure as 151.5 ((\$155.5 + 1.3 + 40.1)/1.3). This amount is primarily due to a large portion of the company's interest expense being noncash expenses.

We have reviewed many financial ratios and how to compute them. Exhibit 6.6 provides a summary listing. Next, let's review how we can use this information

**Exhibit 6.6**
Summary Table of Ratios

$$\text{ROE} = \frac{\text{Net Income}}{\text{Average Stockholders' Equity}}$$

$$\text{ROA} = \frac{\text{Net Income}}{\text{Sales}} \times \frac{\text{Sales}}{\text{Average Assets}}$$

$$\text{ROC} = \frac{\text{Net Income} + \text{Interest Expense} \times (1 - \text{tax rate})}{\text{Average Debt} + \text{Average Stockholders' Equity}}$$

$$\text{Receivables Turnover} = \frac{\text{Sales}}{\text{Average Receivables}}$$

$$\text{Days Receivables} = \frac{365}{\text{Receivables Turnover}}$$

$$\text{Inventory Turnover} = \frac{\text{Cost of Goods Sold}}{\text{Average Inventories}}$$

$$\text{Days Inventory} = \frac{365}{\text{Inventory Turnover}}$$

$$\text{Payables Turnover} = \frac{\text{Cost of Goods Sold}}{\text{Average (Accounts) Payable}}$$

$$\text{Days Payables} = \frac{365}{\text{Payables Turnover}}$$

$$\text{Working Capital Turnover} = \frac{\text{Sales}}{\text{Average Current Assets} - \text{Average Current Liabilities}}$$

$$\text{Capital Assets Turnover} = \frac{\text{Sales}}{\text{Average Plant, Property, and Equipment}}$$

$$\text{Current Ratio} = \frac{\text{Current Assets}}{\text{Current Liabilities}}$$

$$\text{Quick Ratio} = \frac{\text{Cash, Marketable Securities, and Receivables}}{\text{Current Liabilities}}$$

$$\text{Cash Ratio} = \frac{\text{Cash and Cash Equivalent Investments}}{\text{Current Liabilities}}$$

$$\text{Interest Coverage} = \frac{\text{Income Before Interest and Tax Expenses}}{\text{Interest Expense}}$$

$$\text{Debt/Equity Ratio} = \frac{\text{Short-term Debt} + \text{Long-term Debt}}{\text{Stockholders' Equity}}$$

to get a better understanding of a firm's past performance as well as make more accurate forecasts of the future.

## USING FINANCIAL RATIOS TO ASSESS COMPARATIVE PERFORMANCE

Ratios can be used to assess comparative performance. To do so, the analyst typically would look for trends in the data both across time (*inter-temporal* comparisons) and across firms (*cross-sectional* comparisons).

### INTER-TEMPORAL COMPARISONS

We use inter-temporal comparisons of financial ratios to help reveal changes in performance as well as identify causes for those changes. For example, AnnTaylor's ROE increased from 4.9 percent (29.1/(612.1 + 574)/2) in fiscal year 2002 to 12.1 percent in 2003. From the common-size income statements (Exhibit 6.3), we find that the major cause of this improvement results from the change in profit margins (from 2.2 percent to 5.8 percent). Further investigation points to a reduction in cost of sales as a percent of sales (from 50.2 percent to 45.9 percent). In turn, from management's discussion and analysis (not included here but available in the 10-K report), we note that the higher percent cost of sales in 2001 is a consequence of an inventory write-down (inventory values written down resulting in a loss) in that year.

Another significant change pertains to AnnTaylor's short-term debt-paying ability. The current ratio, quick ratio, and cash ratio all increased significantly during fiscal year 2003. Most of the change in these ratios relates to an increase in cash, as reflected in the cash ratio that went from 0.2 at the end of fiscal year 2002 to 1.4 at the end of fiscal year 2003. Offsetting some of the increase in the current and quick ratios due to cash is the decline in the accounts receivable. Again, management's discussion and analysis provide an explanation: the company sold its proprietary credit card receivables during fiscal year 2003. Further, we observe that the company's receivables turnover increased from 21 (1,299.6/(65.6 + 58)/2) to 36.3 during that year.

### CROSS-SECTIONAL COMPARISONS

Another dimension in the use of financial ratios to evaluate performance lies in cross-sectional comparisons with other companies, especially those in the same industry. In order to illustrate, we calculated similar ratios from the Talbots' financial statements (Exhibits 6.7 and 6.8). Talbots, like AnnTaylor, is also a women's clothing retailer specializing in classic styles.

Exhibit 6.9 provides a comparison of the ratios for AnnTaylor and Talbots. Looking first at profitability:

| | AnnTaylor | Talbots |
|---|---|---|
| ROE | 12.1% | 21.3% |
| ROA | 8.5% | 14.2% |
| ROC | 10.3% | 18.0% |

Exhibit 6.7
Statement of Net Income

THE REAL WORLD

Talbots

| | 02/01/2003 | 02/01/2002 | 02/01/2001 |
|---|---|---|---|
| Net sales | $1,595,325,000 | $1,612,513,000 | $1,594,996,000 |
| Costs and expenses: | | | |
| Cost of sales, buying, and occupancy | 963,501,000 | 967,163,000 | 936,009,000 |
| Selling, general, and administrative | 435,757,000 | 435,334,000 | 467,324,000 |
| Operating income: | 196,067,000 | 210,016,000 | 191,663,000 |
| Interest | | | |
| Interest expense | 3,262,000 | 6,102,000 | 7,706,000 |
| Interest income | 409,000 | 927,000 | 3,364,000 |
| Interest expense, net | 2,853,000 | 5,175,000 | 4,342,000 |
| Income before taxes | 193,214,000 | 204,841,000 | 187,321,000 |
| Income taxes | 72,455,000 | 77,840,000 | 72,119,000 |
| Net Income | $120,759,000 | $127,001,000 | $115,202,000 |

| | 02/01/2003 | 02/01/2002 | 02/01/2001 |
|---|---|---|---|
| Net sales | 100.0% | 100.0% | 100.0% |
| Costs and expenses: | | | |
| Cost of sales, buying, and occupancy | 60.4% | 60.0% | 58.7% |
| Selling, general, and administrative | 27.3% | 27.0% | 29.3% |
| Operating income: | 12.3% | 13.0% | 12.0% |
| Interest | | | |
| Interest expense | 0.2% | 0.4% | 0.5% |
| Interest income | 0.0% | 0.1% | 0.2% |
| Interest expense, net | 0.2% | 0.3% | 0.3% |
| Income before taxes | 12.1% | 12.7% | 11.7% |
| Income taxes | 4.5% | 4.8% | 4.5% |
| Net Income | 7.6% | 7.9% | 7.2% |

Talbots surpasses AnnTaylor on all the above measures of profitability. We can trace a major cause of this higher performance to selling, general, and administrative expenses from a common size income statement (shown in Exhibit 6.7). These expenses are only 27.3 percent for Talbots as compared to 44.3 percent for AnnTaylor. Total asset turnover provides another contributing factor to the difference in these rates of return (1.9 for Talbots versus 1.5 for AnnTaylor). AnnTaylor does a better job of collecting on its receivables but is less efficient with regard to its inventory turnover.

From a debt-repayment point of view, Talbots also has an advantage in the long-run in that its interest coverage ratio is 60. However, it does have a slightly higher debt-to-equity ratio at 0.28 and its current, quick, and cash ratios are all less favorable than AnnTaylor's at 2.95, 1.4, and 0.17, respectively.

**Exhibit 6.8**
Balance Sheet

THE REAL WORLD

**Talbots**

| | 02/01/2003 | 02/01/2002 |
|---|---|---|
| Current assets: | | |
| Cash and cash equivalents | $ 25,566,000 | $ 18,306,000 |
| Customer accounts receivable, net | 181,189,000 | 172,183,000 |
| Merchandise inventories | 175,289,000 | 183,803,000 |
| Deferred catalog costs | 5,877,000 | 8,341,000 |
| Due from affiliates | 8,793,000 | 9,618,000 |
| Deferred income taxes | 10,255,000 | 8,222,000 |
| Prepaid and other current assets | 28,929,000 | 29,089,000 |
| Total current assets | 435,898,000 | 429,562,000 |
| Property and equipment, net | 315,227,000 | 277,576,000 |
| Goodwill, net | 35,513,000 | 35,513,000 |
| Trademarks, net | 75,884,000 | 75,884,000 |
| Deferred income taxes | 0 | 3,595,000 |
| Other assets | 9,403,000 | 8,934,000 |
| Total Assets | $871,925,000 | $831,064,000 |
| Current liabilities: | | |
| Accounts payable | $ 48,365,000 | $ 49,645,000 |
| Accrued income taxes | 11,590,000 | 1,019,000 |
| Accrued liabilities | 87,986,000 | 79,628,000 |
| Total current liabilities | 147,941,000 | 130,292,000 |
| Long-term debt | 100,000,000 | 100,000,000 |
| Deferred rent under lease commitments | 20,688,000 | 19,542,000 |
| Deferred income taxes | 2,921,000 | 0 |
| Other liabilities | 32,699,000 | 13,354,000 |
| Commitments | | |
| Stockholders equity: | | |
| Common stock, $0.01 par value; 200,000,000 authorized; 75,270,013 shares and 74,935,856 share issued, respectively, and 57,505,802 shares and 60,382,406 shares outstanding, respectively | 753,000 | 749,000 |
| Additional paid-in capital | 389,402,000 | 378,955,000 |
| Retained earnings | 572,741,000 | 472,594,000 |
| Accumulated other comprehensive income (loss) | (15,437,000) | (5,508,000) |
| Restricted stock awards | (78,000) | (697,000) |
| Treasury stock, at cost:17,764,211 shares and 14,553,450 shares, respectively | (379,705,000) | (278,217,000) |
| Total stockholders' equity | 567,676,000 | 567,876,000 |
| Total liabilities and stockholders' equity | $871,925,000 | $831,064,000 |

While the assessment of past performance is useful, analysts are primarily concerned with forecasting the future. To that end, analysts often use their analysis of past performance to assist them in the forecasting of the future results of the firm. We now turn to a discussion of forecasting.

**Exhibit 6.9**
Ratio Comparison of Ann Taylor and Talbots

THE REAL WORLD

**Ann Taylor and Talbots**

| Ratio | Ann Taylor | Talbots |
|---|---|---|
| ROE | 12.1% | 21.3% |
| ROA | 8.5% | 14.2% |
| Profit Margin | 5.8% | 7.6% |
| Total Asset Turnover | 1.46 | 1.90 |
| ROC | 10.3% | 18.0% |
| Receivables Turnover | 36.3 | 9.0 |
| Days of Receivables | 10.0 | 40.4 |
| Inventory Turnover | 3.4 | 5.4 |
| Days of Inventory | 107.3 | 68.0 |
| Accounts Payable Turnover | 11.6 | 19.7 |
| Days of Accounts Payable | 31.4 | 18.6 |
| Working Capital Turnover | 5.6 | 5.4 |
| Capital Asset Turnover | 5.5 | 5.4 |
| Current Ratio | 3 | 2.95 |
| Quick Ratio | 1.5 | 1.4 |
| Cash Ratio | 1.4 | 0.17 |
| Interest Coverage | 20 | 60 |
| Debt/Equity | 0.2 | 0.28 |

## FORECASTING

The financial analyst's principal stock-in-trade lies in forming estimates of firm values based on forecasts of future earnings or cash flows. In developing forecasts, analysts may use their understanding of markets for the firm's products or services to model supply and demand, formal statistical methods to exploit past observations in characterizing time series behavior, experience and judgment to determine future trends, or some combination of these approaches. The value of a forecast ultimately is derived from improved decision making based on the estimates that the forecast produces.

Evidence indicates that the market may react differentially to whether a firm meets or fails to meet analysts' forecasts, although the evidence is mixed as to the direction. See Skinner and Sloan, *Review of Accounting Studies* (2002) and Payne and Thomas, *The Accounting Review* (2003).

Forecasting future operating performance usually begins with predicting sales. There are many ways in which to approach this task. An economist might form a set of equations that models industry supply and demand (called *structural* equations as they describe the structure of market supply and demand conditions faced by the firm). Economists may then use estimates of these equations to predict the future price of a firm's output, which, when combined with projected production, would lead to a forecast of sales. The data required by such a model might include wages of workers and income of consumers, implying the need to forecast these factors.

An alternative modeling approach looks for a functional relationship between sales and time. By examining past observations of sales, analysts may detect a systematic relationship between sales and the passage of time that can be reasonably portrayed by a mathematical equation. For example, sales might be growing at a fixed rate such as 2 percent a year or it might be growing at a certain percentage of another variable, such as population growth.

Less-formal approaches to forecasts rely on analysts' intuition and judgment. The simplest approach would be to predict that next period's sales would equal this period's sales. Another approach might be to portray future sales as a weighted average of current sales and the previous forecast. Last, but not least, rather than rely on economic or mathematical models or simply intuition, we can instead build a statistical model of time series behavior from an analysis of past observations based only on the data. In other words, an analyst might statistically examine the properties of the data themselves to specify a forecasting model. Let's look at this approach in more detail.

## TIME SERIES ANALYSIS

Time series analysis basically estimates a model of the process generating the variable of interest (in our case, sales) from past observations. Typically, the initial step in identifying such a model is to estimate the *statistical correlations* (how one variable behaves relative to another) between lagged observations. For example, current sales might be correlated with sales of the previous period, sales of two periods ago, sales of three periods ago, and so on. These correlations allow analysts to determine a tentative model. For example, some firms display seasonal variations in quarterly sales such that, say, fourth quarter sales are more highly correlated with fourth quarter sales of the previous year than with third quarter sales of the current year (e.g., holiday-season sales for toy manufacturers). Accordingly, a suitable forecasting model of quarterly sales would likely take that correlation information into account.

Once we formulate a model, we then check how well the estimated model captures the time series behavior of the data. This might involve a measure of *forecast errors* (deviations between actual sales and sales predicted by the model). If necessary, we repeat the process until the measure used to check the model indicates that it fits the data sufficiently well.

However, analysts want to forecast earnings, so providing a sales forecast using time series analysis is only half the battle. Analysts must also forecast expenses for the firm, usually by relating them to sales. For example, analysts might employ common-size ratios under the assumption that expenses would remain a constant percentage of sales. Some expenses may also depend on planned investments in working capital and long-term assets, such as plant, property, and equipment. Thus, a comprehensive approach toward forecasting earnings or cash flows often involves projecting a full set of financial statements including successive balance sheets. These forecasted financial statements are called the **pro forma statements.**

## PRO FORMA STATEMENTS

Firms sometimes prepare pro forma statements to depict the consequences of a future financing event. For example, an initial public offering (IPO) of stock for sale to the public requires the preparation of a *prospectus* (a document filed with the SEC) containing financial statements that reflect the disposition of the anticipated proceeds from the sale of stock and the pro forma changes to assets, liabilities, and stockholders' equity that would result.

Exhibit 6.10
Intel Corporation

THE REAL WORLD
Intel Corporation

Pro forma information is required by SFAS No. 123 as if the company had accounted for its employee stock options (including shares issued under the Stock Participation Plan, collectively called "options") granted subsequent to December 31, 1994 under the fair value method of that statement.

For purposes of pro forma disclosures, the estimated fair value of the options is amortized to expense over the options' vesting periods. The company's pro forma information follows:

| (In millions-except per share amounts) | 2001 | 2000 | 1999 |
|---|---|---|---|
| Net income | $254 | $9,699 | $6,860 |

To judge the significance of these adjustments, note that the reported net income for Intel was $1,291, $10,535, and $7,314 (in millions) for the years 2001, 2000, and 1999, respectively. Therefore, the effect of this adjustment was less than 10 percent of net income in 1999 and 2000 but was an 80 percent decline in income in 2001. This could have a significant influence on an analyst's forecast of the future income on the company.

Firms also use pro forma statements to depict the consequences of an alternative accounting treatment when more than one method is allowed. For example, accounting rules for employee stock options (considered in Chapter 12) allow firms to either recognize compensation expense associated with those options or not recognize compensation expense but disclose pro forma net income as if the compensation expense had been recorded. Exhibit 6.10 illustrates the disclosure for Intel.

Although our principal perspective in developing forecasts of operating data is at the firm level, analysts must also characterize the future prospects of the industry and economy at large. Business cycles and industry trends often factor prominently in forming predictions regarding the outlook for firms susceptible to the influence of those factors. In such cases, we might begin to build a forecast for the firm by first developing or obtaining forecasts at an industry- or economy-wide level. An integrated approach might involve joint analyses of firm, industry, and economy data with the objective of improving estimates at the firm level.

A risk to forecasting models that focus only on time series data is that analysts might be ignoring changes in competitive strategy and changes in organizational structure. For example, how would analysts handle a firm's merger with another company? This event might fundamentally alter the basic statistical properties of a the firm's sales or earnings. In this case, analysts can capture this change with a more encompassing model. Or, analysts might modify pre-merger operating data as if both firms had always been a single entity (an example of employing pro forma statements) and then apply one of the forecasting approaches described above.

## TIME VALUE OF MONEY

Analysts utilize forecasts of future results to help them value the stock of a company today. Before we explain more fully how analysts incorporate their forecasts of future results to arrive at these value estimates, it is important to talk about the concepts of the time value of money, specifically the *present value* of money.

A standard question in an effort to convey the concept of time value of money is to ask whether you would prefer to receive a dollar today or a dollar tomorrow. Most people will respond by saying that they would prefer to receive the dollar today. When asked why, many observe that if they had the dollar today then they would be at least as well off as if they waited until tomorrow because they could always choose to hold the dollar rather than spend it. Moreover, they would have the option not to hold the dollar and spend it if they so chose, which implies more value. It often occurs to at least some that if they had the dollar today, then they could immediately deposit it in their bank and, given that their bank pays interest on a daily basis, they would have more than a dollar tomorrow. In other words, there is a time value to money.

There are many familiar examples of the time value of money. TV ads for automobiles often present prospective buyers with a low interest rate on funds borrowed to pay for a car or a lump sum reduction in the purchase price if they pay in cash. Bank statements may show interest earned on funds held on deposit, copies of information returns filed by insurance companies and brokerage houses also report interest earned, while similar filings by mortgage companies report interest paid. It is hard to escape some exposure to the notion of interest and a time value to money.

In virtually all of the situations where time value of money is relevant, the problem is to somehow compare a dollar amount today, known as **present value,** with an amount in the future, known as **future value.** The calculations that we often employ to compare values at different points in time are referred to as **time value of money** calculations and they all involve the time value of money being expressed as an **interest rate** or **discount rate.** Next we consider the process of converting a present value into a future value and vice versa.

## FUTURE VALUE

A useful way to approach the concept of the present value of a future value (sometimes referred to as a **future sum**) is to turn the issue around and ask what an investment of cash today would yield in terms of cash in the future if, in the interim, that investment earned interest. Suppose that one could invest $1,000 in a bank savings account that pays interest at a rate of 5 percent for one year. At the end of the year, the account would contain $1,050, the initial investment of $1,000 plus interest of $50 ($1,000 × 0.05). Now, suppose that the $1,050 was left in the savings account for a second year and the interest was allowed to also earn interest (called **compounding of interest**). At the end of that year the account would contain $1,102.50 ($1,050 + $1,050 × 0.05 or $1,000 × $(1 + 0.05)^2$). Note that the $50 of interest earned in the first year then earned $2.50 of interest in the second year, reflecting the compounding of interest. Mathematically, the future value of $C$ dollars at the end of two years at an interest rate of $r$, compounded annually, can be expressed as follows (where **FV** is referred to as a **future value factor**):

$$\text{Future Value}(2) = C + rC + r(C + rC) = C + 2rC + r^2C = C(1 + r)^2 = \text{C} \times \text{FV}_{2r}$$

Generalizing in the above to $n$ years at rate $r$, we obtain

$$FV_{n,r} = (1 + r)^n$$
$$\text{Future Value}(n) = C \times FV_{n,r}$$

Note that many books, this one included, contain a table of such future value factors arranged by the number of periods ($n$) and the interest rate per period ($r$). Such tables are often referred to as **future value of $1** tables. Functions that calculate these factors are also incorporated into handheld financial calculators and spreadsheet programs such as Microsoft Excel™.

## PRESENT VALUE

The concept of present value reverses the exercise by posing the question: what is an amount to be received in the future worth now? Intuitively, one would expect present value to be less than the future amount because, if we had the cash now, then it could be invested, earn interest, and be worth more in the future.

In the numerical example above, the present value of $1,050 to be received in one year given an interest rate (discount rate) of 5 percent and annual compounding would be $1,050 ÷ 1.05 or $1,000. Similarly, the present value of $1,102.50 to be received two years hence would be $1,102.50 ÷ $(1.05)^2$, or $1,000 again. It should be fairly clear that mathematically, the present value of $C$ dollars to be received in two years at a discount rate of $r$, compounded annually, can be expressed as follows (where **PV** is the **present value factor**):

$$\text{Present Value}(2) = \frac{C}{(1 + r)(1 + r)} = \frac{C}{(1 + r)^2} = C \times PV_{2,r}$$

Again, generalizing to $n$ years, results in:

$$PV_{n,r} = \frac{1}{(1 + r)^n}$$
$$\text{Present Value}(n) = C \times PV_{n,r}$$

## ADJUSTING FOR UNCERTAINTY

In applying time value of money concepts to an investor's decisions, the interest rate (discount rate) that the investor would use should reflect their own personal time preference for money. Typically this rate will be a function of the other opportunities available to the investor for return on investment and some adjustment for the risk or uncertainty associated with the investment opportunity. The issue of risk is that if one waits until tomorrow to receive the dollar, then something may happen between today and tomorrow such that tomorrow's dollar (or some portions of the dollar) might not materialize. All else held constant, the interest rate required by an investor when there is uncertainty about the outcome of the investment might be higher than the interest rate on a sure thing, depending on the risk preferences of the investor. If the investor is risk averse, then the discount rate employed by that investor would likely be higher to compensate for bearing the risk. By risk averse we mean that the individual strictly prefers a sure thing to a gamble for which the expected payoff is the same as the payoff on the sure thing. For example, risk averse individuals often buy insurance. They prefer to pay a certain premium to an insurance company for coverage of a possible loss when the expected loss is less than the premium.

# MODELS FOR VALUING EQUITY

One application of both forecasting and the time value of money is to estimate the value of the equity of a firm. The two basic approaches used by analysts for estimating the value of equity are the **discounted cash flow (DCF)** and **residual income (RI)** models. Both approaches begin with forecasts of operating results. In the DCF approach, forecasting techniques are used to estimate future free cash flows to equity (discussed in Chapter 5); in the RI approach, a quantity known as *future abnormal earnings* is estimated rather than cash flows.

## DCF APPROACH

Under the DCF approach, operating income is transformed into cash from operations by adding back noncash expenses including depreciation and amortization of operating assets, and subtracting changes in operating working capital. This is the same format used in the cash flow statement to produce cash from operations under GAAP. Cash from operations is then reduced by cash used in investment activities and increased by net borrowings (or reduced by net repayments of borrowings) to arrive at an amount known as **free cash flow** to equity holders (i.e., stockholders). Free cash flows must then be forecasted over the future life of the firm. Typically, DCF analysis also establishes a **time horizon** for the analysis, and the firm's value at the end of that time period (known as the **terminal value**) is estimated. This terminal value is then discounted along with the estimates of free cash flow, using the present value techniques described earlier, to obtain the estimate of the value for the firm's stock. The discount rate employed reflects the rate of return investors require in order to buy the firm's stock. This rate is sometimes called the firm's equity **cost of capital.**

To illustrate, let $FCF_1$, $FCF_2$, and $FCF_n$ denote free cash flows received at the end of future periods 1, 2, and so forth, up to the end of the life of the firm in period $n$. The terminal period is $n$, and let $TV_n$ be the estimated terminal value. We can calculate the present value of the firm and the estimated value of stockholders' equity as follows:

$$\text{Value of Stockholders' Equity} = \frac{FCF_1}{(1+r)} + \frac{FCF_2}{(1+r)^2} + \cdots\cdots\cdots + \frac{FCF_n}{(1+r)^n} + \frac{TV_n}{(1+r)^n}$$

Exhibit 6.11 provides condensed financial data for a hypothetical firm in the form of pro forma financial statements over an assumed remaining firm life (investment horizon) of four years. The initial balance sheet at time 0 reflects

Exhibit 6.11
Pro forma Financial Statements Hypothetical Firm

| Balance Sheet Period | 0 | 1 | 2 | 3 | 4 |
|---|---|---|---|---|---|
| Equipment, Net | 1,000 | 750 | 500 | 250 | 0 |
| Total Assets | 1,000 | 750 | 500 | 250 | 0 |
| Common Stock | 1,000 | 1,000 | 1,000 | 1,000 | 0 |
| Retained Earnings | 0 | −250 | −500 | −750 | 0 |
| Total Liability and Owners' Equity | 1,000 | 750 | 500 | 250 | 0 |
| **Income Statement Period** | | 1 | 2 | 3 | 4 |
| Revenue | | 500 | 500 | 500 | 500 |
| Depreciation | | −250 | −250 | −250 | −250 |
| Net Income | | 250 | 250 | 250 | 250 |
| **Cash Flow Statement Period** | | 1 | 2 | 3 | 4 |
| Net Income | | 250 | 250 | 250 | 250 |
| Depreciation | | 250 | 250 | 250 | 250 |
| Operating Cash Flow | | 500 | 500 | 500 | 500 |
| Dividends | | −500 | −500 | −500 | −500 |
| Change in Cash | | 0 | 0 | 0 | 0 |

equipment of $1,000 purchased from the proceeds of a common stock issue for that amount. The equipment will last four years, at which point it becomes valueless. To keep the calculation simple we will assume that the terminal value is zero at that point in time. Revenues are forecasted to be $500 per year. The only expense is depreciation, which we assume is $250 per year. All available cash each year is distributed in the form of a dividend to common stockholders. The cost of equity is assumed to be 10 percent.

In this example, free cash flows are equivalent to cash from operations on the cash flow statement as there are no investment or debt cash flows. Because free cash flow is the same in all four years, the present value of those cash flows, our estimate of equity value, can be calculated as follows:

Value of Stockholders' Equity

$$= 500 \times \left(\frac{1}{1+.10} + \left(\frac{1}{1+.10}\right)^2 + \left(\frac{1}{1+.10}\right)^3 + \left(\frac{1}{1+.10}\right)^4\right)$$

$$= 500 \times \left(\frac{1-(1+.10)^{-4}}{.10}\right) = 1{,}585$$

where the last term contained in parentheses is a shorthand way of expressing the present value factor for a series of constant amounts received each year. This stream of cash flows (the four $500 payments) is called an **annuity,** and the factor in the last equation would be called a *present value of an annuity factor.* A more detailed description of present value and annuities, along with related tables of present value factors, is provided in Appendix B.

Observe that the value of stockholders' equity derived from the free cash flows of $1,585 is also the present value of the stream of future dividends. Thus, a value of stockholders' equity of $1,585 makes sense when one looks at firm value from an investor's perspective. The interpretation would be that if you purchased the stock in this company for $1,585 and received the four dividends of $500 each, you would have received a return of 10 percent on your investment, due to the fact that we used a discount rate of 10 percent to present value the cash flows.

## RI APPROACH

Under the RI approach, a quantity known as **abnormal earnings** is calculated. Abnormal earnings are simply those earnings that are above or below the earnings currently expected by investors, given their investment in the firm and their required (expected) rate of return. Abnormal earnings are calculated by deducting a charge for the use of capital provided by stockholders from net income. This **capital charge** is determined by multiplying the book value of stockholders' equity at the start of the year by cost of equity capital (rate). The present value of abnormal earnings projected over the life of the firm is then added to the initial book value of stockholders' equity to arrive at an estimate of the value of stockholders' equity. To put this in simple terms, if the firm issued stock for $1,000 and invested the proceeds in operating assets and stockholders expected to earn 10 percent on their investment, then they would expect $100 in earnings every period. If earnings were above or below $100 then they would be viewed as abnormal earnings.

Let $AE_1$, $AE_2$ and $AE_K$ denote abnormal earnings for future periods 1, 2, k, and so on over the remaining life of the firm. The value of stockholders' equity is then:

$$\text{Value of Stockholder's Equity} = \text{Book Value of Stockholder's Equity} + \frac{AE_1}{(1 + r)} + \frac{AE_2}{(1 + r)^2} + \cdots\cdots + \frac{AE_k}{(1 + r)^k} + \cdots\cdots$$

Using the data from Exhibit 6.11, the cost of capital charge is calculated by multiplying stockholders' equity at the beginning of each period by the cost of capital (10 percent). Abnormal earnings are then calculated as the reported net income minus the capital charge:

Year 1: $150 = $250 − (10% × $1,000)
Year 2: $175 = $250 − (10% × $750)
Year 3: $200 = $250 − (10% × $500)
Year 4: $225 = $250 − (10% × $250)

The book value of stockholders' equity is the $1,000 of common stock at the start of the forecast horizon. Accordingly, the value of stockholders' equity can be determined from accounting numbers as follows:

$$\text{Value of Stockholders' Equity} = 1{,}000 + 150 \times \left(\frac{1}{1.10}\right) + 175 \times \left(\frac{1}{1.10}\right)^2 + 200 \times \left(\frac{1}{1.10}\right)^3 + 225 \times \left(\frac{1}{1.10}\right)^4 = 1{,}585$$

Not surprisingly, the value of stockholders' equity is the same under both a DCF and an RI approach. It should also not be surprising that this asset is worth more than the $1,000 paid to acquire it given that the investor is expecting a 10 percent return. If you just consider the first year, the asset would be expected to return only $100 in income, yet it returns $250 or $150 more than expected. This is true in each of the four years of the asset's life, as shown in the calculation of abnormal earnings. Therefore, the $1,000 asset is worth more ($1,585) than its cost.

## SUMMARY AND TRANSITION

Financial statement analysis encompasses many dimensions. Because companies often employ different methods of accounting, it may be necessary to transform financial statements to reflect common accounting practices when making cross-sectional comparisons. Fortunately, accounting reports often contain sufficient information, either in the statements themselves or in accompanying footnotes and supporting schedules, to make these transformations.

A further problem in working from data contained in financial statements for purposes of both time series and cross-sectional comparisons is adjusting for differences in size. To remedy this problem, analysts construct financial ratios that place accounting numbers on a common scale. Besides controlling for differences in size, financial ratios are useful in assessing operating performance. Two broad classes of financial ratios for use in this respect are ratios that measure profitability and ratios that measure debt-repayment ability.

One of the more common ratios for assessing profitability from the stockholders' perspective is rate of return on equity (ROE), determined by dividing net income by stockholders' equity. ROE can be usefully broken down into rate of return on assets (ROA) and leverage, as measured by the ratio of total assets-to-debt. In turn, ROA can be broken down into profit margin and asset turnover, measures of the company's efficiency in converting sales into profits and assets into sales, respectively. The company's ability to generate a higher return on stockholders' equity through the use of financial leverage can be determined by comparing ROE to the rate of return on capital (ROC), where capital is defined as debt plus stockholders' equity, and interest, net of taxes, is added to net income in the numerator of this ratio.

Indicators of a company's short-term debt repayment ability include liquidity ratios, such as the current ratio (current assets divided by current liabilities), quick ratio (current assets other than inventories and prepaid expenses divided by current liabilities), and cash ratio (cash divided by current liabilities). Common ratios for assessing long-term debt-repayment ability include interest coverage (income before interest expense and taxes divided by interest expense) and debt to total debt and equity.

Financial analysts are principally concerned with predicting future performance. This typically begins with a forecast of sales. Sales forecasts might be based on economic models of supply and demand facing the firm, mathematical models that relate sales to time, models based on subjective judgment, and statistical models that extrapolate past sales behavior. Projections of future operating expenses often involve common-size ratios and an assumption that costs will remain proportional to sales. Industry- and economy-wide data may also be useful in forming predictions concerning how the company will fare. The company's strategies in meeting its competition may be relevant as well.

Analysts may then use the forecasted data to provide an estimate of the market value of equity using time value of money techniques. Two basic models are used in this process: the discounted cash flow model and the residual income model.

At this point in the book, we have provided an overview of the basics of financial reporting and financial statement analysis. In the next several chapters, we will return to the balance sheet and focus on more detailed accounting issues related to each of the major types of assets, liabilities, and owners' equity accounts.

# END OF CHAPTER MATERIAL

## KEY TERMS

Abnormal Earnings
Annuity
Capital Asset Turnover
Capital Charge
Cash Ratio
Common Size Balance Sheet
Common Size Income Statement
Compounding of Interest
Cost of Capital
Cross-sectional
Current Ratio
Debt/Equity Ratio
Discount Rate
Discounted Cash Flow Model (DCF)
Financial Leverage
Financial Statement Analysis
Free Cash Flow
Future Sum
Future Value
Future Value Factor
Interest Coverage
Interest Rate
Inter-temporal
Inventory Turnover
Operating Forecasts
Present Value
Present Value Factor
Pro Forma Statements
Profit Margin
Quick Ratio
Receivables Turnover
Residual Income Model (RI)
Return on Assets (ROA)
Return on Capital (ROC)
Return on Equity (ROE)
Terminal Value
Time Horizon
Time Value of Money
Total Asset Turnover
Trading on Equity
Weighted Average Cost of Capital (WACC)
Working Capital Turnover

# ASSIGNMENT MATERIAL

## REVIEW QUESTIONS

1. Compare and contrast inter-temporal and cross-sectional analysis.
2. For each of the following ratios, reproduce the formula for their calculation:
   a. ROA
   b. ROC
   c. ROE
   d. Receivable Turnover
   e. Inventory Turnover
   f. Payables Turnover
   g. Current
   h. Quick
   i. Debt/Equity
   j. Interest Coverage
3. Describe leverage and explain how it is evidenced in the ROA, ROC, and ROE ratios.
4. Explain, using the profit margin and total asset turnover ratios, how two companies in the same industry can earn the same ROA, yet may have very different operating strategies.
5. What is the advantage of preparing common-size statements in financial statement analysis?
6. Explain why the current ratio is subject to manipulation as a measure of liquidity.
7. Explain how as-if restatements might be used in financial statement analysis.
8. Explain how mandated and discretionary accounting method changes can affect financial statement analysis.
9. What is the purpose of adjusting for scale?
10. Describe the discounted cash flow approach to estimating the value of stockholders' equity.
11. Describe how free cash flow would be calculated.
12. Describe the residual income approach to estimating the value of stockholders' equity.

## APPLYING YOUR KNOWLEDGE

13. Discuss the implications that different country accounting standards have for the statement analysis of foreign competitor companies.
14. Suppose that you are analyzing two competitor companies, one a U.S. company and the other a company in the United Kingdom, whose statements are expressed in pounds. Discuss whether it is necessary to convert the statements of the UK company into U.S. dollars before computing ratios.

15. Auditors typically conduct a preliminary review of a firm's financial statements using analytical procedures, which include ratio analysis. As an auditor, why would ratio analysis be useful in auditing the financial statements?

16. Contracts with lenders, such as bonds, typically place restrictions on the financial statement ratios. Two commonly used ratios are the current ratio and the debt/equity ratio. Explain why these might appear as restrictions; in other words, do they protect the lender?

17. Management compensation plans typically specify performance criteria in terms of financial statement ratios. For instance, a plan might specify that management must achieve a certain level of return on investment (e.g., ROA). If management were trying to maximize their compensation, how could they manipulate the ROA ratio to achieve this maximization?

18. The financial data for Nova Electronics Company and Pulsar Electricals for the current year is as follows:

| | Annual Sales | Accounts Receivable Jan 1 | Accounts Receivable Dec 31 |
|---|---|---|---|
| Nova Electronics | 3,893,567 | 1,103,879 | 1,140,251 |
| Pulsar Electricals | 1,382,683 | 357,934 | 243,212 |

a. Compute the Accounts Receivable Turnover for each company.

b. Compute the average number of days required by each company to collect the receivables.

c. Which company is more efficient in terms of handling its accounts receivable policy?

19. Information regarding the activities of Polymer Plastics Corporation is as follows:

| | Year 1 | Year 2 | Year 3 | Year 4 | Year 5 |
|---|---|---|---|---|---|
| Cost of Goods Sold | 363,827 | 411,125 | 493,350 | 579,686 | 608,670 |
| Average Inventory | 60,537 | 76,560 | 107,338 | 156,672 | 202,895 |

a. Do a time series analysis for the inventory turnover for each year and also compute the average number of days that inventories are held for the respective years.

b. Is Polymer Plastics Corporation efficiently managing its inventories?

20. The following financial information relates to Delocro Mechanical, Inc. (amounts in thousands):

| | Year 1 | Year 2 | Year 3 | Year 4 |
|---|---|---|---|---|
| Sales | 2,000 | 2,200 | 2,420 | 2,662 |
| Average Total Assets | 1,111 | 1,222 | 1,344 | 1,479 |
| Average Owners' Equity | 620 | 682 | 750 | 825 |
| Net Income | 200 | 230 | 264 | 304 |
| Interest Expense | 50 | 55 | 61 | 67 |
| Tax Rate | 40% | 40% | 40% | 30% |

For each year calculate:

a. Return on Owners' Equity (ROE)

b. ROI

   i. Profit Margin Ratio

   ii. Total Asset Turnover

c. Comment on the profitability of Delocro Mechanical, Inc.

21. Empire Company's balance sheet is as follows:

| | | | |
|---|---|---|---|
| Total Assets | $500,000 | Liabilities | $100,000 |
| | | Owner's Equity | 400,000 |
| | $500,000 | | $500,000 |

The interest rate on the liabilities is 10 percent, and the income tax rate is 30 percent.

a. If the ROE is equal to the ROI, compute the Net Income.

b. Compute the ROE, taking the Net Income determined in part a.

c. Compute the income before interest and taxes for the net income derived in part a.

d. Assume that total assets remain the same (i.e., at $500,000) and that loans increase to $300,000, while Owners' Equity decreases to $200,000. The interest rate is now 8 percent, and the income tax rate remains at 30 percent. What is the ROE if you require the same ROA as calculated in part b?

e. Compare the ROE in both situations and comment.

22. Spectrum Associates' financial data is as follows (amounts in thousands):

| | | Year 1 | Year 2 | Year 3 | Year 4 |
|---|---|---|---|---|---|
| Current Assets | | | | | |
| | Accounts Receivable | $ 700 | $ 800 | $ 600 | $ 650 |
| | Cash | 200 | 100 | 200 | 150 |
| | Other Current Assets | 100 | 100 | 250 | 100 |
| | Inventories | 500 | 1,000 | 1,450 | 2,100 |
| | | $1,500 | $2,000 | $2,500 | $3,000 |
| Current Liabilities | | | | | |
| | Accounts Payable | $ 600 | $ 700 | $ 825 | $ 800 |
| | Accrued Salaries | 300 | 400 | 495 | 400 |
| | Other Current Liabilities | 100 | 150 | 165 | 300 |
| | | $1,000 | $1,250 | $1,475 | $1,500 |

a. Compute the current and quick ratios for years 1 through 4.

b. Comment on the short-term liquidity position of Spectrum Associates.

23. Artscan Enterprises' financial data is as follows:

| | Year 1 | Year 2 | Year 3 |
|---|---|---|---|
| Income before Interest and Taxes | $ 400 | $ 600 | $ 800 |
| Interest | 70 | 100 | 135 |
| Current Liabilities | 375 | 475 | 750 |
| Noncurrent Liabilities | 625 | 1,125 | 1,600 |
| Owners' Equity | $1,000 | $1,500 | $2,000 |

a. Compute the Debt/Equity and Times Interest Earned Ratio.

b. Comment on the long-term liquidity position of Artscan Enterprises.

24. State the immediate effect (increase, decrease, no effect) of the following transactions on:

a. Current Ratio

b. Quick Ratio

c. Working Capital

d. ROE

e. Debt/Equity Ratio

Transaction:

1. Inventory worth $25,000 is purchased on credit.
2. Inventory worth $125,000 is sold on account for $158,000.
3. Payments of $65,000 are made to suppliers.
4. A machine costing $120,000 is purchased. $30,000 is paid in cash, and the balance will be paid in equal installments for the next three years.
5. Shares of common stock worth $100,000 are issued.
6. Equipment costing $80,000 with accumulated depreciation of $50,000 is sold for $40,000 in cash.
7. Goods worth $35,000 were destroyed by fire. Salvage value of some of the partly burnt goods was $3,000, which is received in cash. The goods were not insured.

25. Calculate the present value of $10,000 to be received ten years from now at 12 percent assuming that interest is compounded:

a. annually

b. quarterly

c. monthly

26. Calculate the present value of an annuity of $100 each year for the next ten years at 12 percent assuming that interest is compounded once a year.

27. Suppose that the free cash flows for a firm are estimated to be $500 per year in each of the next ten years and that the terminal value at the end of the ten years is expected to be $2,000. If your desired rate of return given the risk of this investment was 15 percent, using the DCF approach, what would be the maximum price you would be willing to pay for the entire firm?

28. Suppose that the abnormal earnings of the firm are estimated to be $200 a year for each of the next ten years and that it has a current book value of

$1,500. Using the residual income approach, what would be the maximum amount you would pay for the entire firm if your desired rate of return given the risk of this investment were 12 percent?

## USING REAL DATA

**29.** Use the data from the financial statements of Dell and Gateway to answer the following questions.

| DELL COMPUTER CORP. Balance Sheet | 01/31/2003 | 01/31/2002 |
|---|---|---|
| Current assets: | | |
| Cash and cash equivalents | $ 4,232,000,000 | $ 3,641,000,000 |
| Short-term investments | 406,000,000 | 273,000,000 |
| Accounts receivable, net | 2,586,000,000 | 2,269,000,000 |
| Inventories | 306,000,000 | 278,000,000 |
| Other | 1,394,000,000 | 1,416,000,000 |
| Total current assets | 8,924,000,000 | 7,877,000,000 |
| Property, plant, and equipment, net | 913,000,000 | 826,000,000 |
| Investments | 5,267,000,000 | 4,373,000,000 |
| Other noncurrent assets | 366,000,000 | 459,000,000 |
| Total assets | $15,470,000,000 | $13,535,000,000 |
| Liabilities and stockholders' equity | | |
| Current liabilities: | | |
| Accounts payable | $ 5,989,000,000 | $ 5,075,000,000 |
| Accrued and other | 2,944,000,000 | 2,444,000,000 |
| Total current liabilities | 8,933,000,000 | 7,519,000,000 |
| Long-term debt | 506,000,000 | 520,000,000 |
| Other | 1,158,000,000 | 802,000,000 |
| Commitments and contingent liabilities (Note 6) | | |
| Total liabilities | 10,597,000,000 | 8,841,000,000 |
| Stockholders equity: | | |
| Preferred stock and capital in excess of $.01 par value; shares issued and outstanding: none | – | – |
| Common stock and capital in excess of $.01 par value; shares authorized: 7,000; shares issued: 2,681 and 2,654, respectively | 6,018,000,000 | 5,605,000,000 |
| Treasury stock, at cost; 102 and 52 shares, respectively | (4,539,000,000) | (2,249,000,000) |
| Retained earnings | 3,486,000,000 | 1,364,000,000 |
| Other comprehensive income (loss) | (33,000,000) | 38,000,000 |
| Other | (59,000,000) | (64,000,000) |
| Total stockholders' equity | 4,873,000,000 | 4,694,000,000 |
| Total liabilities and stockholders' equity | $15,470,000,000 | $13,535,000,000 |

| DELL COMPUTER CORP. Income Statement | 01/31/2003 | 01/31/2002 | 01/31/2001 |
|---|---|---|---|
| Net revenue | $35,404,000,000 | $31,168,000,000 | $31,888,000,000 |
| Cost of revenue | 29,055,000,000 | 25,661,000,000 | 25,445,000,000 |
| Gross margin | 6,349,000,000 | 5,507,000,000 | 6,443,000,000 |
| Operating expenses: | | | |
| Selling, general, and administrative | 3,050,000,000 | 2,784,000,000 | 3,193,000,000 |
| Research, development, and engineering | 455,000,000 | 452,000,000 | 482,000,000 |
| Special charges | – | 482,000,000 | 105,000,000 |
| Total operating expenses | 3,505,000,000 | 3,718,000,000 | 3,780,000,000 |
| Operating income | 2,844,000,000 | 1,789,000,000 | 2,663,000,000 |
| Investment and other income (loss), net | 183,000,000 | (58,000,000) | 531,000,000 |
| Income before income taxes and cumulative effect of change in accounting principle | 3,027,000,000 | 1,731,000,000 | 3,194,000,000 |
| Provision for income taxes | 905,000,000 | 485,000,000 | 958,000,000 |
| Income before cumulative effect of change in accounting principle | 2,122,000,000 | 1,246,000,000 | 2,236,000,000 |
| Cumulative effect of change in accounting principle, net | – | – | 59,000,000 |
| Net income | $ 2,122,000,000 | $ 1,246,000,000 | $ 2,177,000,000 |

| DELL COMPUTER CORP. Cash Flow Statement | 01/31/2003 | 01/31/2002 | 01/312/001 |
|---|---|---|---|
| Cash flows from operating activities: | | | |
| Net income | $2,122,000,000 | $1,246,000,000 | $2,177,000,000 |
| Adjustments to reconcile net income to net cash provided by operating activities: | | | |
| Depreciation and amortization | 211,000,000 | 239,000,000 | 240,000,000 |
| Tax benefits of employee stock plans | 260,000,000 | 487,000,000 | 929,000,000 |
| Special charges | – | 742,000,000 | 105,000,000 |
| (Gains)/losses on investments | (67,000,000) | 17,000,000 | (307,000,000) |
| Other, primarily effects of exchange rate changes on monetary assets and liabilities denominated in foreign currencies | (410,000,000) | 178,000,000 | 135,000,000 |
| Changes in: | | | |
| Operating working capital | 1,210,000,000 | 826,000,000 | 642,000,000 |
| Noncurrent assets and liabilities | 212,000,000 | 62,000,000 | 274,000,000 |
| Net cash provided by operating activities | 3,538,000,000 | 3,797,000,000 | 4,195,000,000 |
| Cash flows from investing activities: | | | |
| Investments: | | | |
| Purchases | (8,736,000,000) | (5,382,000,000) | (2,606,000,000) |
| Maturities and sales | 7,660,000,000 | 3,425,000,000 | 2,331,000,000 |
| Capital expenditures | (305,000,000) | (303,000,000) | (482,000,000) |
| Net cash used in investing activities | (1,381,000,000) | (2,260,000,000) | (757,000,000) |

| | 01/31/2003 | 01/31/2002 | 01/312/001 |
|---|---|---|---|
| Cash flows from financing activities: | | | |
| Purchase of common stock | (2,290,000,000) | (3,000,000,000) | (2,700,000,000) |
| Issuance of common stock under employee plans | 265,000,000 | 298,000,000 | 395,000,000 |
| Net cash used in financing activities | (2,025,000,000) | (2,702,000,000) | (2,305,000,000) |
| Effect of exchange rate changes on cash | 459,000,000 | (104,000,000) | (32,000,000) |
| Net increase (decrease) in cash | 591,000,000 | (1,269,000,000) | 1,101,000,000 |
| Cash and cash equivalents at beginning of period | 3,641,000,000 | 4,910,000,000 | 3,809,000,000 |
| Cash and cash equivalents at end of period | $4,232,000,000 | $3,641,000,000 | $4,910,000,000 |

| GATEWAY, INC. Balance Sheet | 12/31/2003 | 12/31/2002 |
|---|---|---|
| ASSETS | | |
| Current assets: | | |
| Cash and cash equivalents | $ 349,101,000 | $ 465,603,000 |
| Marketable securities | 739,936,000 | 601,118,000 |
| Accounts receivable, net | 210,151,000 | 197,817,000 |
| Inventory | 114,136,000 | 88,761,000 |
| Other, net | 250,153,000 | 602,073,000 |
| Total current assets | 1,663,477,000 | 1,955,372,000 |
| Property, plant, and equipment, net | 330,913,000 | 481,011,000 |
| Intangibles, net | 13,983,000 | 23,292,000 |
| Other assets, net | 20,065,000 | 49,732,000 |
| | $2,028,438,000 | $2,509,407,000 |
| Liabilities and equity | | |
| Current liabilities: | | |
| Accounts payable | $ 415,971,000 | $ 278,609,000 |
| Accrued liabilities | 277,455,000 | 364,741,000 |
| Accrued royalties | 48,488,000 | 56,684,000 |
| Other current liabilities | 257,090,000 | 240,315,000 |
| Total current liabilities | 999,004,000 | 940,349,000 |
| Other long-term liabilities | 109,696,000 | 127,118,000 |
| Total liabilities | 1,108,700,000 | 1,067,467,000 |
| Commitments and contingencies (Note 5) | | |
| Series C redeemable convertible preferred stock, \$.01 par value, \$200,000 liquidation value, 50 shares authorized, issued and outstanding in 2003 and 2002 | 197,720,000 | 195,422,000 |
| Stockholders' equity: | | |
| Series A convertible preferred stock, \$.01 par value, \$200,000 liquidation value, 50 shares authorized, issued and outstanding in 2003 and 2002 | 200,000,000 | 200,000,000 |
| Preferred stock, \$.01 par value, 4,900 shares authorized; none issued and outstanding | – | – |
| Class A common stock, nonvoting, \$.01 par value, 1,000 shares authorized; none issued and outstanding | – | – |

| | 12/31/2003 | 12/31/2002 |
|---|---|---|
| Common stock, $.01 par value, 1,000,000 shares authorized; 324,392 shares and 324,072 shares issued and outstanding in 2003 and 2002, respectively | 3,244,000 | 3,240,000 |
| Additional paid-in capital | 734,550,000 | 732,760,000 |
| Retained earnings (Accumulated deficit) | (218,571,000) | 307,379,000 |
| Accumulated other comprehensive income | 2,795,000 | 3,139,000 |
| Total stockholders' equity | 722,018,000 | 1,246,518,000 |
| | $2,028,438,000 | $2,509,407,000 |

GATEWAY, INC. Income Statement

| | 12/31/2003 | 12/31/2002 | 12/31/2001 |
|---|---|---|---|
| Net sales | $3,402,364,000 | $4,171,325,000 | $ 5,937,896,000 |
| Cost of goods sold | 2,938,800,000 | 3,605,120,000 | 5,099,704,000 |
| Gross profit | 463,564,000 | 566,205,000 | 838,192,000 |
| Selling, general, and administrative expenses | 974,139,000 | 1,077,447,000 | 2,022,122,000 |
| Operating loss | (510,575,000) | (511,242,000) | (1,183,930,000) |
| Other income (loss), net | 19,328,000 | 35,496,000 | (94,964,000) |
| Loss before income taxes and cumulative effect of change in accounting principle | (491,247,000) | (475,746,000) | (1,278,894,000) |
| Provision (benefit) for income taxes | 23,565,000 | (178,028,000) | (271,683,000) |
| Loss before cumulative effect of change in accounting principle | (514,812,000) | (297,718,000) | (1,007,211,000) |
| Cumulative effect of change in accounting principle, net of tax | – | – | (23,851,000) |
| Net loss | (514,812,000) | (297,718,000) | (1,031,062,000) |
| Preferred stock dividends and accretion | (11,138,000) | (11,323,000) | – |
| Net loss attributable to common stockholders | $ (525,950,000) | $ (309,041,000) | $(1,031,062,000) |

GATEWAY, INC. Cash Flow

| | 12/31/2003 | 12/31/2002 | 12/31/2001 |
|---|---|---|---|
| Cash flows from operating activities: | | | |
| Net loss | $(514,812,000) | $(297,718,000) | $(1,031,062,000) |
| Adjustments to reconcile net loss to net cash provided by (used in) operating activities: | | | |
| Depreciation and amortization | 163,973,000 | 159,458,000 | 199,976,000 |
| Provision for uncollectible accounts receivable | 11,297,000 | 11,139,000 | 23,151,000 |
| Deferred income taxes | 6,000,000 | 257,172,000 | (27,282,000) |
| Loss on investments | 808,000 | 30,272,000 | 186,745,000 |
| Write-down of long-lived assets | 66,397,000 | 52,975,000 | 418,304,000 |
| Gain on settlement of acquisition liability | – | (13,782,000) | – |
| Loss on sale of property | 6,052,000 | – | – |
| Cumulative effect of change in accounting principle | – | – | 23,851,000 |
| Gain on extinguishment of debt | – | – | (6,890,000) |
| Other, net | 1,941,000 | (1,929,000) | (1,707,000) |
| Changes in operating assets and liabilities: | | | |
| Accounts receivable | (23,633,000) | 11,020,000 | 301,630,000 |

| | 12/31/2003 | 12/31/2002 | 12/31/2001 |
|---|---|---|---|
| Inventory | (25,375,000) | 31,505,000 | 194,799,000 |
| Other assets | 306,258,000 | (76,975,000) | 21,729,000 |
| Accounts payable | 137,716,000 | (59,856,000) | (442,312,000) |
| Accrued liabilities | (95,117,000) | (103,868,000) | (87,714,000) |
| Accrued royalties | (8,196,000) | (79,014,000) | (2,747,000) |
| Other liabilities | 39,382,000 | 54,924,000 | (40,810,000) |
| Net cash provided by (used in) operating activities | 72,691,000 | (24,677,000) | (270,339,000) |
| Cash flows from investing activities: | | | |
| Capital expenditures | (72,978,000) | (78,497,000) | (199,493,000) |
| Proceeds from sale of investment | – | 11,100,000 | – |
| Purchases of available-for-sale securities | (530,323,000) | (614,023,000) | (638,869,000) |
| Sales of available-for-sale securities | 401,109,000 | 436,316,000 | 356,071,000 |
| Proceeds from the sale of financing receivables | – | 9,896,000 | 569,579,000 |
| Purchase of financing receivables, net of repayments | – | – | (28,476,000) |
| Proceeds from notes receivable | 20,045,000 | – | 50,000,000 |
| Other, net | – | – | 189,000 |
| Net cash provided by (used in) investing activities | (182,147,000) | (235,208,000) | 109,001,000 |
| Cash flows from financing activities: | | | |
| Proceeds from issuance of notes payable | – | – | 200,000,000 |
| Principal payments on long-term obligations and notes payable | – | – | (3,984,000) |
| Proceeds from stock issuance | – | – | 200,000,000 |
| Payment of preferred dividends | (8,840,000) | (5,878,000) | – |
| Stock options exercised | 1,794,000 | 367,000 | 9,431,000 |
| Net cash provided by (used in) financing activities | (7,046,000) | (5,511,000) | 405,447,000 |
| Foreign exchange effect on cash and cash equivalents | – | – | 2,893,000 |
| Net increase (decrease) in cash and cash equivalents | (116,502,000) | (265,396,000) | 247,002,000 |
| Cash and cash equivalents, beginning of year | 465,603,000 | 730,999,000 | 483,997,000 |
| Cash and cash equivalents, end of year | $ 349,101,000 | $ 465,603,000 | $ 730,999,000 |

**a.** Calculate the following ratios:

ROE, ROC, ROA, Profit Margin, Total Asset Turnover, Receivable Turnover, Inventory Turnover, Payables Turnover Current, Quick, Debt/Equity

**b.** Calculate the common-size balance sheet and income statement.

**c.** Comment on the financial health of the two organizations from the point of view of a lender who has been asked to make a $200 million loan to each of the companies.

**d.** Estimate Dell's and Gateway's 2003 net sales if sales were recognized as cash is collected rather than on the accrual basis. Comment on the significance of the difference between your estimate and reported sales.

**e.** Suppose you are interested in forecasting future sales for Dell and Gateway. Describe methods that can be used. Forecast Dell's and Gateway's sales for 2006. Justify your answer.

30. Use the data from the financial statement of Home Depot and Lowes to answer the following questions.

| HOME DEPOT, INC. Balance Sheet | 02/01/2004 | 02/01/2003 |
|---|---|---|
| Assets | | |
| Current assets: | | |
| Cash and cash equivalents | $ 2,826,000,000 | $ 2,188,000,000 |
| Short-term investments, including current maturities of long-term investments | 26,000,000 | 65,000,000 |
| Receivables, net | 1,097,000,000 | 1,072,000,000 |
| Merchandise inventories | 9,076,000,000 | 8,338,000,000 |
| Other current assets | 303,000,000 | 254,000,000 |
| Total current assets | 13,328,000,000 | 11,917,000,000 |
| Property and equipment, at cost: | | |
| Land | 6,397,000,000 | 5,560,000,000 |
| Buildings | 10,920,000,000 | 9,197,000,000 |
| Furniture, fixtures, and equipment | 5,163,000,000 | 4,074,000,000 |
| Leasehold improvements | 942,000,000 | 872,000,000 |
| Construction in progress | 820,000,000 | 724,000,000 |
| Capital leases | 352,000,000 | 306,000,000 |
| | 24,594,000,000 | 20,733,000,000 |
| Less accumulated depreciation and amortization | 4,531,000,000 | 3,565,000,000 |
| Net property and equipment | 20,063,000,000 | 17,168,000,000 |
| Notes receivable | 84,000,000 | 107,000,000 |
| Cost in excess of the fair value of net assets acquired, net of accumulated amortization of $54 at February 1, 2004 and $50 at February 2, 2003 | 833,000,000 | 575,000,000 |
| Other assets | 129,000,000 | 244,000,000 |
| Total assets | $34,437,000,000 | $ 30,011,000,000 |
| Liabilities and stockholders' equity | | |
| Current liabilities: | | |
| Accounts payable | $ 5,159,000,000 | $ 4,560,000,000 |
| Accrued salaries and related expenses | 801,000,000 | 809,000,000 |
| Sales taxes payable | 419,000,000 | 307,000,000 |
| Deferred revenue | 1,281,000,000 | 998,000,000 |
| Income taxes payable | 175,000,000 | 227,000,000 |
| Current installments of long-term debt | 509,000,000 | 7,000,000 |
| Other accrued expenses | 1,210,000,000 | 1,127,000,000 |
| Total current liabilities | 9,554,000,000 | 8,035,000,000 |

| | 02/01/2004 | 02/01/2003 |
|---|---|---|
| Long-term debt, excluding current installments | 856,000,000 | 1,321,000,000 |
| Other long-term liabilities | 653,000,000 | 491,000,000 |
| Deferred income taxes | 967,000,000 | 362,000,000 |
| Stockholders' equity | | |
| Common stock, par value $0.05; authorized: 10,000 shares, issued and outstanding 2,373 shares at February 1, 2004 and 2,362 shares at February 2, 2003 | 119,000,000 | 118,000,000 |
| Paid-in capital | 6,184,000,000 | 5,858,000,000 |
| Retained earnings | 19,680,000,000 | 15,971,000,000 |
| Accumulated other comprehensive income (loss) | 90,000,000 | (82,000,000) |
| Unearned compensation | (76,000,000) | (63,000,000) |
| Treasury stock, at cost, 116 shares at February 1, 2004 and 69 shares at February 2, 2003 | (3,590,000,000) | (2,000,000,000) |
| Total stockholders' equity | 22,407,000,000 | 19,802,000,000 |
| Total liabilities and stockholders' equity | $34,437,000,000 | $30,011,000,000 |

| HOME DEPOT, INC. Income Statement | 02/01/2004 | 02/01/2003 | 02/01/2002 |
|---|---|---|---|
| Net sales | $64,816,000,000 | $58,247,000,000 | $53,553,000,000 |
| Cost of merchandise sold | 44,236,000,000 | 40,139,000,000 | 37,406,000,000 |
| Gross profit | 20,580,000,000 | 18,108,000,000 | 16,147,000,000 |
| Operating expenses: | | | |
| Selling and store operating | 12,502,000,000 | 11,180,000,000 | 10,163,000,000 |
| Pre-opening | 86,000,000 | 96,000,000 | 117,000,000 |
| General and administrative | 1,146,000,000 | 1,002,000,000 | 935,000,000 |
| Total operating expenses | 13,734,000,000 | 12,278,000,000 | 11,215,000,000 |
| Operating income | 6,846,000,000 | 5,830,000,000 | 4,932,000,000 |
| Interest income (expense): | | | |
| Interest and investment income | 59,000,000 | 79,000,000 | 53,000,000 |
| Interest expense | (62,000,000) | (37,000,000) | (28,000,000) |
| Interest, net | (3,000,000) | 42,000,000 | 25,000,000 |
| Earnings before provision for income taxes | 6,843,000,000 | 5,872,000,000 | 4,957,000,000 |
| Provision for income taxes | 2,539,000,000 | 2,208,000,000 | 1,913,000,000 |
| Net earnings | $ 4,304,000,000 | $3,664,000,000 | $3,044,000,000 |

| HOME DEPOT, INC. Cash Flow | 02/01/2004 | 02/01/2003 | 02/01/2002 |
|---|---|---|---|
| Cash flows from operations: | | | |
| Net earnings | $4,304,000,000 | $3,664,000,000 | $3,044,000,000 |
| Reconciliation of net earnings to net | | | |
| Cash provided by operations: | | | |
| Depreciation and amortization | 1,076,000,000 | 903,000,000 | 764,000,000 |
| Decrease (increase) in receivables, net | 25,000,000 | (38,000,000) | (119,000,000) |
| Increase in merchandise inventories | (693,000,000) | (1,592,000,000) | (166,000,000) |
| Increase in accounts payable and accrued liabilities | 790,000,000 | 1,394,000,000 | 1,878,000,000 |
| Increase in deferred revenue | 279,000,000 | 147,000,000 | 200,000,000 |
| (Decrease) increase in income taxes payable | (27,000,000) | 83,000,000 | 272,000,000 |
| Increase (decrease) in deferred income taxes | 605,000,000 | 173,000,000 | (6,000,000) |
| Other | 186,000,000 | 68,000,000 | 96,000,000 |
| Net cash provided by operations | 6,545,000,000 | 4,802,000,000 | 5,963,000,000 |
| Cash flows from investing activities: | | | |
| Capital expenditures, net of $47, $49, and $5 of noncash capital expenditures in fiscal 2003, 2002 and 2001, respectively | (3,508,000,000) | (2,749,000,000) | (3,393,000,000) |
| Purchase of assets from off-balance sheet financing arrangement | (598,000,000) | – | – |
| Payments for businesses acquired, net | (215,000,000) | (235,000,000) | (190,000,000) |
| Proceeds from sales of businesses, net | – | 22,000,000 | 64,000,000 |
| Proceeds from sales of property and equipment | 265,000,000 | 105,000,000 | 126,000,000 |
| Purchases of investments | (159,000,000) | (583,000,000) | (85,000,000) |
| Proceeds from maturities of investments | 219,000,000 | 506,000,000 | 25,000,000 |
| Other | 0 | 0 | (13,000,000) |
| Net cash used in investing activities | (3,996,000,000) | (2,934,000,000) | (3,466,000,000) |
| Cash flows from financing activities: | | | |
| Repayments of commercial paper obligations, net | – | – | (754,000,000) |
| Proceeds from long-term debt | – | 1,000,000 | 532,000,000 |
| Repayments of long-term debt | (9,000,000) | – | – |
| Repurchase of common stock | (1,554,000,000) | (2,000,000,000) | – |
| Proceeds from sale of common stock, net | 227,000,000 | 326,000,000 | 445,000,000 |
| Cash dividends paid to stockholders | (595,000,000) | (492,000,000) | (396,000,000) |
| Net cash used in financing activities | (1,931,000,000) | (2,165,000,000) | (173,000,000) |
| Effect of exchange rate changes on cash and cash equivalents | 20,000,000 | 8,000,000 | (14,000,000) |
| Increase (decrease) in cash and cash equivalents | 638,000,000 | (289,000,000) | 2,310,000,000 |
| Cash and cash equivalents at beginning of year | 2,188,000,000 | 2,477,000,000 | 167,000,000 |
| Cash and cash equivalents at end of year | 2,826,000,000 | 2,188,000,000 | 2,477,000,000 |
| Supplemental disclosure of cash payments made for: | | | |
| Interest, net of interest capitalized | 70,000,000 | 50,000,000 | 18,000,000 |
| Income taxes | $2,037,000,000 | $1,951,000,000 | $1,685,000,000 |

Lowe's Companies, Inc.
Consolidated Balance Sheets
(In Millions, Except Par Value Data)

| | Jan-30-04 | Jan-31-03 |
|---|---|---|
| Assets | | |
| Current assets: | | |
| Cash and cash equivalents | $ 1,446,000,000 | $ 853,000,000 |
| Short-term investments (note 3) | 178,000,000 | 273,000,000 |
| Accounts receivable, net (note 1) | 131,000,000 | 172,000,000 |
| Merchandise inventory (note 1) | 4,584,000,000 | 3,968,000,000 |
| Deferred income taxes (note 13) | 59,000,000 | 58,000,000 |
| Other current assets | 289,000,000 | 244,000,000 |
| Total current assets | 6,687,000,000 | 5,568,000,000 |
| Property, less accumulated depreciation (notes 4 and 5) | 11,945,000,000 | 10,352,000,000 |
| Long-term investments (note 3) | 169,000,000 | 29,000,000 |
| Other assets (note 5) | 241,000,000 | 160,000,000 |
| Total assets | $19,042,000,000 | $16,109,000,000 |
| Liabilities and shareholders' equity | | |
| Current liabilities: | | |
| Short-term borrowings (note 6) | $ – | $ 50,000,000 |
| Current maturities of long-term debt (note 7) | 77,000,000 | 29,000,000 |
| Accounts payable | 2,366,000,000 | 1,943,000,000 |
| Employee retirement plans (note 12) | 74,000,000 | 88,000,000 |
| Accrued salaries and wages | 335,000,000 | 306,000,000 |
| Other current liabilities (note 5) | 1,516,000,000 | 1,162,000,000 |
| Total current liabilities | 4,368,000,000 | 3,578,000,000 |
| Long-term debt, excluding current maturities (notes 7, 8, and 11) | 3,678,000,000 | 3,736,000,000 |
| Deferred income taxes (note 13) | 657,000,000 | 478,000,000 |
| Other long-term liabilities | 30,000,000 | 15,000,000 |
| Total liabilities | 8,733,000,000 | 7,807,000,000 |
| Shareholders' equity (note 10): | | |
| Preferred stock $5 par value, none issued | – | – |
| Common stock –$.50 par value; shares issued and outstanding January 30, 2004 – 787 January 31, 2003 – 782 | 394,000,000 | 391,000,000 |
| Capital in excess of par value | 2,237,000,000 | 2,023,000,000 |
| Retained earnings | 7,677,000,000 | 5,887,000,000 |
| Accumulated other comprehensive income | 1,000,000 | 1,000,000 |
| Total shareholders' equity | 10,309,000,000 | 8,302,000,000 |
| Total liabilities and shareholders' equity | $19,042,000,000 | $16,109,000,000 |

| Lowe's Companies, Inc. Consolidated Statements of Earnings Years Ended on | Jan-30-04 | Jan-31-03 | Feb-1-02 |
|---|---|---|---|
| Net sales | $30,838,000,000 | $26,112,000,000 | $21,714,000,000 |
| Cost of sales | 21,231,000,000 | 18,164,000,000 | 15,427,000,000 |
| Gross margin | 9,607,000,000 | 7,948,000,000 | 6,287,000,000 |
| Expenses: | – | – | – |
| Selling, general, and administrative (note 5) | 5,543,000,000 | 4,676,000,000 | 3,857,000,000 |
| Store opening costs | 128,000,000 | 129,000,000 | 140,000,000 |
| Depreciation | 758,000,000 | 622,000,000 | 513,000,000 |
| Interest (note 15) | 180,000,000 | 182,000,000 | 174,000,000 |
| Total expenses | 6,609,000,000 | 5,609,000,000 | 4,684,000,000 |
| Pre-tax earnings | 2,998,000,000 | 2,339,000,000 | 1,603,000,000 |
| Income tax provision (note 13) | 1,136,000,000 | 880,000,000 | 593,000,000 |
| Earnings from continuing operations | 1,862,000,000 | 1,459,000,000 | 1,010,000,000 |
| Earnings from discontinued operations, net of tax (note 2) | 15,000,000 | 12,000,000 | 13,000,000 |
| Net earnings | $ 877,000,000 | $ 1,471,000,000 | $ 1,023,000,000 |

| LOWES COMPANIES, INC. Cash Flow | 01/30/2004 | 01/30/2003 | 01/30/2002 |
|---|---|---|---|
| Cash Flows from operating activities: | | | |
| Net earnings | $1,877,000,000 | $1,471,000,000 | $1,023,000,000 |
| Earnings from discontinued operations, net of tax | (15,000,000) | (12,000,000) | (13,000,000) |
| Earnings from continuing operations | 1,862,000,000 | 1,459,000,000 | 1,010,000,000 |
| Adjustments to reconcile net earnings to net cash provided by operating activities: | | | |
| Depreciation and amortization | 781,000,000 | 641,000,000 | 530,000,000 |
| Deferred income taxes | 178,000,000 | 208,000,000 | 42,000,000 |
| Loss on disposition/write-down of fixed and other assets | 31,000,000 | 18,000,000 | 39,000,000 |
| Stock-based compensation expense | 41,000,000 | – | – |
| Tax effect of stock options exercised | 31,000,000 | 29,000,000 | 35,000,000 |
| Changes in operating assets and liabilities: | | | |
| Accounts receivable, net | 2,000,000 | (9,000,000) | (5,000,000) |
| Merchandise inventory | (648,000,000) | (357,000,000) | (326,000,000) |
| Other operating assets | (45,000,000) | (41,000,000) | (37,000,000) |
| Accounts payable | 423,000,000 | 228,000,000 | 1,000,000 |
| Employee retirement plans | (14,000,000) | 40,000,000 | 114,000,000 |
| Other operating liabilities | 399,000,000 | 461,000,000 | 193,000,000 |

| | 01/30/2004 | 01/30/2003 | 01/30/2002 |
|---|---|---|---|
| Net cash provided by operating activities from continuing operations | 3,041,000,000 | 2,677,000,000 | 1,596,000,000 |
| Cash flows from investing activities: | | | |
| Decrease (increase) in investment assets: | | | |
| Short-term investments | 139,000,000 | (203,000,000) | (30,000,000) |
| Purchases of long-term investments | (381,000,000) | (24,000,000) | (1,000,000) |
| Proceeds from sale/maturity of long-term investments | 193,000,000 | – | 3,000,000 |
| Increase in other long-term assets | (95,000,000) | (33,000,000) | (14,000,000) |
| Fixed assets acquired | (2,444,000,000) | (2,359,000,000) | (2,196,000,000) |
| Proceeds from the sale of fixed and other long-term assets | 45,000,000 | 44,000,000 | 42,000,000 |
| Net cash used in investing activities from continuing operations | (2,543,000,000) | (2,575,000,000) | (2,196,000,000) |
| Cash flows from financing activities: | | | |
| Net decrease in short-term borrowings | (50,000,000) | (50,000,000) | (150,000,000) |
| Long-term debt borrowings | – | – | 1,087,000,000 |
| Repayment of long-term debt | (29,000,000) | (63,000,000) | (63,000,000) |
| Proceeds from employee stock purchase plan | 52,000,000 | 50,000,000 | 38,000,000 |
| Proceeds from stock options exercised | 97,000,000 | 65,000,000 | 77,000,000 |
| Cash dividend payments | (87,000,000) | (66,000,000) | (60,000,000) |
| Net cash provided by (used in) financing activities from continuing operations | (17,000,000) | (64,000,000) | 929,000,000 |
| Net cash provided by discontinued operations | 112,000,000 | 16,000,000 | 14,000,000 |
| Net increase (decrease) in cash and cash equivalents | 593,000,000 | 54,000,000 | 343,000,000 |
| Cash and cash equivalents, beginning of year | 853,000,000 | 799,000,000 | 456,000,000 |
| Cash and cash equivalents, end of year | $1,446,000,000 | $ 853,000,000 | $ 799,000,000 |

**a.** Calculate the following ratios:

ROE, ROC, ROA, Profit Margin, Total Asset Turnover, Receivable Turnover, Inventory Turnover, Payables Turnover Current, Quick, Debt/Equity

**b.** Calculate the common-size balance sheet and income statement.

**c.** Comment on the financial health of the two organizations from the point of view of a lender who has been asked to make a $200 million loan to each of the companies.

**d.** Estimate Lowe's and Home Depot's sales for the year ending February 1, 2004 if sales had been recorded as cash is collected rather than on the accrual basis. Comment on the significance of the difference between your estimate and reported sales.

Suppose you are interested in forecasting future sales for Lowes and Home Depot. Describe methods that can be used. Forecast Lowe's and Home Depot's sales for 2006. Justify your answer.

Assuming that the amount forecast for 2006 will continue indefinitely into the future, estimate the market value of Lowes and Home Depot using the free cash flow and residual income approaches. Assume a required rate of return of 10 percent. Hint: The present value of a stream of cash flows that continues into infinity is computed as the amount divided by the required rate of return. For example, the present value of $10 to be received annually forever is 10/.1 = $100 (assuming a 10 percent required rate of return).

## BEYOND THE BOOK

**31.** Prepare a comparative ratio analysis of two competitor companies. At the direction of your instructor, pick either two domestic or one domestic and one foreign competitor. At a minimum, use the set of ratios discussed in the text and at least three years of data. Use any additional ratios that might be commonly used in the industry that you select (you may also need to drop some of the ratios discussed in the book if they are not relevant).

Required: Prepare a written report summarizing your comparative analysis. For the purpose of this report, assume some sort of decision perspective; for instance, you might assume that you are a bank loan officer evaluating the two competitors to decide which has the best lending risk profile.

## Outline

# Part II: Evaluating Economic Performance of Companies and Projects

- Lecture slides on ratio analysis, discounted cash flows and transform techniques

- Chapters 2 and 3 of "Advanced Engineering Economics" by Park and Sharp-Bette

- Lecture slides on figures of merit

- Chapters 6 and 7 of "Advanced Engineering Economics" by Park and Sharp-Bette

# Evaluating Financial Performance

## Profitability ratios

- **Return on Equity (ROE) =** Net income / Shareholders' Equity
- **Return on Assets (ROA) =** Net income / Assets

- **Return on Invested Capital (ROIC) =** EBIT ( 1- Tax rate) / (Interest-bearing debt + Shareholders' equity)

- **Profit Margin (PM) =** Net income / Sales
- **Gross Margin (GM) =** Gross profit / Sales
- **Price to Earnings (P/E ratio) =** Price per share / Earnings per share

# Evaluating Financial Performance

## Return on Equity

**ROE** = Net income/ Shareholders' Equity

**= (Net income/Sales) x (Sales/Assets) x (Assets/Shareholders' Equity)**

| = | Profit margin | x Asset Turnover x | Financial Leverage |
|---|---|---|---|
| | **I.S.** | **Left B.S.** | **Right B.S.** |

➢ **ROE is not a reliable financial yardstick:**

- **Timing problem**
- **Risk problem**
- **Value problem**

## Evaluating Financial Performance

Turnover-control ratios

- **Asset Turnover =** Sales / Assets

- **Fixed-Asset Turnover =** Sales / Net property, plant and equipment

- **Inventory Turnover =** Cost of goods sold / Ending inventory

- **Collection Period =** Accounts receivable / Credit sales per day

(Use sales if credit sales unavailable)

- **Days' Sales in Cash =** Cash and securities / Sales per day

- **Payables Period =** Accounts payable / Credit purchases per day

(Use COGS if credit purchases unavailable))

# Evaluating Financial Performance

## Leverage & liquidity ratios

- **Assets to Equity** = Assets / Shareholders' equity

- **Debt to Assets** = Total liabilities / Assets

- **Debt to Equity** = Total liabilities / Shareholders' equity

- **Times Interest Earned** = EBIT / Interest expense

- **Current Ratio** = Current assets / Current liabilities

- **Acid Test** = (Current assets – Inventory) / Current liabilities

# Compounding, Equivalence and Transform Techniques

- ➢Payback period and accounting rate of return
- ➢Time value of money
- ➢Interest rates
- ➢Useful formulas
- ➢Discrete compounding
- ➢Continuous compounding
- ➢Equivalence of cash flows
- ➢Effect of inflation on cash flow equivalence
- ➢Z-transforms and discrete cash flows
- ➢Laplace transforms and continuous cash flows

## Compounding, Equivalence and Transform Techniques

Interest rates

- **Simple interest**
  - $F_N = P + I = P(1 + Ni)$
- **Compound interest**
  - $F_N = P + I = P(1 + i)^N$
- **Nominal and effective interest rates**
  - Annual percentage rate (APR) vs. Effective annual rate (EAR)
    - ✓ $m$: number of interest periods per year
    - ✓ $\text{EAR} = (1 + APR / m)^m - 1$

# Compounding, Equivalence and Transform Techniques

## Discrete Compounding

- **4 major types of discrete payments**

  - **Single payment**

$$F_N = F \quad \text{and} \quad F_n = 0, \ \forall n \in \{1, \ldots, N-1\}$$

  - **Uniform series or equal-payment series**

$$F_n = A, \ \forall n \in \{1, \ldots, N\}$$

  - **Arithmetic gradient series**

$$F_n = (n-1)G, \ \forall n \in \{1, \ldots, N\}$$

  - **Geometric gradient series**

$$F_n = F_1(1+g)^{n-1}, \ \forall n \in \{1, \ldots, N\}$$

## Compounding, Equivalence and Transform Techniques

### Discrete Compounding

#### Uniform Series

- **Compound amount:** $(F/A, i, N)$

$$F = A\left[\frac{(1+i)^N - 1}{i}\right]$$

- **Sinking fund:** $(A/F, i, N)$

$$A = F\left[\frac{i}{(1+i)^N - 1}\right]$$

- **Present worth:** $(P/A, i, N)$

$$P = \frac{A}{i}\left[1 - \frac{1}{(1+i)^N}\right]$$

- **Capital recovery:** $(A/P, i, N)$

$$A = P\frac{i}{1 - \frac{1}{(1+i)^N}}$$

➢ **Present worth:** $(P/G,i,N)$

$$P = G\left[\frac{1-\dfrac{(1+Ni)}{(1+i)^N}}{i^2}\right]$$

➢ **Uniform gradient series conversion factor:**
$(A/G,i,N)$

$$A = G\left[\frac{1}{i} - \frac{N}{(1+i)^N - 1}\right]$$

➢ **Future worth equivalent of a gradient series:**
$(F/G,i,N)$

$$(F/G,i,N) = \frac{G}{i}[(F/A,i,N) - N]$$

➢ **Present worth:**

$$P = F_1 \frac{1 - \left(\frac{1+g}{1+i}\right)^N}{i - g}$$

Using $g' = \frac{1+i}{1+g} - 1$, we also obtain

$$P = \frac{F_1}{1+g}(P/A, g', N)$$

## ➢Continuous compounding at rate *r*

- **The effective interest rate $i$ is:**
  - ✓ $i = e^{r} - 1$
- **Use the formulas of discrete compounding**

➢ **Continuous compounding at rate $r$ with flow rate at time $t$ of $F_t$**

- **Present value**

$$P = \int_0^N F_t e^{-rt} dt$$

- **Future value**

$$F = \int_0^N F_t e^{r(N-t)} dt$$

➢ **Special case: $F_t = B$**

- **Funds flow present worth factor**

$$P = B\int_0^N e^{-rt}\,dt = B\left(\frac{1-e^{-rN}}{r}\right)$$

- **Funds flow compound amount factor**

$$F = B\int_0^N e^{rt}\,dt = B\left(\frac{e^{rN}-1}{r}\right)$$

- **Two cash flows are equivalent *at interest i* if we can convert one cash flow into the other using proper compound interest factors**

- **Cash flow equivalence is used a lot in the stock market and is the basis of the "absence of arbitrage" principle**

## Effect of Inflation on Cash Flow Equivalence

- **Measures of inflation:**
  - CPI (Consumer Price Index) based on market basket
  - GNPIPD (Gross National Product Implicit Price Deflator)
  - PPI (Producer Price Index)

- **These measures tend to overstate inflation as they do not take into account:**
  - Improvements in quality
  - Opportunities for substitution

- **Explicit and implicit treatments of inflation in discounting**
  - Actual dollars (current dollars, future dollars, inflated dollars, nominal dollars)
  - Constant dollars (real dollars, deflated dollars, todays dollars)
  - Market interest rate $i$
  - Inflation-free interest rate $i'$ (real interest rate, true interest rate, constant-dollar interest rate)
  - General inflation rate $f$

$$i' = \frac{i-f}{1+f}$$

- **Z- transform of an infinite cash flow $\{f(n)\}$ is:**

$$F(z) = Z\{f(n)\} \equiv \sum_{n=0}^{\infty} f(n) z^{-n}$$

$$F(1+i) = \sum_{n=0}^{\infty} f(n)(1+i)^{-n}$$

- **Properties:**
  - **There is a one to one mapping between an infinite cash flow and its Z-transform**
  - **Linear combinations of cash flows correspond to the same linear combinations of their Z-transforms**
- **Z-transforms have been pre-computed for a large number of cash flows**

## Laplace Transforms for Continuous Cash Flows

- **Laplace transform of an infinite continuous cash flow $\{f(t)\}$ is:**

$$PV(r) = F(z) \equiv \int_0^\infty f(t)e^{-rt}\,dt$$

- **Properties:**
  - **There is a one to one mapping between an infinite cash flow and its Laplace transform**
  - **Linear combinations of cash flows correspond to the same linear combinations of their Laplace transforms**
- **Laplace transforms have been pre-computed for a large number of cash flows**

## Outline

**Part II: Evaluating Economic Performance of Companies and Projects**

- Lecture slides on ratio analysis, discounted cash flows and transform techniques

- Chapters 2 and 3 of "Advanced Engineering Economics" by Park and Sharp-Bette

- Lecture slides on figures of merit

- Chapters 6 and 7 of "Advanced Engineering Economics" by Park and Sharp-Bette

# 2

# Interest and Equivalence

## 2.1 INTRODUCTION

Engineering economic analysis is primarily concerned with the evaluation of economic investment alternatives. We often describe these investment alternatives by a cash flow diagram showing the amount and timing of estimated future receipts and disbursements that will result from each decision. Because the time value of money is related to the effect of time and interest on monetary amounts, we must consider both the timing and the magnitude of cash flow. When comparing investment alternatives, we must consider the expected receipts and disbursements of these investment alternatives on the same basis. This type of comparison requires understanding of the concepts of equivalence and the proper use of various interest formulas. In this chapter we will examine a number of mathematical operations that are based on the time value of money, with an emphasis on modeling cash flow profiles.

## 2.2. CASH FLOW PROFILE

An investment project can be described by the amount and timing of expected costs and benefits in the planning horizon. (We will use the terms *project* and *proposal* interchangeably throughout this book.) The terms *costs* and *benefits* represent *disbursements* and *receipts*, respectively. We will use the term *payment* (or *net cash flow*) to denote the receipts less the disbursements that occur at the same point in time. The stream of disbursements and receipts for an investment project over the planning horizon is said to be the *cash flow profile* of the project.

To facilitate the description of project cash flows, we classify them in two categories: (1) discrete-time cash flows and (2) continuous-time flows. The discrete-time cash flows are those in which cash flow occurs at the end of, at the start of, or within discrete time periods. The continuous flows are those in which money flows at a given rate and continuously throughout a given time period. The following notation will be adopted:

$F_n$ = discrete payment occurring at period $n$,

$F_t$ = continuous payment occurring at time $t$.

If $F_n < 0$, $F_n$ represents a net disbursement (cash outflow). If $F_n > 0$, $F_n$ represents a net receipt (cash inflow). We can say the same for $F_t$.

## 2.3 TIME PREFERENCE AND INTEREST

### 2.3.1 Time Preference

Cash flows that occur at different points in time have different values and cannot be compared directly with one another. This fact is often stated simply as "money has a time value." There are several reasons why we must assess cash flows in different periods in terms of time preference.

First, money has a potential *earning power,* because having a dollar now gives us an opportunity to invest this dollar in the near future. In other words, equal dollar amounts available at different points in time have different values based on the opportunity to profit from investment activity.

Second, money has a time value because a user may have a different utility of consumption of dollars (i.e., consider them more or less desirable to use) at different times. The preference for consumption in different periods is measured by the rate of time preference. For example, if we have a rate of time preference of $i$ per time period, we are indifferent toward the prospect of either consuming $P$ units now or consuming $P(1 + i)$ units at the end of the period. The rate of time preference is often called the *interest rate* (or *discount rate*) in economic analysis.

Third, money has time value because the *buying power* of a dollar changes through time. When there is inflation, the amount of goods that can be bought for a certain amount of money decreases as the time of purchase is further in the future. Although this change in the buying power of money is important, we limit our concept of time preference to the fact that money has an *earning power,* or utility of consumption. We will treat the effects of inflation explicitly in a later section, and any future reference to the time value of money will be restricted to the first two aspects. Before considering the actual effect of this time value, we will review the types of interest and how they are calculated.

### 2.3.2 Types of Interest

If an amount of money is deposited in a financial institution, interest accrues (accumulates) at regular time intervals. Each time interval represents an *interest period.* Then the interest earned on the original amount is calculated according to a specified interest rate at the end of the interest period. Two approaches are in use in calculating the earned interest: *simple interest* and *compound interest.*

The first approach considers that the interest earned in any present activity is a linear function of time. Consider the situation in which a present amount $P$ is borrowed from the bank, to be repaid $N$ periods hence by a future amount $F$. The difference, $F - P$, is simply the interest payment $I$ owed to the bank for the use of the principal $P$ dollars. Because the interest earned is directly proportional to the principal, the interest $i$ is called *simple interest* and is computed from

$$\begin{aligned} I &= F - P \\ &= (Pi)N \\ F &= P + (Pi)N \\ &= P(1 + iN) \end{aligned} \tag{2.1}$$

The second approach assumes that the earned interest is not withdrawn at the end of an interest period and is automatically redeposited with the original sum in the next interest period. The interest thus accumulated is called *compound interest.* For example, if we deposit $100 in a bank that pays 5% compounded annually and leave the interest in the account, we will have

| | | |
|---|---|---|
| after 1 year | $100 (1.05) = | $105.00 |
| after 2 years | $105.00 (1.05) = | $110.25 |
| after 3 years | $110.25 (1.05) = | $115.7625 |

The amount $115.7625 is greater than the original $100 plus the simple interest of $100(0.05)(3), which would be $115.00, because the interest earned during the first and second periods earns additional interest. Symbolically, we can represent a future amount $F$ at time $N$ in terms of a present amount $P$ at time 0, assuming i% interest per period:

$$\begin{aligned} F_1 &= P(1 + i) && \text{after 1 year} \\ F_2 &= F_1(1 + i) = P(1 + i)^2 && \text{after 2 years} \\ &\vdots \\ F_N &= F_{N-1}(1 + i) = P(1 + i)^N && \text{after } N \text{ years} \end{aligned}$$

or

$$F = P[(1 + i)^N] \tag{2.2}$$

From Eq. 2.2, the total interest earned over $N$ periods with the compound interest is

$$I = F - P = P[(1 + i)^N - 1] \tag{2.3}$$

The additional interest earned with the compound interest is

$$\begin{aligned} \Delta I &= P[(1 + i)^N - 1] - PiN \\ &= P[(1 + i)^N - (1 + iN)] \end{aligned} \tag{2.4}$$

As either $i$ or $N$ becomes large, $\Delta I$ also becomes large, so the effect of compounding is further pronounced.

### *Example 2.1*

Compare the interest earned by $1,000 for 10 years at 9% simple interest with that earned by the same amount for 10 years at 9% compounded annually.

$$\Delta I = 1000[(1 + 0.09)^{10} - (1 + 0.09(10))] = \$467.36$$

The difference in interest payments is $467.36. □

Unless stated otherwise, practically all financial transactions are based on compound interest; however, the length of the interest period for compounding and the interest rate per period must be specified for individual transactions. In the next section we discuss the conventions used in describing the interest period and the compounding period in business transactions.

### 2.3.3 Nominal and Effective Interest Rates

In engineering economic analysis, a year is usually used as the interest period, because investments in engineering projects are of long duration and a calendar year is a convenient period for accounting and tax computation. In financial transactions, however, the interest period may be of any duration—a month, a quarter, a year, and so on. For example, the interest charge for the purchase of a car on credit may be compounded monthly, whereas the interest accrued from a savings account in a credit union may be compounded quarterly. Consequently, we must introduce the terms nominal interest rate and effective interest rate to describe more precisely the nature of compounding schemes.

***Nominal Interest.*** If a financial institution uses more than one interest period per year in compounding the interest, it usually quotes the interest on an annual basis. For example, a year's interest at 1.5% compounded each month is typically quoted as "18% (1.5% × 12) compounded monthly." When the interest rate is stated in this fashion, the 18% interest is called a *nominal interest rate* or *annual percentage rate.* The nominal interest rate, while convenient for a financial institution to use in quoting interest rates on its transactions, does not explain the effect of any compounding during the year. We use the term effective interest rate to describe more precisely the compounding effect of any business transaction.

***Effective Interest Rate.*** The effective interest rate represents the actual interest earned or charged for a specified time period. In specifying such a time period, we may use the convention of either a year or a time period identical to the payment period. The effective interest rate based on a year is referred to as the *effective annual interest rate* $i_a$. The effective interest rate based on the payment period is called the *effective interest rate per payment period* $i$.

We will first look at the expression of the effective annual interest rate. Suppose a bank charges an interest rate of 12% compounded quarterly. This means that the interest rate per period is 3% (12%/4) for each of the 3-month periods during the year. Then interest for a sum of $1 accrued at the end of the year (see Eq. 2.3) is

$$\left(1 + \frac{0.12}{4}\right)^4 - 1 = 0.1255$$

Thus, the effective annual interest rate is 12.55%. Similarly, an interest rate of 12% compounded monthly means that the interest rate per period is 1% (12%/12) for each month during the year. Thus, the effective annual interest rate is

$$\left(1 + \frac{0.12}{12}\right)^{12} - 1 = 0.1268 = 12.68\%$$

Now we can generalize the result as

$$i_a = \left(1 + \frac{r}{M}\right)^M - 1 \tag{2.5}$$

where $i_a$ = the effective annual interest rate,
$r$ = the nominal interest rate per year,
$M$ = the number of interest (compounding) periods per year,
$r/M$ = the interest rate per interest period.

For the special case where $M = 1$ (i.e., one interest period per year, or annual compounding) and $r/M = r$, Eq. 2.5 reduces to $i_a = r = i$. This simply means that with annual compounding we do not need to distinguish between the nominal and effective interest rates.

The result of Eq. 2.5 can be further generalized to compute the effective interest rate in *any payment period.* This results in

$$\begin{aligned} i &= \left(1 + \frac{r}{M}\right)^C - 1 \\ &= \left(1 + \frac{r}{CK}\right)^C - 1 \end{aligned} \tag{2.6}$$

where $i$ = the effective interest rate per payment period,
$C$ = the number of interest periods per payment period,
$K$ = the number of payment periods per year,
$r/K$ = the nominal interest rate per payment period.

In deriving Eq. 2.6, we should note the relationships $M \geq C$ and $M = CK$. Obviously, when $K = 1$, $C$ is equal to $M$, and therefore $i = i_a$. Figure 2.1 illustrates the relationship between the nominal and effective interest rates.

Some financial institutions offer a large number of interest periods per year, such as $M = 365$ (daily compounding). As the number of interest periods $M$ becomes very large, the interest rate per interest period, $r/M$, becomes very small. If $M$ approaches infinity and $r/M$ approaches zero as a limit, the limiting

Situation: Interest is calculated on the basis of 12% compounded monthly. Payments are made quarterly.

$K$ = 4, 4 quarterly payment periods per year
$C$ = 3, 3 interest (compounding) periods per quarter
$r$ = 12%
$M$ = 12, 12 monthly interest (compounding) periods per year
$r/M$ = 1%, the interest rate per month
$r/K$ = 3%, the nominal interest rate per quarter

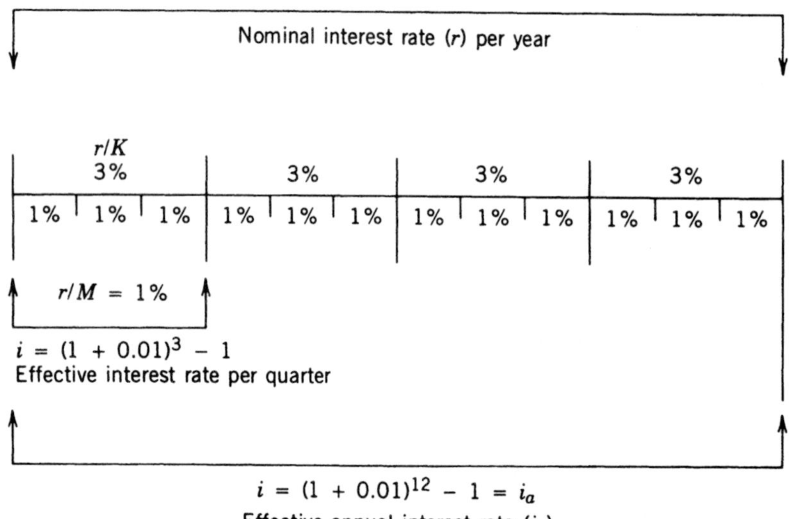


**FIGURE 2.1 Functional relationships of $r$, $i$, and $i_a$ for monthly compounding with quarterly payments.**

condition is equivalent to continuous compounding. By taking limits on both sides of Eq. 2.6, we obtain

$$
\begin{aligned}
i &= \lim_{M\to\infty}\left[\left(1 + \frac{r}{M}\right)^{M} - 1\right] \\
&= \lim_{CK\to\infty}\left[\left(1 + \frac{r}{CK}\right)^{C} - 1\right] \\
&= \lim_{CK\to\infty}\left(1 + \frac{r}{CK}\right)^{C} - 1 \\
&= \lim_{CK\to\infty}\left[\left(1 + \frac{r}{CK}\right)^{CK}\right]^{1/K} - 1 \\
&= (e^{r})^{1/K} - 1 \\
&= e^{r/K} - 1 \qquad (2.7)
\end{aligned}
$$

For the effective annual interest rate for continuous compounding, we simply evaluate Eq. 2.7 by setting $K$ to 1. This gives us

$$i_a = e^r - 1 \tag{2.8}$$

## *Example 2.2*

Find the effective interest rate per quarter at a nominal rate of 18% compounded (1) quarterly, (2) monthly, and (3) continuously.

**1.** Quarterly compounding

$$r = 18\%, \quad M = 4, \quad C = 1, \quad K = 4$$

$$i = \left(1 + \frac{0.18}{4}\right)^1 - 1 = 4.5\%$$

**2.** Monthly compounding

$$r = 18\%, \quad M = 12, \quad C = 3, \quad K = 4$$

$$i = \left(1 + \frac{0.18}{12}\right)^3 - 1 = 4.568\%$$

**3.** Continuous compounding

$$r = 18\%, \quad K = 4, \quad (M = \infty, C = \infty)$$

$$i = e^{0.18/4} - 1 = 4.603\%$$

If we deposit \$1,000 in a bank for just one quarter at the interest rate and compounding frequencies specified, our balance at the end of the quarter will grow to \$1,045, \$1,045.68, and \$1,046.03, respectively. □

In Example 2.2 we examined how our deposit balance would grow for a time period of one quarter, but these results can be generalized for deposits of any duration. In the sections ahead, we will develop interest formulas that facilitate the interest compounding associated with various types of cash flow and compounding frequencies. For this presentation, we will group the compound interest formulas into four categories by the type of compounding and type of cash flow. We will first consider discrete compounding in which compounding occurs at a discrete point in time: annual compounding, monthly compounding, and so forth.

## 2.4 DISCRETE COMPOUNDING

### 2.4.1 Comparable Payment and Compounding Periods

We first consider the situations for which the payment periods are identical to the compounding periods (annual payments with annual compounding, quarterly payments with quarterly compounding, monthly payments with monthly compounding, and so forth).

***Single Sums.*** In the simplest situation we deposit a single sum of money $P$ in a financial institution for $N$ interest periods. To determine how much can be accumulated by the end of $N$ periods, we may use the result developed in Eq. 2.2,

$$F = P(1 + i)^N \tag{2.9}$$

The factor $(1 + i)^N$ is called the *single-payment compound amount factor* and is available in tables indexed by $i$ and $N$. It is represented symbolically by $(F/P, i, N)$. Note that where payment and compounding periods are identical, the effective interest rate is simply $i = r/M$. This transaction can be portrayed by the cash flow diagram shown in Figure 2.2. (Note the time scale convention: the first period begins at $n = 0$ and ends at $n = 1$.)

For example, consider a deposit of $1,000 for 8 years in an individual retirement account (IRA) that earns an interest rate of 11% compounded annually. The balance of the account at the end of 8 years will be

$$F = \$1000(1 + 0.11)^8 = \$2,304.54$$

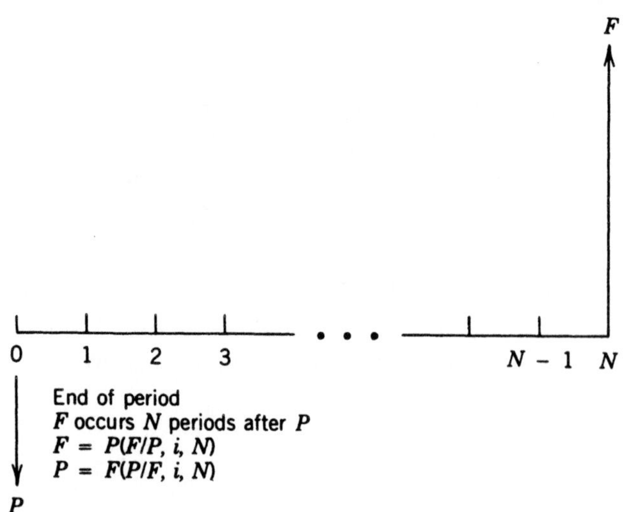


**FIGURE 2.2** Cash flow diagram for a single payment.

If the account earns the interest at the rate of 11% compounded quarterly, the balance becomes

$$F = \$1000\left(1 + \frac{0.11}{4}\right)^{32} = \$2,382.42$$

If we wish to know what sum $P$ we must deposit with a bank now, at $i$% compounded periodically, in order to have a future sum $F$ in $N$ periods, we can solve Eq. 2.9 for $P$.

$$P = F[(1 + i)^{-N}] \tag{2.10}$$

The bracketed term is called the *single-payment present-worth factor,* designated by $(P/F, i, N)$.

For example, we will have \$100 at the end of 3 years if we deposit \$86.38 in a 5% interest-bearing account:

$$P = \$100(\overset{P/F,5\%,3}{0.8638}) = \$86.38$$

***Uniform Series.*** Most transactions with a financial institution involve more than two flows. If we have equal, periodic flows, we can develop formulas for determining beginning and ending balances. For example, an amount $A$ deposited at the *end* of each compounding period in an account paying $i$% will grow to an amount after $N$ periods of

$$A \sum_{n=1}^{N} (1 + i)^{N-n} = A\left[\frac{(1 + i)^N - 1}{i}\right] \tag{2.11}$$

The term in brackets is called the *uniform-series compound amount factor,* or *equal-series compound amount factor,* and is represented by $(F/A, i, N)$. The transaction can be portrayed by the cash flow diagram shown in Figure 2.3. In deriving the summation results in Eq. 2.11, we refer the reader to Table 2.1, which contains closed-form expressions for selected finite summations that are useful in developing interest formulas.

The inverse relationship to Eq. 2.11 yields the *uniform-series sinking-fund factor,* or *sinking-fund factor,*

$$A = F\left[\frac{i}{(1 + i)^N - 1}\right] \tag{2.12}$$

designated by $(A/F, i, N)$. The name derives from a historical practice of depositing a fixed sum at the end of each period into an interest-bearing account (a sinking fund) to provide for replacement moneys for fixed assets.

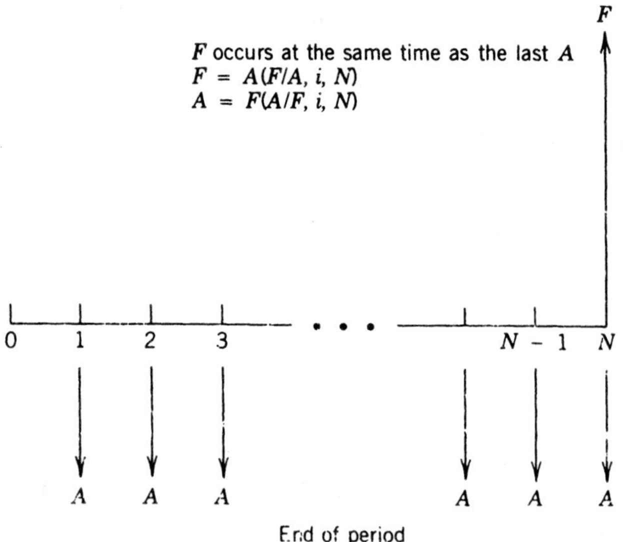


**FIGURE 2.3** Cash flow diagram of the relationship between $A$ and $F$.

**Table 2.1** ***Summations Useful in Deriving Interest Formulas***

Geometric series

$$\sum_{n=0}^{N} x^n = 1 + x + x^2 + \cdots + x^N = \frac{1 - x^{N+1}}{1 - x}$$

where $x \neq 1$

If $-1 < x < 1$, then

$$\sum_{n=0}^{\infty} x^n = 1 + x + x^2 + x^3 + \cdots = \frac{1}{1 - x}$$

Arithmetic–geometric series

$$\sum_{n=0}^{N} nx^n = 0 + x + 2x^2 + \cdots + Nx^N = \frac{x[1 - (N + 1)x^N + Nx^{N+1}]}{(1 - x)^2}$$

where $x \neq 1$

If $-1 < x < 1$, then

$$\sum_{n=0}^{\infty} nx^n = 0 + x + 2x^2 + 3x^3 + \cdots = \frac{x}{(1 - x)^2}$$

Educational endowment funds can be constructed conveniently by using the sinking-fund factor: to build a \$12,000 fund in 18 years at 5% compounded annually requires

$$A = \$12{,}000\overset{A/F,5\%,18}{(0.0356)} = \$427.20 \quad \text{at the end of each year}$$

The relationships among *P, F,* and *A* can be manipulated to relate a series of equal, periodic flows (defined by *A*) to a present amount *P*. Substituting Eq. 2.11 into Eq. 2.9 yields

$$P = A\left[\frac{(1 + i)^N - 1}{i(1 + i)^N}\right] \tag{2.13}$$

and its inverse

$$A = P\left[\frac{i(1 + i)^N}{(1 + i)^N - 1}\right] \tag{2.14}$$

The bracketed term in Eq. 2.13 is the *uniform-series present worth factor,* designated by (*P/A, i, N*). The term in Eq. 2.14 is the *uniform-series capital recovery factor,* or simply the *capital recovery factor,* represented by (*A/P, i, N*). Figure 2.4 shows the cash flow transactions associated with these factors. The latter factor can be used to determine loan repayment schedules so that principal and interest are repaid over a given time period in equal end-of-period amounts.

To illustrate the use of *A/P* and *P/A* factors, consider a commercial mortgage at 8% over 20 years, with a loan principal of \$1 million. If equal year-end payments are desired, each annual payment must be

$$\$1{,}000{,}000\overset{A/P,8\%,20}{(0.10185)} = \$101{,}850$$

The loan schedule can then be constructed as in Table 2.2. The interest due at $n = 1$ is 8% of the \$1 million outstanding during the first year. The \$21,850 left over is applied to the principal, reducing the amount outstanding in the second year to \$978,150. The interest due in the second year is 8% of \$978,150, or \$78,252, leaving \$23,598 for repayment of the principal. At $n = 20$, the last \$101,850 payment is just sufficient to pay the interest on the outstanding loan principal and to repay the outstanding principal.

Such an equal-payments scheme is also common for home mortgages and automobile loans. In each period a decreasing amount of interest is paid, leaving a larger amount to reduce the principal. Each reduction of loan principal increases an owner's equity in the item by a corresponding amount.

The series present worth factor can be useful for determining the outstanding balance of a loan at any time, as portrayed in Table 2.2. At the end of the fifth year, for example, we still owe 15 payments of \$101,850. The value of those

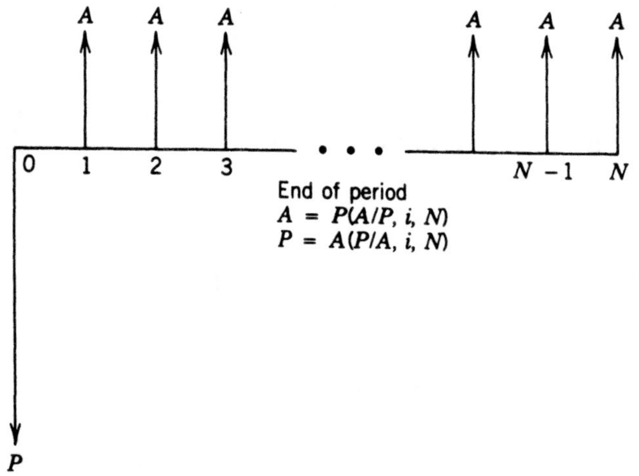


**FIGURE 2.4** Equal-payment series and single present amount.

**Table 2.2** ***A Loan Repayment Schedule Showing Principal and Interest Payments***

| Year | Beginning Loan Balance | Interest Payment | Principal Payment | Total Payment |
|---|---|---|---|---|
| 1 | 1,000,000* | 80,000 | 21,850 | 101,850 |
| 2 | 978,150 | 78,252 | 23,598 | 101,850 |
| 3 | 954,552 | 76,364 | 25,486 | 101,850 |
| 4 | 929,066 | 74,325 | 27,525 | 101,850 |
| 5 | 901,541 | 72,123 | 29,727 | 101,850 |
| 6 | 871,814 | 69,745 | 32,105 | 101,850 |
| 7 | 839,709 | 67,177 | 34,673 | 101,850 |
| 8 | 805,036 | 64,403 | 37,447 | 101,850 |
| 9 | 767,589 | 61,407 | 40,443 | 101,850 |
| 10 | 727,146 | 58,172 | 43,678 | 101,850 |
| 11 | 683,468 | 54,677 | 47,173 | 101,850 |
| 12 | 636,295 | 50,904 | 50,946 | 101,850 |
| 13 | 585,349 | 46,828 | 55,022 | 101,850 |
| 14 | 530,327 | 42,426 | 59,424 | 101,850 |
| 15 | 470,903 | 37,672 | 64,178 | 101,850 |
| 16 | 406,725 | 32,538 | 69,312 | 101,850 |
| 17 | 337,413 | 26,993 | 74,857 | 101,850 |
| 18 | 262,556 | 21,005 | 60,845 | 101,850 |
| 19 | 181,711 | 14,537 | 87,313 | 101,850 |
| 20 | 94,398 | 7,452 | 94,398 | 101,850 |

*All figures are rounded to nearest dollars.

NOTE: Loan Amount = $1,000,000
Loan life = 20 years
Loan interest = 8% compounded annually
Equal annual payment size = $1,000,000(*A*/*P*, 8%, 20)
= $1,000,000(0.10185)
= $101,850

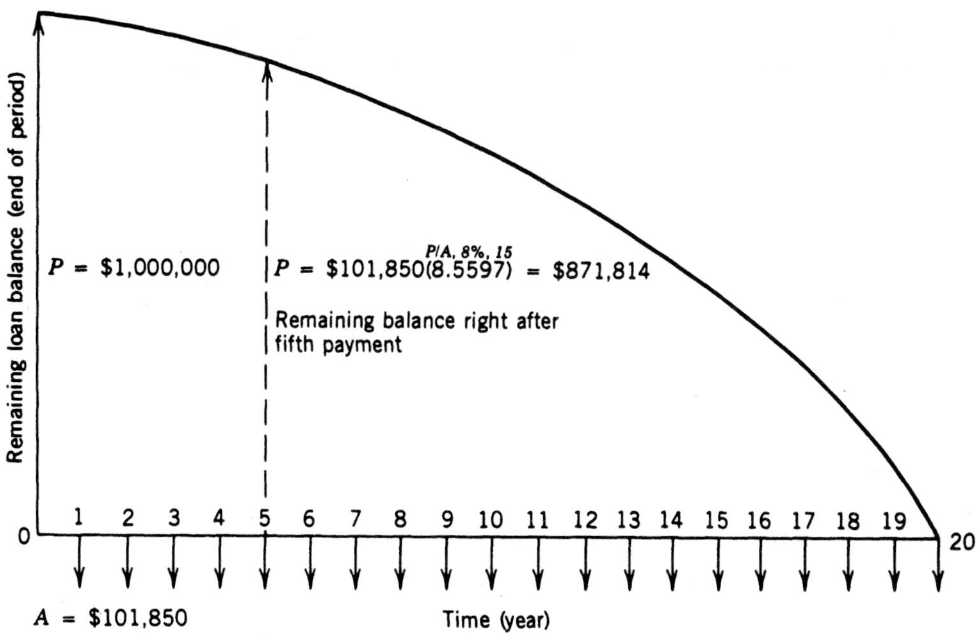


**FIGURE 2.5** loan balance as a function of time ($n$).

payments at time 5 can be represented as in Figure 2.5 with the time scale shifted by 5 and is found from the equation to be

$$P = \$101{,}850\overset{P/A,8\%,15}{(8.5595)} = \$871{,}785$$

which is the same as the $871,814 in Table 2.2.

## *Example 2.3*

Suppose we are in the market for a medium-sized used car. We have surveyed the dealers' advertisements in the newspaper and have found a car that should fulfill our needs. The asking price of the car is $7,500, and the dealer proposes that we make a $500 down payment now and pay the rest of the balance in equal end-of-month payments of $194.82 each over a 48-month period. Consider the following situations.

1. Instead of using the dealer's financing, we decide to make a down payment of $500 and borrow the rest from a bank at 12% compounded monthly. What would be our monthly payment to pay off the loan in 4 years? To find $A$,

$$i = \frac{12\%}{12 \text{ periods}} = 1\% \text{ per month}$$

$$N = (4 \text{ years})(12 \text{ periods per year}) = 48 \text{ periods}$$

$$A = P(A/P,\ i,\ N) = (\$7{,}500 - \$500)\overset{A/P,1\%,48}{(0.0263)} = \$184.34$$

2. We are going to accept the dealer's offer but we want to know the effective rate of interest per month that the dealer is charging. To find $i$, let $P$ = \$7,000, $A$ = \$194.82, and $N$ = 48.

$$\$194.82 = \$7{,}000(A/P,\ i,\ 48)$$

The satisfying value $i$ can be found by trial and error from

$$(A/P,\ i,\ 48) = \frac{i(1+i)^{48}}{(1+i)^{48}-1} = 0.0278$$

to be $i$ = 1.25% per month. This value is used to find the nominal annual interest rate used by the dealer.

$$\begin{aligned} r = (i)(M) &= (1.25\% \text{ per month})(12 \text{ months per year}) \\ &= 15\% \text{ per year} \end{aligned}$$

Then the effective annual interest used by the dealer is simply

$$i_a = \left(1 + \frac{0.15}{12}\right)^{12} - 1 = 16.08\% \quad \square$$

***Linear Gradient Series.*** Many engineering economy problems, particularly those related to equipment maintenance, involve cash flows that change by a constant amount ($G$) each period. We can use the gradient factors to convert such gradient series to present amounts and equal annual series. Consider the series

$$F_n = (n-1)G, \qquad n = 1, 2, \ldots, N \tag{2.15}$$

As shown in Figure 2.6, the gradient $G$ can be either positive or negative. If $G >$ 0, we call the series an increasing gradient series. If $G < 0$, we have a decreasing gradient series. We can apply the single-payment present-worth factor to each term of the series and obtain the expression

$$P = \sum_{n=1}^{N} (n-1)G(1+i)^{-n} \tag{2.16}$$

Using the finite summation of a linear function in Table 2.1, we obtain

$$P = G\left[\frac{1-(1+Ni)(1+i)^{-N}}{i^2}\right] \tag{2.17}$$

The resulting factor in brackets is called the ***gradient series present-worth factor*** and is designated $(P/G,\ i,\ N)$.

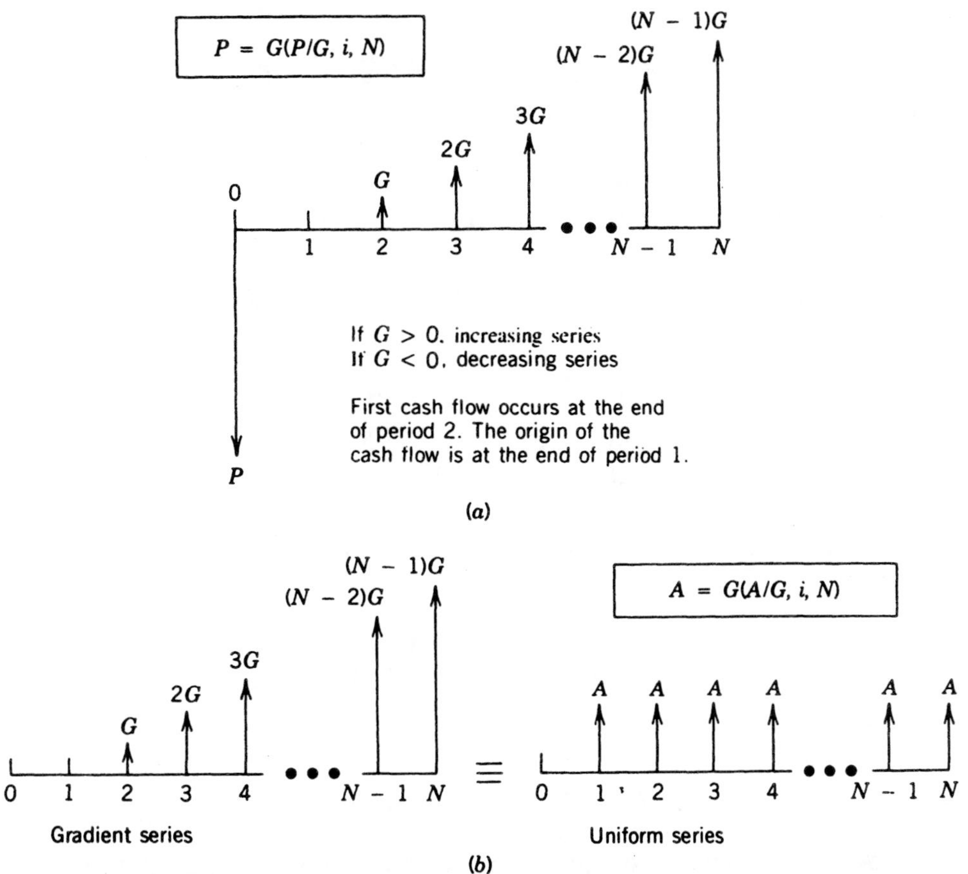


**FIGURE 2.6 Cash flow diagram for a gradient series. (*a*) A strictly gradient series. (*b*) Conversion factor from a gradient series to a uniform series.**

A uniform series equivalent to the gradient series can be obtained by substituting Eq. 2.17 into Eq. 2.14 for $P$,

$$A = G\left[\frac{1}{i} - \frac{N}{(1+i)^N - 1}\right] \tag{2.18}$$

where the resulting factor in brackets is referred to as the *gradient-to-uniform-series conversion factor* and is designated $(A/G, i, N)$.

To obtain the future-worth equivalent of a gradient series, we substitute Eq. 2.18 into Eq. 2.14 for $A$

$$F = \frac{G}{i}\left[\frac{(1+i)^N - 1}{i} - N\right]$$

$$= \frac{G}{i}\left[(F/A, i, N) - N\right] \tag{2.19}$$

### *Example 2.4*

An example of the use of a gradient factor is to find the future amount of the following series with $i = 10\%$ per period.

| $n$ | 0 | 1 | 2 | 3 | 4 | 5 | 6 | 7 | 8 |
|---|---|---|---|---|---|---|---|---|---|
| $F_n$ | 0 | 100 | 106 | 112 | 118 | 124 | 130 | 136 | 142 |

The constant portion of 100 is separated from the gradient series of 0,0,6,12, . . . , 42.

| $n$ | 0 | 1 | 2 | 3 | 4 | 5 | 6 | 7 | 8 |
|---|---|---|---|---|---|---|---|---|---|
| $F_n$ | 0 | 100 | 100 | 100 | 100 | 100 | 100 | 100 | 100 |
| | 0 | 0 | 6 | 12 | 18 | 24 | 30 | 36 | 42 |

We can quickly verify that the portion of the strict gradient series will accumulate to $206.15.

$$F = 100\overset{F/A,10\%,8}{(11.436)} + \frac{6}{0.1}[\overset{F/A,10\%,8}{(11.436)} - 8]$$

$$= 1{,}143.60 + 206.15$$

$$= 1{,}349.76 \quad \square$$

***Geometric Series.*** In many situations periodic payments increase or decrease over time, not by a constant amount (gradient) but by a constant percentage (geometric growth). If we use $g$ to designate the percentage change in the payment from one period to the next, the magnitude of the $n$th payment, $F_n$, is related to the first payment, $F_1$, by

$$F_n = F_1(1 + g)^{n-1}, \qquad n = 1, 2, \ldots, N \tag{2.20}$$

As illustrated in Figure 2.7, $g$ can be either positive or negative, depending on the type of cash flow. If $g > 0$ the series will increase, and if $g < 0$ the series will decrease.

To find an expression for the present amount $P$, we apply the single-payment present-worth factor to each term of the series

$$P = \sum_{n=1}^{N} F_1(1 + g)^{n-1}(1 + i)^{-n} \tag{2.21}$$

Bringing the term $F_1(1 + g)^{-1}$ outside the summation yields

$$P = \frac{F_1}{1 + g}\sum_{n=1}^{N}\left(\frac{1 + g}{1 + i}\right)^n \tag{2.22}$$

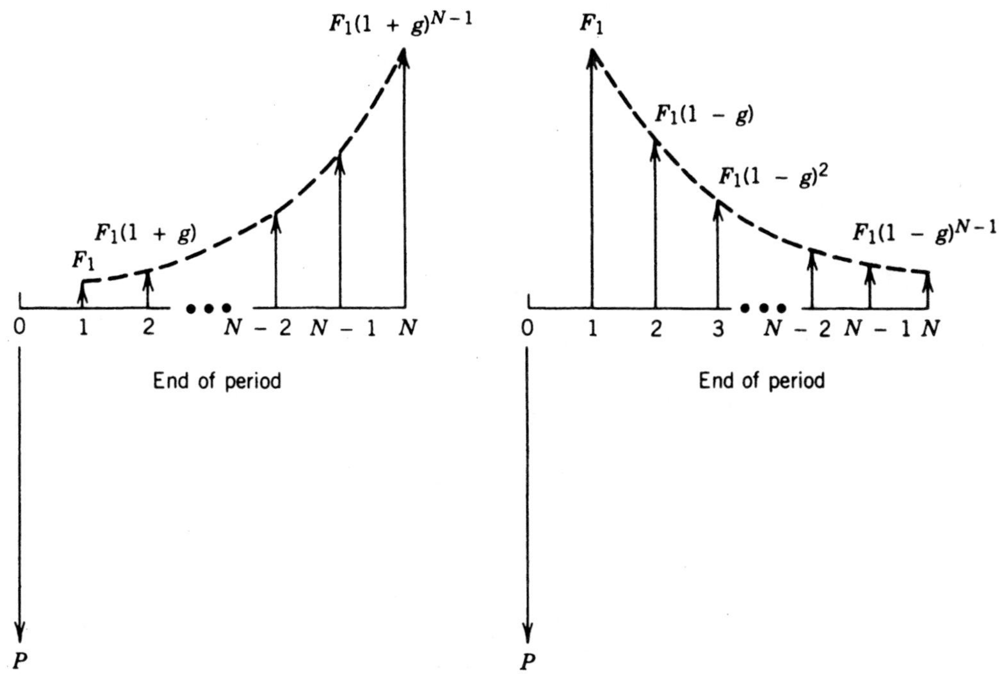


**FIGURE 2.7** Cash flow diagram of the geometric series.

The summation in Eq. 2.22 represents the first $N$ terms of a geometric series, and the closed-form expression for the partial geometric summation yields the following relationship.

$$P = \begin{cases} F_1\left[\dfrac{1-(1+g)^N(1+i)^{-N}}{i-g}\right] & i \neq g \\ \dfrac{NF_1}{1+i} & i = g \end{cases} \tag{2.23}$$

This present-worth factor is designated $(P/A, g, i, N)$.

The future-worth equivalent of the geometric series is obtained by substituting Eq. 2.23 into Eq. 2.5 to find $(F/A, g, i, N)$.

$$F = \begin{cases} F_1\left[\dfrac{(1+i)^N(1+i)^{-N}}{i-g}\right] & i \neq g \\ NF_1(1+i)^{N-1} & i = g \end{cases} \tag{2.24}$$

We may use an alternative expression of Eq. 2.23 as shown in [4]. In Eq. 2.22 we may rewrite the term $(1+g)/(1+i)$ as

$$\frac{1+g}{1+i} = \frac{1}{1+g'} \tag{2.25}$$

or

$$g' = \frac{1 + i}{1 + g} - 1$$

We then substitute Eq. 2.25 back into Eq. 2.22 to obtain

$$P = \frac{F_1}{1 + g} \sum_{n=1}^{N} (1 + g')^{-n} \tag{2.26}$$

The summation term constitutes the uniform-series present-worth factor for $N$ periods. Therefore,

$$P = \frac{F_1}{1 + g}\left[\frac{g'(1 + g')^N}{(1+g') - 1}\right]$$

$$= \frac{F_1}{1 + g}(P/A, g', N), g \neq i \tag{2.27}$$

If $g < i$, then $g' > 0$, and we can use the $(P/A, g', N)$ factor to find $P$. If $g = i$, then $g' = 0$, and the value of $(P/A, g', N)$ will be $N$. The geometric-series factor thus reduces to $P = F_1N/(1 + g)$. If $g > i$, then $g' < 0$. In this case, no table values can be used to evaluate the $P/A$ factor, and it will have to be calculated directly from a formula. Table 2.3 summarizes the interest formulas developed in this section and the cash flow situations in which they should be used.

### *Example 2.5*

A mining company is concerned about the increasing cost of diesel fuel for their mining operation. A special piece of mining equipment, a tractor-mounted ripper, is used to loosen the earth in open-pit mining operations. The company thinks that the diesel fuel consumption will escalate at the rate of 10% per year as the efficiency of the equipment decreases. The company's records indicate that the ripper averages 18 gallons per operational hour in year 1, with 2,000 hours of operation per year. What would the present worth of the cost of fuel for this ripper be for the next five years if the interest rate is 15% compounded annually?

Assuming that all the fuel costs occur at the end of each year, we determine the present equivalent fuel cost by calculating the fuel cost for the first year:

$$F_1 = (\$1.10/\text{gal})(18\ \text{gal/hr})(2{,}000\ \text{hr/year}) = \$39{,}600/\text{year}$$

$$(g = 0.10, N = 5, i = 0.15)$$

Then, using the appropriate factors in Eq. 2.23, we compute

$$P = \$39{,}600\left[\frac{1 - (1 + 0.10)^5(1 + 0.15)^{-5}}{0.15 - 0.10}\right] = \$157{,}839.18$$

**Table 2.3** ***Summary of Discrete Compounding Formulas with Discrete Payments***

| Flow Type | Factor Notation | Formula | Cash Flow Diagram |
|---|---|---|---|
| Single | Compound amount $(F/P, i, N)$ | $F = P(1 + i)^N$ |  0 … N; P at 0, F at N |
| Single | Present worth $(P/F, i, N)$ | $P = F(1 + i)^{-N}$ | |
| Equal payment series | Compound amount $(F/A, i, N)$ | $F = A\left[\frac{(1 + i)^N - 1}{i}\right]$ | 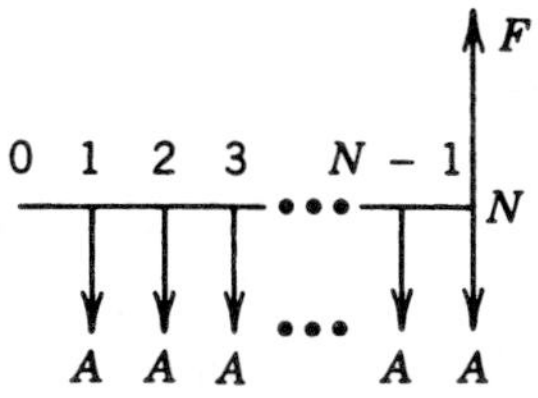 0 1 2 3 … N − 1 N; A A A … A A; F at N |
| Equal payment series | Sinking fund $(A/F, i, N)$ | $A = F\left[\frac{i}{(1 + i)^N - 1}\right]$ | |
| Equal payment series | Present worth $(P/A, i, N)$ | $P = A\left[\frac{(1 + i)^N - 1}{i(1 + i)^N}\right]$ | 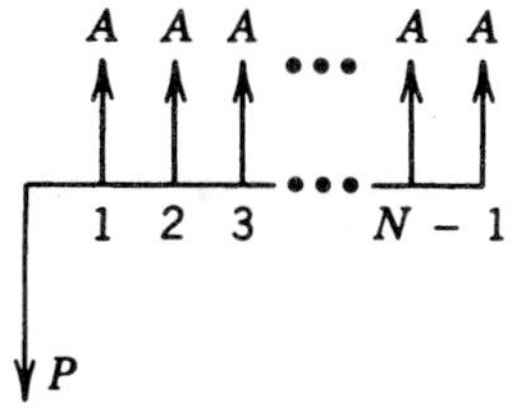 A A A … A A; 1 2 3 … N − 1; P |
| Equal payment series | Capital recovery $(A/P, i, N)$ | $A = P\left[\frac{i(1 + i)^N}{(1 + i)^N - 1}\right]$ | |
| Gradient series | Uniform gradient Present worth $(P/G, i, N)$ | $P = G\left[\frac{(1 + i)^N - iN - 1}{i^2(1 + i)^N}\right]$ | 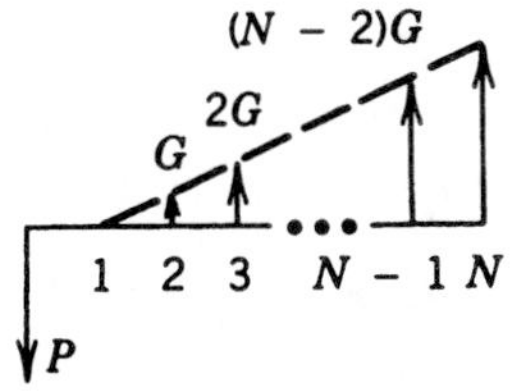 G, 2G, … (N − 2)G; 1 2 3 … N − 1 N; P |
| Gradient series | Geometric gradient Present worth $(P/A, g, i, N)$ | $P = \begin{cases} F_1\left[\frac{1 - (1 + g)^N(1 + i)^{-N}}{i - g}\right] \\ \frac{NF_1}{1 + i} \quad (\text{if } i = g) \end{cases}$ | 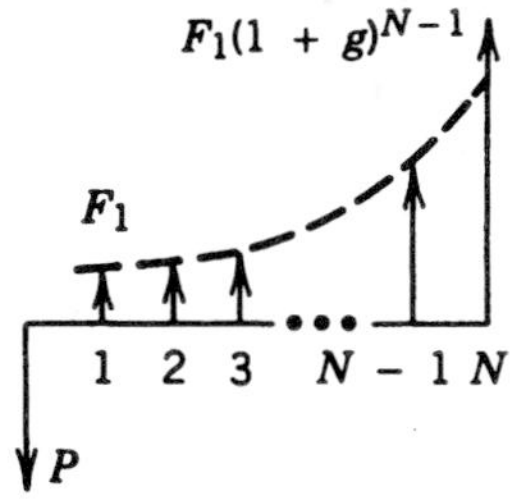 $F_1$, … $F_1(1 + g)^{N-1}$; 1 2 3 … N − 1 N; P |

Source: Park [3].

Using the alternative formula in Eq. 2.27, we first compute

$$g' = \frac{1.15}{1.10} - 1 = 0.04545$$

We then obtain

$$P = \frac{39{,}600}{1.10} \overset{P/A,\ 4.545\%,5}{(4.38442)} = 157{,}839.20$$

Although Eq. 2.27 looks more compact than Eq. 2.23, it does not provide any computational advantage in this example. □

All the interest formulas developed in Table 2.3 are applicable only to situations in which the compounding period coincides with the payment period. In the next section we discuss situations in which we have noncomparable payment and compounding periods.

### 2.4.2 Noncomparable Payment and Compounding Periods

Whenever the payment period and the compounding period do not correspond, we approach the problem by finding the effective interest rate based on the payment period and then using this rate in the compounding interest formulas in Table 2.3.

The specific computational procedure for noncomparable compounding and payment periods is as follows.

1. Identify the number of compounding periods per year ($M$), the number of payment periods per year ($K$), and the number of interest periods per payment period ($C$).
2. Compute the effective interest rate per payment period, using Eq. 2.6.

$$i = \left(1 + \frac{r}{M}\right)^C - 1$$

3. Find the total number of payment periods.

$$N = K(\text{number of years})$$

4. Use $i$ and $N$ in the appropriate formula given in Table 2.3.

#### *Example 2.6*

What is the present worth of a series of equal quarterly payments of $1,000 that extends over a period of 5 years if the interest rate is 8% compounded monthly? The variables are

$K = 4$ payment periods per year

$M = 12$ compounding periods per year

$C = 3$ interest periods per payment period (quarter)

$r = 8\%$

$$i = \left(1 + \frac{r}{M}\right)^C - 1 = \left(1 + \frac{0.08}{12}\right)^3 - 1 = 2.0133\% \text{ per quarter}$$

$N = (5)(4) = 20$ payment periods

Then the present amount is

$$\begin{aligned} P &= A(P/A, i, N) \\ &= \$1000(P/A, 2.0133\%, 20) = \$16{,}330.37 \quad \square \end{aligned}$$

In certain situations the compounding periods occur *less* frequently than the payment periods. Depending on the financial institution involved, no interest may be paid for funds deposited during an interest period. The accounting methods used by most firms record cash transactions at the end of the period in which they have occurred, and any cash transactions that occur within a compounding period are assumed to have occurred at the end of that period. Thus, when cash flows occur daily but the compounding period is monthly, we sum the cash flows within each month (ignoring interest) and place them at the end of each month. The modified cash flows become the basis for any calculations involving the interest factors.

In the extreme situation in which payment occurs more frequently than compounding, we might find that the cash flows continuously throughout the planning horizon on a somewhat uniform basis. If this happens, we can also apply the approach discussed earlier (integrating instead of summing all cash flows that occur during the compounding period and placing them at the end of each compounding period) to find the present worth of the cash flow series. In practice, we avoid this cumbersome approach by adopting the funds flow concept, which is discussed in the next section.

### *Example 2.7*

Consider the cash flow diagram shown in Figure 2.8*a*, where the time scale is monthly. If interest is compounded quarterly, the cash flows can be relocated as shown in Figure 2.8*b*. The cash flow shown in Figure 2.8*b* is equivalent to the cash flow in Figure 2.8*a* for quarterly compounding. After the equivalent cash flow is determined, we can proceed as previously discussed for the situation in which the compounding periods and the payment periods coincide.

Let $i = 3\%$ per quarter. Then the present worth of cash flow given in Figure 2.8*a* is equivalent to the present worth of cash flow given in Figure 2.8*b*. Since $G = \$90$,

$$P = \$330\overset{P/A,3\%,8}{(7.0197)} + \$90\overset{P/G,3\%,8}{(23.4806)} = \$4{,}429.76 \quad \square$$

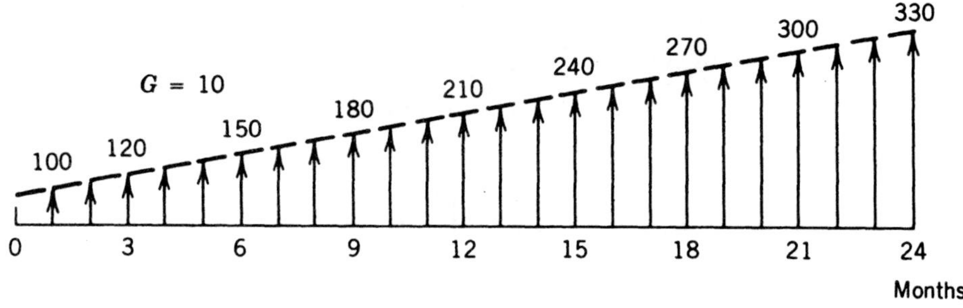


(a)

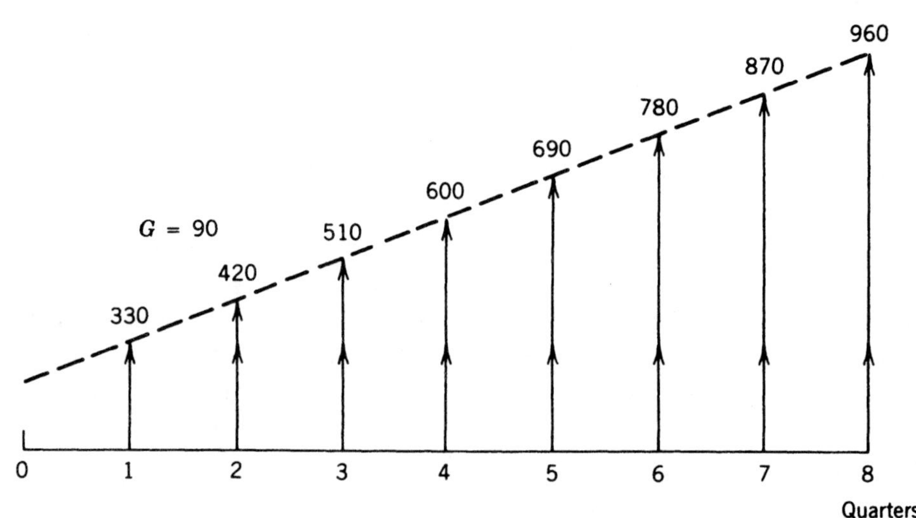


(b)

**FIGURE 2.8** **Example of cash flows where compounding is less frequent than payment. (*a*) Original cash flows. (*b*) Equivalent quarterly cash flows.**

## 2.5 CONTINUOUS COMPOUNDING

### 2.5.1 Discrete Payments

When payments occur at discrete points in time but interest is permitted to compound an infinite number of times per year (that is, continuously in time), we have the special instance of more frequent compounding than payments discussed in Section 2.4.2. Therefore, we approach the problem in the following way.

1. Identify the payment periods per year ($K$).
2. Compute $i = e^{r/K} - 1$ by using Eq. 2.7.
3. Find the total number of payment periods.

$$N = K \quad \text{(number of years)}$$

4. Use $i$ and $N$ in the appropriate interest formulas given in Table 2.3.

We can derive a new family of interest factors under continuous compounding by substituting $e^r - 1$ for $i$ when payments are annual and $e^{r/K} - 1$

**Table 2.4** ***Summary of Continuous Compounding Formulas with Annual Payments***

| Flow Type | Factor Notation | Formula | Cash Flow Diagram |
|---|---|---|---|
| Single | Compound amount $(F/P, r, N)$ | $F = P(e^{rN})$ | |
| | Present worth $(P/F, r, N)$ | $P = F(e^{-rN})$ | |
| Equal payment series | Compound amount $(F/A, r, N)$ | $F = A\left(\dfrac{e^{rN} - 1}{e^{r} - 1}\right)$ | |
| | Sinking fund $(A/F, r, N)$ | $A = F\left(\dfrac{e^{r} - 1}{e^{rN} - 1}\right)$ | |
| | Present worth $(P/A, r, N)$ | $P = A\left[\dfrac{e^{rN} - 1}{e^{rN}(e^{r} - 1)}\right]$ | |
| | Capital recovery $(A/P, r, N)$ | $A = P\left[\dfrac{e^{rN}(e^{r} - 1)}{e^{rN} - 1}\right]$ | |
| Gradient series | Uniform gradient Present worth $(P/G, r, N)$ | $P = G\left[\dfrac{e^{rN} - 1 - N(e^{r} - 1)}{e^{rN}(e^{r} - 1)^2}\right]$ | |
| | Geometric gradient Present worth $(P/A, g, r, N)$ | $P = \begin{cases} F_1\left[\dfrac{1 - e^{(g-r)N}}{e^{r} - e^{g}}\right] \\ \dfrac{NF_1}{e^{r}} \quad (\text{if } g = e^{r} - 1) \end{cases}$ | |

Source: Park [3].

for $i$ when payments are more frequent than annual. Table 2.4 summarizes the resulting compound interest factors for annual payments.

### *Example 2.8*

What is the present worth of a uniform series of year-end payments of $500 each for 10 years if the interest rate is 8% compounded continuously?

$$\text{Let } r = 0.08$$
$$i = e^r - 1 = 8.33\%$$
$$N = 10$$
$$A = \$500$$

Then

$$P = A\left[\frac{e^{rN} - 1}{e^{rN}(e^r - 1)}\right] = \$500(6.6117) = \$3{,}305.85$$

Using the discrete compounding formula with $i = 8.33\%$, we also find that

$$P = A\overset{P/A,8.33\%,10}{(6.6117)} = \$3{,}305.85 \quad \square$$

### *Example 2.9*

A series of equal quarterly payments of $1,000 extends over a period of 5 years. What is the present worth of this quarterly time series at 8% interest compounded continuously?

Since the payments are quarterly, the calculations must be quarterly. The required calculations are

$$\frac{r}{K} = \frac{8\%}{4 \text{ quarters}} = 2\% \text{ per quarter compounded continuously}$$

$$i = e^{r/K} - 1 = e^{0.02} - 1 = 0.0202 = 2.02\% \text{ per quarter}$$

$$N = (4 \text{ payment periods per year})(5 \text{ years}) = 20 \text{ periods}$$

$$P = A\left[\frac{e^{(r/K)N} - 1}{e^{(r/K)N}(e^{r/K} - 1)}\right] = \$1{,}000(15.3197) = \$16{,}319.70$$

Using the discrete compounding formula with $i = 2.02\%$, we also find that

$$\text{P} = \text{A}\overset{P/A,2.02\%,20}{(16.3197)} = \$16{,}319.70 \quad \square$$

### **2.5.2 Continuous Cash Flows**

It is often appropriate to treat cash flows as though they were continuous rather than discrete. An advantage of the continuous flow representation is its

**Table 2.5** ***Summary of Interest Factors for Continuous Cash Flows with Continuous Compounding***

| Type of Cash Flow | Cash Flow Function | Parameters: To Find | Parameters: Given | Algebraic Notation | Factor Notation |
|---|---|---|---|---|---|
| Uniform (step) | 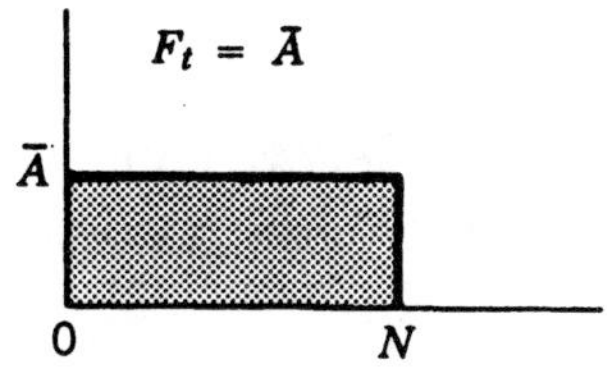 $F_t = \bar{A}$ | $P$ | $\bar{A}$ | $\bar{A}\left(\frac{e^{rN}-1}{re^{rN}}\right)$ | $(P/\bar{A}, r, N)$ |
| | | $\bar{A}$ | $P$ | $P\left(\frac{re^{rN}}{e^{rN}-1}\right)$ | $(\bar{A}/P, r, N)$ |
| | | $F$ | $\bar{A}$ | $\bar{A}\left(\frac{e^{rN}-1}{r}\right)$ | $(F/\bar{A}, r, N)$ |
| | | $\bar{A}$ | $F$ | $F\left(\frac{r}{e^{rN}-1}\right)$ | $(\bar{A}/P, r, N)$ |
| Gradient (ramp) | 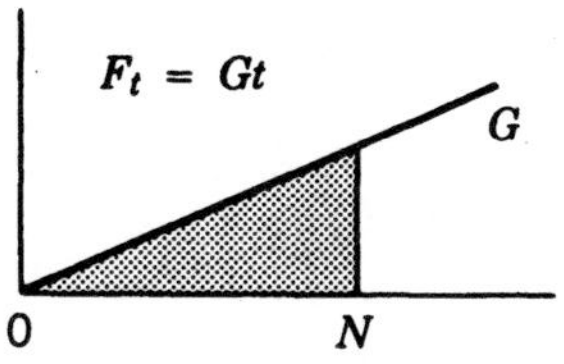 $F_t = Gt$ | $P$ | $G$ | $\frac{G}{r^2}(1-e^{-rN}) - \frac{G}{r}(Ne^{-rN})$ | |
| Decay | 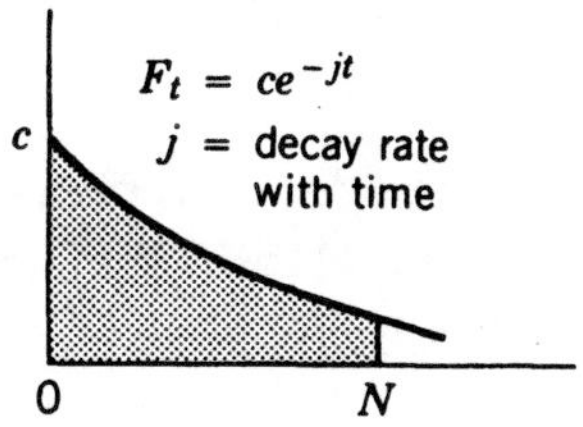 $F_t = ce^{-jt}$; $j$ = decay rate with time | $P$ | $c, j$ | $\frac{c}{r+j}(1-e^{-(r+j)N})$ | |
| Exponential | 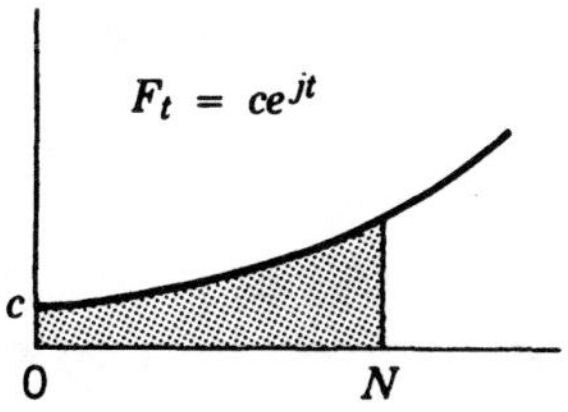 $F_t = ce^{jt}$ | $P$ | $c, j$ | $\frac{c}{r-j}(1-e^{-(r-j)N})$ | |
| Growth | 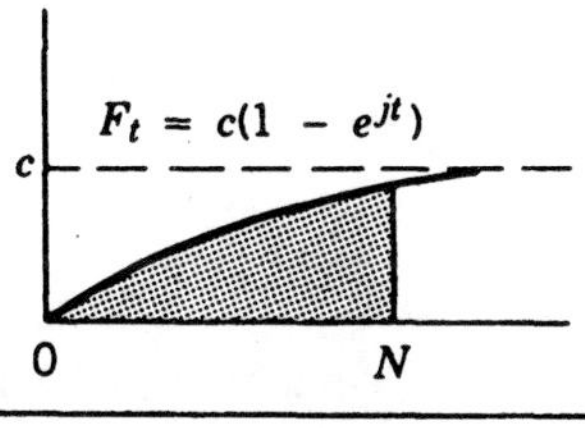 $F_t = c(1-e^{jt})$ | $P$ | $c, j$ | $\frac{c}{r}(1-e^{-rN}) - \frac{c}{r+j}(1-e^{-(r+j)N})$ | |

flexibility for dealing with patterns other than the uniform and gradient ones. Some of the selected continuous cash flow functions are shown in Table 2.5.

To find the present worth of a continuous cash flow function under continuous compounding, we first recognize that the present-worth formula for a discrete series of cash flows with discrete compounding is

$$P = \sum_{n=0}^{N} F_n(1 + i)^{-n}$$

Since $F_n$ becomes a continuous function $F_t$ and the effective annual interest rate $i$ for continuous compounding is $e^r - 1$, integration of the argument instead of summation yields

$$P = \int_0^N (F_t)e^{-rt}\,dt \tag{2.28}$$

[Note that $n \to t$, $F_n \to F_t$, $\sum_{n=0}^{N} \to \int_0^N$, and $(1 + i)^{-n} \to e^{-rt}$.] Then the future value equivalent of $F_t$ over $N$ periods is simply

$$F = \int_0^N F_t e^{r(N-t)}dt \tag{2.29}$$

To illustrate the continuous flow concept, consider $F_t$ to be a uniform flow function when an amount flows at the rate $\bar{A}$ per period for $N$ periods. (This cash flow function is presented in Table 2.5 and is expressed as $F_t = \bar{A}$, $0 \leq t \leq N$.) Then the present-worth equivalent is

$$P = \int_0^N \bar{A}e^{-rt}\,dt = \bar{A}\left(\frac{e^{rN} - 1}{re^{rN}}\right) = \bar{A}\left(\frac{1 - e^{-rN}}{r}\right) \tag{2.30}$$

The resulting factor in parenthesis in (2.30) is referred to as the *funds flow present-worth factor* and is designated $(P/\bar{A}, r, N)$. The future-worth equivalent is obtained from

$$F = \int_0^N \bar{A}e^{rt}\,dt = \bar{A}\left(\frac{e^{rN} - 1}{r}\right) \tag{2.31}$$

The resulting factor $(e^{rN} - 1)/r$ is called the *funds flow compound amount factor* and is designated $(F/\bar{A}, r, N)$. Since the relationships of $\bar{A}$ to $P$ and $F$ are given by Eqs. 2.30 and 2.31, we can easily solve for $\bar{A}$ if $P$ or $F$ is given. Table 2.5 summarizes all the funds flow factors necessary to find present-worth and future-worth equivalents for a variety of cash flow functions.

As a simple example, we compare the present-worth figures obtained in two situations. We deposit \$10 each day for 18 months in a savings account that has an interest rate of 12% compounded daily. Assuming that there are 548 days in the 18-month period, we compute the present worth.

$$P = 10\overset{P/A,0.032877\%,548}{(501.4211)} = \$5{,}014.21$$

Now we approximate this discrete cash flow series by a uniform continuous cash flow profile (assuming continuous compounding). In doing so, we may define $\bar{A}$ as

$$\bar{A} = 10(365) = \$3{,}650/\text{year}$$

Note that our time unit is a year. Thus, an 18-month period is 1.5 years. Substituting these values back into Eq. 2.30 yields

$$P = \int_0^{1.5} 3{,}650e^{-0.12t} = \frac{3{,}650}{0.12}\left(1 - e^{-0.18}\right)$$

$$= \$5{,}010.53$$

The discrepancy between the values obtained by the two methods is only \$3.68.

### *Example 2.10*

A county government is considering building a road from downtown to the airport to relieve congested traffic on the existing two-lane divided highway. Before allowing the sale of a bond to finance the road project, the court has requested an estimate of future toll revenues over the bond life. The toll revenues are directly proportional to the growth of traffic over the years, so the following growth cash flow function (with units in millions of dollars) is assumed to be reasonable.

$$F_t = 5(1 - e^{-0.10t})$$

Find the present worth of toll revenues at 6% interest compounded continuously over a 25-year period.

Expanding $F_t$ gives us

$$F_t = 5 - 5e^{-0.10t}$$

If we let $f(t)_1 = 5$ and $f(t)_2 = -5e^{-0.10t}$, the present-worth equivalent for each function would be

$$P_1 = \int_0^{25} 5e^{-0.06t}\,dt = 5\left[\frac{e^{0.06(25)} - 1}{(0.06)e^{0.06(25)}}\right] = \$64.74$$

$$P_2 = \int_0^{25} -5e^{-(0.10 + 0.06)t}\,dt = -5\left[\frac{e^{0.16(25)} - 1}{(0.16)e^{0.16(25)}}\right] = -\$30.68$$

and

$$P = P_1 + P_2 = \$34.06$$

The present worth of toll revenues over a 25-year period amounts to \$34.06 million. This figure could be used for bond validation. □

## 2.6 EQUIVALENCE OF CASH FLOWS

### 2.6.1 Concept of Equivalence

When we compare two cash flows, we must compare their characteristics on the same basis. By definition, two cash flows are equivalent if they have the same economic effect. More precisely, two cash flows are equivalent at interest $i$ if we can convert one cash flow into the other by using the proper compound interest factors. For example, if we deposit \$100 in a bank for 3 years at 8% interest compounded annually, we will accumulate \$125.97. Here we may say that, at 8% interest, \$100 at time 0 is equivalent to \$125.97 at time 3.

Consider another example in which an individual has to choose between two options. Option I is to receive a lump sum of \$1,000 now. Option II is to receive \$600 at the end of each year for 2 years, which provides \$1,200 over the 2-year period. Our question is what interest rate makes these two options equivalent. To answer the question, we need to establish a common base in time to convert the cash flows. Three common bases are the equivalent future value $F$, the equivalent present value $P$, and the equivalent annual value $A$. Future value is a measure of the cash flow relative to some "future planning horizon," considering the earning opportunities of the intermediate cash receipts. The present value represents a measure of future cash flow relative to the time point "now" with provisions that account for earning opportunities. The annual equivalent value determines the equal payments on an annual basis. The uniform cash flow equivalent might be the more appropriate term to use. The conceptual transformation from one type of cash flow to another is depicted in Figure 2.9.

For our example, we will use $F$ as a base of reference value and set the planning horizon at the end of year 2. To find the future value of option I, we may use an $(F/P, i, A)$ factor.

$$F_{\text{I}} = 1000(F/P, i, 2) = 1000(1 + i)^2$$

For option II, we may use an $(F/A, i, n)$ factor.

$$F_{\text{II}} = 600(F/A, i, 2) = 600(1 + i) + 600$$

If we specify $i$, we can easily evaluate $F_{\text{I}}$ and $F_{\text{II}}$. Table 2.6 summarizes these values at selected interest rates. We observe from the table that $F_{\text{I}} = F_{\text{II}} = \$1{,}278$ at $i = 13\%$. In other words, the two options are equivalent if the individual can earn a 13% interest from the investment activity. We also observe that at $i = 13\%$ $P_{\text{I}} = P_{\text{II}}$ and $A_{\text{I}} = A_{\text{II}}$. This is not surprising, because the present value amount is merely the future amount times a constant. The same can be said for the annual

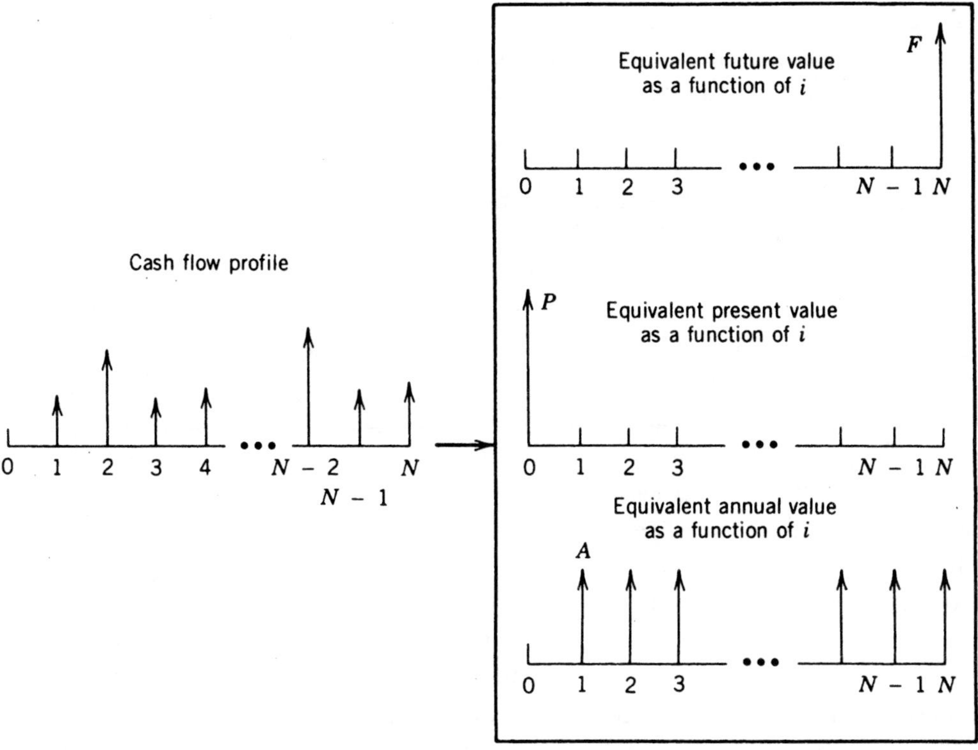


**FIGURE 2.9** Conversion to equivalent bases.

## Table 2.6 *Equivalence Calculations*

| $i$ (%) | Option I $F_I = 1{,}000(1 + i)^2$ | Option II $F_{II} = 600(1 + i) + 600$ | Equivalence |
|---|---|---|---|
| 0 | $1,000 | $1,200 | |
| 5 | 1,103 | 1,230 | |
| 7 | 1,145 | 1,242 | $F_I < F_{II}$ |
| 12 | 1,254 | 1,272 | |
| 13 | 1,277 | 1,277 | $F_I = F_{II}$ |
| 15 | 1,323 | 1,290 | $F_I > F_{II}$ |
| 20 | 1,440 | 1,320 | |

Option I

$1,000

0 1 2

Option II

$600 $600

0 1 2

equivalent value amount. Therefore, we should expect that any equivalent value that directly compares future value amounts could just as well compare present value amounts or annual equivalent amounts without affecting the selection outcome.

### 2.6.2 Equivalence Calculations with Several Interest Factors

Thus far we have used only single factors to perform equivalence calculations. In many situations, however, we must use several interest factors to obtain an equivalent value. To show this, we will take an example from home financing instruments offered by many banks. The particular financing method to be considered is called the graduated-payment method (GPM). This mortgage financing is designed for young people with low incomes but good earning prospects. (The term mortgage refers to a special loan for buying a piece of property such as a house.) The Department of Housing and Urban Development (HUD) initiated the GPM with a fixed interest rate for 30 years. During the first 5 or 10 years the monthly payments increase in stair-step fashion each year, allowing buyers to make a lower monthly payment in the beginning; the payments then level off at an amount higher than those of a comparable conventional fixed-rate mortgage. The monthly payment is applied to both principal and interest and can carry negative amortization. (The loan balance actually grows instead of decreasing under negative amortization when monthly payments are lower than monthly loan interests.) Our question is how the monthly payments are computed for a certain loan amount, interest rate, and life of the loan.

Let

$P$ = loan amount,

$A$ = monthly payment for the first year,

$i$ = loan interest rate per month,

$g$ = annual rate of increase in the monthly payment,

$K$ = number of years the payment will increase,

$N$ = number of months to maturity of the loan.

Figure 2.10*a* illustrates the cash flow transactions associated with the GPM. From the lender's view, lending the amount $P$ now should be equivalent to a transaction in which the monthly payments are as shown in Figure 2.10*a*. To establish the equivalence relation between $P$ and $A$ with fixed values of $i$, $g$, $K$, and $N$, we convert each group of 12 equal monthly payments to a single present equivalent amount at the beginning of each year. Then the remaining $(N - 12K)$ equal payments are converted to a single present equivalent amount at $n = 12K$. The equivalent cash flow after this transformation should look like Figure 2.10*b*. To find the present equivalent value of this transformed cash flow, we simply calculate

$$P = A(P/A, i, 12) + A(1 + g)(P/A, i, 12)(P/F, i, 12)$$
$$+ A(1 + g)^2(P/A, i, 12)(P/F, i, 24) + \cdots$$

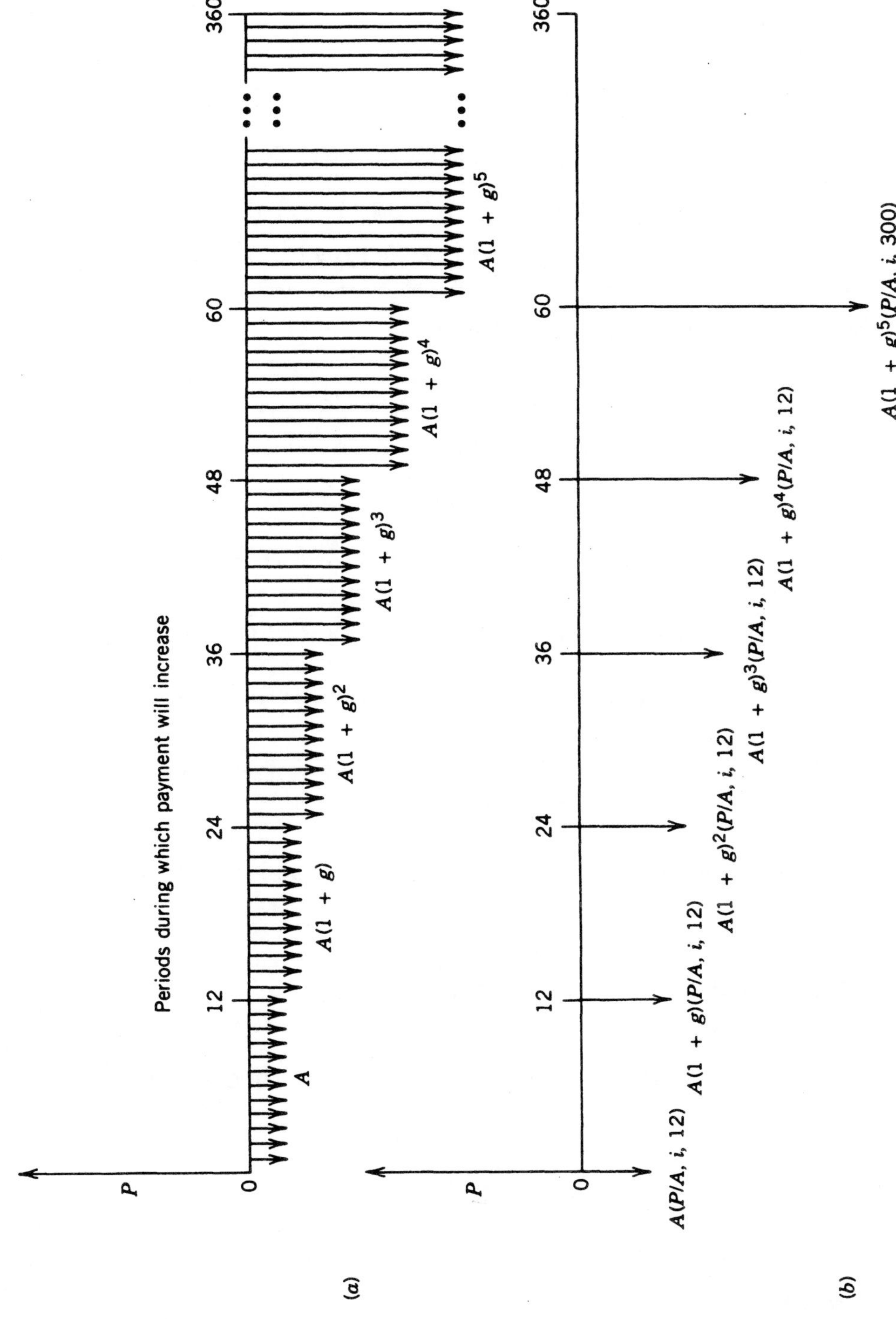


**FIGURE 2.10** **Cash flow diagram of a typical GPM loan.** ***(a)*** **Loan transactions (monthly).** ***(b)*** **Equivalent transactions.**

$$+ A\{(1 + g)^{K-1} (P/A, i, 12)[P/F, i, 12(K - 1)]\}$$
$$+ A(1 + g)^{K}(P/A, i, N - 12K)(P/F, i, 12K) \tag{2.32}$$

We multiply each term by $(1 + i)^{12}$ or $(F/P, i, 12)$.

$$\begin{aligned} P(1 + i)^{12} = {} & A(P/A, i, 12)(1 + i)^{12} + A(1 + g)(P/A, i, 12) \\ & + A(1 + g)^{2}(P/A, i, 12)(1 + i)^{-12} + \cdots \\ & + A(1 + g)^{K-1}(P/A, i, 12)(1 + i)^{-12(K-2)} \\ & + A(1 + g)^{K}(P/A, i, N - 12K)(1 + i)^{-12(K+1)} \end{aligned} \tag{2.33}$$

We multiply each term in Eq. 2.32 by $1 + g$.

$$\begin{aligned} P(1+g) = {} & A(1+g)(P/A, i, 12) + A(1+g)^{2}(P/A, i, 12)(1+i)^{-12} \\ & + A(1 + g)^{3}(P/A, i, 12)(1 + i)^{-24} + \cdots \\ & + A(1 + g)^{K}(P/A, i, 12)(1 + i)^{-12(K-1)} \\ & + A(1 + g)^{K+1}(P/A, i, N - 12K)(1 + i)^{-12K} \end{aligned} \tag{2.34}$$

Now we subtract Eq. 2.34 from Eq. 2.33 and solve for $A$ to get

$$\begin{aligned} A = {} & P[(1 + i)^{12} - (1 + g)]\{(1 + g)^{K}(1 + i)^{-12(K+1)}[(P/A, i, N - 12K) \\ & - (P/A, i, 12)] + [(P/A, i, 12)(1 + i)^{12} \\ & - (1 + g)^{K+1}(P/A, i, N - 12K)(1 + i)^{-12K}]\}^{-1} \end{aligned} \tag{2.35}$$

For an example of such an equivalence calculation, consider the following data:

$P$ = \$45,000,
$i = \frac{3}{4}\%$ per month (9% compounded monthly),
$g$ = 5% per year,
$K$ = 5 years (no further increase in monthly payment after the sixth year),
$N$ = 360 months (30 years).

Evaluating Eq. 2.35 with these figures yields

$$\begin{aligned} A &= 45{,}000[0.04387]\{0.8916\,[107.7267] + 12.5076 - 101.9927\}^{-1} \\ &= \$300.18/\text{month} \end{aligned}$$

Then the monthly payment will increase the second year to \$315.19, the third year to \$330.95, the fourth year to \$347.50, the fifth year to \$364.87, and for the remaining years to \$383.11.

***Example 2.11***

The following two cash flow transactions are said to be equivalent in terms of economic desirability at an interest rate of 10% compounded annually. Determine the unknown value $A$.

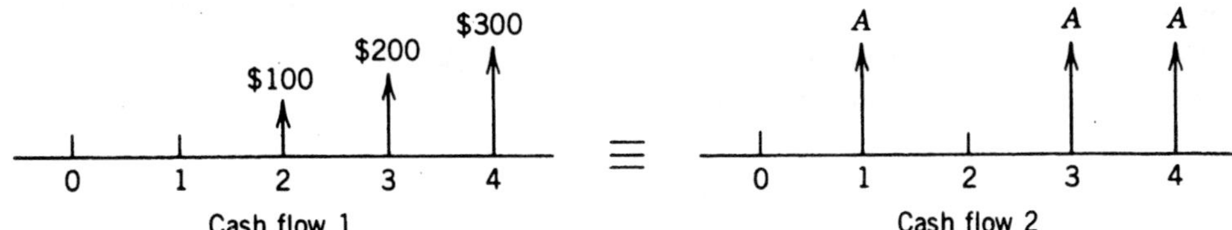


We will first use the present equivalent as the basis of comparison. Cash flow 1 represents a strict gradient series, whereas cash flow 2 can be viewed as an equivalent payment series with the second payment missing. Therefore, the equivalence would be expressed by

$$100\overset{P/G,10\%,4}{(4.3781)} = A\left[\overset{P/F,10\%,1}{(0.9091)} + \overset{P/F,10\%,3}{(0.7513)} + \overset{P/F,10\%,4}{(0.6830)}\right]$$

Solving for $A$ yields

$$A = \$186.83$$

If we use the annual equivalent as the basis of comparison, we compute

$$100\overset{A/G,10\%,4}{(1.3812)} = A - A\overset{P/F,10\%,2}{(0.8264)}\ \overset{A/P,10\%,4}{(0.3155)}$$

Solving for $A$ yields $A = \$186.83$ again. The second approach should be computationally more attractive because it takes advantage of the cash flow pattern and thus requires fewer interest factors in the computation. □

## 2.7 EFFECT OF INFLATION ON CASH FLOW EQUIVALENCE

Up to this point we have shown how we properly account for the time value of money in equivalence calculations in the absence of inflation. In this section we present methods that incorporate the effect of inflation in our equivalence calculations.

### 2.7.1 Measure of Inflation

***Definition.*** Before discussing the effect of inflation on equivalence calculations, we need to discuss how we measure inflation. In simple terms, the results of investment activity are stated in dollars, but the dollar is an imperfect unit of measure because its value changes from time to time. Inflation is the term used to describe a decline in the value of the dollar. For example, if we deposit $1,000 in a one-year savings certificate and withdraw $1,090 a year later, we say that our rate of return has been 9%—and it has, as long as those dollars we withdraw at year's end actually purchase 9% more. If inflation has reduced the value of the dollar by 10%, our 9% positive investment return in dollars is actually about a 1% loss in economic value or purchasing power. Inflation is thus a measure of the decline in the purchasing power of the dollar.

***Measure.*** The decline in purchasing power can be measured in many ways. Consumers may judge inflation in terms of the prices they pay for food and other goods; economists record this measure in the form of the consumer price index (CPI), which is based on sample prices in a "market basket" of purchases. We should note that consumer prices do not always behave like wholesale prices or commodity prices, and as a result, a dollar's worth varies depending on what is bought.

There is another measure of the dollar's value that reflects the average purchasing power of the dollar as it applies to all goods and services in the economy—the gross national product implicit price deflator (GNPIPD). The GNPIPD is computed and published quarterly by the U.S. Department of Commerce, Bureau of Economic Analysis.

Various cost indices are also available to the estimator. A government index listing is given by the *Statistical Abstract of the United States,* a yearly publication that includes material, labor, and construction costs. The Bureau of Labor Statistics publishes the monthly *Producer Price Index* and covers some 3,000 product groupings.

***Average Inflation Rate.*** To account for the effect of inflation, we utilize an annual percentage rate that represents the annual increase in prices over a one-year period. Because the rate each year is based on the previous year's price, this inflation rate has a compounding effect. For example, prices that increase at the rate of 5% per year in the first year and 8% per year in the second year, with a starting base price of $100, will increase at an average inflation rate of 6.49%.

$$\underbrace{\underbrace{100(1 + 0.05)}_{\text{first year}}(1 + 0.08)}_{\text{second year}} = 113.40$$

Let $f$ be the average annual inflation rate. Then we equate

$$100(1 + f)^2 = 113.40$$

$$f = 6.49\%$$

The inflation rate itself may be computed from any of the several available indices. With the CPI value, the annual inflation rate may be calculated from the expression

$$\text{Annual inflation rate for year } n = \frac{\text{CPI}_n - \text{CPI}_{n-1}}{\text{CPI}_{n-1}} \tag{2.36}$$

For example, with $\text{CPI}_{1990} = 270$ and $\text{CPI}_{1989} = 260$, the annual inflation rate for year 1990 is

$$\frac{270 - 260}{260} = 0.0385 \text{ or } 3.85\%$$

As just indicated, we can easily compute the inflation rates for the years with known CPI values. However, most equivalence calculations for projects require the use of cash flow estimates that depend on expectations of *future* inflation rates. The methods used by economists to estimate future inflation rates are many and varied. Important factors to consider may include historical trends in rates, predicted economic conditions, professional judgment, and other elements of economic forecasting. The estimation of future inflation rates is certainly a difficult task; a complete discussion of this subject is beyond the scope of this text but can be found elsewhere [1]. Our interest here is in how we use these rates in equivalence calculations, when they are provided.

### 2.7.2 Explicit and Implicit Treatments of Inflation in Discounting

We will present three basic approaches for calculating equivalence values in an inflationary environment that allow for the simultaneous consideration of changes in earning power and changes in purchasing power. The three approaches are consistent and, if applied properly, should result in identical solutions. The first approach assumes that cash flow is estimated in terms of *actual dollars,* and the second uses the concept of *constant dollars.* The third approach uses a combination of actual and constant dollars and is discussed in Section 2.7.3.

***Definition of Inflation Terminology.*** To develop the relationship between actual-dollar analysis and constant-dollar analysis, we will give precise definitions of several inflation-related terms, borrowed from Thuesen and Fabrycky [4].

> *Actual dollars* represent the out-of-pocket dollars received or expended at any point in time. Other names for them are then-current dollars, current dollars, future dollars, inflated dollars, and nominal dollars.
>
> *Constant dollars* represent the hypothetical purchasing power of future receipts and disbursements in terms of the purchasing dollars in some base year. (The base year is normally time zero, the beginning of the investment.) We will assume that the base year is always time zero unless specified otherwise. Other names are real dollars, deflated dollars, and today's dollars.

*Market interest rate* ($i$) represents the opportunity to earn as reflected by the actual rates of interest available in the financial market. The interest rates used in previous sections are actually market interest rates. (The designation $i$ is used consistently throughout this book to represent interest rates available in the marketplace.) When the rate of inflation increases, there is a corresponding upward movement in market interest rates. Thus, the market interest rates include the effects of both the earning power and the purchasing power of money. Other names are combined interest rate, nominal interest rate, minimum attractive rate of return, and inflation-adjusted discount rate.

*Inflation-free interest rate* ($i'$) represents the earning power of money isolated from the effects of inflation. This interest rate is not quoted by financial institutions and other investors and is therefore not generally known to the public. This rate can be computed, however, if the market interest rate and inflation rate are known. Naturally, if there is no inflation in an economy, $i$ and $i'$ should be identical. Other names are real interest rate, true interest rate, and constant-dollar interest rate.

*General inflation rate* ($f$) represents the average annual percentage of increase in prices of goods and services. The market inflation rate is expected to respond to this general inflation rate. *Escalation rate* ($e$) represents a specific inflation rate applicable to a specific segment of the economy. It is sometimes used in contracts.

It is important to recognize that there is a relationship between inflation and interest rate. For example, the historical rate on AAA bonds is about 2.5% to 3% above the general inflation rate as measured by the CPI [1]. In addition, the rate of return (ROR) required by well-managed companies on their investments must be at some level above the inflation rate. In the next section we will derive the mathematical relationships of $i$, $i'$, and $f$.

***Relationships of $i$, $i'$, and $f$.*** We must first establish the relationship between actual dollars and constant dollars. Suppose we estimate a future single payment $F'$ that occurs at the end of the $n$th period in terms of constant dollars (primes indicate constant dollars). To translate this constant-dollar amount into the actual dollars at the end of the $n$th period, we use

$$F = F'(1 + f)^n$$

Solving for $F'$ yields

$$F' = F(1 + f)^{-n} \tag{2.37}$$

where $F'$ = constant-dollar expression for the cash flow at the end of the $n$th period,

$F$ = actual-dollar expression for the cash flow at the end of the $n$th period.

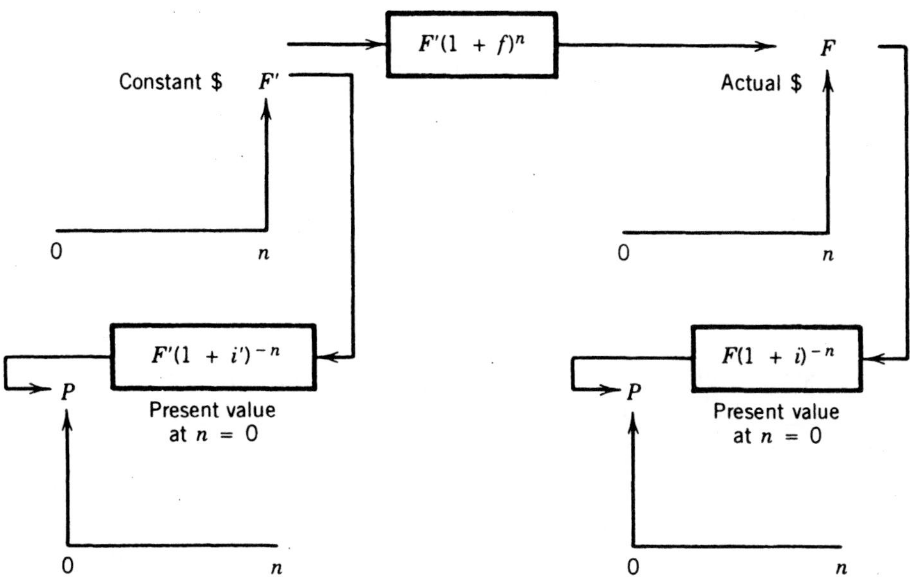


**FIGURE 2.11** Relationships of $i$, $i^1$ and $f$.

As shown in Figure 2.11, to find the present value equivalent of this actual dollar, we should use the market interest rate $i$ in

$$P = F(1 + i)^{-n} \tag{2.38}$$

If the cash flow is already given in constant dollars with the inflation effect removed, we should use $i'$ to account for only the earning power of the money. To find the present value equivalent of this constant dollar at $i'$, we use

$$P = F'(1 + i')^{-n} \tag{2.39}$$

The $P$ values must be equal at time zero, and equating the results of Eqs. 2.38 and 2.39 yields

$$\begin{aligned}
F(1 + i)^{-n} &= F'(1 + i')^{-n} \\
&= F(1 + f)^{-n}(1 + i')^{-n} \\
(1 + i)^{-n} &= (1 + f)^{-n}(1 + i')^{-n} \\
(1 + i) &= (1 + f)(1 + i') \\
&= 1 + f + i' + i'f
\end{aligned}$$

or

$$i = i' + f + i'f \tag{2.40}$$

Solving for $i'$ yields

$$i' = \frac{i - f}{1 + f} \tag{2.41}$$

As an example, say that the inflation rate is 6% per year and the market interest rate is known to be 15% per year. Calculating $i'$ gives us

$$i' = \frac{0.15 - 0.06}{1 + 0.06} = 8.49\%$$

To summarize, the interest rate that is applicable in equivalence calculations depends on the assumptions used in estimating the cash flow. If the cash flow is estimated in terms of actual dollars, the market interest rate ($i$) should be used. If the cash flow is estimated in terms of constant dollars, the inflation-free interest rate ($i$) should be used. In subsequent sections we will give more detailed examples of how the two interest rates are used in equivalence calculations.

***Actual-Dollar versus Constant-Dollar Analysis.*** If cash flow is represented in constant dollars (such as 1990 dollars), an inflation-free discount rate $i$ (say 5% to 15%) may be appropriate for a profitable business. If cash flow is represented in inflated dollars, a market interest rate (say 15% to 25%) may be appropriate. Often, the difficulty lies in determining the nature of the cash flow. In this section, we will consider two cases and explain how the analyses in terms of actual and constant dollars can be used.

**Case 1:** Projections in physical units can often be translated into constant-dollar projections by using a constant-dollar price per unit and then converted to present value by using an inflation-free discount rate.

## *Example 2.12*

SM Manufacturing Company makes electric meters of the type with which utility companies measure electricity consumption by users. SM has projected the sale of its meters by using data on new housing starts and deterioration and replacement of existing units. The price per unit should keep up with the wholesale price index (WPI). In 1990 the price per unit is $25. To achieve the production and sales projected in the following, SM needs to invest $75,000 now (in 1990). Other costs remain unchanged.

| $n$ | 0 | 1 | 2 | 3 | 4 | 5 | 6 | 7 |
|---|---|---|---|---|---|---|---|---|
| Unit Sales | — | 1,000 | 1,100 | 1,200 | 1,200 | 1,300 | 1,300 | 1,200 |
| $ Inflow | — | 25,000 | 27,500 | 30,000 | 30,000 | 32,500 | 32,500 | 30,000 |

SM thinks it should earn a 5% inflation-free rate of return (ROR) on any investment.

This is an easy problem because all figures are in constant (1990) dollars. Just discount the dollar inflows at 5%. For example, present value would be

$$\begin{aligned} P &= -75{,}000 + 25{,}000(1/1.05) + 27{,}500(1/1.05)^2 \\ &\quad + 30{,}000(1/1.05)^3 + 30{,}000(1/1.05)^4 + 32{,}500(1/1.05)^5 \\ &\quad + 32{,}500(1/1.05)^6 + 30{,}000(1/1.05)^7 \\ &= 95{,}386 \text{ in 1990 dollars} \quad \square \end{aligned}$$

**Case 2:** If projections in dollars are made with numerical and statistical techniques, they will very likely reflect some inflationary trend. If they do, we should use a market interest rate or a two-step approach in which we first convert to constant dollars and then compute present value by using an inflation-free discount rate.

### *Example 2.13*

U.S. Cola Company (USCC) is studying a new marketing scheme in southeast Georgia. By examining a similar project conducted from 1977 to 1989 and using nonlinear statistical regression, the analysts have projected additional dollar profits from this new marketing practice as follows.

| Year | 1 (1991) | 2 | 3 | 4 | 5 | 6 |
|---|---|---|---|---|---|---|
| Additonal Profit | 100,000 | 120,000 | 150,000 | 200,000 | 150,000 | 100,000 |

An investment of $500,000 is required now (1990) to fund the project. USCC is accustomed to obtaining a 20% ROR on its projects during these inflation-ridden times.

Statistical regression on dollar sales inevitably reflects any inflationary trends during the study period (1977 to 1989 in this example), so we may conclude that the dollar profits are represented in inflated, actual dollars. The 20% discount rate was developed for today's inflationary economy, so it can be used to compute a present value:

$$\begin{aligned} P &= -500{,}000 + 100{,}000(1/1.2) + 120{,}000(1/1.2)^2 \\ &\quad + 150{,}000(1/1.2)^3 + 200{,}000(1/1.2)^4 \\ &\quad + 150{,}000(1/1.2)^5 + 100{,}000(1/1.2)^6 \\ &= -56{,}306 \text{ in 1990 dollars} \end{aligned}$$

(Note that in the sign convention used a minus sign means cash outflow.) □

## *Example 2.14*

The scenario is the same as in example 2.13, but we assume that inflation is projected to be 9% per year, and we do the analysis by first converting to constant dollars. USCC expects at least a 10% inflation-free return on its investments. Noting that

$$(1 + 0.1)(1 + 0.09) = 1.990 \cong (1 + 0.2)$$

we judge this to be a reasonable translation. We first deflate the cash flow at 9%.

| $n$ | 1 | 2 | 3 | 4 | 5 | 6 |
|---|---|---|---|---|---|---|
| $F'_n$ | 91,743 | 101,002 | 115,828 | 141,685 | 97,490 | 59,627 |

Now we compute a present value using the constant-dollar cash flow with appropriate interest rate of 10%:

$$\begin{aligned} P &= -500{,}000 + 91{,}743(1/1.1) + 101{,}002(1/1.1)^2 \\ &\quad + 115{,}828(1/1.1)^3 + 141{,}685(1/1.1)^4 \\ &\quad + 97{,}490(1/1.1)^5 + 59{,}627(1/1.1)^6 \\ &= -55{,}137 \text{ in 1990 dollars} \end{aligned}$$

This value agrees closely with that obtained by using actual dollars and the market interest rate of 20%; the discrepancy comes from the fact that $1.199 \neq 1.200$. □

***Composite Cash Flow Elements with Different Escalation Rates.*** The equivalence calculation examples in the previous sections were all based on the assumption that all cash flows respond to the inflationary trend in a uniform manner. Many project cash flows, however, are composed of several cash flow elements with different degrees of responsiveness to the inflationary trend. For example, the net cash flow elements for a certain project may comprise sales revenue, operating and maintenance costs, and taxes. Each element may respond to the inflationary environment to a varying degree. In computing the tax element alone, we need to isolate the depreciation element. With inflation, sales and operating costs are assumed to increase accordingly. Depreciation would be unchanged, but taxes, profits, and thus the net cash flow usually would be higher. (A complete discussion of the effect of inflation on the after-tax cash flow will be given in Chapter 4.) Now we will discuss briefly how we compute the equivalence value with such cash flows.

In complex situations there may be several inflation rates. For example, an apartment developer might project physical unit sales, building costs in actual dollars using a building cost index, and sales revenue in actual dollars using a real estate price index, and then find the equivalent present value using an interest rate that reflects the consumer price index.

### *Example 2.15*

This more complex example illustrates the apartment building project. Base year cost per unit is $15,000 and selling price per unit is $20,000. The building cost index is projected to increase 11% next year and 10% more the following year. The real estate price index is expected to jump 15% next year and then level off at a 13% increase per year. We will use a market interest rate of 15%, hoping that it will yield an inflation-free return of 5% when the general inflation rate is 9% to 10% (to be precise, $f = 9.52\%$).

| Item | $n$: 0 | 1 | 2 | 3 |
|---|---|---|---|---|
| Units built | 200 | 250 | 200 | — |
| Units sold | — | 200 | 250 | 200 |
| Costs (thousands) | 3,000 | 3,750(1.11) | 3,000(1.11)(1.1) | — |
| Revenues (thousands) | — | 4,000(1.15) | 5,000(1.15)(1.13) | $4{,}000(1.15)(1.13)^2$ |
| Net flow (thousands) (actual $) | −3,000 | +438 | +2,835 | +5,874 |
| ($P/F$, 15%, $n$) | 1 | 0.8696 | 0.7561 | 0.6575 |

$$P = -3{,}000 + 438(0.8696) + 2{,}835(0.7561) + 5{,}874(0.6575)$$

$$P = \$3{,}387{,}000 \text{ in base year (time 0) dollars} \quad \square$$

### 2.7.3 Home Ownership Analysis during Inflation

A personal decision of wide and continuing interest is whether it is more economical to buy a home or to rent during an inflationary environment. In this section we will illustrate how this decision can be made on a rational basis by applying the concepts of actual and constant dollars.

***Renting a House.*** To make a meaningful comparison, let's estimate the current rent of a two-bedroom apartment as $400 per month plus $60 per month for basic utilities (heating and cooling but not telephone, water, and sewer). Both costs have a tendency to increase with inflation, so let's project a 10% inflation rate, which gives us the following monthly costs per year.

| $n$ | 1 | 2 | 3 | | 10 |
|---|---|---|---|---|---|
| Rent | 400 | 440 | 484 | . . . | 943 |
| Utilities | 60 | 66 | 73 | . . . | 141 |

We selected a planning period of 10 years because realtors tell us that very few people live in the same house for the period of a home mortgage (typically 25 to 30 years). Of course, when you rent an apartment you are free to switch every year, and we'll assume a fairly uniform market of rents with no rent control (this situation occurs when the vacancy rate is 5% to 10%). Let's use a market interest rate of 15% (annual compounding) to compute the present value of apartment living costs (approximate, since we collapse all monthly flows to the year's end).

$$P = (-460)(12)/1.15 + (-506)(12)/(1.15)^2 + \cdots + (-1{,}084)(12)/(1.15)^{10}$$
$$= -39{,}610 \text{ in time 0 dollars}$$

Alternatively, we can compute an inflation-free discount rate $i'$ to be used with constant dollars by applying Eq. 2.40.

$$0.15 = i' + 0.1 + 0.1i'$$
$$i' = 0.0455$$

We must also convert 460 to 460/1.1 = 418.18. Thus, a present value using the constant-dollar cash flow is

$$P = (-418.18)(12)(P/A,\ 4.55\%,10)$$

and

$$(P/A,\ 4.55\%,\ 10) = \left[\frac{(1.0455)^{10} - 1}{0.0455(1.0455)^{10}}\right] = 7.8933$$

so

$$P = (-418.18)(12)(7.8933)$$
$$= -39{,}610 \text{ in time 0 dollars}$$

***Buying a House.*** Now we must estimate the cash flow for a house or condominium. The purchase cost will be $60,000. "Wait a minute!" you say. "I've seen those $60,000 units and they're too old, too small, or too far away, or built like apartments." Right. It's difficult to compare the space and quality of an apartment with those of a house, but it is not fair to compare a two-bedroom apartment with a new, close-in home or condominium containing 1,500 or more square feet. Therefore, the $60,000 home is a more appropriate comparison. If you finally decide to spend $80,000, you're allocating more money to your residence than when you lived in apartments, but you'll get more space, privacy, convenience, return, and so forth.

We will try for 95% financing, which means that we need a $3,000 down payment plus about another $3,000 for closing costs, for a cash requirement of about $6,000.

The mortgage interest rate might be 14.5% (total 14.5/12 = 1.208% per month) on a fixed-rate 30-year mortgage. So the monthly payment is

$$57{,}000\ (A/P,\ 1.208\%,\ 360) = (57{,}000)\left[\frac{0.01208(1.01208)^{360}}{(1.01208)^{360} - 1}\right]$$

$$= (57{,}000)(0.012242)$$

$$= \$697.815 = \$698/\text{month}$$

The mortgage balance remaining after our 10-year comparison period is

$$697.815(P/A,\ 1.208\%,\ 240) = 697.815\left[\frac{(1.01208)^{240} - 1}{0.01208(1.1208)^{240}}\right]$$

$$= (697.815)(78.143) = \$54{,}529$$

We will have paid off less than 5% of the loan in 10 years, which is not unusual for these mortgages. Approximately 97% of our monthly payments will be interest, which is tax deductible:

| | | | |
|---|---|---|---|
| (698)(12)(10) | = | \$83,760 | total payments |
| 57,000 − 54,529 | = | \$ 2,471 | principal repayments |
| | | \$81,289 | interest payments |

We will assume a 40%[1] marginal income tax rate (federal plus state) and sufficient other deductions to make the interest reduce our tax by

$$(698)(0.97)(0.40) = \$271/\text{month}$$

So the after-tax cost of the mortgage is only \$698 − \$271 = \$427.

Real estate taxes are estimated to be \$600 per year, or \$50/month, and these are also tax deductible, which saves us \$20/month for an after-tax cost of \$30/month. These taxes will increase at about 10% per year.

Basic taxes and utilities will be about \$60/month for a condominium and \$100/month for a house, so let's use \$80/month, with 10% inflation. Homeowner's insurance is slightly higher than renter's insurance, so we allow \$100 per year. Maintenance can be another \$300 per year. The monthly total of these items is \$33/month, inflating at 10%. Our home will appreciate in value at about 7% per year and sell at

$$60{,}000(1.07)^{10} = \$118{,}029$$

After paying a 6% realtor's commission and the mortgage balance, we keep

$$(118{,}029)(0.94) - 54{,}529 = \$56{,}418$$

[1]A 30% tax rate may be more reasonable for many homeowners. We will leave this for the reader to do as an exercise (see Problem 2.23).

(We assume no capital gain tax on this amount.) Now we're ready to compute $P$.

$$\begin{aligned}
P = & -6{,}000 && \text{constant dollars} \\
& -(427)(12)(P/A,\ 15\%,\ 10) && \text{actual dollars} \\
& \left.\begin{aligned} & -(30/1.1)(12)(P/A,\ 4.55\%,\ 10) \\ & -(80/1.1)(12)(P/A,\ 4.55\%,\ 10) \\ & -(33/1.1)(12)(P/A,\ 4.55\%,\ 10) \end{aligned}\right\} && \text{constant dollars} \\
& +56{,}418(P/F,\ 15\%,\ 10) && \text{actual dollars}
\end{aligned}$$

Note carefully that we use 15% for actual-dollars expenses and 4.55% for constant-dollars expenses. We could convert the real estate taxes, utilities, incremental insurance, and maintenance to actual dollars by using 10% and then using 15% for discounting, but that is too much work. Our method produces the same numerical results.

$$\begin{aligned}
P = & -6{,}000 \\
& -(427)(12)(5.0188) \\
& -(130)(12)(7.8933) \\
& +(56{,}418)(0.2472) \\
= & -30{,}080 \text{ in constant dollars}
\end{aligned}$$

This cost is $9,530 *less* than renting. In this example the present value costs in constant dollars for home ownership are about 76% of the present value costs for renting. The big difference comes from the fact that you are using $57,000 of someone else's money to buy an asset that resells at two times its purchase price. You pay interest on the loan, but this is partly offset by the rent you would pay in an apartment.

Notice that the house was assumed to appreciate at 7%, compared with a mortgage interest rate of 14.5% nominal (15.5% effective per year). Many people think home ownership makes sense only if the mortgage interest rate is below the real estate appreciation rate. This is not true, as the example demonstrates.

We also used a 15% market interest rate, versus 10% general inflation and 7% real estate inflation. We might question the sensitivity of the results to these factors. In Table 2.7 we show some results of a sensitivity analysis in which we vary the inflation rate, the real estate appreciation rate, and the rent. We can see that there is a wide range of parameter values where buying is better. In fact, many people have benefited financially from home ownership during inflation. The home ownership analysis could be based on the principle of monthly payment and monthly compounding without collapsing all monthly flows to year end. We will leave this for the reader to do as an exercise (see Problem 2.22).

**Table 2.7** ***Sensitivity Analysis: Buy versus Rent Decision***

| Inflation $f$: | 5% | | | 10% | | | 15% | | |
|---|---|---|---|---|---|---|---|---|---|
| Market Interest $i$: | 10% | | | 15% | | | 20% | | |
| Real Estate Appreciation Rate: Rent | 0% | 2.5% | 5% | 5% | 7.5% | 10% | 5% | 10% | 15% |
| 350 | −36.6 | −36.6 | −36.6 | −35.3 | −35.3 | −35.3 | −34.1 | −34.1 | −34.1 |
| | −49.6 | −43.5 | −35.9 | −34.8 | −28.8 | −21.4 | −33.4 | −24.6 | −11.4 |
| | <u>136</u> | <u>119</u> | <u>98</u> | <u>99</u> | <u>82</u> | <u>61</u> | <u>98</u> | <u>72</u> | <u>33</u> |
| 400 | −41.1 | −41.1 | −41.1 | −39.6 | −39.6 | −39.6 | −38.3 | −38.3 | −38.3 |
| | −49.6 | −43.5 | −35.9 | −34.8 | −28.8 | −21.4 | −33.4 | −24.6 | −11.4 |
| | <u>121</u> | <u>106</u> | <u>87</u> | <u>88</u> | <u>73</u> | <u>54</u> | <u>87</u> | <u>64</u> | <u>30</u> |
| 450 | −45.5 | −45.5 | −45.5 | −43.9 | −43.9 | −43.9 | −42.4 | −42.4 | −42.4 |
| | −49.6 | −43.5 | −35.9 | −34.8 | −28.8 | −21.4 | −33.4 | −24.6 | −11.4 |
| | <u>109</u> | <u>96</u> | <u>79</u> | <u>79</u> | <u>66</u> | <u>49</u> | <u>79</u> | <u>58</u> | <u>27</u> |

NOTES: Each triplet of entries consists of present value of rental cash flow in thousands, present value of ownership cash flow in thousands, and percentage ratio of ownership flow to rental flow.

Other parameters:

| | | | |
|---|---|---|---|
| 5% down | $60,000 home cost | $80/month utilities (home) | $300/year maintenance (home) |
| 5% closing costs | 14.5% mortgage rate | $600/year real estate taxes | 6% realtor's commission |
| 30-year mortgage | 40% marginal tax rate | $100/year incremental insurance | 10-year planning period |

## 2.8 SUMMARY

In this chapter we have examined the concept of the time value of money and the equivalence of cash flows. Discrete compound interest formulas have been derived for converting present sums, future sums, uniform series, gradient series, and geometric series to specified points in time. We also discussed the concepts of nominal interest rate and effective interest rate, which led to the idea of continuous compounding. Continuous-compounding formulas were then derived for both discrete and continuous cash flows.

We discussed the measures of inflation and the effects of inflation on equivalence calculations. We presented two basic approaches that may be used in equivalence calculations to offset the effects of changes in purchasing power. In the actual-dollar analysis, we include an inflation component in estimating cash flows so that a market interest rate is used to find the equivalence value. In the constant-dollar approach we express the cash flows in terms of base-year dollars and use an inflation-free interest rate to compute the equivalent value at the specified points in time. We also showed that if these approaches are applied correctly, they should lead to identical results.

## REFERENCES

1. Buck, J. R., and C. S. Park, *Inflation and Its Impact on Investment Decisions,* Industrial Engineering and Management Press, Institute of Industrial Engineers, Norcross, Ga., 1984.
2. Fleischer, G. A., and T. L. Ward, "Classification of Compound Interest Models in Economic Analysis," *The Engineering Economist,* Vol. 23, No. 1, pp. 13–29, Fall 1977.
3. Park, C. S., *Modern Engineering Economic Analysis,* Addison–Wesley, Reading, Mass., 1990.
4. Thuesen, G. J., and W. J. Fabrycky, *Engineering Economy,* 7th edition, Prentice–Hall, Englewood Cliffs, N.J., 1989.
5. White, J. A., M. H. Agee, and K. E. Case, *Principles of Engineering Economic Analysis,* 3rd edition, Wiley, New York, 1989.

## PROBLEMS

**2.1.** A typical bank offers you a Visa credit card that charges interest on unpaid balance at a 1.5% per month compounded monthly. This means that the nominal interest (annual percentage) rate for this account is $A$ and the effective annual interest rate is $B$. Suppose your beginning balance was \$500 and you make only the required minimum *monthly* payment (payable at the end of each month) of \$20 for next 3 months. If you made no new purchases with this card during this period, your unpaid balance will be $C$ at the end of 3 months. What are the values of $A$, $B$, and $C$?

**2.2.** In January 1989, C&S, the largest mutual savings bank in Georgia, published the following information: interest, 7.55%; effective annual yield, 7.842%. The bank did not explain how the 7.55% is connected to the 7.842%, but you can figure out that the compounding scheme used by the bank should be ______.

**2.3.** How many years will it take an investment to double if the interest rate is 12% compounded (a) annually, (b) semiannually, (c) quarterly, (d) monthly, (e) weekly, (f) daily, and (g) continuously?

**2.4.** Suppose that \$1,000 is placed in a bank account at the end of each *quarter* over the next 10 years. Determine the total accumulated value (future worth) at the end of 10 years where the interest rate is 8% compounded *quarterly*.

**2.5.** What equal-payment series is required to repay the following present amounts?

a. \$10,000 in 4 years at 10% interest compounded annually with 4 annual payments.
b. \$5,000 in 3 years at 12% interest compounded semiannually with 6 semiannual payments.
c. \$6,000 in 5 years at 8% interest compounded quarterly with 20 quarterly payments.
d. \$80,000 in 30 years at 9% interest compounded monthly with 360 monthly payments.

**2.6.** Suppose that \$5,000 is placed in a bank account at the end of each quarter over the next 10 years. Determine the total accumulated value (future worth) at the end of 10 years when the interest rate is

a. 12% compounded annually.
b. 12% compounded quarterly.
c. 12% compounded monthly.
d. 12% compounded continuously.

**2.7.** What equal *quarterly* payments will be required to repay a loan of \$10,000 over 3 years if the rate of interest is 8% compounded *continuously?*

**2.8.** Compute the present worth of cash flow that has a triangular pattern with 12% interest compounded continuously.

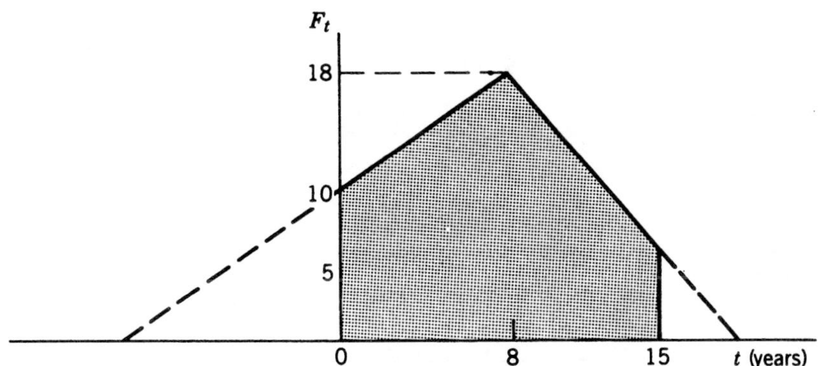


**2.9.** Suppose a uniformly increasing continuous cash flow (a ramp) accumulates \$600 over 3 years. Find the present worth of this cash flow under continuous compounding at $r = 12\%$.

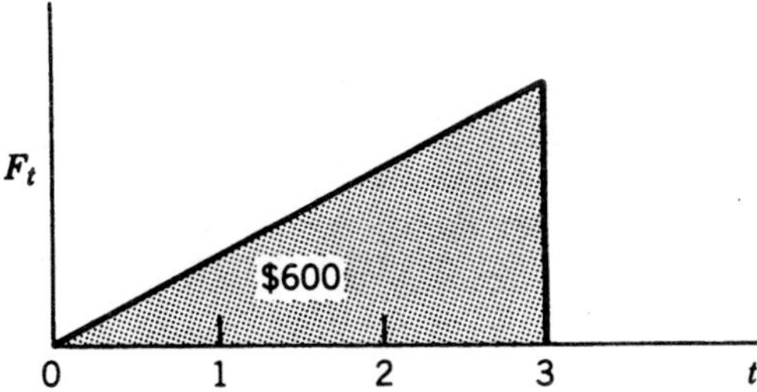

**2.10.** For computing the equivalent equal-payment series ($A$) of the following cash flow with $i = 10\%$, which of the following statements is (are) correct?

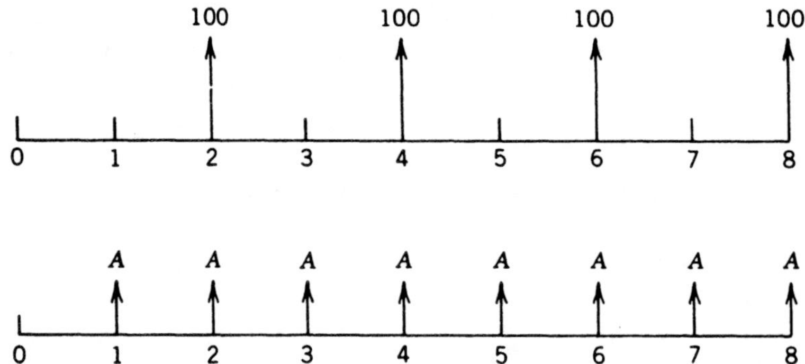


a. $A = 100(P/A, 10\%, 4)(A/P, 10\%, 8)$
b. $A = [100(P/F, 10\%, 2) + 100(P/F, 10\%, 4) + 100(P/F, 10\%, 6) + 100(P/F, 10\%, 8)](A/P, 10\%, 8)$
c. $A = 100(A/F, 10\%, 2)$
d. $A = 100(P/A, 21\%, 4)(A/P, 10\%, 8)$
e. $A = 100(F/A, 10\%, 4)(A/F, 10\%, 8)$
f. $A = 100(F/A, 21\%, 4)(A/F, 10\%, 8)$

**2.11.** The following equation describes the conversion of a cash flow into an equivalent equal-payment series with $n = 8$. Draw the original cash flow diagram. Assume an interest rate of 10% compounded annually.

$$A = [-1{,}000 - 1{,}000(P/F, 10\%, 1)](A/P, 10\%, 8)$$
$$+ [3{,}000 + 500(A/G, 10\%, 4)](P/A, 10\%, 4)(P/F, 10\%, 1)(A/P, 10\%, 8)$$
$$+ 750(F/A, 10\%, 2)(A/F, 10\%, 8)$$

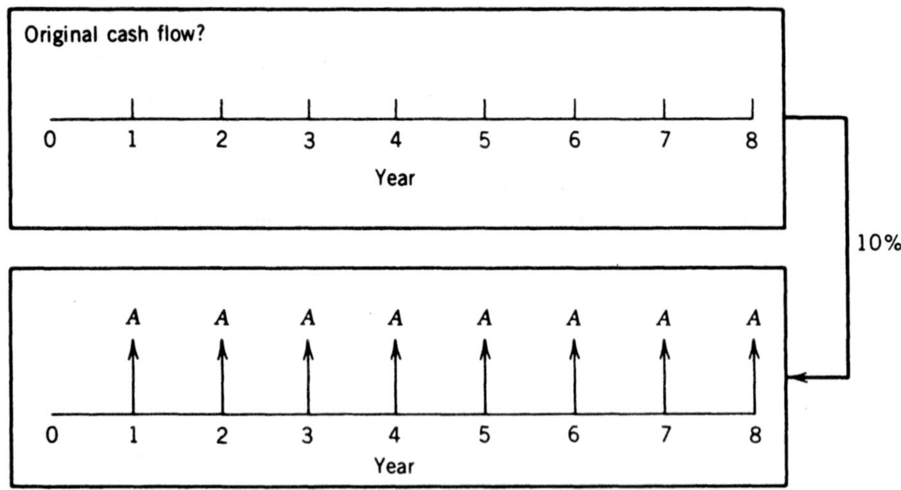

**2.12.** The following two cash flow transactions are said to be equivalent at 10% interest compounded annually. Find the unknown value $X$ that satisfies the equivalence.

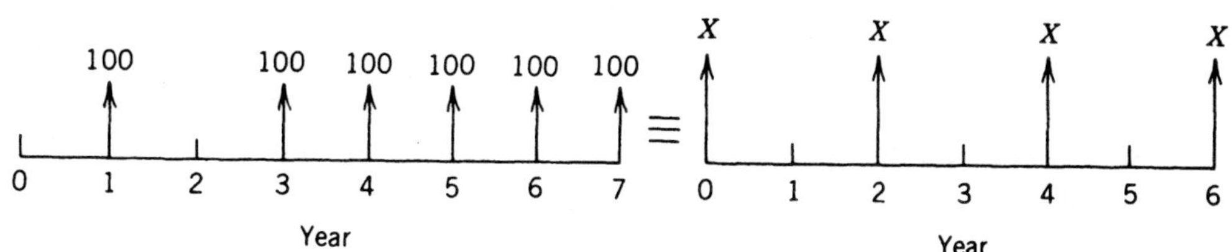


**2.13.** Suppose you have the choice of investing in (1) a zero-coupon bond that costs \$513.60 today, pays nothing during its life, and then pays \$1,000 after 5 years or (2) a municipal bond that costs \$1,000 today, pays \$67 in interest *semiannually,* and matures at the end of 5 years. Which bond would provide the higher *yield to maturity* (or return on your investment)?

**2.14.** You borrow $B$ dollars from your bank, which adds on the total interest before computing the monthly payment (add-on interest). Thus, if the quoted nominal interest rate (annual percentage rate) is $r$% and the loan is for $N$ months, the total amount that you agree to repay is

$$B + B(N/12)(r/100)$$

This is divided by $N$ to give the amount of each payment, $A$.

$$A = B(1/N + r/1200)$$

This is called an add-on loan. But the true rate of interest that you are paying is somewhat more than $r$%, because you do not hold the amount of the loan for the full $N$ months.

a. Find the equation to determine the true rate of interest $i$ per month.
b. Plot the relationship between $r$ and $i$ as a function of $N$.
c. For $B$ = \$10,000, $N$ = 36 months, and $r$ = 8%, find the effective annual borrowing rate per year.
d. Identify the lending situation in which the true interest rate $i$ per month approaches to $r/12$.

**2.15.** John Hamilton is going to buy a car worth \$10,000 from a local dealer. He is told that the add-on interest rate is only 1.25% per month, and his monthly payment is computed as follows:

Installment period = 30 months
Interest = 30(0.0125)(\$10,000) = \$3,750
Credit check, life insurance, and processing fee = \$50
Total amount owed = \$10,000 + \$3,750 + \$50 = \$13,800
Monthly payment size = \$13,800/30 = \$460 per month

What is the effective rate that John is paying for his auto financing?

a. Effective interest rate per month?
b. Effective annual interest rate?
c. Suppose that John bought the car and made 15 such monthly payments (\$460). Now he decides to pay off the remaining debt with one lump sum payment at the time of the sixteenth payment. What should the size of this payment be?

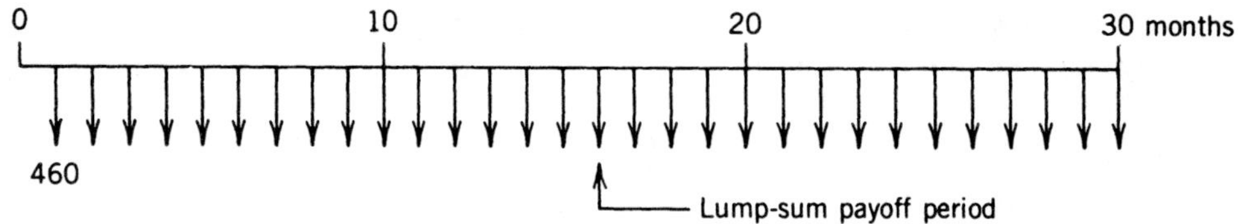


**2.16.** A pipeline was built 3 years ago to last 6 years. It develops leaks according to the relation

$$\log N = 0.07T - 2.42, \qquad T > 30$$

where $N$ is the total number of leaks from installation and $T$ is the time in months from installation. It costs $500 to repair a leak. If money is worth 8% per year, and without considering any tax effect, how much can be spent now for a cathodic system that will reduce leaks by 75%? (Adapted from F. C. Jelen and J. H. Black, *Cost and Optimization,* McGraw–Hill, New York, 1983.)

**2.17.** A market survey indicates that the price of a 10-oz jar of instant coffee has fluctuated over the last few years as follows:

| Period | −4 | −3 | −2 | −1 | 0 | 1 |
|---|---|---|---|---|---|---|
| Price ($) | 2.83 | 3.13 | 3.47 | 4.67 | 5.83 | ? |

a. Assuming that the base period (price index = 100) is period −4 (four periods ago), compute the average price index for this instant coffee.

b. Estimate the price at time period 1, if the current price trend is expected to continue.

**2.18.** The annual operating costs of a small electrical generating unit are expected to remain the same ($200,000) if the effects of inflation are not considered. The best estimates indicate that the annual inflation-free rate of interest ($i'$) will be 5% and the annual inflation rate ($f$) 6%. If the generator is to be used 3 more years, what is the present equivalent of its operating costs using *actual-dollar analysis?*

**2.19.** You want to know how much money to set aside now to pay for 1,000 gallons of home heating oil each year for 10 years. The current price of heating oil is $1.00 per gallon, and the price is expected to increase at a 10% compound price change each year for the next 10 years. The money to pay for the fuel oil will be set aside now in a bank savings account that pays 6% annual interest. How much money do you have to place in the savings account now, if payment for the fuel is made by end-of-year withdrawals?

**2.20.** An investment of $100,000 is required to expand a certain production facility in a manufacturing company. The firm estimates that labor costs will be $150,000 for the first year but will increase at the rate of 8% over the previous year's expenditure. Material costs, on the other hand, will be $400,000 for the first year but will increase at the rate of 10% per year due to inflation. If the firm's inflation-free interest rate ($i'$) is 10% and the average general inflation rate ($f$) is expected to be 5% over the next 5 years, determine the total present equivalent operating expenses (with no tax consideration) for the project.

**2.21.** A couple with a 7-year-old daughter want to save for their child's college expenses in advance. Assuming that the child enters college at age 18, they estimate that an amount of $20,000 per year in terms of today's dollars will be required to support the child's college expenses for 4 years. The future inflation rate is estimated to be

6% per year and they can invest their savings at 8% compounded quarterly.

a. Determine the equal quarterly amounts the couple must save until they send their child to college.

b. If the couple has decided to save only $500 each quarter, how much will the child have to borrow each year to support her college education?

**2.22.** Consider the problem of renting versus buying a home given in Section 2.7.3. Recall that the analysis was performed on the basis of annual payments with annual compounding. Repeat the analysis using monthly payments and monthly compounding.

**2.23.** Consider again the problem of renting versus buying a home given in Section 2.7.3. Recall that the tax rate used in the analysis was 40%, which seems too high. Repeat the analysis using a tax rate of 30%. Does a lower tax rate make the buying option more attractive?

# 3

# Transform Techniques in Cash Flow Modeling

## 3.1 INTRODUCTION

In Chapter 2 equivalence calculations were made by the proper use of the various interest formulas. In particular, with the interest rate and the compounding schemes specified, we showed how to convert various cash flow profiles into equivalent present values. In many situations, however, the cash flow patterns may take more complex forms than those discussed in Chapter 2. If they do, transform methods are often used to accomplish the same equivalence calculations with less computational effort and in a more routine manner. These methods are the $Z$-transform and Laplace transform methods. We will show in this chapter how they may be used in the modeling and analysis of economic situations involving either a discrete or a continuous time series of cash flow.

We will first discuss the concept of present value and its relationship to transform theory. Some useful properties of transforms will be presented, and their applications to economic model building will be discussed. Many examples are offered to aid the reader in understanding these powerful techniques. The reader will see that application of these transform formulas eliminates many of the calculations that are required when conventional interest formulas are used in complicated equivalence calculations.

## 3.2 Z-TRANSFORMS AND DISCRETE CASH FLOWS

### 3.2.1 The Z-Transform and Present Value

Consider that the function $f(n)$ describes the cash flow magnitude at the discrete point in time $n$. Then the equivalent present value of this cash flow series over an infinite time horizon at an interest rate $i$, assuming a discrete compounding principle, is

$$PV(i) = \sum_{n=0}^{\infty} f(n)(1 + i)^{-n} \tag{3.1}$$

Hill and Buck [6] recognized that the general form of the summation in (3.1) bears a striking resemblance to the definition of $Z$-transforms, the only difference being a definition of variables. That is, when a general discrete time series is described by a function $f(nT)$, where $T$ is an equidistant time interval and $n$ is an integer, the $Z$-transform of the time series $f(nT)$ is defined as

$$F(z) = \sum_{n=0}^{\infty} f(nT)z^{-n} \tag{3.2a}$$

With $T = 1$,

$$F(z) = \sum_{n=0}^{\infty} f(n)z^{-n} = Z\{f(n)\} \tag{3.2b}$$

where $z$ is a complex variable. If we replace $z$ with the interest rate $1 + i$ and set the constant-length time interval $T$ to unity (that is, the compounding period is the unit of time, monthly or yearly), Eq. 3.2 becomes

$$F(z) = \sum_{n=0}^{\infty} f(n)(1 + i)^{-n} \tag{3.3}$$

where $i$ is the interest rate for a compounding period. Throughout this chapter the value of $T$ will be set to unity so that the compounding period can be assumed to be the unit of time. In the literature of mathematics, we find a transformation essentially the same as our $Z$-transform but expressed in positive powers of $z$:

$$F'(z) = \sum_{n=0}^{\infty} f(n)z^{n} \tag{3.4}$$

In this book we use the definition in (3.2) because the expressions for the corresponding $Z$-transform are analogous to those for present values. It should be obvious, however, that both transformations have the same purpose and application, and that one transform is converted to the other by the relations

$$F'(z) = F\left(\frac{1}{z}\right), \qquad F(z) = F'\left(\frac{1}{z}\right) \tag{3.5}$$

In the construction of $Z$-transforms, the following notation will be used. If $f(n)$ represents the discrete $f$ function, $F(z)$ will represent the transform. In addition, as a shorthand notation, the transform pair will be denoted by $f(n) \leftrightarrow F(z)$. This double arrow is symbolic of the uniqueness of the one-to-one correspondence between $f(n)$ and $F(z)$. Thus, if $Z\{g(n)\} = G(z)$, we write $g(n) \leftrightarrow G(z)$. This lowercase–uppercase correspondence will be adhered to throughout this chapter.

For a cash flow sequence of infinite duration, the resulting $Z$-transform will be an infinite series involving inverse powers of $z$. This series can be expressed as a rational fraction in $z$, provided that the series converges. These so-called closed-form expressions will be especially convenient for our computations. For expressing a $Z$-transform as a ratio of polynomials in $z$, two important identities of infinite series will be needed:

$$\sum_{n=0}^{\infty} a^n = \frac{1}{1-a} \quad \text{provided } |a| < 1 \tag{3.6}$$

and

$$\sum_{n=0}^{\infty} (1+n)a^n = \frac{1}{(1-a)^2} \quad \text{provided } |a| < 1 \tag{3.7}$$

Now consider the sequence of function $f(n) = a^n$. The $Z$-transform is

$$F(z) = \sum_{n=0}^{\infty} f(n)z^{-n} = \sum_{n=0}^{\infty} a^n z^{-n} = \sum_{n=0}^{\infty} \left(\frac{a}{z}\right)^n$$

Using Eq. 3.6, we obtain

$$F(z) = \frac{1}{1-a/z} = \frac{z}{z-a} \quad \text{if } \left|\frac{a}{z}\right| < 1 \tag{3.8}$$

In other words, the infinite geometric series $a^n$ converges to $z/(z-a)$ if $|z| > |a|$. For ease of conversion, the table of transform pairs of $f(n)$ and $F(z)$ is provided (see Table 3.1).

Many cash flow transactions have a finite time duration. Because transforms are defined for series with infinite time horizons, it is necessary to introduce additional techniques to provide a methodology that is applicable to finite time horizons. We will examine some properties of the $Z$-transform in the following section.

### 3.2.2 Properties of the Z-Transform

Many useful properties of the $Z$-transform are discussed in the literature of mathematics, probability theory, and operations research [4,5,7]. We will focus on two important properties that are most relevant in equivalence calculations: linearity and translation.

**Table 3.1** ***A Short Table of Z-Transform Pairs***

| Standard Pattern | Original Function, $f(n)$ | Z-Transform, $F(z)$ | Present Value of $f(n)$ Starting at $n=0$ and Continuous over the Infinite Time Horizon |
|---|---|---|---|
| Step (uniform series) | $C$ | $C\left(\frac{z}{z-1}\right)$ | $C\left(\frac{1+i}{i}\right)$ |
| Ramp (gradient series) | $Cn$ | $C\left[\frac{z}{(z-1)^2}\right]$ | $C\left(\frac{1+i}{i^2}\right)$ |
| Geometric | $Ca^n$ | $C\left(\frac{z}{z-a}\right)$ | $C\left(\frac{1+i}{1+i-a}\right)$ |
| Decay | $Ce^{-jn}$ | $C\left(\frac{z}{z-e^{-j}}\right)$ | $C\left(\frac{1+i}{1+i-e^{-j}}\right)$ |
| Growth | $C(1-e^{-jn})$ | $C\left(\frac{z}{z-1}-\frac{z}{z-e^{-j}}\right)$ | $C\left(\frac{1+i}{i}-\frac{1+i}{1+i-e^{-j}}\right)$ |
| Impulse (single payment) | $C\delta(n-k)$ | $C\left(z^{-k}\right)$ | $C(1+i)^{-k}$ |

NOTE: $C$ = pattern scale factor
$n$ = time index for compounding periods
$i$ = effective interest rate for a compounding period.
$a$ = pattern base factor
$j$ = pattern rate factor
$\delta$ = impulse function
$k$ = number of time periods before the impulse occurs

***Linearity.*** The $Z$-transform is a linear operation. Thus, when a sequence can be expressed as a sum of other sequences, the following result will be useful.

$$f(n) = C_1 f_1(n) + C_2 f_2(n) \leftrightarrow F(z)$$
$$f_1(n) \leftrightarrow F_1(z)$$
$$f_2(n) \leftrightarrow F_2(z)$$

then

$$F(z) = C_1\,F_1\,(z) + C_2 F_2\,(z) \tag{3.9}$$

This linearity property makes it possible to combine component time forms and to amplify general time patterns by the scale factor $C$ to represent the

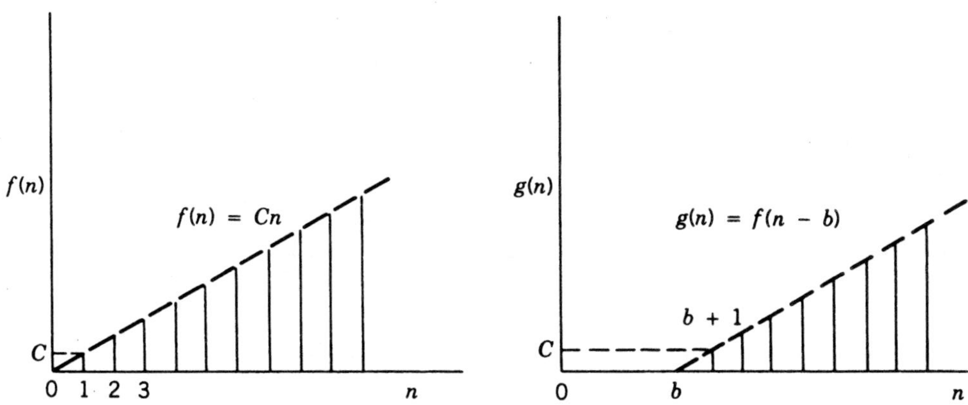


**FIGURE 3.1** Ramp pattern transaction (gradient series).

proportion of the component. By adding it to or subtracting it from the scaled transforms of other components, we are able to describe the composite Z-transform of the entire stream of components.

***Translation with Time Advance.*** To consider a composite of cash flows that start at various points in time, we seek the relation between the Z-transform of sequences and their shifted version. Consider the sequence $g(n)$ obtained from $f(n)$ by shifting $f(n)$ to the right by $b$ units of time. This situation is illustrated in Figure 3.1, in which the function $f(n)$ takes a ramp pattern. Since the sequence $g(n)$ is 0 for $n < b$, we can define the sequence $g(n)$ in terms of $f(n)$ as

$$g(n) = \begin{cases} f(n-b) & \text{for } n \geq b \\ 0 & \text{for } n < b \end{cases} \tag{3.10}$$

To find the transform of this time-shifted function, we use the property of the unit step function. If we take the unit step function and translate it $b$ units to the right to get $u(n - b)$, we obtain the function shown in Figure 3.2*a*. Mathematically, we denote this by

$$u(n-b) = \begin{cases} 1 & \text{for } n \geq b \\ 0 & \text{for } n < b \end{cases} \tag{3.11}$$

Notice that the shifted unit step function in Figure 3.2*a* has no values for $n < b$ but is equal to 1 for $n \geq b$. The product $f(n - b)u(n - b)$ will be zero for $n < b$ and will equal $f(n - b)$ for $n \geq b$. This product form shown in Figure 3.2*c* defines precisely the shifted ramp function we defined in Figure 3.1*b*. More generally, we define such a function as

$$g(n) = f(n-b)u(n-b) = \begin{cases} f(n-b) & \text{for } n \geq b \\ 0 & \text{for } n < b \end{cases} \tag{3.12}$$

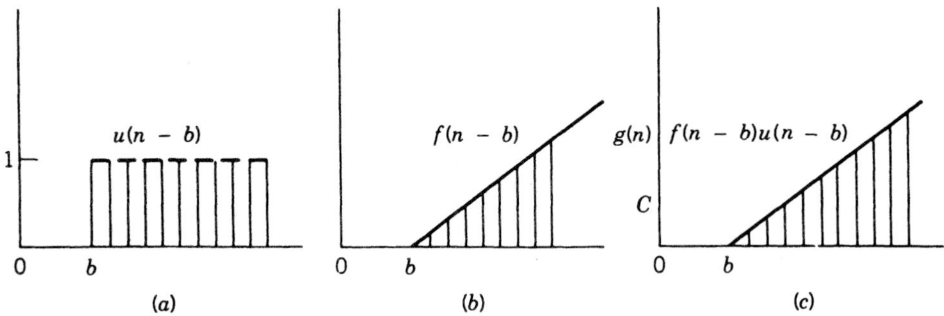


**FIGURE 3.2** Graph of the ramp function with translation and cutoff.

Then the $Z$-transform of the above expression is defined as

$$G(z) = z^{-b} F(z) = (1 + i)^{-b} F(z) \tag{3.13}$$

The quantity $z^{-b}$ in the $Z$-transform simply reflects the fact that the start of the function $f(n)$ has been shifted forward in time by $b$ units. Thus, if $f(n) = Cn$, shifting $f(n)$ to the right by $b$ units and taking its $Z$-transform generates $z^{-b}[Cz/(z - 1)^2]$. Expressing this in terms of the present value and replacing $z$ with $(1 + i)$, we obtain $PV(i) = [C(1 + i)^{1-b}]/i^2$.

***Translation with Cutoff.*** Many realistic cash flow functions extend over finite time horizons. Another scheme of translation property is useful in finding the $Z$-transforms for these translated cash flow functions. Consider the function $g(n)$ shown in Figure 3.3*c*. This function is basically the truncated ramp function $f(n)$ in Figure 3.3*b* with the added feature of a delayed turn-on at time $h$, where $h$ is an integer. By using the translation property discussed in the last section and multiplying the ramp function $f(n)$ by a unit step, we can express the desired truncated function $g(n)$ as

$$g(n) = f(n)u(n - h) = \begin{cases} f(n) & \text{for } h \leq n \\ 0 & \text{otherwise} \end{cases} \tag{3.14}$$

and the $Z$-transform of this product expression is

$$G(z) = z^{-h} Z\{f(n + h)\} \tag{3.15}$$

Unlike the situation in Figure 3.2*c*, the origin of the function $f(n)$ remains unchanged, but the first transaction begins at time $h$. Thus, it is important to recognize the functional distinction between $f(n)u(n - h)$ and $f(n - h)u(n - h)$. That is, an expression $f(n - h)u(n - h)$ similar to the one illustrated by Figure 3.2*c* will appear in shifting the sequence $f(n)$ to the right by $h$ units in time; and its first transaction also starts at time $h$.

Now the $Z$-transform and present value expression for the ramp function

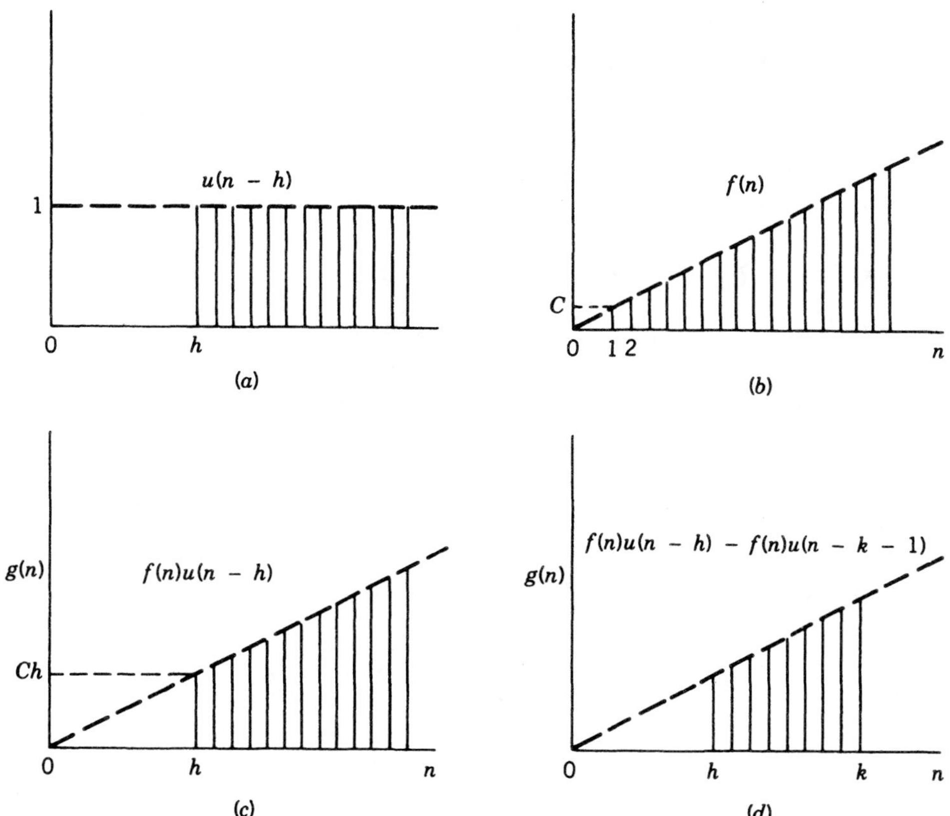


**FIGURE 3.3** Ramp function with translation and cutoff.

with a delayed turn-on at time $h$ shown in Figure 3.3$c$ can easily be found. Since $f(n) = Cn$, the transform of $g(n)$ is

$$G(z) = z^{-h}Z\{f(n + h)\}$$
$$= z^{-h}Z\{Cn + Ch\}$$
$$= Cz^{-h}\left[\frac{z}{(z-1)^2} + \frac{hz}{z-1}\right]$$
$$= \frac{Cz^{1-h}}{(z-1)^2}[1 + h(z-1)] \tag{3.16}$$

By replacing $z$ with $(1 + i)$, we obtain the present value expression

$$PV(i) = \frac{C(1+i)^{1-h}}{i^2}(1 + hi) \tag{3.17}$$

Suppose we want to find the present value of the series shown in Figure 3.3$d$. This function is the same ramp function with the delayed turn-on at time $h$ but also with a turn-off at time $k$, where $h$ and $k$ are integers. By using the property of the unit step function, we can express the desired ramp translation with turn-on and turn-off as follows.

$$g(n) = f(n)u(n - h) - f(n)u(n - k - 1) \tag{3.18}$$

The transform of this function will be

$$\begin{aligned} G(z) &= z^{-h}Z\{f(n + h)\} - z^{-(k+1)}Z\{f(n + k + 1)\} \\ &= z^{-h}Z\{Cn + Ch\} - z^{-(k+1)}Z\{Cn + C(k + 1)\} \\ &= Cz^{-h}\left[\frac{z}{(z-1)^2} + \frac{hz}{z-1}\right] - Cz^{-(k+1)}\left[\frac{z}{(z-1)^2} + \frac{(k+1)z}{z-1}\right] \\ &= \frac{C}{(z-1)^2}(z^{1-h} - z^{-k}) + \frac{C}{z-1}[hz^{1-h} - (k+1)z^{-k}] \end{aligned} \tag{3.19}$$

In terms of the present value expression, we have

$$PV(i) = \frac{C}{i^2}[(1 + i)^{1-h} - (1 + i)^{-k}] + \frac{C}{i}[h(1 + i)^{1-h} - (k + 1)(1 + i)^{-k}] \tag{3.20}$$

### *Example 3.1*

As an example of the use of Eq. 3.20, suppose that estimates of certain end-of-year expenses are \$300 for the third year, \$400 for the fourth year, and \$500 for the fifth year. If the effective interest rate is 15%, what is the equivalent present value?

The gradient series can be expressed as

$$f(n) = 100n \quad \text{where } 3 \leq n \leq 5$$

With $C = 100$, $h = 3$, $k = 5$, and $i = 0.15$, we obtain

$$\begin{aligned} PV(15\%) &= \frac{100}{(0.15)^2}[(1.15)^{-2} - (1.15)^{-5}] + \frac{100}{0.15}[3(1.15)^{-2} - 6(1.15)^{-5}] \\ &= \$674.54 \quad \square \end{aligned}$$

***Translation with Impulses.*** Suppose we want to find the transform of an impulse function $g(n)$ as given in Figure 3.4*c*. This type of impulse function may represent the salvage value of an item at time $h$, when the salvage value $f(n)$ decreases exponentially over time. To obtain the transforms of such impulse functions, we need to define a Kronecker delta function that corresponds to a unit impulse function as shown in Figure 3.4*c*. That is,

$$\delta(n - h) = \begin{cases} 1 & \text{for } n = h \\ 0 & \text{otherwise} \end{cases} \tag{3.21}$$

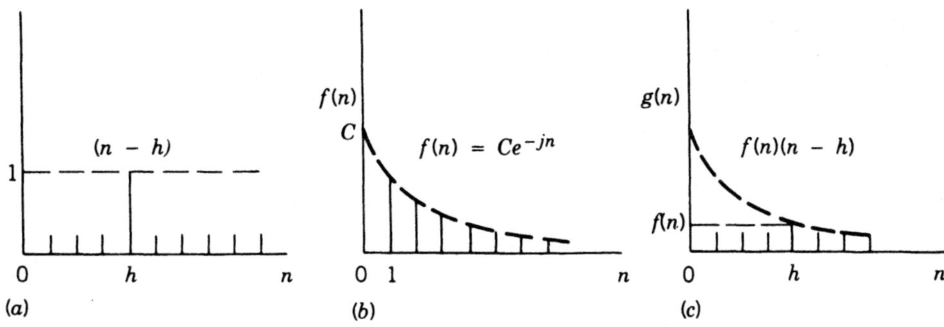


**FIGURE 3.4** Kronecker delta function and translation with impulse.

By multiplying the salvage value function $f(n)$ by the unit impulse function, we obtain an expression in which the salvage value occurs only at time $h$, as desired. Formally, we may write this product expression as

$$g(n) = f(n)\delta(n - h) = \begin{cases} f(h) & \text{for } n = h \\ 0 & \text{otherwise} \end{cases} \tag{3.22}$$

Since $f(h)$ is a constant and the transform of the shifted unit impulse function $\delta(n - h)$ is $z^{-h}$, the transform of the product form yields

$$G(z) = z^{-h}f(h) = f(h)(1 + i)^{-h} \tag{3.23}$$

and this is exactly the present value expression for a single payment. If we define $f(h) = Ce^{-jh}$, we can find the present value expression

$$PV(i) = Ce^{-jh}(1 + i)^{-h} \tag{3.24}$$

where $j$ is the pattern rate factor for a decay function.

The linearity and translation properties just discussed provide many of the necessary analytical tools for finding the $Z$-transforms of realistic discrete time series encountered in economic analysis. Table 3.2 summarizes some other useful operational rules for the $Z$-transform. (See [7].)

### 3.2.3 Development of Present Value Models

We develop two types of present value models that correspond to the timing of the start of the original cash flow function. They are the extensive models and the simplified models.

***Extensive Present Value Models.*** The extensive models represent cash flow functions that are shifted forward in time but switched on only at time $h$ ($h \geq b$) and then terminated at time $k$ ($k > h$) (see Figure 3.5). This function is basically the shifted ramp (gradient series) in Figure 3.1$b$ with a delayed turn-on at time $h$ and a turn-off at time $k$, where $h$ and $k$ are integers.

**Table 3.2** ***Some Properties of the Z-Transform***

| Operational Rule | Original Function, $f(n)$ | Z-Transform, $F(z)$ |
|---|---|---|
| Linearity | $C_1f_1(n) + C_2f_2(n)$ | $C_1F_1(z) + C_2F_2(z)$ |
| Damping | $a^{-n}f(n)$ | $F(az)$ |
| Shifting to the right | $f(n-k)u(n-k),\ k \geq 0$ | $z^{-k}F(z)$ |
| Shifting to the left | $f(n+k),\ k \geq 0$ | $z^k\left[F(z)-\sum_{n=0}^{k-1} f(n)z^{-n}\right]$ |
| Differencing of $f(n)$ | $\Delta f(n) = f(n+1) - f(n)$ | $(z-1)F(z) - zf(0)$ |
| | $\nabla f(n) = f(n) - f(n-1)u(n-1)$ | $\frac{z-1}{z}F(z)$ |
| Summation of $f(n)$ | $\sum_{j=0}^{n} f(j)$ | $\frac{z}{z-1}F(z)$ |
| Periodic sequences | $f(n+k) = f(n)$, period $k$ | $\frac{z^k}{z^k-1}\sum_{n=0}^{k-1} f(n)z^{-n}$ |
| Convolution | $f(n) * g(n)$ | $F(z) * G(z)$ |

To find the correct transform, we use the translation properties of Eqs. 3.12 and 3.14. The function $g(n)$ can then be expressed by multiplying the shifted gradient series by a unit step function. The resulting functional expression is

$$g(n) = [u(n-b) - u(n-k-1)]f(n-b) \tag{3.25}$$

Since $f(n) = Cn$ (gradient series), we may rewrite $f(n-b)$ as

$$f(n-b) = C(n-b) = Cn - Cb = f(n) - f(b)$$

Thus, we may also rewrite $g(n)$ as

$$g(n) = f(n)[u(n-b) - u(n-k-1)] + f(b)[u(n-k-1) - u(n-b)] \tag{3.26}$$

Note that $f(b)$ is a constant $Cb$. Using the transform results of Eq. 3.18, we obtain

$$G(z) = \frac{C}{(z-1)^2}(z^{1-b} - z^{-k}) + \frac{C}{z-1}[(b-b)z^{1-b} - (k+1-b)z^{-k}] \tag{3.27}$$

By replacing $z$ with $1 + i$, we obtain the present value expression of this extensive model.

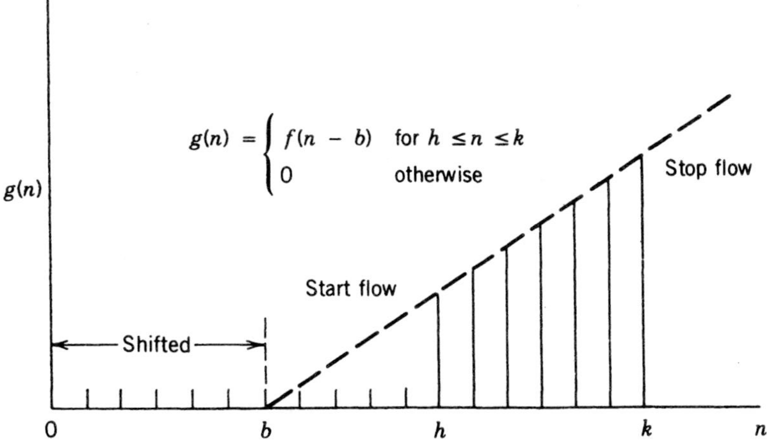


**FIGURE 3.5** Extensive model of ramp time pattern.

$$PV(i) = \frac{C}{i^2}[(1 + i)^{1-h} - (1 + i)^{-k}] + \frac{C}{i}[(h - b)(1 + i)^{1-h}] - (k + 1 - b)(1 + i)^{-k}] \quad (3.28)$$

If we use the conventional engineering economy notation, the present value of this shifted-gradient series is

$$PV(i) = [Cb(P/A, i, k - h + i) + C(P/G, i, k - h + 1)]\,(P/F, i, h - 1) \quad (3.29)$$

If we converted these factor notations to algebraic form, the final form would be as long an expression as Eq. 3.28. Table 3.3 provides the extensive models of other discrete cash flow patterns.

## *Example 3.2*

A 20-MW oil-burning power plant now under construction is expected to be in full commercial operation in 4 years from now. The fuel cost for this new plant is a function of plant size, thermal conversion efficiency (heat rate), and plant utilization factor. Because of inflation, the future price of oil will increase. The annual fuel cost is then represented by the following expression,

$$f(n) = (S)(H)(U)\left(\frac{8{,}760\text{ hr/year}}{10^6}\right)P_0\,(1 + f)^{n-1}$$

where $f(n)$ = annual fuel cost at the end of the $n$th operating year,
$S$ = plant size in kW (1 MW = 1,000 kW),
$H$ = heat rate (Btu/kW·hr),
$U$ = plant utilization factor,
$f$ = average annual fuel inflation rate,
$P_0$ = starting price of fuel per million Btu during the first year of operation.

## Table 3.3 *Extensive Discrete Present Value Models*

| Cash Flow Pattern | Function | Typical Cost Example | Present Value, $PV(i)$ |
|---|---|---|---|
| $C$, $g(n)$; $b$ $h$ $k$ | Step<br>$g(n) = f(n-b)$<br>$= C$ | Operating costs | $\frac{C}{i}[(1+i)^{1-h} - (1+i)^{-k}]$ |
| slope = $C$; $g(n)$; $b$ $h$ $k$ | Ramp<br>$g(n) = f(n-b)$<br>$= C(n-b)$ | Maintenance and deterioration | $\frac{C}{i^2}[(1+i)^{1-h} - (1+i)^{-k}]$<br>$+ \frac{C}{i}[(h-b)(1+i)^{1-h} - (k+1-b)(1+i)^{-k}]$ |
| Slope = $-C$; $A$, $g(n)$; $b$ $h$ $k$ | Decreasing Ramp<br>$g(n) = f(n-b)$<br>$= A - C(n-b)$ | Value depreciation costs | $\frac{(1+i)^{1-h}}{i}\left[A - \frac{C}{i} - C(h-b)\right]$<br>$- \frac{(1+i)^{-k}}{i}\left[A - \frac{C}{i} - C(k+1-b)\right]$ |
| $g(n)$; $b$ $h$ $k$ | Geometric series<br>$g(n) = f(n-b)$<br>$= Ca^{(n-b)}$ | Inflationary costs | $\frac{Ca^{h-b}}{1+i-a}[(1+i)^{1-h} - a^{k+1-b}(1+i)^{-k}]$ |
| $C$, $g(n)$; $b$ $h$ $k$ | Decay<br>$g(n) = f(n-b)$<br>$= Ce^{-j(n-b)})$ | Start-up and learning costs | $\frac{C(1+i)}{1+i-e^{-j}}\left[\frac{e^{-j(h-b)}}{(1+i)^h} - \frac{e^{-j(k+1-b)}}{(1+i)^{k+1}}\right]$ |
| $C$, $g(n)$; $b$ $h$ $k$ | Growth<br>$g(n) = C(1 - e^{-j(n-b)})$ | Wear-in maintenance costs | $\frac{C(1+i)}{i(1+i-e^{-j})}\left[\frac{(1+i-e^{-j}) - ie^{-j(h-b)}}{(1+i)^h}\right.$<br>$\left.- \frac{(1+i-e^{-j}) - ie^{-j(k+1-b)}}{(1+i)^{k+1}}\right]$ |

Assume that $S = 20{,}000$ kW, $H = 10{,}000$ Btu/kW·hr, $U = 0.20$, $f = 0.07$, and $P_0 =$ \$4.5 per million Btu during year 4. The expected life of the plant is 15 years. What is the present value of the total fuel cost at the beginning of construction (now) if the annual market rate of interest is 18%?

With the parameters as specified, the annual fuel cost function is

$$f(n) = 1{,}576{,}800\,(1 + 0.07)^{n-1}, \qquad 1 \le n \le 15$$

To find the present value of the total fuel cost at the beginning of construction, we rewrite $f(n)$ to obtain $g(n)$.

$$\begin{aligned} g(n) &= f(n - 4) \\ &= 1{,}576{,}800\,(1 + 0.07)^{n-5}, \qquad 5 \le n \le 19 \\ &= 1{,}473{,}645(1.07)^{n-4} \end{aligned}$$

Now we can use the geometric series formula given in Table 3.3. We identify $C = 1{,}473{,}645$, $a = 1.07$, $b = 4$, $h = 5$, $k = 19$, and $i = 0.18$, which yield

$$\begin{aligned} PV(18\%) &= \frac{1{,}473{,}645(1.07)}{0.11}[(1.18)^{-4} - (1.07)^{15}\,(1.18)^{-19}] \\ &= \$5{,}689{,}941 \quad \square \end{aligned}$$

***Simplified Present Value Models.*** The simplified models are defined as those with cash flows that have no delayed turn-on ($b = 0$) and that terminate after $k$ time units. The procedure for finding the $Z$-transform for this type of simplified form was illustrated in the previous section (see Figure 3.3*d*). Table 3.4 summarizes the present value models for some other common cash flow patterns. These simplified present value models correspond, in fact, to the traditional tabulated interest factors found in engineering economy textbooks. They simplify the use of this transform methodology when the modified features of cash flow patterns are not required.

### 3.2.4 Extension to Future and Annual Equivalent Models

The future equivalent values at the end of period $N$ can easily be obtained from the present values shown in Tables 3.3 and 3.4 by multiplying through by $(1 + i)^N$. Similarly, annual equivalent values over period $N$ are determined by multiplying the present values by the factor $i/[1 - (1 + i)^{-N}]$.

$$FV(i) = PV(i)[(1 + i)^N]$$

$$AE(i) = PV(i)\left[\frac{i}{1 - (1 + i)^{-N}}\right]$$

Consequently, all the $Z$-transforms in Tables 3.3 and 3.4 may be directly converted to a future or annual equivalent value by applying these elementary algebraic

## Table 3.4 *Simplified Discrete Present Value Models*

| Cash Flow Pattern | Function | Typical Cost Example | Present Value, $PV(i)$ |
|---|---|---|---|
| $f(n)$; 0, $h = 1$, $k$ | $f(n) = C$ | Operating costs | $\frac{C}{i}[1 - (1 + i)^{-k}]$ |
| $f(n)$; 0, $h = 1$, $k$ | $f(n) = Cn$ | Maintenance and deterioration | $\frac{C}{i^2}[1 - (1 + i)^{-k}]$ $+ \frac{C}{i}[1 - (k + 1)(1 + i)^{-k}]$ |
| $f(n)$; 0, $h = 1$, $k$ | $f(n) = A - Cn$ | Value depreciation costs | $\frac{1}{i}\left(A - \frac{C}{i} - C\right)$ $- \frac{(1 + i)^{-k}}{i}\left[A - \frac{C}{i} - C(k + 1)\right]$ |
| $f(n)$; $b = h = 1$, $k$ | $f(n) = Ca^n$ | Inflationary costs | $\frac{Ca}{1 + i - a}[1 - a^k(1 + i)^{-k}]$ |
| $f(n)$; 0, $h = 1$, $k$ | $f(n) = Ce^{-jn}$ | Start-up and learning costs | $\frac{C(1 + i)}{1 + i - e^{-j}}\left[\frac{e^{-j}}{1 + i} - \frac{e^{-j(k+1)}}{(1 + i)^{k+1}}\right]$ |
| $f(n)$; 0, $h = 1$, $k$ | $f(n) = C(1 - e^{-jn})$ | Wear-in maintenance costs | $\frac{C(1 + i)}{1 + i - e^{-j}}\left[\frac{1 - e^{-j}}{i} - \frac{1 + i - e^{-j} - ie^{-j(k+1)}}{i(1 + i)^{k+1}}\right]$ |

manipulations as needed. All the Z-transforms derived in the previous sections are based on the assumption that the compounding periods and the payment occurrences coincide. In situations in which the compounding periods occur more frequently than the receipt of payments, one can find the effective interest rate for the payment period and use it in the Z-transforms developed in Tables 3.3 and 3.4 (see Section 2.4.2).

### 3.2.5 Applications of Z-Transforms

In this section we will demonstrate the application of the Z-transform to the solution of equivalence problems. Two uses will be illustrated: profit margin analysis and calculation of the present value of interest payments.

***Profit Margin Analysis.*** Consider that a new production facility under construction is expected to be in full commercial operation 2 years from now. The plant is expected to have an initial profit margin of \$5 million per year. Find the present value of the total profit margin at 10% interest compounded annually for 20 years of operation if

i. Profit margin and plant performance stay level.

$$g(n) = 5, \qquad 3 \leq n \leq 22$$

ii. Performance traces a learning curve whereby the profit margin grows in each year.

$$g(n) = 5(2 - e^{-0.10(n-3)}), \qquad 3 \leq n \leq 22$$

iii. Performance traces the same growth curve, but the profit margin shrinks at a rate of $e^{-0.03(n-3)}$ so that

$$g(n) = 5e^{-0.03(n-3)}(2 - e^{-0.10(n-3)}), \qquad 3 \leq n \leq 22$$

These three cases are illustrated in Figure 3.6.

For case i, the cash flow diagram is a shifted step function with $C = 5$, $b = 3$, $h = 3$, and $k = 22$. From Table 3.3 the equivalent present value for this shifted step function is

$$PV(i) = \frac{5}{0.1}[(1.1)^{-2} - (1.1)^{-22}] = 50(0.7036) = \underline{\$35.18}$$

For case ii, the growth cash flow function may be regarded as a linear combination of a shifted step function and a shifted decay function. That is,

$$\begin{array}{ccccc} \text{Growth function} & = & \text{Step function} & - & \text{Decay function} \\ g(n) & = & 5(2) & - & 5e^{-0.10(n-3)} \end{array}$$

Thus, for the step function, the corresponding parameters would be $C = 10$, $b = 3$, $h = 3$, and $k = 22$, and for the decay function they would be $C = 5$, $j = 0.10$,

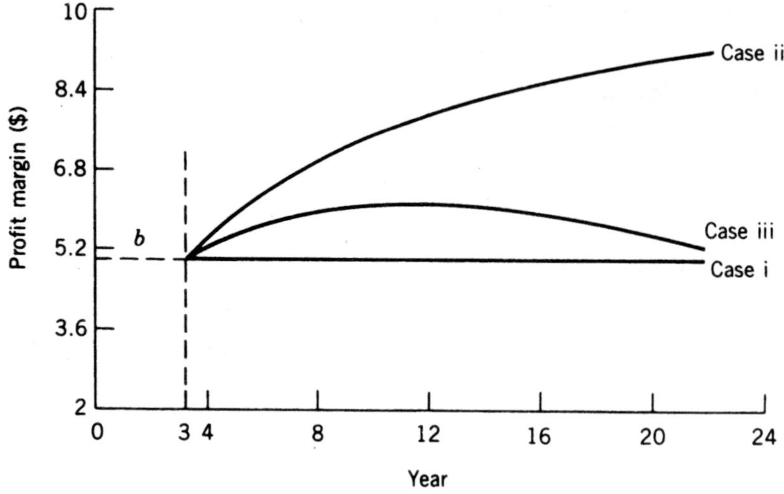


| $n$ | Case i | Case ii | Case iii |
|---|---|---|---|
| 3 | 5 | 5 | 5 |
| 4 | 5 | 5.475813 | 5.313978 |
| 5 | 5 | 5.906346 | 5.562387 |
| 6 | 5 | 6.295909 | 5.754028 |
| 7 | 5 | 6.6484 | 5.896602 |
| 8 | 5 | 6.967347 | 5.996851 |
| 9 | 5 | 7.255942 | 6.060672 |
| 10 | 5 | 7.517073 | 6.093221 |
| 11 | 5 | 7.753355 | 6.099005 |
| 12 | 5 | 7.967152 | 6.08196 |
| 13 | 5 | 8.160603 | 6.045523 |
| 14 | 5 | 8.335645 | 5.992693 |
| 15 | 5 | 8.494029 | 5.926083 |
| 16 | 5 | 8.637341 | 5.847972 |
| 17 | 5 | 8.767016 | 5.76034 |
| 18 | 5 | 8.884349 | 5.664912 |
| 19 | 5 | 8.990518 | 5.563184 |
| 20 | 5 | 9.086582 | 5.456453 |
| 21 | 5 | 9.173506 | 5.345845 |
| 22 | 5 | 9.252158 | 5.232331 |

**FIGURE 3.6** Profit margin analysis.

$b = 3$, $h = 3$, and $k = 22$. From Table 3.3 we obtain the $Z$-transform of this composite function as follows.

$$PV(i) = \frac{10}{0.1}\left[(1.1)^{-2} - (1.1)^{-22}\right] - \frac{5(1.1)}{1.1 - e^{-0.1}}\left[\frac{1}{(1.1)^3} - \frac{e^{-2.0}}{(1.1)^{23}}\right]$$

$$= 70.36 - 20.74 = \underline{\$49.61}$$

As expected, the total profit margin has increased significantly compared with case i, where no learning effect is appreciable.

For case iii, $g(n)$ is also a linear combination of two similar types of decay function. That is,

$$g(n) = 10e^{-0.03(n-3)} - 5e^{-0.13(n-3)}$$

The first decay function has parameter values of $C = 10, b = 3, h = 3, j = 0.03$, and $k = 22$. The second decay function has $C = 5, b = 3, h = 3, j = 0.13$, and $k = 22$. Thus, from Table 3.3 the $Z$-transform of this combination yields

$$\begin{aligned} PV(i) &= \frac{10(1.1)}{1.1 - e^{-0.03}}\left[\frac{1}{(1.1)^3} - \frac{e^{-0.60}}{(1.1)^{23}}\right] \\ &\quad - \frac{5(1.1)}{1.1 - e^{-0.13}}\left[\frac{1}{(1.1)^3} - \frac{e^{-2.60}}{(1.1)^{23}}\right] \\ &= 58.58 - 18.41 = \underline{\$40.17} \end{aligned}$$

***Analysis of Loan Transactions.*** The repayment schedule for most loans is made up of a portion for the payment of principal and a portion for the payment of interest on the unpaid balance. In economic analysis the interest paid on borrowed capital is considered as a deductible expense for income tax computation. Therefore, it is quite important to know how much of each payment is interest and how much is used to reduce the principal amount borrowed initially. To illustrate this situation, suppose that we want to develop an expression for the present value of the interest components of a uniform repayment plan. Let

$A$ = the equal annual repayment amount,

$B$ = the amount borrowed,

$i_b$ = the borrowing interest rate per period,

$N$ = the maturity of the loan (period).

Then the annual payments will be

$$A = B(A/P, i_b, N) = B\,\frac{i_b(1 + i_b)^N}{(1 + i_b)^N - 1} \tag{3.30}$$

Each payment is divided into an amount that is interest and a remaining amount for reduction of the principal. Let

$I_n$ = portion of payment $A$ at time $n$ that is interest,

$B_n$ = portion of payment $A$ at time $n$ that is used to reduce the remaining balance,

$A = I_n + B_n$, where $n = 1, 2, \ldots, N$,
$U_n$ = unpaid balance at the end of period $n$, with $U_0 = B$.

The relation of these parameters is illustrated in Figure 3.7. Since the interest payment is based on the unpaid principal that remains at the end of each period, the interest accumulation in the first year is simply $i_bB$. Thus, the first payment $A$ consists of an interest payment $i_bB$ and a principal payment of $A - i_bB$. The unpaid balance remaining after the first payment would be $U_1 = B - (A - i_bB) = B(1 + i_b) - A$. Consequently, the interest charge for the second year would be $i_bU_1$, and the size of the net principal reduction associated with the second payment would be $A - i_bU_1$. In other words, the unpaid balance remaining after the second payment would be

$$\begin{aligned} U_2 &= U_1 - (A - i_bU_1) \\ &= U_1(1 + i_b) - A \end{aligned} \tag{3.31}$$

The amount of principal remaining to be repaid right after making the $n$th payment can be found with the recursive relationship

$$U_n = U_{n-1}(1 + i_b) - A$$

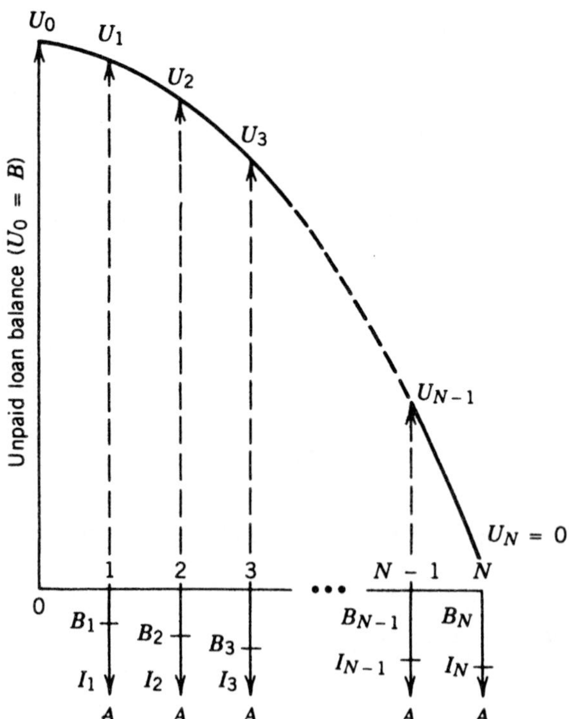


**FIGURE 3.7** Loan transactions—unpaid balance as functions of $B_n$ and $I_n$.

It follows immediately that

$$U_n = B(1 + i_b)^n - A[(1 + i_b)^{n-1} + (1 + i_b)^{n-2} + \cdots + 1]$$
$$= B(1 + i_b)^n - \frac{A}{i_b}[(1 + i_b)^n - 1]$$
$$= \left(B - \frac{A}{i_b}\right)(1 + i_b)^n + \frac{A}{i_b}, \qquad n = 0, 1, \ldots, N - 1 \qquad (3.32)$$

Now we can express the amount of interest payment required at the end of period $n + 1$.

$$I_{n+1} = i_b U_n$$
$$= \underbrace{(Bi_b - A)(1 + i_b)^n}_{\text{geometric series}} + \underbrace{A}_{\text{step function}}, \qquad n, = 0,1,\ldots, N - 1 \qquad (3.33)$$

Finally, the total present value of these interest payments at an interest rate of $i$ over the loan life of $N$ periods is defined as

$$PV(i) = \sum_{n=0}^{N-1} I_{n+1}(1 + i)^{-(n+1)} \qquad (3.34)$$

Let $g(n) = I_{n+1}$, where $g(n)$ is the sum of a geometric and a uniform series. From Table 3.4, the $Z$-transform of the geometric series portion is obtained by letting $a = (1 + i_b)$, $C = Bi_b - A$, $b = h = 1$, and $k = N$.

$$PV_1(i) = \frac{Bi_b - A}{i - i_b}[1 - (1 + i_b)^N(1 + i)^{-N}], \quad \text{where } i \neq i_b \qquad (3.35)$$

The transform of the step function portion is found by substituting $C = A$, $b = h = 1$, and $k = N$.

$$PV_2(i) = \frac{A}{i}[(1 - (1 + i)^{-N}] \qquad (3.36)$$

Finally, the transform of $g(n)$ *is found to be*

$$PV(i) = PV_1(i) + PV_2(i)$$
$$= \frac{Bi_b - A}{i - i_b}\left[1 - \left(\frac{1 + i_b}{1 + i}\right)^N\right] + \frac{A}{i}[1 - (1 + i)^{-N}] \qquad (3.37)$$

To illustrate the use of this formula, suppose that \$50,000 is borrowed at 8% annual interest and is to be repaid in ten equal annual payments. Determine the total present value of these interest payments associated with the loan transaction at a discount rate of 15%. Since we have $B = \$50{,}000$, $i_b = 8\%$, $N = 10$ years, and $i = 15\%$, the payment size $A$ is

$$A = \$50{,}000(A/P,\ 8\%,\ 10) = \$7{,}451.47$$

Then the total present value is

$$\begin{aligned} PV(15\%) &= \frac{\$50{,}000(0.08) - \$7{,}451.57}{0.15 - 0.08}\left[1 - \left(\frac{1.08}{1.15}\right)^{10}\right] \\ &\quad + \frac{\$7{,}451.47}{0.15}\left[1 - \frac{1}{(1.15)^{10}}\right] \\ &= -\$49{,}306.70(1 - 0.53365) + \$49{,}676.47(1 - 0.24718) \\ &= \$14{,}403.26 \end{aligned}$$

It may be of interest to compare the use of Eq. 3.37 with that of the conventional discounting formula developed by Brooking and Burgess [1]. They use the expression

$$\begin{aligned} PV(i) &= B\left\{(A/P,\ i_b,\ N)\left[[(P/A,\ i,\ N) - \frac{(P/F,\ i_b,\ N) - (P/F,\ i,\ N)}{i - i_b}\right]\right\} \\ &= A\left[\frac{1 - (1 + i)^{-N}}{i} - \frac{(1 + i_b)^{-N} - (1 + i)^{-N}}{i - i_b}\right] \end{aligned} \qquad (3.38)$$

Our method may be numerically verified with the traditional method as follows.

$$\begin{aligned} PV(15\%) &= \$7{,}451.47(5.0188 - \frac{0.4632 - 0.2472}{0.07}) \\ &= \$7{,}451.47(5.0188 - 3.0857) \\ &= \$14{,}404.47 \end{aligned}$$

The slight difference is due to rounding errors.

## 3.3 LAPLACE TRANSFORMS AND CONTINUOUS CASH FLOWS

Up to this point we have discussed only discrete cash flow functions. In this section we will extend the modeling philosophy to continuous cash flow functions. The Laplace transform method offers a modeling flexibility similar to that of the $Z$-transform for computing present values for many forms of continuous cash flow functions.

### 3.3.1 Laplace Transform and Present Value

As shown in Section 2.5.2, the present value of the infinite continuous cash flow streams, assuming continuous compounding, is given by the expression

$$PV(r) = \int_0^\infty f(t)e^{-rt}\,dt \tag{3.39}$$

where $f(t)$ = continuous cash flow function of the project,
$r$ = nominal interest rate $[r = \ln(1 + i)]$,
$t$ = time expressed in years,
$e^{-rt}$ = discount function.

As Buck and Hill [2] recognized, the general form of this integral bears a close resemblance to the definition of the Laplace transforms. That is, if the function $f(t)$ is considered to be piecewise continuous, then the Laplace transform of $f(t)$, written $L\{f(t)\}$, is defined as a function $F(s)$ of the variable $s$ by the integral

$$L\{f(t)\} = F(s) = \int_0^\infty f(t)e^{-st}\,dt \tag{3.40}$$

over the range of values of $s$ for which the integral exists. Replacing $s$ in Eq. 3.40 with the continuous compound interest rate $r$ simply generates Eq. 3.39; thus, taking a Laplace transform on the cash flow function $f(t)$ is equivalent to computing the present value of the cash flow streams over an infinite horizon time.

In the construction of Laplace transforms, we will use the following notation. If $f(t)$ represents the time domain continuous function, then $F(s)$ will represent its transform. As for the $Z$-transform, this lowercase–uppercase correspondence will be used throughout the text. As a shorthand notation, the transform pair will be denoted by

$$f(t) \leftrightarrow F(s)$$

For example, to find the transform of a linear function $f(t) = t$, $t > 0$, we directly evaluate Eq. 3.40.

$$F(s) = \int_0^\infty te^{-st}\,dt = \frac{1}{s^2} \tag{3.41}$$

and find that the transform pair is

$$t \leftrightarrow \frac{1}{s^2}$$

The transforms of some causal time functions that are typically encountered are shown in Table 3.5. The function $u(t)$ in this table represents the unit

## Table 3.5 *A Short Table of Laplace Transform Pairs**

| Standard Cash Flow Pattern | Cash Flow Function, $f(t)$ | Laplace Transform, $F(s)$ | Present Value, (Infinite), $PV(r)$ |
|---|---|---|---|
| Unit step ($f(t)$, 1, $t$) | $f(t) = u(t) = \begin{cases} 1 & t > 0 \\ 0 & \text{otherwise} \end{cases}$ | $1/s$ | $1/r$ |
| Delayed unit step ($f(t)$, $b$, $t$) | $f(t) = u(t - b) \quad b > 0$ | $e^{-bs}/s$ | $e^{-br}/r$ |
| Ramp ($f(t)$, $t$) | $f(t) = t$ | $1/s^2$ | $1/r^2$ |

## Table 3.5 (*Continued*)

| Standard Cash Flow Pattern | Cash Flow Function, $f(t)$ | Laplace Transform, $F(s)$ | Present Value, (Infinite), $PV(r)$ |
|---|---|---|---|
| Decay | $f(t) = e^{-jt}$ | $1/(s + j)$ | $1/(r + j)$ |
| Exponential | $f(t) = e^{jt}$ | $1/(s - j)$ | $1/(r - j)$ |
| Growth | $f(t) = 1 - e^{-jt}$ | $\frac{1}{s} - \frac{1}{s + j}$ | $j/r(r + j)$ |

*See [7] for a complete Laplace function table.

step function with jump at $t = 0$, and $u(t - a)$ denotes the unit step function with jump at $t = a$. The special property of this function is discussed in the next section.

### 3.3.2 Properties of Laplace Transforms

In this section we will examine some useful operational properties of the Laplace transform. As in the $Z$-transform analysis, the properties most relevant to modeling cash flows are linearity and translation.

***Linearity.*** If we define

$$f_1(t) \leftrightarrow F_1(s) \quad \text{and} \quad f_2(t) \leftrightarrow F_2(s)$$

then

$$c_1 f_1(t) + c_2 f_2(t) \leftrightarrow c_1 F_1(s) + c_2 F_2(s) \tag{3.42}$$

This follows from the linearity property of integrals of Eq. 3.40. Suppose we define $f(t)$ as

$$f(t) = 1 + t + \tfrac{1}{2}t^2$$

The transform is

$$L\{f(t)\} = L\{1\} + L\{t\} + L\{\tfrac{1}{2}t^2\}$$

Using Eqs. 3.42 and 3.40 along with the transform results in Table 3.5, we obtain

$$F(s) = \frac{1}{s} + \frac{1}{s^2} + \frac{1}{s^3}$$

***Translation with Time Delay.*** Consider Figure 3.8, in which the function $g(t)$ is obtained from $f(t)$ by shifting the graph of $f(t)$ $b$ units on the time scale to the right. Mathematically, we define such a function as

$$g(t) = \begin{cases} f(t - b) & \text{for } t \geq b \\ 0 & \text{for } t < b \end{cases} \tag{3.43}$$

To find the transform of this type of cash flow function that starts after a delay of $b$ time units, we utilize the property of the unit step function $u(t)$. If we take the unit step function and translate it $b$ units to the right to get $u(t - b)$, we obtain the function shown in Table 3.5. Mathematically, we denote this by

$$u(t - b) = \begin{cases} 1 & \text{for } t \geq b \\ 0 & \text{for } t < b \end{cases} \tag{3.44}$$

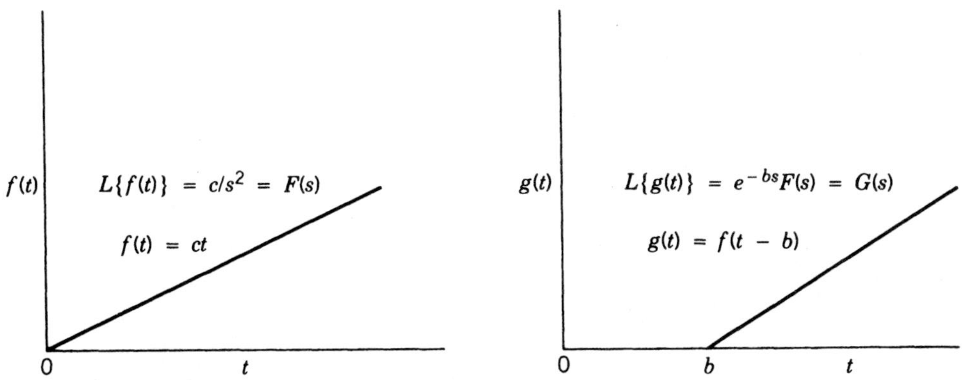


**FIGURE 3.8** Translation of continuous ramp pattern.

Then the product $g(t)u(t - b)$ or $f(t - b)u(t - b)$ will be defined as

$$g(t) = f(t - b)u(t - b) = \begin{cases} f(t - b) & \text{for } t \geq b \\ 0 & \text{for } t < b \end{cases} \tag{3.45}$$

The Laplace transform of $g(t)$ given by Eq. 3.45 is

$$L\{g(t)\} = e^{-bs}F(s) \tag{3.46}$$

Accordingly, a cash flow that starts later than $t = 0$ can be treated as if it started immediately and then a correction for the delayed start can be made with the discount factor $e^{-sb}$ $(= e^{-rb})$. This feature proves to be very useful when developing present value models with a composite of delayed turn-on cash flows.

***Translation with Cutoff.*** Another translation property of interest is turning cash flow streams on and off as desired. To illustrate the concept, suppose we wish to find the Laplace transform of a ramp function with features of a delayed turn-on at time $b$ and a turn-off at time $k$. This function is illustrated in Figure 3.9. Mathematically, we denote such a function by

$$g(t) = f(t)[u(t - b) - u(t - k)] \tag{3.47}$$

The first unit step begins the transactions at $t = b$ and the second stops the transactions at $t = k$. The Laplace transform of this $g(t)$ is defined by

$$G(s) = (e^{-bs} - e^{-ks})\left[F(s) + \frac{f(b)}{s}\right] \tag{3.48}$$

Some care must be exercised in using the time delay theorem. The reader should note the subtle functional difference that $f(t)u(t - b)$ is not a simple time-shifted function $[f(t - b)u(t - b)]$.

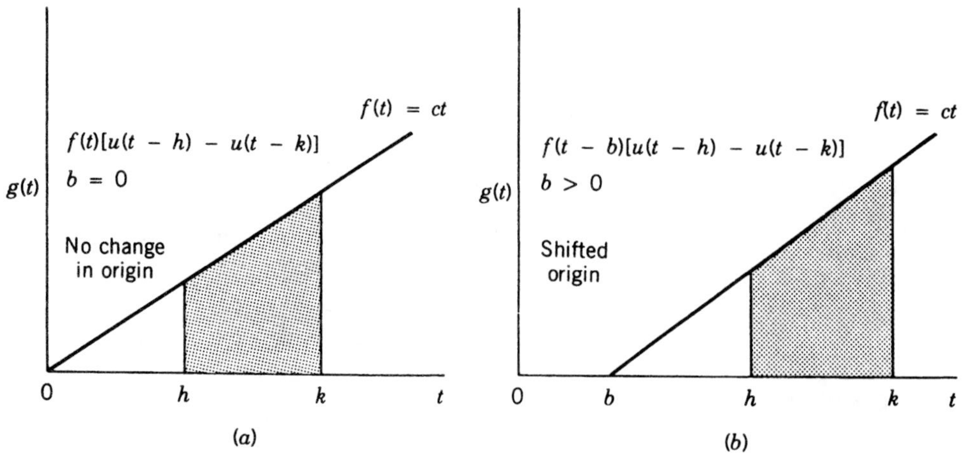


**FIGURE 3.9** A continuous ramp function with translation and cutoff.

$$f(t)u(t-b) \neq f(t-b)u(t-b)$$

This difference is illustrated in Fig. 3.10. We can rewrite the function as

$$f(t)u(t-b) = f(t-b)u(t-b) + f(b)u(t-b) \tag{3.49}$$

Since $f(b)$ is a constant, the Laplace transform of Eq. 3.49 is found by using Eq. 3.46:

$$\begin{aligned} L\{f(t)u(t-b)\} &= e^{-bs}F(s) + \frac{f(b)e^{-bs}}{s} \\ &= e^{-bs}L\{f(t+b)\} \end{aligned} \tag{3.50}$$

Therefore, the transform of Eq. 3.47 can be expressed as

$$L\{g(t)\} = G(s) = e^{-bs}L\{f(t+b\} - e^{-ks}L\{f(t+k)\} \tag{3.51}$$

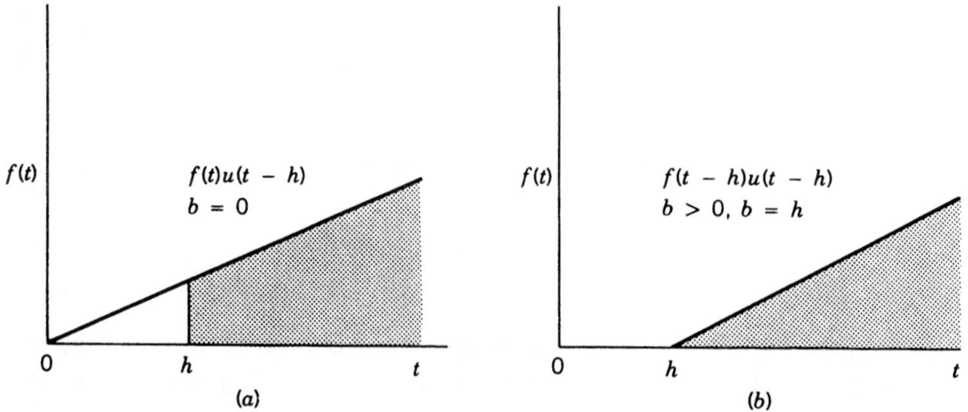


**FIGURE 3.10** Functional difference between $f(t)u(t-b)$ and $f(t-b)u(t-b)$.

## *Example 3.3*

Suppose a cash flow function is given by

$$f(t) = 5t, \qquad 10 \le t \le 20$$

Using Eq. 3.48 and Table 3.5, we obtain

$$\begin{aligned} G(s) &= e^{-10s}L\{5(t+10)\} - e^{-20s}L\{5(t+20)\} \\ &= e^{-10s}\left(\frac{5}{s^2} + \frac{50}{s}\right) - e^{-20s}\left(\frac{5}{s^2} + \frac{100}{s}\right) \\ &= \frac{5}{s^2}\left(e^{-10s} - e^{-20s}\right) + \frac{50}{s}\left(e^{-10s} - 2e^{-20s}\right) \end{aligned}$$

With a nominal interest rate of 10% ($r = s = 0.1$), the total present value is

$$\begin{aligned} PV(10\%) &= \frac{5}{(0.1)^2}(e^{-1} - e^{-2}) + \frac{50}{0.1}(e^{-1} - 2e^{-2}) \\ &= 116.27 + 48.60 = \$164.87 \end{aligned}$$

Our method may be numerically verified by direct integration of the cash flow function.

$$PV(10\%) = \int_{10}^{20} 5te^{-0.1t}\,dt = \$165$$

Once again, the slight difference is due to rounding errors. □

***Translations with Impulses.*** Suppose we want to find the transform of an impulse function $f(t)$ shown in Figure 3.11. This type of impulse function may represent the salvage value of an asset at $t = h$ when the salvage value $f(t)$ decreases exponentially over time. To obtain the transform of such an impulse function, we need to define a Kronecker delta function that corresponds to a unit impulse at $t = h$. That is,

$$\delta(t-h) = \begin{cases} 1 & \text{for } t = h \\ 0 & \text{otherwise} \end{cases} \tag{3.52}$$

By multiplying the salvage value function $f(t)$ by the unit impulse function, we obtain

$$g(t) = f(t)\delta(t-h) = \begin{cases} f(h) & \text{for } t = h \\ 0 & \text{otherwise} \end{cases} \tag{3.53}$$

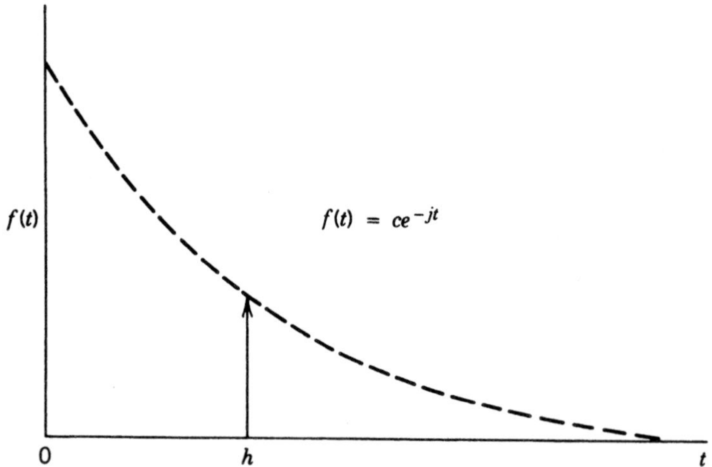


**FIGURE 3.11** Example of an impulse cash flow function—decay.

Since $f(h)$ is a constant, the transform of the product form yields

$$g(s) = e^{-hs}f(h) \tag{3.54}$$

which is the present value expression for a single payment.

Many other useful operational rules can be used in modeling continuous cash flow functions, such as scaling, periodic functions, and convolutions. These are summarized in Table 3.6. (See also Muth [7].)

### 3.3.3 Development of Continuous Present Value Models

Two types of present value models are needed, corresponding to the start of the original cash flow function. These are the extensive models and the simplified models. Figure 3.12 illustrates the modeling concept of both the extensive and the simplified forms of the ramp time form.

***Extensive Present Value Models.*** The computational procedure for finding the correct extensive present value model was discussed in the previous section. Formulas for directly computing the present values of these extensive models of five common cash flow time forms are presented in Table 3.7. To examine the modeling concept again, consider the exponential time forms of cash flow given in Table 3.7.

Let $f(t) = ce^{jt}$, where $c$ is the scale factor and $j$ is the growth rate with time. To obtain a geometric time form shifted to the right by $h$ time units, we define $g(t) = f(t - h)$. To denote the added feature of a delayed turn-on at $t = h$ and a turn-off at $t = k$, we write

$$g(t) = f(t - h)[u(t - h) - u(t - k)]$$

**Table 3.6** ***Summary of Operational Rules of the Laplace Transform***

| Operational Rule | Original Function | Laplace Transform |
|---|---|---|
| Linearity | $C_1 f_1(t) + C_2 f_2(t)$ | $c_1 F_1(s) + c_2 F_2(s)$ |
| Change of scale | $f(at),\ a > 0$ | $\frac{1}{a} F(s)$ |
| Shifting to the right | $f(t - a)u(t - a),\ a > 0$ | $e^{-as}F(s)$ |
| Shifting to the left | $f(t + a),\ a < 0$ | $e^{as}\left[F(s) - \int_0^a e^{-st}f(t)\,dt\right]$ |
| Damping | $e^{-at}f(t)$ | $F(s + a)$ |
| Differentiation of $F(s)$ function | $tf(t)$ | $-\frac{d}{ds} F(s)$ |
| Integration of $F(s)$ function | $\frac{f(t)}{t}$ | $\int_s^\infty F(u)\,du$ |
| Differentiation of $f(t)$ | $\frac{d}{dt} f(t)$ | $sF(s) - f(0^+)$ |
| | $\frac{d^n}{dt^n} f(t)$ | $s^nF(s) - s^{n-1}f(0^+) - s^{n-2}fE(0^+) - \cdots - f^{(n-1)}(0^+)$ |
| Integration of f(t) | $\int_0^t f(u)\,du$ | $\frac{1}{s} F(s)$ |
| Periodic function | $f(t) = f(t + T),\ T = \text{period}$ | $F(s) = \frac{1}{1 - e^{-sT}}\int_0^T e^{-st}f(t)dt$ |
| Convolution | $f_1(t) * f_2(t)$ | $F_1(s)F_2(s)$ |

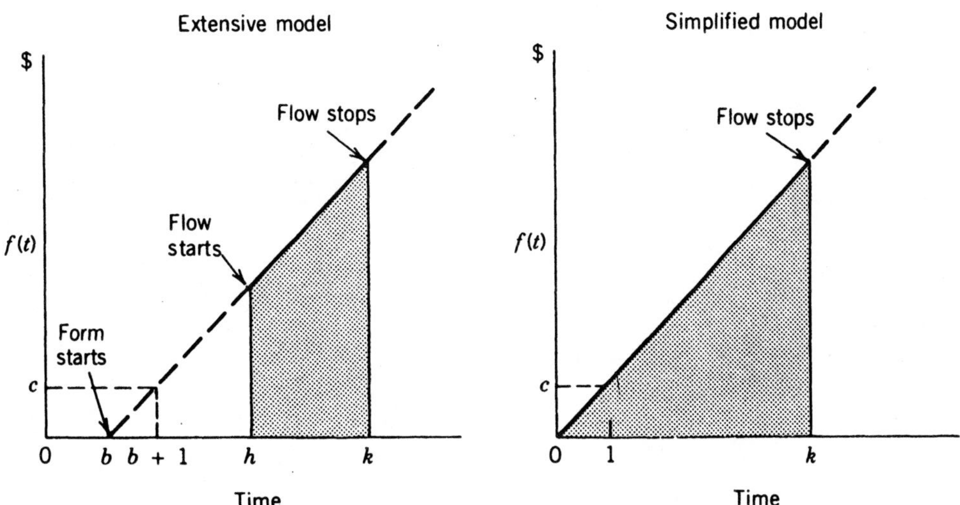


**FIGURE 3.12 Features of extensive and simplified continuous models.**

**Table 3.7** ***Extensive Continuous Present Value Models***

| Time Form | $f(t)$ | $PV(r)$ |
|---|---|---|
| Step |  $c$ | $\frac{c}{r}(e^{-hr} - e^{-kr})$ |
| Ramp | 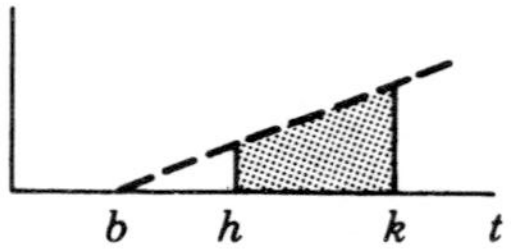 $ct$ | $\frac{c}{r^2}(e^{-hr} - e^{-kr}) + \frac{c}{r}[(h - b)e^{-hr} - (k - b)e^{-kr}]$ |
| Decay | 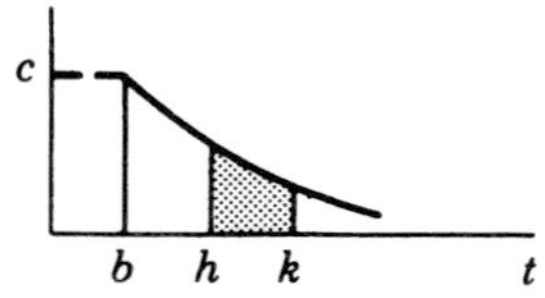 $ce^{-jt}$ | $\frac{ce^{+bj}}{r + j}(e^{-h(j+r)} - e^{-k(j+r)})$ |
| Growth | 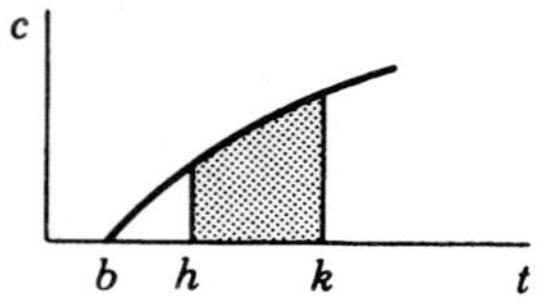 $c(1 - e^{-jt})$ | $\frac{c}{r}(e^{-hr} - e^{-kr}) - \frac{ce^{bj}}{r + j}(e^{-h(j+r)} - e^{-k(j+r)})$ |
| Exponential | 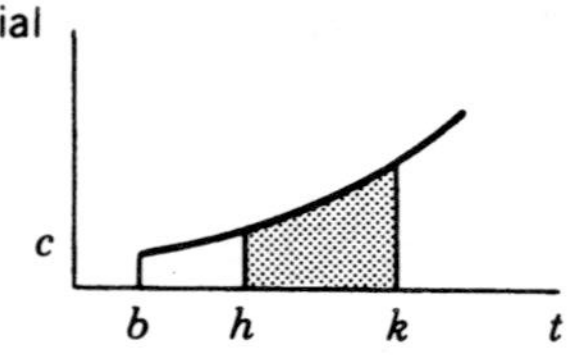 $ce^{jt}$ | $\frac{ce^{-bj}}{r - j}(e^{h(j-r)} - e^{k(j-r)}),\ j \neq r$ |

Since $f(t) = ce^{jt}$, $f(t - b) = ce^{j(t-b)}$. Therefore, we may rewrite $g(t)$ as

$$\begin{aligned} g(t) &= ce^{j(t-b)}[u(t - h) - u(t - k)] \\ &= (e^{-bj})(ce^{jt})[u(t - h) - u(t - k)] \\ &= (e^{-bj})f(t)[u(t - h) - u(t - k)] \end{aligned} \tag{3.55}$$

From Eq. 3.47, the transform of $g(t)$ yields

$$L\{g(t)\} = e^{-bj}[e^{-hs}L\{f(t + h) - e^{-ks}L\{f(t + k)\}\}]$$

To evaluate $L\{f(t + h)\}$ and $L\{f(t + k)\}$, we simply expand the original function $f(t) = ce^{jt}$

$$L\{f(t + h)\} = \{ce^{j(t+h)}\} = ce^{jh}L\{f(t)\} = ce^{jh}F(s)$$

$$L\{f(t + k)\} = \{ce^{j(t+k)}\} = ce^{jk}L\{f(t)\} = ce^{jk}F(s)$$

Since $F(s) = 1/(s - j)$ for $f(t) = e^{jt}$, but with $s = r$, we have

$$L\{g(t)\} = \frac{ce^{-bj}}{r - j}\left(e^{h(j-r)} - e^{k(j-r)}\right) \tag{3.56}$$

## *Example 3.4*

Consider a cash inflow stream that starts at $t = 2$ (years) and increases \$1,000 per year uniformly until $t = 10$. Table 3.7 reveals that the ramp is the proper time form for the cash flow. This time form has the scale parameter of $c = \$1{,}000$. Assume that the pattern starts at $b = 2$, the cash flow begins immediately after that at $h = 2$, and the flow stops at $k = 10$. The present value at the nominal rate of interest 10% is

$$\begin{aligned} PV(10\%) &= \frac{\$1{,}000}{(0.1)^2}(e^{-0.2} - e^{-1}) + \frac{\$1{,}000}{0.1}(0 - 8e^{-1}) \\ &= \$45{,}085.13 - \$29{,}430.35 = \$15{,}654.78 \quad \square \end{aligned}$$

***Simplified Present Value Models.*** When there is no shift in time form and no delayed turn-on, the extra factors in the extensive model become cumbersome. In other words, if $b = h = 0$, we can further simplify the formulas in Table 3.7. The reader may notice that the simplified models correspond to the traditional tabulated interest factors (funds flow factors) used in most engineering economy textbooks. These are summarized in Table 3.8.

***Present Values of Impulse Cash Flows.*** Single instantaneous cash flows are referred to as "impulses" to distinguish them from the continuous flow streams examined in the previous sections. Frequently, it is necessary to describe a cash

**Table 3.8** ***Simplified Continuous Present Value Models***

| Time Form | $f(t)$ | $PV(r)$ |
|---|---|---|
| 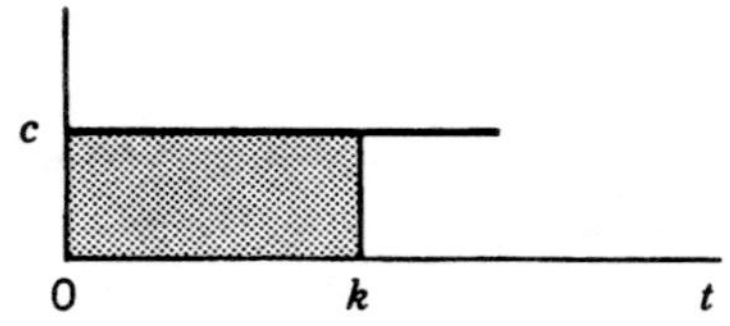 Step (c; 0, k, t) | $c$ | $\frac{c}{r}(1 - e^{-kr})$ |
| Ramp (0, k, t) | 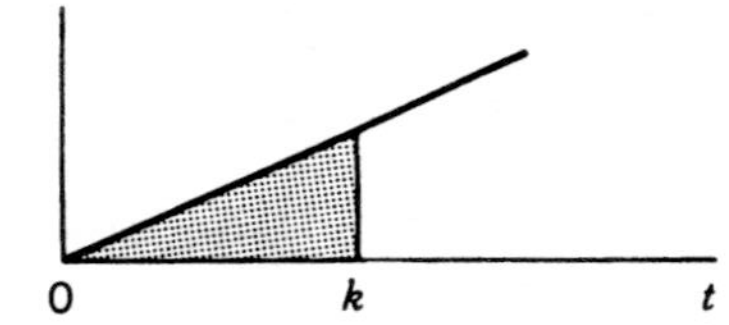 $ct$ | $\frac{c}{r^2}(1 - e^{-kr} - rke^{-kr})$ |
| Decay (c; 0, k, t) | 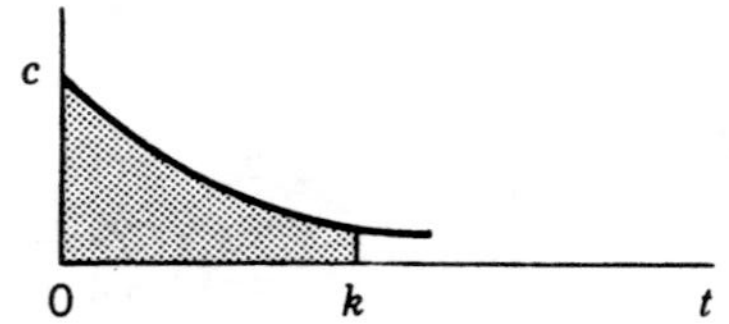 $ce^{-jt}$ | $\frac{c}{r+j}(1 - e^{-k(j+r)})$ |
| Growth (c; 0, k, t) | 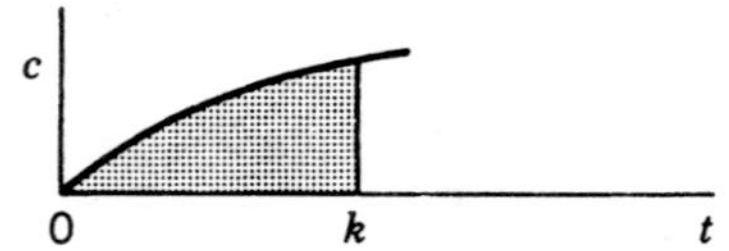 $c(1 - e^{-jt})$ | $\frac{c}{r}(1 - e^{-kr}) - \frac{c}{r+j}(1 - e^{-k(j+r)})$ |
| Exponential (c; 0, k, t) | 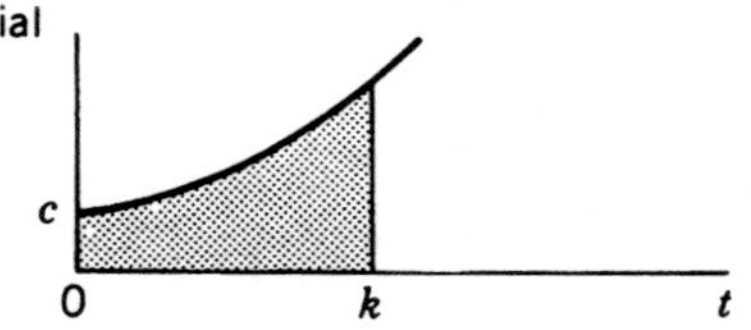 $ce^{jt}$ | $\frac{c}{r-j}(1 - e^{k(j-r)})$ |

impulse that changes in magnitude over time according to some time form. As an example, a salvage value from the sale of a machine decreases gradually with the age of the machine, but the actual value received is a single flow at the time of disposal. Present value formulas corresponding to such a cash impulse, following the four time forms but occurring only at time $T$, are summarized in Table 3.9. These present value formulas are derived from Eq. 3.54.

### *Example 3.5*

Suppose that the salvage value of an automobile can be described by a decay time form with an initial value of \$6,000. The decay rate with time is given as 0.3. Find the present value of the salvage value that occurs at the end of 5 years at a nominal interest rate of 10% compounded continuously. Let $c = 6{,}000$, $r = 0.3$, $j = 0.1$, and $T = 5$. Then

$$PV(10\%) = ce^{-(j + r)T} = \$6{,}000e^{-2.0} = \$812.01 \quad \square$$

**Table 3.9** ***Present Values of Impulse Cash Flows***

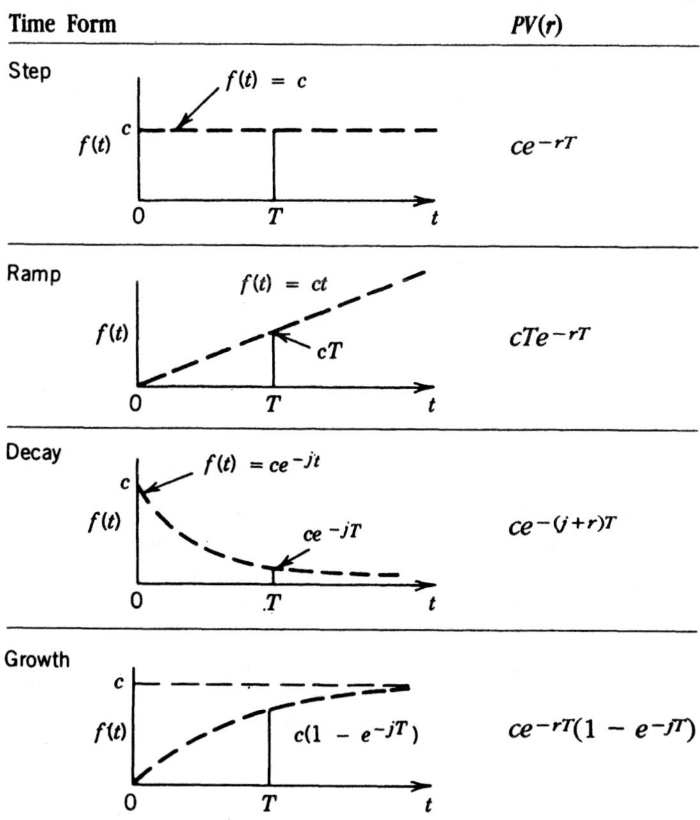

### 3.3.4 Extension to Future and Annual Equivalent Models

The future equivalent values at the end of period $T$ can easily be obtained from the present value formulas shown in Tables 3.7, 3.8, and 3.9 simply by multiplying through by $e^{rT}$. Similarly, annual values of equivalent cash flow streams are defined here as the annual cash flow of a step time form starting immediately, terminating at the same time as the equivalent stream, and possessing equal present value. Accordingly, the present value of a step (uniform) time form with the annual cash flow of $\bar{A}$ dollars may be equated to the present value formulas of the other time forms. Solving for $\bar{A}$ gives us the equivalent annual value.

***Example 3.6***

Consider Example 3.5 and find the equivalent annual value at a nominal interest rate of 10% compounded continuously. Since the present value of the ramp time form that extends over a 10-year period is \$15,654.78, the annual equivalent cash flow stream of $\bar{A}$ dollars per year is determined as follows. From Table 3.8, the present value of the step time form with $b = h = 0$, $c = \bar{A}$, $k = 10$, and $r = 0.1$ yields

$$\frac{\bar{A}}{0.1}(1 - e^{-1}) = \$15{,}654.78$$

The satisfying value of $\bar{A}$ is the equivalent annual value, which is $\bar{A} =$ \$2,476.55. □

### 3.3.5 Application of the Laplace Transform

***Description of the Basic Inventory System.*** Consider the simplest imaginable type of inventory system in which there is only a single item. The demand rate for this item is assumed to be deterministic and a constant $\lambda$ units per year. The fixed cost of placing an order in dollars is $A$. The unit cost of the item in dollars is $C$. Let $I_0$ be the inventory carrying charge (measured in the units of dollars per year per dollar of investment in inventory) exclusive of the rate of return (i.e., of the opportunity cost). We will further assume that the procurement lead time is a constant and that the system is not allowed to be out of stock at any point in time. Orders for the item are received in lots of $Q$ units. The problem is to determine the optimal value of $Q$.

Figure 3.13 depicts the inventory behavior of this model with respect to time. Since the order quantity $Q$ and the demand rate $\lambda$ are constant, the inventory level of the first cycle $T$ is

$$I(t) = Q - \lambda t, \qquad 0 \le t \le T \tag{3.57}$$

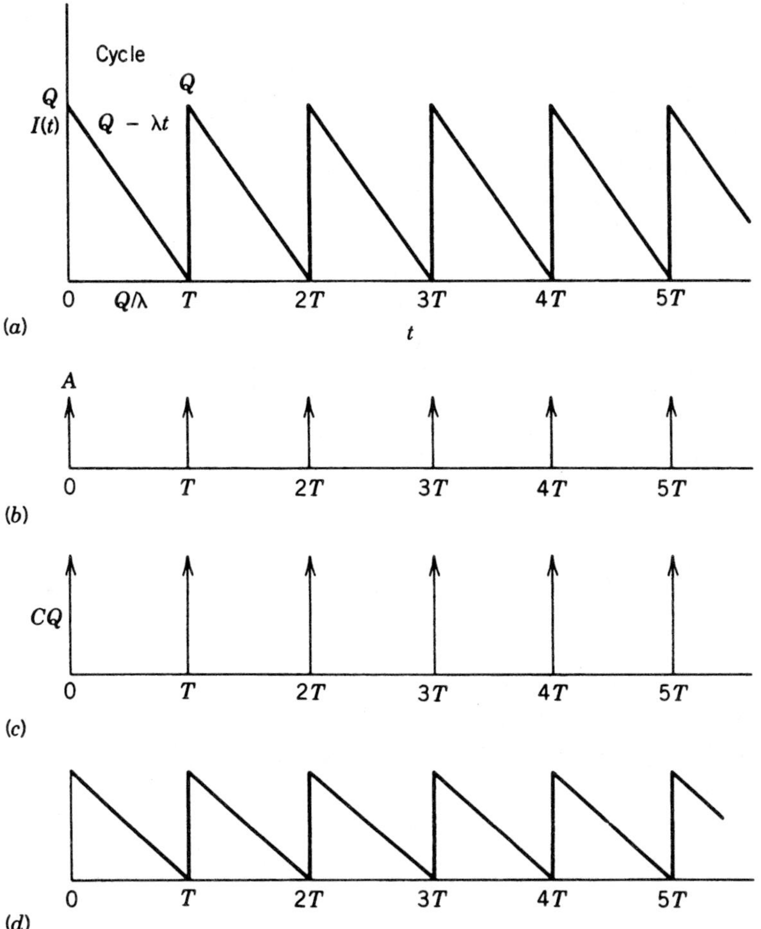


**FIGURE 3.13** Inventory behavior: quantity and const as functions of time. (*a*) Inventory positions. (*b*) Ordering costs. (*c*) Purchase costs. (*d*) Inventory costs.

Note that $I(t) = 0$ at $t = T$ and $T = Q/\lambda$. Let

$$\begin{aligned} r &= \text{the nominal interest rate,} \\ f(t)_1 &= \text{the ordering cost per cycle,} \\ f(t)_2 &= \text{the purchase cost per cycle,} \\ f(t)_3 &= \text{the inventory carrying cost per cycle.} \end{aligned}$$

Then the inventory cost for the first cycle is given by

$$f(t) = f(t)_1 + f(t)_2 + f(t)_3 \tag{3.58}$$

where

$$\begin{aligned} f(t)_1 &= A, \\ f(t)_2 &= CQ, \\ f(t)_3 &= I_0 C \int_0^T (Q - \lambda t)\, dt. \end{aligned}$$

Equation 3.58 represents the inventory cost per cycle *without* considering the effect of the time value of money.

To find the present value of the inventory cost for the first cycle, we assume that the ordering and purchase costs will occur only at the beginning of the cycle, but that the inventory carrying cost will occur continuously over the cycle. With these assumptions, the Laplace transform of the inventory cost function is

$$\begin{aligned} F(s) &= A + CQ + L\{I_0C(Q - \lambda t)\} \\ &= A + CQ + I_0C\left[\frac{Q}{s} - \frac{\lambda}{s^2}(1 - e^{-sT})\right] \end{aligned} \tag{3.59}$$

After substituting $s = r$ and $T = Q/\lambda$ back into Eq. 3.59, we find that the present value expression is

$$PV(r)_{\text{cycle}} = A + CQ + I_0C\left[\frac{Q}{r} - \frac{\lambda}{r^2}(1 - e^{-rQ/\lambda})\right] \tag{3.60}$$

Since the cycle repeats itself forever, we can use the Laplace transform property of periodic functions. If we denote the total inventory cost over infinite cycles as $g(t)$, $G(s)$ can be expressed in terms of the transform of the first cycle $F(s)$.

$$G(s) = F(s)\frac{1}{1 - e^{-sT}} \tag{3.61}$$

$$\begin{aligned} PV(r)_{\text{total}} &= PV(r)_{\text{cycle}}\left(\frac{1}{1 - e^{-rQ/\lambda}}\right) \\ &= \frac{1}{1 - e^{-rQ/\lambda}}\left(A + CQ + \frac{I_0CQ}{r}\right) - \frac{I_0C\lambda}{r^2} \end{aligned} \tag{3.62}$$

Differentiating $PV(r)_{\text{total}}$ with respect to $Q$ and equating the result to zero gives us

$$(1 - e^{-rQ/\lambda})\left(C + \frac{I_0C}{r}\right) - \left(A + CQ + \frac{I_0CQ}{r}\right)\left(\frac{r}{\lambda}e^{-rQ/\lambda}\right) = 0 \tag{3.63}$$

An exact analytical solution of (3.63) for $Q$ is not normally possible, but a numerical solution may be obtained by using the Newton–Raphson method [8]. An approximate solution (within about 2%) can be obtained more easily, however, by using a second-order approximation for the exponential term.

$$\begin{aligned} e^{-rQ/\lambda} &= 1 - \left(\frac{r}{\lambda}\right)Q + \left(\frac{r}{\lambda}\right)^2 Q^2\frac{1}{2!} \\ &\quad - \left(\frac{r}{\lambda}\right)^3 Q^3\frac{1}{3!} + \cdots \end{aligned} \tag{3.64}$$

Since $0<r<1$ (in general), we can ignore the terms $(r/\lambda)^3$ and higher. Then, substituting the first three terms into Eq. 3.63 and solving for $Q$, we obtain

$$Q^* \triangleq \left[\frac{2A}{(I_0 + r)C}\right]^{1/2} \tag{3.65}$$

With $A$ = \$10, $C$ = \$5/unit, $I_0 = 0.1$, $r = 0.1$, and $\lambda = 100$ units per year, the optimal order quantity is about

$$Q^* \triangleq \left[\frac{2(15)(100)}{(0.1 + 0.2)5}\right]^{1/2} = 36.51$$

The numerical solution obtained by the Newton–Raphson method would be $Q^* = 36.23$.

## 3.4 SUMMARY

The $Z$-transform and the Laplace transform can be used in a wide variety of cash flow models, and in many situations these methodologies are more efficient than the traditional approach. This chapter was intended to (1) introduce the transform methodologies, (2) provide alternative techniques for modeling cash flows that are interrupted or impulses that follow a particular time form, and (3) demonstrate the use of this methodology in equivalence calculations. We do not recommend the transform analysis for modeling simple cash flow transactions because there is not much savings in computation. The transform analysis will provide definite computational advantages, however, for complex cash flow functions.

## REFERENCES


1. Brooking, S. A., and A. R. Burgess, "Present Worth of Interest Tax Credit," *The Engineering Economist*, Vol. 21, No. 2, Winter 1976, pp. 111–117.
2. Buck, J. R., and T. W. Hill, "Laplace Transforms for the Economic Analysis of Deterministic Problems in Engineering," *The Engineering Economist*, Vol. 16, No. 4, 1971, pp. 247–263.
3. Buck, J. R., and T. W. Hill, "Additions to the Laplace Transform Methodology for Economic Analysis," *The Engineering Economist*, Vol. 20, No. 3, 1975, pp. 197–208.
4. Giffin, W. C., *Transform Techniques for Probability Modeling*, Academic Press, New York, 1975.
5. Grubbstrom, R. W., "On the Application of the Laplace Transform to Certain Economic Problems," *Management Science*, Vol. 13, No. 7, 1967, pp. 558–567.
6. Hill, T. W., and J. R. Buck, "Zeta Transforms, Present Value, and Economic Analysis," *AIIE Transactions*, Vol. 6, No. 2, 1974, pp. 120–125.
7. Muth, E. J., *Transform Methods with Applications to Engineering and Operations Research*, Prentice–Hall, Englewood Cliffs, N.J., 1977.

8. PARK, C. S., and Y. K. SON, "The Effect of Discounting on Inventory Lot Sizing Models," *Engineering Costs and Production Economics,* Vol. 16, No. 1, 1989, pp. 35–48.

9. REMER, D. S., J. C. TU, D. E. CARSON, and S. A. GANIY, "The State of the Art of Present Worth Analysis of Cash Flow Distributions," *Engineering Costs and Production Economics,* Vol. 7, No. 4, 1984, pp. 257–278.

## PROBLEMS

**3.1.** Consider a cash flow stream for which the monthly profits are \$1,000$e^{-0.1n}$ for $n$ = 1, 2, 3, . . . , 12 months and the nominal interest rate is 12%. Find the present value under

a. 12% compounded annually.
b. 12% compounded quarterly.
c. 12% compounded monthly.
d. 12% compounded continuously.

**3.2.** Consider the discrete cash flow patterns shown in the accompanying illustration.

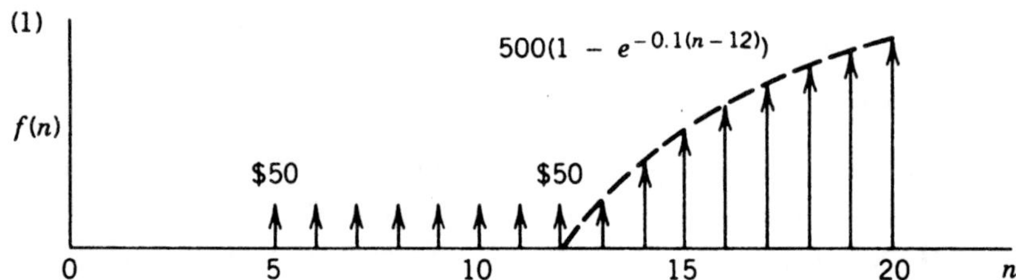


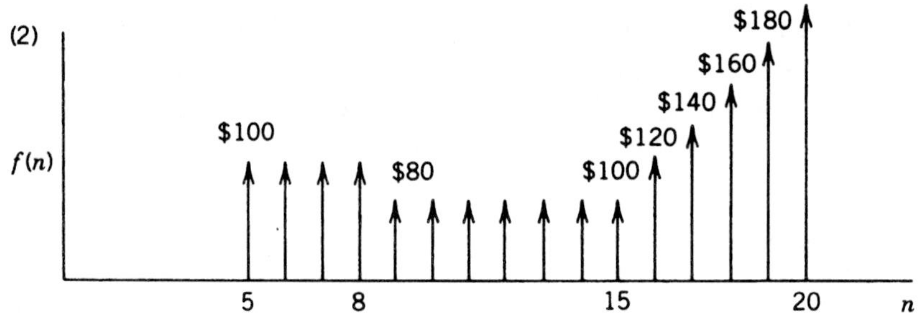


a. Compute the present value of each cash flow series using the conventional interest formulas at $i$ = 10%.
b. Compute the present value of each cash flow series using the discrete transform results at $i$ = 10%.
c. Compute the annual equivalent value of each cash flow series over 20 years.

**3.3.** Consider the retirement schedule for a \$100,000 bond issue by a city, which is to be proportional to the city's anticipated growth. If this anticipated growth tends to follow the general growth pattern of

$$f(n) = C(1 - e^{-0.087n})$$

and the bond interest rate is 5%, find an increasing repayment over 20 years.

**3.4.** Suppose you borrow \$100,000 at an interest rate of 9% compounded monthly over 30 years to finance a home. If your interest rate is 1% per month, compute the present value of the total interest payment of the loan.

**3.5.** Consider the following cost and return components of a machine tool.

a. The initial cost of \$8,000.

b. A uniform operating cost of \$800 each year.

c. Maintenance costs, which increase at a rate of \$400 each year.

d. Annual start-up costs, which decay at the rate of 1.0 from an upper limit of \$1,000 initially.

e. A single salvage value return, which decays at the rate of 0.5 with age from the initial cost of \$8,000. Assume $i = 8\%$.

Compute the present value of these five cash flow components over 10 years.

**3.6.** Consider a machine that now exists in condition $j$ and generates earnings at the uniform continuous rate of $A_j$ dollars per year. If at some time $T$ the machine's condition changes from $j$ to $k$, its earning rate will instantaneously change from $A_j$ to $A_k$. We will inspect the machine exactly one year from now. You may treat the time value of money in terms of a nominal interest rate of $r$ compounded continuously.

a. If the machine's condition changes to $k$ at time $T$, where $T$ is in time interval between 0 and 1, what is the present value of its earnings for the year?

b. If the machine remains in condition $j$ for the entire year, what is the present value of its earnings for the year?

**3.7.** Suppose a uniformly increasing continuous cash flow (a ramp) accumulates \$1,000 over 4 years. The continuous cash flow function is expressed as

$$f(t) = ct, \qquad 0 \le t \le 4$$

Assume that $r = 12\%$ compounded continuously.

a. Find the slope $c$.

b. Compute the present equivalent of this continuous series.

c. Compute the future value of this continuous series.

**3.8.** Find the present value of the following quadratic cash flow at 10% interest compounded continuously,

$$f(t) = \$200 + 45t - 3t^2$$

a. if $0 \le t \le 10$.

b. if $0 \le t \le \infty$.

**3.9.** A chemical process for an industrial solvent generates a continuous after-tax cash flow $f(t)$ of \$250,000 per year for a 10-year planning horizon.

a. Find the present value of this cash flow stream over 10 years if money is worth 12% compounded continuously.

b. The profit per year is expected to increase continuously because of increased productivity and can be expressed as

$$f(t) = 250{,}000(2.0 - e^{-0.2t})$$

where $t$ is time in years. Find the present value of this cash flow stream.

c. Productivity increases as in part b, but competition reduces the profit continuously by 8% per year. Find the present value of the cash flow.

**3.10.** Consider the following simple inventory system. A stock of $Q$ units is produced at a rate of $a_p$ units per day for a period $T_p$. It is then necessary to leave the batch in stock for a period of $T_d$, during which sorting, inspection, and painting are carried out. A quantity $Q_1$ is then supplied to the assembly line at the rate of $a$ units per day for a period $T_c$. The supply to the assembly is intermittent, so that after a supply period $T_c$ there is an interval $T_0$ before supply is resumed for another period $T_c$, and so on. Assuming that the relationship between $Q$ and $a$ is defined as $Q = ka$, $k$ is an integer, and $h$ stands for a holding cost of one unit per unit time, answer the following questions.

a. Draw the level of inventory position as a function of time $t$.
b. Assuming continuous compounding at a nominal rate of $r$, find the expression of present value of the total inventory cost over one complete cycle. (One cycle is defined as a time interval in which the entire stock $Q$ is depleted.)
c. With $Q$ = 1,000 units, $a_p$ = 10 units/day, $T_p$ = 100 days, $T_d$ = 50 days, $a$ = 5 units/day, $T_c$ = 80 days, $T_0$ = 55 days, $h$ = \$5 per unit per year, and $r$ = 12% compounded continuously, find the total present value using the formula developed in part b.

**3.11.** Consider an inventory system in which an order is placed every $T$ units of time. It is desired to determine the optimal value of $Q$ by maximizing the average annual profit. This profit is the revenue less the sum of the ordering, purchasing, and inventory carrying costs. All demands will be met from inventory so that there are never any back orders or lost sales. We assume that the demand rate $\lambda$ is known with certainty and does not change with time. If the on-hand inventory does not continually increase or decrease with each period, the quantity ordered each time will be $Q = \lambda T$. To minimize carrying charges, the on-hand inventory when a procurement arrives should be zero. Suppose that $A$ is the fixed cost of placing an order, $C$ is the cost of one unit, $I$ is the inventory carrying charge, and $R$ is the unit sales price. For simplicity, we select the time origin as a point just prior to the arrival of an order so that nothing is on hand at the time origin.

a. If $r$ is the nominal interest compounded continuously, find the optimal $Q$ that maximizes the present value of all future profits.
b. As a specific example, consider a situation in which $A$ = \$15, $C$ = \$35, $I$ = 0.10, $r$ = 10%, $\lambda$ = 1,500 units per year, and $R$ = \$60 per unit.

**3.12.** Develop the $Z$-transform result for the decay function, $g(n) = Ce^{-j(n-b)}$, shown in Table 3.3.

**3.13.** Develop the $Z$-transform result for the growth function, $g(n) = C(1 - e^{-j(n-b)})$, shown in Table 3.3. Knowing that this growth function is the sum of $C$ and $-Ce^{-j(n-b)}$, use the linearity property.

**3.14.** Develop the Laplace transform result for the growth function shown in Table 3.7.

## Outline

# Part II: Evaluating Economic Performance of Companies and Projects

- Lecture slides on ratio analysis, discounted cash flows and transform techniques

- Chapters 2 and 3 of "Advanced Engineering Economics" by Park and Sharp-Bette

- Lecture slides on figures of merit

- Chapters 6 and 7 of "Advanced Engineering Economics" by Park and Sharp-Bette

## Figures of Merit

- The Net Present Value Criterion
- The Future Value Criterion
- The Annual Equivalence Criterion
- The Internal Rate of Return Criterion
- Solomon's Average Rate of Return Criterion
- The Modified Internal Rate of Return Criterion
- The Benefit-Cost Ratios Criteria
- The Discounted Payback Period
- The Project Balance Concept
- Conventional, Potentially Profitable, Pure and Mixed Investments

# Figures of Merit

## The Net Present Value Criterion

➢ **A project net present value (NPV) is:**

$$NPV(i) = \sum_{n=0}^{N} \frac{F_n}{(1+i)^n}$$

- **NPV Criterion:**
  - ➢ Accept the project if $NPV(i) > 0$
  - ➢ Remain indifferent if $NPV(i) = 0$
  - ➢ Reject the project if $NPV(i) < 0$

## Figures of Merit

The Internal Rate of Return Criterion

- "The" internal rate of return (IRR) of a project is "the" rate $i^*$ for which:

$$NPV(i^*) = 0$$

- **IRR Criterion:**
  - Accept the project if $i^* > MARR$
  - Remain indifferent if $i^* = MARR$
  - Reject the project if $i^* < MARR$

## Figures of Merit

### The Benefit-Cost Ratios Criteria

➢ **A project NPV is:**

$$NPV(i) = \sum_{n=0}^{N} \frac{F_n}{(1+i)^n} = \sum_{n=0}^{N} \frac{b_n}{(1+i)^n} - \sum_{n=0}^{N} \frac{c_n}{(1+i)^n} = B - C$$

- **Aggregate B/C Ratio:**

$$R_A = \frac{B}{C}$$

- **Aggregate B/C Ratio Criterion:**
  - ➢ Accept the project if $R_A > 1$
  - ➢ Remain indifferent if $R_A = 1$
  - ➢ Reject the project if $R_A < 1$

## Figures of Merit

The Benefit-Cost Ratios Criteria

➢ **A project's outflows can be decomposed into two parts:**

- **I : the initial investment**
- **O = C – I : consists of annual operating and maintenance costs**

- **Netted B/C Ratio:**

$$R_N = \frac{B - O}{I}$$

- **Netted B/C Ratio Criterion:**
  - ➢ Accept the project if $R_N > 1$
  - ➢ Remain indifferent if $R_N = 1$
  - ➢ Reject the project if $R_N < 1$

- **Lorie-Savage Ratio:**

$$L-S=\frac{B-C}{I}$$

- **Lorie-Savage Ratio Criterion:**
  - Accept the project if $L\text{-}S > 0$
  - Remain indifferent if $L\text{-}S = 0$
  - Reject the project if $L\text{-}S < 0$

## Figures of Merit

The Project Balance Concept

- **Generalized Project balance (PB):**

$$PB(i,j)_0 = F_0$$

$$PB(i,j)_n = \begin{cases} PB(i,j)_{n-1}(1+i) + F_n, \text{if } PB(i,j)_{n-1} \leq 0 \\ PB(i,j)_{n-1}(1+j) + F_n, \text{if } PB(i,j)_{n-1} > 0 \end{cases}$$

Where ***j*** is a conservative rate at which a company can invest recovered balances

- **GPB Criterion:**
  - Accept the project if $PB(i,j)_N > 0$
  - Remain indifferent if $PB(i,j)_N = 0$
  - Reject the project if $PB(i,j)_N < 0$

## Potentially Profitable Conventional Investments

- **Investment:** $F_0 < 0$

- **Conventional (or simple) Investment:** investment with only one change in the sign of the cash flows

- **Potentially Profitable Investment:** investment with a positive sum of net cash flows

- **Proposition:** a **potentially profitable conventional investment has a unique positive root**

## Conventional, Potentially Profitable, Pure and Mixed Investments

### Potentially Profitable Conventional Investments

- **Pure Investment:** no over-recovered balances at its largest root

  ➢ NPV ( $i^*$ ) = 0 , NPV ( $i$ ) $<>$ 0 for $i > i^*$ and PB ( $i^*$ )$_{\text{n}}$ $\leq$ 0 for n=0,1,…,N-1

  $\Rightarrow$ All conventional investments are pure

- **Mixed Investment:** investment that is not pure

  ➢ Let $j$ be the investment rate for over-recovered balances

  ➢ Let $i\,(j\,)$ ) be the interest rate at which the ending balance is zero: PB ( $i\,(j\,), j$ )$_{\text{N}}$ = 0

- **Generalized IRR criterion:**

  ➢Accept the project if $i\ (j\,) >$ **MARR**

  ➢Remain indifferent if $i\ (j\,) =$ **MARR**

  ➢Reject the project if $i\ (j\,) <$ **MARR**

## Decision Rules for Selecting Among Multiple Alternatives

### Incremental Approach

- **Rule:**
  - ➢ Sort potentially profitable conventional investments by increasing order of the sum of their cash flows
  - ➢ Compute incremental IRR and use IRR criterion to switch projects

## Outline

# Part II: Evaluating Economic Performance of Companies and Projects

- Lecture slides on ratio analysis, discounted cash flows and transform techniques

- Chapters 2 and 3 of "Advanced Engineering Economics" by Park and Sharp-Bette

- Lecture slides on figures of merit

- Chapters 6 and 7 of "Advanced Engineering Economics" by Park and Sharp-Bette

# 6 Measures of Investment Worth —Single Project

## 6.1 INTRODUCTION

In this chapter we focus primarily on evaluating individual projects by the application of various numerical criteria. In our analysis we treat investment projects as almost the same as securities (stocks, bonds, and so on). Both investment projects and securities normally require initial outlays in orger to provide a later sequence of cash receipts. The major difference is that investment projects are not marketable and securities are. When it is necessary to distinguish between projects and securities in our discussion, it will be done. Otherwise, the assumption can be made that the analyses are identical.

Ten different criteria are discussed in this chapter. The net present value (*PV*) criterion is considered the standard measure of investment, and the other measures are discussed and compared with it. The *PV* criterion and its economic interpretation by means of the project balance concept are discussed in Section 6.2. The internal rate of return (*IRR*) criterion, Solomon's average rate of return (*ARR*) criterion, and modified internal rate of return (*MIRR*) criterion are defined in Section 6.3 and are compared with the *PV* criterion. In Section 6.4 alternative measures, benefit–cost ratios, are presented, and again they are compared with the *PV* criterion. The payback period of an investment is discussed in Section 6.5. Finally, the time-dependent measure of investment worth is developed in Section 6.6. In discussing the various measures, we need to make certain assumptions about the investment settings.

### 6.1.1 Initial Assumptions

In the following investment worth analysis, we assume that the *MARR* (or cost of capital) is known to the decision maker. We also assume a stable, perfect capital market and complete certainty about investment outcomes. In a perfect capital market a firm can raise as much cash as it wants at the going rate of interest, or the firm has sufficient funds to accept all profitable investments. A perfect capital market makes it possible for a firm to invest as much cash as it wants at the market rate of interest. Since the firm may already have undertaken all profitable investments, the market rate of interest is assumed to measure the return on the firm's marginal investment opportunities. Having complete certainty about an investment means that the firm has perfect knowledge of the present and future cash flows associated with the project. Because of this knowledge, the firm finds it unnecessary to make any allowance for uncertainty in project evaluation.

These assumptions describe what might be called the ideal investment situation, quite different from the real-world situation. By setting aside certain complications, however, these assumptions will allow us to introduce the topic of investment analysis at a much simpler level than we otherwise could. In later chapters these assumptions will be removed and the analysis extended to more realistic situations, in which none of these assumptions is fully satisfied.

### 6.1.2 Notation

To discuss the various evaluation criteria, we will use the following common notation for cash flow representation.

- $n$ time, measured in discrete compounding periods
- $i$ opportunity interest rate (*MARR*), or market interest rate
- $C_0$ initial investment at time 0, a positive amount
- $b_n$ revenue at end of period $n$, $b_n \geq 0$
- $c_n$ expense at the end of period $n$, $c_n \geq 0$
- $N$ project life
- $F_n$ net cash flow at the end of period $n$ ($F_n = b_n - c_n$; if $b_n \geq c_n$, then $F_n \geq 0$; if $b_n < c_n$, then $F_n < 0$)

Figure 6.1 illustrates this notation with a cash flow diagram. Additional notation pertaining to a specific criterion will be defined later as necessary. It must be emphasized that all cash flows represent the *cash flows after taxes.*

## 6.2 THE NET PRESENT VALUE CRITERION

We will use the concept of equivalence to develop the net present value (*PV*) criterion for evaluating investment worth. The future value and annual equivalent criteria are variations of the *PV* criterion found by converting the *PV* into either the future value or the annual equivalent by using the same interest rate. In this section we define and discuss the interpretation of these three criteria.

### 6.2.1 Mathematical Definition

***The PV Criterion.*** Consider a project that will generate cash receipts of $b_n$ at the end of each period $n$. The present value of cash receipts over the project life, $B$, is expressed by

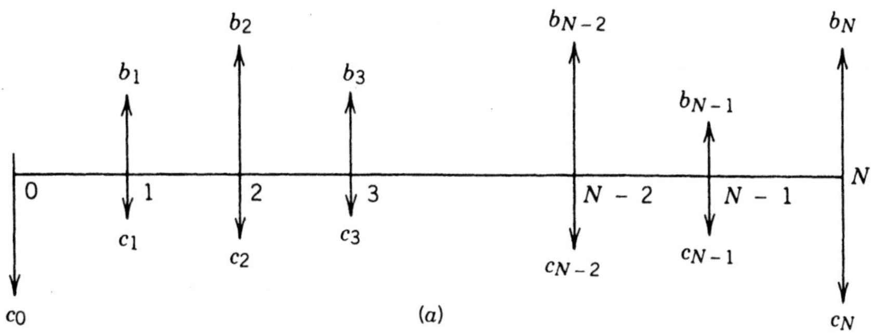


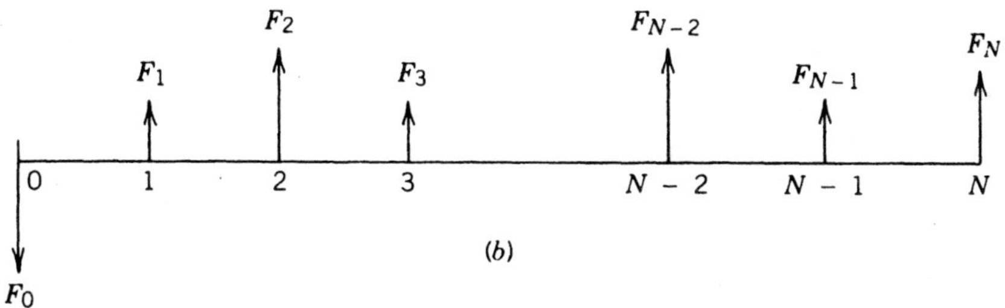


**FIGURE 6.1.** Notation conventions. (a) Gross cash flow. (b) Net cash flow.

$$B = \sum_{n=0}^{N} \frac{b_n}{(1 + i)^n} \tag{6.1}$$

Assume that the cash expenses (including the initial outlay associated with the project) at the end of each period are $c_n$. The present value expression of cash expenses, $C$, is

$$C = \sum_{n=0}^{N} \frac{c_n}{(1 + i)^n} \tag{6.2}$$

Then the *PV* of the project [denoted by *PV*($i$)] is defined by the difference between $B$ and $C$; that is,

$$PV(i) = \sum_{n=0}^{N} \frac{b_n - c_n}{(1 + i)^n} = \sum_{n=0}^{N} \frac{F_n}{(1 + i)^n} \tag{6.3a}$$

The $F_n$ will be positive if the corresponding period has a net cash inflow and negative if there is a net cash outflow. The foregoing computation of the *PV* is based on a rate of interest that remains constant over time. The *PV* could be computed with different rates of interest over time, in which case we would label the $n$th period's rate of interest as $i_n$. The *PV* expression is then

$$PV(i_n, n) = F_0 + \frac{F_1}{1 + i_1} + \frac{F_2}{(1 + i_1)(1 + i_2)} + \cdots \tag{6.3b}$$

For simplicity, we assume here a single rate of interest in computing the *PV*. We further assume compounding at discrete points in time. A continuous compounding process or continuous cash flows can be handled according to the procedures outlined in Chapter 2.

A positive *PV* for a project represents a positive surplus, and we should accept the project if sufficient funds are available for it. A project with a negative *PV* should be rejected, because we could do better by investing in other projects at the opportunity rate or outside the market. The decision rule expressed simply is

| |
|---|
| If $PV(i) > 0$, accept. |
| If $PV(i) = 0$, remain indifferent. |
| If $PV(i) < 0$, reject. |

***Future Value Criterion.*** As a variation of the *PV* criterion, the future value (*FV*) criterion measures the economic value of a project at the end of the project's life, *N*. Converting the project cash flows into a single payment concentrated at period *N* produces a cash flow equal to *FV*.

$$FV(i) = \sum_{n=0}^{N} F_n(1 + i)^{N-n}$$

$$= PV(i)(1 + i)^N \tag{6.4}$$

From another view, if we borrowed and lent at *i*, operated the project, and left all extra funds to accumulate at *i*, we would have a value equal to $FV(i)$ at the end of period *N*. If this value is positive, the project is acceptable. If it is negative, the project should be rejected. As expected, the decision rule for the *FV* criterion is the same as that for the *PV* criterion.

| |
|---|
| If $FV(i) > 0$, accept. |
| If $FV(i) = 0$, remain indifferent. |
| If $FV(i) < 0$, reject. |

***Annual Equivalent Criterion.*** The annual equivalent (*AE*) criterion is another basis for measuring investment worth that has characteristics similar to those of the *PV* criterion. This similarity is evident when we consider that any cash flow can be converted into a series of equal annual payments by first finding the *PV* for the original series and then multiplying the *PV* by the capital recovery factor.

$$AE(i) = PV(i)\left[\frac{i(1 + i)^N}{(1 + i)^N - 1}\right] = PV(i)(A/P, i, N) \tag{6.5}$$

Because the factor $(A/P, i, N)$ is positive for $-1 < i < \infty$, the *AE* criterion should provide a consistent basis for evaluating an investment project as the previous criteria have done.

| |
|---|
| If $AE(i) > 0$, accept. |
| If $AE(i) = 0$, remain indifferent. |
| If $AE(i) < 0$, reject. |

## *Example 6.1*

This example will serve to illustrate the use of the *PV* criterion. Consider a project that requires a $1,000 initial investment with the following patterns of cash flow.

| | End of Period $n$ | | | | | |
|---|---|---|---|---|---|---|
| Cash Flow | 0 | 1 | 2 | 3 | 4 | 5 |
| Receipt ($b_n$) | $0 | 500 | 500 | 500 | 500 | 500 |
| Expense ($c_n$) | $1,000 | 100 | 140 | 180 | 220 | 260 |
| Net Flow ($F_n$) | −$1,000 | 400 | 360 | 320 | 280 | 240 |

The cash flow diagram is shown in Figure 6.2. Assume the firm's *MARR* is 10%. Substituting $F_n$ values into Eq. 6.3 and varying $i$ values ($0 \leq i \leq 40\%$), we obtain Table 6.1 and Figure 6.3. We then find that the project's *PV* decreases monoto-

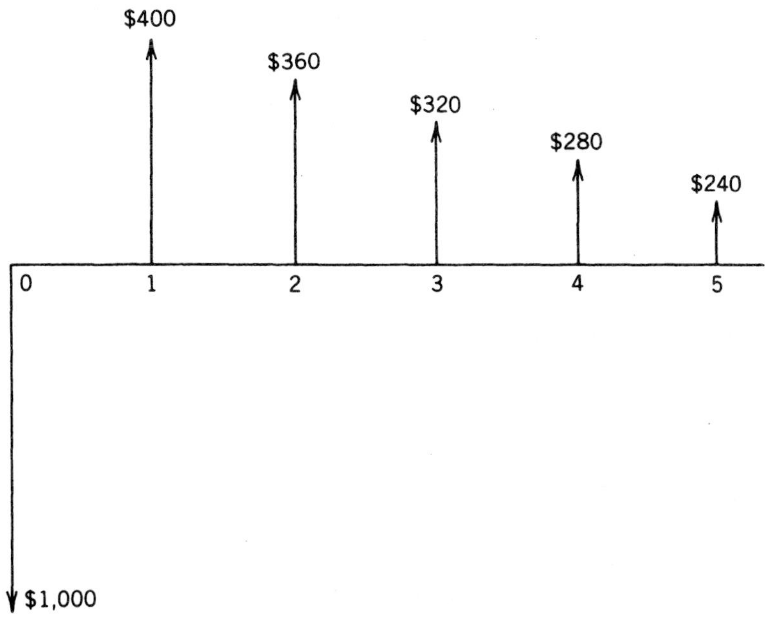


**FIGURE 6.2. Cash flow diagram for Example 6.1.**

**Table 6.1** ***Net Present Values PV(i) at Varying Interest Rate i, Example 6.1***

| *i* (%) | *PV(i)* | *i* (%) | *PV(i)* |
|---|---|---|---|
| 0 | $600.00 | 21% | −$19.5 |
| 1 | 556.96 | 22 | −38.84 |
| 2 | 515.77 | 23 | −57.30 |
| 3 | 476.33 | 24 | −75.15 |
| 4 | 438.54 | 25 | −92.43 |
| 5 | 402.31 | 26 | −109.15 |
| 6 | 367.56 | 27 | −125.34 |
| 7 | 334.21 | 28 | −141.03 |
| 8 | 302.19 | 29 | −156.23 |
| 9 | 271.42 | 30 | −170.96 |
| 10 | 241.84 | 31 | −185.25 |
| 11 | 213.40 | 32 | −199.11 |
| 12 | 186.03 | 33 | −212.56 |
| 13 | 159.68 | 34 | −225.61 |
| 14 | 134.31 | 35 | −238.29 |
| 15 | 109.86 | 36 | −250.60 |
| 16 | 86.29 | 37 | −262.56 |
| 17 | 63.55 | 38 | −274.19 |
| 18 | 41.62 | 39 | −285.49 |
| 19 | 20.45 | 40 | −296.48 |
| 20 | 0 | | |

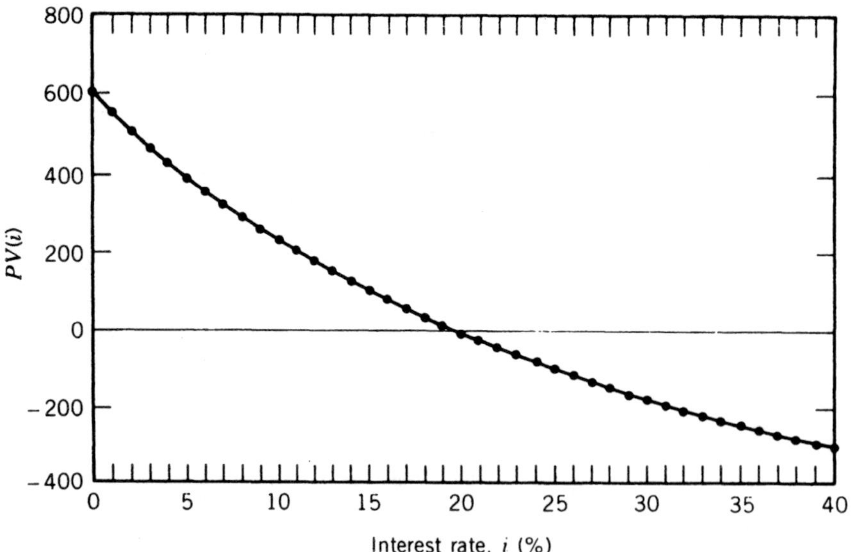


**FIGURE 6.3.** Plot of $PV(i)$ as a function of $i$, Example 6.1.

nically with the firm's $i$. The project has a positive *PV* if the firm's interest rate (*MARR*) is below 20% and a negative *PV* if the *MARR* is above 20%. At $i = 10\%$, the *PV* (the equivalent present value to the firm of the total surplus) is \$241.84.

Using Eqs. 6.4 and 6.5, we find

$$FV(10\%) = \$241.84(F/P,\ 10\%,\ 5) = \$389.49$$

$$AE(10\%) = \$241.84(A/P,\ 10\%,\ 5) = \$58.0$$

Since both $FV(10\%)$ and $AE(10\%)$ are positive, the project is considered viable under these criteria. □

### 6.2.2 Economic Interpretation Through Project Balance

An alternative way to interpret the economic significance of these criteria is through the project balance concept. In this section we define the project balance concept and then explain how these criteria are related to the terminal project balance.

***Project Balance Concept.*** The *project balance* describes the net equivalent amount of dollars tied up in or committed to the project at each point in time over the life of the project. We will use $PB(i)_n$ to denote the project balance at the end of period $n$ computed at the opportunity cost rate (*MARR*) of $i$. We will assume that the cost of having money tied up in the project is not incurred unless it is committed for the entire period. To show how the $PB(i)_n$ are computed, we consider the project described in Example 6.1. (See Figure 6.2.)

The project balance at the present time ($n = 0$) is just the investment itself.

$$PB(10\%)_0 = -\$1{,}000$$

At $n = 1$, the firm has an accumulated commitment of \$1,100, which consists of the initial investment and the associated cost of having the initial investment tied up in the project for one period. However, the project returns \$400 at $n = 1$. This reduces the firm's investment commitment to \$700, so the project balance at $n = 1$ is

$$PB(10\%)_1 = -\$1{,}000(1 + 0.1) + \$400 = -\$700$$

This amount becomes the net amount committed to that project at the beginning of period 2. The project balance at the end of period 2 is

$$PB(10\%)_2 = -\$700(1 + 0.1) + \$360 = -\$410$$

This represents the cost of having \$700 committed at the beginning of the second year along with the receipt of \$360 at the end of that year.

We compute the remaining project balances similarly.

$$PB(10\%)_3 = -\$410(1.1) + \$320 = -\$131.00$$
$$PB(10\%)_4 = -\$131(1.1) + \$280 = \$135.90$$
$$PB(10\%)_5 = \$135.90(1.1) + \$240 = \$389.49$$

Notice that the firm fully recovers its initial investment and opportunity cost at the end of period 4 and has a profit of \$135.90. Assuming that the firm can reinvest this amount at the same interest rate ($i$ = 10%) in other projects or outside the market, the project balance grows to \$389.49 with the receipt of \$240 at the end of period 5. The project is then terminated with a net profit of \$389.49.

If we compute the present value equivalent of this net profit at time 0, we obtain

$$PV(10\%) = \$389.49(P/F, 10\%, 5) = \$241.84$$

The result is the same as that obtained when we directly compute the present value of the project at $i$ = 10%. Table 6.2 summarizes these computational results.

***Mathematical Derivation.*** Defining the project balance mathematically based on the previous example yields the recursive relationship

$$PB(i)_n = (1 + i)PB(i)_{n-1} + F_n \tag{6.6}$$

where $PB(i)_0 = F_0$ and $n = 0, 1, 2, \ldots, N$.

We can develop an alternative expression for the project balance from Eq. 6.6 by making substitutions as follows.

$$\begin{aligned} PB(i)_0 &= F_0 \\ PB(i)_1 &= (1 + i)F_0 + F_1 \\ PB(i)_2 &= (1 + i)[(1 + i)F_0 + F_1] + F_2 \\ &= F_0(1 + i)^2 + F_1(1 + i) + F_2 \end{aligned}$$

so that at any period $n$

$$PB(i)_n = F_0(1 + i)^n + F_1(1 + i)^{n-1} + \cdots + F_n \tag{6.7}$$

The terminal project balance is then expressed by

$$\begin{aligned} PB(i)_N &= F_0(1 + i)^N + F_1(1 + i)^{N-1} + \cdots + F_N \\ &= \sum_{n=0}^{N} F_n(1 + i)^{N-n} \\ &= FV(i) \end{aligned} \tag{6.8}$$

Note that $PB(i)_N$ is the future value of the project.

**Table 6.2** ***Project Balance Computations for the Project in Example 6.1***

| Item | *n*: 0 | 1 | 2 | 3 | 4 | 5 |
|---|---|---|---|---|---|---|
| Beginning project balance, $PB(i)_{n-1}$ | \$0 | −1,000 | −700 | −410 | −131 | +135.90 |
| Interest owed, $i[PB(i)_{n-1}]$ | \$0 | −100 | −70 | −41 | −13.10 | 13.59 |
| Cash receipt, $F_n$ | −1,000 | 400 | 360 | 320 | 280 | 240 |
| Ending project balance, $PB(i)_n$ | −\$1,000 | −\$700 | −\$410 | −\$131 | \$135.90 | \$389.49 $PB(i)_N$ |

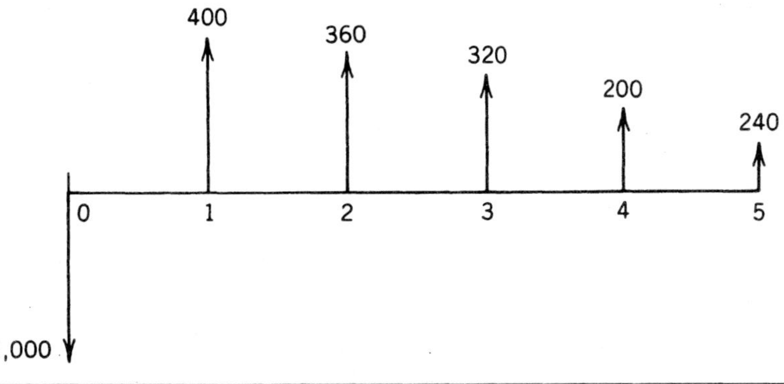


$$PV(10\%) = PB(10\%)_5(1 + 0.1)^{-5} = \$389.49(P/F, 10\%, 5) = \$241.84$$

$$PV(10\%) = -\$1{,}000 + 400(1.1)^{-1} + 360(1.1)^{-2} + 320(1.1)^{-3} + 280(1.1)^{-4} + 240(1.1)^{-5} = \$241.84$$

***Economic Interpretation.*** If $PB(i)_N > 0$, we can say that the firm recovers the initial investment plus any interest owed, with a profit at the end of the project. If $PB(i)_N = 0$, the firm recovers only the initial investment plus interest owed and breaks even. If $PB(i)_N < 0$, the firm ends up with a loss by not being able to recover even the initial investment and interest owed. Naturally, the firm should accept a project only if $PB(i)_N > 0$. The present equivalent amount of this terminal profit is

$$PV(i) = \frac{PB(i)_N}{(1+i)^N} = \frac{FV(i)_N}{(1+i)^N} \tag{6.9}$$

The factor $1/(1 + i)^N$ is always positive for $-1 < i < \infty$. This implies that the $PV(i)$ will be positive if and only if $PB(i)_N > 0$ [14].

Now the meaning of the *PV* criterion should be clear; accepting a project with $PV(i) > 0$ is equivalent to accepting a project with $PB(i)_N > 0$. Because the *PV* and the future value are measures of equivalence that differ only in the times at which they are stated, they should provide identical results. The analysis and discussion should also make clear why we consider *PV* as the baseline, or correct, criterion to use in a stable, perfect capital market with complete certainty.

## 6.3 INTERNAL RATE-OF-RETURN CRITERION

### 6.3.1 Definition of IRR

***Mathematical Definition.*** The internal rate of return (*IRR*) is another time-discounted measure of investment worth similar to the *PV* criterion. The *IRR* of a project is defined as the rate of interest that equates the *PV* of the entire series of cash flows to zero. The project's *IRR*, $i^*$, is defined mathematically by

$$PV(i^*) = \sum_{n=0}^{N} \frac{F_n}{(1 + i^*)^n} = 0 \tag{6.10}$$

Multiplying both sides of Eq. 6.10 by $(1 + i^*)^N$, we obtain

$$PV(i^*)(1 + i^*)^N = \sum_{n=0}^{N} F_n(1 + i^*)^{N-n}$$

$$= FV(i^*) = 0 \tag{6.11}$$

The left-hand side of Eq. 6.11 is, by definition, the future value (terminal project balance) of the project.

If we multiply both sides of Eq. 6.10 by the capital recovery factor, we obtain the relationship $AE(i^*) = 0$ (see Eq. 6.9). Alternatively, the *IRR* of a project may be defined as the rate of interest that equates the future value, terminal project balance, and annual equivalent value of the entire series of cash flows to zero.

$$PV(i^*) = FV(i^*) = PB(i^*)_N = AE(i^*) = 0 \tag{6.12}$$

***Computational Methods.*** Note that Eq. 6.11 is a polynomial function of $i^*$. A direct solution for such a function is not generally possible except for projects with a life of four periods or fewer. Instead, two approximation techniques are in general use, one using iterative procedures (a trial-and-error approach) and the other using Newton's approximation to the solution of a polynomial.

An iterative procedure requires an initial guess. To approximate the *IRR*, we calculate the *PV* for a certain interest rate (initial guess). If this *PV* is not zero, another interest rate is tried. A negative *PV* usually indicates that the choice is too high. We continue approximating until we reach the two bounds that contain the answer. We then interpolate to find the closest approximation to the *IRR(s)*.

The Newton approximation to a polynomial $f(X) = 0$ is made by starting with an arbitrary approximation of $X$ and forming successive approximations by the formula

$$X_{j+1} = X_j - \frac{f(X_j)}{f'(X_j)} \tag{6.13}$$

where $f'(X_j)$ is the first derivative of the polynomial evaluated at $X_j$. *The process is continued until we observe* $X_j \cong X_{j-1}$.

### *Example 6.2*

Consider a project with cash flows −\$100, 50, and 84 at the end of periods 0, 1, and 2, respectively. The present value expression for this project is

$$PV(i) = -\$100 + \frac{50}{1+i} + \frac{84}{(1+i)^2}$$

Let $X = 1/(1 + i)$. Our polynomial, the present value function, is then

$$f(X) = -100 + 50X + 84X^2$$

The derivative of this polynomial is

$$f'(X) = 50 + 168X$$

Suppose the first approximation we make is

$$X_1 = 0.8696 \qquad (i = 0.15)$$

The second approximation is

$$\begin{aligned} X_2 &= 0.8696 - \frac{-100 + 50(0.8696) + 84(0.8696)^2}{50 + 168(0.8696)} \\ &= 0.8339 \end{aligned}$$

The third approximation is

$$\begin{aligned} X_3 &= 0.8339 - \frac{-100 + 50(0.8339) + 84(0.8339)^2}{50 + 168(0.8339)} \\ &= 0.8333 \end{aligned}$$

Further iterations indicate that $X = 0.8333$ or $i^* = 20\%$. (With any approximation we are limited by rounding, so when we get the same answer twice in the sequence of approximations, we stop. □

Although the calculations in Newton's method are relatively simple, they are time-consuming if many iterations are required. The use of a computer is eventually necessary. (When we program the computer, it is wise to set tolerance limits on the degree of accuracy required to avoid unnecessary iterations.)

***Uniqueness of* i*.** The existence of a unique *IRR* is of special interest in applying the *IRR* investment worth criterion. Consider a project with cash flows of −\$10, \$47, −\$72, and \$36 at the end of periods 0, 1, 2, and 3, respectively. Applying Eq. 6.10 and solving for $i$ gives us three roots: 20%, 50%, and 100%. This really should not surprise us, since Eq. 6.10 is a third-degree polynomial for the project. Here the plot of *PV* as a function of interest rate crosses the $i$ axis several times, as illustrated in Figure 6.4. As we will see in later sections, multiple *IRR*s hinder the application of the *IRR* criterion, and we do not recommend the *IRR* criterion in such cases. In this section we will focus on the problem of whether a unique *IRR* for a project can be predicted by the cash flow stream.

One way to predict an upper limit on the number of positive roots of a polynomial is to apply Descartes' rule of signs.

> ***Descartes' Rule.*** The number of real positive roots of an $n$th-degree polynominal with real coefficients is never greater than the number of sign changes in the sequence of the coefficients.

Letting $X = 1/(1 + i)$, we can write Eq. 6.10 as

$$F_0 + F_1X + F_2X^2 + \cdots + F_NX^N = 0 \tag{6.14}$$

Thus, we need examine only the sign changes in $F_n$ to apply the rule. For example, if the project has outflows followed by inflows, there is only one sign change and hence at most one real positive root.

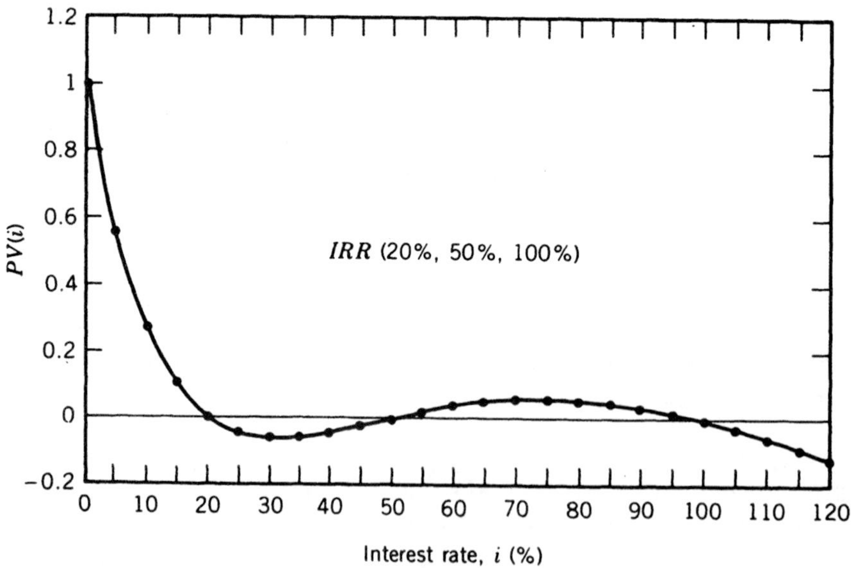


**FIGURE 6.4. Multiple internal rates of return.**

The Norstrom criterion [5] provides a more discriminating condition for the uniqueness of the root in the interval ($0 < i^* < \infty$).

> ***Norstrom Criterion.*** Consider a cash flow series $F_0, F_1, F_2, \ldots, F_N$. Form the auxiliary series $S_n = \sum_{j=0}^{n} F_j$, $n = 0, 1, \ldots, N$. If the series $S_n$ starts negative and changes sign only once, there exists a unique positive real root. (6.15)

Additional criteria for the uniqueness of roots do exist, but they are rather tedious to apply and will not be discussed here. Bernhard [5] discusses these additional criteria and provides another general method for detecting the uniqueness of *IRR*.

## *Example 6.3*

To illustrate the use of both Descartes' rule and the Norstrom criterion, consider the following pattern of cash flows.

| $n$ | 0 | 1 | 2 |
|---|---|---|---|
| $F_n$ | −\$100 | \$140 | −\$10 |

Descartes' rule implies that the maximum number of positive real roots is less than or equal to two, which indicates that there may be multiple roots. There are two sign changes in $F_n(-, +, -)$.

To apply the Norstrom criterion, we first compute the cumulative cash flow stream, $S_n$.

$$S_0 = F_0 = -\$100$$

$$S_1 = F_0 + F_1 = -\$100 + \$140 = \$40$$

$$S_2 = F_0 + F_1 + F_2 = \$40 - \$10 = \$30$$

The criterion indicates a unique positive, real root for the problem because there is only one sign change in the $S_n$ series $(-, +, +)$. In fact, the project has a unique *IRR* at $i^* = 32.45\%$. □

### 6.3.2 Classification of Investment Projects

In discussing the *IRR* criterion, we need to distinguish between simple and nonsimple investments. Investment projects are further classified as pure or mixed investments.

***Simple versus Nonsimple.*** A *simple* investment is defined as one in which there is only one sign change in the net cash flow ($F_n$). A *nonsimple* investment is one whose net cash outflows are not restricted to the initial period but are interspersed with net cash inflows throughout the life of the project. In other

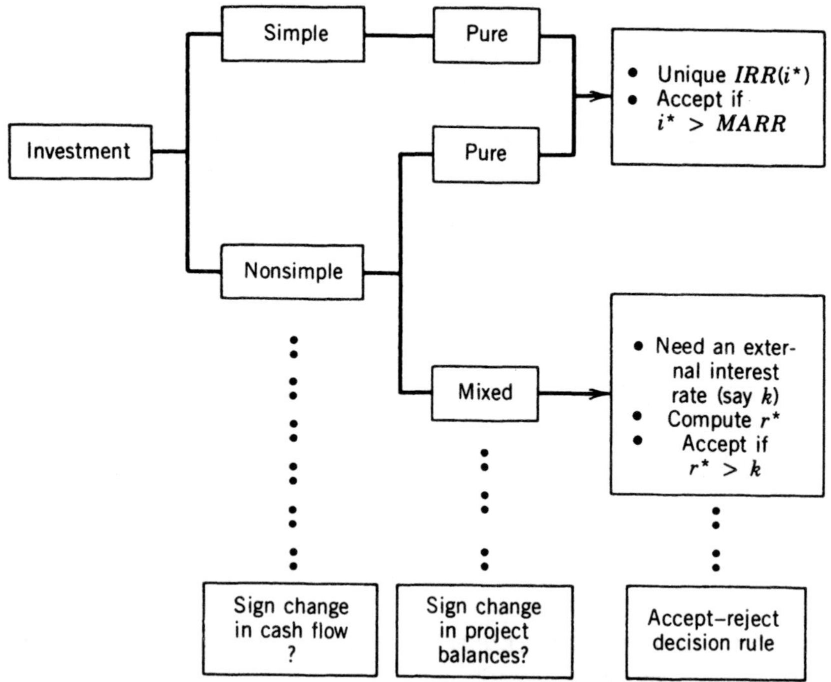


**FIGURE 6.5.** Classification of investment projects.

words, when there is more than one sign change in the net cash flow, the project is called a nonsimple project.

***Pure versus Mixed.*** A *pure* investment is defined as an investment whose project balances computed at the project's *IRR*, $PB(i^*)_n$, are either zero or negative throughout the life of the project (with $F_0 < 0$). The implication of nonpositivity of $PB(i^*)_n$ for all values of $n$ is that the firm has committed (or "lent") funds in the amount of $PB(i^*)_n$ dollars to the project for time $n$ to time $n + 1$. In other words, the firm does not "borrow" from the project at any time during the life of the project.

A *mixed* investment, in contrast, is defined as any investment for which $PB(i^*)_n > 0$ for some values of $n$ and $PB(i^*)_n \leq 0$ for the remaining values of $n$. These sign changes in $PB(i^*)_n$ indicate that at some times during the project's life $[PB(i^*)_n < 0]$ the firm acts as an "investor" in the project and at other times $[PB(i^*)_n > 0]$ the firm acts as a "borrower" from the project.

***Classification by $i_{min}$.*** An alternative way of distinguishing between pure and mixed investments is to compute the value of $i_{\text{min}}$, the smallest interest rate that makes $PB(i)_n \leq 0$ for $n = 0, 1, 2, \ldots, N - 1$. Then we evaluate the sign of $PB(i_{\text{min}})_N$, the terminal project balance. If $PB(i_{\text{min}})_N \geq 0$, the project is a pure investment. If $PB(i_{\text{min}})_N < 0$, the project is a mixed investment.

If $PB(i_{\text{min}})_N > 0$, we can find some *IRR*, $i^* > i_{\text{min}}$, that will set $PB(i^*)_N$ to zero. Then use of a higher interest rate will simply magnify the negativity of $PB(i)_n$. Thus, the condition of $i^* \geq i_{\text{min}}$ will ensure the nonpositivity of $PB(i^*)_n$ for $0 \leq n \leq N - 1$. This is the definition of a pure investment.

If $PB(i_{\text{min}})_N < 0$, we can expect that $i^* < i_{\text{min}}$, which will set $PB(i^*)_N$ to zero. Because $i_{min}$ is the minimum rate at which the nonpositivity condition $[PB(i_{min}) \leq 0]$ satisfies $0 \leq n \leq N-1$, we know that $PB(i^*)_n$ is not always zero or negative for $0 \leq n \leq N-1$. This implies that the project is a mixed investment.

Figure 6.5 illustrates the final classification scheme that provides the basis for the analysis of investments under the *IRR* criterion. Note that simple investments are always classified as pure investments. (See the proof in Bussey [6].) As we will see, the phenomenon of multiple *IRR*s occurs only in the situation of a mixed investment. Although a simple investment is always a pure investment, a pure investment is not necessarily a simple investment, as we will see in Example 6.4.

## *Example 6.4*

We will illustrate the distinction between pure and mixed investments with numerical examples. Consider the following four projects with known $i^*$ values.

| End of Period | Project | | | |
|---|---|---|---|---|
| $n$ | A | B | C | D |
| 0 | −\$100 | −\$100 | −\$100 | −\$100 |
| 1 | −100 | 140 | 50 | 470 |
| 2 | 200 | −10 | −50 | −720 |
| 3 | 200 | | 200 | 360 |
| *IRR* | $i^*$ = 41.42% | $i^*$ = 32.45% | $i^*$ = 29.95% | $i^*$ = 20%, 50%, 100% |

Table 6.3 summarizes the project balances from these projects at their respective *IRR*s. Project A is the only simple project; the rest are nonsimple. Projects A and C are pure investments, whereas projects B and D are mixed investments. As seen in project B, the existence of a unique *IRR* is a necessary but not a sufficient condition for a pure investment.

**Table 6.3** ***Project Balances, Example 6.4***

| Project | *IRR* | | End of Period $n$ | | | |
|---|---|---|---|---|---|---|
| | | | 0 | 1 | 2 | 3 |
| | | $F_n$ | −\$100 | −100 | 200 | 200 |
| A | 41.42% | $PB(i^*)_n$ | −\$100 | −241.42 | −141.42 | 0 |
| | | $F_n$ | −\$100 | 140 | −10 | |
| B | 32.45% | $PB(i^*)_n$ | −\$100 | 7.55 | 0 | |
| | | $F_n$ | −\$100 | 50 | −50 | 200 |
| C | 29.95% | $PB(i^*)_n$ | −\$100 | −79.95 | −153.90 | 0 |
| | | $F_n$ | −\$100 | 470 | −720 | 360 |
| | 20% | $PB(20\%)$ | −\$100 | 350 | −300 | 0 |
| | 50% | $PB(50\%)$ | −\$100 | 320 | −240 | 0 |
| D | 100% | $PB(100\%)$ | −\$100 | 270 | −180 | 0 |

In distinguishing pure and mixed investments, we could use the $i_{min}$ test. We will show how this is done for project D. Since $N = 3$, we need to consider $PB(i)_0$, $PB(i)_1$, and $PB(i)_2$.

$$PB(i)_0 = -100$$
$$PB(i)_1 = PB(i)_0(1 + i) + 470 = -100i + 370$$
$$PB(i)_2 = PB(i)_1(1 + i) - 720 = -100i^2 + 270i - 350$$

Since $PB(i)_0 < 0$, we find the smallest value of $i$ that makes both $PB(i)_1$ and $PB(i)_2$ nonpositive. The minimum value is 370%. Now we evaluate $PB(i_{min})_3$ to find

$$PB(370\%)_3 = -720(4.70) + 360 = -\$3024 < 0$$

Since $PB(i_{min})_3 < 0$, project D is a mixed investment. □

### 6.3.3 IRR and Pure Investments

According to the *IRR* criterion, a pure investment should be accepted if its *IRR* is above the *MARR* (or cost of capital) to the firm. We will show why this decision rule can produce an accept–reject decision consistent with the *PV* criterion.

Recall that pure investments have the following characteristics.

1. Net investment throughout the life of the project.
2. Existence of unique $i^*$.
3. $PB(i^*)_n \leq 0$ for $0 \leq n \leq N - 1$, and $PB(i^*)_N = 0$.
4. $PB(i)_N\left[\dfrac{1}{(1 + i)^N}\right] = PV(i)$

and if $i = i^*$,

$$PB(i)_N = 0 \rightarrow PV(i) = 0$$

We will first consider computing $PB(i)_N$ with $i > i^*$. Here $i$ is the *MARR* (or cost of capital) to the firm. Since $PB(i^*)_n \leq 0$ for $0 \leq n \leq N - 1$ and $PB(i^*)_N = 0$, the effect of a higher compounding rate is to magnify the negativity of these project balances. This implies that $PB(i)_N < PB(i^*)_N = 0$. From Eq. 6.9, this also implies that $PV(i) < 0$. If $i = i^*$, then $PB(i)_N = PB(i^*)_N = 0$ so that $PV(i) = 0$. If $i < i^*$, then $PB(i)_N > 0$, indicating that $PV(i) > 0$. Hence we accept the investment. This proves the equivalence of the *PV* and *IRR* criteria for accept–reject decisions concerning simple investments. These relationships are illustrated in Figure 6.6.

| |
|---|
| If $i < i^*$, accept. |
| If $i = i^*$, remain indifferent. |
| If $i > i^*$, reject. |

When a firm makes a pure investment, it has funds committed to the project over the life of the project and at no time takes a loan from the project. Only in such a

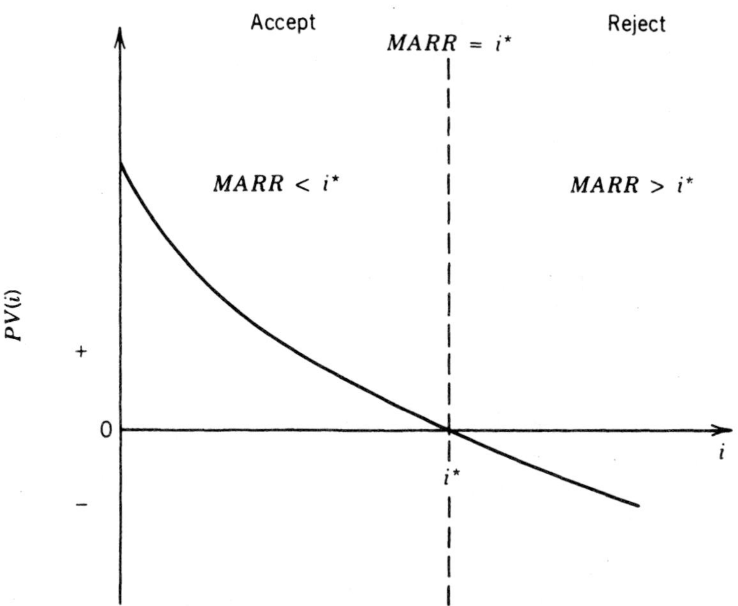


**FIGURE 6.6.** ***PV(i)*** **of simple investment as a function of** ***i*****.**

situation is a rate of return concept *internal* to the project. Then the *IRR* can be viewed as the interest rate *earned* on the committed project balance (unrecovered balance, or negative project balance) of an investment, *not* the interest earned on the initial investment. The reader should keep this in mind, since it is a point not generally understood by many practitioners.

## *Example 6.5*

Consider the project described in Example 6.1. (Note that the project is a simple and pure investment.) The project was acceptable at $i = 10\%$ by the *PV* criterion. We find that the *IRR* of this project is 20% by solving for $i^*$ in Eq. 6.10.

$$PV(i^*) = -\$1{,}000 + \frac{\$400}{1 + i^*} + \frac{\$360}{(1 + i^*)^2} + \frac{\$320}{(1 + i^*)^3} + \frac{\$280}{(1 + i^*)^4} + \frac{\$240}{(1 + i^*)^5} = 0$$

Since $i^* > 10\%$, the project should be acceptable. The economic interpretation of the 20% is that the investment under consideration brings in enough cash to pay for itself in 5 years and also to provide the firm with a return of 20% on its invested capital over the project life.

Expressed another way, suppose that a firm obtains all its capital by borrowing from a bank at the interest rate of exactly 20%. If the firm invests in the project and uses the cash flow generated by the investment to pay off the principal and interest on the bank loan, the firm should come out exactly even on the transaction. If the firm can borrow the funds at a rate lower than 20%, the project should be profitable. If the borrowing interest rate is greater than 20%, acceptance of the project would result in losses. This break-even characteristic makes the *IRR* a popular criterion among many practitioners. □

### 6.3.4 *IRR* and Mixed Investments

Recall that the mixed investments have the following characteristics.

1. More than one sign change in cash flow.
2. Possibility of multiple rates of return.
3. Mixed signs in $PB(i^*)_n$.

The difficulty in mixed investments is determining which rate to use for the acceptance test, if any. The mixed signs in $PB(i^*)_n$ indicate that the firm has funds committed to the project part of the time [$PB(i^*)_n < 0$ for some values of $n$] and takes a "loan" from the project the rest of the time [$PB(i^*)_n > 0$ for some value of $n$]. Because of this lending and borrowing activity, there is no rate of return concept internal to the project. The return on such mixed investments tends to vary with the external interest rate (i.e., cost of capital) to the firm.

To circumvent this conceptual difficulty, we may modify the procedure for computation by compounding positive project balances at the cost of borrowing capital, $k$, and negative project balances at the return on invested capital (*RIC*), $r$. (We use the symbol $r$ because the return on invested capital of a mixed project is generally not equal to the *IRR*, $i^*$, of the project.) Since the firm is never indebted to the project for pure investment, it is clear that $k$ does not enter into the compounding process; hence this *RIC* is independent of $k$, the cost of capital to the firm. Two approaches may be used in computing $r$: the trial-and-error approach and the analytical approach.

***Trial-and-Error Approach.*** The trial-and-error approach is similar to finding a project's internal rate of return. For a given cost of capital, $k$, we first compute the project balances from an investment with a somewhat arbitrarily selected $r$ value. Since it is hoped that projects will promise a return of at least the cost of capital, a value of $r$ close to $k$ is a good starting point for most problems. For a given pair of $(k, r)$, we calculate the last project balance and see whether it is positive, negative, or zero. Suppose the last project balance $PB(r, k)_N$ is negative—what do we do then? A nonzero terminal project balance indicates that the guessed $r$ value is not the true $r$ value. We must lower the $r$ value and go through the process again. Conversely, if the $PB(r, k)_N > 0$, we raise the $r$ value and repeat the process.

## *Example 6.6*

To illustrate the method described, consider the following cash flow of a project.

| $n$ | 0 | 1 | 2 |
|---|---|---|---|
| $F_n$ | −$1,000 | 2,900 | −2,080 |

Suppose that the cost of capital, $k$, is known to be 15%. For $k$ = 15%, we must compute $r^*$ by trial and error.

For $k$ = 15% and trial $r$ = 16%,

$$PB(16, 15)_0 = -1{,}000 \qquad\qquad = -\$1{,}000$$

$$PB(16, 15)_1 = -1{,}000(1 + 0.16) + 2{,}900 = \$1{,}300 \quad [\text{use } r, \text{ since } PB(16, 15)_0 < 0]$$

$$PB(16, 15)_2 = 1{,}300(1 + 0.15) - 2{,}080 = -\$585 \quad [\text{use } k, \text{ since } PB(16, 15)_1 > 0]$$

The terminal project balance is not zero, indicating that $r^*$ is not equal to our 16% trial $r$. The next trial value should be smaller than 16% because the terminal balance is negative (−585). After several trials, we conclude that for $k$ = 15%, $r^*$ is approximately at 9.13%. To verify the results,

$$PB(9.13, 15)_0 = -1{,}000 \qquad\qquad = -\$1{,}000$$

$$PB(9.13, 15)_1 = -1{,}000(1 + 0.0913) + 2{,}900 = \$1{,}808.70$$

$$PB(9.13, 15)_2 = 1{,}808.70(1 + 0.15) - 2{,}080 = 0$$

Since $r^* < k$, the investment is not profitable. Note that the project would also be rejected under the $PV$ analysis at $MARR = i = k = 15\%$.

$$\begin{aligned} PV(15\%) &= -1{,}000 + 2{,}900(P/F, 15\%, 1) - 2{,}080(P/F, 15\%, 2) \\ &= -\$51.04 < 0 \quad \square \end{aligned}$$

***Analytical Approach.*** The most direct procedure for determining the functional relationship between $r$ and $k$ of a mixed investment is to write out the expression for the future value of the project. Since the project balance of a mixed investment is compounded at either $r$ or $k$, depending on the sign of the project balance, the terminal (future) balance of the project, denoted by $PB(r, k)_N$, is a function of two variables. The following steps can be used to determine the $RIC$, $r$.

**Step 1:** Find $i_{min}$ by solving for the smallest real rate for which all $PB(i_{min})_n \le 0$, for $n = 1, \ldots, N - 1$. This is usually done by a trial-and-error method.

**Step 2:** Find $PB(i_{min})_N$.

a. If $PB(i_{min})_N \ge 0$, the project is a pure investment.

(1) Find the $IRR$, $i^*$, for which $PB(i^*)_N = 0$; $i^* = r^*$ for a pure investment.

(2) Apply the decision rules given in step 5.

b. If $PB(i_{min})_N < 0$, the project is a mixed investment and it is necessary to proceed with step 3.

**Step 3:** Calculate $PB(r, k)_n$ according to the following.

$$PB(r, k)_0 = F_0$$

$$PB(r, k)_1 = \begin{cases} PB(r, k)_0(1 + r) + F_1 & \text{if } PB(r, k)_0 \le 0 \\ PB(r, k)_0(1 + k) + F_1 & \text{if } PB(r, k)_0 > 0 \end{cases}$$

$$\vdots$$

$$PB(r, k)_n = \begin{cases} PB(r, k)_{n-1}(1 + r) + F_n & \text{if } PB(r, k)_{n-1} \le 0 \\ PB(r, k)_{n-1}(1 + k) + F_n & \text{if } PB(r, k)_{n-1} > 0 \end{cases}$$

To determine the positivity or negativity of $PB(r, k)_n$ at each period, set $r = i_{min}$, knowing that $r \leq i_{min}$. (See Problem 6.10.)

**Step 4:** Determine the value of $r^*$ by solving the equation $PB(r, k)_N = 0$.

**Step 5:** Apply the following set of decision rules to accept or reject the project.

> If $r^* > k$, accept.
> If $r^* = k$, remain indifferent.
> If $r^* < k$, reject.

### *Example 6.7*

Consider the project cash flows given in Example 6.6.

| End of Period $n$ | 0 | 1 | 2 |
|---|---|---|---|
| Cash Flow $F_n$ | −\$1,000 | 2,900 | −2,080 |

There are two sign changes in the ordered sequence of cash flows (−, +, −). The project has two *IRR*s, corresponding to $i^*_1 = 30\%$ and $i^*_2 = 60\%$. To derive the functional relationship between the return on invested capital, $r$, and the cost of capital, $k$, we apply the algorithm described in the preceding section.

**Step 1:** Find the $i_{min}$ that satisfies the following two equations ($N = 2, N - 1 = 1$).

$$PB(i)_0 = -1{,}000 < 0$$

$$PB(i)_1 = -1{,}000(1 + i) + 2{,}900$$

$$= -1{,}000i + 1{,}900 \leq 0$$

Since $PB(i)_0 < 0$, we need only find the smallest $i$ that satisfies $PB(i)_1 \leq 0$. The value of $i_{min}$ is 190%.

**Step 2:** Calculate $PB(i_{min})_N$.

$$PB(i_{min})_2 = (-1{,}000i_{min} + 1900)(1 + i_{min}) - 2{,}080$$

$$= -2{,}080$$

Since $PB(i_{min})_2 < 0$, the project is a mixed investment.

**Step 3:** Calculate $PB(r, k)_n$.

$$PB(r, k)_0 = -1{,}000$$

Since $PB(r, k)_0 < 0$, we use $r$.

$$PB(r, k)_1 = -1{,}000(1 + r) + 2{,}900$$

$$= -1{,}000r + 1{,}900$$

Since $r$ cannot exceed $i_{\min}$, $PB(r, k)_1 \geq 0$. Then we use $k$.

$$PB(r, k)_2 = (-1{,}000r + 1{,}900)(1 + k) - 2{,}080$$

**Step 4:** Find the solution of $PB(r, k)_2 = 0$.

$$r = 1.9 - \frac{2.08}{1 + k} \tag{6.16}$$

The graph of Eq. 6.16 is shown in Figure 6.7. We observe the following characteristics.

1. First, since $\frac{dr}{dk} = \frac{2.08}{(1 + k)^2} > 0$, $r$ is a monotonically increasing function of $k$. This means that the higher the cost that the firm places on borrowing funds from the project, the higher the return it will require on the invested capital.
2. Second, if we set $r = k$ in Eq. 6.16, we have $r = k = i^*$. Equation 6.16 intersects the 45° line $r = k$ twice, once at $k = 30\%$ and again at $k = 60\%$. With $r = k = i^*$, the terminal project balance $PB(r, k)_2$ decreases to $PB(i^*)_2 = 0$. Solving $PB(i^*)_2 = 0$ for $i^*$ yields the *IRR* of the project. In other words, this mixed investment has multiple rates of return ($i_1{}^* = 30\%$, $i_2{}^* = 60\%$). Therefore, the roots $i^*$ for mixed investment are the values of the return on invested capital, $r$, when the cost of borrowed money, $k$, is assumed to be equal to $r$.
3. Third, applying the decision rule, we have

| | |
|---|---|
| If $30\% < k < 60\% \rightarrow r^* > k$, | accept the project. |
| If $k = 30\%$ or $k = 60\% \rightarrow r^* = k$, | remain indifferent. |
| If $k < 30\%$ or $k > 60\% \rightarrow r^* < k$, | reject the project. |

4. Fourth, the decision we make will be consistent with the decision derived from applying the *PV* criterion when $i = MARR = k$. The *PV* of the project at an interest rate of $k$ can be expressed as

$$PV(k) = -\$1{,}000 + \frac{\$2{,}900}{1 + k} - \frac{\$2{,}080}{(1 + k)^2} \tag{6.17}$$

which is also depicted in Figure 6.7.

The following comments about the *PV* function are in order. First, the *IRR* is by definition the solution to the equation $PV(k) = 0$. Therefore, we observe that $PV(k)$ intersects the horizontal axis at $k = 30\%$ and at $k = 60\%$. Second, since $PV(k)$ is positive only in the range $30\% < k < 60\%$, the *PV* criterion gives the same accept–reject signal as the *IRR* criterion. □

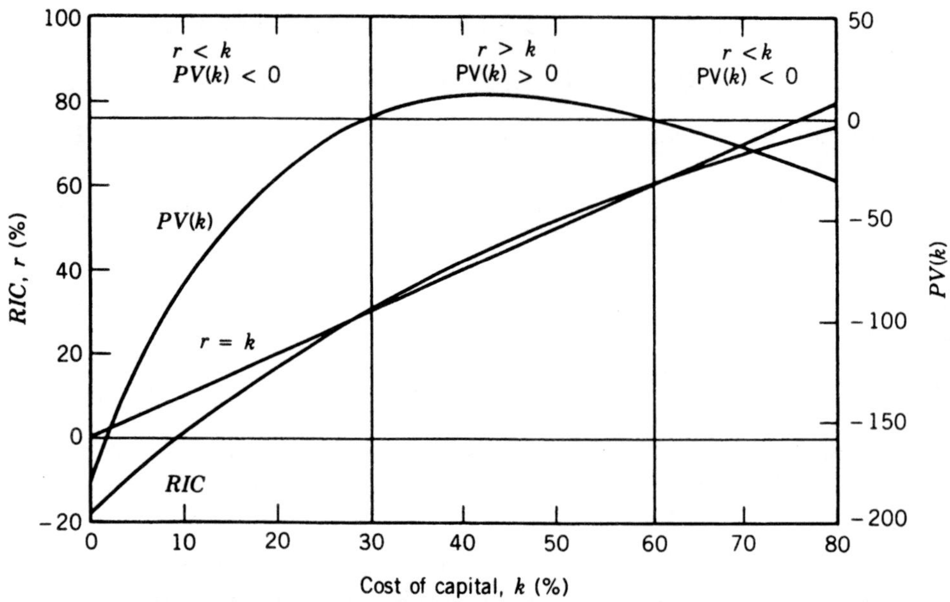


**FIGURE 6.7.** *RIC* **and** *PV* **as functions of** *k***, Example 6.7.**

## 6.3.5 Modified Rate of Return

An alternative way of approaching mixed investments is to modify the procedure for computing the rate of return by making explicit and consistent assumptions about the interest rate at which intermediate receipts from projects may be reinvested. This reinvestment could be either in other projects or in the outside market. This procedure is similar to the previous use of two different rates $(r, k)$ in the computation of the *project balance*. This section reviews some of the methods for applying the procedure.

***Solomon's Average Rate of Return (ARR).*** A different way of looking at a project is to ask the following question. Suppose we take the net revenues $F_n (F_n > 0)$ and reinvest them each year at $i$, letting them accumulate until time $N$. What rate of interest does investment $C_0$ have to earn to reach the same accumulated value in $N$ periods [15]?

Mathematically, we wish to find $s$ to solve the equation

$$\underbrace{C_0(1+s)^N}_{\substack{\text{alternative}\\\text{investment}}} = \underbrace{\sum_{n=1}^{N} F_n(1+i)^{N-n}}_{\text{current investment}} \tag{6.18}$$

With known $s$, the acceptance rule is

| |
|---|
| If $s > i = MARR$, accept. |
| If $s = i$, remain indifferent. |
| If $s < i$, reject. |

We can easily show that the *ARR* criterion is completely consistent with the *PV* criterion [2]. Recall that for a given project with $F_0 < 0$ but $F_n > 0$ for $1 \leq n \leq N$, the *PV* acceptance rule is

$$\sum_{n=0}^{N} F_n(1 + i)^{-n} > 0 \tag{6.19}$$

Substituting $C_0$ for $F_0$ (note that $F_0 = -C_0$) gives us

$$C_0 < \sum_{n=1}^{N} F_n(1 + i)^{-n} \tag{6.20}$$

Multiplying both sides of Eq. 6.18 by $(1 + i)^{-N}$ yields

$$C_0(1 + s)^N(1 + i)^{-N} = \sum_{n=1}^{N} F_n(1 + i)^{-n} \tag{6.21}$$

By comparing Eqs. 6.20 and 6.21, we can deduce that

$$C_0(1 + s)^N(1 + i)^{-N} > C_0$$

or

$$(1 + s)^N > (1 + i)^N \tag{6.22}$$

This implies that $s > i$, which is the *ARR* acceptance condition.

### *Example 6.8*

Consider the cash flows shown in Figure 6.2, where $C_0$ = \$1,000, $F_1$ = \$400, $F_2$ = \$360, $F_3$ = \$320, $F_4$ = \$280, and $F_5$ = \$240. Substituting these values into Eq. 6.18, we obtain

$$\begin{aligned} 1{,}000(1 + s)^5 &= 400(1.1)^4 + 360(1.1)^3 + 320(1.1)^2 + 280(1.1) + 240 \\ &= \$2{,}000 \end{aligned}$$

Solving for $s$ yields 15%. This tells us that we can invest \$1,000 in the project, reinvest the proceeds at our opportunity rate (*MARR*) of 10%, and have \$2,000 at time 5. If we do not wish to invest in the project but still wish to earn \$2,000, the original \$1,000 would have to earn 15% per period. Since the *MARR* is 10%, we are clearly better off accepting the project. If $s$ had been less than $i$ = 10%, we would have rejected the project. □

***Modified Internal Rate of Return (MIRR).*** As a variation of the *ARR* procedure, we may make explicit the expected reinvestment rate of intermediate incomes

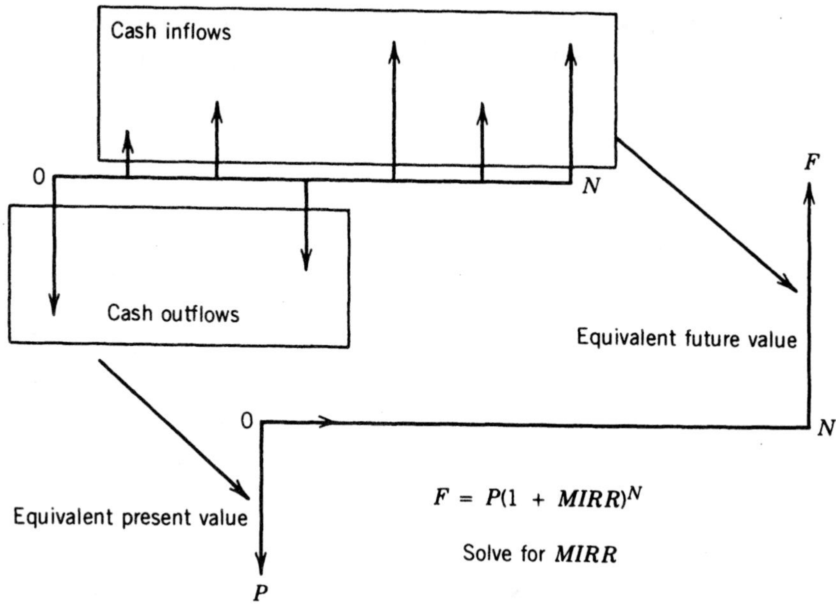


**FIGURE 6.8.** Illustration of the *MIRR* concept.

and costs and reduce them to an equivalent initial cost and a terminal project balance, a procedure known as the modified internal rate of return (*MIRR*) [12] or the external rate of return. In this way a unique *IRR* can be computed. This *MIRR* is defined by

$$\frac{\text{Future value of net cash inflow}}{\text{Present value of net cash outflow}}$$

$$= \frac{\sum_{n=0}^{N} \max(F_n, 0)(1+i)^{N-n}}{-\sum_{n=0}^{N} \min(F_n, 0)(1+i)^{-n}} = (1 + MIRR)^N \tag{6.23}$$

where $\max(F_n, 0) = F_n$ if $F_n > 0$, otherwise $F_n = 0$; $\min(F_n, 0) = F_n$ if $F_n < 0$, otherwise $F_n = 0$; and $i$ is the *MARR* to the firm. The meaning of the *MIRR* is illustrated in Figure 6.8.

By rearranging terms in Eq. 6.23, we can rewrite it as

$$\sum_{n=0}^{N} \max(F_n, 0)(1+i)^{N-n} = \left[-\sum_{n=0}^{N} \min(F_n, 0)(1+i)^{-n}\right](1 + MIRR)^N \tag{6.24}$$

If the cash outflow is restricted to the first period, $n = 0$, the *MIRR* is exactly the same as the *ARR, s.* The acceptance rule is then

| |
|---|
| If $MIRR > i$, accept.<br>If $MIRR = i$, remain indifferent.<br>If $MIRR < i$, reject. |

The *MIRR* will always give a unique solution and is also consistent with the *PV* criterion. The *MIRR* will always exceed the alternative rate whenever the investment sequence has a positive *PV* at *i.* This can be visualized from the following equations.

The project acceptance condition by the *PV* criterion is

$$\sum_{n=0}^{N} \max(F_n, 0)(1+i)^{-n} \quad > \quad -\sum_{n=0}^{N} \min(F_n, 0)(1+i)^{-n} \tag{6.25}$$

Present value of net cash inflow > Present value of net cash outflow

Multiplying both sides of Eq. 6.24 by $(1+i)^{-N}$ yields

$$\sum_{n=0}^{N} \max(F_n, 0)(1+i)^{-n}$$
$$= \left[-\sum_{n=0}^{N} \min(F_n, 0)(1+i)^{-n}\right](1+MIRR)^N(1+i)^{-N} \tag{6.26}$$

From the relation given in Eq. 6.25, we can say

$$\left[-\sum_{n=0}^{N} \min(F_n, 0)(1+i)^{-n}\right](1+MIRR)^N(1+i)^{-N}$$
$$> -\sum_{n=0}^{N} \min(F_n, 0)(1+i)^{-n} \tag{6.27}$$

Simplifying the terms above gives

$$(1+MIRR)^N > (1+i)^N \tag{6.28}$$

which indicates that $MIRR > i$.

There are three other variations of the *MIRR* [4], but these indices (including *ARR* and *MIRR*) have numerical values distinctly different from one another, and without additional information provided, these rates are considerably more complex to use than the simple *PV* criterion.

### *Example 6.9*

Using an example from [4], we will illustrate the method of computing the *MIRR*. Assume that $i = 6\%$, and the cash flow components are

| Cash Flow | *n*: 0 | 1 | 2 | 3 |
|---|---|---|---|---|
| $b_n$ | \$0 | 3 | 2 | 25 |
| $c_n$ | \$10 | 1 | 5 | 2 |
| $F_n$ | −\$10 | 2 | −3 | 23 |

$$\text{Present value of net cash outflow} = +10 + 3(1 + 0.06)^{-2} = \$12.67$$

$$\text{Future value of net cash inflow} = 2(1 + 0.06)^2 + 23 = \$25.25$$

Using Eq. 6.24, we find

$$25.25 = 12.67(1 + MIRR)^3$$

$$MIRR = 25.84\%$$

Since $MIRR > 6\%$, the project should be acceptable. Note that $PV(6\%) = \$8.53 > 0$, so the *MIRR* result is consistent with the *PV* criterion. □

## 6.4 BENEFIT–COST RATIOS

Another way to express the worthiness of a project is to compare the inflows with the investment. This leads to three types of benefit–cost ratios: the aggregate benefit–cost ratio (Eckstein $B/C$), the netted benefit–cost ratio (simple $B/C$), and the Lorie–Savage ratio.

Let $B$ and $C$ be the present values of cash inflows and outflows defined by Eqs. 6.1 and 6.2. We will split the equivalent cost $C$ into two components, the initial capital expenditure and the annual costs accrued in each successive period. Assuming that an initial investment is required during the first $m$ periods, while annual costs accrue in each period following, the components are defined as

$$I = \sum_{n=0}^{m} c_n(1 + i)^{-n} \tag{6.29}$$

$$C' = \sum_{n=m+1}^{N} c_n(1 + i)^{-n} \tag{6.30}$$

and $C = I + C'$.

The following example will be used to demonstrate the application of different $B/C$ ratio criteria.

| Cash Flow | $n$: 0 | 1 | 2 | 3 | 4 | 5 |
|---|---|---|---|---|---|---|
| $b_n$ | \$0 | 0 | 10 | 10 | 20 | 20 |
| $c_n$ | \$10 | 5 | 5 | 5 | 5 | 10 |
| $F_n$ | −\$10 | −5 | 5 | 5 | 15 | 10 |

With $i =$ 10%, we define

$$N = 5$$

$$m = 1$$

$$B = 10(1.1)^{-2} + 10(1.1)^{-3} + 20(1.1)^{-4} + 20(1.1)^{-5} = \$41.86$$

$$C = 10 + 5(1.1)^{-1} + 5(1.1)^{-2} + 5(1.1)^{-3} + 5(1.1)^{-4} + 10(1.1)^{-5} = \$32.06$$

$$I = 10 + 5(1.1)^{-1} = \$14.55$$

$$C' = 5(1.1)^{-2} + 5(1.1)^{-3} + 5(1.1)^{-4} + 10(1.1)^{-5} = \$17.51$$

$$PV(10\%) = B - C = \$9.80$$

### 6.4.1 Benefit–Cost Ratios Defined

***Aggregate B/C Ratio.*** The aggregate $B/C$ ratio introduced by Eckstein [7] is defined as

$$R_A = \frac{B}{C} = \frac{B}{I + C'}, \qquad I + C' > 0 \tag{6.31}$$

To accept a project, the $R_A$ must be greater than 1. Historically, this ratio was developed in the 1930s in response to the fact that in public projects the user is generally not the same as the sponsor. To have a better perspective on the user's benefits, we need to separate them from the sponsor's costs. If we assume that for a project $b_n$ represents the user's benefits and $c_n$ the sponsor's costs, the ratio is

$$R_A = \frac{41.86}{14.55 + 17.51} = 1.306$$

The ratio exceeds 1, which implies that the user's benefits exceed the sponsor's costs. Public projects usually also have benefits that are difficult to measure, whereas costs are more easily quantified. In this respect, the Eckstein $B/C$ ratio lends itself readily to sensitivity analysis with respect to the value of benefits. We will discuss this measure in greater detail in Chapter 14.

***Netted B/C Ratio.*** As an alternative expression in defining their terms, some analysts consider only the initial capital expenditure as a cash outlay, and equivalent benefits become net benefits (i.e., revenues minus annual outlays). This alternative measure is referred to as the *netted benefit–cost ratio,* $R_N$, and is expressed by

$$R_N = \frac{B - C'}{I}, \qquad I > 0 \tag{6.32}$$

The advantage of having the benefit–cost ratio defined in this manner is that it provides an index indicating the net benefit expected per dollar invested, sometimes called a *profitability index*. Again, for a project to remain under consideration, the ratio must be greater than 1. For our example, the $R_N$ is

$$R_N = \frac{41.86 - 17.51}{14.55} = 1.674$$

Note that this is just a comparison of the present value of net revenues ($F_n$) with the present value of investment. Since $R_N > 1$, there is a surplus at time 0 and the project is favorable. The use of this criterion also had its origin in the evaluation of public projects in the 1930s.

***Lorie–Savage Ratio.*** As a variation on $R_N$, the Lorie–Savage ($L$–$S$) ratio is defined as

$$L\text{–}S = \frac{B - C}{I} = \frac{B - C'}{I} - 1 = R_N - 1 > 0 \tag{6.33}$$

Here the comparison is between the surplus at time 0 and the investment itself. If the ratio is greater than 0, the project is favorable. Clearly, the $R_N$ $B/C$ and the $L$–$S$ $B/C$ ratios will always yield the same decision for a project, since both the ratios and their respective cutoff points differ by 1.0. For our example, $L$–$S$ = $1.674 - 1 = 0.674 > 0$. Thus the $L$–$S$ ratio also indicates acceptance of the project.

### 6.4.2 Equivalence of B/C Ratios and PV

Using the notation in Section 6.4.1, we can state the $PV$ criterion for project acceptance as

$$\begin{aligned} PV(i) &= B - C \\ &= B - (I + C') > 0. \end{aligned} \tag{6.34}$$

By transposing the term $(I + C')$ to the right-hand side and dividing both sides by $(I + C')$, we have

$$\frac{B}{I + C'} > 1 \qquad (I + C' > 0)$$

which is exactly the decision rule for accepting a project with the $R_A$ criterion. On the other hand, by transposing the term $I$ to the right-hand side and dividing both sides of the equation by $I$, we obtain

$$\frac{B - C'}{I} > 1 \qquad (I > 0)$$

which is exactly the decision rule for accepting a project with the $R_N$ criterion. In other words, use of $R_A$ or use of $R_N$ will lead to the same conclusion about the initial acceptability of a single project, as long as $I > 0$ and $I + C' > 0$. Notice that these $B/C$ ratios will always agree with each other for an individual project, since $I$ and $C'$ are nonnegative.

$$\frac{B}{I + C'} > 1 \longleftrightarrow B > I + C' \longleftrightarrow B - C' > I$$

$$B > I + C' \;\updownarrow\; PV(i) = B - (I + C') > 0$$

$$B - C' > I \;\updownarrow\; \frac{B - C'}{I} > 1 \;\updownarrow\; \frac{B - C'}{I} - 1 > 0$$

Although $ARR$ does not appear to be related to the benefit–cost ratios, it does, in fact, yield the same decisions for a project. From Eq. 6.18 we have

$$C_0(1 + s)^N = \sum_{n=1}^{N} F_n(1 + i)^{N-n}$$

Expressed differently,

$$\begin{aligned} I(1 + s)^N(1 + i)^{-N} &= \sum_{n=1}^{N} F_n(1 + i)^{-n} \\ &= B - C' \end{aligned}$$

$$\frac{B - C'}{I} = \left(\frac{1 + s}{1 + i}\right)^N \tag{6.35}$$

We require $s > i$ for project acceptance, so we must have

$$\frac{B - C'}{I} > 1$$

## 6.5 PAYBACK PERIOD

A popular rule-of-thumb method for evaluating projects is to determine the number of periods needed to recover the original investment. In this section we present two procedures for assessing the payback period of an investment.

### 6.5.1 Payback Period Defined

***Conventional Payback Period.*** The payback period ($PP$) is defined as the number of periods it will take to recover the initial investment outlay. Mathematically, the payback period is computed as the smallest value of $n$ that satisfies the equation

$$\sum_{n=0}^{n_p} F_n \geqslant 0 \tag{6.36}$$

This payback period ($n_p$) is then compared with the maximum acceptable payback period ($n_{max}$) to determine whether the project should be accepted. If $n_{max} > n_p$, the proposed project will be accepted. Otherwise, the project will be rejected.

Obviously the most serious deficiencies of the payback period are that it fails to consider the time value of money and that it fails to consider the consequences of the investment after the payback period.

***Discounted Payback Period.*** As a modification of the conventional payback period, one may incorporate the time value of money. The method is to determine the length of time required for the project's equivalent receipts to exceed the equivalent capital outlays.

Mathematically, the discounted payback period $Q$ is the smallest $n$ that satisfies the expression

$$\sum_{n=0}^{Q} F_n(1 + i)^{-n} \geqslant 0 \tag{6.37}$$

where $i$ is the *MARR*.

If we multiply both sides of Eq. 6.37 by $(1 + i)^Q$, we should obtain

$$\sum_{n=0}^{Q} F_n(1 + i)^{Q-n} \geqslant 0 \tag{6.38}$$

Notice that Eq. 6.38 is the definition of project balance $PB(i)_n$. Thus, the discounted payback period is alternatively defined as the smallest $n$ that makes $PB(i)_n \geq 0$.

### 6.5.2 Popularity of the Payback Period

Clearly, the payback period analysis is simple to apply and, in some cases, may give answers approximately equivalent to those provided by more sophisticated methods. A number of authors have tried to show an equivalence between the payback period and other criteria, such as *IRR*, under special circumstances [11]. For example, Gordon [8] interpreted the payback period as an indirect, though quick, measure of return. With a uniform stream of receipts, the reciprocal of the payback period is the *IRR* for a project of infinite life and is a good approximation to this rate for a long-lived project.

Weingartner [19] analyzed the basic reasons why the payback period measure is so popular in business. One reason is that the payback period can function like many other rules of thumb to shortcut the process of generating information and then evaluating it. Payback reduces the information search by focusing on the time when the firm expects to "be made whole again." Hence, it allows the decision maker to judge whether the life of the project past the breakeven (bench mark) point is sufficient to make the undertaking worthwhile.

In summary, the payback period gives some measure of the rate at which a project will recover its initial outlay. This piece of information is not available from either the *PV* or the *IRR*. The payback period may not be used as a direct figure of merit, but it may be used as a constraint: no project may be accepted unless its payback period is shorter than some specified period of time.

### *Example 6.10*

Suppose that a firm is considering a project costing $10,000, the life of the project is 5 years, and the expected net annual cash flows at the end of the year are as follows (assume *MARR* = 10%).

| Cash Flow | *n*: 0 | 1 | 2 | 3 | 4 | 5 |
|---|---|---|---|---|---|---|
| $F_n$ | −$10,000 | $3,000 | $3,000 | $4,000 | $3,000 | $3,000 |
| Cumulative $F_n$ | −$10,000 | −7,000 | −4,000 | 0 | 3,000 | 6,000 |
| *PV*(10%) | −$10,000 | 2,727 | 2,479 | 3,005 | 2,049 | 1,862 |
| Cumulative present value | −$10,000 | −7,273 | −4,794 | −1,789 | 260 | 2,122 |

The conventional payback period is 3 years, whereas the discounted payback period is 3.87 years. This example demonstrates how consideration of the time value of money in payback analysis can produce different results. Clearly, this discounted measure is conceptually better than the conventional one, but both measures fail to indicate the overall profitability of the project. □

## 6.6 TIME-DEPENDENT MEASURE OF INVESTMENT WORTH

The project balance, which measures the equivalent loss or profit of an investment project as a function of time, is a recent development that provides additional insight into investment decisions. In Section 6.2.2 we defined the project balance and demonstrated its calculation both mathematically and through examples. This section presents particular characteristics of project balance profiles and their economic interpretation. We also discuss some possible measures of investment desirability based on these profiles. (The material presented in this section is based on the analysis given by Park and Thuesen [14].)

### 6.6.1 Areas of Negative and Positive Balances

Recall that the project balance is defined by

$$PB(i)_n = \sum_{j=0}^{n} F_j(1 + i)^{n-j}, \qquad n = 0, 1, 2, \ldots, N$$

By plotting $PB(i)_n$ as a function of time $n$, we can trace the time path of project balance as shown in Figure 6.9. This time path is referred to as the *project balance pattern*, and it provides the basic information about the attractiveness of a particular investment proposal as a function of its life. The shaded area represents the period of time during which the project balance has negative values, that is, the time during which the initial investment plus interest is not fully recovered. This area is referred to as the *area of negative balance* (*ANB*). Mathematically, the area is represented by

$$ANB = \sum_{n=0}^{Q-1} PB(i)_n \tag{6.39}$$

where $Q$ is the discounted payback period [the first period in which $PB(i)_n \geq 0$]. Since the value $PB(i)_n$ for $n < Q$ represents the magnitude of negative balance

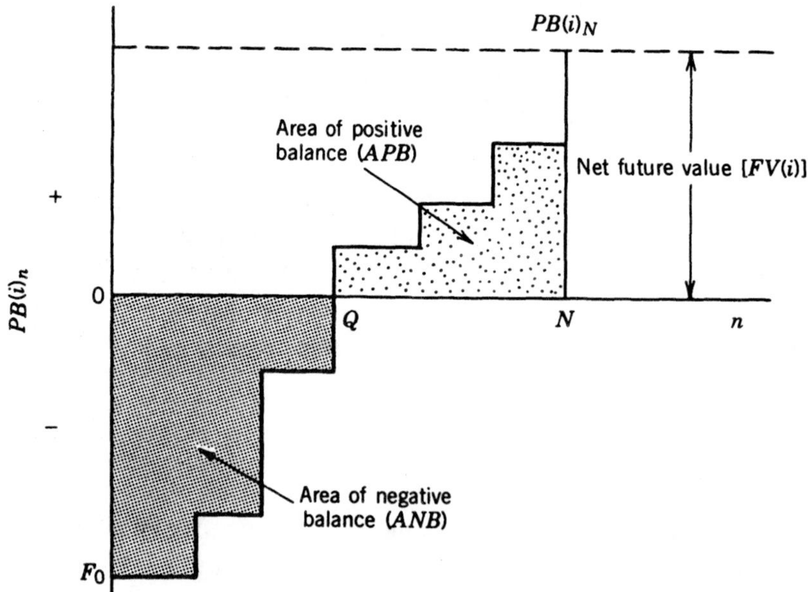


**FIGURE 6.9. A general project balance diagram.**

of the project at the end of period $n$, it is equivalent to the amount of possible loss if the project is terminated at this time. With certainty, the *ANB* can be interpreted as the total amount of dollars to be tied up for the particular investment option. The smaller the *ANB*, the more flexible the firm's future investment options. Therefore, the smaller the *ANB* for a project, the more attractive the project is considered, assuming that the expected terminal profits for other projects are the same.

Point $Q$ on the horizontal axis in Figure 6.9 represents the discounted payback period, which indicates how long it will be before the project breaks even. Therefore, the smaller the $Q$ for a project, the more desirable the project is considered, if other things are equal. (See the mathematical definition in Eq. 6.38.)

The stippled area in Figure 6.9 represents the period of time during which the $PB(i)_n$ maintains a positive project balance. This area is referred to as the *area of positive balance* (*APB*). The initial investment of the project has been fully recovered, so receipts during this time period contribute directly to the final profitability of the project. Symbolically, the area is represented by

$$APB = \sum_{n=Q}^{N-1} PB(i)_n \tag{6.40}$$

The project balance diagram during these periods can be interpreted as the rate at which the project is expected to accumulate profits. This is certainly an important parameter which affects project desirability when decisions are made about the retirement of projects. Since the values $PB(i)_n$ for $n > Q$ represent the magnitude of positive project balance, there is no possible loss even though the project is terminated in a period before the end of its life or no additional receipts are received. Thus, $PB(i)_n$ becomes the net equivalent dollars earned.

Finally, the last project balance $PB(i)_N$ represents the net future value of the project (or terminal profit) at the end of its life. The *PV* of the project can be found easily by a simple transformation, shown in Eq. 6.9.

### 6.6.2. Investment Flexibility

To illustrate the basic concept of investment flexibility and its discriminating ability compared with the traditional measures of investment worth (e.g., *PV*), we consider the hypothetical investment situation shown in Figure 6.10*a*. Projects 1 and 2 have single-payment and uniform-series cash flows, respectively. Projects 3 and 4 are gradient series, one being an increasing gradient series and the other a decreasing gradient series. All the projects require the same initial investment and have a service life of 3 years. All the projects would have an equivalent future value of \$63.40 at a *MARR* of 10% [or *PV*(10%) = \$47.63]. This implies that no project is preferable to the others when they are compared on the basis of present value.

Plotting the project balance pattern for each project provides additional information that is not revealed by computing only present value equivalents

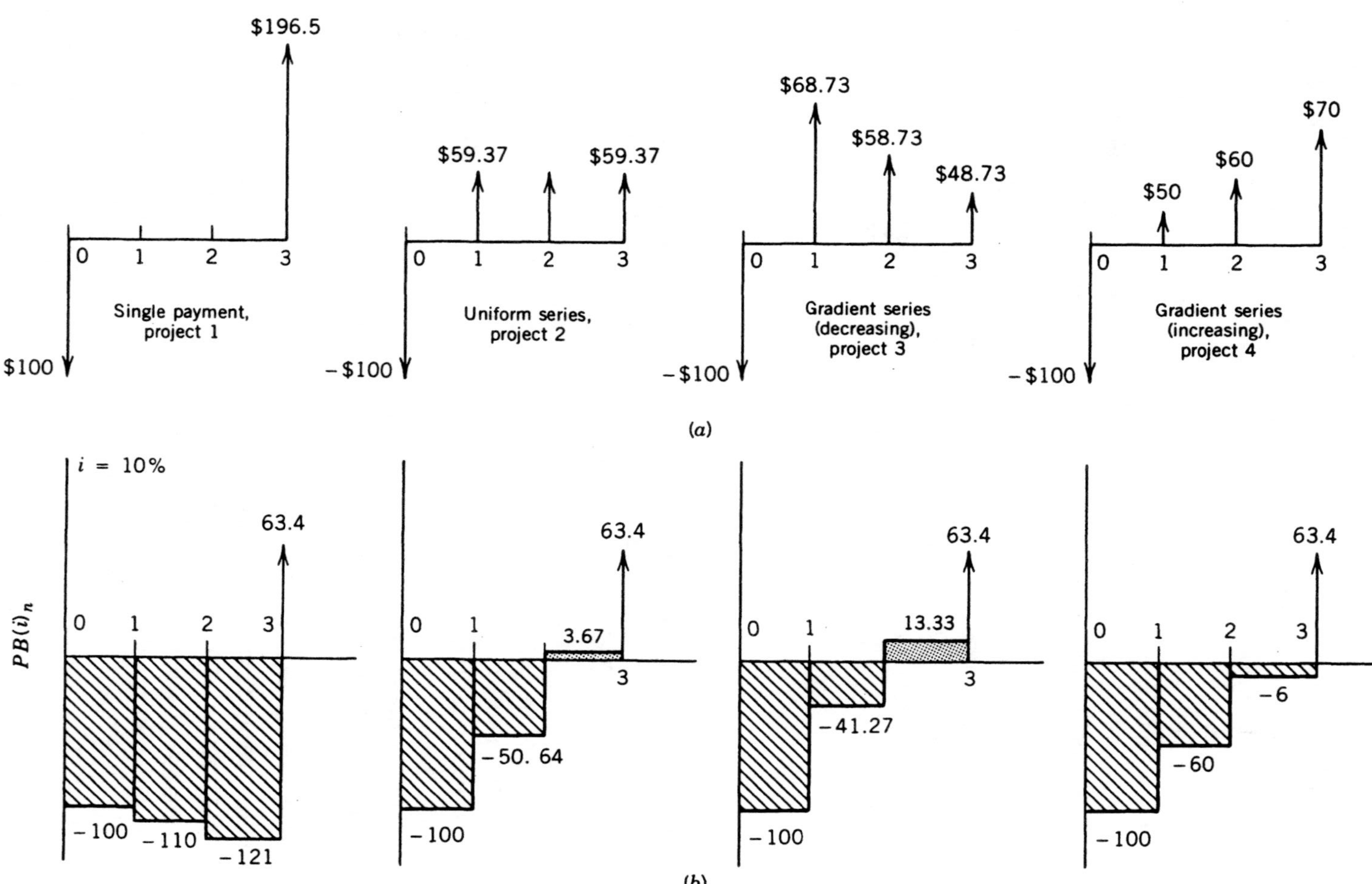


**FIGURE 6.10.** Project balance for four cash flow patterns.

**Table 6.4** ***Statistics of Project Balance Patterns for Projects 1, 2, 3, and 4***

| Project Number | Cash Flow Pattern | Future Value *FV*(10%) | *ANB* | *APB* | *Q* |
|---|---|---|---|---|---|
| 1 | Single payment | \$63.4 | 331.00 | 0 | 3 |
| 2 | Uniform series | \$63.4 | 150.63 | 3.67 | 2 |
| 3 | Gradient series (decreasing) | \$63.4 | 141.27 | 13.33 | 2 |
| 4 | Gradient series (increasing) | \$63.4 | 166.00 | 0 | 3 |

(see Figure 6.10*b*). For example, a comparison of project 1 with project 3 in terms of the shape of the project balance pattern shows that project 3 recovers its initial investment within 2 years, whereas project 1 takes 3 years to recover the same initial investment. This, in turn, indicates that project 3 would provide more flexibility in future investment activity to the firm than project 1. By selecting project 3, the investor can be sure of being restored to his or her initial position within a short span of time. Similar one-to-one comparisons can be made among all four projects. Table 6.4 summarizes the statistics obtained from the balance patterns for each project shown in Figure 6.10*b*.

Table 6.4 shows that project 3 appears to be most desirable, even though its terminal profitability is equal to those of the other projects, because its *ANB* is the smallest and its *APB* is the largest among the projects. As discussed in Section 6.6.1, the small value of *ANB* implies more flexibility in the firm's future investment activity. In other words, an early resolution of the negative project balance would make funds available for attractive investment opportunities that become

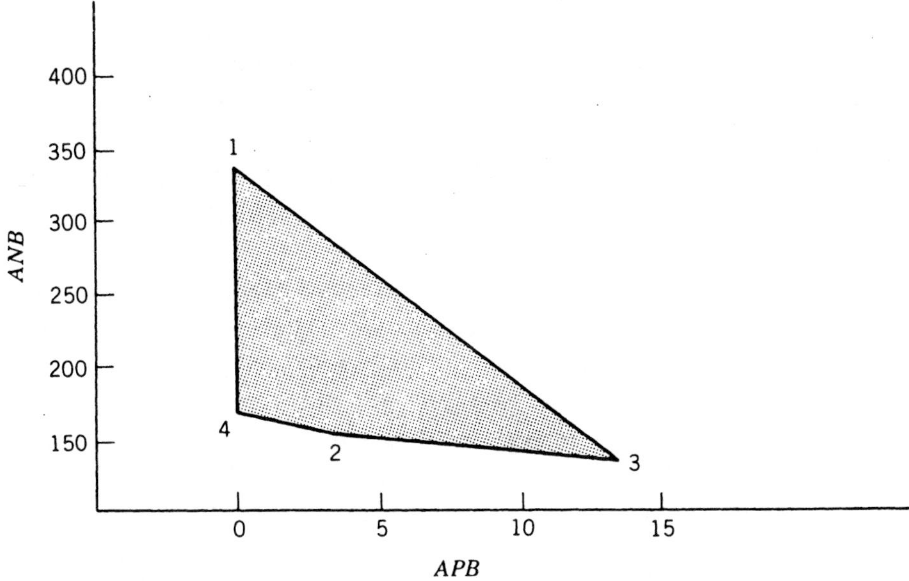


**FIGURE 6.11.** Plot of *APB* against *ANB* for different cash flow patterns.

available in the subsequent decision periods. One-to-one comparisons of the projects in terms of *ANB* and *APB* can be depicted graphically (see Figure 6.11). From Figure 6.9, it becomes evident that the project balance parameters such as *ANB* and *APB* reflect the changes in the cash flow patterns over time. Since project 3 represents the highest *APB* with the smallest *ANB*, project 3 appears to be the most desirable. Of course, the environment in which the decision is made and individual preferences will dictate which of these parameters should be used so that the economic implications of an investment project are fully understood.

## 6.7 SUMMARY

In this chapter we showed the following.

1. The *PV*, *FV*, and *AE* will always yield the same decision for a project. We consider *PV* as the baseline, or "correct," criterion to use in a stable, perfect capital market with complete certainty about investment outcomes.
2. The distinction between pure and mixed investments is needed to determine whether the return on invested capital is independent of the cost of capital.
3. Only for a pure investment is there a rate of return concept internal to the project. For pure investments, the *IRR* and *PV* criteria result in identical acceptance and rejection decisions.
4. The return on invested capital for a mixed project varies directly with the cost of capital. The phenomenon of multiple *IRR*s, which occurs only in the situation of a mixed investment, is actually a manifestation of the existence of this basic functional relationship. The *RIC* is consistent with the *PV* criterion.
5. *ARR* and *MIRR* will also always yield the same decision for a project, consistent with the *PV* criterion.
6. $R_A$, $R_N$, and $L$–$S$ ratios will give the same accept–reject decisions for an individual project. The *PV* and these $B/C$ ratios will always agree.
7. Neither the payback period nor the discounted payback period should be considered as a criterion, since they may not agree with *PV*. They may be used as additional constraints in the decision-making process, but they should be used with caution.
8. The project balance diagram provides quantitative information about four important characteristics associated with the economic desirability of an investment project. Two of these characteristics, net future value (terminal project balance) and discounted payback period, have generally been a part of conventional economic analyses. However, the other two characteristics, *ANB* and *APB*, have not been considered. Possible applications of the project balance indicate that a variety of measurements can be devised that reflect particular characteristics of the investment project under consideration. The project balance at the end of a project, $PB(i)_N$, is identical to the *FV* criterion.

In conclusion, we can say that the *PV* criterion is superior among the traditional measures of investment worth because of its ease of use, robustness, and consistency.

## REFERENCES


1. Baldwin, R. H., "How to Assess Investment Proposals," *Harvard Business Review,* Vol. 27, No. 3, pp. 98–104, May–June 1959.
2. Bernhard, R. H., "Discount Methods for Expenditure Evaluation—A Clarification of Their Assumptions," *Journal of Industrial Engineering,* Vol. 18, No. 1, pp. 19–27, January–February 1962.
3. Bernhard, R. H., "A Comprehensive Comparison and Critique of Discounting Indices Proposed for Capital Investment Evaluation," *The Engineering Economist,* Vol. 16, No. 3, pp. 157–186, Spring 1971.
4. Bernhard, R. H., "Modified Rates of Return for Investment Project Evaluation—A Comparison and Critique," *The Engineering Economist,* Vol. 24, No. 3, pp. 161–167, Spring 1979.
5. Bernhard, R. H., "Unrecovered Investment, Uniqueness of the Internal Rate and the Question of Project Acceptability," *Journal of Financial and Quantitative Analysis,* Vol. 12, No. 1, pp. 33–38, March 1977.
6. Bussey, L. E., *The Economic Analysis of Industrial Projects,* Prentice–Hall, Englewood Cliffs, N.J., 1978.
7. Eckstein, O., *Water Resource Development: The Economics of Project Evaluation,* Harvard University Press, Cambridge, Mass., 1958.
8. Gordon, M., "The Payoff Period and the Rate of Profit," *Journal of Business,* Vol. 28, No. 4, pp. 253–260, October 1955.
9. Kaplan, S., "A Note on a Method for Precisely Determining the Uniqueness or Nonuniqueness of the Internal Rate of Return for a Proposed Investment," *Journal of Industrial Engineering,* Vol. 26, No. 1, pp. 70–71, January–February 1965.
10. Kaplan, S., "Computer Algorithms for Finding Exact Rates of Return," *Journal of Business,* Vol. 40, No. 4, pp. 389–392, October 1967.
11. Levy, H., and M. Sarnat, *Capital Investment and Financial Decisions,* 2nd edition, Prentice–Hall, Englewood Cliffs, N.J., 1983.
12. Lin, S., "The Modified Internal Rate of Return and Investment Criterion," *The Engineering Economist,* Vol. 21, No. 4, pp. 237–248, Summer 1976.
13. Mao, J. C. T., *Quantitative Analysis of Financial Decisions,* Macmillan, Toronto, 1969.
14. Park, C. S., and G. J. Thuesen, "Combining Concepts of Uncertainty Resolution and Project Balance for Capital Allocation Decisions," *The Engineering Economist,* Vol. 24, No. 2, pp. 109–127, Winter 1979.
15. Solomon, E., "The Arithmetic of Capital-Budgeting Decision," *Journal of Business,* Vol. 29, No. 2, pp. 124–129, April 1956.
16. Teichroew, D., A. A. Robichek, and M. Montalbano, "Mathematical Analysis of Rates of Return under Certainty," *Management Science,* Vol. 11, No. 3, pp. 395–403, January 1965.
17. Teichroew, D., A. A. Robichek, and M. Montalbano, "An Analysis of Criteria for Investment and Financing Decisions under Certainty," *Management Science,* Vol. 12, No. 3, pp. 151–179, November 1965.

18. WEINGARTNER, H. M., "The Excess Present Value Index: A Theoretical Basis and Critique," *Journal of Accounting Research,* Vol. 1, No. 2, pp. 213–224, Autumn 1963.

19. WEINGARTNER, H. M., "Some New Views on the Payback Period and Capital Budgeting Decision," *Management Science,* Vol. 15, No. 12, pp. B594–B607, August 1969.

## PROBLEMS

All cash flows given in this problem set represent the cash flows after taxes, unless otherwise mentioned.

**6.1.** Consider the following sets of investment projects.

| | After-Tax Cash Flows | | | |
|---|---|---|---|---|
| Project | $n$: 0 | 1 | 2 | 3 |
| A | −$10,000 | 0 | 0 | 19,650 |
| B | −$10,000 | 5,937 | 5,937 | 5,937 |
| C | −$10,000 | 6,873 | 5,873 | 4,873 |
| D | −$10,000 | 5,000 | 6,000 | 7,000 |

a. Compute the net present value of each project at $i = 10\%$.
b. Compute the project balance of each project as a function of the project year.
c. Compute the future value of each project at $i = 10\%$.
d. Compute the annual equivalent of each project at $i = 10\%$.

**6.2.** In Problem 6.1

a. Graph the net present value of each project as a function of $i$.
b. Graph the project balances (at $i = 10\%$) of each project as a function of $n$.
c. From the graphical results in part b of Problem 6.1, which project appears to be the safest to undertake if there is some possibility of premature termination of the projects at the end of year 2?

**6.3.** Consider the following set of independent investment projects.

| | $F_n$ | | | | | | |
|---|---|---|---|---|---|---|---|
| Project | $n$: 0 | 1 | 2 | 3 | 4 | 5 | 6–20 |
| 1 | −100 | 50 | 50 | 50 | 50 | −750 | 100 |
| 2 | −100 | 30 | 30 | 30 | 10 | 10 | |
| 3 | −16 | 92 | −170 | 100 | | | |

Assume $MARR(i) = 10\%$ for the following questions.

a. Compute the present value for each project and determine the acceptability of each project.
b. Compute the future value of each project at the end of each project period and determine its acceptability.
c. Compute the annual equivalent of each project and determine the acceptability of each project.
d. Compute the project value of each project at the end of 20 years with variable *MARR*s: 10% for $n = 0$ to $n = 10$ and 15% for $n = 11$ to $n = 20$.
e. Compute the project balance as a function of $n$ for project 2.
f. Compute Solomon's average rate of return (*ARR*) for project 2, and determine the acceptability of the project.

g. Compute the modified internal rate of return (*MIRR*) for project 3 and determine the project's acceptability.

**6.4.** Consider the following project balance profiles for proposed investment projects.

| | | Project Balance (End of Year) | | | | | |
|---|---|---|---|---|---|---|---|
| Project | $i$ | $PB(i)_0$ | $PB(i)_1$ | $PB(i)_2$ | $PB(i)_3$ | $PB(i)_4$ | $PB(i)_5$ |
| A | 10% | −$1,000 | −1,000 | −900 | −690 | −359 | 105 |
| B | 0 | −$1,000 | −800 | −600 | −400 | −200 | 0 |
| C | 15 | −$1,000 | −650 | −348 | −100 | 85 | 198 |
| D | 18 | −$1,000 | −680 | −302 | −57 | 233 | 575 |
| E | 20 | −$1,000 | −1,200 | −1,440 | −1,328 | −1,194 | −1,000 |
| F | 12.9 | −$1,000 | −530 | −99 | −211 | −89 | 0 |

Project balance figures are rounded to dollars.

a. Compute the present value of each investment.
b. Determine the cash flows for each project.
c. Identify the future value of each project.
d. What would the internal rates of return be for projects B and F?

**6.5.** Consider the following sequence of cash flows.

| Project | $n$: 0 | 1 | 2 | 3 |
|---|---|---|---|---|
| A | −10 | 5 | −5 | 20 |
| B | 100 | −216 | 116 | |

a. Descartes' rule of sign indicates _____ possible rates of return for project A, but the Norstrom rule indicates _____ real root(s) because there are _____ sign change(s) in the $S_n$ series. The rates of return is are _____.
b. For project B, determine the range of *MARR* for which the project would be acceptable.
c. Compute the *MIRR* for both projects. ($i = 6\%$)
d. Compute $i_{\min}$ for both projects and compute the return on invested capital at $k = 6\%$.

**6.6.** Consider the following set of investment projects.

| | | After-Tax Cash Flow | | | | |
|---|---|---|---|---|---|---|
| Project | $n$: 0 | 1 | 2 | 3 | 4 | 5 |
| 1 | −$10 | 60 | −120 | 80 | | |
| 2 | −$225 | 100 | 100 | 100 | 100 | |
| 3 | | 100 | 50 | 0 | −230 | |
| 4 | −$100 | 50 | 50 | 50 | −100 | 600 |
| 5 | −$100 | 300 | −100 | 500 | | |

a. Classify each project as either simple or nonsimple.
b. Compute the internal rate(s) of return for each project.
c. Classify each project as either a pure or a mixed investment.
d. Assuming that $MARR = i = k = 10\%$, determine the acceptability of each project based on the rate-of-return principle.
e. For all mixed projects, compute the *MIRR*s.

**6.7.** Consider the following set of investment projects.

| Project | After-Tax Cash Flow $n$: 0 | 1 | 2 | 3 | 4 | 5 |
|---|---|---|---|---|---|---|
| 1 | −60 | 70 | −20 | 240 | | |
| 2 | −100 | 50 | 100 | | | |
| 3 | −800 | 400 | −100 | 400 | 400 | −100 |
| 4 | −160 | 920 | −1,700 | 1,000 | | |
| 5 | −450 | −200 | 700 | −60 | 2,000 | −500 |

a. Compute the *PV* for each project. ($i$ = 12%).
b. Classify each project as either simple or nonsimple.
c. Compute the internal rate(s) of return for each project.
d. Classify each project as either a pure or a mixed investment.
e. Assuming that $MARR = i = k = 12\%$, determine the acceptability of each project based on the rate-of-return principle.

**6.8.** Consider the following set of investment projects.

| Project | After-Tax Cash Flow $n$: 0 | 1 | 2 | 3 | 4 |
|---|---|---|---|---|---|
| 1 | −$10 | −30 | 80 | −30 | |
| 2 | −$70 | 50 | 23 | 11 | |
| 3 | −$50 | 25 | 102 | −100 | 392 |
| 4 | −$100 | 500 | −600 | | |
| 5 | −$110 | 10 | 100 | 50 | |
| 6 | −$10 | 60 | −110 | 60 | |

a. Classify each project as either simple or nonsimple.
b. Compute the internal rate(s) of return for each project.
c. Classify each project as either a pure or a mixed investment.
d. Assuming that $MARR = i = k = 10\%$, determine the acceptability of each project based on the rate-of-return principle.

**6.9.** Consider the following series of cash flows for an investment project.

| $n$ | 0 | 1 | 2 | 3 |
|---|---|---|---|---|
| $F_n$ | −$500 | 1,000 | 3,000 | −4,000 |

a. Find $i_{min}$ for this investment.
b. Determine whether this is a mixed investment.
c. If this is a mixed investment, derive the functional relationship between the *RIC*, $r^*$, and the cost of capital, $k$.
d. Assume $k$ = 10%. Determine the value of $r^*$ and the acceptability of this investment.

**6.10.** Prove that $r \leq i_{min}$, in relation to the project balance.

**6.11.** Consider the following set of investment projects.

| Project | After-Tax Cash Flow $n$: 0 | 1 | 2 |
|---|---|---|---|
| 1 | −$1,000 | 500 | 840 |
| 2 | −$2,000 | 1,560 | 944 |
| 3 | −$1,000 | 1,400 | −100 |

Assume $MARR = i = 12\%$ in the following questions.

a. Compute the internal rate of return for each project. If there is more than one rate of return, identify all the rates.

b. Determine the acceptability of each project based on the rate-of-return principle.

**6.12.** Consider the projects described in Problem 6.3.

a. Compute the rate of return (internal rate of return) for each project.

b. Plot the present value as a function of interest rate ($i$) for each project.

c. Classify each project as either simple or nonsimple. Then reclassify each project as either a pure or a mixed investment.

d. Now determine the acceptability of each project by using the rate-of-return principle. Use $MARR(i) = 10\%$.

**6.13.** Consider the following investment project at $MARR = 10\%$.

| Cash Flow | $n$: 0 | 1 | 2 | 3 | 4 | 5 | 6 | 7 | 8 | 9 | 10 |
|---|---|---|---|---|---|---|---|---|---|---|---|
| $b_n$ | | | | 100 | 100 | 200 | 300 | 300 | 200 | 100 | 50 |
| $c_n$ | \$200 | 100 | 50 | 20 | 20 | 100 | 100 | 100 | 50 | 50 | 30 |
| $F_n$ | −\$200 | −100 | −50 | 80 | 80 | 100 | 200 | 200 | 150 | 50 | 20 |

a. Identify the values of $N$, $m$, $B$, $C$, $I$, and $C'$.

b. Compute $R_A$, $R_N$, and the $L$–$S$ ratio.

c. Compute the $PV(10\%)$.

**6.14.** Consider the investment situation in which an investment of $P$ dollars at $n = 0$ is followed by a series of equal annual positive payments $A$ over $N$ periods. If it is assumed that $A$ dollars are recovered each year, with $A$ being a percentage of $P$, the number of years required for payback can be found as a function of the rate of return of the investment. That is, knowing the relationship $A = P(A/P,i^*,N)$, or

$$A = P\left[\frac{i^*(1 + i^*)^N}{(1 + i^*)^N - 1}\right]$$

we can rewrite the relationship as

$$i^* = \frac{A}{P} - \frac{A}{P}\left(\frac{1}{1 + i^*}\right)^N$$

Note that $A/P$ is the payback reciprocal, $R_p = 1/n_p$. Rearranging terms yields

$$R_p = \frac{i^*}{1 - (1 + i^*)^{-N}}$$

This relationship provides a convenient equation for carrying out a numerical analysis of the general relation between the payback reciprocal and the internal rate of return.

a. Develop a chart that estimates the internal rate of return of a project as a function of payback reciprocal.

b. Consider a project that requires an initial investment of \$1,000 and has annual receipts of \$500 for 5 years. This project has a payback period of 2 years, giving $R_p = 0.5$. Verify that the project has the internal rate of return of 41.04% from the chart developed in part a.

**6.15.** Johnson Chemical Company is considering investing in a new composite material processing project after a 3-year period of research and process development.

*R&D cost:* $3 million over a 3-year period, with an annual R&D growth rate of 50%/year ($0.63 million at the beginning of year 1, $0.95 million at the beginning of year 2, and $1.42 million at the beginning of year 3). These R&D expenditures will be expensed rather than amortized for tax purposes.

*Capital investment:* $5 million at the beginning of year 4, depreciated over a 7-year period using MACRS percentages.

*Process life:* 10 years.

*Salvage value:* 10% of initial capital investment at the end of year 10.

*Total sales:* $100 million (at the end of year 4) with a sales growth rate of 10%/year (compound growth) during the first 6 years and −10% (negative compound growth)/year for the remaining process life.

*Out-of-pocket expenditures:* 80% of annual sales.

*Working capital:* 10% of annual sales (considered as an investment at the beginning of each year and recovered fully at the end of year 10)

*Marginal tax rate:* 40%.

*Minimum attractive rate of return (MARR):* 18%.

a. Compute the net present value of this investment and determine whether the project should be pursued.
b. Compute the rate of return on this investment.
c. Compute the benefit–cost ratio for this investment.
d. Compute the annual equivalent for this project.

# 7

# Decision Rules for Selecting among Multiple Alternatives

## 7.1. INTRODUCTION

In the previous chapter we presented ten different criteria for measuring the investment worth of an individual project. For an individual project all ten criteria yield consistent answers for the accept–reject decision. Which one to use is therefore a question of convenience and habit. When we *compare* projects, however, the situation is quite different. Naive or improper application of various criteria can lead to conflicting results. Fortunately, the *proper use of any of the ten criteria will always result in decisions consistent with PV analysis, which we consider the baseline, or "correct," criterion.*

In Section 7.2 we present some preliminary steps that must be taken before analysis can begin: formulating mutually exclusive alternatives and ordering them. Section 7.3 is the main part of the chapter, and here we present the criteria and decision rules for comparing alternatives. In Section 7.4 we examine some of the more detailed aspects of the "assumptions" behind the decision criteria and consider other writings on the subject. Section 7.5 treats the subject of unequal lives, which becomes important in service projects; benefits of service projects are unknown or not measured. Finally, there is a brief discussion of investment timing in Section 7.6.

As in Chapter 6, we assume that the *MARR* is known and that we operate in a stable, perfect capital market with complete certainty about the outcome of investments. The firm can therefore borrow funds at the *MARR* and invest any excess funds at the same rate. The firm's ability to borrow may be *limited,* however, which differs from the situation assumed in Chapter 6.

## 7.2. FORMULATING MUTUALLY EXCLUSIVE ALTERNATIVES

We need to distinguish between projects that are independent of one another and those that are dependent. We say that two or more projects are *independent* if the accept–reject decision of one has no influence, except for a possible budgetary reason, on the accept–reject decision of any of the others. We call this a *set of independent projects*. Typical examples are projects that derive revenues from different markets and require different technical resources.

Two or more projects are *mutually exclusive* if the acceptance of any one precludes the acceptance of any of the others. We call this a *set of mutually exclusive projects*. An example is a set of projects, each of which requires full-time use of a single, special-purpose machine. If we select a particular project, the machine becomes unavailable for any other use.

Two projects are *dependent* if the acceptance of one requires the acceptance of another. For example, the decision to add container ship dock facilities in an existing harbor may require a decision to increase the depth of the harbor channel. The container ship dock project is dependent on the channel project. Notice that the channel project does *not* depend on the dock project, however, since an increase in channel depth can benefit the conventional docks. If the channel project also depended on the container dock project, we would combine the two into one project.

Before applying any investment criterion to selecting among projects, we follow this procedure.

1. Reject any individual project that fails to meet the criterion acceptance test, *unless* some other project that passes the test depends on it. This step is not absolutely necessary, but it speeds later computations.
2. Form all possible, feasible *combinations* with the remaining projects. We call this step formulating mutually exclusive alternatives.
3. *Order* the alternatives formed in step 2, usually, but not always, by the investment required at time 0, $c_0$. If there is an overall budget limit, we may at this step eliminate any alternatives that exceed the limit.

### *Example 7.1*

A chemical company is considering the manufacture of two products, A and B. The market demand for each of these products is independent of the demand for the other. Product A may be produced by either process x or process y, and product B by either process y or process z. It is inefficient to use more than one process to manufacture a particular product, and no process may be used to manufacture more than one product. *Formulate* all mutually exclusive investment alternatives. Table 7.1 presents the eight alternatives. The first one is the *do-nothing* alternative, which should always be included. We then list all alternatives that consist of a single product for manufacture, followed by all feasible combinations of two products. Since Ay and By are inherently mutually exclusive, we do not consider the combination. Nor do we consider combinations such as Ax, Ay, since they are mutually exclusive according to the problem statement. □

**Table 7.1** ***Mutually Exclusive Investment Alternatives, Example 7.1***

| Alternative | Product–Process Combinations Included |
|---|---|
| 1 | None |
| 2 | Ax |
| 3 | Ay |
| 4 | By |
| 5 | Bz |
| 6 | Ax, By |
| 7 | Ax, Bz |
| 8 | Ay, Bz |

## *Example 7.2*

A marketing manager is evaluating strategies for three market areas, A, B, and C. The strategy selected in any one area is independent of that in any other area. Only one strategy is to be selected for each area. There are two strategies for A, 1 and 2; three for B, 1, 2, and 3; and three for C, 1, 2, and 3. Strategy 1 for any area is a do-nothing strategy. *Formulate* all mutually exclusive investment alternatives. Table 7.2 presents the $(2)(3)(3) = 18$ alternatives. □

After formulating all possible, feasible combinations, we *treat* them as a set of mutually exclusive alternatives. The cash flow for any alternative is simply the sum of the cash flows of the included projects. Since we consider all possible, feasible combinations, we must obtain the optimal combination. The reason for defining mutually exclusive alternatives is related to the properties of an invest-

**Table 7.2** ***Mutually Exclusive Investment Alternatives, Example 7.2***

| | Strategy Selected for Each Market Area | | | | Strategy Selected for Each Market Area | | |
|---|---|---|---|---|---|---|---|
| Alternative | A | B | C | Alternative | A | B | C |
| 1 | 1 | 1 | 1 | 10 | 2 | 1 | 1 |
| 2 | 1 | 1 | 2 | 11 | 2 | 1 | 2 |
| 3 | 1 | 1 | 3 | 12 | 2 | 1 | 3 |
| 4 | 1 | 2 | 1 | 13 | 2 | 2 | 1 |
| 5 | 1 | 2 | 2 | 14 | 2 | 2 | 2 |
| 6 | 1 | 2 | 3 | 15 | 2 | 2 | 3 |
| 7 | 1 | 3 | 1 | 16 | 2 | 3 | 1 |
| 8 | 1 | 3 | 2 | 17 | 2 | 3 | 2 |
| 9 | 1 | 3 | 3 | 18 | 2 | 3 | 3 |

ment worth criterion. If we are considering the projects as wholly or partially independent, can we be sure our criterion will always lead to the best combination, no matter which project we examine first? With mutually exclusive alternatives we avoid this type of problem, because we have specific rules for ordering the alternatives before applying the investment worth criterion.

The *ordering* of the alternatives depends on which criterion is to be applied. There are four classifications.

1. Time 0 investment, $c_0$: order the alternatives by increasing $c_0$. Applies to *PV, FV, AE, PB,* and *ARR.*
2. $I$, the $PV(i)$ of initial investments $c_0, c_1, ..., c_m$: order by increasing $I$. Here $i$ is the *MARR.* Applies to $R_N$ and *L–S.*
3. $C$, the $PV(i)$ of all expenditures, consisting of initial investment plus annual expenses: order by increasing $C$. Again, $i$ is the *MARR.* Applies to $R_A$ and *MIRR.*
4. $PV(0\%)$ of all cash flows: order by increasing $PV(0\%)$. When there are ties, order by increasing first derivative of $PV(0\%)$. Applies to *IRR* and *RIC.*

These ordering rules are designed to facilitate the application of the criteria, as shown in the next section. They are not the only rules. For example, *any* ordering rule will work with *PV, FV, AE,* and *PB.* In addition, we can sometimes use ordering rule 1, based on $c_0$, with the other criteria, provided we modify the decision rules. These modifications often result in cumbersome variations and thus are usually avoided.

## 7.3 APPLICATION OF INVESTMENT WORTH CRITERIA

### 7.3.1 Total Investment Approach

This approach applies the investment criterion separately to each mutually exclusive alternative. Example 7.3 illustrates the approach.

### *Example 7.3*

Two mutually exclusive alternatives, $j$ and $k$, are being considered as shown in Table 7.3. Apply the various criteria to each alternative, using *MARR* = 10%. The results are shown in the lower part of Table 7.3. (The derivation of the results in the table is left as an exercise; see Problem 7.3.) □

***Opposite Ranking Phenomenon.*** Four of the criteria seem to indicate that alternative $k$ is the better choice, whereas the other six give numerically higher ratings for $j$. We have here an example of the *opposite ranking phenomenon.* The cause of the discrepancy is that some of the criteria are *relative* measures of investment worth and others are *absolute* measures. The resolution of this conflict, for the situation of perfect capital markets and complete certainty, is given by the *incremental approach* in Section 7.3.2.

**Table 7.3** ***Total Investment Approach, Example 7.3***

| | Alternative $j$ | | | Alternative $k$ | | |
|---|---|---|---|---|---|---|
| Time | Outflow | Inflow | Net Flow | Outflow | Inflow | Net Flow |
| 0 | \$1,000 | 0 | −\$1,000 | \$2,000 | 0 | −\$2,000 |
| 1 | 2,000 | 2,475 | 475 | 5,000 | 5,915 | 915 |
| 2 | 1,000 | 1,475 | 475 | 6,000 | 6,915 | 915 |
| 3 | 500 | 975 | 475 | 7,000 | 7,915 | 915 |

| Criterion* | Value for $j$ | Value for $k$ | Alternative with Larger Value |
|---|---|---|---|
| $PV$ | \$181 | \$275 | $k$ |
| $FV$ | \$241 | \$367 | $k$ |
| $AE$ | \$ 73 | \$111 | $k$ |
| $PB_N$ | \$242 | \$367 | $k$ |
| $IRR$ | 20% | 18% | $j$ |
| $ARR$ | 16% | 15% | $j$ |
| $MIRR$ | 12% | 11% | $j$ |
| $R_A$ | 1.045 | 1.016 | $j$ |
| $R_N$ | 1.182 | 1.138 | $j$ |
| $L–S$ | 0.182 | 0.138 | $j$ |

*$i$ = 10% for all criteria.

At this point, we argue that *when we apply the total investment approach*, the $PV$, $FV$, $AE$, and $PB_N$ give the *correct answer*. This is so because maximizing these criteria maximizes the future wealth of the firm. This point is proved in detail in Section 7.4.1. Before we resolve the discrepancies between $PV$ and the other criteria, some special cases are considered.

***Consistency Within Groups.*** The consistency within groups of the criteria is not coincidence but rather a fundamental characteristic. If the lifetimes of all alternatives are the same and $-100\% < i$, it is easy to show that the following groups will always show internal consistency in ranking mutually exclusive alternatives.

*$PV$, $FV$, $AE$ and $PB_N$.* The four criteria, $PV$, $FV$, $AE$, and $PB$, will always agree among themselves.

If

$$PV(i)_j < PV(i)_k$$

then

$$(F/P, i, N)PV(i)_j < (F/P, i, N)PV(i)_k$$

and

$$FV(i)_j < FV(i)_k$$

In addition,

$$(A/P, i, N)PV(i)_j < (A/P, i, N)PV(i)_k$$

and

$$AE(i)_j < AE(i)_k \tag{7.1}$$

The $PB_N(i)$ is the same as $FV(i)$, so we complete the proof.

These criteria measure the surplus in an investment alternative over and above investment of $i = MARR$. It does not matter when we measure the surplus in comparing alternatives—at time 0, at time $N$, or spread equally over the life of the alternative. If one alternative has a greater time 0 surplus than another, its time $N$ surplus will also be greater, and so forth. The surplus is measured in dollars (or other currency unit), and hence these criteria are ***absolute*** measures of investment worth. This argument again reinforces the *correctness of using PV, FV, AE, and $PB_N$ with the total investment approach.*

For example, the addition of alternative $m$ to $j$, where $PV(10\%)_m$ equals 0, does not change the $PV$ measure of $j$:

| Net Cash Flow | $n$: 0 | 1 | 2 | 3 | $PV(10\%)$ |
|---|---|---|---|---|---|
| Alternative $m$ | −\$5,000 | 0 | 0 | 6,655 | 0 |
| Alternative $j$ | −\$1,000 | 475 | 475 | 475 | 181 |
| Alternative $j + m$ | −\$6,000 | 475 | 475 | 7,130 | 181 |

*$R_N$, L–S, and ARR.* The Lorrie–Savage ratio $L$–$S$ is simply the netted benefit–cost ratio minus one, or $L\text{–}S = R_N - 1$, so we need only compare Solomon's average rate of return, $ARR$, with $R_N$. In addition to equal lifetimes and $-100\% < i$, we assume the initial investment occurs only at time 0 (other outlays are annual operating expenses). Then $I = c_0$, and $R_N = (B - C')/c_0$.
Assume

$$R_{Nj} > R_{Nk}$$

Then

$$\frac{B_j - C'_j}{c_{0j}} > \frac{B_k - C'_k}{c_{0k}}$$

or

$$\sum_{n=1}^{N} \frac{F_{nj}(1 + i)^{-n}}{c_{0j}} > \sum_{n=1}^{N} \frac{F_{nj}(1 + i)^{-n}}{c_{0k}}$$

where $F_{nj}$ is the net cash flow for alternative $j$ at the end of period $n$. In addition,

$$\sum_{n=1}^{N} \frac{F_{nj}(1 + i)^{N-n}}{c_{0j}} > \sum_{n=1}^{N} \frac{F_{nk}(1 + i)^{N-n}}{c_{0k}}$$

Substituting from Eq. 6.18, we have

$$(1 + s_j)^N > (1 + s_k)^N$$

and

$$s_j > s_k \tag{7.2}$$

If the initial investment extends beyond time 0, the result need not hold (see Problem 7.16 at the end of the chapter).

*$R_A$, MIRR.* The aggregate benefit–cost ratio, $R_A$, and the modified internal rate of return as defined by Eq. 6.23, *MIRR*, will always agree. Assume

$$R_{Aj} > R_{Ak}$$

or

$$\frac{B_j}{I_j + C'_j} > \frac{B_k}{I_k + C'_k}$$

From the definitions of *B*, *I*, and *C'*, Eqs. 6.1, 6.29, and 6.30, we substitute and obtain

$$\frac{\sum_{n=0}^{N} b_{nj}(1 + i)^{-n}}{\sum_{n=0}^{N} c_{nj}(1 + i)^{-n}} > \frac{\sum_{n=0}^{N} b_{nk}(1 + i)^{-n}}{\sum_{n=0}^{N} c_{nk}(1 + i)^{-n}}$$

Then

$$\frac{\sum_{n=0}^{N} b_{nj}(1 + i)^{N-n}}{\sum_{n=0}^{N} c_{nj}(1 + i)^{N-n}} > \frac{\sum_{n=0}^{N} b_{nk}(1 + i)^{N-n}}{\sum_{n=0}^{N} c_{nk}(1 + i)^{N-n}}$$

Using Eq. 6.23, we obtain

$$(1 + MIRR_j)^N > (1 + MIRR_k)^N$$

$$MIRR_j > MIRR_k \tag{7.3}$$

*IRR.* The internal rate of return, *IRR*, or return on invested capital, *RIC*, for mixed investments does not necessarily agree with any of the other criteria.

***Special Cases.*** In some special cases there will be agreement across some of the groups [2]. If each alternative has the same initial investment, the *PV* and $R_N$ groups will give consistent rankings. If each alternative has a constant net cash flow during its lifetime, *IRR* (or *RIC*) will agree with the $R_N$ group.

***Modification of Criteria To Include Unspent Budget Amounts.*** Some authors advocate a modification of the investment criteria to include the effects of left-over funds [8,12]. Applying this concept to alternatives $j$ and $k$ with *IRR*, we would add to alternative $j$ an additional investment of \$1,000 earning interest at $MARR = 10\%$ and returning $1{,}000(A/P, 10\%, 3) = \$402$ each year. The argument is that we have \$2,000 to invest at time 0; otherwise we would not consider alternative $k$. The augmented cash flow, designated by some as a *total cash flow,* becomes for alternative $j$

| Time | Original Net Flow, Alternative $j$ | Unspent 1,000 Earning 10% | Total Flow |
|---|---|---|---|
| 0 | −\$1,000 | −\$1,000 | −\$2,000 |
| 1 | 475 | 402 | 877 |
| 2 | 475 | 402 | 877 |
| 3 | 475 | 402 | 877 |

The *IRR* for the total flow is 15%, which is less than the 18% for $k$. Thus, *IRR,* applied to the total cash flow, agrees with *PV.* Notice that this agreement between the criteria can be derived from the special cases just mentioned.

A similar approach has been proposed for benefit–cost ratios [8]. The extent to which the total cash flow approach ensures consistent ranking by the various criteria does not appear to have been fully examined. (See Problem 7.20 at the end of the chapter.) The following example illustrates opposite ranking with the same initial investment.

## *Example 7.4*

Relevant summary data for alternatives $p$ and $q$ are given below. Evaluate the alternatives by using $R_A$ and $R_N$. Here $I$ is assumed to be $c_0$.

| Item | Alternative $p$ | Alternative $q$ |
|---|---|---|
| Time 0 investment, $c_0$ | \$100 | \$100 |
| *PV* of annual expenses, $C'$ | 10 | 0 |
| *PV* of annual receipts, $B$ | 220 | 205 |

Computing $R_A$ and $R_N$, we have

| Ratio | Alternative $p$ | Alternative $q$ |
|---|---|---|
| $R_A$ | 2.00 | 2.05 |
| $R_N$ | 2.10 | 2.05 |

□

In Example 7.4 alternative $p$ has a smaller $R_A$ value but a larger $R_N$ value. Since the classification of a cash flow element as a user benefit or a sponsor cost is often arbitrary, the use of a total cash flow approach is questionable.

### 7.3.2 Incremental Analysis

Investment alternatives can have opposite ranking because some criteria are *relative* measures of investment worth. The resolution of the discrepancy requires incremental analysis. The general approach is as follows.

1. *Order* the investment alternatives by the ordering rule specified for the criterion in Section 7.2.
2. Apply the criterion to the cash flow of the first alternative.
3. a. If the criterion value is favorable, go to step 4.
   b. If the criterion value is unfavorable, select the next alternative in order. Continue until an alternative with a favorable criterion value is obtained. (If none is obtained, reject all alternatives.) Go to step 4.
4. Apply the criterion to the cash flow *difference* between the next alternative in order and the one most recently evaluated favorably.
5. Repeat step 4 until no more alternatives exist. Accept the last alternative for which the cash flow difference was evaluated favorably.

See Example 7.6 at the end of Section 7.3 for a comprehensive application of these rules.

***Irrelevance of Ordering for PV, FV, AE, and*** $PB_N$. The ordering rule for criteria $PV$, $FV$, $AE$, and $PB_N$ is by increasing time 0 investment, $c_0$. This rule is based on convention but is not required. For these four *absolute* measures of investment worth, the *ordering is irrelevant; furthermore, the incremental analysis always agrees with the total investment approach, which is optimal for perfect capital markets and complete certainty.*

If

$$PV(i)_j < PV(i)_k$$

then

$$PV(i)_{k-j} > 0 \tag{7.4}$$

by the definition of $PV$ and the distributive rule of multiplication. In addition,

$$PV(i)_{k-j} = -PV(i)_{j-k} \tag{7.5}$$

and since the other three criteria always agree with $PV$, the ordering of alternatives is irrelevant for this group.

Applying these rules to Example 7.3, we obtain the ordering based on $c_0$: $j$, $k$. We have $PV(10\%)_j = \$181$, which is favorable.

We than examine the cash flow difference between *k* and *j*.

| $n$ | Net Flow Alt. *j* | Alt. *k* | $k - j$ |
|---|---|---|---|
| 0 | −\$1,000 | −\$2,000 | −\$1,000 |
| 1 | 475 | 915 | 440 |
| 2 | 475 | 915 | 440 |
| 3 | 475 | 915 | 440 |

We have

$$PV(10\%)_{k-j} = -1{,}000 + 440\overset{P/A,\ 10\%,\ 3}{(2.4869)} = \$94$$

There are no more alternatives, and we accept *k*, the last one for which the cash flow difference was evaluated favorably.

*If we had started with the larger* time 0 investment, we would have evaluated *k* and found it favorable with a *PV* of \$275. The cash flow difference between *j* and *k* is

| $n$ | 0 | 1 | 2 | 3 |
|---|---|---|---|---|
| $j - k$, Cash Flow | \$1,000 | −440 | −440 | −440 |

The $PV(10\%)_{j-k} = -\$94$, and we again accept *k*.

***Agreement on Increments Between PV and Other Criteria.*** Let us compare with *PV* any *one* of the other criteria, from the set *IRR* (or *RIC*), *ARR*, *MIRR*, $R_A$, $R_N$, *L–S*. We will use the ordering rule for the other criterion, since we just showed that for *PV* the ordering is irrelevant. The ordering rules are designed so that each increment appears to be an investment when evaluated by the criterion, as

**Table 7.4** ***Incremental Analysis, Example 7.3***

| Criterion | Value for *j* | Favorable? | Next Increment | Value for Increment | Favorable? | Final Choice |
|---|---|---|---|---|---|---|
| *PV* | \$181 | Yes | *k–j* | \$94 | Yes | *k* |
| *FV* | \$241 | Yes | *k–j* | \$125* | Yes | *k* |
| *AE* | \$73 | Yes | *k–j* | \$38 | Yes | *k* |
| $PB_N$ | \$242 | Yes | *k–j* | \$125 | Yes | *k* |
| *IRR* | 20% | Yes | *k–j* | 15% | Yes | *k* |
| *ARR* | 16% | Yes | *k–j* | 14% | Yes | *k* |
| *MIRR* | 12% | Yes | *k–j* | 10.3% | Yes | *k* |
| $R_A$ | 1.045 | Yes | *k–j* | 1.007 | Yes | *k* |
| $R_N$ | 1.182 | Yes | *k–j* | 1.093 | Yes | *k* |
| *L–S* | 0.182 | Yes | *k–j* | 0.093 | Yes | *k* |

*Values do not add to 367 because of rounding.

opposed to a loan, for example. Examining each increment by both criteria will yield the *identical sequence of accept–reject decisions,* because the other criterion *always agrees with PV for an individual project, or cash flow,* as shown in Chapter 6. Therefore, using *incremental analysis with any of the ten criteria will result in optimal decisions.* Some of the ordering rules may give different *sequences* of increments, but since each criterion agrees step by step with *PV*, and since *PV* is indifferent to ordering, the *final decisions will be the same.*

Table 7.4 contains the relevant data for all ten criteria as applied to Example 7.3. For each the ordering is *j, k*. Again, the derivation of table entries is left as an exercise; see Problem 7.4.

***Alternative Derivations.*** In this section we provide some alternative algebraic derivations to show the correctness of incremental analysis. Space limits prevent us from presenting all of them, and some are left as chapter problems. These proofs also illustrate the logic behind the ordering rules.

$R_N$. If

$$R_{N,k-j} > 1$$

then

$$(B_{k-j} - C'_{k-j})/I_{k-j} > 1$$

and

$$B_{k-j} - C'_{k-j} > I_{k-j}$$

Since

$$I_{k-j} > 0 \quad \text{by the ordering rule,}$$

$$B_k - C'_k - I_k > B_j - C'_j - I_j$$

or

$$PV_k > PV_j \tag{7.6}$$

We can also reverse the step sequence. Thus, the netted benefit–cost ratio, when used with incremental analysis, always agrees with *PV*.

$R_A$. If

$$R_{A,k-j} > 1$$

then

$$B_{k-j}/C_{k-j} > 1$$

and

$$B_{k-j} > C_{k-j}$$

Since

$$C_{k-j} > 0 \quad \text{by the ordering rule}$$

$$B_k - C_k > B_j - C_j$$

or

$$PV_k > PV_j \tag{7.7}$$

***Detailed Rules for IRR.*** Many practitioners apply *IRR* by using incremental analysis and ordering based on time 0 investment, $c_0$. Most of the time this presents no difficulties. Figure 7.1 shows the *PV* functions of the two alternatives *j* and *k* in Example 7.3. The ordering of alternatives by $c_0$ is first *j*, then *k*. If *MARR* $= i_1$, then $i_j^* >$ *MARR,* so alternative *j* is favorable. The difference cash flow ($k - j$) has an *IRR* of $i_F >$ *MARR,* so we accept *k*. (We call the *IRR* $i_F$ for Fisher's intersection, described in Section 7.4.) From the graph in Figure 7.1, it is clear that $PV(i_1)_k > PV(i_1)_j$, so we are consistent with *PV.* If *MARR* $= i_2$, then again $i_j^* >$ *MARR.* But the *IRR* for ($k - j$) is less than *MARR,* so our final choice is alternative *j.* Again, we have consistency with *PV,* since $PV(i_2)_k < PV(i_2)_j$.

But what if the ordering is first *k,* then *j,* and the *PV* functions are similar to those in Figure 7.1? The next example illustrates this situation.

## *Example 7.5*

Compare the following two alternatives by using *IRR* with incremental analysis based on ordering by $c_0$, with *MARR* = 10%.

| | Net Flow | | |
|---|---|---|---|
| *n* | Alt. *w* | Alt. *j* | $j - w$ |
| 0 | −\$900 | −\$1,000 | −\$100 |
| 1 | −350 | 475 | 825 |
| 2 | 915 | 475 | −440 |
| 3 | 915 | 475 | −440 |

The ordering by $c_0$ is first *w,* then *j.*

Examining *w,* we have $i_w^* = 19\% > 10\%$, so it is favorable. The difference cash flow has multiple sign changes, so multiple roots are possible. However, in the range 0 to 100% there is only one *IRR*: 16%. This value exceeds *MARR,* so we would accept *j.* However, $PV(10\%)_j = 181$, which is *less* than $PV(10\%)_w = 225$!

The explanation is that the cash flow difference ($j - w$) represents a borrowing activity, despite the negative time 0 flow. The *PV* function for ($j - w$) begins negative (which is characteristic of borrowing activities), crosses the horizontal axis near 16%, and then continues upward. The other root is at $i$ = 660%. (Applying *RIC,* we obtain $r_{j-w}^* = -38.64\%$ at $k = i = 10\%$, so we accept *w.*)

| $i$ | 0 | 10 | 16 | 20 | 50 | 100 | 200 | 500 | 660 | 700 |
|---|---|---|---|---|---|---|---|---|---|---|
| $PV(i)_{j-w}$ | −155 | −44 | 2 | 27 | 124 | 148 | 110 | 23 | 0 | −5 |

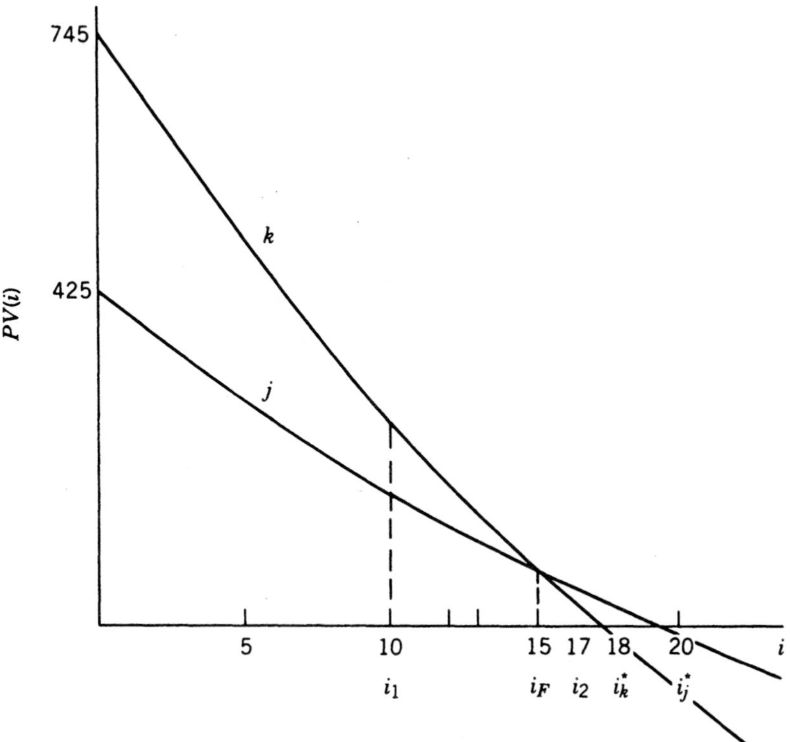


**FIGURE 7.1.** ***IRR*** **for cash flow difference (*k* - *j*), Example 7.3.**

From this example, it is clear that *ordering by* $c_0$ for *IRR* can lead to *incorrect* results.

Various other circumstances can cause problems for the practitioner accustomed to ordering by $c_0$. These include the situations in which the time 0 investment is the same for two alternatives. To remedy these difficulties, Wohl has recently developed a set of strict rules for applying *IRR* with incremental analysis [1, 13]. These rules result in complete consistency with *PV*.

For many applications the ordering rule based on *PV*(0%) clears up any inconsistencies between *IRR* and *PV*. When there are multiple roots, the *IRR* criterion can be replaced by return on invested capital, *RIC*. Multiple roots inevitably cause more computational work, whether we use *RIC*, the strict rules for *IRR* that require obtaining all roots, or plotting of the *PV* function. Plotting the *PV* function need be neither difficult nor time-consuming, and the plot contains at least as much information as is obtained by the other methods. In essence, we have argued for use of the *PV* criterion.

## *Example 7.6*

We end this section with a comprehensive example that demonstrates the incremental analysis technique for several of the criteria. Three independent projects, A, B, and C, are to be evaluated by using *PV*, $R_N$, $R_A$, and *IRR*, with *MARR* = 10%. (Note that each of the four groups is represented.) There is a time 0 expenditure budget of $4,000. The cash flows for the three projects are given in the upper left portion of Table 7.5. Select the best project or projects.

**Table 7.5** ***Preliminary Data for Example 7.6***

| Alternative: | 1 | 2 | 3 | 4 | 5 | 6 |
|---|---|---|---|---|---|---|
| Project: | A | B | C | A + B | A + C | B + C |
| Outflows, $n = 0$ | \$1,000 | 900 | 3,000 | 1,900 | 4,000 | 3,900 |
| 1 | \$2,000 | 1,265 | 5,000 | 3,265 | 7,000 | 6,265 |
| 2 | \$1,000 | 6,000 | 5,000 | 7,000 | 6,000 | 11,000 |
| 3 | \$500 | 7,000 | 5,000 | 7,500 | 5,500 | 12,000 |
| Inflows, $n = 0$ | \$0 | 0 | 0 | 0 | 0 | 0 |
| 1 | \$2,475 | 915 | 6,336 | 3,390 | 8,811 | 7,251 |
| 2 | \$1,475 | 6,915 | 6,336 | 8,390 | 7,811 | 13,251 |
| 3 | \$975 | 7,915 | 6,336 | 8,890 | 7,311 | 14,251 |
| Net flows, $n = 0$ | −\$1,000 | −900 | −3,000 | −1,900 | −4,000 | −3,900 |
| 1 | \$475 | −350 | 1,336 | 125 | 1,811 | 986 |
| 2 | \$475 | 915 | 1,336 | 1,390 | 1,811 | 2,251 |
| 3 | \$475 | 915 | 1,336 | 1,390 | 1,811 | 2,251 |
| $c_0$ | \$1,000 | 900 | 3,000 | 1,900 | 4,000 | 3,900 |
| $m$ | 0 | 2 | 0 | 0,2 | 0 | 2,0 |
| $I(10\%)$ | \$1,000 | 7,009 | 3,000 | 8,009 | 4,000 | 10,009 |
| $C'(10\%)$ | \$3,020 | 5,259 | 12,434 | 8,279 | 15,455 | 17,693 |
| $C(10\%)$ | \$4,020 | 12,268 | 15,434 | 16,288 | 19,455 | 27,702 |
| $PV(0\%)$ | \$425 | 580 | 1,008 | 1,005 | 1,433 | 1,588 |
| $B(10\%)$ | \$4,202 | 12,493 | 15,757 | 16,695 | 19,958 | 28,250 |
| $PV(10\%)$ | \$181 | 225 | 322 | 407 | 504 | 548 |
| $R_N$ | 1.182 | 1.032 | 1.108 | NA | NA | NA |
| $R_A$ | 1.045 | 1.018 | 1.021 | NA | NA | NA |
| $IRR$, % | 20.0 | 18.8 | 16.0 | NA | NA | NA |

NOTE: $m$ is the period of the initial investments $c_0, c_1, ..., c_m$.

**Preliminary screening.** The lower left portion of Table 7.5 shows the relevant data for screening the projects individually. Each of the three projects, A, B, and C, is acceptable by each of the four criteria, $PV$, $R_N$, $R_A$, and $IRR$, using $MARR$ = 10%. (We expected the agreement on the individual projects by the criteria.)

**Form investment alternatives.** Since we know that the budget is \$4,000 and that A, B, and C are independent, we can form three combinations: (A + B), (A + C), and (B + C). We thus have six investment alternatives (in addition to the do-nothing alternative). For the three alternatives composed of combinations of projects, the cash flows are shown in the upper right portion of Table 7.5, and the data needed for applying the criteria are shown in the lower right.

**Order the alternatives.** Here we apply the ordering rules specified in Section 7.2.

| | |
|---|---|
| For $PV$, order by $c_0$: | alternatives 2, 1, 4, 3, 6, 5. |
| For $R_N$, order by $I$: | alternatives 1, 3, 5, 2, 4, 6. |

For $R_A$, order by $C$: alternatives 1, 2, 3, 4, 5, 6.
For *IRR*, order by $PV(0\%)$: alternatives 1, 2, 4, 3, 5, 6.

We are now ready to apply the incremental method with the four criteria.

***PV*(10%)**

Alt. 2 vs. do nothing, or B vs. do nothing: $PV(10\%)_{2-0} = \$225 > 0$, so alt. 2 is *favorable.*

Alt. 1 vs. alt. 2, or A vs. B: $PV(10\%)_{1-2} = -\$44 < 0$, so alt. 1 is *not* favored over alt. 2. Note that we are using the relation $PV(i)_{x-y} = PV(i)_x - PV(i)_y$ to save ourselves some work. The cash flow difference (1 − 2) is the same as (A − B).

Alt. 4 vs. alt. 2, or (A + B) vs. A: $PV(10\%)_{4-2} = \$182 > 0$, so alt. 4 is *favored* over alt. 2. Note that the difference (4 − 2) is just the cash flow for A.

Alt. 3 vs. alt. 4, or C vs. (A + B): $PV(10\%)_{3-4} = -\$85 < 0$, so alt. 3 is *not* favored over 4.

Alt. 6 vs. alt. 4, or (B + C) vs. (A + B): $PV(10\%)_{6-4} = \$141 > 0$, so alt. 6 is *favored* over alt. 4. The difference (6 − 4) is the same as (C − B).

Alt. 5 vs. alt. 6, or (A + C) vs. (B + C): $PV(10\%)_{5-6} = -\$44 < 0$, so alt. 5 is *not* favored over alt. 6. The difference (5 − 6) is the same as (A − B), which was evaluated earlier.

The last alternative favorably evaluated is 6, so we accept projects B and C with a total *PV* of $548.

**$R_N$, the netted benefit–cost ratio**

Alt. 1 vs. do nothing, or A vs. do nothing: $R_{N,1-0} = 1.182 > 1$, so alt. 1 is *favorable.*

Alt. 3 vs. alt. 1, or C vs. A:

$$R_{N,3-1} = \frac{(\$15{,}757 - 4{,}202) - (\$12{,}434 - 3{,}020)}{\$3{,}000 - 1{,}000} = 1.071 > 1$$

so alt. 3 is *favored* over alt. 1.

Alt. 5 vs. alt. 3, or (A + C) vs. C: The difference (5 − 3) is the same as the cash flow for A. So $R_{N,5-3} = 1.182 > 1$, and alt. 5 is *favored* over alt. 3.

Alt. 2 vs. alt. 5, or B vs. (A + C):

$$R_{N,2-5} = \frac{(\$12{,}493 - 19{,}958) - (\$5{,}259 - 15{,}455)}{\$7{,}009 - 4{,}000} = 0.908 < 1$$

so alt. 2 is *not* favored over alt. 5.

Alt. 4 vs. alt. 5, or (A + B) vs. (A + C):

$$R_{N,4-5} = \frac{(\$16{,}695 - 19{,}958) - (\$8{,}279 - 15{,}455)}{\$8{,}009 - 4{,}000} = 0.976 < 1$$

so alt. 4 is *not* favored over 5. The difference (4 − 5) is the same as (B − C).

Alt. 6 vs. alt. 5, or (B + C) vs. (A + C):

$$R_{N,6-5} = \frac{(\$28{,}250 - 19{,}958) - (\$17{,}693 - 15{,}455)}{\$10{,}009 - 4{,}000} = 1.007 > 1$$

so alt. 6 is *favored* over alt. 5. The difference (6 − 5) is the same as (B − A).

We accept projects B and C, which constitute alternative 6, the last one favorably accepted. This decision agrees with *PV* analysis, as expected.

***$R_A$*, The aggregate benefit–cost ratio**

Alt. 1 vs. do nothing, or A vs. do nothing: $R_{A,1-0} = 1.045 > 1$, so alt. 1 is *favorable.*

Alt. 2 vs. alt. 1, or B vs. A:

$$R_{A,2-1} = \frac{\$12{,}493 - 4{,}202}{\$12{,}268 - 4{,}020} = 1.005 > 1$$

so alt. 2 is *favored* over alt. 1.

Alt. 3 vs. alt. 2, or C vs. B:

$$R_{A,3-2} = \frac{\$15{,}757 - 12{,}493}{\$15{,}434 - 12{,}268} = 1.031 > 1$$

so alt. 3 is *favored* over alt. 2.

Alt. 4 vs. alt. 3, or (A + B) vs. C:

$$R_{A,4-3} = \frac{\$16{,}695 - 15{,}757}{\$16{,}288 - 15{,}434} = 1.098 > 1$$

so alt. 4 is *favored* over alt. 3.

Alt. 5 vs. alt. 4, or (A + C) vs. (A + B): The difference (5 − 4) is the same as (C − B), which was evaluated in the comparison of alt. 3 vs. alt. 2. So $R_{A,5-4} = 1.031 > 1$, and alt. 5 is *favored* over alt. 4.

Alt. 6 vs. alt. 5, or (B + C) vs. (A + C): The difference (6 − 5) is the same as (B − A), which was evaluated in the comparison of alt. 2 vs. alt. 1. So $R_{A,6-5} = 1.005 > 1$, and alt. 6 is *favored* over alt. 5.

Again, our final selection is alternative 6, or projects B and C.

***IRR*, internal rate of return, and *RIC*, return on invested capital**

Alt. 1 vs. do nothing, or A vs. do nothing: $i^*_{1-0} = 20.0\% > 10\%$, so alt. 1 is *favorable.*

Alt. 2 vs. alt. 1, or B vs. A: The difference cash flow is +\$100, −825, +440, +440. The multiple sign changes suggest two roots, and if we refer to

Example 7.5, we see that the roots are 16% and 660%. Applying *RIC*, we obtain $r^* = 15.03\%$, so alt. 2 is *favored* over alt. 1.

As an alternative, consider a more fundamental approach to the analysis of the cash flow for alt. 2 vs. alt. 1. In Example 7.5 the opposite cash flow, that is, −$100, +825, −440, −440, was determined to be a borrowing activity. The cash flow +100, −825, +440, +440 is an investment activity, despite the initial inflow.

| $i$ | 0 | 10 | 16 | 20 | 50 | 100 |
|---|---|---|---|---|---|---|
| $PV(i)_{2-1}$ | $155 | 44 | −2 | −27 | −124 | −148 |

Notice that our decision here to accept the cash flow +$100, −825, +440, +440 using $i = 10\%$ is consistent with the decision in Example 7.5 to reject the opposite cash flow using $i = 10\%$. With $i^*_{2-1}$ near 16% > 10%, alt. 2 is *favored* over alt. 1.

Alt. 4 vs. alt. 2, or (A + B) vs. B: The difference cash flow is just that for A. So $i^*_{2-1} = 20.0\% > 10\%$, and alt. 4 is *favored* over alt. 2.

Alt. 3 vs. alt. 4, or C vs. (A + B): The difference cash flow is −$1,100, +1,211, −54, −54. Again, we have multiple sign changes, but Norstrom's auxiliary series $S_n$ is −$1,100, +111, +57, +3. This guarantees a unique, positive, real root (see Section 6.3.1). With $i^*_{3-4} = 0.3\% < 10\%$, alt. 3 is ***not*** favored over alt. 4.

Alt. 5 vs. alt. 4, or (A + C) vs. (A + B): The difference cash flow is the same as (C − B), or −$2,100, +1,686, +421, +421. This is a pure investment with a unique root of $i^*_{5-4} = 13.5\% > 10\%$, so alt. 5 is *favored* over alt. 4.

Alt. 6 vs. alt. 5, or (B + C) vs. (A + C): We have a repeat of the cash flow for alt. 2 vs. alt. 1, and $i^*_{6-5} = 16\% > 10\%$, so alt. 6 is *favored over alt. 5*.

Again, but after considerable work, our final selection is alternative 6, or projects B and C.

We thus arrive at the same final selection by using incremental analysis with each of the four criteria. □

Several conclusions are drawn from Example 7.6.

1. Correct ordering for evaluation is essential for all criteria except *PV* and the related *FV*, *AE*, and $PB_N$.
2. Although the ordering is different for each of the criteria used here, the final results are consistent with the fundamental criterion of *PV*.
3. The *IRR* criterion is particularly troublesome to apply, especially when we take differences between combination alternatives. The *RIC* concept is difficult to apply, and sometimes it is easier to obtain the *PV(i)* function.
4. *PV* with the *total investment approach* is by far the *easiest method* to apply. In this example we need to compute the *PV* of each of the three projects, add the appropriate *PVs* to obtain the *PV* of each combination alternative, and simply select the alternative with the largest *PV*.

## 7.4 REINVESTMENT ISSUES

We will begin this section with a simple example that puzzles most students when they encounter it for the first time.

### *Example* 7.7.

Given projects A and B, which is preferred, project A with *MARR* = 5% or project B with *MARR* = 10%?

| | Cash Flows | | | |
|---|---|---|---|---|
| Project | $n$: 0 | 1 | 2 | 3 |
| A | −$1,000 | 600 | 500 | 300 |
| B | −$1,000 | 300 | 200 | 1,000 |

If we compute *PV*s, we obtain $PV(5\%)_A$ = $284, $PV(10\%)_B$ = $189. Most students (and practitioners, too) select project A because of its higher *PV*.

But how can we compare a *PV* computed at 5% with one computed at 10%? The interest rate used for discounting certainly implies something about reinvestment opportunities, as discussed in Chapter 5. Trying to compare the two projects as stated in the example is tantamount to trying to compare projects in different economic environments. Projects A and B might represent investment opportunities in two different countries, with different reinvestment rates and restrictions on repatriating cash flows. Or perhaps projects A and B occur in different regulatory environments, and the decision maker assumes that after project selection the firm will reinvest its cash flows in the chosen environment.

If we are eventually to recover the reinvested cash, by repatriating it in the one situation or by returning it to the firm's treasury in the second, it does not make sense to compare A and B by using *PV*. *PV* measures the surplus of funds a project generates over and above a minimum rate, and in this example the minimum rates differ. Instead, let's compute the total cash available at time 3 for each option.

**Direct computation**

Project A: $600(1.05)^2 + 500(1.05)^1 + 300 = \$1{,}487$

Project B: $300(1.1)^2 + 200(1.1)^1 + 1{,}000 = \$1{,}583$

**Computation from *PV***

Project A: $(284 + 1{,}000)(1.05)^3 = \$1{,}486 \approx \$1{,}487$

Project B: $(189 + 1{,}000)(1.1)^3 = \$1{,}583$

We see that project B produces more cash at time 3, which is a direct result of the higher reinvestment rate, 10% for project B versus 5% for project A. It is clear that the reinvestment rate plays a crucial role in the analysis. □

### 7.4.1 Net Present Value

Virtually all writers on engineering economics agree that the *PV* criterion is based on the assumption of reinvestment at the interest rate used for calculating *PV*. In Section 6.2 we assumed that positive cash flows would be reinvested at the outside, or market, interest rate, the same rate used for obtaining *PV*. In Chapter 5 we explained that the equity interest rate is the outside rate from the view of the equity holder. Whichever assumptions we make, we represent the rate by $i$.

In a perfect capital market we can borrow and lend unlimited amounts at the market interest rate. In this chapter we have modified that assumption to reflect a limited borrowing ability. But we still assume that we can *lend unlimited amounts* by investing at a market interest rate. This is the same as assuming reinvestment at the market interest rate. In this situation, maximizing *PV* is the same as maximizing the future cash of the firm.

Assume that we have two mutually exclusive alternatives, $j$ and $k$, with cash flows $F_{nj}$, $n = 0, ..., N_j$, and $F_{nk}$, $n = 0, ..., N_k$. Further, assume that outlays occur only at time 0 and that we have a budget of $M$, which is greater than either time 0 outlay. The $MARR = i$. Select a horizon time $N$ as the greater of $N_j$ and $N_k$.

We have by definition

$$PV(i)_j = \sum_{n=0}^{N_j} F_{nj}(1 + i)^{-n}, \qquad PV(i)_k = \sum_{n=0}^{N_k} F_{nk}(1 + i)^{-n} \tag{7.8}$$

Now let's obtain the future cash at time $N$ for the three possible decisions. Say $N = N_j$, for example.

*Decision 1, do nothing*

$$\text{Future cash at time } N = M(1 + i)^N \tag{7.9}$$

Unspent amounts are invested at $i$, which is consistent with the reinvestment assumption.

*Decision 2, select j*

Future cash at time $N$

$$= (M + F_{0j})(1 + i)^N + \sum_{n=1}^{N} F_{nj}(1 + i)^{N-n}$$

$$= M(1 + i)^N + \sum_{n=0}^{N} F_{nj}(1 + i)^{N-n}$$

$$= M(1 + i)^N + (1 + i)^N \sum_{n=0}^{N} F_{nj}(1 + i)^{-n}$$

$$= M(1 + i)^N + PV(i)_j(1 + i)^N \tag{7.10}$$

The future cash is the same as for do nothing plus the $PV(i)_j$ shifted to time $N$. For $j$ the $N_j = N$, so the shifted *PV* is the *FV*.

*Decision 3, select k*

Future cash at time $N$

$$= (M + F_{0k})(1 + i)^N + \sum_{n=1}^{N_k} F_{nk}(1 + i)^{N_k - n}(1 + i)^{N - N_k}$$

$$= M(1 + i)^N + \sum_{n=0}^{N} F_{nk}(1 + i)^{N-n}$$

$$= M(1 + i)^N + PV(i)_k(1 + i)^N \tag{7.11}$$

At the end of the project life the accumulated cash from reinvesting project inflows is left to earn interest until time $N$.

The $PV$ of the do-nothing alternative is zero. In each case the future cash at time $N$ is equal to the initial amount $M$ times $(F/P, i, N)$ plus $PV(i)(F/P, i, N)$. Thus, by selecting the alternative with maximum $PV(i)$, we maximize future cash, assuming reinvestment at $i$.

Let us return to Example 7.7 and evaluate A and B with $i = 5\%$.

$$PV(5\%)_A = \$284, \qquad PV(5\%)_B = \$331$$

Here project B is preferred. Computing future cash amounts, we have

Project A: $(1{,}000 + 284)(1.05)^3 = \$1{,}486$

Project B: $(1{,}000 + 331)(1.05)^3 = \$1{,}541$

Again, project B is preferred, in agreement with our theoretical analysis.

### 7.4.2 Internal Rate of Return

Some authors have argued that implicit in the use of the *IRR* is an assumption of reinvestment at the project *IRR* [1, 3, 4]. It is difficult to prove or disprove what someone had in mind in stating the *IRR* criterion or using it. Instead, we show in this section the results of selecting alternatives with *IRR* under some special circumstances.

Let us first compute *IRR* for the projects in Example 7.7.

$$\text{Project A: } -\$1{,}000 + \frac{600}{1 + i} + \frac{500}{(1 + i)^2} + \frac{300}{(1 + i)^3} = 0$$

$$i^*_A = 21.48\%$$

$$\text{Project B: } -\$1{,}000 + \frac{300}{1 + i} + \frac{200}{(1 + i)^2} + \frac{1{,}000}{(1 + i)^3} = 0$$

$$i^*_B = 18.33\%$$

If we simply select A over B on the basis of its higher *IRR*, we would be in conflict with the *PV*s calculated at 5%: \$1,486 for A and \$1,541 for B.

We might ask whether there is a value $i$ for which $PV$ favors project A. The

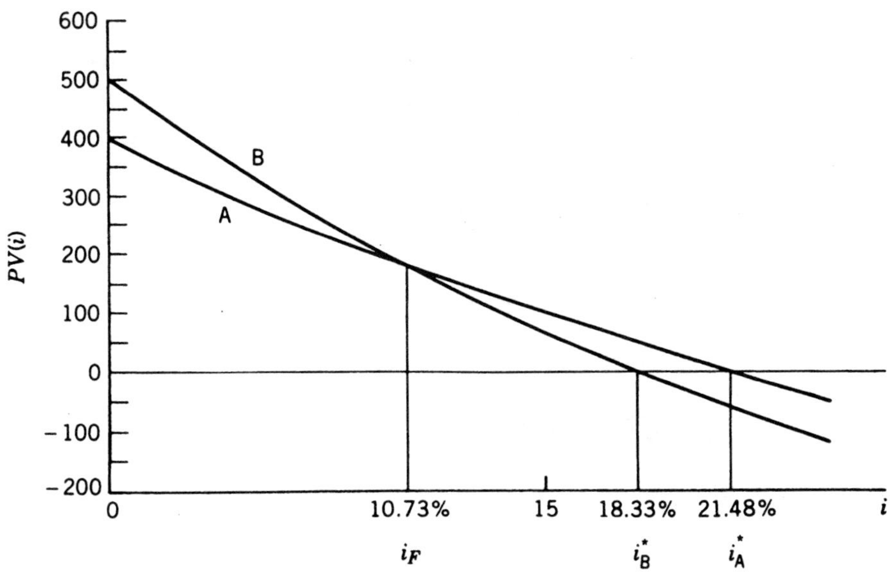


**FIGURE 7.2.** Fisher's intersection, Example 7.7.

*PV* curves for A and B are similar to those in Figure 7.1, with B starting higher than A but crossing the horizontal axis sooner. Figure 7.2 shows the curves for A and B. Clearly, *PV*(21.48%) is greater for A than for B. The point of intersection is at 10.73%. This point is also called ***Fisher's intersection*** or the ***rate of return over cost*** [5]. For any value of $i$ equal to or greater than 10.73%, the *PV* criterion prefers project A. Fisher's intersection is also the *IRR* of the difference cash flow between A and B: $0, 300, 300, −700.

If we are uncertain about the reinvestment rate in selecting one of two alternatives, calculating Fisher's intersection can be useful. In our example any reinvestment rate greater than 10.73% would lead us to prefer A over B, and B would be favored at rates lower than 10.73%. This approach becomes cumbersome when more than two alternatives are compared.

Let us now examine the consequences of ***assuming reinvestment at IRR***. If each investment alternative has its excess cash reinvested at its *IRR*, we could select among alternatives by choosing the one with the highest *IRR*. Say that alternative $j$ has the highest *IRR*, $i_j^*$. Then for all others $PV(i_j^*)$ must be less than zero. (If we also have borrowing alternatives with upward-sloping *PV* curves, we must modify the acceptance rules.)

But how sensible is the assumption of reinvestment at *IRR*? Not very sensible at all. Do different *IRR*s imply different reinvestment rates? We don't think so. And with what should we compare the *IRR* if reinvestment is at that rate? The entire discussion is rather fruitless and provides little help for decision making.

The *IRR*, along with *RIC*, is a useful criterion when it is used with correct ordering and the incremental method. Capital that remains invested in a project grows at the *IRR* of the project, and cash released would be invested to grow at the *MARR* (or the cost of capital when this rate is used in *PV* calculation) [9]. When two alternatives are compared, Fisher's intersection is useful if the reinvestment rate is not known with certainty.

### 7.4.3 Benefit–Cost Ratio

A similar argument can be presented for the aggregate $B/C$ ratio in relation to Fisher's intersection when we are comparing two alternatives [3]. We can demonstrate the logic by applying it to Example 7.7. We assume for simplicity that all investment and operating expenditures occur at time 0 and that the flows from time 1 to time 3 are benefits. Thus, we have

$$B_A = \frac{\$600}{1+i} + \frac{500}{(1+i)^2} + \frac{300}{(1+i)^3}$$

$$I_A + C'_A = 1{,}000$$

$$B_B = \frac{\$300}{1+i} + \frac{200}{(1+i)^2} + \frac{1{,}000}{(1+i)^3}$$

$$I_B + C'_B = 1{,}000$$

The $i$ value for which the $B/(I + C')$ ratios are equal must satisfy the following expression.

$$\frac{\dfrac{\$600}{1+i} + \dfrac{500}{(1+i)^2} + \dfrac{300}{(1+i)^3}}{1{,}000} = \frac{\dfrac{\$300}{1+i} + \dfrac{200}{(1+i)^2} + \dfrac{1{,}000}{(1+i)^3}}{1{,}000}$$

or

$$\frac{\$300}{1+i} + \frac{300}{(1+i)^2} - \frac{700}{(1+i)^3} = 0$$

But this last expression simply yields the *IRR* of the difference cash flow between A and B.

We conclude this section on reinvestment issues by observing that much has been written on the subject, but not all is of use in decision making. The reinvestment rate assumed is critical for alternative selection, and the assumed value should be based on the concepts in Chapter 5. Use of the *PV* criterion implies reinvestment at the rate used for *PV* calculations. Fisher's intersection is useful when comparing two alternatives, but it becomes cumbersome with more than two.

In the real world the reinvestment rates may depend on the time period and on which investments have been accepted. In Chapter 8 we present some mathematical programming approaches that can be used to model such problems.

## 7.5 COMPARISON OF PROJECTS WITH UNEQUAL LIVES

Comparing projects with unequal lives can be particularly troublesome, for a number of different situations must be considered. Furthermore, many of the methods presented in textbooks have underlying assumptions that are not always clearly stated. Unfortunately, competing projects often have unequal lives, especially in engineering studies for which only costs (not benefits) are known. Problems in this class are more difficult than those for which all benefits are known, and they require more assumptions to be made. Another aspect of the unequal-lives situation is that of repeatability. Decisions involving projects that are likely to be repeated can often be made conveniently by easier methods.

We thus have the following classifications of cases:

1. *Service projects,* for which no revenues or benefits are estimated, or the revenues or benefits do not depend on the project. Here we must select a *study period* common to all alternatives. There are two general cases.
   a. Repeatability is likely.
   b. Repeatability is unlikely.
2. *Revenue projects,* for which all benefits and costs are known. Here the *study period* may be different for each alternative, provided we have a well-specified reinvestment rate.
   a. Repeatability is likely.
   b. Repeatability is unlikely.

These four cases will lead to (and in some instances force us into making) various assumptions concerning reinvestment, salvage values, and characteristics of the repeated projects.

Notice that in this section we are not trying to determine the best life of any individual project that is likely to be repeated. This type of decision is covered in detail in Chapter 16. We now present some of the more common ways of treating unequal lives.

### 7.5.1 Common Service Period Approach

If the benefit from a project is needed for a much longer period than the individual life of the project, it may be convenient to assume repeatability of identical projects.

## *Example 7.8.*

The Historical Society of New England must repaint its showcase headquarters building. The choice is between a latex paint that costs $12.00/gallon and an oil paint that costs $26.00/gallon. Each gallon would cover 500 square feet; labor is the same for both, 1 hour per 100 square feet at $18.00/hour. The latex paint has an estimated life of 5 years, compared with 8 years for the oil paint. With $i = 8\%$, which paint should be selected?

Let us assume that after either the 5- or the 8-year period the building would be repainted repeatedly with the same paint and that the same costs would apply, as shown in Figure 7.3. The lowest common multiple of 5 and 8 is 40, so we will use 40 as the *common service period.* This becomes the *study period.*

For latex paint, we have the initial painting and seven repaintings.

$$PV(8\%) = \left(\frac{\$12.00}{500} + \frac{\$18.00}{100}\right)[1 + (P/F, 8\%, 5) + (P/F, 8\%, 10) + \cdots + (P/F, 8\%, 35)]$$

$$= (\$0.204)[1 + \overset{P/A,\ 46.9\%,\ 7}{(1.9866)}] = \$0.609 \text{ per square foot}$$

Note: $1.469 = (1.08)^5$.

For oil paint, there are four repaintings plus the initial painting.

$$PV(8\%) = \left(\frac{\$26.00}{500} + \frac{\$18.00}{100}\right)[1 + (P/F, 8\%, 8) + (P/F, 8\%, 16) + \cdots + (P/F, 8\%, 32)]$$

$$= (\$0.232)[1 + \overset{P/A,\ 85.1\%,\ 4}{(1.0751)}] = \$0.481 \text{ per square foot}$$

Note: $1.851 = (1.08)^8$.

The *PV* of the oil paint per square foot is considerably less, so the oil paint should be the choice. □

In Example 7.8 a service period of 40 years seem reasonable. The number of repaintings needed with each type of paint will depend on the technology of paint, so we may or may not need exactly seven (latex) or four (oil) repaintings. The validity of the analysis also depends on the costs of paint and labor remaining constant. If we assume constant-dollar prices, this may be a reasonable assumption. But then our interest rate of 8% must represent an inflation-free rate $i'$. Thus, many assumptions are necessary to make the approach valid.

An easier way to solve Example 7.8 is to use annual equivalents. The *AE* of each 40-year cash flow is the same as that of the corresponding 5- or 8-year cash flow.

For latex paint, computing from a 5-year life, we have

$$AE(8\%) = \left(\frac{\$12.00}{500} + \frac{\$18.00}{100}\right)\overset{A/P,\ 8\%,\ 5}{(0.2505)} = \$0.0511 \text{ per square foot}$$

Computing from a 40-year period, we have

$$AE(8\%) = \$0.609\overset{A/P,\ 8\%,\ 40}{(0.0839)} = \$0.0511 \text{ per square foot}$$

For oil paint, computing from an 8-year life, we have

$$AE(8\%) = \left(\frac{\$26.00}{500} + \frac{\$18.00}{100}\right)\overset{A/P,\ 8\%,\ 8}{(0.1740)} = \$0.0403 \text{ per square foot}$$

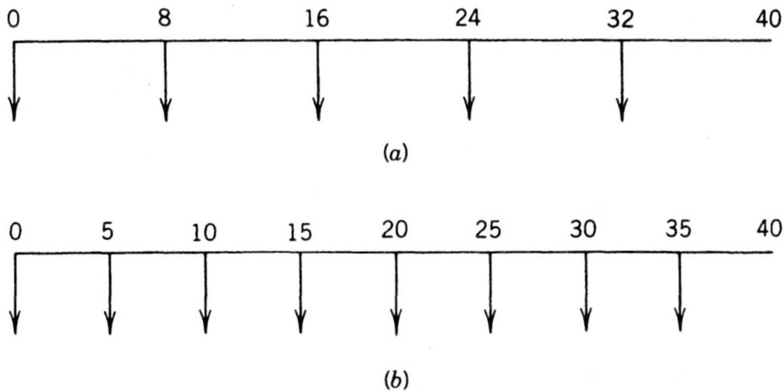


**FIGURE 7.3.** Common service period approach, Example 7.8: (*a*) oil, five paintings, (*b*) latex, eight paintings.

Computing from a 40-year period, we have

$$AE(8\%) = \$0.481\overset{A/P,\ 8\%,\ 40}{(0.0839)} = \$0.0403 \text{ per square foot}$$

With annual equivalents there is another possible interpretation regarding a common service period. We could assume that after the initial period, either 5 or 8 years, the building would be repainted with the type of paint that has the lower *AE* cost. Thus, if oil paint had the lower *AE* cost, the sequences would be

Latex paint (0 → 5), oil paint (5 → )

Oil paint (0 → 8), oil paint (8 → )

After time 5 the *AE* costs are the same. If latex paint had the lower *AE* cost, the sequences would be

Latex paint (0 → 5), latex paint (5 → )

Oil paint (0 → 8), latex paint (8 → )

After time 8 the *AE* costs are the same.

What circumstances would allow us to ignore the costs beyond time 5 when oil paint has the lower *AE* cost or time 8 when latex had the lower *AE* cost? An infinite service period with unchanging costs! Then we could simply look at the first 8 years; thereafter, costs would be identical. Actually, we do not need all these assumptions for reasonable accuracy in decision making. A long service period, say 30 years, and gradual changes in costs and technology will usually lead to the same decision about the initial choice of paint. Thus, we can minimize the *PV* of a long service period by selecting the alternative with the lower *AE* cost for an initial life.

The common service period approach is often used for analyzing *service projects,* for which no revenues or benefits are estimated or whose revenues or benefits are independent. The approach also can be applied to *revenue projects,* whose costs *and* benefits are known. In this situation we must be even more careful about our assumptions, especially regarding benefits.

### 7.5.2 Estimating Salvage Value of Longer-Lived Projects

If repeatability of projects is not likely for service projects, we must assume something about the salvage value of the longer-lived project. The next example shows how we can *explicitly* incorporate salvage values for assets with value remaining beyond the *required service period.*

## *Example 7.9*

A highway contractor requires a ripper–bulldozer for breaking loose rock without the use of explosives, for a period of 3 years at about 2,000 hours/year. The smaller model, A, costs $300,000, has a life of 8,000 hours, and costs $40,000/year to operate. The larger model, B, costs $450,000, has a life of 12,000 hours, and costs $50,000/year to operate. Model B will perform adequately under all circumstances, whereas for model A some extra drilling is expected at an annual cost of $35,000. With a marginal tax rate of 40%, units of production depreciation, and $i = 15\%$, which model should be purchased?

Since either model's lifetime exceeds the required service period (also the *study period*) of 3 years, we must assume something about the used equipment at that time. Let us assume that after 3 years model A would be sold for $60,000 and model B for $190,000. The after-tax cash flows for each alternative are given in Table 7.6 and shown in Figure 7.4. Model A has the lower *PV* of costs and would be preferred. □

**Table 7.6** ***Explicit Salvage Values, Example 7.9***

| Model | After-Tax Cash Flows (thousands) | | | |
|---|---|---|---|---|
| | *n*: 0 | 1 | 2 | 3 |
| Model A | | | | |
| Investment | −$300 | | | |
| Depreciation, (300/8,000) (2,000) (0.4) | | +$30 | +30 | +30 |
| Operating costs, (40) (0.6) | | −$24 | −24 | −24 |
| Drilling costs, (35) (0.6) | | −$21 | −21 | −21 |
| Salvage value | | | | +60 |
| Tax credit on salvage, (75 − 60) (0.4) | | | | +6 |
| Totals | −$300 | −15 | −15 | +51 |
| Model B | | | | |
| Investment | −$450 | | | |
| Depreciation, (450/12,000) (2,000) (0.4) | | +30 | +30 | +30 |
| Operating costs, (50) (0.6) | | −30 | −30 | −30 |
| Salvage value | | | | +190 |
| Tax credit on salvage, (225 − 190) (0.4) | | | | +14 |
| Totals | −$450 | 0 | 0 | +$204 |

$PV(15\%)_A = -\$291$, $PV(15)_B = -\$316$

The outcome of Example 7.9 depends very much on the salvage values received for the used equipment. We estimated these values by using 1 − (hours used/lifetime in hours)$^{0.8}$. What effect would higher salvage values have, say with an exponent of 1.5 instead of 0.8?

*Model A:*

$$[1 - (0.75)^{1.5}](300{,}000) = \$105{,}000 \text{ salvage value}$$

$$\text{Change in cash flow} = (105{,}000 - 60{,}000)(0.6) = +\$27{,}000$$

$$\text{New } PV = -291{,}000 + 27{,}000/(1.15)^3 = -\$273{,}000$$

*Model B:*

$$[1 - (0.5)^{1.5}](450{,}000) = \$291{,}000 \text{ salvage value}$$

$$\text{Change in cash flow} = (291{,}000 - 190{,}000)(0.6) = +\$61{,}000$$

$$\text{New } PV = -316{,}000 + 61{,}000/(1.15)^3 = -\$276{,}000$$

The numbers have changed to the point that intangible factors are likely to determine the selection.

What would happen if we evaluate models A and B by using *AE*s for their respective lives? First, we need some terminal salvage values; assume 10%, which gives $30,000 and $45,000, respectively. Second, we need to make some assumption about the extra drilling costs for model A; assume they would continue during the fourth year. The annual cash flows would be, as in Table 7.6, −$15,000 for model A and and $0 for model B. The positive salvage values

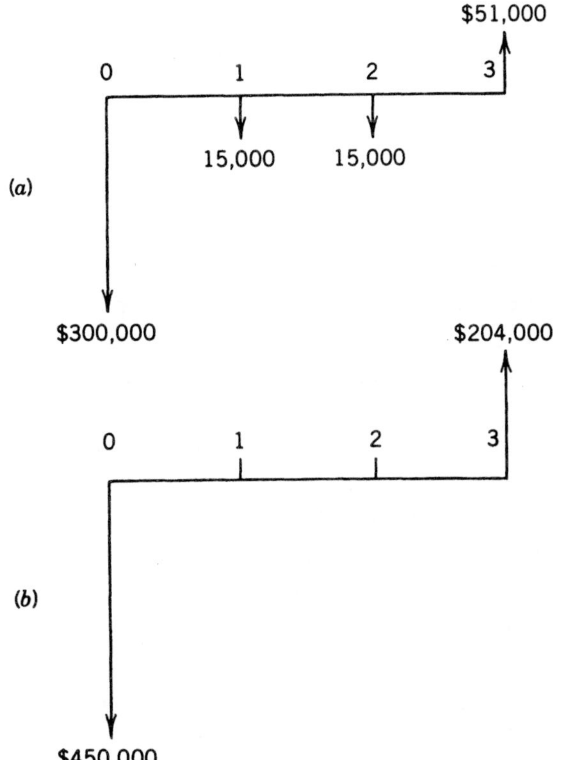


**FIGURE 7.4. After-tax cash flows using explicit salvage value estimates, Example 7.9: (*a*) model A, (*b*) model B.**

would result in depreciation recapture, so the net salvage proceeds would be (30,000)(0.6) = \$18,000 for model A and (45,000)(0.6) = \$27,000 for model B. Thus

$$AE(15\%)_A = -300{,}000\overset{A/P,\,15\%,\,4}{(0.3503)} - 15{,}000 + 18{,}000\overset{A/F,\,15\%,\,4}{(0.2003)}$$
$$= -\$116{,}485$$

$$AE(15\%)_B = -450{,}000\overset{A/P,\,15\%,\,6}{(0.2642)} + 0 + 27{,}000\overset{A/F,\,15\%,\,6}{(0.1142)}$$
$$= -\$115{,}807$$

The question at this point is not whether the foregoing analysis is valid, for the problem statement in Example 7.9 implies that it is not. (Many analysts use this method, nevertheless). Rather, we pose this question: Are there 3-year salvage values for models A and B that, when used in a 3-year analysis, yield these *AE* costs?

The answer is yes, and we can calculate the values as follows [7].

$$AE(15\%)_A = -300{,}000(A/P,\ 15\%,\ 3) - 15{,}000 + F_A(A/F,\ 15\%,\ 3)$$
$$= -116{,}485$$

or

$$AE(15\%)_A = -(300{,}000 - F_A)(0.4380) - 15{,}000 - F_A(0.15)$$
$$= -116{,}485$$

This gives $F_A$ = \$103,872, net proceeds after taxes, which implies a selling price of [103,872 − (0.4)(75,000)]/(0.6) = <u>\$123,120</u>. Similarly,

$$AE(15\%)_B = -(450{,}000 - F_B)\overset{A/P,\,15\%,\,3}{(0.4380)} - F_B(0.15) = -\$115{,}807$$

and $F_B$ = \$282,267, net proceeds after taxes, giving a selling price of [282,267 − (0.4)(225,000)]/(0.6) = <u>\$320,445</u>. (The derivation of the expression for selling price before depreciation recapture is left as an exercise; see Problem 7.24.)

These 3-year salvage values of \$123,120 and \$320,445 for models A and B, respectively, will result in *AE* costs of −\$116,485 and −\$115,807. From another point of view, if we make the selection decision between A and B by using *AE*s over 4 and 6 years, respectively, we are ***implicitly*** assuming these 3-year salvage values. Figure 7.5 shows these conversions. In Example 7.9 the contractor needs the equipment for only 3 years and will either sell the selected equipment after the 3-year period or use it elsewhere. If the equipment is sold, the contractor will receive a salvage value. If it is used elsewhere, the contractor considers the ***unused value*** to be equivalent to the implied salvage value [7, 10]. In this example we might be skeptical of 3-year salvage value ratios of 41% and 71% for bulldozer models A and B, respectively.

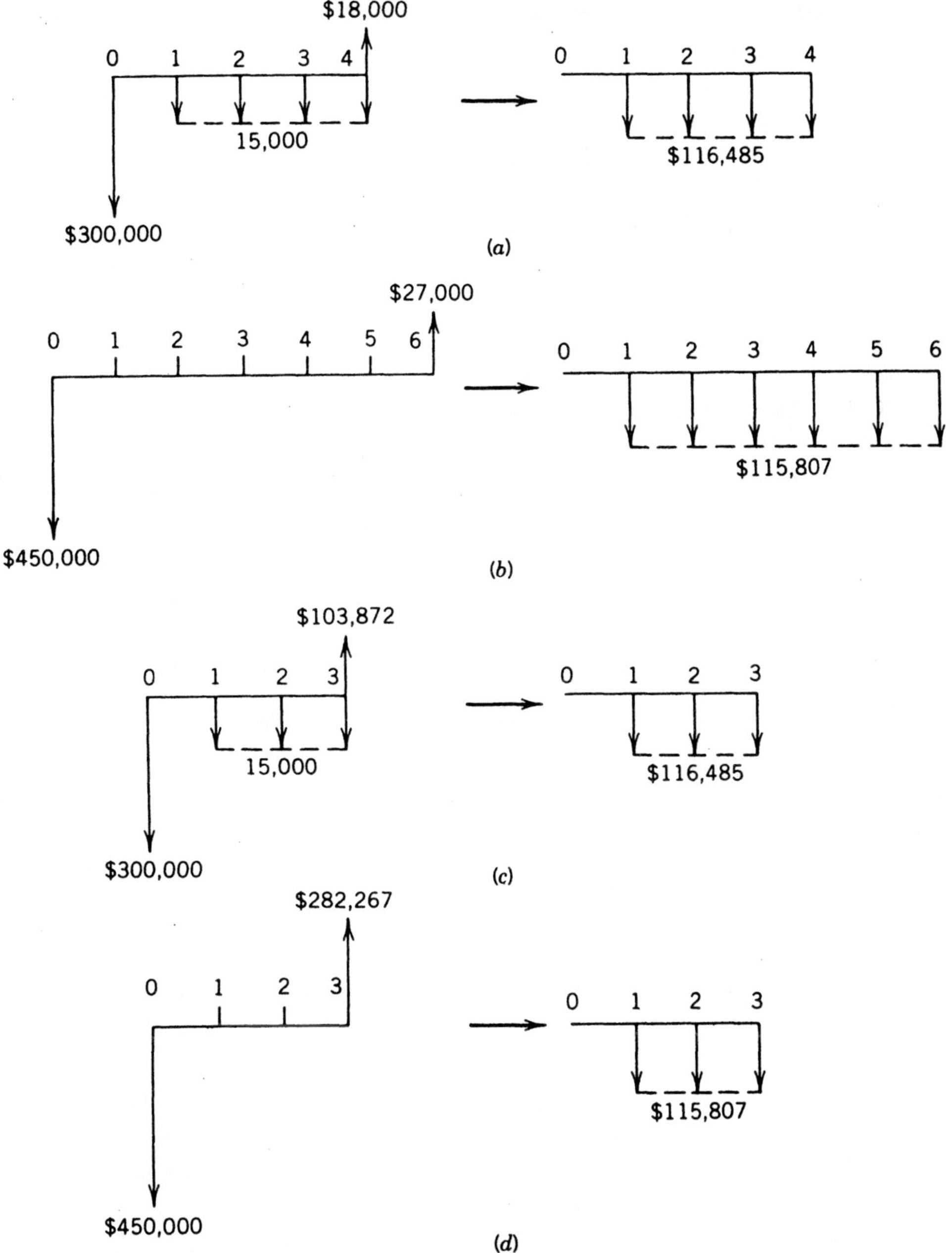


**FIGURE 7.5.** **Conversions to annual equivalents, Example 7.9: (*a*) model A, original life; (*b*) model B, original life; (*c*) model A, 3-year life with implied salvage value; (*d*) model B, 3-year life with implied salvage value.**

Sometimes one or more of the projects will have a life shorter than the required service period. One way to analyze such a situation is to *assume explicitly* how the requirement would be satisfied, for instance, by leasing an asset or by subcontracting. The *study period* then coincides with the *required service period,* which is desirable. If we use *AE* over the short life, we are *assuming explicitly* that we can lease an asset or subcontract for the remainder of the required service period at an annual cost equal to the *AE*.

In summary, when using *AE*s over the original, unequal lifetimes of projects, we are making *implicit* assumptions about salvage values or leasing costs at the end of the study period. Because most analysts do not understand these assumptions clearly and calculation of the implied values is not straightforward (especially for an after-tax analysis), we recommend that any salvage values and leasing costs used be *estimated explicitly*. The study period should equal the required service period. We do not recommend using *AE*s over unequal lifetimes for comparing service projects or using a study period different from the required service period.

### 7.5.3 Reinvestment Issues When Revenues Are Known

The presentation in Section 7.4.1 proved that, when cash inflows are reinvested at $i$, we will maximize future cash by using $PV(i)$ as a selection criterion. That proof applies for comparing projects with unequal lives as well as of those with equal lives. We thus have a way to compare revenue projects with unequal lives: use $PV(i)$. (If the reinvestment rate is not known, we must use the techniques presented in later chapters.)

### 7.5.4 Summary, Treatment of Unequal Lives

We summarize this section in terms of the classification given at the beginning.

1. Service projects
   a. Repeatability is likely.
      i. Use *AE* for each project's life. This is the easy method and is applicable in a greater variety of circumstances than the following method.
      ii. Use *PV* with a common service period. This is a tedious method and it requires or implies stricter assumptions than those in part i.
   b. Repeatability is not likely.
      i. *Explicitly* estimate salvage values for any assets with a remaining value at the end of the required service period. If an asset life falls short of the required service period, explicitly estimate the cost of leasing an asset or subcontracting.
      ii. Using *AE* for each project's life involves *implicit* estimates of salvage value or of the value of productive use after the required service period or both. This method should be used *only* if these implicit values are calculated and judged realistic.
2. Revenue projects
   a. Repeatability is likely.
      i. Use *AE* for each project's life.
      ii. Alternatively, use *PV* with a common service period.
   b. Repeatability is not likely. Use *PV* for each project's life.

It is particularly important to understand the assumptions underlying each of these methods.

## 7.6 DECISIONS ON THE TIMING OF INVESTMENTS

Sometimes it is possible to change the implementation timing of an investment. There are various reasons why this could occur, related to technology, marketing, production costs, financing costs, and so forth. We discuss briefly some of these situations and indicate how they can be treated analytically. For each situation it is understood that the same investment project with different implementation times should be treated as a set of mutually exclusive projects (a project would be implemented only once, if at all).

A rapidly *changing technology* may be a good reason to consider a timing change. Computer equipment, electronic instrumentation, aircraft, and the like change fast enough that a delay of one or two years in acquiring assets may result in significant differences in operating costs and performance capabilities. Such situations must be evaluated individually.

When the investment involves producing and marketing a product, the *product life cycle* should be considered [6].

| PERIOD | CHARACTERISTICS |
|---|---|
| Early years | Product still being developed.<br>High unit costs.<br>Relatively small market. |
| Middle years | Product design is stable.<br>Production economies have been achieved.<br>Peak annual sales for product. |
| Late years | Product is being replaced by new ones.<br>Annual sales are declining. |

Companies with technological strengths try to be leaders and hope to get a marketing advantage by producing an item during its early years. Companies with production and marketing strengths avoid the high development costs and wait until the product design is stable; they will then attempt to produce and market the product at a lower price. During the late years of the product life cycle, the advantage rests with low-cost producers who have widespread marketing organizations. By evaluating its own capabilities, a company can decide how best to utilize its strengths.

*Differential inflation* rates for first cost have been used to argue for earlier construction of civil works and power plants. For methods for dealing with inflation, see Chapter 2. In the case of nuclear power plants, a positive differential inflation rate combined with more complex technology (related to safety measures) has brought about the cancellation of many planned facilities. Had they been constructed five or ten years earlier, they might have been successful investments.

*Changing financing costs* are often cited for delaying planned investments. Here we must be careful to separate the effects of raising more capital, perhaps by borrowing, from those of investment in a project. If the financing is not tied directly to the proposed project, a high borrowing cost should be viewed in the context of the company's overall cost of capital and capital structure; see Chapter 5. Viewed in this way, a high current borrowing cost may or may not raise the weighted-average cost of capital sufficiently to make a project undesirable. When borrowing costs are high, a company with financial strength may gain a significant market advantage by investing in new products and services. Delaying investments because of high rates may be shortsighted. Again, each situation must be evaluated by itself.

When we compare different timing decisions for the same project, a common point in time should be selected for the comparison. For example, *PV* at time 0 (a specific date) can be used. Here it is particularly important to have a good estimate of *MARR*, because different lateral time shifts of cash flows for two or more projects may distort the comparison if the *MARR* does not accurately reflect reinvestment opportunities.

## 7.7 SUMMARY

In this chapter we have shown how the proper use of any of the ten decision criteria presented in Chapter 6 will lead to correct decisions when we select among competing projects. The final selection will be consistent with *PV*, which is the correct, or baseline, criterion to use in a stable, perfect capital market with complete certainty. The necessary steps for proper use of a criterion are

1. Preliminary screening to eliminate unfavorable projects.
2. Forming mutually exclusive alternatives.
3. Ordering the alternatives (not always by the time 0 investment).
4. Applying the incremental procedure.

The total investment approach is guaranteed to work only with *PV*, *FV*, *AE*, and *PB*. Moreover, for these four criteria one can use arbitrary ordering with the incremental procedure. Detailed rules apply to *IRR* and make it particularly difficult to use properly.

Use of *PV* implies reinvestment at the rate used for computing *PV*. Since the other criteria, when used properly, give the same project selection, it can be argued that their use also implies reinvestment at the same rate. It is clear that the discount rate, designated *MARR*, must be selected carefully; see Chapter 5. Much has been written about the reinvestment rate implied by use of other criteria, especially *IRR*, but this criterion is of relatively little use for decision making, with the exception of Fisher's intersection.

When comparing projects with unequal lives, one must distinguish between service projects and revenue projects. The likelihood of repeatability affects the analysis techniques to be used. Finally, any salvage value assumptions should be stated clearly and treated explicitly.

This chapter is the last one dealing with "traditional" engineering economic analysis techniques. The next chapter considers more complex decision environments, still assuming certainty. Later chapters deal with variable cash flows and other uncertainties.

## REFERENCES


1. AU, T., and T. P. AU, *Engineering Economics for Capital Investment Analysis,* Allyn and Bacon, Boston, 1983.
2. BERNHARD, R. H., "A Comprehensive Comparison and Critique of Discounting Indices Proposed for Capital Investment Evaluation," *The Engineering Economist,* Vol. 16, No. 3, pp. 157–186, Spring 1971.
3. BUSSEY, L. E., *The Economic Analysis of Industrial Projects,* Prentice–Hall, Englewood Cliffs, N.J., 1978 (see Ch. 8).
4. DEGARMO, E. P., W. G. SULLIVAN, and J. R. CANADA, *Engineering Economy,* 7th edition, Macmillan, New York, 1984 (see Chs. 5 and 6).
5. FISHER, I., *The Theory of Interest,* Macmillan, New York, 1930.
6. KAMIEN, M. I., and N. L. SCHWARTZ,"Timing of Innovations under Rivalry," *Econometrica,* Vol. 40, No. 1, pp. 43–59, 1972.
7. KULONDA, D. J., "Replacement Analysis with Unequal Lives," *The Engineering Economist,* Vol. 23, No. 3, pp. 171–179, Spring 1978.
8. LEVY, N. S.,"On the Ranking of Economic Alternatives by the Total Opportunity ROR and B/C Ratios—A Note," *The Engineering Economist,* Vol. 26, No. 2, pp. 166–171, Winter 1981.
9. LOHMANN, J. R., "The IRR, NPV and the Fallacy of the Reinvestment Rate Assumptions," *The Engineering Economist,* Vol. 33, No. 4, pp. 303–330, Summer 1988.
10. SAXENA, U., and A. GARG,"On Comparing Alternatives with Different Lives," *The Engineering Economist,* Vol. 29, No. 1, pp. 59–70, Fall 1983.
11. THEUSEN, G. J., and W. J. FABRYCKY, *Engineering Economy,* 7th edition, Prentice–Hall, Englewood Cliffs, N.J., 1989 (see Ch. 7, Sec. 8.3).
12. WHITE, J. A., M. H. AGEE, and K. E. CASE, *Principles of Engineering Economic Analysis,* 3rd edition, Wiley, New York, 1989 (see Ch. 5).
13. WOHL, M., "A New Ordering Procedure and Set of Decision Rules for the Internal Rate of Return Method," *The Engineering Economist,* Vol. 30, No. 4, pp. 363–386, Summer 1985.


## PROBLEMS

**7.1.** A company has the capability of manufacturing four products. There are three plants, with product capabilities as follows.

| | |
|---|---|
| Plant A | Products 1, 2, 4 |
| Plant B | Products 2, 3 |
| Plant C | Products 1, 3, 4 |

For various reasons, the company does not produce the *same* product in more than *two* plants. In addition, any particular plant is used to produce only *one* product. Form all possible combinations of plants and products that the company should consider.

**7.2.** If there are four independent investment proposals A, B, C, and D, form all possible investment alternatives with them.

**7.3.** Apply the ten investment criteria to projects $j$ and $k$ in Example 7.3 to derive the results in Table 7.3.

**7.4.** Apply the incremental procedure to projects *j* and *k* in Example 7.3 to derive the results in Table 7.4.

**7.5.** Consider the four projects with cash flows as shown.

| Project | *n*: 0 | 1 | 2 | 3 |
|---|---|---|---|---|
| A | −1,000 | 900 | 500 | 100 |
| B | −1,000 | 600 | 500 | 500 |
| C | −2,000 | 900 | 900 | 800 |
| D | +1,000 | −402 | −402 | −402 |

Before proceeding to the questions, we will need to obtain *FV* for each project by using *MARR* = 10%, 20%.

a. Explain why the *FV* criterion prefers A over B at 20% when it prefers B over A at 10%.

b. With *MARR* = 10%, how much money would you have at time 3 if you invested $1,000 of your own money in A? In B?

c. Which of the following situations would you prefer?
   i. *MARR* = 10%; you invest $1000 in B.
   ii. *MARR* = 20%; you invest $1000 in A.
   Explain your answer.

d. With *MARR* = 10%, how much money would you have at time 3 if you invested $2,000 of your own money in C?

e. Explain why the *FV* criterion prefers A over C at 10%, even though in situation d the cash at time 3 is greater than that in situation b (for project A).

f. What is the *IRR* for D? Would you accept D with *MARR* = 20%? How would you modify the *IRR* acceptance rule when examining project D?

g. Suppose A and B are mutually exclusive projects. Which project would you select using *MARR* of 10% and the *IRR* criterion?

**7.6.** Your company is faced with three independent proposals:

| Project | *n*: 0 | 1 | 2 | 3 |
|---|---|---|---|---|
| A | −1,000 | 500 | 500 | 500 |
| B | −1,500 | 1,000 | 200 | 1,000 |
| C | −3,000 | 1,300 | 1,300 | 1,300 |

a. With a budget of $3,000 at time 0 and *MARR* = 8%, which project or projects should you choose? Use *FV*.

b. How much cash would you have at time 3? Answer this part by performing a minimum of computations.

c. Could you use *IRR* to obtain the answer to part a? Do you foresee any potential difficulties?

**7.7.** Consider the following three mutually exclusive projects. Each has a lifetime of 20 years and *MARR* = 15%.

| Project | Investment | Annual User Benefits | Annual Sponsor Costs |
|---|---|---|---|
| A | 1,000 | 400 | 160 |
| B | 800 | 300 | 110 |
| C | 1,500 | 360 | 50 |

a. Select the best project, using the *PV* criterion.
b. Select the best project, using the aggregate benefit–cost ratio.

**7.8.** Consider the following four mutually exclusive projects. Use the incremental method with *PV* and the aggregate cost–benefit ratio to select the best project. Each has a lifetime of 20 years, and *MARR* = 8%.

| Project | Investment | Annual User Benefits | Annual Sponsor Costs |
|---|---|---|---|
| A | 978 | 500 | 100 |
| B | 1,180 | 492 | 60 |
| C | 1,390 | 550 | 120 |
| D | 1,600 | 630 | 140 |

**7.9.** Use *IRR* to select the best of the following three mutually exclusive projects. Each has a lifetime of 10 years, and *MARR* = 15%.

| Project | Investment | Annual Net Cash Flow |
|---|---|---|
| A | 5,000 | 1,400 |
| B | 10,000 | 2,500 |
| C | 8,000 | 1,900 |

**7.10.** Use *IRR* to select the best of the following three independent projects. Each has a lifetime of 5 years, and *MARR* = 8%. The investment budget is $13,000.

| Project | Investment | Annual Net Cash Flow |
|---|---|---|
| A | 5,000 | 1,319 |
| B | 7,000 | 1,942 |
| C | 8,500 | 2,300 |

**7.11.** Use the netted benefit–cost ratio to select the best of the following four mutually exclusive projects. Each has a lifetime of 5 years, and *MARR* = 12%.

| Project | Investment | Annual Net Cash Flow |
|---|---|---|
| A | 10,000 | 4,438 |
| B | 14,000 | 5,548 |
| C | 12,000 | 5,048 |
| D | 5,000 | 2,774 |

**7.12.** Rework Problem 7.11 with the assumption that the projects are independent and the investment budget is $16,000.

**7.13.** Listed are cash flows for three independent proposals. Use the netted benefit–cost ratio to select the best proposal or proposals with *MARR* = 12% and an investment budget of $34,000.

| Project | *n*: 0 | 1 | 2 | 3 | 4 |
|---|---|---|---|---|---|
| A | −10,000 | 4,175 | 4,175 | 4,175 | 4,175 |
| B | −17,500 | 10,025 | 3,025 | 7,025 | 7,025 |
| C | −15,000 | 6,025 | 6,025 | 6,025 | 6,025 |

**7.14.** Listed are data for three mutually exclusive proposals. Use the aggregate benefit–cost ratio to select the best proposal with *MARR* = 10%.

| | Proposal A | | Proposal B | | Proposal C | |
|---|---|---|---|---|---|---|
| *n* | Costs | Benefits | Costs | Benefits | Costs | Benefits |
| 0 | 10,000 | — | 14,000 | — | 17,000 | — |
| 1 | 1,000 | 5,500 | 4,000 | 10,000 | 1,000 | 10,000 |
| 2 | 1,000 | 5,500 | 4,000 | 10,000 | 1,000 | 3,000 |
| 3 | 1,000 | 5,500 | 4,000 | 10,000 | 1,000 | 10,000 |
| 4 | 1,000 | 5,500 | 4,000 | 10,000 | 1,000 | 10,000 |

**7.15.** Apply *IRR* to the selection in problem 7.14.

**7.16.** Construct an example in which Solomon's average rate of return yields an answer inconsistent with the netted benefit–cost ratio. Use the total investment approach.

**7.17.** Prove that if each investment alternative has the same initial investment, then *PV* agrees with the netted benefit–cost ratio. Use the total investment approach.

**7.18.** Prove that if each investment alternative has a constant net cash flow during its lifetime, then *IRR* agrees with the netted benefit–cost ratio. Use the total investment approach. (Assume a common life).

**7.19.** What modifications are needed in the accept–reject rules for the aggregate benefit–cost ratio if the ordering for the incremental procedure is by the time 0 investment?

**7.20.** Prove, or disprove by counterexample, that consistency is obtained across all four groups of investment criteria. Use the total investment approach:

a. When the total invested in each alternative is the same.

b. When the total invested in each alternative is the same, and the lifetimes of all alternatives are the same.

**7.21.** Prove that incremental analysis with Solomon's average rate of return yields the same answer as *PV* analysis.

**7.22.** Use the *common service period* approach to compare the following two options. *MARR* = 12%; ignore taxes.

i. Initial cost of $1,000, annual costs of $300, salvage value of $100, 10-year lifetime.

ii. Initial cost of $1,300, annual costs of $270, salvage value of $200, 12-year lifetime.

Is the length of the common service period plausible?

**7.23.** A manufacturer requires a chemical finishing process for a product produced under contract for a period of 4 years. Three options are available.

i. Process device A, which costs $100,000, has annual operating and labor costs of $60,000 and an estimated salvage value of $10,000 after 4 years.

ii. Process device B, which costs $150,000, has annual operating and labor costs of $50,000 and an estimated salvage value of $30,000 after 6 years.

iii. Subcontracting at $100,000 per year.

a. Which option would you recommend? *MARR* = 10%.

b. What is the salvage value of process device B after 4 years that would cause the manufacturer to be indifferent in choosing between it and process device A?

c. What options should the manufacturer consider if the required service period is 5 years? 7 years?

**7.24.** Derive the selling price before depreciation recapture for the assets in Example 7.9.

# Index

# Tables

CPSIA information can be obtained
at www.ICGtesting.com
Printed in the USA
EDOW021136290513
1708ED